The Family History of a Lot of POUNDS

and Their Travels

by
Walter C. Pounds, Jr.

HERITAGE BOOKS
2008

HERITAGE BOOKS

AN IMPRINT OF HERITAGE BOOKS, INC.

Books, Cds, and more—Worldwide

For our listing of thousands of titles see our website
at
www.HeritageBooks.com

Published 2008 by
HERITAGE BOOKS, INC.
Publishing Division
100 Railroad Ave. #104
Westminster, Maryland 21157

International Standard Book Numbers
Paperbound: 978-0-7884-0128-2
Clothbound: 978-0-7884-7739-3

This populous clan's southern ancestors originated in Virginia in the 1600s and has migrated throughout the south. This genealogical history aims to show family connections for all the progeny thus far researched from the 1600s to the present day. Inevitably there will be families that are not included. The greatest bulk of descendants seem to stem from the second child and first son of John Pound and Elizabeth Joy, named John Pound, Jr. Recognizing that a genealogical work is never done, this book was written with the data available at the time of its' publication.

ACKNOWLEDGEMENTS

It is with deep appreciation that the author acknowledges the considerable contributions of other dedicated compilers. It is truly the collective networking of all individuals who made this work possible. Each researcher seemed to collect at least one gem of information that other researchers were unable to find. Without giving any favoritism to any one researcher, they are therefore presented in alphabetical order:

1. Col. Frank L. Adams (ret)
   Tampa, Florida
2. M. Otto Burgett
   Ft. Lauderdale, Florida
3. D. Clyde Cribbs
   Millington, Tennessee
4. Doyle Hinton
   Pasadena, Texas
5. Donna Britton Johnston
   Jackson, Louisiana

6. Nancy Pounds Long
   Torrance, California
7. Carla Gross Machate
   Oklahoma City, Oklahoma
8. Linda Ward Meadows
   Adel, Georgia
9. Edward C. Miles
   Rossville, Georgia
10. Carl Robert Pounds
    Miami, Florida
11. Cleburne G. Pound
    Seminole, Oklahoma
12. George Pounds
    Bradford, Tennessee
13. James Pounds
    Pensacola, Florida
14. Leland Pound
    Irvine, California
15. Thomas W. Pounds
    St. Petersburg, Florida
16. Rachel Reid
    Palatka, Florida
17. Marine Snyder
    Cottondale, Alabama
18. Maurene Wahlquist
    Salt Lake City, Utah

IN MEMORIAM
Willie Pounds Cook
Lloyd C. Hicks,Jr.
Clarence Odell Kennedy
Carl Robert Pounds
Sudie Irene Pounds
Silas Brown Wright

Pounds Surname Origin

The surname Pounds or variants; Pound, de la Pound, Pund, Pundler, Pounder, Pounde, Pounte, Poundes or any other variant is derived from the "Old English" word Pund, meaning an enclosure or one who has charge of the pinfold or enclosure for animals. The surname also had an early meaning of pound weights. And as well, it meant a unit of currency. So, the origin of the surname had a trifold beginning.

The following were probably makers of the pound weights: Henry Pund of County Kent; William Pund of County Northumberland and Stephen Pound of Cambridgeshire, all living in the period 1206-1279 in England. Ralph de (of) Punda lived in Oxfordshire in 1270. Adam atte (at the) Pounde lived in Somersetshire in 1327. Ralph Proby and Alice Pounte were issued a marriage license in London in 1579. The foregoing were either dwellers at the pound where domestic straying cattle were impounded or they could have been the ones who impounded the cattle.

As surnames came to be used commonly in the beginning of the thirteenth century, and as the population grew, the surname became a necessity to distinguish between more than one person with the same given name. Already there were several variations of the Pounds name encountered in various regions and time periods.

There are numerous records of the Pounds families in Somerset County and other counties in England. Some of the Somerset records go back as far as the 1300s. Other counties in England with listings of Pounds surnames include: Kent, Lancashire, Leicester, Lincoln, Oxford, Shropshire, Stafford, Surrey, Warwick, Wiltshire and Worcester. Some of the Pounds families were quite prominent and as late as 1904, there was a John Pound who was Lord Mayor of London.

The following information was originally compiled by Sister M. Aloysius, the only sister of Jerome Balaam Pound, great-great-grandson of Reuben Pound, who himself was the great-grandson of the second known Pound (Pownd) family member (John Pownd) known to emigrate to America. "In England, the Pounds were subjects of the Lancastrian King, Henry VI, whose coat-of-arms was a red rose. Then the entire family held a large estate, and all were devout Catholics. Under Henry VIII, and later under Queen Elizabeth, persecution and heavy fines forced the family to sell the land, acre by acre, until little remained except the old home built in the sixteenth century. Poverty, caused by persecution, influenced the family to accept the new religion."

Father Thomas Pounde, Jesuit lay affiliate and confessor, b. Belmont, near Winchester, England, May 29, 1539; d. Belmont, March 5, 1615. Thomas was the elder son of William Pounde, wealthy country gentleman, and Anne Wriothesley, sister of Thomas, Earl of Southampton. Until c. 1562 he was educated at Winchester, and then, at Lincoln's Inn, London. Thomas, admitted to Elizabeth's court and appointed esquire of the body, outwardly remained a Protestant until, following a humiliation at court (c. 1569-70), he retired to Belmont and was reconciled to the Church. Four years of spiritual preparation followed: two as a hermit, two with Thomas Stephens. In 1574 while preparing to leave for Rome, he was arrested in London. According to Pounde's own reckoning, over the succeeding 30 years, there followed 15 imprisonments of varying lengths and in numerous prisons. During this time he was also fined 4000 pounds for recusancy. He was admitted to the Jesuits in 1579 by a letter from General Everard Mercurian, which was smuggled to his prison cell in the Tower of London. His brief treatise "The Six Reasons" (1580), an attack on the scriptura sola position, was circulated in manuscript among English Catholics. In 1604 following James I's accession, he was released, and retired to the seclusion of his Belmont home until his death. His lengthy imprisonment may well be the longest for any English Catholic layman of the period.

As yet, no single record has been found of any Pound(s) family who came directly from Europe, but in the year 1635 there were two single men with Pound(s) surnames who emigrated to America. In the list of Emigrants to America 1600-1700 by Hotten, printed by the Baltimore Genealogical Publishing Company, there is mentioned:

29 Apr 1635 - to be transported to New England embarqued in the ELIZABETH AND ANN, Roger Cooper, Master;

Tho. Pond (Pound) age 21. Certificates were brought from the Minister of the Parish and Justice of the Peace, Church of England.

4 Jul 1635 - to be transported to Virginia aboard TRANSPORT OF LONDON, Edward Walker, Master;

John Pownd (Pound) age 20. The parties have brought certificate from the Minister of Gravesend of their conformitie of the Church of England.

So, naturally the first question that pops to mind is; are these two men related? The answer is YES!. Both were sons of John Pound and Jone Clarke in England. They had one other brother, named Henry Isham Pound; he, too, emigrated to America. But coincidentally, the progeny of

these first two men seems to have been aligned
into northern and southern groups. Thomas Pound,
who emigrated to New England, seems to have been
responsible for those branches of the Pounds
families who populated the northern tier of states
and John Pound seems to have been responsible for
those branches of the Pounds families who
populated the southern tier of states.

So little mention has been found of the
Thomas Pound who emigrated to New England in 1635
that there is much uncertainty about him, since we
have a fifty-two year gap from 1635 to 1687 where
the next mention is made about Thomas Pound, if we
indeed do have the right one. It is believed that
he married a woman named Elizabeth --- and had a
son named after him. At this time, this is
conjecture, with no solid evidence to back it up.
In the book "Blackbeard and Other Pirates of the
Atlantic Coast" by Nancy Roberts, published by
John Blair in Winston-Salem, North Carolina, is an
article that might be the aforementioned Thomas.
The pirate Thomas was forgiven of his sins by the
King of England and appointed captain of the
frigate Sally Rose of the Royal Navy. In 1699 he
retired to live the life of a country squire at
Isleworth, Middlesex, England and died there in
1703, honored and respected by all. Also, his
piratical adventures are mentioned in the book
"The Pirates' Who's Who', page 248-249. So, when
or where he married in America is not known, or if
in fact he did leave male heirs. In addition, in
the Dictionary of American Biography vol XV,
Thomas Pound is given the credit for producing the
first map of Boston Harbor to be engraved. Made
probably about 1691 or 1692 and entitled 'A Mapp
of New England from the Cape Codd to Cape Sables,
Describing All the Sands, Shoals, Rocks and
Difficultyes together with a Sand Draft of the
Massachusetts Bay', dedicated to his friend the
Earl of Macclesfield. It was engraved at
Cheapside, London, by John Harris and sold by
Phillip Lea.

The third son of John Pound and Jone Clarke
in England, Henry Isham Pound, born in 1626 in
England emigrated to America, but the year in
which he did this is not known. It is believed
that he settled on the Bermuda Hundred in Henrico

County, Virginia, where he died in 1676. It is not certain that he left any male heirs.

According to one family researcher, an American branch of the Pound family came from Lancashire, England, near the Irish Sea, probably in the surrounding area of Prescot, and settled in Canada. Three sons of the family crossed the boundary and joined the American Revolution. One settled in New England (was this John Pound who was among the early settlers of Piscataway, Middlesex County, New Jersey and died there February 21, 1690?). It is not known from where he came nor when he arrived at Piscataway, but the town records show that he was residing there as early as September 17, 1686. The John Pound of New Jersey has well-publicized genealogical histories (Pound and Kester families). This is pure speculation, but wouldn't it be great if this John Pound was a son of Thomas Pound, who emigrated from England? It is possible within this time frame. The names John and Thomas seem to be eternally popular. The second son settled in North Carolina; the other in the west, either in Kansas or Nebraska. Further research is needed to connect any of these family members to other families in this populous clan.

In "An Account of Servants That sent to Virginia in the ship called the ELEANOR OF LIVERPOOLE, Nicholas Reynolds, Master;

was:
September 5, 1698 - one of the passengers

Susanna Pound of Devon, widdowe 4 years

No further records of emigrants have yet been uncovered for the early colonial period. Further research may develop more emigrants from England and while it is generally agreed that the Pound(s) families did indeed originate in England, the main problem is to definitively prove a genealogical connection from one branch to the others with sufficient documentation for verification.

From the second generation in America, the Pounds men developed "itchy" feet and began their migrations into other areas of this mostly undeveloped country. Their journeys along the eastern seaboard and into other wildernesses are amazing in retrospect, when you consider the difficulties involved in traversing these huge primitive territories. Each generation seemed to continue this wanderlust as they found what was just around the next bend.

EXPLANATION OF THE
NUMBERING SYSTEM

The numbering system for the Pound(s) family descendants begins with the four children of John Pound and Elizabeth Joy: Margaret, John, Thomas and Samuel; each being given alphabetical designators. Each successive generation has been identified with the alphabetical prefix and a numberical identifier in sequence, in order of birth in each family.

For example, Margaret's children are A1 through A6; John's grandchildren are B41 through B46; Thomas's great-grandchildren are C611 through C619 and Samuel's great-great-grandchildren are D4151 through D4156. Each further generation continues in this manner.

Each child in each generation of each family is given a progressive number.

JOHN POUND (POWND)

John Pound (Pownd) - second known immigrant of Pound(s) surname from England. This second known record of a member of the Pound(s) family is that of John Pound (Pownd) who came to this country in 1635 aboard the ship TRANSPORT OF LONDON, captained by Edward Walker. All parties aboard had to have certificates from the Minister of Gravesend of their conformity with the Church of England. In retrospect, this is all the more amazing when you consider that he was probably uneducated and illiterate, but apparently possessed of much courage to make such a trip to an unknown country, still in its' primitive stages. Most of this new country was still undeveloped with no roads as such, only rivers or Indian or animal trails to get you from one point to another.

Since the record of this second known immigrant showed that he was 20 years old when he arrived here, it is believed that he must have married a woman whose name is unknown, and that he fathered a son, also named John, born about 1663, probably in Virginia. This son married on 28 Oct 1683 in North Farnham Parish, Richmond County, Virginia to Elizabeth Joy, born about 1662. This marriage probably took place with the arrival of a "circuit" preacher to their parish. John and Elizabeth had a daughter born 5 August 1683, in North Farnham Parish, Richmond, County, Virginia; named Margaret Pound. After their marriage, John and Elizabeth had three more children; John Pound Jr., Thomas Pound and Samuel Pound.

So, the first known Pound(s) family of the southern branches of the Pounds families originated in Virginia comprised John Pound and Elizabeth Joy as parents, with their issue being the third generation in America:

A. Margaret Pound   born 5 August 1683
   North Farnham Parish, Richmond County, Virginia

B. John Pound, Jr.   born 1685
   North Farnham Parish, Richmond County, Virginia

C. Thomas Pound   born 1687

2

North Farnham Parish, Richmond County, Virginia

D. Samuel Pound   born 1690
   North Farnham Parish, Richmond County, Virginia

On January 26, 1717, John Pound died in North Farnham Parish and is believed to be buried in Richmond County, Virginia. It is not known when Elizabeth Joy, his wife, died.

In 1717, in Richmond County, Virginia, North Farnham Parish, John Pound made his WILL, which was proved in open court a few days later in the same year. In this WILL, he names his oldest son, John Pound, Jr., and his daughter Margaret Smith. He also mentioned his grandchildren, the children of John Pound, Jr. and since his wife is not mentioned, it is assumed that she was already dead. John Pound made his WILL on 26 January 1717, recorded 5 February 1717, in North Farnham Parish, Richmond County, Virginia. The WILL was proved in open court by oaths of Zachariah Hefford and John Newman; witnesses were Sarah Pound, his son Thomas Pound, his son Samuel Pound and his daughter Margaret Smith.

WILL of JOHN POUND
Richmond County, Virginia
Farnham Parish

To my eldest son John, one shilling; my son Thomas, my daughter Margaret Smith, to my son Samuel. To my grandchildren by my son John, my son Thomas, my son Samuel Pound and my daughter Margaret Smith, my sole estate.
          26 Jan 1717

[From the wording of the will, it appears that he left his holdings to his grandchildren collectively].

A. Margaret Pound

A. Margaret Pound, first child and only daughter of John Pound and Elizabeth Joy, born 5 August 1683 in North Farnham Parish, Richmond County, Virginia, married Robert Smith. They had issue, which was the fourth generation in America:

A1. Anne Smith, first child and first daughter of Margaret Pound and Robert Smith, born 6 Feb 1715 in North Farnham Parish, Richmond County, Virginia.

A2. Margaret Smith, second child and second daughter of Margaret Pound and Robert Smith, born 6 Sep 1718 in North Farnham Parish, Richmond County, Virginia.

A3. Elizabeth Smith, third child and third daughter of Margaret Pound and Robert Smith, born 28 Jan 1721 in North Farnham Parish, Richmond County, Virginia.

A4. William Smith, fourth child and first son of Margaret Pound and Robert Smith, born 16 May 1724 in North Farnham Parish, Richmond County, Virginia.

A5. Thomas Smith, fifth child and second son of Margaret Pound and Robert Smith, born 18 Jul 1726 in North Farnham Parish, Richmond County, Virginia.

A6. John Smith, sixth child and third son of Margaret Pound and Robert Smith, born 6 Aug 1729 in North Farnham Parish, Richmond County, Virginia.

B. JOHN POUND, Jr.

B. John Pound, Jr. was born about 1685 in North Farnham Parish, Richmond County, Virginia. He was the second child and first son of John Pound and Elizabeth Joy. John Pound, Jr. married about 1708 in Richmond County, Virginia to Deborah Lewis, daughter of Thomas Lewis and Mary ---. born about 1691 in Virginia and died 19 Apr 1726. John and Deborah had issue, which was the fourth generation in America. John Pound, Jr. died in Richmond County, Virginia 7 November 1718, leaving four small children orphaned. His wife, Deborah, died in 1726, making total orphans of the children. The widow Deborah Pound administered her husband's estate. When she died 19 April 1726, her orphan son John Pound IV was apprenticed to Daniel Hornby "to learn the trade of shoemaker, until he reached the age of 21". John had turned 11 on 2 Aug 1726. John Pound, Jr. and his wife, Deborah Lewis, apparently named two sons John; with the reason thought to have been that the first son John died very early in infancy or early childhood. But there are no clues to support this theory.

B1. Elizabeth Pound, first child and first daughter of John Pound, Jr. and Deborah Lewis, born 12 Oct 1709 in North Farnham Parish, Richmond County, Virginia. No further information has yet been developed about her subsequent life.

B2. Lewis Pound, second child and first son of John Pound, Jr. and Deborah Lewis, born 4 Jun 1712 in North Farnham Parish, Richmond County, Virginia. No further information has yet been developed about his subsequent life.

B3. John Pound, third child and second son of John Pound, Jr. and Deborah Lewis, born 2 Aug 1713 in North Farnham Parish, Richmond County, Virginia. This son died before 1715 in infancy.

B4. John Pound, fourth child and third son of John Pound, Jr. and Deborah Lewis, born 4 Nov 1715 in North Farnham Parish, Richmond County, Virginia. This son survived to adulthood, married a native American as his wife and he died in 1752 in Richmond County, Virginia. There was no stigma in this era for white men to marry Indians. They had issue, which was the fifth generation in America:

B41. Reuben Pound, first child and first son of John Pound and his Indian Wife, born 1730 in Orange County, Virginia; died in 1797 in Greene County, Georgia. Married Frances Merriman. Reuben was a soldier in the War for Independence, fighting as a corporal in the 2nd Georgia Battalion, commanded by Colonel Samuel Elbert, Continental Army. Joseph Pannill was Lieutenant Colonel of this outfit, and they were a part of the army of General Nathaniel Greene. It is evident that Reuben Pound left Virginia and lived for a while in Orange County, North Carolina. His bachelor son John (Jack) Pound died in Orange County in 1791 and his daughter Sarah (Sallie) Pound married John Chism there 22 Nov 1781. They, too, went to Georgia later. The Chisholms had a family and raised them there. Reuben and Frances Merriman and had issue, which was the sixth generation in America:

B411. John (Jack) Pound born about 1756 in Virginia, first child and first son of Reuben and Frances, never married; he died 22 Sep 1791 in Orange County, North Carolina. John (Jack) Pound was a soldier in the Revolution and he gave the powder horn he carried in the war to his brother, Merriman Pound, with the request it be passed to the eldest son in each succeeding generation. The powder horn today is in the possession of Dr. Hannon Pound of Tallahassee, Florida (a prominent surgeon and a member of the National College of Surgeons). Dr. Pound is a great-grandson of Merriman Pound.

B412. Catherine (Katy) Pound born 1763 in Virginia, second child and first daughter of Reuben and Frances, born 1763 in Virginia and died before 1857 in Marshall County, Mississippi. Buried in Mississippi. Katy married 1790 in

6

Clarke County, Georgia to Julius Saunders, born about 1760 in North Carolina and died 24 Apr 1786 in White County, Tennessee; son of John and Susannah --- Saunders. John Saunders was a Revolutionary War soldier in the North Carolina Continental Line. He was deceased by 24 Apr 1875. The Saunders family moved from Georgia to White County, Tennessee. From there, they moved to Mississippi after 1835 where Catherine (Katy) Pound Saunders died, probably prior to 1857. Robert Uriah Saunders died that year and did not mention his mother in his will, indicating that she had died before him in Marshall County, Mississippi. There is no record of a marked grave for her. The Saunders family had raised horses and supplied fresh horses for the Jefferson Stage Coach Lines before the business moved its' operation to Texas. Julius Saunders and Katy Pound had four sons and three daughters; their issue being the seventh generation in America:

B4121. John L. Saunders, first child and first son of Katy Pound and Julius Saunders, born 1783 in North Carolina and married Elizabeth Hathorn 7 Mar 1811 in Putnam County, Georgia.

B4122. Susan Saunders, second child and first daughter of Katy Pound and Julius Saunders, born 1793 in Georgia where she married William J. Harlowe. Susan Saunders and William Harlowe had issue, which was the eighth generation in America:

B41221. Barney Harlowe, first child and first son of Susan Saunders and William Harlowe, date and place of birth unknown.

B41222. Nancy Harlowe, second child and first daughter of Susan Saunders and William Harlowe, date and place of birth unknown.

B41223. John Harlowe, third child and second son of Susan Saunders and William Harlowe, date and place of birth unknown.

B4123. Sarah (Sally) Saunders, third child and second daughter of Katy Pound and Julius Saunders, born 1805 in Georgia.

B4124. Robert Uriah Saunders, fourth child and second son of Katy Pound and

7

Julius Saunders, born 1810 in Georgia; died 1857 in Mississippi. Married 1828 White County, Tennessee to Nancy Simpson, born in White County, Tennessee. Robert Saunders and Nancy Simpson had issue, which was the eighth generation in America:

B41241.   William   C. Saunders, first child and first son of Robert Saunders and Nancy Simpson, born 1830 in White County, Tennessee.

B41242. Angela Saunders, second child and first daughter of Robert Saunders and Nancy Simpson, born 1832 in White County, Tennessee. Married Rufus B. Ragan.

B4125.   Julius C. Saunders, fifth child and third son of Katy Pound and Julius Saunders, born 1812 in Georgia and died about 1852 in Mississippi; married 17 Apr 1837 in Mississippi to Susan Hudson.

B4126.   Elizabeth Saunders, sixth child and third daughter of Katy Pound and Julius Saunders, born 1818 in Tennessee.

B4127.   Martha   Saunders, seventh child and fourth daughter of Katy Pound and Julius Saunders, born 1820 in Tennessee; married 1860 in Marshall County, Mississippi to John L. Hensley. Martha Saunders and John Hensley had issue, which was the eighth generation in America:

B41271.   Sally Hensley, first child and first daughter of Martha Saunders and John Hensley, date and place of birth unknown.

B41272.   Mary Hensley, second child and second daughter of Martha Saunders and John Hensley, date and place of birth unknown.

B41273.   Merriman Hensley, third child and first son of Martha Saunders and John Hensley, date and place of birth unknown.

B41274. John M. Hensley, fourth child and second son of Martha Saunders and John Hensley, date and place of birth unknown.

B41275.   Alexander Hensley, fifth child and third son of Martha Saunders and John Hensley, date and place of birth unknown.

B41276. Thomas Hensley, sixth child and fourth son of Martha Saunders and John Hensley, date and place of birth unknown.

B413. Richard Eli Pound, sixth child and fourth son of Reuben Pound and Frances Merriman, born about 1763 in Virginia and died 6 Jun 1807 in Jefferson, Jackson County, Georgia. Richard is buried in Watkinsville, Clarke County, Georgia. Richard married about 1785 Mary (Molly) Ann Davidson, daughter of John Davidson and Sarah ---, born about 1765 in Rockingham County, North Carolina and died 1865 in Cleburne County, Alabama. Richard and Mary lived for several years in North Carolina before they moved to South Carolina, and then on to Georgia, where they settled first in Hancock County, later moving to Clarke County, Georgia, near Watkinsville, which is now in Oconee County, Georgia. He was living on Barbor's Creek, not far from the town of Watkinsville, in Clarke County at the time of his tragic death, being killed by a man who mistook him for another man, in the new town of Jefferson, Georgia in Jackson County. According to Jackson County, Georgia Superior Court Minutes between 1803 and 1808, a George Cooper was found guilty of manslaughter. No mention of the man he murdered, but he could have been Richard's murderer. Richard's tragic death left his wife Mary Ann a widow with eight children to care for, ranging in age from 1 year to about 21 years of age. Proceedings on the estate of Richard Eli Pound was dated 6 Jun 1807. William Pounds and Richard's widow Mary Pound were the administrators of the estate. Mary rented the plantation and home and hire of negroes in Clarke County, Georgia. On 6 Sep 1819 in Clarke County, Mary was made guardian of Catherine, Elizabeth and Mary Pounds, orphans of Richard Pound. Newman Pounds was surety. Mary and her young children lived in the home of William Pounds (Administrator of Richard's Will). According to the Estate Inventory of Richard Pound's estate, Mary sold the property in Clarke County, when she moved to Gwinnett County, Georgia. The sale was sworn to in open court 4 Feb 1822. In about 1820, Mary moved with her minor children to Gwinnett County, Georgia's

Berkshire District, where she lived for about 10 years. Mary moved to neighboring DeKalb County, Georgia with her son Newman Pounds. They are enumerated in the 1830 DeKalb County Census, Mary living in his household. It is not known how long they lived in DeKalb County, but both Mary and her son Newman are enumerated in the 1840 Benton (now Calhoun) County, Alabama census. Mary was living next door to Newman. Mary was enumerated in the 1850 Benton County and 1860 Calhoun County censuses. Mary had various pieces of property consisting of approximately 161.53 acres in Benton County, Alabama in Township 15, Range 12 and Township 16, Range 12 between Abernathy and Lebanon. Sometime in 1856, Mary's son John Pound came to Benton County, Alabama from Gwinnett County, Georgia to visit his mother while she was living with a daughter. Not far away lived Newman. To John she said, "John, order your horse, I want to go with you to Newman's!" "Mother, how will you go?" he asked. "Your horse will carry double and I can ride behind you," and thus they went. A novel scene to see a man of 70 and his mother of 90 riding on the same horse. Mary died about 1865 and is buried at Old Lebanon Cemetery, Cleburne County, Alabama. Over the years Old Lebanon Cemetery has slowly deteriorated, partly by weather and partly by human hands. Since 1989 there is nothing left of this cemetery. Richard and Mary's issue was the seventh generation in America:

B4131. Merriman Pound, first child and first son of Richard Eli Pound and Mary Davidson, born 30 Jul 1785 in Clarke County, Georgia and died 21 May 1883 at Tuscaloosa, Tuscaloosa County, Alabama. Buried in Hopewell cemetery, Tuscaloosa County, Alabama Married 1815 in Clarke County, Georgia to Mary (Polly) A. White, born Sep 1791 in South Carolina and died Aug 1869 in Tuscaloosa, Tuscaloosa County, Alabama. Buried in Hopewell cemetery, Tuscaloosa County, Alabama. Merriman and Mary had issue, which was the eighth generation in America:

B41311. Martha Patsey Pounds, first child and first daughter of Merriman Pound and Mary White, born about 1815 in Georgia.

Married 24 Feb 1834 in Tuscaloosa, Tuscaloosa County, Alabama to Jesse P. Garner. Martha Pounds and Jesse Garner had issue, which was the ninth generation in America:

B413111. Marion Garner, first child and first son of Martha Pounds and Jesse Garner, date and place of birth unknown.

B413112. Mary E. Garner, second child and first daughter of Martha Pounds and Jesse Garner, date and place of birth unknown.

B413113. Oregon Garner, third child and second daughter of Martha Pounds and Jesse Garner, date and place of birth unknown.

B413114. James Garner, fourth child and second son of Martha Pounds and Jesse Garner, date and place of birth unknown.

B41312. Raleigh W. Pounds, second child and first son of Merriman Pound and Mary White, born 30 Jul 1818 in Tuscaloosa County, Alabama and died 1911 in Tuscaloosa County, Alabama. Married 14 Jan 1846 in Tuscaloosa County, Alabama to Martha Matilda Scales Otey, daughter of Thomas Scales and Mary (Polly) Hanes, born 1817 in Georgia. Martha had married firstly to Richard Otey and their marriage had issue: Richard Otey, born 1838 in Alabama; Thomas Otey, born 1840 in Alabama; and Mary Ann Otey, born 1842 in Tuscaloosa County, Alabama. Raleigh Pounds and Martha Otey had issue, which was the ninth generation in America:

B413121. Alexander M. Pounds, first child and first son of Raleigh Pounds and Martha Otey, born 1847 in Tuscaloosa County, Alabama. Married Amanda Gillen.

B413122. Matilda Pounds, second child and first daughter of Raleigh Pounds and Martha Otey, born about 1849 in Tuscaloosa County, Alabama.

B413123. Oregon Pounds, third child and second daughter of Raleigh Pounds and Martha Otey, born 1852 in Tuscaloosa County, Alabama. Married 12 Jan 1876 in Alabama at Raleigh Pounds residence in Tuscaloosa County,

Alabama to William Moore. Married secondly to James S. McGee. Oregon and William Moore had issue, which was the tenth generation in America:

B4131231. Raleigh Moore, first child and first son of Oregon Pounds and William Moore, born 1877 in Tuscaloosa County, Alabama.

B413124. George Washington Pounds, fourth child and second son of Raleigh Pounds and Martha Otey, born 11 Jun 1854 in Tuscaloosa County, Alabama and died 12 Dec 1935 in Walker County, Alabama. Buried at Oakman, Earnest Chapel cemetery, Alabama. Married 22 Feb 1896 in Tuscaloosa County, Alabama to Mary Ellen Kelly, born Jan 1863. Married secondly to Addie Watts. Married thirdly 22 Feb 1896 to Alice Day, born 2 Aug 1876 and died 13 Feb 1862 in Walker County, Alabama. Buried at Oakman, Day cemetery. George Washington Pounds and Alice Day Pounds are buried at separate places because a son was buried at Earnest Chapel and he wanted to be buried there. Grandmother Alice Day Pounds wanted to be buried by her daughters at Day cemetery. No issue is known by George's marriage to Addie Watts, but there was issue from the first and third marriages. George Washington Pounds and Mary Ellen Kelly had issue, which was the tenth generation in America:

B4131241. William E. Pounds, first child and first son of George Pounds and Mary Kelly, born 23 Feb 1880 in Alabama.

B413124. George Washington Pounds married thirdly to Alice Day, born 2 Aug 1876 and died 13 Feb 1962 in Walker County, Alabama. Buried at Oakman, Day cemetery, Alabama. George Pounds and Alice Day had issue, which was the tenth generation in America:

B4131241. Annie Pounds, first child and first daughter of George Washington Pounds and Alice Day, born 10 Dec 1896 in Walker County, Alabama.

B4131242. Irene Pounds, second child and second daughter of George Washington Pounds and Alice Day, born 24 Aug 1898 in Walker County, Alabama and died 10 May 1899 in Walker County, Alabama.

B4131243. Laura Ethel Pounds, third child and third daughter of George Washington Pounds and Alice Day, born 29 Aug 1900 in Walker County, Alabama and died 7 Sep 1900 in Walker County, Alabama.

B4131244. Griffin Pounds, fourth child and first son of George Washington Pounds and Alice Day, born 7 Aug 1901 in Walker County, Alabama and died 13 Jun 1926. Married in Walker County, Alabama to Louvena Windham. Griffin Pounds and Louvena Windham had issue, which was the eleventh generation in America:

B41312441. Raleigh Malcolm Pounds, first child and first son of Griffin Pounds and Louvena Windham, born 30 Jul 1926.

B41312442. Eloise Pounds, second child and first daughter of Griffin Pounds and Louvena Windham, date and place of birth unknown.

B41312443. O.C. Pounds, third child and second son of Griffin Pounds and Louvena Windham, date and place of birth unknown.

B41312444. Evelyn Pounds, fourth child and second daughter of Griffin Pounds and Louvena Windham, date and place of birth unknown.

B41312445. James Ray Pounds, fifth child and third son of Griffin Pounds and Louvena Windham, date and place of birth unknown.

B41312446. George Pounds, sixth child and fourth son of Griffin Pounds and Louvena Windham, date and place of birth unknown.

B41312447. Charlotte Pounds, seventh child and third daughter of Griffin Pounds and Louvena Windham, date and place of birth unknown.

B4131245. Clarence Pounds, fifth child and second son of George Washington Pounds and Alice Day, born 26 Apr 1903 in Walker County, Alabama and died Aug 1877 at Jasper, Walker County, Alabama. Married about 1925 in

13

Alabama to Annie Woods, daughter of Wiley Woods and Vergie Fuller, born 13 Mar 1907 in Alabama. Clarence Pounds and Annie Woods had issue, which was the eleventh generation in America:

B41312451. Juelette Charlotte Pounds, first child and first daughter of Clarence Pounds and Annie Woods, born 29 Jun 1926 in Walker County, Alabama. Married Howard Carr.

B41312452. Irene Merle Pounds, second child and second daughter of Clarence Pounds and Annie Woods, born 15 Feb 1928 in Walker County, Alabama. Married M.J. Philips.

B41312453. Shirley Ann Pounds, third child and third daughter of Clarence Pounds and Annie Woods, born 22 Jan 1936 in Walker County, Alabama and died 20 Feb 1936 in Walker County, Alabama.

B41312454. Connie Jo Pounds, fourth child and fourth daughter of Clarence Pounds and Annie Woods, born 30 Nov 1947 in Walker County, Alabama. Married Larry Thompson.

B4131246. George Murry Pounds, sixth child and third son of George Washington Pounds and Alice Day, born 17 Aug 1911 in Walker County, Alabama and died 2 Jan 1919 in Walker County, Alabama.

B413125. Ann Pounds, fifth child and third daughter of Raleigh Pounds and Martha Otey, born 10 Nov 1856 in Tuscaloosa County, Alabama.

B413126. Benjamin Pounds, sixth child and third son of Raleigh Pounds and Martha Otey, born 1864 in Alabama.

B41312. Raleigh W. Pounds, second child and first son of Merriman Pound and Mary White, born 30 Jul 1818 in Tuscaloosa County, Alabama and died 1911 in Tuscaloosa County, Alabama married secondly Elizabeth Riley. Raleigh Pounds and Elizabeth Riley had issue, which was the ninth generation in America:

B413121. Charley Pounds, first child and first son of Raleigh Pounds and Elizabeth Riley, born 1864 in Tuscaloosa County, Alabama. Married Angie Daniel. Charley Pounds and Angie Daniel had issue, which was the tenth generation in America:

B4131211. Lecil T. Pounds, first child and first son of Charley Pounds and Angie Daniel, date and place of birth unknown. Married Myrtle Beck.

B4131212. Lillian Pounds, second child and first daughter of Charley Pounds and Angie Daniel, date and place of birth unknown. Married Jack Knight.

B4131213. Richard Simpson Pounds, third child and second son of Charley Pounds and Angie Daniel, date and place of birth unknown.

B4131214. James Garland Pounds, Sr., fourth child and third son of Charley Pounds and Angie Daniel, date and place of birth unknown. Married Lois Tuggle. James Pounds and Lois Tuggle had issue, which was the eleventh generation in America:

B41312141. Betty G. Pounds, first child and first daughter of James Pounds and Lois Tuggle, date and place of birth unknown.

B41312142. Lora Elouise Pounds, second child and second daughter of James Pounds and Lois Tuggle, date and place of birth unknown. Married Jimmy Bagwell.

B41312143. Laura Joan Pounds, third child and third daughter of James Pounds and Lois Tuggle, date and place of birth unknown. Married L.T. Gurganus, Jr.

B41312144. Charlie Wheeler Pounds, fourth child and first son of James Pounds and Lois Tuggle, date and place of birth unknown. Married Judith Wasilevich.

B41312145. James Kenneth Pounds, fifth child and second son of James Pounds and Lois Tuggle, date and place of birth unknown. Married Doris Ann Evans.

B41312146. James Garland Pounds, Jr., sixth child and second son of James Pounds and Lois Tuggle, date and place of birth unknown. Married Janice Key.

B41312147. Roy Gale Pounds, seventh child and third son of James

15

Pounds and Lois Tuggle, date and place of birth unknown. Married Denise Olene Moore.

B41312148. Kathern Ann Pounds, eighth child and fourth daughter of James Pounds and Lois Tuggle, date and place of birth unknown.

B413121. Charley Pounds, first child and first son of Raleigh Pounds and Elizabeth Riley, date and place of birth unknown. Married secondly Janie Allen, date and place of birth unknown. Charley Pounds and Janie Allen had issue, which was the tenth generation in America:

B4131211. Gaby Bedford Pounds, first child and first son of Charley Pounds and Janie Allen, date and place of birth unknown.

B413122. Raleigh Pounds, Jr., second child and second son of Raleigh Pounds and Elizabeth Riley, date and place of birth unknown. Married Ann Lisenba.

B413123. Richard Pounds, third child and third son of Raleigh Pounds and Elizabeth Riley, date and place of birth unknown.

B413124. Gertrude Pounds, fourth child and first daughter of Raleigh Pounds and Elizabeth Riley, date and place of birth unknown. Married John Robertson. Married secondly Charlie Yates. Married thirdly Si Yagle.

B413125. Mary Elizabeth Pounds, fifth child and second daughter of Raleigh Pounds and Elizabeth Riley, date and place of birth unknown. Married Ed Ryan. They had issue, which was the tenth generation in America:

B4131251. Edward Ryan, first child and first son of Mary Pounds and Ed Ryan, date and place of birth unknown.

B4131252. Mildred E. Ryan, second child and first daughter of Mary Pounds and Ed Ryan, date and place of birth unknown.

B4131253. Minnie Alice Ryan, third child and second daughter of Mary Pounds and Ed Ryan, date and place of birth unknown.

B4131254. Raleigh J. Ryan, fourth child and second son of Mary Pounds and Ed Ryan, date and place of birth unknown.

B4131255. Newbern Ryan, fifth child and third son of Mary Pounds and Ed Ryan, date and place of birth unknown.

B413126. Dewey Pounds, sixth child and fourth son of Raleigh Pounds and Elizabeth Riley, date and place of birth unknown.

B41313. Eliza Pounds, third child and second daughter of Merriman Pound and Mary White, born 16 Jul 1820 in Clarke County, Georgia and died 24 Sep 1902. Buried Hopewell cemetery, Tuscaloosa County, Alabama. Married Alexander Simpson, born Aug 1817 in South Carolina and died Dec 1897.

B41314. Benjamin Pounds, fourth child and second son of Merriman Pound and Mary White, born about 1824 in Clarke County, Georgia and died about 1865. Married Emeline Dodson. Benjamin Pounds and Emeline Dodson had issue, which was the ninth generation in America:

B413141. Thomas Pounds, first child and first son of Benjamin Pounds and Emeline Dodson, date and place of birth unknown.

B413142. Henry Pounds, second child and second son of Benjamin Pounds and Emeline Dodson, date and place of birth unknown.

B413143. Sarah Pounds, third child and first daughter of Benjamin Pounds and Emeline Dodson, date and place of birth unknown.

B413144. William Pounds, fourth child and third son of Benjamin Pounds and Emeline Dodson, date and place of birth unknown.

B413145. Merryman Pounds, fifth child and fourth son of Benjamin Pounds and Emeline Dodson, date and place of birth unknown.

B413146. Benjamin Pounds, sixth child and fifth son of Benjamin Pounds and Emeline Dodson, date and place of birth unknown.

B41315. Mary Elizabeth Pounds, fifth child and third daughter of Merriman

Pound and Mary White, born Feb 1829 in Clarke County, Georgia and died about 1902. Married 15 Sep 1852 in Tuscaloosa County, Alabama to Durel L. Abston, born 1831 and died 1878 in Franklin County, Alabama. Buried Belgreen cemetery in Alabama. Mary Pounds and Durel Abston had issue, which was the ninth generation in America:

B413151. Joseph Alva Abston, first child and first son of Mary Pounds and Durel Abston, born 1855 and died 28 Feb 1946 in Franklin County, Alabama. Married 15 Aug 1876 to Mary Elizabeth Taylor. Married secondly 9 Dec 1897 to Annie Brewer. Joseph Abston and Mary Taylor had issue, which was the tenth generation in America:

B4131511. William Arthur Durel Abston, first child and first son of Joseph Abston and Mary Taylor, date and place of birth unknown. Married Georgia Ann Craven. William Abston and Georgia Craven had issue, which was the eleventh generation in America:

B41315111. Stella Abston, first child and first daughter of William Abston and Georgia Craven, date and place of birth unknown. Married Adell Epps. Stella Abston and Adell Epps had issue, which was the twelth generation in America:

B413151111. Glen Epps, first child and first son of Stella Abston and Adell Epps, date and place of birth unknown.

B413151112. Bob Epps, second child and second son of Stella Abston and Adell Epps, date and place of birth unknown.

B413151113. Bud Epps, third child and third son of Stella Abston and Adell Epps, date and place of birth unknown.

B413151114. Steve Epps, fourth child and fourth son of Stella Abston and Adell Epps, date and place of birth unknown.

B413151115. Jessie Mae Epps, fifth child and first daughter of Stella Abston and Adell Epps, date and place of birth unknown.

B413151116. Vera Epps, sixth child and second daughter of Stella Abston and Adell Epps, date and place of birth unknown.

B413151117. Melvin Epps, seventh child and fifth son of Stella Abston and Adell Epps, date and place of birth unknown.

B413151118. JoAnn Epps, eighth child and third daughter of Stella Abston and Adell Epps, date and place of birth unknown.

B413151119. Joyce Epps, ninth child and fourth daughter of Stella Abston and Adell Epps, date and place of birth unknown.

B4131511110. Venie Epps, tenth child and fifth daughter of Stella Abston and Adell Epps, date and place of birth unknown.

B41315112. Clarence Abston, second child and first son of William Abston and Georgia Craven, date and place of birth unknown. Married Dona Ray.

B41315113. Fred Abston, third child and second son of William Abston and Georgia Craven, date and place of birth unknown. Married Carrie ---. Fred Abston and Carrie --- had issue, which was the twelth generation in America:

B413151131. Martha Jean Abston, first child and first daughter of Fred Abston and Carrie ---, date and place of birth unknown.

B41315114. Lillie Abston, fourth child and second daughter of William Abston and Georgia Craven, date and place of birth unknown. Married Lesley English. Lillie Abston and Lesley English had issue, which was the twelth generation in America:

B413151141. James English, first child and first son of Lillie Abston and Lesley English, date and place of birth unknown.

B413151142. Bill English, second child and second son of Lillie Abston and Lesley English, date and place of birth unknown.

B413151143. Dan English, third child and third son of Lillie Abston and Lesley English, date and place of birth unknown.

B41315115. Thomas Denver Abston, fifth child and third son of William Abston and Georgia Craven, date and place of birth unknown. Married Martha B. Murphy. Thomas Abston and Martha Murphy had issue, which was the twelth generation in America:

B413151151. James A. Abston, first child and first son of Thomas Abston and Martha Murphy, date and place of birth unknown.

B413151152. Martha Geneva Abston, second child and first daughter of Thomas Abston and Martha Murphy, date and place of birth unknown.

B413151153. Sarah Ann Abston, third child and second daughter of Thomas Abston and Martha Murphy, date and place of birth unknown.

B41315116. Marvin Abston, sixth child and fourth son of William Abston and Georgia Craven, date and place of birth unknown. Married Rona Wilkes. Marvin Abston and Rona Wilkes had issue, which was the twelth generation in America.

B413151161. Gloria Abston, first child and first daughter of Marvin Abston and Rona Wilkes, date and place of birth unknown.

B413151162. Dorothy Abston, second child and second daughter of Marvin Abston and Rona Wilkes, date and place of birth unknown.

B413151163. James E. Abston, third child and first son of Marvin Abston and Rona Wilkes, date and place of birth unknown.

B413151164. William Abston, fourth child and second son of Marvin Abston and Rona Wilkes, date and place of birth unknown.

B41315117. Ollie Abston, seventh child and fifth daughter of William Abston and Georgia Craven, date and place of birth unknown. Married J.C. Jackson. Ollie Abston and J.C. Jackson had issue, which was the twelth generation in America:

B413151171. Jerry Jackson, first child and first son of Ollie Abston and J.C. Jackson, date and place of birth unknown.

B413151172. Fred Jackson, second child and second son of Ollie Abston and J.C. Jackson, date and place of birth unknown.

B413151173. William L. Jackson, third child and third son of Ollie Abston and J.C. Jackson, date and place of birth unknown.

B41315118. Ralph Abston, eight child and sixth son of William Abston and Georgia Craven, date and place of birth unknown. Married

Inez Cummings. Ralph Abston and Inez Cummings had issue, which was the twelth generation in America:

B413151181. Ralph Abston, first child and first son of Ralph Abston and Inez Cummings, date and place of birth unknown.

B41315119. Willow Dean Abston, ninth child and third daughter of William Abston and Georgia Craven, date and place of birth unknown. Married Forbes Shelmut. Willow Abston and Forbes Shelmut had issue, which was the twelth generation in America:

B413151191. Oscar W. Shelmut, first child and first son of Willow Abston and Forbes Shelmut, date and place of birth unknown.

B413151192. Jane Shelmut, second child and first daughter of Willow Abston and Forbes Shelmut, date and place of birth unknown.

B4131512. Leonard Abston, second child and second son of Joseph Abston and Mary Taylor, date and place of birth unknown. Married Lois Lawler. Leonard Abston and Lois Lawler had issue, which was the eleventh generation in America:

B41315121. Alva Abston, first child and first son of Leonard Abston and Lois Lawler, date and place of birth unknown.

B41315122. Della Mae Abston, second child and first daughter of Leonard Abston and Lois Lawler, date and place of birth unknown.

B4131513. Nannie Bell Abston third child and first daughter of Joseph Abston and Mary Taylor, date and place of birth unknown. Married Thomas Nix.

B4131514. John Henry Abston, third child and third son of Joseph Abston and Mary Taylor, date and place of birth unknown. Married Eula Zann. John Abston and Eula Zann had issue, which was the eleventh generation in America:

B41315141. Laverne Abston, first child and first daughter of John Abston and Eula Zann, date and place of birth unknown.

B413152.   Sarah Allie Abston, second child and first daughter of Mary Pounds and Durel Abston, born 1858 and died 1941.   Married 30 Jun 1903 at Wade Pounds residence in Tuscaloosa County, Alabama to N.J. Waldrop.

B413153.   Mary Jane Abston, third child and second daughter of Mary Pounds and Durel Abston, born 15 Jan 1861 and died 6 Aug 1946 in Franklin County, Alabama.   Buried in Russellville, Franklin County, Alabama.   Married James Henry Hargett.   Mary Abston and James Hargett had issue, which was the tenth generation in America:

B4131531.   William M. Hargett, first child and first son of Mary Abston and James Hargett, date and place of birth unknown.

B4131532.   Hilmar Hargett, second child and first daughter of Mary Abston and James Hargett, date and place of birth unknown.

B4131533.   Durel Hargett, third child and second son of Mary Abston and James Hargett, date and place of birth unknown.

B4131534.   Ocie Lee Hargett, fourth child and second daughter of Mary Abston and James Hargett, date and place of birth unknown.

B4131535.   Lillian L. Hargett, fifth child and third daughter of Mary Abston and James Hargett, date and place of birth unknown.

B4131536.   Arthur Plas Hargett, sixth child and third son of Mary Abston and James Hargett, date and place of birth unknown.

B4131537.   Celestial L. Hargett, seventh child and fourth daughter of Mary Abston and James Hargett, date and place of birth unknown.

B4131538.   Mary E. Hargett, eighth child and fifth daughter of Mary Abston and James Hargett, date and place of birth unknown.

B413154.   John Henry Abston, fourth child and second son of Mary Pounds and Durel Abston, born Jan 1875 and died 11 Nov 1939. Buried Big Hurricane cemetery, Alabama.   Married 22 Oct 1897 in Tuscaloosa County, Alabama to Nancy Pratt Abston, born 1865 and died 19 Nov 1961. Buried Big Hurricane cemetery, Alabama.   John Abston and Nancy Abston had issue, which was the tenth generation in America:

B4131541. Lera Abston, first child and first daughter of John Abston and Nancy Abston, born 22 Sep 1899. Married Roy McCoy. Lera Abston and Roy McCoy had issue, which was the eleventh generation in America:

B41315411. Wyman Eschol McCoy, first child and first son of Lera Abston and Roy McCoy, date and place of birth unknown. Married Ollie Stephens. Wyman McCoy and Ollie Stephens had issue, which was the twelth generation in America:

B413154111. Larry McCoy, first child and first son of Wyman McCoy and Ollie Stephens, date and place of birth unknown. Married Mary Hamilton. Larry McCoy and Mary Hamilton had issue, which was the thirteenth generation in America:

B41315141111. Michael Hamilton McCoy, first child and first son of Larry McCoy and Mary Hamilton, date and place of birth unknown.

B413154112. Brenda McCoy, second child and first daughter of Wyman McCoy and Ollie Stephens, date and place of birth unknown. Married Norman Smith. Brenda McCoy and Norman Smith had issue, which was the thirteenth generation in America:

B4131541121. Regina Ann Smith, first child and first daughter of Brenda McCoy and Norman Smith, date and place of birth unknown.

B4131541122. Norman Smith, Jr., second child and first son of Brenda McCoy and Norman Smith, date and place of birth unknown.

B4131541123. Joseph Bryan Smith, third child and second son of Brenda McCoy and Norman Smith, date and place of birth unknown.

B4131541124. Stephen Smith, fourth child and third son of Brenda McCoy and Norman Smith, date and place of birth unknown.

B4131541125. Rhonda L. Smith, fifth child and second daughter of Brenda

McCoy and Norman Smith, date and place of birth unknown.

B4131541126. Terri L. Smith, sixth child and third daughter of Brenda McCoy and Norman Smith, date and place of birth unknown.

B413154113. Susan Ray McCoy, third child and second daughter of Wyman McCoy and Ollie Stephens, date and place of birth unknown. Married Larry Melton. Married secondly Joseph W. Taglavore. Susan McCoy and Larry Melton had issue, which was the thirteenth generation in America:

B4131541131. Kenneth W. Melton, first child and first son of Susan McCoy and Larry Melton, date and place of birth unknown.

B413154113. Susan Ray McCoy, third child and second daughter of Wyman McCoy and Ollie Stephens, date and place of birth unknown. Married secondly to Joseph W. Taglavore. Susan McCoy and Joseph Taglavore had issue, which was the thirteenth generation in America:

B4131541131. Lisa Taglavore, first child and first daughter of Susan McCoy and Joseph Taglavore, date and place of birth unknown.

B4131541132. Dianna Taglavore, second child and second daughter of Susan McCoy and Joseph Taglavore, date and place of birth unknown.

B413154114. Margaret Ann McCoy, fourth child and third daughter of Wyman McCoy and Ollie Stephens, date and place of birth unknown. Married Bobby Hankins. Margaret McCoy and Bobby Hankins had issue, which was the thirteenth generation in America:

B4131541141. Renae Hankins, first child and first daughter of Margaret McCoy and Bobby Hankins, date and place of birth unknown.

B4131541142. Cory Hankins, second child and second daughter of Margaret McCoy and Bobby Hankins, date and place of birth unknown.

B41315412. Evelyn L. McCoy, second child and first daughter of Lera Abston and Roy McCoy, date and place of birth unknown. Married Lessie

Walker, Jr. Evelyn McCoy and Lessie Walker had issue, which was the twelth generation in America:

B413154121. Linda C. Walker, first child and first daughter of Evelyn McCoy and Lessie Walker, date and place of birth unknown. Married Robert Pettitt. Linda Walker and Robert Pettitt had issue, which was the thirteenth generation in America:

B4131541211. Dennis Pettitt, first child and first son of Linda Walker and Robert Pettitt, date and place of birth unknown.

B4131541212. Darryl Pettitt, second child and second son of Linda Walker and Robert Pettitt, date and place of birth unknown.

B4131541213. Duane Pettitt, third child and third son of Linda Walker and Robert Pettitt, date and place of birth unknown.

B4131541214. Darlene Pettitt, fourth child and first daughter of Linda Walker and Robert Pettitt, date and place of birth unknown.

B4131541215. Donna Pettitt, fifth child and second daughter of Linda Walker and Robert Pettitt, date and place of birth unknown.

B4131541216. Kathryn Pettitt, sixth child and third daughter of Linda Walker and Robert Pettitt, date and place of birth unknown.

B413154122. Sandra Gail Walker, second child and second daughter of Evelyn McCoy and Lessie Walker, date and place of birth unknown. Married Whitley Ridenour, Jr. Sandra Walker and Whitley Ridenour had issue, which was the thirteenth generation in America:

B4131541221. Steven Ridenour, first child and first son of Sandra Walker and Whitley Ridenour, date and place of birth unknown.

B4131541222. Suzanne Ridenour, second child and first daughter of Sandra Walker and Whitley Ridenour, date and place of birth unknown.

B413154123. Sharon L. Walker, third child and third daughter of Evelyn McCoy and Lessie Walker, date and place of birth unknown. Married Dennis Sterk. Sharon Walker and Dennis Sterk had issue, which was the thirteenth generation in America:

25

B4131541231. Stephanie Sterk, first child and first daughter of Sharon Walker and Dennis Sterk, date and place of birth unknown.

B4131541232. Danny Sterk, second child and first son of Sharon Walker and Dennis Sterk, date and place of birth unknown.

B4131541233. Matthew Sterk, third child and second son of Sharon Walker and Dennis Sterk, date and place of birth unknown.

B413154124. Paula Ann Walker, fourth child and fourth daughter of Evelyn McCoy and Lessie Walker, date and place of birth unknown. Married Kent Thompson. Paula Walker and Kent Thompson had issue, which was the thirteenth generation in America:

B4131541241. Shane Thompson, first child and first son of Paula Walker and Kent Thompson, date and place of birth unknown.

B41315413. Lillian E. McCoy, third child and second daughter of Lera Abston and Roy McCoy, date and place of birth unknown. Married Raiford M. Griffin. Lillian McCoy and Raiford Griffin had issue, which was the twelth generation in America:

B413154131. Steven Griffin, first child and first son of Lillian McCoy and Raiford Griffin, date and place of birth unknown. Married Joan Campora. Steven Griffin and Joan Campora had issue, which was the thirteenth generation in America:

B4131541311. Steven Griffin, first child and first son of Steven Griffin and Joan Campora, date and place of birth unknown.

B4131541312. Lauren Griffin, second child and first daughter of Steven Griffin and Joan Campora, date and place of birth unknown.

B4131541313. Lesa Griffin, third child and second daughter of Steven Griffin and Joan Campora, date and place of birth unknown.

B4131541314. Shawn Griffin, fourth child and second son of Steven Griffin and Joan Campora, date and place of birth unknown.

B413154132. Gary Griffin, second child and second son of Lillian McCoy and Raiford Griffin, date and place of birth unknown.

B41315414. Roy Maye McCoy, fourth child and third daughter of Lera Abston and Roy McCoy,

date and place of birth unknown. Married Adrian
Yoder. Roy Maye McCoy and Adrian Yoder had issue,
which was the twelth generation in America:
B413154141. Cynthia Yoder, first
child and first daughter of Roy Maye McCoy and
Adrian Yoder, date and place of birth unknown.
Married Randy Horton. Cynthia Yoder and Randy
Horton had issue, which was the thirteenth
generation in America:
B4131541411. Marcus Horton,
first child and first son of Cynthia Yoder and
Randy Horton, date and place of birth unknown.
B4131541412. John
Horton, second child and first son of Cynthia
Yoder and Randy Horton, date and place of birth
unknown.
B4131541413. Billy Horton,
third child and third son of Cynthia Yoder and
Randy Horton, date and place of birth unknown.
B413154142. Pamela Yoder,
second child and second daughter of Roy Maye McCoy
and Adrian Yoder, date and place of birth unknown.
Married John Lillard. Pamela Yoder and John
Lillard had issue, which was the thirteenth
generation in America:
B4131541421. Matthew Lillard,
first child and first son of Pamela Yoder and John
Lillard, date and place of birth unknown.
B4131542. William Abston, second child
and first son of John Abston and Nancy Abston,
born 26 Dec 1900. Married Pearl Price. William
Abston and Pearl Price had issue, which was the
eleventh generation in America:
B41315421. Elmer Hargrove Abston,
first child and first son of William Abston and
Pearl Price, born 30 Jul 1923 at Tuscaloosa,
Tuscaloosa County, Alabama. Married 12 Feb 1950
to Martha Emily Tissier, daughter of Henry P.
Tissier and Margaret Marciowski, born 14 Oct 1925.
Elmer Abston and Martha Tissier did not have
issue, but they did adopt a son, who was regarded
as the twelfth generation in America:
B413154211. Jim Abston
(adopted), first child and first son of Elmer
Abston and Martha Tissier, born 31 Oct 1957 in
Birmingham, Jefferson County, Alabama. Married 25

Aug 1978 in Birmingham, Jefferson County, Alabama to Laura Mundie. Jim Abston and Laura Mundie had issue, which was the thirteenth generation in America:

B4131542111. Valerie Abston, first child and first daughter of Jim Abston and Laura Mundie, date and place of birth unknown.

B4131542112. Rachel Abston, second child and second daughter of Jim Abston and Laura Mundie, date and place of birth unknown.

B41315422. Howell Abston, second child and second son of William Abston and Pearl Price, born 7 Aug 1925 in Tuscaloosa County, Alabama. Married Helen Watts Travis, date and place of birth unknown and died 26 Jun 1984 in Tuscaloosa, Tuscaloosa County, Alabama. Howell Abston and Helen Travis had issue, which was the twelth generation in America:

B413154221. Sheila Abston, first child and first daughter of Howell Abston and Helen Travis, born 23 Jun 1951 in Tuscaloosa, Tuscaloosa County, Alabama. Married 27 Jun 1969 to Sonny Owens. Sheila Abston and Sonny Owens had issue, which was the thirteenth generation in America:

B4131542211. Carrie Owens, first child and first daughter of Sheila Abston and Sonny Owens, date and place of birth unknown.

B4131542212. Amy Owens, second child and second daughter of Sheila Abston and Sonny Owens, date and place of birth unknown.

B413154222. Robert Abston, second child and first son of Howell Abston and Helen Travis, born 2 Dec 1949 in Tuscaloosa County, Alabama. Married Joann ---. Robert Abston and Joann --- had issue, which was the thirteenth generation in America:

B4131542221. Heath Abston, first child and first son of Robert Abston and Joann ---, date and place of birth unknown.

B413154223. Kenneth Abston, third child and second son of Howell Abston and Helen Travis, born 12 Jun 1953 in Tuscaloosa

County, Alabama. Married Debra Barger. Kenneth Abston and Debra Barger had issue, which was the thirteenth generation in America:

B4131542231. Lorie Abston, first child and first daughter of Kennth Abston and Debra Barger, date and place of birth unknown.

B4131542232. Dustin Abston, second child and first son of Kenneth Abston and Debra Barger, date and place of birth unknown.

B41315423. Mearline Abston, third child and first daughter of William Abston and Pearl Price, born 2 Jun 1927. Married 24 Feb 1946 to James Simmons, son of Ed Simmons and Erdeal ---, born 23 Apr 1926. Mearline Abston and James Simmons had issue, which was the twelth generation in America:

B413154231. Jimmy Simmons, first child and first son of Mearline Abston and James Simmons, born 11 Oct 1948 in Portsmouth, Virginia. Married Dorothy J. Hittle. Married secondly Anna Smith. Jimmy Simmons and Dorothy Hittle had issue, which was the thirteenth generation in America:

B4131542311. Michelle Simmons, first child and first daughter of Jimmy Simmons and Dorothy Hittle, date and place of birth unknown.

B413154231. Jimmy Simmons, first child and first son of Mearline Abston and James Simmons, born 11 Oct 1948 in Portsmouth, Virginia. Married secondly to Anna Smith, date and place of birth unknown. Jimmy Simmons and Anna Smith had issue, which was the thirteenth generation in America:

B4131542311. Bryan Simmons, first child and first son of Jimmy Simmons and Anna Smith, date and place of birth unknown.

B413154232. Teresa Simmons, second child and first daughter of Mearline Abston and James Simmons, born 12 Jul 1950 in Tuscaloosa County, Alabama. Married Wayne N. Langely. Teresa Simmons and Wayne Langely had issue, which was the thirteenth generation in America:

B4131542321. Ann Langely, first child and first daughter of Teresa Simmons and Wayne Langely, date and place of birth unknown.

B4131542322. Nicholas Langely, second child and first son of Teresa Simmons and Wayne Langely, date and place of birth unknown.

B4131542323. Jennifer Langely, third child and second daughter of Teresa Simmons and Wayne Langely, date and place of birth unknown.

B4131542324. Michael Langely, fourth child and second son of Teresa Simmons and Wayne Langely, date and place of birth unknown.

B413154233. David Simmons, third child and second son of Mearline Abston and James Simmons, born 12 Jul 1952 in Washington, D.C. Married Renee Ferguson. David Simmons and Renee Ferguson had issue, which was the thirteenth generation in America:

B4131542331. Christopher Simmons, first child and first son of David Simmons and Renee Ferguson, date and place of birth unknown.

B413154234. Bradford Simmons, fourth child and third son of Mearline Abston and James Simmons, born 3 Apr 1953 in Tuscaloosa County, Alabama. Married Vickie Avery. Bradford Simmons and Vickie Avery had issue, which was the thirteenth generation in America:

B4131542341. Heath Simmons, first child and first son of Bradford Simmons and Vickie Avery, date and place of birth unknown.

B4131542342. Jessie Simmons, second child and first daughter of Bradford Simmons and Vickie Avery, date and place of birth unknown.

B4131543. Carl Alvie Lee Abston, third child and second son of John Abston and Nancy Abston, born 9 Feb 1903. Married Lillie Mae Sartain. Carl Abston and Lillie Sartain had issue, which was the eleventh generation in America:

B41315431. James Dale Abston, first child and first son of Carl Abston and Lillie Sartain, born 4 Feb 1937 in Tuscaloosa County, Alabama. Married 2 Jun 1957 in Macon, Bibb County, Georgia to Barbara Ann Hopper, born 5 Jun 1935 in Macon, Bibb County, Georgia. James Abston and Barbara Hopper had issue, which was the twelfth generation in America:

B413154311. Sheri Lee Abston, first child and first daughter of James Abston and Barbara Hopper, born 20 Dec 1961 at Warner Robins, Houston County, Georgia.

B413154312. Laura Kimberly Abston, second child and second daughter of James Abston and Barbara Hopper, born 12 May 1965 at Warner Robins, Houston County, Georgia.

B41315432. Alvie Lee Abston, second child and second son of Carl Abston and Lillie Sartain, born 3 Jan 1930 in Tuscaloosa County, Alabama. Married 25 Jun 1950 in Columbus, Lowndes County, Mississippi to Betty Jean Phillips, daughter of Horace G. Phillips and Mary Lou Kerr. born 28 Dec 1933 at Gordo, Pickens County, Alabama. Alvie Abston and Betty Phillips had issue, which was the twelfth generation in America:

B413154321. Linda Gail Abston, first child and first daughter of Alvie Abston and Betty Phillips, born 17 Apr 1951 in Tuscaloosa County, Alabama. Married Barry Frank Sorrow. Linda Abston and Barry Sorrow had issue, which was the thirteenth generation in America:

B4131543211. David Allen Sorrow, first child and first son of Linda Abston and Barry Sorrow, date and place of birth unknown.

B413154322. Sharon Diane Abston, second child and second daughter of Alvie Abston and Betty Phillips, born 8 Nov 1954 at Oakland, Alameda County, California. Married George Brannen. Sharon Abston and George Brannen had issue, which was the thirteenth generation in America:

B4131543221. Lisa Danielle Brannen, first child and first daughter of Sharon Abston and George Brannen, date and place of birth unknown.

31

B413154323. James Michael Abston, third child and first son of Alvie Abston and Betty Phillips, born 4 Feb 1957 at Perry, Houston County, Alabama. Married Theresa J. Larkin.

B4131544. Eschol Elisha Abston, fourth child and third son of John Abston and Nancy, Abston, born 5 Oct 1905 in Tuscaloosa, Tuscaloosa County, Alabama and died 8 Apr 1968. Buried at Brookwood, Big Hurricane cemetery, Alabama. Married 18 Dec 1924 at Cedar Cove, Alabama to Flossie Gay Linebarger, daughter of William Alexander Linebarger and Dora Bell Gardner, born 3 Apr 1903 in Pickens County, Alabama and died 10 Jan 1981 in Tuscaloosa, Tuscaloosa County, Alabama. Buried at Memory Hill Gardens. Eschol Abston and Flossie Linebarger had issue, which was the eleventh generation in America:

B41315441. Emerlon Marine Abston, first child and first daughter of eschol Abston and Flossie Linebarger, born 26 Jan 1926 at Gilmore, Tuscaloosa County, Alabama. Married 3 Apr 1948 at Columbia, Houston County, Alabama to Revice Howell Snider. Emerlon Abston and Revice Snider had issue, which was the twelth generation in America:

B413154411. Caroll R. Snider, first child and first son of Emerlon Abston and Revice Snider, date and place of birth unknown. Married Nancy Boyd Rogers. Caroll Snider and Nancy Rogers had issue, which was the thirteenth generation in America:

B4131544111. Kim Snider, first child and first daughter of Caroll Snider and Nancy Rogers, date and place of birth unknown.

B4131544112. Tommy Rogers (stepson), date and place of birth unknown.

B4131544113. Tammy Rogers (stepdaughter), date and place of birth unknown.

B413154412. Debra K. Snider, second child and first daughter of Emerlon Abson and Revice Snider, date and place of birth unknown. Married Ronnie R. Britton. Debra Snider and Ronnie Britton had issue, which was the thirteenth generation in America:

B4131544121. Amy Britton, first child and first daughter of Debra Snider and Ronnie Britton, date and place of birth unknown. B4131544122. Lorie Britton, second child and second daughter of Debra Snider and Ronnie Britton, date and place of birth unknown.

B41315442. Lowell Abston, second child and second daughter of Eschol Abston and Flossie Linebarger, born 7 Dec 1927 at Howton, Tuscaloosa County, Alabama. Married 18 May 1958 at Columbus, Lowndes County, Mississippi to John Aubrey Craft, son of Dudley Craft and Cora Colson, born 13 Oct 1921 at Aliceville, Pickens County, Alabama and died 10 Aug 1982 at Eutaw, Greene County, Mississippi. Lowell Abston and John Craft had issue, which was the twelth generation in America:

B413154421. Lowell Virginia Craft, first child and first daughter of Lowell Abston and John Craft, born 21 Nov 1960 at Tuscaloosa, Tuscaloosa County, Alabama.

B413154422. John Aubrey Craft, second child and first son of Lowell Abston and John Craft, born 23 Dec 1962 at Tuscaloosa, Tuscaloosa County, Alabama. Married 22 Dec 1991 to Danah Cornett.

B413154423. Linda Suzanne Craft, third child and second daughter of Lowell Abston and John Craft, born 6 Oct 1965 at Tuscaloosa, Tuscaloosa County, Alabama. Married 18 Oct 1983 to George Kennard. Married secondly 6 Jun 1992 to Robert J. Hagan III.

B41315443. Rayburn Young Abston, third child and first son of Eschol Abston and Flossie Linebarger, born 8 Oct 1934 at Howton, Tuscaloosa County, Alabama and died 29 Dec 1934 at Howton, Tuscaloosa County, Alabama. Buried in Brookwood, Big Hurricane cemetery, Alabama.

B41316. Andrew Pounds, sixth child and third son of Merriman Pound and Mary White, born 5 Dec 1834 in Clarke County, Georgia. Married 5 Dec 1854 to Mary Black.

B41317. Wade A. Pounds, seventh child and fourth son of Merriman Pound and Mary White, born 16 Jan 1836 in Calhoun County, Alabama and died 30

Jan 1910 in Tuscaloosa, Tuscaloosa County, Alabama. Buried in Hopewell cemetery, Tuscaloosa County, Alabama. Married 28 Feb 1867 to Margaret Albright. Wade Pounds and Margaret Albright had issue, which was the ninth generation in America:

B413171. George Ann Pounds, first child and first daughter of Wade Pounds and Margaret Albright, date and place of birth unknown.

B413172. Nancy J. Pounds, second child and second daughter of Wade Pounds and Margaret Albright, date and place of birth unknown. Married John Holleyhand. Nancy Pounds and John Holleyhand had issue, which was the tenth generation in America:

B4131721. Steve Holleyhand, first child and first son of Nancy Pounds and John Holleyhand, date and place of birth unknown.

B4131722. William Holleyhand, second child and second son of Nancy Pounds and John Holleyhand, date and place of birth unknown.

B413173. Alex Dock Pounds, third child and first son of Wade Pounds and Margaret Albright, date and place of birth unknown. Married Ruhamie Crowder. Married secondly to unknown spouse. Alex Pounds and Ruhamie Crowder had issue, which was the tenth generation in America:

B4131731. A.D. Pounds, first child and first son of Alex Pounds and Ruhamie Crowder, date and place of birth unknown.

B4131732. Billy Gene Pounds, second child and second son of Alex Pounds and Ruhamie Crowder, date and place of birth unknown.

B4131733. Robert Pounds, third child and third son of Alex Pounds and Ruhamie Crowder, date and place of birth unknown.

B4131734. Myrtle Lee Pounds, fourth child and first daughter of Alex Pounds and Ruhamie Crowder, date and place of birth unknown.

B4131735. George Pounds, fifth child and fourth son of Alex Pounds and Ruhamie Crowder, date and place of birth unknown.

B4131736. Newbern Pounds, sixth child and fifth son of Alex Pounds and Ruhamie Crowder, date and place of birth unknown.

B4131737. L.V. Pounds, seventh child and sixth son of Alex Pounds and Ruhamie Crowder, date and place of birth unknown.

B413173. Alex Dock Pounds, third child and first son of Wade Pounds and Margaret Albright, married secondly to --- ---. Alex Pounds and his unknown spouse had issue, which was the tenth generation in America:

B4131731. Lester Pounds, first child and first son of Alex Pounds and --- ---, date and place of birth unknown.

B4131732. Chester Pounds, second child and second son of Alex Pounds and --- ---, born 19 Oct 1898 in Alabama and died Aug 1775 at Woodstock, Bibb County, Alabama.

B413174. William Wade L. Pounds, fourth child and second son of Wade Pounds and Margaret Albright, born 19 Mar 1876 and died 6 Dec 1953. Buried at Evergreen cemetery in Tuscaloosa, Tuscaloosa County, Alabama. Married 24 May 1903 in Tuscaloosa, Tuscaloosa County, Alabama to Daisy Agnes Cribbs. William Pounds and Daisy Cribbs had issue, which was the tenth generation in America:

B4131741. Jessie Jewell Pounds, first child and first daughter of William Pounds and Daisy Cribbs, date and place of birth unknown. Married M. Gifford.

B4131742. Arvill Ray Pounds, second child and first son of William Pounds and Daisy Cribbs, born 1906 and died 2 Mar 1949. Buried at Fulton, Enon Church cemetery, Georgia. Married 13 May 1930 to Tommie Norwood. Arvill Pounds and Tommie Norwood had issue, which was the eleventh generation in America:

B41317421. Don Pounds, first child and first son of Arvill Pounds and Tommie Norwood, date and place of birth unknown. Married Sara Ivey. Don Pounds and Sara Ivey had issue, which was the twelth generation in America:

B413174211. Janet Pounds, first child and first daughter of Don Pounds and Sara Ivey, date and place of birth unknown.

B413174212. Van Pounds, second child and first son of Don Pounds and Sara Ivey, date and place of birth unknown.

B413174213.   Lynn
Pounds, third child and second daughter of Don
Pounds and Sara Ivey, date and place of birth
unknown.

B4131743.   William   Wade   L.
Pounds, Jr., third child and second son of William
Wade Pounds, Sr., and Daisy Cribbs, date and place
of birth unknown. Married 7 Apr 1929 to Mildred
---.

B4131744. Thurman Pounds, fourth
child and third son of William Pounds and Daisy
Cribbs, date and place of birth unknown. Married
Alva Heniger.

B4131745. Ormand Pounds, fifth
child and fourth son of William Pounds and Daisy
Cribbs, date and place of birth unknown.

B41318.   Alva (Alley) P. Pounds, eighth
child and fifth son of Merriman Pound and Mary
White, born 22 Mar 1837 and died 30 Jul 1863 at
Gettysburg, Pennsylvania in the Civil War.

B41319. Victorine Pounds, ninth child and
fourth daughter of Merriman Pound and Mary White,
born Apr 1840 in Tuscaloosa, Tuscaloosa County,
Alabama and died 1941. Married 12 Jan 1871 in
Tuscaloosa, Tuscaloosa County, Alabama to Francis
J. Keene. Victorine Pounds and Francis Keene had
issue, which was the ninth generation in America:

B413191. Sidnie Simpson Keene, first
child and first son of Victorine Pounds and
Francis Keene, date and place of birth unknown.
Married Annie Lou Herring. Sidnie Keene and Annie
Herring had issue, which was the tenth generation
in America:

B4131911.   Edith Keene, first
child and first daughter of Sidnie Keene and Annie
Herring, date and place of birth unknown.

B4131912.   Emmett Keene, second
child and first son of Sidnie Keene and Annie
Herring, date and place of birth unknown.

B4131913.   Sydnia Keene, third
child and second daughter of Sidnie Keene and
Annie Herring, date and place of birth unknown.

B413192. William August Keene, second
child and second son of Victorine Pounds and
Francis Keene, date and place of birth unknown.

B413193. Ociola Keene, third child and first daughter of Victorine Pounds and Francis Keene, date and place of birth unknown. B413194. Francis Lee Keene, fourth child and third son of Victorine Pounds and Francis Keene, date and place of birth unknown. B413195. Malcolm Kemp Keene, fifth child and fourth son of Victorine Pounds and Francis Keene, date and place of birth unknown. Married Belle Green. Malcolm Keene and Belle Green had issue, which was the tenth generation in America:

B4131951. Ola Merle Keene, first child and first daughter of Malcolm Keene and Belle Green, date and place of birth unknown. B4131952. Lorene Keene, second child and second daughter of Malcolm Keene and Belle Green, date and place of birth unknown. B4131953. Velma Keene, third child and third daughter of Malcolm Keene and Belle Green, date and place of birth unknown.

B4131910. Sarah Harriet Pounds, tenth child and fifth daughter of Merriman Pound and Mary White, born about 1845 in Tuscaloosa County, Alabama. Married 26 Aug 1847 to an unknown spouse.

B4132. John T. (Jackey) Pound, second child and second of Richard Eli Pound and Mary Davidson, born 20 Dec 1786 in North Augusta, Aiken County, South Carolina and died 25 Dec 1881 in Gwinnett County, Georgia. Jackey is buried in the Old Pounds cemetery in Gwinnett County, Georgia. Married in Clarke County, Georgia to Christianna (Anna) Rainey, born in Georgia and died before 1840. John T. (Jackey) Pound was named after Richard's brother who died at an early age. Jackey married first Anna Rainey and then Marian Caldwell Mar 1824 in Gwinnett County, Georgia. Jackey Pound and Anna Rainey had issue, which was the eighth generation in America:

B41321. Marion Pounds, first child and first daughter of Jackey Pound and Anna Rainey, born 20 Dec 1811 Clarke County, Georgia and died 17 Apr 1877 in Georgia. Buried Pounds cemetery, Gwinnett County, Georgia. Married John Burney.

B41322. Mary Pounds, second child and second daughter of Jackey Pound and Anna Rainey, born about 1813 Clarke County, Georgia. Married Clayton Caldwell.

B41323. Eleanor Pounds, third child and third daughter of Jackey Pound and Anna Rainey, born about 1815 Clarke County, Georgia. Married Andrew Millican.

B41324. Attallia Pounds, fourth child and fourth daughter of Jackey Pound and Anna Rainey, date and place of birth unknown. Married Thomas Williams.

B41325. Richard Davis Pounds, fifth child and first son of Jackey Pound and Anna Rainey, born 5 Dec 1818 in South Carolina and died 15 Aug 1888 in Gwinnett County, Georgia. Buried in Pounds cemetery, Gwinnett County, Georgia. Married Nancy Norcepa Cordia, born 1 Sep 1822 in Georgia and died 9 Aug 1900 in Gwinnett County, Georgia. Buried in Pounds cemetery in Gwinnett County, Georgia. Richard Pounds and Nancy Cordia had issue, which was the ninth generation in America:

B413251. Pauline Ann Pounds, first child and first daughter of Richard Pounds and Nancy Cordia, born 1841 in Gwinnett County, Georgia.

B413252. Sylvester Pounds, second child and first son of Richard Pounds and Nancy Cordia, born 1842 in Gwinnett County, Georgia and died 1926 at Stone Mountain, Gwinnett County, Georgia. Married 8 Jun 1865 in DeKalb County, Georgia to Mary Elizabeth Ragsdale, born 25 Dec 1836 and died 23 Nov 1933. Sylvester Pounds and Mary Ragsdale had issue, which was the tenth generation in America:

B4132521. Ida Victoria Pounds, first child and first daughter of Sylvester Pounds and Mary Ragsdale, born 22 Jun 1866 in Georgia and died 5 Jun 1959 in Georgia. Married 1879 in Georgia to Benson (Bensie) Bolton, son of David Bolton and Margaret Ross, born 10 Aug 1845 in Georgia and died 1 Jan 1921 in Georgia. Ida Pounds and Bensie Bolton had issue, which was the eleventh generation in America:

B41325211.   Ruby
(twin) Bolton, first child and first daughter of
Ida Pounds and Bensie Bolton, born 3 Feb 1901 in
Georgia. Married 1927 in Georgia to Orville Akins
(Kit) McGee, son of John William McGee and Nancy
Caroline Russell, born 28 Oct 1887 in Georgia.
Ruby Bolton and Orville McGee had issue, which was
the twelth generation in America:
                    B413252111. Harold Victor
McGee, first child and first son of Ruby Bolton
and Orville Mcgee, born 1 Sep 1929. Married 1954
to Candis Ada Jackson, born 4 Sep 1935 in DeKalb
County, Georgia.
                    B413252112.. Loyd Orville
McGee, second child and second son of Ruby Bolton
and Orville McGee, born 21 Dec 1931. Married 1952
to Marilyn Bell Mewborn.
                    B413252113. Ruth Caroline
McGee, third child and first daughter of Ruby
Bolton and Orville McGee, born 10 Jan 1938.
Married 1956 to Roy Darrell Mullinax.
                    B41325212.   Julia   (twin)
Bolton, second child and second daughter of Ida
Pounds and Bensie Bolton, born 3 Feb 1901 in
Georgia. Married Frank Hamilton. Julia Bolton and
Frank Hamilton had issue, which was the twelth
generation in America:
                    B413252121.   Chester
Hamilton, first child and first son of Julia
Bolton and Frank Hamilton, date and place of birth
unknown.
                    B4132522. Eddie Pounds, second
child and first son of Sylvester Pounds and Mary
Ragsdale, date and place of birth unknown.
                    B4132523. John David Pounds,
third child and second son of Sylvester Pounds and
Mary Ragsdale, born 1869 and died 7 Feb 1925.
Married Leila Morris. John Pounds and Leila
Morris had issue, which was the eleventh
generation in America:
                    B41325231. Sadie Pounds,
first child and first daughter of John Pounds and
Leila Morris, date and place of birth unknown.
Married Curtis Adcock.

B4132524. Delia Amanda Pounds, fourth child and second daughter of Sylvester Pounds and Mary Ragsdale, born 1870 and died 1943.

B4132525. James W. Pounds, fifth child and third son of Sylvester Pounds and Mary Ragsdale, born 31 Aug 1874 and died 1 Apr 1951. Married Maggie Lauretta Corley, born 14 Mar 1882 in Gwinnett County, Georgia and died 16 Feb 1920. Married secondly 8 Jan 1921 to Ida Bray. James Pounds and Maggie Corley had issue, which was the eleventh generation in America:

B41325251. James Tilly Pounds, first child and first son of James Pounds and Maggie Corley, born 18 Aug 1906 and died Sep 1912.

B41325252. Georgia Pounds, second child and first daughter of James Pounds and Maggie Corley, born 8 Apr 1908. Married Eddie Warnock. Georgia Pounds and Eddie Warnock had issue, which was the twelth generation in America:

B413252521. Jimmie Lou Warnock, first child and first daughter of Georgia Pounds and Eddie Warnock, born 23 Feb 1932. Married --- Poss. Jimmie Warnock and --- Poss had issue, which was the thirteenth generation in America:

B4132525211. Jerry David Poss, first child and first son of Jimmie Warnock and --- Poss, born 10 Mar 1952.

B4132525212. Beverly Jean Poss, second child and first daughter of Jimmie Warnock and --- Poss, born 5 Jan 1956.

B41325253. Myrtice Pounds, third child and second daughter of James Pounds and Maggie Corley, born 9 Oct 1910. Married 27 Sep 1946 to Charles William West. Myrtice Pounds and Charles West had issue, which was the twelfth generation in America:

B413252531. Nancy Carol West, first child and first daughter of Myrtice Pounds and Charles West, born and died 5 Jun 1947.

B413252532. Charles William West, Jr., second child and first son of Myrtice Pounds and Charles West, born 17 May 1948.

B413252533. Gloria Jean West, third child and second daughter of Myrtice Pounds and Charles West, born 13 Jan 1950. Married --- Odom.

B4132525. James W. Pounds, fifth child and third son of Sylvester Pounds and Mary Ragsdale, born 31 Aug 1874 and died 1 Apr 1951. Married secondly 8 Jan 1921 to Ida Bray, born 22 Aug 1889 and died 28 Jul 1970. James Pounds and Ida Bray had issue, which was the eleventh generation in America:

B41325251. James Donald Pounds, first child and first son of James Pounds and Ida Bray, born 11 Aug 1923. Married 30 Jun 1946 to Teresita Blardondy. James Pounds and Teresita Blardondy had issue, which was the twelth generation in America:

B413252511. Caroline Charlotte Pounds, first child and first daughter of James Pounds and Teresita Blardondy, born 2 Jul 1947. Married Robert Russell Taylor. Caroline Pounds and Robert Taylor had issue, which was the thirteenth generation in America:

B4132525111. Robert Russell Taylor, Jr., first child and first son of Caroline Pounds and Robert Taylor, born 14 Apr 1972.

B4132525112. Dawn Lorraine Taylor, second child and first daughter of Caroline Pounds and Robert Taylor, born 17 Nov 1974.

B413252512. James Donald Pounds, Jr., second child and first son of James Pounds and Teresita Blardondy, born 5 Dec 1948. Married 31 May 1968 to Helen Diana Storey. James Pounds and Helen Storey had issue, which was the thirteenth generation in America:

B4132525121. James Donald Pounds III, first child and first son of James Pounds and Helen Storey, born 30 Nov 1969.

B4132525122. Jonathan Edward Pounds, second child and second son of James Pounds and Helen Storey, born 24 May 1974.

B413252513. Rebecca Elaine Pounds, third child and second daughter of James Pounds and Teresita Blardondy, born 22 Aug 1952.

B413252514. Michael Lester Pounds, fourth child and second son of James Pounds and Teresita Blardondy, born 8 Sep 1957.

B413252515. Christina Rene Pounds, fifth child and third daughter of James Pounds and Teresita Blardondy, born 26 Nov 1972.

B41325252. Elton Ray Pounds, second child and second son of James Pounds and Ida Bray, born 1 Dec 1924. Married 4 Jan 1947 to Lucille Thomas. Elton Pounds and Lucille Thomas had issue, which was the twelth generation in America:

B413252521. Marcia Louise Pounds, first child and first daughter of Elton Pounds and Lucille Thomas, born 20 Jan 1951. Married 6 Jun 1971 to Olen Neal Malone.

B413252522. Elton Ray Pounds, Jr., second child and first son of Elton Pounds and Lucille Thomas, born 25 Jul 1954.

B413252523. Raymond Harrold Pounds, third child and second son of Elton Pounds and Lucille Thomas, born 7 Jul 1964.

B41325253. Charlotte Inez Pounds, third child and first daughter of James Pounds and Ida Bray, born 7 Oct 1926. Married 12 Jan 1951 to Arthur Ireland. Charlotte Pounds and Arthur Ireland had issue, which was the twelfth generation in America:

B413252531. David Wayne Ireland, first child and first son of Charlotte Pounds and Arthur Ireland, born 20 Apr 1953.

B413252532. Susan May Ireland, second child and first daughter of Charlotte Pounds and Arthur Ireland, born 11 Oct 1955. Married 5 Apr 1975 to James Terry Wright.

B41325254. Betty Sue Pounds, fourth child and second daughter of James Pounds and Ida Bray, born 7 Oct 1928. Married 21 Dec 1946 to John Marlowe. Betty Pounds and John Marlowe had issue, which was the twelfth generation in America:

B413252541. John Pierce Marlowe, first child and first son of Betty Pounds and John Marlowe, born 23 May 1962.

B413252542. William Lance Marlowe, second child and second son of Betty Pounds and John Marlowe, born 3 Jan 1965.

B4132526. Charlie Pounds, sixth child and fourth son of Sylvester Pounds and Mary Ragsdale, born 1877 in Georgia and died 1930.

B4132527. Jenny Pounds, seventh child and third daughter of Sylvester Pounds and Mary Ragsdale, born 1878 and died 1902.

B4132528. Mary Elizabeth Pounds, eighth child and fourth daughter of Sylvester Pounds and Mary Ragsdale, born 25 Feb 1881 in Gwinnett County, Georgia and died 7 Oct 1957. Married 14 Oct 1906 in Fulton County, Georgia to Arthur T. Harris, Sr., born 28 Oct 1881 and died 26 Jul 1962. Buried at Decatur, DeKalb County, Georgia. Mary Pounds and Arthur Harris had issue, which was the eleventh generation in America:

B41325281. Arthur T. Harris, Jr., first child and first son of Mary Pounds and Arthur Harris, born 21 Jul 1907 in Bibb County, Georgia. Married 17 Jan 1931 in Fulton County, Georgia to Nell Miner, born 3 Mar 1906. Arthur Harris and Nell Miner had issue, which was the twelth generation in America:

B413252811. Betty Lake Harris, first child and first daughter of Arthur Harris and Nell Miner, born 14 Mar 1932. Married 5 Feb 1956 to Lt. John H. Fellerhoff. Betty Harris and John Fellerhoff had issue, which was the thirteenth generation in America:

B4132528111. Gretchen Fellerhoff, first child and first daughter of Betty Harris and John Fellerhoff, born 2 Dec 1956.

B4132528112. Karen Fellerhoff, second child and second daughter of Betty Harris and John Fellerhoff, born 15 Jul 1959.

B413252812. Patricia Harris, second child and second daughter of Arthur Harris and Nell Miner, born 23 Sep 1937. Married 3 Jun 1960 to William K. Noland. Patricia Harris and William Noland had issue, which was the thirteenth generation in America:

B4132528121. Nancy Noland, first child and first daughter of Patricia Harris and William Noland, born 15 Apr 1963.

B4132528122. Catherine Noland, second child and second daughter of Patricia Harris and William Noland, born 11 May 1965.

B4132528123. Suzanne Noland, third child and third daughter of Patricia Harris and William Noland, born 11 Feb 1971.

B41325282. Evelyn Harris, second child and first daughter of Mary Pounds and Arthur Harris, born 15 Oct 1909 and died 2 Sep 1962. Married 5 Apr 1930 to Lewis Parr, date of birth unknown, but he died in 1972. Evelyn Harris and Lewis Parr had issue, which was the twelth generation in America:
B413252821. Evelyn E. Parr, first child and first daughter of Evelyn Harris and Lewis Parr, born 12 Jul 1932. Married B.J. Gladden. Evelyn Parr and B.J. Gladden had issue, which was the thirteenth generation in America:
B4132528211. Cindy (twin) Gladden, first child and first daughter of Evelyn Parr and B.J. Gladden, born 2 Oct 1957.
B4132528212. Tandy (twin) Gladden, second child and second daughter of Evelyn Parr and B.J. Gladden, born 2 Oct 1957.
B41325283. Ethlyn Kate Harris, third child and second daughter of Mary Pounds and Arthur Harris, born 3 Jun 1912 in Fulton County, Georgia. Married 20 Nov 1933 to John E. Ashworth, date of birth unknown, but he died 11 Apr 1960. Ethlyn Harris and John Ashworth had issue, which was the twelth generation in America:
B413252831. Robert A. (twin) Ashworth, first child and first son of Ethlyn Harris and John Ashworth, born 11 Apr 1934. Married 29 Jul 1962 to Julie Webb. Robert Ashworth and Julie Webb had issue, which was the thirteenth generation in America:
B4132528311. Kathryn Ashworth, first child and first daughter of Robert Ashworth and Julie Webb, born 5 Oct 1963.
B4132528312. John W. Ashworth, second child and first son of Robert Ashworth and Julie Webb, born 15 May 1965.
B413252832. Richard W. (twin) Ashworth, second child and second son of Ethlyn Harris and John Ashworth, born and died 11 Apr 1934.
B413252833. June Ethlyn Ashworth, third child and first daughter of Ethlyn Harris and John Ashworth, born 29 Oct 1941.
B41325284. Dorothy Marie Harris, fourth child and third daughter of Mary Pounds and Arthur Harris, born 10 Jan 1915 in Fulton County, Georgia. Married 6 Jan 1939 to George

Lallerstedt, date of birth unknown, but he died 31 May 1964. Married secondly 9 Jan 1969 to Benjamin L. Winkles. Dorothy Harris and George Lallerstedt had issue, which was the twelth generation in America:

B413252841. George Lawson Lallerstedt, first child and first son of Dorothy Harris and George Lallerstedt, born 7 Feb 1942. Married 30 Jun 1964 to Linda McGinnis. George Lallerstedt and Linda McGinnis had issue, which was the thirteenth generation in America:

B4132528411. Troy Lallerstedt, first child and first son of George Lallerstedt and Linda McGinnis, date and place of birth unknown.

B4132528412. Terry Lallerstedt, second child and second son of George Lallerstedt and Linda McGinnis, date and place of birth unknown.

B413252842. Jackson Lewis Lallerstedt, second child and second son of Dorothy Harris and George Lallerstedt, born 2 Aug 1944. Married 14 May 1962 to Susan Gardner. Jackson Lallerstedt and Susan Gardner had issue, which was the thirteenth generation in America:

B4132528421. Donna Lallerstedt, first child and first daughter of Jackson Lallerstedt and Susan Gardner, date and place of birth unknown.

B4132528422. Beth Lallerstedt, second child and second daughter of Jackson Lallerstedt and Susan Gardner, date and place of birth unknown.

B413252843. John Lamar Lallerstedt, third child and third son of Dorothy Harris and George Lallerstedt, born 1 Feb 1952.

B413252844. Mack Harris Lallerstedt, fourth child and fourth son of Dorothy Harris and George Lallerstedt, born 24 May 1954. Married 19 Oct 1974 to Anne M. Waters. Mack Lallerstedt and Anne Waters had issue, which was the thirteenth generation in America:

B4132528441. Patricia Anne Lallerstedt, first child and first daughter of Mack Lallerstedt and Anne Waters, date and place of birth unknown.

B41325285. Sarah Helen Harris, fifth child and fourth daughter of Mary Pounds and Arthur Harris, born 3 Jan 1920 in Fulton County, Georgia. Married 9 Jan 1940 in DeKalb County, Georgia to Carl Vanek. Sarah Harris and Carl Vanek had issue, which was the twelth generation in America:

B413252851. Carl Vanek, Jr., first child and first son of Sarah Harris and Carl Vanek, date and place of birth unknown.

B41325286. Sylvia Lucile Harris, sixth child and fifth daughter of Mary Pounds and Arthur Harris, born 26 Sep 1923 in DeKalb County, Georgia. Married 17 Jan 1942 in DeKalb County, Georgia to John T. Avera, born 18 Dec 1917 in Dooly County, Georgia. Sylvia Harris and John Avera had issue, which was the twelth generation in America:

B413252861. Sylvia E. Avera, first child and first daughter of Sylvia Harris and John Avera, born 17 Jan 1943. Married 10 Oct 1964 to Ronald I. Bailey. Sylvia Avera and Ronald Bailey had issue, which was the thirteenth generation in America:

B4132528611. Rhonda F. Bailey, first child and first daughter of Sylvia Avera and Ronald Bailey, born 4 Aug 1965.

B413252862. Tandy L. Avera, second child and second daughter of Sylvia Harris and John Avera, born 19 Dec 1945. Married 24 Oct 1964 to James R. Moore. Tandy Avera and James Moore had issue, which was the thirteenth generation in America:

B4132528621. Christa Anne Moore, first child and first daughter of Tandy Avera and James Moore, born 23 Apr 1972.

B4132528622. Linda Elizabeth Moore, second child and second daughter of Tandy Avera and James Moore, born 5 Oct 1973.

B413252863. Deborah Anne Avera, third child and third daughter of Sylvia Harris and John Avera, born 15 Oct 1954.

B4132529. Lula Mae Pounds, ninth child and fifth daughter of Sylvester Pounds and Mary Ragsdale, born 1882 and died 1914. Married 8 May 1908 to Charlie Henry Mauldin. Lula Pounds and Charlie Mauldin had issue, which was the eleventh generation in America:

B41325291. Henry Sylvester Mauldin, first child and first son of Lula Pounds and Charlie Mauldin, born 5 Jul 1909 and died Nov 1974. Married 1 Sep 1972 to Emma Rhodes.

B41325292. Lula Lois Mauldin, second child and first daughter of Lula Pounds and Charlie Mauldin, born 1911 and died 1913.

B4132530. Richard Eli Pounds, tenth child and fifth son of Sylvester Pounds and Mary Ragsdale, born 18 May 1885. Married 10 Nov 1907 to Henri Gradie Jackson, born 29 May 1891. Richard Pounds and Henri Jackson had issue, which was the eleventh generation in America:

B41325301. Bertha Rebecca Pounds, first child and first daughter of Richard Pounds and Henri Jackson, born 6 Feb 1910. Married 27 Feb 1927 to Charles Nicholas Bray, born 2 Apr 1908. Bertha Pounds and Charles Bray had issue, which was the twelth generation in America:

B413253011. Joe Nicholas Bray, first child and first son of Bertha Pounds and Charles Bray, born 10 May 1929. Married 4 Jun 1950 at Clayton, Rabun County, Georgia to Betty Williamson.

B413253012. Bobby Dean Bray, second child and second son of Bertha Pounds and Charles Bray, born 13 Jul 1934. Married 14 Dec 1952 in Fulton County, Georgia to Beverly Smith.

B413253013. Rebecca Annette Bray, third child and first daughter of Bertha Pounds and Charles Bray, born 27 Aug 1936. Married 11 Jun 1955 at Clayton, Rabun County, Georgia to Benny Chambers. Rebecca Bray and Benny Chambers had issue, which was the thirteenth generation in America:

B4132530131. Greg Chambers, first child and first son of Rebecca Bray and Benny Chambers, date and place of birth unknown.

B4132530132. Keith Chambers, second child and second son of Rebecca Bray and Benny Chambers, date and place of birth unknown.

B413253014. Larry Eli Bray, fourth child and third son of Bertha Pounds and Charles

Bray, born 25 Aug 1938. Married in Fulton County, Georgia to Ruth Mitchell.

B413253015. Charles Kenneth Bray, fifth child and fourth son of Bertha Pounds and Charles Bray, born 2 Jan 1940. Married 11 Jun 1961 in Clayton County, Georgia to Martha Cash.

B413253016. Grady Jackson Bray, sixth child and fifth son of Bertha Pounds and Charles Bray, date and place of birth unknown.

B41325302. Gradie Louise Pounds, second child and second daughter of Richard Pounds and Henri Jackson, born 16 Sep 1911. Married 3 Apr 1931 to Charles Douglas Garner, born 10 Jul 1909 and died 20 Nov 1957. Gradie Pounds and Charles Garner had issue, which was the twelth generation in America:

B413253021. Betty Louise Garner, first child and first daughter of Gradie Pounds and Charles Garner, born 18 Oct 1931. Married Jun 1951 to Robert A. Townley. Betty Garner and Robert Townley had issue, which was the thirteenth generation in America:

B4132530211. Grace Ann Townley, first child and first daughter of Betty Garner and Robert Townley, date and place of birth unknown.

B413253022. Charles Douglas Garner, Jr., second child and first son of Gradie Pounds and Charles Garner, date and place of birth unknown. Married Sep 1958 to Elizabeth Jannett Bennett. Charles Garner and Elizabeth Bennett had issue, which was the thirteenth generation in America:

B4132530221. Beth Garner, first child and first daughter of Charles Garner and Elizabeth Bennett, date and place of birth unknown.

B4132530222. Cynthia (twin) Garner, second child and second daughter of Charles Garner and Elizabeth Bennett, date and place of birth unknown.

B4132530223. Cathy (twin) Garner, third child and third daughter of Charles Garner and Elizabeth Bennett, date and place of birth unknown.

B4132530224. Mark Garner, fourth child and first son of Charles Garner and

Elizabeth Bennett, date and place of birth unknown.

B413253023. Brenda Ann Garner, third child and second daughter of Gradie Pounds and Charles Garner, born 14 Sep 1944. Married Jul 1962 to Troy E. Bailey. Brenda Garner and Troy Bailey had issue, which was the thirteenth generation in America:

B4132530231. Mike Bailey, first child and first son of Brenda Garner and Troy Bailey, date and place of birth unknown.

B41325303. Mary Elizabeth Pounds, third child and third daughter of Richard Pounds and Henri Jackson, born 24 Dec 1914. Married 11 Mar 1933 to Henry Grady Lyon, born 16 Oct 1909. Mary Pounds and Henry Lyon had issue, which was the twelth generation in America:

B413253031. Peggy Elizabeth Lyon, first child and first daughter of Mary Pounds and Henry Lyon, born 4 Mar 1935.

B413253032. Ethel Maye Lyon, second child and second daughter of Mary Pounds and Henry Lyon, born 17 Jan 1939. Married 23 Jul 1960 to Clyde Jackson Eaton, born 31 Mar 1938. Ethel Lyon and Clyde Eaton had issue, which was the thirteenth generation in America:

B4132530321. Jackson Lyon Eaton, first child and first son of Ethel Lyon and Clyde Eaton, born 19 Apr 1962.

B4132530322. Todd Richard Eaton, second child and second son of Ethel Lyon and Clyde Eaton, born 3 Jun 1965.

B4132530323. Merrie Beth Eaton, third child and first daughter of Ethel Lyon and Clyde Eaton, born 26 Apr 1967.

B41325304. Richard Everett Pounds, fourth child and first son of Richard Pounds and Henri Jackson, born 3 Mar 1916. Married 15 Jul 1934 to Mary Gibbs Coker, born 4 May 1918. Married secondly 25 Jan 1941 to Edna Cofer. Richard Pounds and Mary Coker had issue, which was the twelth generation in America:

B413253041. Richard Gib Pounds, first child and first son of Richard Pounds and Mary Coker, born 17 Oct 1935. Married 22 Dec 1956 to Rachel Crumbley. Richard Pounds and Rachel

Crumbley had issue, which was the thirteenth generation in America:

B4132530411. Richard Gib Pounds, Jr., first child and first son of Richard Pounds and Rachel Crumbley, born 8 Feb 1958.

B4132530412. Charles Randall Pounds, second child and second son of Richard Pounds and Rachel Crumbley, born 30 Jan 1961.

B4132530413. James Russell Pounds, third child and third son of Richard Pounds and Rachel Crumbley, born 19 Dec 1963.

B4132530414. Mary Robin Pounds, fourth child and first daughter of Richard Pounds and Rachel Crumbley, born 10 Oct 1973.

B413253042. Ronald Sylvester Pounds, second child and second son of Richard Pounds and Mary Coker, born 8 Feb 1939. Married 8 Mar 1958 to Angel Davenport. Ronald Pounds and Angel Davenport had issue, which was the thirteenth generation in America:

B4132530421. Rhonda Lee Pounds, first child and first daughter of Ronald Pounds and Angel Davenport, born 29 Jun 1959.

B4132530422. Ronald Sylvester Pounds, Jr., second child and first son of Ronald Pounds and Angel Davenport, born 8 Aug 1960.

B413253043. Mary Pounds, third child and first daughter of Richard Pounds and Mary Coker, date and place of birth unknown.

B41325304. Richard Everett Pounds, fourth child and first son of Richard Pounds and Henri Jackson, born 3 Mar 1916. Married secondly 25 Jan 1941 to Edna Cofer, born 12 Jul 1923. Richard Pounds and Edna Cofer had issue, which was the twelth generation in America:

B413253041. Jerry Everett Pounds, first child and first son of Richard Pounds and Edna Cofer, born 4 May 1943. Married Carol Sorrowes. Married secondly 1968 to Beth Storey. Jerry Pounds and Beth Storey had issue, which was the thirteenth generation in America:

B4132530411. Jason Pounds, first child and first son of Jerry Pounds and Beth Storey, born 24 Jul 1970.

B413253042. Shelia Pounds, second child and first daughter of Richard Pounds and

Edna Cofer, born 20 Nov 1950. Married Ray Wasson. Married secondly to Jim Skelton. Shelia Pounds and Ray Wasson had issue, which was the thirteenth generation in America:

B4132530421. Shelia Marlean Wasson, first child and first daughter of Shelia Pounds and Ray Wasson, date and place of birth unknown.

B413253043. Gloria Denise Pounds, third child and second daughter of Richard Pounds and Edna Cofer, born 24 Apr 1961.

B41325305. Robert Sylvester Pounds, fifth child and second son of Richard Pounds and Henri Jackson, born 1 Feb 1921. Married 28 May 1939 to Barbara Anderson, born 12 Feb 1922. Robert Pounds and Barbara Anderson had issue, which was the twelth generation in America:

B413253051. Barbara Olivia Pounds, first child and first daughter of Robert Pounds and Barbara Anderson, born 20 Nov 1940. Married 21 Jul 1960 to Norman Gene Richards, born 1 Jul 1939. Married secondly 4 Aug 1972 to Wendell I. Parker. Barbara Pounds and Norman Richards had issue, which was the thirteenth generation in America:

B4132530511. Gina Olivia Richards, first child and first daughter of Barbara Pounds and Norman Richards, born 23 May 1961.

B413253052. Robert Sylvester Pounds, Jr., second child and first son of Robert Pounds and Barbara Anderson, born 27 Mar 1944. Married 27 Apr 1962 to Sandra Lee Burton, born 28 Oct 1945. Robert Pounds and Sandra Burton had issue, which was the thirteenth generation in America:

B4132530521. Deborah Lee Pounds, first child and first daughter of Robert Pounds and Sandra Burton, born 25 Apr 1963.

B4132530522. Heather Lee Pounds, second child and second daughter of Robert Pounds and Sandra Burton, born 15 Feb 1971.

B413253053. Richard Thomas Pounds, third child and second son of Robert Pounds and Barbara Anderson, born and died 29 Jul 1948.

B4132531. Grover Franklin Pounds, eleventh

51

child and sixth son of Sylvester Pounds and Mary Ragsdale, born 1887 and died 1932.

B4132532. Albert Pounds, twelfth child and seventh son of Sylvester Pounds and Mary Ragsdale, born 19 Sep 1893 in Georgia and died Aug 1973 at Doraville, DeKalb County, Georgia. Married 1918 to Ina Womack, born 1898 and died 15 Feb 1957.

B413253. Lavicy Jane Pounds, third child and second daughter of Richard Pounds and Nancy Cordia, born 1846 in Gwinnett County, Georgia.

B413254. Mary Elizabeth (twin) Pounds, fourth child and third daughter of Richard Pounds and Nancy Cordia, born 25 Oct 1849 in Gwinnett County, Georgia and died 3 Sep 1919 in Georgia. Buried at Liberty Baptist cemetery in Georgia. Married 12 Dec 1867 in Gwinnett County, Georgia to John Richard Cain, born 19 Aug 1848 in Gwinnett County, Georgia and died 18 Dec 1920 in Georgia. Buried in Liberty Baptist cemetery in Georgia. Mary Pounds and John Cain had issue, which was the tenth generation in America:

B4132541. Thomas Leonard Cain, first child and first son of Mary Pounds and John Cain, born 14 Feb 1869 in Georgia and died 16 Nov 1939 in Georgia. Married 1889 to Lillier A. Minor, date and place of birth unknown and died 1941 in Brunswick, Glynn County, Georgia. Thomas Cain and Lillier Minor had issue, which was the eleventh generation in America:

B41325411. Arthur B. Cain, first child and first son of Thomas Cain and Lillier Minor, date and place of birth unknown.

B41325412. Era Cain, second child and first daughter of Thomas Cain and Lillier Minor, date and place of birth unknown. Married Wiley Williams.

B41325413. Verlon Cain, third child and second son of Thomas Cain and Lillier Minor, date and place of birth unknown.

B41325414. Lester Cain, fourth child and third son of Thomas Cain and Lillier Minor, date and place of birth unknown.

B41325415. Hoyt Cain, fifth child and fourth son of Thomas Cain and Lillier Minor, date and place of birth unknown.

B41325416. Thomas Leonard Cain, Jr., sixth child and fifth son of Thomas Cain and Lillier Minor, born 14 Feb 1869 in Georgia and died 16 Nov 1939 in Georgia.

B41325417. Willie Cain, seventh child and sixth son of Thomas Cain and Lillier Minor, date and place of birth unknown and died 1979. Married --- Remer. Married secondly Eula ------.

B41325418. Bernice Cain, eighth child and second daughter of Thomas Cain and Lillier Minor, date and place of birth unknown. Married Alex Lee McPherson.

B41325419. Aldora Cain, ninth child and third daughter of Thomas Cain and Lillier Minor, date and place of birth unknown. Married Wilbur Dunman.

B4132542. John Davis Cain, second child and second son of Mary Pounds and John Cain, born 15 Oct 1870 in Georgia and died 14 Sep 1936 in Georgia. Married 1892 to Margaret (Maggie) Minor, born 21 Apr 1874 in Georgia and died 29 Jan 1966 at Norcross, Fulton County, Georgia. John Cain and Margaret Minor had issue, which was the eleventh generation in America:

B41325421. Annie Belle Cain, first child and first daughter of John Cain and Margaret Minor, date and place of birth unknown.

B41325422. Ethel Cain, second child and second daughter of John Cain and Margaret Minor, date and place of birth unknown. Married John Miller Ivey, born 3 Oct 1899 in Baker County, Georgia and died 17 Sep 1900 in Baker County, Georgia. Buried Ivey cemetery.

B41325423. Thelma C. Cain, third child and third daughter of John Cain and Margaret Minor, date and place of birth unknown. Married Robert B. Logan.

B41325424. Lillier Cain, fourth child and fourth daughter of John Cain and Margaret Minor, date and place of birth unknown. Married Walter M. Pepper.

B41325425. Walter Davis Cain, fifth child and first son of John Cain and Margaret Minor, date and place of birth unknown. Married Cecile Ivy. Walter Cain and Cecile Ivy had issue, which was the twelth generation in America:

B413254251. Walter D. Cain, first child and first son of Walter Cain and Cecile Ivy, date and place of birth unknown.

B413254252. Gloria Jeanne Cain, second child and first daughter of Walter Cain and Cecile Ivy, date and place of birth unknown.

B41325426. Margaret Cain, sixth child and fifth daughter of John Cain and Margaret Minor, date and place of birth unknown. Married J.D. Prince.

B41325427. Lula Ina Cain, seventh child and sixth daughter of John Cain and Margaret Minor, date and place of birth unknown.

B4132543. James Andrew Cain, third child and third son of Mary Pounds and John Cain, born 21 Dec 1872 in Georgia and died 1 Sep 1923 in Georgia. Married 1893 in Gwinnett County, Georgia to Camie Forrester, born 9 Dec 1876 in Georgia and died 4 Nov 1956 in Gwinnett County, Georgia. Buried Libert Baptist Church cemetery. James Cain and Camie Forrester had issue, which was the eleventh generation in America:

B41325431. Arlie Cain, first child and first son of James Cain and Camie Forrester, born Gwinnett County, Georgia and died Dec 1950 in Gwinnett County, Georgia.

B41325432. Avva Cain, second child and first daughter of James Cain and Camie Forrester, born in Gwinnett County, Georgia.

B41325433. Lathan Cain, third child and second son of James Cain and Camie Forrester, born in Gwinnett County, Georgia. Married Bunnie ---.

B413255. Eleanor Louisa (twin) Pounds, fifth child and fourth daughter of Richard Pounds and Nancy Cordia, born 25 Oct 1849 in Gwinnett County, Georgia. Married 20 Nov 1866 in Gwinnett County, Georgia to William Augustus Carroll, son of Thomas Carroll and Rhoda Blake, born 13 Oct 1842 in Georgia and died 2 Jul 1924 in Gwinnett County, Georgia. Eleanor Pounds and William Carroll had issue, which was the eleventh generation in America:

B4132551. Thomas R. Carroll, first child and first son of Eleanor Pounds and William Carroll, born 10 Jul 1867 in Georgia and died 13 Mar 1930

54

in Georgia. Married Maggie Matthews, born 6 Dec 1876 in Georgia and died 29 Sep 1927 in Georgia. Thomas Carroll and Maggie Matthews had issue, which was the eleventh generation in America:

B41325511. James T. Carroll, first child and first son of Thomas Carroll and Maggie Matthews, died in infancy.

B41325512. Clyde B. Carroll, second child and second son of Thomas Carroll and Maggie Matthews, died in infancy.

B41325513. William Glad Carroll, third child and third son of Thomas Carroll and Maggie Matthews, date and place of birth unknown. Married Lucy Mae Pittard. William Carroll and Lucy Pittard had issue, which was the twelth generation in America:

B413255131. Eloise Carroll, first child and first daughter of William Carroll and Lucy Pittard, date and place of birth unknown

B413255132. Jacqueline Carroll, second child and second daughter of William Carroll and Lucy Pittard, date and place of birth unknown.

B41325514. Codell Carroll, fourth child and first daughter of Thomas Carroll and Maggie Matthews, date and place of birth unknown. Married Dudley L. Grosson. Codell Carroll and Dudley Grosson had issue, which was the twelth generation in America:

B413255141. Dudley Grosson, Jr., first child and first son of Codell Carroll and Dudley Grosson, date and place of birth unknown.

B41325515. Eleanor Carroll, fifth child and second daughter of Thomas Carroll and Maggie Matthews, date and place of birth unknown. Married Anthony Creamer.

B41325516. William T. Carroll, sixth child and fourth son of Thomas Carroll and Maggie Matthews, date and place of birth unknown. Married Alberta Epps. William Carroll and Alberta Epps had issue, which was the twelth generation in America:

B413255161. Donnie Carroll, first child and first son of William Carroll and Alberta Epps, born Carrollton, Carroll County, Georgia.

B413255162. William T. Carroll, Jr., second child and second son of William T.

Carroll, Sr. and Alberta Epps, born Carrollton, Carroll County, Georgia.

B4132552. Amma Carroll, second child and first daughter of William Augustus Carroll and Eleanor Pounds, born 19 Nov 1869 in Georgia and died 26 Dec 1945 in Georgia. Married Oliver T. Kelley, born 12 Jul 1868 in Georgia and died 24 Jul 1949 in Georgia. Buried Lilburn 1st Baptist cemetery, Gwinnett County, Georgia. Amma Carroll and Oliver Kelley had issue, which was the eleventh generation in America:

B41325521. Thomas Charles Kelley, first child and first son of Amma Carroll and Oliver Kelley, date and place of birth unknown. Married Ily Deemery.

B41325522. Lillian Vesta Kelley, second child and first daughter of Amma Carroll and Oliver Kelley, date and place of birth unknown. Married John Robert Pickens. Lillian Kelley and John Pickens had issue, which was the twelth generation in America:

B413255221. Doris Eloise Pickens, first child and first daughter of Lillian Kelley and John Pickens, date and place of birth unknown. Married Hayden Zimmerman. Doris Pickens and Hayden Zimmerman had issue, which was the thirteenth generation in America:

B4132552211. Carol Zimmerman, first child and first daughter of Doris Pickens and Hayden Zimmerman, date and place of birth unknown. Married Gene Cargile. Carol Zimmerman and Gene Cargile had issue, which was the fourteenth generation in America:

B41325522111. Karen Lawanna Cargile, first child and first daughter of Carol Zimmerman and Gene Cargile, date and place of birth unknown.

B41325523. William Amos Kelley, third child and second son of Amma Carroll and Oliver Kelley, date and place of birth unknown. Married Ineal Heard. William Kelley and Ineal Heard had issue, which was the twelth generation in America:

B413255231. Neal Kelley, first child and first son of William Kelley and Ineal Heard, born Atlanta, Fulton County, Georgia.

B413255232. Jane Kelley, second child and first daughter of William Kelley and Ineal Heard, born Atlanta, Fulton County, Georgia.

B413255524. Tip Kelley, fourth child and third son of Amma Carroll and Oliver Kelley, date and place of birth unknown.

B41325553. James Darling Carroll, third child and second son of Eleanor Pounds and William Carroll, born 24 May 1872 and died 14 Oct 1948. Married Annie Laura Cowan, born 18 Jun 1884 and died 28 Feb 1958. James Carroll and Annie Cowan had issue, which was the eleventh generation in America:

B413255531. Mary Eleanor Carroll, first child and first daughter of James Carroll and Annie Cowan, date and place of birth unknown.

B41325554. Sarah (Sally) Carroll, fourth child and second daughter of William Carroll and Eleanor Pounds, born 11 Dec 1875 and died 7 Aug 1955. Married Robert Stephen Nash, born 5 May 1871 and died 13 Jan 1947. Sarah Carroll and Robert Nash had issue, which was the eleventh generation in America:

B413255541. Lucille Nash, first child and first daughter of Sarah Carroll and Robert Nash, date and place of birth unknown. Married Seth Greer.

B41325555. Floy Jane Carroll, fifth child and third daughter of William Carroll and Eleanor Pounds, born 25 Mar 1882 and died 8 Apr 1960. Married Henry B. Harmon.

B413256. Evaline Pounds, sixth child and fifth daughter of Richard Pounds and Nancy Cordia, born 1855 in Gwinnett County, Georgia.

B413257. John R. Pounds, seventh child and second son of Richard Pounds and Nancy Cordia, born 1857 in Gwinnett County, Georgia. Married Mattie L. --- born 1860 in Georgia. John Pounds and Mattie --- had issue, which was the twelth generation in America:

B4132571. Lilly Pounds, first child and first daughter of John Pounds and Mattie ---, born in Georgia.

B4132572. Nora Pounds, second child and second daughter of John Pounds and Mattie ---, born in Georgia.

B4132573. James (Jim) Pounds, third child and first son of John Pounds and Mattie ---, born in Georgia.

B4132574. Frank Richard Pounds, fourth child and second son of John Pounds and Mattie ---, born 11 Dec 1885 in Stone Mountain, Gwinnett County, Georgia, and died 1935 in Orlando, Orange County, Florida. Buried in Orlando, Orange County, Florida. Married in Lousiana to Arlie Davis, born 11 Jun 1887 in Orlando, Orange County, Florida and died 27 Nov 1989 in Winter Garden, Orange County, Florida. Buried in Orlando, Greenwood cemetery, Florida. Frank Pounds and Arlie Davis had issue, which was the eleventh generation in America:

B41325741. Roger Pounds, first child and first son of Frank Pounds and Arlie Davis, born 7 Dec 1913 in west Orange County, Florida. Married 13 May 1933 at Sanford, Seminole County, Florida to Ruth Johnson. Roger Pounds and Ruth Johnson had issue, which was the twelth generation in America:

B413257411. Peggy Jo Pounds, first child and first daughter of Roger Pounds and Ruth Johnson, born 11 Dec 1933 at Orlando, Orange County, Florida. Married Egerton King van den Berg, from whom she later divorced. Peggy Pounds and Egerton van den Berg had issue, which was the thirteenth generation in America:

B4132574111. David Andrew van den Berg, first child and first son of Peggy Pounds and Egerton van den Berg, born 8 Oct 1967 at Orlando, Orange County, Florida.

B4132575. Clyde Pounds, fifth child and third son of John Pounds and Mattie ---, born in Georgia.

B4132576. William (Will) S. Pounds, sixth child and fourth son of John Pounds and Mattie --- , born 1879 in Georgia.

B41325761. Richard Pounds, first child and first son of William Pounds and --- ---.

B41325762. Phillip Clyde Pounds, second child and second son of William Pounds and --- --- . Phillip Pounds married --- ---. Phillip Pounds and --- --- had issue, which was the twelth generation in America:

B413257621. Phillip Clyde Pounds, Jr., first child and first son of Phillip Pounds and --- ---, born 30 Jul 1929 in Miami, Dade County, Florida. Married 30 Dec 1948 in DeLand, Volusia County, Florida to Blondell Thompson, born 4 Mar 1929 in DeLand, Volusia County, Florida. Phillip Pounds and Blondell Thompson had issue, which was the thirteenth generation in America:

B4132576211. Richard Edwin Pounds, first child and first son of Phillip Pounds and Blondell Thompson, born 9 Apr 1951 in DeLand, Volusia County, Florida. Married Diana Sidmore.

B4132576212. Francine Blondell Pounds, second child and first daughter of Phillip Pounds and Blondell Thompson, born 27 May 1953 at Millington, Shelby County, Tennessee. Married 1st Terry Jimines. Married secondly to Kevin Johnson. Francine Pounds and Terry Jimines had issue, which was the fourteenth generation in America:

B41325762121. Tina Jimines, first child and first daughter of Francine Pounds and Terry Jimines, born 12 Jul 1966 at Pensacola, Santa Rosa County, Florida.

B41325763. William Pounds, third child and third son of William Pounds and --- ---.

B4132577. Hoyle Pounds, seventh child and fifth son of John Pounds and Mattie ---, born 6 Dec 1893 in Florida and died 6 Mar 1981 in Florida. Married in 1913 to Lucy Agnes New, daughter of Patrick J. New and Lenora Parker. Hoyle Pounds and Lucy New had issue, which was the eleventh generation in America:

B41325771. Donald Emerson Pounds, first child and first son of Hoyle Pounds and Lucy New, born 28 Aug 1915 in Florida. Married Donna Conybear, born 22 Sep 1926 in Chicago, Cook County, Illinois. Donald Pounds and Donna Conybear had issue, which was the twelth generation in America:

B413257711. Judy Pounds, first child and first daughter of Donald Pounds and Donna Conybear, born 13 May 1940 in Florida.

B413257712. Dona Pounds, second child and second daughter of Donald Pounds and Donna Conybear, born 9 May 1943 in Florida.

B413257713. Barbara (Bo) Pounds, third child and third daughter of Donald Pounds and Donna Conybear, born 11 Feb 1949 in Florida.

B413257714. Donald Pounds, Jr., fourth child and first son of Donald Pounds and Donna Conybear, born 20 Aug 1950 in Florida.

B413257715. John Pounds, fifth child and second son of Donald Pounds and Donna Conybear, born 21 Oct 1952 in Florida.

B413257716. William (Will) Pounds, sixth child and third son of Donald Pounds and Donna Conybear, born 29 Jul 1954 in Florida.

B41325772. James Herbert Pounds, second child and second son of Hoyle Pounds and Lucy New, born 29 Nov 1917 in Florida. Married Jess ---. Married secondly to --- ---. James Pounds and Jess --- had issue, which was the twelth generation in America:

B413257721. James (Jimmy) Pounds, first child and first son of James Pounds and Jess ---, born 28 Jun 1949 in Florida.

B413257722. Steven (Steve) Pounds, second child and second son of James Pounds and Jess ---, born 13 Mar 1951 in Florida.

B41325773. Russell Stevenson Pounds, third child and third son of Hoyle Pounds and Lucy New, born 20 Jun 1920 in Florida and died 12 Dec 1989 in Florida. Russell Pounds married --- ---. Russell Pounds and --- --- had issue, which was the twelth generation in America:

B413257731. Russell Stevenson Pounds, Jr., first child and first son of Russell Pounds and --- ---, born 18 Dec 1943.

B413257732. Rice Pounds, second child and second son of Russell Pounds and --- --, born 11 Jan 1945 in Florida.

B413257733. Mary Dial Pounds, third child and first daughter of Russell Pounds and --- ---, born 26 Sep 1952.

B41325774. Harriet Pounds, fourth child and first daughter of Hoyle Pounds and Lucy New, born 12 Aug 1922 in Florida and died 13 Sep 1975. Married Jack Zeiss. Harriet Pounds and Jack Zeiss had issue, which was the twelth generation in America:

B413257741. Lucy Zeiss, first child and first daughter of Harriet Pounds and Jack Zeiss, born 12 Jul 1949 in Florida.

B413257742. Debbie Zeiss, second child and second daughter of Harriet Pounds and Jack Zeiss, born 8 Jun 1953 in Florida.

B413257743. David Zeiss, third child and first son of Harriet Pounds and Jack Zeiss, born 23 Jul 1954 in Florida.

B413258. Narcissus Ophelia Pounds, eighth child and sixth daughter of Richard Pounds and Nancy Cordia, born 31 Mar 1859 in Gwinnett County, Georgia, and died 1 Apr 1951. Married about 1876 in Georgia to Dr. Allen Green Carroll, son of James C. Carroll and Milda A. McDaniel, born 6 Oct 1857 in Georgia and died 7 Aug 1910 at Alpharetta, Fulton County, Georgia. Narcissus Pounds and Allen Carroll had issue, which was the tenth generation in America:

B4132581. William Mack Carroll, first child and first son of Narcissus Pounds and Allen Carroll, born 8 Dec 1877 and died 21 May 1945. Married Carrie Rickett. William Carroll and Carrie Rickett had issue, which was the eleventh generation in America:

B41325811. James Clifford Carroll, first child and first son of William Carroll and Carrie Rickett, date and place of birth unknown.

B4132581. William Mack Carroll, first child and first son of Narcissus Pounds and Allen Carroll, born 8 Dec 1877 and died 21 May 1945. Married secondly Daisy Bell Wyley, born 31 Mar 1888 in Georgia and died 3 Jun 1947 in Georgia. William Carroll and Daisy Wyley had issue, which was the eleventh generation in America:

B41325811. Richard Eugene Carroll, first child and first son of William Carroll and Daisy Wyley, date and place of birth unknown.

B41325812. Ruby Ophelia Carroll, second child and first daughter of William Carroll and Daisy Wyley, date and place of birth unknown.

B4132582. Allie Ozola Carroll, second child and first daughter of Narcissus Pounds and Allen Carroll, born 31 Dec 1880 and died 16 Dec 1952. Married Argus Raymond Waters, born 4 Jun 1882 in Georgia and died Jun 1955 in Georgia. Allie

Carroll and Argus Waters had issue, which was the eleventh generation in America:

B41325821. Raymond Dewitt Waters, first child and first son of Allie Carroll and Argus Waters, date and place of birth unknown.

B41325822. Allen Elford Waters, second child and second son of Allie Carroll and Argus Waters, date and place of birth unknown.

B41325823. Ben Eva Waters, third child and first daughter of Allie Carroll and Argus Waters, date and place of birth unknown.

B41325824. Dorothy Waters, fourth child and second daughter of Allie Carroll and Argus Waters, date and place of birth unknown.

B41325825. Margaret Waters, fifth child and third daughter of Allie Carroll and Argus Waters, date and place of birth unknown.

B4132583. James Overton Carroll, third child and second son of Narcissus Pounds and Allen Carroll, born 23 Mar 1883 at Alpharetta, Fulton County, Georgia and died 23 Aug 1918.

B4132584. Raymie Eleanor Carroll, fourth child and second daughter of Narcissus Pounds and Allen Carroll, born 12 Mar 1883 and died 27 Sep 1968. Married Dana Henry Lee, born 1876 at Alpharetta, Fulton County, Georgia and died 1932 in Georgia. Raymie Carroll and Dana Lee had issue, which was the eleventh generation in America:

B41325841. Evelyn Ophelia Lee, first child and first daughter of Raymie Carroll and Dana Lee, date and place of birth unknown.

B41325842. Eleanor Eugenia Lee, second child and second daughter of Raymie Carroll and Dana Lee, date and place of birth unknown.

B41325843. Jemmie Lou Lee, third child and third daughter of Raymie Carroll and Dana Lee, date and place of birth unknown.

B4132585. John Richard Carroll, fifth child and third son of Narcissus Pounds and Allen Carroll, born 12 Mar 1888 at Alpharetta, Fulton County, Georgia and died 31 Oct 1971. Married Ruby Odessa Buchanan, born 2 Aug 1893 in Georgia and died 8 Dec 1973 in Georgia. John Carroll and Ruby Buchanan had issue, which was the eleventh generation in America:

B41325851. Mary Frances Carroll, first child and first daughter of John Carroll and Ruby Buchanan, date and place of birth unknown.

B4132586. Eva Evelyn Carroll, sixth child and third daughter of Narcissus Pounds and Allen Carroll, born 7 Sep 1890 at Alpharetta, Fulton County, Georgia and died 2 May 1963 in Georgia. Married William H. Swords, born 1888 in Georgia and died 1972 in Georgia.

B413259. Bastian Pounds, ninth child and third son of Richard Pounds and Nancy Cordia, born 1861 in Gwinnett County, Georgia.

B4132510. James Pounds, tenth child and fourth son of Richard Pounds and Nancy Cordia, born 1863 in Gwinnett County, Georgia.

B4132511. Augustus Young Pounds, eleventh child and fifth son of Richard Pounds and Nancy Cordia, born 1866 in Gwinnett County, Georgia. Married 1880 in Gwinnett County, Georgia to Ida Mae Bracewell, born about 1868 in Georgia and died 28 Oct 1918 at Stone Mountain, Gwinnett County, Georgia. Augustus Pounds and Ida Bracewell had issue, which was the tenth generation in America:

B41325111. James Carlus Pounds, first child and first son of Augustus Pounds and Ida Bracewell, born 25 Jul 1902 in Gwinnett County, Georgia. Married Mary Pauline Minor, daughter of William Arthur Minor and Martha Wood, born 27 Sep 1905 at Lilburn, Gwinnett County, Georgia. James Pounds and Mary Minor had issue, which was the eleventh generation in America:

B413251111. James Carlus Pounds, Jr., first child and first son of James Carlus Pounds, Sr. and Mary Minor, born 5 Nov 1931 in Georgia and died 23 Jul 1955.

B413251112. Leslie Young Pounds, second child and second son of James Pounds and Mary Minor, born 23 Jan 1935 in Georgia. Married 1959 in Georgia to Beverly Davis.

B413251113. Mary Sue Pounds, third child and first daughter of James Pounds and Mary Minor, born 11 Aug 1939 in Gwinnett County, Georgia. Married 1958 in Georgia to Clement Latimer Harper III.

B41325111. James Carlus Pounds, first child and first son of Augustus Pounds and Ida

Bracewell, born 25 Jul 1902 at Stone Mountain, Gwinnett County, Georgia. Married secondly Ada Kelley. James Pounds and Ada Kelley had issue, which was the eleventh generation in America:

B413251111. Rosie Pounds, first child and first daughter of James Pounds and Ada Kelley, date and place of birth unknown. Married Rufus Dorsey Sanders. Rosie Pounds and Rufus Sanders had issue, which was the twelth generation in America:

B4132511111. Rufus Dorsey Sanders, Jr., first child and first son of Rosie Pounds and Rufus Sanders, date and place of birth unknown.

B4132511112. James Brittain Sanders, second child and second son of Rosie Pounds and Rufus Sanders, date and place of birth unknown.

B4132511113. Sarah Sanders, third child and first daughter of Rosie Pounds and Rufus Sanders, date and place of birth unknown.

B413251112. Annie Pounds, second child and second daughter of James Pounds and Ada Kelley, date and place of birth unknown.

B413251113. Henry Pounds, third child and first son of James Pounds and Ada Kelley, date and place of birth unknown. Buried at Atlanta, Westview cemetery, Georgia.

B413251114. Carlos (Shug) Pounds, fourth child and second son of James Pounds and Ada Kelley, date and place of birth unknown.

B413251115. Edna Pounds, fifth child and third daughter of James Pounds and Ada Kelley, date and place of birth unknown.

B413251116. Corrine Pounds, sixth child and fourth daughter of James Pounds and Ada Kelley, date and place of birth unknown. Married Sidney Washington. Corrine Pounds and Sidney Washington had issue, which was the thirteenth generation in America:

B4132511161. Sidney Washington, Jr., first child and first son of Corrine Pounds and Sidney Washington, date and place of birth unknown.

B41326. William Newman Pounds, sixth child and second son of Jackey Pound and Marian Caldwell,

born 1828 in Gwinnett County, Georgia. Married
Milly E. ---, born 1821 in Georgia. William
Pounds and Milly --- had issue, which was the
ninth generation in America:

B413261. Letha Ann Pounds, first child and
first daughter of William Pounds and Milly ---,
born 1849 in Gwinnett County, Georgia.

B413262. John William Pounds, second child
and first son of William Pounds and Milly ---,
born 1851 in Gwinnett County, Georgia and died
1917. Buried in Gwinnett County, Georgia.
Married 1875 in Gwinnett County, Georgia to Sara
J. Braden, born 1855 in Georgia and died 1915
Gwinnett County, Georgia. John Pounds and Sara
Braden had issue, which was the tenth generation
in America:

B4132621. William M. Pounds, first
child and first son of John Pounds and Sara
Braden, born 1880 in Georgia.

B4132622. Lonie Rufus Pounds, second
child and second son of John Pounds and Sara
Braden, born 26 Sep 1897 in Georgia and died 27
Sep 1932 in Georgia. Buried in Gwinnett County,
Georgia. Married Marvie M. Lee, born 28 Jul 1898
in Georgia and died 5 Oct 1958 in Georgia. Buried
in Gwinnett County, Georgia.

B413263. Miles J. Pounds, third child and
third son of William Pounds and Milly ---, born 22
Mar 1852 in Georgia and died 22 Jan 1914 in
Georgia. Married 1884 in Gwinnett County, Georgia
to Perlina Hortense Brooks, born 6 Jun 1862 in
Georgia and died 9 Aug 1900 in Georgia. Buried in
Gwinnett County, Georgia. Miles Pounds and
Hortense Brooks had issue, which was the tenth
generation in America:

B4132631. James Edward Pounds, first
child and first son of Miles Pounds and Hortense
Brooks, date and place of birth unknown. Married
--- Carroll. James Pounds and --- Carroll had
issue, which was the eleventh generation in
America:

B41326311. Mildred Louise Pounds,
first child and first daughter of James Pounds and
--- Carroll, date and place of birth unknown.
Married at Decatur, DeKalb County, Georgia to
Jackson Phillips, born in North Carolina.

B41326312. Hortense Pounds, second child and second daughter of James Pounds and --- Carroll, date and place of birth unknown. Married Frank J. Suslavich, born Darien, Fairfield County, Connecticutt.

B41326313. --- Pounds, third child, sex undetermined, of James Pounds and --- Carroll, born 1916 in Gwinnett County, Georgia and died 1916 in Gwinnett County, Georgia.

B413264. Frances Pounds, fourth child and second daughter of William Pound and Milly ---, born 1855 in Georgia.

B413265. Richard N. Pounds, fifth child and third son of William Pound and Milly ---,born 1858 in Georgia and died 7 Dec 1891 in Georgia. Buried in Gwinnett County, Georgia. Married 15 Jan 1885 in Georgia to Dollie Isabella Luckie, born 10 Nov 1860 in Georgia and died 5 May 1921 in Georgia. Buried in Gwinnett County, Georgia.

B413266. Martha Pounds, sixth child and third daughter of William Pound and Milly ---, born 1862 in Georgia.

B4132. John T. (Jackey) Pound, second child and second of Richard Eli Pound and Mary Davidson, born 20 Dec 1786 in North Augusta, Aiken County, South Carolina and died 25 Dec 1881 in Gwinnett County, Georgia. Buried in Old Pounds cemetery. Married secondly Mar 1824 in Gwinnett County, Georgia to Marian Caldwell, born 20 Dec 1811 in North Carolina and died 17 Apr 1877 in Gwinnett County, Georgia. Jackey Pound and Marian Caldwell had issue, which was the eighth generation in America:

B41321. Martha Ann Pounds, first child and first daughter of Jackey Pound and Marian Caldwell, born 1840 Gwinnett County, Georgia.

B41322. John L. Pounds, second child and first son of Jackey Pound and Marian Caldwell, born 22 Nov 1842 in Gwinnett County, Georgia and died 22 Dec 1885 in Gwinnett County, Georgia. Married Edna Edson, born 1851 in Georgia. John Pounds and Edna Edson had issue, which was the ninth generation in America:

B413221. Ophelia C. Pounds, first child and first daughter of John Pounds and Edna Edson, born 1868 in Gwinnett County, Georgia.

B413222. Minor B. Pounds, second child and first son of John Pounds and Edna Edson, born 24 Jun 1869 in Gwinnett County, Georgia and died 14 Jan 1939. Buried in Gwinnett County, Georgia. Married Martha C. ---, born 1 Sep 1871 in Georgia and died 10 Apr 1948 in Georgia. Buried in Gwinnett County, Georgia. Minor Pounds and Martha --- had issue, which was the tenth generation in America:

B4132221. Verdie Lou Pounds, first child and first daughter of Minor Pounds and Martha ---, born 13 May 1902 in Georgia and died 1 Oct 1903 in Georgia.

B4132222. Jessie Pounds, second child and second daughter of Minor Pounds and Martha ---, born 2 Dec 1904 in Georgia and died 30 Mar 1917 in Georgia. Buried in Gwinnett County, Georgia.

B4132223. Doris Pounds, third child and third daughter of Minor Pounds and Martha ---, born 30 Jul 1912 in Georgia and died 3 Aug 1956 in Georgia. Buried in Gwinnett County, Georgia.

B413223. John W. Pounds, third child and second son of John Pounds and Edna Edson, born 1871 in Gwinnett County, Georgia and died 1941. Buried in Gwinnett County, Georgia. Married Jessie M. McClain, born 5 Jul 1874 in Georgia and died 27 Dec 1904 in Georgia. Buried in Gwinnett County, Georgia.

B413224. Anna Pearl Pounds, fourth child and second daughter of John Pounds and Edna Edson, born 25 Nov 1873 in Gwinnett County, Georgia and died 1968. Buried in Gwinnett County, Georgia. Married Charles Elery Britt, born 1873 in Georgia and died 1968. Buried in Gwinnett County, Georgia. Anna Pounds and Charles Britt had issue, which was the tenth generation in America:

B4132241. Julian Britt, first child and first son of Anna Pounds and Charles Britt, born 1903 in Gwinnett County, Georgia. Married Vera Armstrong. Julian Britt and Vera Armstrong had issue, which was the eleventh generation in America:

B41322411. Mary Britt, first child and first daughter of Julian Britt and Vera Armstrong, born 1931 in Georgia. Married Hubert Nix.

B4132242. Bonnie Britt, second child and first daughter of Anna Pounds and Charles Britt, born 1932 in Georgia. Married Art DeLoach.

B413225. Nancy M. Pounds, fifth child and third daughter of John Pounds and Edna Edson, born 1874 in Gwinnett County, Georgia. Married Robert Riley Jackson, born 1869 in Georgia.

B413226. George M. Pounds, sixth child and third son of John Pounds and Edna Edson, born 1875 in Gwinnett County, Georgia.

B413227. Thomas T. Pounds, seventh child and fourth son of John Pounds and Edna Edson, born 11 Aug 1876 in Gwinnett County, Georgia and died 24 Ded 1922 in Gwinnett County, Georgia. Married Emma ---.

B413228. Minerva M. Pounds, eighth child and fourth daughter of John Pounds and Edna Edson, born 1878 in Gwinnett County, Georgia.

B413229. Verdie H. Pounds, ninth child and fifth daughter of John Pounds and Edna Edson, born 15 Oct 1884 in Gwinnett County, Georgia and died 14 Jan 1969. Buried Corinth cemetery, Gwinnett County, Georgia. Married Daniel Elbert Lanford, born 13 Aug 1881 in Georgia and died 30 Apr 1935 in Georgia.

B4133. Newman Madison Pound, third child and third son of Richard Eli Pound and Mary Davidson, born Nov 1795 in Clarke County, Georgia and died 9 Sep 1871 in Cleburne County, Alabama. Married 11 Oct 1831 in Henry County, Georgia to Mary A. (Polly) Albright, daughter of William Albright and Catherine Margaret Reid, born 1803 in Henry County, Georgia and died 22 Apr 1872 in Cleburne County, Alabama. Newman Pound and Mary Albright had issue, which was the eighth generation in America:

B41331. Richard Franklin Pounds, first child and first son of Newman Pound and Mary Albright, born 19 Apr 1832 in Clarke County, Georgia and died 10 Jan 1887 in Cleburne County, Alabama. Buried in Shiloh Church cemetery, Cleburne County,

Alabama. Married 13 Feb 1753 in Benton County, Alabama to Nancy Reed, daughter of Reicy Reed and --- Kidd, born 16 Mar 1834 in Georgia and died 20 Mar 1918 in Cleburne County, Alabama. Buried at Shiloh Church cemetery, Cleburne County, Alabama. Richard Pounds and Nancy Reed had issue, which was the ninth generation in America:

B413311. Newman R.A. Pounds, first child and first son of Richard Pounds and Nancy Reed, born 30 Oct 1853 in Cleburne County, Alabama and died 13 Nov 1913 in Cleburne County, Alabama. Buried in Shiloh Church cemetery in Cleburne County, Alabama. Married 26 Sep 1875 in Cleburne County, Alabama to Anna E. (Annie) Harris, born 4 Sep 1857 in Georgia and died 8 Oct 1926 in Cleburne County, Alabama. Buried in Shiloh Church cemetery in Cleburne County, Alabama. Newman R.A. Pounds and Anna Harris had issue, which was the tenth generation in America:

B4133111. Buny Olley Pounds, first child and first daughter of Newman Pounds and Anna Harris, born Oct 1878 in Cleburne County, Alabama.

B4133112. Christie M. Pounds, second child and second daughter of Newman Pounds and Anna Harris, born 25 May 1882 in Cleburne County, Alabama and died 18 Aug 1944 in Cleburne County, Alabama. Married --- Munroe.

B4133113. Carsie Lee Pounds, third child and third daughter of Newman Pounds and Anna Harris, born 17 Aug 1886 in Cleburne County, Alabama and died 25 Jun 1959 in Cleburne County, Alabama. Married 10 Nov 1901 in Alabama to K.N. Clayton.

B4133114. James Cleveland Pounds, fourth child and first son of Newman Pounds and Anna Harris, born 10 Jul 1888 in Cleburne County, Alabama and died 3 Dec 1947 in Cleburne County, Alabama. Married 22 Dec 1907 in Alabama to Pearl Gentry.

B4133115. Jettie Pounds, fifth child and fourth daughter of Newman Pounds and Anna Harris, born Nov 1889 in Cleburne County, Alabama. Married 26 Dec 1906 in Alabama to J.A. Stephens.

B4133116. Richard S. Pounds, sixth child and second son of Newman Pounds and Anna

Harris, born 10 Nov 1891 in Cleburne County, Alabama and died 10 Mar 1968 in Cleburne County, Alabama.

B4133117. Lona Pounds, seventh child and fifth daughter of Newman Pounds and Anna Harris, born Apr 1893 in Cleburne County, Alabama. Married 23 Dec 1910 in Alabama to A.G. Todd.

B4133118. Newman Leroy Pounds, eighth child and third son of Newman Pounds and Anna Harris, born 3 Oct 1894 in Cleburne County, Alabama and died 29 Apr 1964 in Cleburne County, Alabama.

B4133119. Edward Spencer Pounds, ninth child and fourth son of Newman Pounds and Anna Harris, born Feb 1896 in Cleburne County, Alabama and died May 1975 at Anniston, Calhoun County, Alabama.

B413312. A.J. Pounds, second child and second son of Richard Pounds and Nancy Reed, born 1858 in Cleburne County, Alabama.

B413313. C.S.U. Pounds, third child and first daughter of Richard Pounds and Nancy Reed, born 1861 in Cleburne County, Alabama.

B413314. Lee J. Pounds, fourth child and third son of Richard Pounds and Nancy Reed, born 1864 in Cleburne County, Alabama.

B413315. James R. Pounds, fifth child and fourth son of Richard Pounds and Nancy Reed, born Oct 1866 in Cleburne County, Alabama. Married about 1897 in Alabama to Annie ---, born Nov 1876 in Georgia. James Pounds and Annie --- had issue, which was the tenth generation in America:

B4133151. Clifford Pounds, first child and first son of James Pounds and Annie ---, born Aug 1899 in Cleburne County, Alabama.

B413316. George W. Pounds, sixth child and fifth son of Richard Pounds and Nancy Reed, born 1869 in Cleburne County, Alabama.

B413317. Marriman Pounds, seventh child and sixth son of Richard Pounds and Nancy Reed, born 1871 in Cleburne County, Alabama.

B413318. Amisan Pounds, eighth child and second daughter of Richard Pounds and Nancy Reed, born 1873 in Cleburne County, Alabama.

B413319. Melvin H. (Kidd) Pounds, ninth child and seventh son of Richard Pounds and Nancy Reed, born Apr 1876 in Cleburne County, Alabama. Married 7 Oct 1897 in Cleburne County, Alabama to Artie Cornelia Owens, born Mar 1880 in Alabama. Melvin Pounds and Artie Owens had issue, which was the tenth generation in America:

B4133191. Lee Davy Pounds, first child and first son of Melvin Pounds and Artie Owens, born May 1898 in Cleburne County, Alabama.

B413320. Arminda Pounds, tenth child and third daughter of Richard Pounds and Nancy Reed, born 1878 in Cleburne County, Alabama. Married 29 May 1910 in Alabama to J.M. Clayton.

B41332. Merriman Pounds, second child and second son of Newman Pound and Mary Albright, born Sep 1833 in Clarke County, Georgia and died 1900. Married 21 Mar 1880 in Alabama to Julia A. Boyd, born Jun 1852 in Georgia. Merriman Pounds and Julia Boyd had issue, which was the ninth generation in America:

B413321. Isila M.C. Pounds, first child and first daughter of Merriman Pounds and Julia Boyd, born 1854 in Alabama.

B413322. Luran A.L. Pounds, second child and second daughter of Merriman Pounds and Julia Boyd, born 1856 in Alabama.

B413323. Georgia A. Pounds, third child and third daughter of Merriman Pounds and Julia Boyd, born 1866 in Alabama. Married 27 Oct 1883 in Alabama to Barto Barnes.

B413324. Matthew J. Pounds, fourth child and first son of Merriman Pounds and Julia Boyd, born May 1863 in Cleburne County, Alabama. Married about 1883 in Alabama to Annie ---, born May 1869 in Alabama. Matthew Pounds and Annie --- had issue, which was the tenth generation in America:

B4133241. Margaret E. Pounds, first child and first daughter of Matthew Pounds and Annie ---, born Dec 1884 in Cleburne County, Alabama.

B4133242. Arminda Pounds, second child and second daughter of Matthew Pounds and Annie ---, born Feb 1887 in Cleburne County, Alabama.

B4133243. Nancy C. Pounds, third child and third daughter of Matthew Pounds and Annie ---, born Jun 1890 in Cleburne County, Alabama.

B4133244. Dora Bell Pounds, fourth child and fourth daughter of Matthew Pounds and Annie ---, born 1 Aug 1892 in Cleburne County, Alabama.

B4133245. Georgia Ann Pounds, fifth child and fifth daughter of Matthew Pounds and Annie ---, born Mar 1895 in Cleburne County, Alabama.

B4133246. Livella Pounds, sixth child and sixth daughter of Matthew Pounds and Annie ---, born Aug 1897 in Cleburne County, Alabama.

B413325. M. Elizabeth Pounds, fifth child and fourth daughter of Merriman Pounds and Julia Boyd, born 1871 in Alabama.

B413326. Ida A. Pounds, sixth child and fifth daughter of Merriman Pounds and Julia Boyd, born Aug 1888 in Cleburne County, Alabama.

B413327. Newman J. Pounds, seventh child and second son of Merriman Pounds and Julia Boyd, born Feb 1890 in Cleburne County, Alabama.

B41333. William Lafayette Pounds, third child and third son of Newman Pound and Mary Albright, born 21 May 1835 in Benton County, Alabama and died 30 Jun 1894 in Muscadine, Cleburne County, Alabama. Married 25 May 1856 in Benton County, Alabama to Mary Ann Williams, daughter of Sydney Williams, born 26 Jun 1840 in Georgia and died 13 Dec 1895 in Cleburne County, Alabama. William Pounds and Mary Williams had issue, which was the ninth generation in America:

B413331. Sydney Lafayette Pounds, first child and first son of William Pounds and Mary Williams, born 29 Nov 1853 in Muscadine, Cleburne County, Alabama and died 22 Aug 1927 in Terrell, Kaufman County, Texas. Married 16 Dec 1882 at James Batson home, Cleburne County, Alabama to Sarah Frances (Fannie) Batson, daughter of James Willis Batson and Polly Ann Willis, born 27 Jun 1868 in Georgia and died 18 Feb 1948 in Anaheim, Orange County, California. Sydney Pounds and

Fannie Batson had issue, which was the tenth generation in America:

B4133311. Lee Pounds, first child and first son of Sydney Pounds and Fannie Batson, born Dec 1884 in Cleburne County, Alabama.

B4133312. Jackson Pounds, second child and second son of Sydney Pounds and Fannie Batson, born Oct 1887 in Cleburne County, Alabama.

B4133313. Effie Pounds, third child and first daughter of Sydney Pounds and Fannie Batson, born Jan 1890 in Cleburne County, Alabama.

B4133314. Grover C. Pounds, fourth child and second son of Sydney Pounds and Fannie Batson, born 30 Oct 1892 in Cleburne County, Alabama and died 22 Feb 1981 in Alabama. Married 1914 in Alabama to Rena Ann Campbell.

B4133315. Marvin Pounds, fifth child and third son of Sydney Pounds and Fannie Batson, born May 1895 in Cleburne County, Alabama.

B4133316. Willie M. Pounds, sixth child and fourth son of Sydney Pounds and Fannie Batson, born Oct 1897 in Cleburne County, Alabama.

B4133317. Henry Dewey Pounds, seventh child and fifth son of Sydney Pounds and Fannie Batson, born 4 Apr 1900 at Muscadine, Cleburne County, Alabama and died 14 Nov 1946 in West Los Angeles, Los Angeles County, California. Married 14 May in Visalia, Tulare County, California to Zora Mae Greenhill, daughter of William Isaac Greenhill and Mary Elizabeth Swiggett, born 8 Jan 1904 at San Bernadino, San Bernadino County, California. Henry Pounds and Zora Greenhill had issue, which was the eleventh generation in America:

B41333171. Nancy Priscilla Pounds, first child and first daughter of Henry Pounds and Zora Greenhill, born 1 Aug 1933 at Bakersfield, Kern County, California. Married at Los Angeles, Los Angeles County, California to --- Long.

B41333172. Lois Ann Pounds, second child and second daughter of Henry Pounds and Zora Greenhill, born 26 Aug 1934 at Bakersfield, Kern County, California. Married 8 May 1965 at Inglewood, Los Angeles County, California to

Thomas Richard Cravets, born 7 Dec 1935 at Cleveland, Cuyahoga County, Ohio. Lois Pounds and Thomas Cravets had issue, which was the twelth generation in America:

B413331721. Pamela Ann Cravets, first child and first daughter of Lois Pounds and Thomas Cravets, born 10 Jun 1967 at Hawthore, Los Angeles County, California.

B413331722. Jeffery Thomas Cravets, second child and first son of Lois Pounds and Thomas Cravets, born 23 Apr 1973 at Lancaster, Los Angeles County, California.

B41333173. Barbara Gayle Pounds, third child and third daughter of Henry Pounds and Zora Greenhill, born 8 Aug 1937 at San Luis Obispo, San Luis Obispo County, California.

B41333174. Linda Ruth Pounds, fourth child and fourth daughter of Henry Pounds and Zora Greenhill, born 29 Oct 1938 at Bakersfield, Kern County, California.

B41333175. Mary Ellen Pounds, fifth child and fifth daughter of Henry Pounds and Zora Greenhill, born 17 May 1944 at Bakersfield, Kern County, California.

B413332. Lutesha B. Pounds, second child and first daughter of William Pounds and Mary Williams, born about 1861 in Alabama.

B413333. Allis J. Pounds, third child and second daughter of William Pounds and Mary Williams, born about 1864 in Alabama.

B413334. Richard T.V. Pounds, fourth child and second son of William Pounds and Mary Williams, born about 1866 in Alabama.

B413335. Newman W. Pounds, fifth child and third son of William Pounds and Mary Williams, born 1869 in Alabama.

B413336. Nancy Pounds, sixth child and third daughter of William Pounds and Mary Williams, born about 1871 in Alabama.

B413337. Irene Pounds, seventh child and fourth daughter of William Pounds and Mary Williams, born about 1874 in Alabama.

B413338. Merriman M. Pounds, eighth child and fourth son of William Pounds and Mary Williams, born about 1876 in Alabama.

B413339. William F. Pounds, ninth child and fifth son of William Pounds and Mary Williams, born about 1878 in Alabama. Married Celia Land.

B41334. Newman Jackson Pounds, fourth child and fourth son of Newman Pound and Mary Albright, born about 1839 in Alabama and died in Comanche County, Texas. Married --- Corrouth.

B41335. Early Andrew Jackson Pounds, fifth child and fifth son of Newman Pound and Mary Albright, born 5 Aug 1840 in Benton County, Alabama and died 6 Oct 1910 in Cleburne County, Alabama. Buried in Cleburne County, Alabama. Married 12 Nov 1868 to Eliza Scott. Early Pounds married secondly 21 Sep 1872 to Odelia Jane Burgess. Early Pounds married thirdly 10 Nov 1895 to Frances Wigley. Early A.J. Pounds and Eliza Scott had issue, which was the ninth generation in America:

B413351. Newman Jesse Pounds, first child and first son of Early Pounds and Eliza Scott, born about 1869 in Alabama.

B413352. Margarette (Tular) Pounds, second child and first daughter of Early Pounds and Eliza Scott, born about 1871 in Alabama.

B41335. Early Andrew Jackson Pounds, fifth child and fifth son of Newman Pound and Mary Albright, born 5 Aug 1840 in Benton County, Alabama and died 6 Oct 1910 in Cleburne County, Alabama. Married secondly 21 Sep 1872 in Cleburne County, Alabama to Odelia Jane Burgess, born 1854 in Alabama and died 1894 in Cleburne County, Alabama. Early Pounds and Odelia Burgess had issue, which was the ninth generation in America:

B413351. John William Pounds, first child and first son of Early Pounds and Odelia Burgess, born 1874 in Alabama.

B413352. Oscar Jackson Pounds, second child and second son of Early Pounds and Odelia Burgess, born 1875 in Alabama. Married Lizar C. ---.

B413353. Nancy Odelia Pounds, third child and first daughter of Early Pounds and Odelia Burgess, born 1877 in Alabama.

B413354. Henry Forney Pounds, fourth child and third son of Early Pounds and Odelia Burgess, born 1879 in Alabama.

B41336. Arminda Catherine Pounds, sixth child and first daughter of Newman Pound and Mary Albright, born 9 May 1842 in Benton County, Alabama and died 15 Jun 1910 in Jayton, Kent County, Texas. Married 2 Aug 1866 in Alabama to Levi Alexander Harrison, born 3 Jul 1833 in Butler County, Alabama and died 28 Jun 1917 in Jayton, Kent County, Texas. Arminda Pounds and Levi Harrison had issue, which was the ninth generation in America:

B413361. George Washington Harrison, first child and first son of Arminda Pounds and Levi Harrison, born 13 Nov 1869 in Cleburne County, Alabama.

B413362. John William Harrison, second child and second son of Arminda Pounds and Levi Harrison, born 4 Jul 1883 in Comanche County, Texas and died 17 Feb 1965 at Rotan, Fisher County, Texas. Married 15 Mar 1915 in Texas to Tessie Lee Laird, born 28 Dec 1892 at Grosbeck, Limestone County, Texas. John Harrison and Tessie Laird had issue, which was the tenth generation in America:

B4133621. William John Harrison, first child and first son of John Harrison and Tessie Laird, born 25 May 1931 at Jayton, Kent County, Texas. Married 20 Sep 1958 in Texas to Janice Sue Long, born 7 Nov 1939 at Girard, Kent County, Texas.

B41337. Eliza Jane Pounds, seventh child and second daughter of Newman Pound and Mary Albright, born 1846 in Alabama. Married L. Green Bennett.

B41338. Mary Ann Pounds, eighth child and third daughter of Newman Pound and Mary Albright, born 1848 in Alabama. Married 5 Apr 1855 in Alabama to John W. Wiggonton.

B41339. Martha A.E. Pounds, ninth child and fourth daughter of Newman Pound and Mary Albright, born 1848 in Alabama. Married 2 Dec 1869 in Alabama to Z.J. Robertson.

B413310. Permilla M.L. Pounds, tenth child and fifth daughter of Newman Pound and Mary Albright, born 1849 in Alabama. Married 15 Nov 1869 in Alabama to William T. Voss.

B413311. Sarah A. Pounds, eleventh child and sixth daughter of Newman Pound and Mary Albright, born about 1852 in Alabama. Married John J. Pollard.

B4134. Sarah Pound, fourth child and first daughter of Richard Eli Pound and Mary Davidson, born in Clarke County, Georgia. Married George Heard.

B4135. Catherine (Katy) Pounds, fifth child and second daughter of Richard Eli Pound and Mary Davidson, born 1798 in Clarke County, Georgia. Married Augustus Young.

B4136. Martha (Patsy) Pound, sixth child and third daughter of Richard Eli Pound and Mary Davidson, born 18 May 1800 in Clarke County, Georgia and died 21 Feb 1876 in Union County, Arkansas. Buried Hillsboro Baptist Church cemetery in Union County, Arkansas. Married 1 Oct 1816 in Clarke County, Georgia to Benjamin Cothran Williams, born 1 Jul 1791 in Georgia and died 25 Jul 1846 at New London, Union County, Arkansas. Buried at New London, Union County, Arkansas. Martha Pound and Benjamin Williams had issue, which was the eighth generation in America:

B41361. Mary Ann Williams, first child and first daughter of Martha Pound and Benjamin Williams, born 15 Feb 1819 in Alabama and died 5 Dec 1833 in Arkansas.

B41362. Thomas Reed Williams, second child and first son of Martha Pound and Benjamin Williams, born 26 Jan 1821 in Alabama and died 10 Apr 1864 in Union County, Arkansas. Married --- Underwood. Married secondly --- Connor.

B41363. Margaret Elizabeth Williams, third child and second daughter of Martha Pound and Benjamin Williams, born 21 Apr 1823 in Alabama and died 9 Sep 1849. Married William Thompson.

B41364. Asenath Reynolds Williams, fourth child and third daughter of Martha Pound and Benjamin Williams, born 15 Mar 1825 in Alabama and died 25 Apr 1870 in Oktibbeha County, Mississippi. Married 31 Aug 1841 in Arkansas to James A. Montgomery.

B41365. Horatio Gates Perry Williams, fifth child and second son of Martha Pound and Benjamin Williams, born 21 Feb 1827 in Alabama and died 19 Nov 1903 in Union County, Arkansas. Married --- Tatum. Married secondly --- Smith.

77

B41366. Nancy Jane Williams, sixth child and fourth daughter of Martha Pound and Benjamin Williams, born 27 Feb 1829 in Arkansas and died 17 Mar 1834 in Arkansas.

B41367. Martha Catherine Williams, seventh child and fifth daughter of Martha Pound and Benjamin Williams, born 23 May 1831 in Arkansas and died 15 Dec 1878 in Arkansas. Married Rupert McHenry.

B41368. Malcombe Williams, eighth child and third son of Martha Pound and Benjamin Williams, born 6 Jul 1833 in Arkansas and died 8 Aug 1833 in Arkansas.

B41369. Susan Ann Williams, ninth child and sixth daughter of Martha Pound and Benjamin Williams, born 27 Jun 1834 in Arkansas and died 1 Aug 1860 in Arkansas. Married William Jonathan Wallace.

B413610. Henry Clay Williams, tenth child and fourth son of Martha Pound and Benjamin Williams, born 10 Aug 1839 in Arkansas and died 22 Feb 1862 in Lavergne, Rutherford County, Tennessee in the Civil War. Buried New London, Union County, Arkansas.

B4137. Eliza (Elizabeth) Pounds, seventh child and fourth daughter of Richard Eli Pound and Mary Davidson, born 1802 in Clarke County, Georgia. Married 30 Jan 1816 in Pittsboro County, North Carolina to Bishop Parker.

B4138. Mary (Polly) Pounds, eighth child and fifth daughter of Richard Eli Pound and Mary Davidson, born 1804 in Clarke County, Georgia. Married Isaac Weeks.

B414. Newman Pound, Sr. born about 1765 in Orange County, Virginia, third child and second son of Reuben and Frances Pound, died 1842 in Kentucky. His first marriage 26 Oct 1831 in Wilkinson County, Georgia was to a woman whose first name was Margaret, but called Peggy and her family name is unknown, but she was born about 1773 and died before 1830. It appears that Newman may have been married at least three times. He married secondly to --- ---, born in Ohio and died in Missouri. Married thirdly to Sarah ---, born about 1795 in Virginia and died about 1842 in Kentucky. Newman's family reconstructed from family records, census schedules, and other sources is believed to have included eight sons and two daughters, with another daughter stillborn and unnamed. Newman Pound, Sr. and Reuben's daughter Frances (Franky) [also his sister] both decided to go west, so either late in 1804 or early in 1805, they loaded up their possessions and migrated to Louisiana Territory, which had just been purchased from France and which had not yet been surveyed and its' true boundaries determined. Franky had married James M. Britton, Sr. and they had several children by the time they came to Missouri. The two families settled southwest of St. Louis in what later became the state of Missouri. Newman's second wife's name is unknown and his third wife was named Sarah, with her family name unknown. Newman's issue was the seventh generation in America:

B4141. Reuben Pound, first child and first son of Newman Pound, Sr. and Margaret ---, born about 1792 in Clarke County, Georgia; died about 1849 in Missouri.

B4142. James A. Pound, second child and first son of Newman Pound, Sr. and Margaret ---, born 24 Feb 1794 in Greene County, Georgia; died 10 Apr 1866 at Morse Mill, Jefferson County, Missouri. Buried at Bethlehem, Jefferson County, Missouri. Married Susan Eveline Evans, born 1795 in Kentucky. James and Susan had issue, which was the eighth generation in America:

B41421. Newman Pounds, first child and first son of James Pound and Susan Evans, born 28 Dec 1812 at Morse Mill, Jefferson County, Missouri. Married 15 Aug 1833 in Jefferson County, Missouri to Lucinda Graham, born 1816 in Missouri. Newman and Lucinda had issue, which was the ninth generation in America:

B414211. Falkland Pound, first child and first son of Newman Pounds and Lucinda Graham, born 1836 in Jefferson County, Missouri. Married Emeline ---.

B414212. Margaret Pounds, second child and first daughter of Newman Pounds and Lucinda Graham, born 1843 in Jefferson County, Missouri.

B414213. Susan Pounds, third child and second daughter of Newman Pounds and

Lucinda Graham, born 1845 in Jefferson County, Missouri. Married --- Woods.

B414214. John Pound, fourth child and second son of Newman Pounds and Lucinda Graham, born 1850 in Jefferson County, Missouri.

B414215. Mary A. Pounds, fifth child and third daughter of Newman Pounds and Lucinda Graham, born 1852 in Jefferson County, Missouri.

B414216. Eva C. Pounds, sixth child and fourth daughter of Newman Pounds and Lucinda Graham, born 1854 in Jefferson County, Missouri.

B414217. Nancy C. Pounds, seventh child and fifth daughter of Newman Pounds and Lucinda Graham, born 1859 in Jefferson County, Missouri.

B41422. Isaac Pounds, second child and second son of James Pounds and Susan Evans, born 8 Sep 1814 at Morse Mill, Jefferson County, Missouri; died 1838 in Missouri. Married Nov 1832 to Elizabeth Ann Stites, born 1814 in Missouri. Isaac and Elizabeth had issue, which was the ninth generation in America:

B414221. Mary Ann Pound, first child and first daughter of Isaac Pounds and Elizabeth Stites, born 2 Dec 1834 in Jefferson County, Missouri; died 1894 in Missouri. Married 2 Apr 1856 in Missouri to Thomas Jefferson Manion.

B414222. James Milton Pounds, second child and first son of Isaac Pounds and Elizabeth Stites, born 4 Sep 1836 at Morse Mill, Jefferson County, Missouri. Married 23 Dec 1858 in Big River Township, Jefferson County, Missouri to Charlotte McCulloch, daughter of William McCulloch and --- Brown, born 1839 in Jefferson County, Missouri. James and Charlotte had issue, which was the tenth generation in America:

B4142221. Judson Boardman Pounds, first child and first son of James Pounds and Charlotte McCulloch, born 1 Feb 1860 at Morse Mill, Jefferson County, Missouri; died 1927 in Jefferson County, Missouri. Married 26 Dec 1880 at Morse Mill, Jefferson County, Missouri to Ardella Thompson.

B4142222.

Newman Freemont Pounds, second child and second son of James Pounds and Charlotte McCulloch, born 1862 at Morse Mill, Jefferson County, Missouri; married Arnette Williams.

B4142223. Lucinda (Lucy) Pounds, third child and first daughter of James Pounds and Charlotte McCulloch, born 11 Dec 1863 at Morse Mill, Jefferson County, Missouri; died 2 Jan 1885 in Jefferson County, Missouri. Married Thomas Degonia.

B4142224. Grant Pounds, fourth child and third son of James Pounds and Charlotte McCulloch, born 1865 at Morse Mill, Jefferson County, Missouri.

B4142225. Sherman J. Pounds, fifth child and fourth son of James Pounds and Charlotte McCulloch, born 11 Nov 1868 at Morse Mill, Jefferson County, Missouri; died 10 Feb 1917 in Jefferson County, Missouri. Married Eugenia H. Boyrie.

B4142226. Dorah Pounds, sixth child and second daughter of James Pounds and Charlotte McCulloch, born 2 Sep 1869 at Morse Mill, Jefferson County, Missouri; died 1 Feb 1890 in Jefferson County, Missouri.

B4142227. Josephine Pounds, seventh child and third daughter of James Pounds and Charlotte McCulloch, born May 1870 at Morse Mill, Jefferson County, Missouri.

B4142228. Cora E. Pounds, eighth child and fourth daughter of James Pounds and Charlotte McCulloch, born 1873 at Morse Mill, Jefferson County, Missouri; died 1946. Married Justus Wilson.

B414223. Nancy Jane Pounds, third child and second daughter of Isaac Pound and Elizabeth Stites, born 10 May 1838 at Morse Mill, Jefferson County, Missouri. Married 20 Nov 1853 in Jefferson County, Missouri to Abraham Evans.

B41423. Thomas Simpson Pounds, third child and third son of James Pounds and Susan Evans, born 27 Jul 1816 at Morse Mill, Jefferson County, Missouri. Married 26 Apr 1836 in Jefferson County, Missouri to Lucretia Turner. They had issue, which was the ninth generation in America:

B414231. Ellender Pounds, first child and first daughter of Thomas Pounds and Lucretia Turner, born 1837 in Jefferson County, Missouri.

B41423. Thomas Simpson Pounds, third child and third son of James Pounds and Susan Evans, born 27 Jul 1816 at Morse Mill, Jefferson County, Missouri married secondly Emily ---, born about 1820 in Tennessee. They also had issue, which was the ninth generation in America:

B414231. Emeline E. Pounds, first child and first daughter of Thomas Pounds and Emily ---. born 1845 in Jefferson County, Missouri.

B414232. Serena Pounds, second child and second daughter of Thomas Pounds and Emily ---born 1847 in Jefferson County, Missouri.

B414233. William (twin) Pounds, third child and first son of Thomas Pounds and Emily ---, born 1849 in Jefferson County, Missouri.

B414234. Francis (twin) Pounds, fourth child and second son of Thomas Pounds and Emily ---, born 1849 in Jefferson County, Missouri.

B414235. Silas Pounds, fifth child and third son of Thomas Pounds and Emily ---, born 1851 in Jefferson County, Missouri.

B41424. Margaret Pounds, fourth child and first daughter of James Pounds and Susan Evans, born 24 Feb 1819 at Morse Mill, Jefferson County, Missouri.

B41425. Reuben Pounds, fifth child and fourth son of James Pounds and Susan Evans, born 14 Feb 1822 at Morse Mill, Jefferson County, Missouri; died 1883 in Jefferson County, Missouri. Married 19 Apr 1841 in Jefferson County, Missouri to Ann Murrell, born 1823 in Kentucky. Reuben and Ann had issue, which was the ninth generation in America:

B414251. Isaac Evans Pounds, first child and first son of Reuben Pounds and Ann Murrell, born 1842 in Jefferson County, Missouri; died 1925. Married 6 Nov 1865 to Amanda J. McColloch. Married secondly 1888 to Martha M.

Trimble, daughter of John Trimble and Margaret Wiley, born 7 Oct 1856 in Cincinnati, Hamilton County, Ohio and died 1932 in Jefferson County, Missouri. Martha had been married previously to his brother, John T. Pounds.

B414252. Elizabeth E. Pounds, second child and first daughter of Reuben Pounds and Ann Murrell, born 1846 in Jefferson County, Missouri; died 11 Feb 1880 in Jefferson County, Missouri. Married William Graham.

B414253. Martha Missouri Pounds, third child and second daughter of Reuben Pounds and Ann Murrell, born 1847 at Morse Mill, Jefferson County, Missouri. Married 8 Apr 1869 in Jefferson County, Missouri to Arthur Howard Brooks.

B414254. Mary A. Pounds, fourth child and third daughter of Reuben Pounds and Ann Murrell, born 1849 at Morse Mill, Jefferson County, Missouri.

B414255. Margaret Pounds, fifth child and fourth daughter of Reuben Pounds and Ann Murrell, born 1851 at Morse Mill, Jefferson County, Missouri. Married 10 Jan 1869 to George W. Forrester.

B414256. John T. Pounds, sixth child and second son of Reuben Pounds and Ann Murrell, born 1854 in Jefferson County, Missouri; died 1883 in Jefferson County, Missouri. Married Dec 1879 to Martha M. Trimble, daughter of John Trimble and Margaret Wiley, born 7 Oct 1856 in Cincinnati, Hamilton County, Ohio; died 1932 at Ware, Jefferson County, Missouri. John T. Pounds and Martha Trimble had issue, which was the tenth generation in America:

B4142561. James William Pounds, first child and first son of John Pounds and Martha Trimble, born 26 Nov 1879 in Jefferson County, Missouri. Married 18 Sep 1904 in Jefferson County, Missouri to Jeanette Wideman, daughter of Patrick Wideman and Anna K. Anderson, born 22 Oct 1886 in Jefferson County, Missouri. James and Jeanette had issue, which was the eleventh generation in America:

B41425611. Bessie Pearl (twin) Pounds, first child and first daughter of James Pounds and

Jeanette Wideman, born 18 Jul 1905 in Jefferson County, Missouri. Married 23 Oct 1937 to Lewis Andrew Peterson.

B41425612. Essie Florence (twin) Pounds, second child and second daughter of James Pounds and Jeanette Wideman, born 18 Jul 1905 in Jefferson County, Missouri.

B41425613. Margaret Edna Pounds, third child and third daughter of James Pounds and Jeanette Wideman, born 29 Nov 1906 in Jefferson County, Missouri. Married 13 Jun 1927 to Dudley Shelton.

B41425614. John William Pounds, fourth child and first son of James Pounds and Jeanette Wideman, born 5 Aug 1908 in Jefferson County, Missouri. Married 22 Nov 1929 to Leona Record.

B41425615. Elizabeth Pounds, fifth child and fourth daughter of James Pounds and Jeanette Wideman, born 24 Feb 1909 in Jefferson County, Missouri. Married 12 Sep 1938 to Stanley McCoy.

B41425616. Lloyd Earl Pounds, sixth child and second son of James Pounds and Jeanette Wideman, born in Jefferson County, Missouri. Married 16 Jan 1932 to Elsie Mary Phelps.

B41425617. Hazel Myrtle Pounds, seventh child and fifth daughter of James Pounds and Jeanette Wideman, born 3 Sep 1912 in Jefferson County, Missouri. Married 27 Jun 1936 to Raymond Sutton.

B41425618. Annie May Pounds, eighth child and sixth daughter of James Pounds and Jeanette Wideman, born 10 Dec 1914 in Jefferson County, Missouri. Married 28 Feb 1936 to Thomas Rowland Schaaf.

B41425619. Robert Francis Pounds, ninth child and third son of James Pounds and Jeanette Wideman, born 16 Mar 1916 in Jefferson County, Missouri; died 10 Oct 1944 in Jefferson County, Missouri.

B41425620. Matilda Pounds, tenth child and seventh daughter of James Pounds and Jeanette Wideman, born 15 Jul 1917 in Jefferson County, Missouri; died 27 Sep 1935 in Jefferson County, Missouri.

B41425621. Stillborn daughter Pounds, eleventh child and eighth daughter of James Pounds and Jeanette Wideman. Born and died 1919 in Jefferson County, Missouri.

B41425622. Wilbert Warren Pounds, twelth child and fourth son of James Pounds and Jeanette Wideman, born 4 Mar 1921 in Jefferson County, Missouri. Married 15 Jun 1940 to Susanne Fisher.

B41425623. Leona May Pounds, thirteenth child and ninth daughter of James Pounds and Jeanette Wideman, born 12 Jan 1926 in Jefferson County, Missouri.

B41425624. Mildred Kathleen Pounds, fourteenth child and tenth daughter of James Pounds and Jeanette Wideman, born 8 Jul 1930 in Jefferson County, Missouri. Married 26 Aug 1949 to Joseph Oglesby.

B4142562. Elizabeth Pounds, second child and first daughter of John Pounds and Martha Trimble, born 29 Sep 1881 in Jefferson County, Missouri; died 12 Nov 1959. Married Allen Johnson.

B414257. Sarah Jane Pounds, seventh child and fifth daughter of Reuben Pounds and Ann Murrell, born 1856 at Morse Mill, Jefferson County, Missouri.

B41425. Reuben Pound, fifth child and fourth son of James Pound and Susan Evans, born 14 Feb 1822 at Morse Mill, Jefferson County, Missouri, had a second wife named Josephine Herrington, born about 1823 in Missouri, whom he married 21 Feb 1861. They had issue, which was the ninth generation in America:

B414251. Angeline Pounds, first child and first daughter of Reuben Pound and Josephine Herrington, born 1861 in Jefferson County, Missouri.

B414252. James Pounds, second child and first son of Reuben Pound and Josephine Herrington, born 1864 in Jefferson County, Missouri.

B414253. William Pounds, third child and second of Reuben Pound and Josephine Herrington, born 1865 in Jefferson County, Missouri.

B41426. Mary Pounds, sixth child and second daughter of James Pounds and Susan Evans, born 14 Dec 1824 at Morse Mill, Jefferson County, Missouri.

B41427. Stephen Pounds, seventh child and fifth son of James Pounds and Susan Evans, born 15 Oct 1828 at Morse Mill, Jefferson County, Missouri; died 1890 in Jefferson County, Missouri. Married 13 Sep 1849 in Jefferson County, Missouri to Martha Margaret Murrell, born 1832. They had issue, which was the ninth generation in America:

B414271. Willis C. Pounds, first child and first son of Stephen Pounds and Martha Murrell, born 1852 at Morse Mill, Jefferson County, Missouri.

B414272. Charles M. Pounds, second child and second son of Stephen Pounds and Martha Murrell, born 1854 in Jefferson County, Missouri.

B414273. Martha Ann Pounds, third child and first daughter of Stephen Pounds and Martha Murrell, born 19 Feb 1857 at Morse Mill, Jefferson County, Missouri.

B414274. William P. Pounds, fourth child and third son of Stephen Pounds and Martha Murrell, born about 1859 at Morse Mill, Jefferson County, Missouri.

B414275. Susan Pounds, fifth child and second daughter of Stephen Pounds and Martha Murrell, born 1862 at Morse Mill, Jefferson County, Missouri.

B414276. John Sidell Pounds, sixth child and fourth son of Stephen Pounds and Martha Murrell, born 1865 at Morse Mill, Jefferson County, Missouri.

B414277. Mary Pounds, seventh child and third daugther of Stephen Pounds and Martha Murrell, born 1870 at Morse Mill, Jefferson County, Missouri.

B414278. Frances Pounds, eighth child and fourth daughter of Stephen Pounds and Martha Murrell, born 1876 at Morse Mill, Jefferson County, Missouri.

B41428. Silas Pounds, eighth child and sixth son of James Pounds and Susan Evans, born 6 Aug 1832 at Morse Mill, Jefferson County, Missouri.

B4143. Lewis Pound, third child and third son of Newman Pound, Sr. and Margaret ---, born about 1796.

B4144. Thomas S. Pound, fourth child and fourth son of Newman Pound, Sr. and Margaret ---, born about 1798. Married 25 Apr 1836 in Jefferson County, Missouri to Lucretia Turner.

B4145. Mary Pound, fifth child and first daughter of Newman Pound, Sr. and Margaret ---, born 1802. Married 29 Mar 1821 in Franklin County, Missouri to William Mitchell.

B4141. Jane Pound, first child and first daughter of Newman Pound, Sr. and his second wife, name unknown, born in 1806. Married 18 Feb 1833 in Franklin County, Missouri to Lewis Collins.

B4142. Richard Kenner Pound, second child and first son of Newman Pound, Sr. and his second wife, name unknown, born 3 Oct 1815 in Crawford County, Missouri; died 3 Mar 1885 in Springdale, Washington County, Arkansas. Married 3 Sep 1833 in Steelville, Crawford County, Missouri to Martha Ann (Patsy) Boydstun, his first of five wives. Martha was born 13 Feb 1818 in Hickman County, Tennessee, daughter of Robert Washington Boydstun and Rachel Griffith, and died about 1850 in Richland Township, Crawford County, Arkansas. Richard Kenner Pound was a Primitive Baptist preacher and was pastor at the old Shiloh Primitive Baptist Church at the time of his death. He is buried in one of the older cemeteries at Springdale, Arkansas. All his five wives died and he fathered sixteen children. Richard and Martha had issue, which was the eighth generation in America:

B41421. Keziah Jane Pound, first child and first daughter of Richard Pound and Martha Boydstun, born 29 Oct 1834 in Crawford County, Missouri; died 1856 in Johnson County, Arkansas. Married 1850 to John Smith.

B41422. Sarah Ann Pound, second child and second daughter of Richard Pound and Martha Boydstun, born 25 Dec 1836 in Carroll County, Arkansas and died after 1880 in Arkansas. Married firstly Calvin Skaggs. Married secondly Samuel Milton Huggins, son of Luke Huggins and Nancy Milton, born 14 Feb 1823 in Tennessee and died after 1900. Sarah Pound and Samuel Huggins had issue, which was the ninth generation in America:

B414221. James Virgil Huggins, first child and first son of Sarah Pound and Samuel Huggins, born 1862 in Arkansas. Married Mary Stratton.

B414222. Pamela Adeline Huggins, second child and first daughter of Sarah Pound and Samuel Huggins, born 1863 in Arkansas and died 5 Sep 1937. Married Javan (Doc) Stewart.

B414223. Richard Monroe Huggins, third child and second son of Sarah Pound and Samuel Huggins, born 1865 in Arkansas. Married Eliza Battles.

B414224. Vernando Lafayette Huggins, fourth child and third son of Sarah Pound and Samuel Huggins, born 5 Dec 1866 in Arkansas and died 25 Apr 1940. Married Rebecca Hicks.

B414225. Alonzo Loranzo Huggins, fifth child and fourth son of Sarah Pound and Samuel Huggins, born 1869 in Arkansas. Married Callie Childers.

B414226. Mary Idella Huggins, sixth child and second daughter of Sarah Pound and Samuel Huggins, born 6 Jan 1871 in Arkansas and died 26 Jan 1916. Married Jim Corzine.

B414227. Samuel Leroy Huggins, seventh child and fifth son of Sarah Pound and Samuel Huggins, born 22 Sep 1872 in Arkansas and died 10 Jan 1949 in Franklin County, Arkansas. Married 15 Dec 1895 to Levania Ozella Huggins, daughter of James Marion Huggins and Susan Caroline Stapp, born Apr 1879 in Arkansas and died 11 Aug 1906. Samuel Huggins and Susan Stapp had issue, which was the tenth generation in America:

B4142271. Allie Huggins, first child and first daughter of Samuel Huggins and Susan Stapp, born Jul 1897 in White Rock, Franklin County, Arkansas.

B4142272. Evie Huggins, second child and second daughter of Samuel Huggins and Susan Stapp, born Jan 1899 in White Rock, Franklin County, Arkansas.

B4142273. Bonnie Ozella Huggins, third child and third daughter of Samuel Huggins and Susan Stapp, born 11 Aug 1906 and died 5 Jun 1990. Married 8 Jul 1922 to James Luke Battles.

B4142274. Essie Huggins, fourth child and fourth daughter of Samuel Huggins and Susan Stapp, date and place of birth unknown.

B4142275. Russell Huggins, fifth child and first son of Samuel Huggins and Susan Stapp, date and place of birth unknown.

B4142276. Milton Huggins, sixth child and second son of Samuel Huggins and Susan Stapp, date and place of birth unknown.

B414228. Isaac Oscar Huggins, eighth child and sixth son of Sarah Pound and Samuel Huggins, born 1875 in Arkansas. Married Lou Cato.

B414229. Lanora Huggins, ninth child and third daughter of Sarah Pound and Samuel Huggins, born 1878 in Arkansas. Married Will Youngblood.

B414230. Elonza Huggins, tenth child and fourth daughter of Sarah Pound and Samuel Huggins, born Feb 1880 in Arkansas.

B41423. Serena Pound, third child and third daughter of Richard Pound and Martha Boydstun, born 2 May 1839 in Carroll County, Arkansas and died in Arkansas.

B41424. Isaac Simpson Pound, fourth child and first son of Richard Pound and Martha Boydstun, born 11 Oct 1842 at Alma, Crawford County, Arkansas and died 20 Apr 1908 at Alma, Crawford County, Arkansas. Married Mary Hunter, born in Illinois; died 1967 in Arkansas. Isaac was a Confederate soldier in the Civil War; served in Co. "G", 22nd Reg. Arkansas Infantry. Isaac and Mary had issue, which was the ninth generation in America:

B414241. Martha Anna Pounds, first child and first daughter of Isaac Pound and Mary Hunter, born 2 Sep 1861 in Arkansas and died in Arkansas. Married Lewis Raines.

B414242. James Pounds, second child and first son of Isaac Pound and Mary Hunter, born about 1863 in Arkansas and died in Arkansas.

B414243. Thomas Henry Pounds, third child and second son of Isaac Pound and Mary Hunter, born Dec 1867 in Arkansas and died 1913 in Oklahoma. Married Rachel Applewhite Crawford.

B41424. Isaac Simpson Pound, fourth child and first son of Richard Pound and Martha Boydstun, married secondly 1867 in Crawford, Boone County, Arkansas to Nancy Jane James, daughter of Jeremiah James and Caroline Huggins, born 23 Jun 1848 in Franklin County, Arkansas; died 21 Nov 1910 at Alma, Crawford County, Arkansas. Isaac and Nancy had issue, which was the ninth generation in America:

B414241. Samuel Kenner Pound, first child and first son of Isaac Pound and Nancy James, born 10 Sep 1868 at Alma, Crawford County, Arkansas; died 22 Nov 1939 in Oklahoma. Married Nelia A. Gowers.

B414242. Nancy Caroline Pound, second child and first daughter of Isaac Pound and Nancy James. born 21 Jan 1870 at Alma, Crawford County, Arkansas; died 9 Nov 1885 in Arkansas.

B414243. Richard Franklin Pound, third child and second son of Isaac Pound and Nancy James born 9 Nov 1871 at Alma, Crawford County, Arkansas; died 18 Nov 1873 in Arkansas.

B414244. Harriet Elizabeth Pound, fourth child and second daughter of Isaac Pound and Nancy James, born 22 Mar 1873 at Alma, Crawford County, Arkansas; died 24 May 1915 in Arkansas. Married Thomas Gowers. Married secondly to William C. Fox.

B414245. Leroy (twin) Pound, fifth child and third son of Isaac Pound and Nancy James, born 26 Nov 1874 at Alma, Crawford County, Arkansas; died 6 Oct 1958 at Fort Smith, Franklin County, Arkansas. Buried at Van Buren, Gracelawn cemetery, Franklin County, Arkansas. Married 23 Nov 1902 in Pope County,

Arkansas to Maude Bullock, daughter of William Green Bullock and Louisa Ervin, born 12 Mar 1886 at Hector, Pope County, Arkansas. Leroy and Maud had issue, which was the tenth generation in America:

B4142451. Wilburn Clive Pound, first child and first son of Leroy Pound and Maude Bullock. born 31 Dec 1903 at Alma, Crawford County, Arkansas. Married 17 Jul 1926 at Fort Smith, Arkansas to Mary Elizabeth Hawkins.

B4142452. Audra Jane Pound, second child and first daughter of Leroy Pound and Maude Bullock, born 17 Apr 1907 at Alma, Crawford County, Arkansas. Married 7 Jun 1926 at Alma, Crawford County, Arkansas to Haskell Roy Ramsey.

B4142453. Julian Haynes Pound, third child and second son of Leroy Pound and Maude Bullock, born 9 Jun 1909 at Alma, Crawford County, Arkansas; died 11 Dec 1952 in Korea. Married 15 Jan 1931 to Etha Mae Pulis. Married secondly 30 Aug 1935 to Hazel Stroud.

B4142454. Cleburne Green Pound, fourth child and third son of Leroy Pound and Maude Bullock, born 23 Nov 1911 at Hector, Pope County, Arkansas. Married 17 Mar 1934 at Coalgate, Coal County, Oklahoma to Chlorine Howell, daughter of Elvis J. Howell and Christeen Blackwood. Cleburne Pound and Chlorine Howell had issue, which was the eleventh generation in America:

B41424541. Norma Jean Pound, first child and first daughter of Cleburne Pound and Chlorine Howell, born 20 Jan 1935 at Non, Hughes County, Oklahoma. Married Freeman Russell Whitlock, son of Russell Joseph Whitlock and Ruth Goss.

B41424542. Mary Ann Pound, second child and second daughter of Cleburne Pound and Chlorine Howell, born 3 Nov 1939 at Non, Hughes County, Oklahoma. Married 27 Jul 1957 at Holdenville, Hughes County, Oklahoma to Jerry Dean McConnell, son of William Carroll McConnell and Essie Hollingshead.

B41424543. Richard Leroy Pound, third child and first son of Cleburne Pound and Chlorine Howell, born 9 Jul 1945 at

Holdenville, Hughes County, Oklahoma. Married 18 Dec 1965 at Oklahoma City, Oklahoma County, Oklahoma to Judy Dyan Davis, daughter of Nealon Davis and Edna Sanders.

B4142455. Glenn Simpson Pound, fifth child and fourth son of Leroy Pound and Maude Bullock, born 7 Mar 1914 at Hector, Pope County, Arkansas. Married 29 Jun 1932 to Daisy Ferrel Cole.

B4142456. Allyn Vernell Pound, sixth child and second daughter of Leroy Pound and Maude Bullock, born 9 Jun 1917 at Iago, Wharton County, Texas. Married 22 Mar 1940 to William Felix Basham.

B4142457. John Leroy Pound, seventh child and fifth son of Leroy Pound and Maude Bullock, born 24 Jul 1919 at Iago, Wharton County, Texas; died 9 Jul 1921 at Pledger, Brazoria County, Texas.

B4142458. James Erwin Pound, eighth child and sixth son of Leroy Pound and Maude Bullock, born 31 Jan 1922 at Pledger, Brazoria County, Texas. Married first Dorothy Claire Roller. Married secondly to Betty Jane Fintoski. Married thirdly to Edith Bailey.

B4142459. Mary Helen Pound, ninth child and third daughter of Leroy Pound and Maude Bullock, born 5 Jun 1924 at Fort Smith, Franklin County, Arkansas. Married 9 Oct 1943 at Alma, Crawford County, Arkansas to Russell Carlisle Bullock.

B41424510. Robert Bullock Pound, tenth child and seventh son of Leroy Pound and Maude Bullock, born 27 Feb 1926 at Alma, Crawford County, Arkansas. Married 4 Apr 1948 at Alma, Crawford County, Arkansas to Eula Lucille Cole.

B414246. Leander (twin) Pound, sixth child and fourth son of Isaac Pound and Nancy James, born 26 Nov 1874 at Alma, Crawford County, Arkansas; died 15 Nov 1963 in Oklahoma. Married Josephine Jones.

B414247. Sarah Catherine Pound, seventh child and third daughter of Isaac Pound and Nancy James, born 10 Mar 1876 at Alma, Crawford County, Arkansas; died 10 Jul 1967 in Arkansas. Married 20 Feb 1898 in Arkansas to David Crockett Cottrell.

B414248. Frances Lucinda Pound, eighth child and fourth daughter of Isaac Pound and Nancy James, born 20 Apr 1880 at Alma, Crawford County, Arkansas; died 1 Nov 1966 in Oklahoma. Married Elbert Ellis Julian. Frances Pound and Elbert Julian had issue, which was the tenth generation in America:

B4142481. Fred Julian, first child and first son of Frances Pound and Elbert Julian, born Apr 1908 in Atwood, Hughes County, Oklahoma. Married Maurine Tims, born at Wetumka, Hughes County, Oklahoma. Fred Julian and Maurine Tims had issue, which was the eleventh generation in America:

B41424811. --- Julian, first child and first son of Fred Julian and Maurine Tims, date and place of birth unknown.

B41424812. Maurice Julian, second child and second son of Fred Julian and Maurine Tims, date and place of birth unknown.

B4142482. Elmer Julian, second child and second son of Frances Pound and Elbert Julian, born in Atwood, Hughes County, Oklahoma. Married Jessie Mae Pool, born in Atwood, Hughes County, Oklahoma. Elmer Julian and Jessie Pool had issue, which was the eleventh generation in America:

B41424821. --- Julian, first child, sex unknown, of Elmer Julian and Jessie Pool, date and place of birth unknown.

B41424822. --- Julian, second child, sex unknown, of Elmer Julian and Jessie Pool, date and place of birth unknown.

B4142483. Houston Julian, third child and third son of Frances Pound and Elbert Julian, born and died in Atwood, Hughes County, Oklahoma.

B4142484. Ethel Frances Julian, fourth child and first daughter of Frances Pound and Elbert Julian, born 14 Nov 1914 in Atwood, Hughes County, Oklahoma.

B4142485. Edgar Ellis Julian, fifth child and fourth son of Frances Pound and Elbert Julian, born 23 Nov 1917 in Atwood, Hughes County, Oklahoma.

B4142486. William Lee Julian, sixth child and fifth son of Frances Pound and Elbert Julian, born 7 Jul 1920 in Atwood, Hughes County, Oklahoma. Married Cecilia L. Willoughby. William Julian and Cecilia Willoughby had issue, which was the eleventh generation in America:

B41424861. Ted L. Julian, first child and first son of William Julian and Cecilia Willoughby, born 1949. Married Shakirey Sarah. Married secondly to Beverly Hatfield.

B41424862. Sondra K. Julian, second child and first daughter of William Julian and Cecilia Willoughby, born 1951. Married Michael Childs. Married secondly Michael Campbell.

B414249. Isaac Van Pound, ninth child and fifth son of Isaac Pound and Nancy James, born 10 Mar 1882 at Alma, Crawford County, Arkansas; died 18 Jun 1967 in Arkansas. Married Emma Sleeper.

B414250. Josephine Emmaline Pound, tenth child and fifth daughter of Isaac Pound and Nancy James, born 16 Feb 1884 at Alma, Crawford County, Arkansas; died 24 Dec 1947 in California. Married Coleman Younger Harris.

B414251. Mary Belle Pound, eleventh child and sixth daughter of Isaac Pound and Nancy James, born 11 Apr 1886 at Alma, Crawford County, Arkansas; died 27 Feb 1900 in Arkansas.

B414252. Albert Monroe Pound, twelfth child and sixth son of Isaac Pound and Nancy James, born 15 Apr 1886 in Arkansas; died 2 Sep 1962 in Arkansas. Married Mellie Burley Cottrell.

B41425. Permelia Catherine Pound, fifth child and fourth daughter of Richard Kenner Pound and Martha Boydstun, born 8 Dec 1845 in Johnson County, Arkansas; died Nov 1927 in Texas. Married 20 Feb 1862 in Franklin County, Arkansas to Benjamin Franklin Milton.

B41426. Newman Lafayette Pound, sixth child and second son of Richard Kenner Pound and Martha Boydstun, born 10 Jun 1847 in Johnson County, Arkansas; died 1918 in Oklahoma. Married Eliza Jane Hunter. Newman married secondly 8 Jan 1879 in Franklin County, Arkansas to Elizabeth Hendricks; married thirdly 28 May 1884 at National Springs, Logan County, Arkansas to Eliza R. Perkins. Newman's fourth wife was Nancy Campbell. Newman and Eliza Jane Hunter had issue, which was the ninth generation in America:

B414261. James Richard Pound, first child and first son of Newman Pound and Eliza Hunter, born 11 Sep 1866 in Crawford County, Arkansas.

B414262. Martha A.C. Pound, second child and first daughter of Newman Pound and Eliza Hunter, born 1868 in Crawford County, Arkansas.

B414263. Louis Lafayette Sibley Pound, third child and second son of Newman Pound and Eliza Hunter, born 10 Jan 1870 in Crawford County, Arkansas. Married Cynthia M. Poole. Louis Pound and Cynthia Poole had issue, which was the tenth generation in America:

B4142631. Oscar Newman Pound, first child and first son of Louis Pound and Cynthia Poole, born 25 Nov 1895 and died 15 Apr 1945 at Tucson, Pima County, Arkansas. Buried at Miller cemetery, Pushmataha County, Oklahoma. Married 24 Nov 1919 at Miller, Pushmataha County, Oklahoma to Annie Lou Holder, daughter of Lorenzo Dow Holder and Leona Isabelle Lovelace, born 8 Feb 1897 at Mt. Vernon, Franklin County, Texas and died 21 Dec 1981 at Antlers, Pushmataha County, Oklahoma. Buried at Miller cemetery, Pushmataha County, Oklahoma. Oscar Pound and Annie Holder had issue, which was the eleventh generation in America:

B41426311. Oscar Lou Pound, first child and first son of Oscar Pound and Annie Holder, born 19 Feb 1922 at Miller, Pushmataha County, Oklahoma and died 18 Nov 1944 in France (World War II).

B41426312. Louis Dall (L.D.) Pound, second child and second son of Oscar Pound and Annie Holder, born 24 Jan 1926 at Miller, Pushmataha County, Oklahoma. Married 20 Dec 1957 to Lois Van Meter Cogburn.

B41426313. Lee Edward Pound, third child and third son of Oscar Pound and Annie Holder, born 19 Aug 1929 at Miller, Pushmataha County, Oklahoma. Married 28 Jul 1948 to Anna Bell O'Keefe.

B41426314. James Lafayette Pound, fourth child and fourth son of Oscar Pound and Annie Holder, born 13 Mar 1931 at Miller, Pushmataha County, Oklahoma. Married 26 Dec 1953 at Jumbo, Pushmataha County, Oklahoma to Clara Sue Smith, daughter of Henry Smith and Ruby Gregg, born 15 Dec 1936 at Jumbo, Pushmataha County, Oklahoma. James Pound and Clara Smith had issue, which was the twelth generation in America:

B414263141. Jimmy Lynn Pound, first child and first son of James Pound and Clara Smith, born 2 Sep 1955 at Wichita, Sedgwick County, Kansas. Married 26 Nov 1976 to Patti Sue Payne, born 16 Mar 1957 at Pawnee, Pawnee County, Oklahoma.

B414264. Mary Pound, fourth child and second daughter of Newman Pound and Eliza Hunter, born 1874 in Crawford County, Arkansas.

B4142. Richard Kenner Pound, second child and first son of Newman Pound, Sr. and his second wife, name unknown, had a total of five wives, but no children are known from his marriages to his second and third wives, who were respectively; a lady whose last name was Moore, but her first name is unknown; followed by a lady whose last name Mobley and her first name is unknown, also. His fourth marriage was to a lady named Hogan and her first name is unknown. Richard and this wife had issue, which was the eighth generation in America:

B41421. Elizabeth Ann Pound, first child and first daughter of Richard Kenner Pound and --- Hogan, born 1 Sep 1855 in Johnson County, Arkansas; died 1925 in Henryetta, Okmulgee County, Oklahoma. Married Greene Clay.

B4142. Richard Kenner Pound, seventh child and fifth son of Newman Pound, Sr. and Margaret --married a fifth time 11 Apr 1860 in Franklin County, Arkansas to Harriet Huggins, daughter of Luke Huggins and Nancy Milton, born 13 Aug 1837 in Arkansas and died in 1907 in Arkansas. Richard and Harriet had issue, which was the eighth generation in America:

B41421. Richard Jefferson Pound, first child and first son of Richard Kenner Pound and Harriet Huggins, born 29 Dec 1861 in Crawford County, Arkansas and died 1918 in Arkansas. Married Mary J. Moore.

B41422. James Franklin Pound, second child and second son of Richard Kenner Pound and Harriet Huggins, born 6 Feb 1863 in Crawford County, Arkansas and died 7 Oct 1882 in Arkansas.

B41423. Mary Lee Pound, third child and first daughter of Richard Kenner Pound and Harriet Huggins, born 16 Jun 1864 in Crawford County, Arkansas and died 1 Dec 1883 in Arkansas. Married Jack Perkins.

B41424. Martha Lillian Pound, fourth child and second daughter of Richard Kenner Pound and Harriet Huggins, born 12 Mar 1866 in Crawford County, Arkansas and died in Arkansas. Married Samuel Ratcliffe.

B41425. Luke Pound, fifth child and third son of Richard Kenner Pound and Harriet Huggins, born 28 Sep 1867 in Crawford County, Arkansas and died 2 Nov 1867 in Arkansas.

B41426. Josephine Bourland Pound, sixth child and third daughter of Richard Kenner Pound and Harriet Huggins, born 20 Dec 1868 in Crawford County, Arkansas and died 30 Apr 1941 in Oklahoma. Married firstly George Huggins. Married secondly Wiliam Bullock.

B41427. John Henderson Kenner Pound, seventh child and fourth son of Richard Kenner Pound and Harriet Huggins, born 22 Feb 1870 in Crawford County, Arkansas and died May 1940 in Oklahoma. Married Effie Cox.

B41428. Nancy Harriet Pound, eighth child and fourth daughter of Richard Kenner Pound and Harriet Huggins, born 12 Oct 1871 in Crawford County, Arkansas and died 1943 in Oklahoma. Married Jack Horner.

B41429. Margaret Jane Pound, ninth child and fifth daughter of Richard Kenner Pound and Harriet Huggins, born 20 May 1877 in Crawford County, Arkansas and died 30 May 1939 in Oklahoma.

Married 4 Aug 1895 in Franklin County, Arkansas to Daniel F. Rosson.

B4141. Joseph K. Pound, first child and first son of Newman Pound and Sarah ---, born 1818 in Missouri, died before 1864 in McDonald County, Missouri. Married 7 Jan 1836 in Jefferson County, Missouri to Mary Ann Weideman, daughter of Jacob Weideman, Sr., and Sarah ---, born about 1817 in South Carolina; died before 1864 in McDonald County, Missouri. Joseph married secondly Jane ---, but no children are known from this marriage. Joseph and Mary Ann had issue, which was the eighth generation in America:

B41411. Susan Pound, first child and first daughter of Joseph Pound and Mary Weideman, born 17 Oct 1736 in Jefferson County, Missouri.

B41412. Reuben C. Pound, second child and first son of Joseph Pound and Mary Weideman, born 15 Sep 1839 in Jefferson County, Missouri and died 30 Oct 1903 in Wise County, Texas. Married Jul 1872 in Wise County, Texas to Amanda Hobson.

B41413. Edna Louise Pound, third child and second daughter of Joseph Pound and Mary Weideman, born 1 Jan 1841 in McDonald County, Missouri and died 12 Jul 1929; is buried at Denison, Grayson County, Texas. Married a man whose first name is unknown but his last name was Jackson. Married secondly 24 Dec 1868 to William Simmons.

B41414. Mary Elizabeth Pound, fourth child and third daughter of Joseph Pound and Mary Weideman, born 1844 in McDonald County, Missouri.

B41415. Lewis Kenneth Pound, fifth child and second son of Joseph Pound and Mary Weideman, born 10 Mar 1846 in McDonald County, Missouri and died 9 Oct 1916. Married Katherine Williams.

B41416. Margaret Susan Adline Ann Pound, sixth child and fourth daughter of Joseph Pound and Mary Weideman, born 6 Sep 1848 in Newton County, Missouri and died 17 Feb 1934 at Nocona, Montague County, Texas. Buried at Nocona cemetery, Montague County, Texas. Married 14 Jan

1866 in Grayson County, Texas to Thomas N. Bradley, born 25 Dec 1824 in Lauderdale, Lauderdale County, Alabama; died 24 Oct 1906 at Nara Visa, Quay County, New Mexico. Buried Nara Visa cemetery, Quay County, New Mexico. They had issue, which was the ninth generation in America:

B414161. Thomas J. Bradley, first child and first son of Margaret Pound and Thomas Bradley, born 1866 in Texas.

B414162. Nancy Bradley, second child and first daughter of Margaret Pound and Thomas Bradley, born 1868 in Texas.

B414163. Josephine Bradley, third child and second daughter of Margaret Pound and Thomas Bradley, born 2 Aug 1871 at Denison, Grayson County, Texas; died 25 Oct 1946 at Portales, Roosevelt County, New Mexico. Married 25 Oct 1885 at Saint Jo, Montague County, Texas to Floyd Hamilton Atha.

B414164. Frankie Bradley, fourth child and third daughter of Margaret Pound and Thomas Bradley, born 1873 in Texas.

B414165. Nora Bradley, fifth child and fourth daughter of Margaret Pound and Thomas Bradley, born Sep 1873 in Texas. Married --- Goldsmith.

B414166. Hattie Bradley, sixth child and fifth daughter of Margaret Pound and Thomas Bradley, born 27 Nov 1874 at Denison, Grayson County, Texas and died 22 Oct 1875 at Denison, Grayson County, Texas.

B41417. James Pound, seventh child and third son of Joseph Pound and Mary Weideman, born 1854 in Missouri.

B41418. Till Pound, eighth child and fourth son of Joseph Pound and Mary Weideman, date and place of birth unknown.

B4149. Willis Bradshaw Pound, ninth child and seventh son of Newman Pound, Sr. and Margaret ---, born 24 Oct 1820 in Franklin or Gasconade Missouri and died Mar 1902 in Cedarville, Crawford County, Arkansas. Married 1 Jun 1845 in Crawford County, Arkansas to Martha Rhodes. After her early death, he married

Martha's sister, Mary Roades. His third wife was Emily Barnard and his fourth and last wife was Mrs. Jennie Ashe, who survived him. Willis Pound and his third wife, Emily Barnard are buried in the Salem cemetery at Cedarville, Crawford County, Arkansas. Willis Pound and Martha Roades had issue, which was the eighth generation in America:

B41491. Jane Pound, first child and first daughter of Willis Pound and Martha Roades, born 1846 in Missouri and died 1887 in Texas.

B41492. Ellen M. Pound, second child and second daughter of Willis Pound and Martha Roades, born 4 Jul 1848 in Missouri and died 5 Mar 1939 in Arkansas.

B4149. Willis Bradshaw Pound, ninth child and seventh son of Newman Pound, Sr., and Margaret ---, married secondly to Mary Roades. Willis Pound and Mary Roades had issue, which was the eighth generation in America:

B41491. Daughter Pound, first child and first daughter of Willis Pound and Mary Roades, born about 1850 in Missouri. Mary Roades died shortly after the baby daughter was born. A neighbor couple had baby born to them at the same time the Pound infant was born, and their baby died. Needing a baby to nurse the mother's breasts, they borrowed the Pound child (a practice not uncommon in those days). Becoming attached to the motherless child, the family secretly moved away by night, taking the Pound baby with them. Willis searched far and wide for his child, even going to Texas, but never found her. The family which kidnapped the baby was named King.

B4149. Willis Bradshaw Pound, ninth child and seventh son of Newman Pound, Sr., and Margaret ---, married thirdly to Emily Barnard, born 9 Nov 1837 in Kentucky and died 1898 in Arkansas. Willis Pound and Emily Barnard had issue, which was the eighth generation in America:

B41491. James Oliver Pound, first child and first son of Willis Pound and Emily Barnard, born 21 Feb 1857 in Missouri and died 5 Jan 1936 in Arkansas. Married Nancy A ---.

B41492.	Barzilla
Franklin Pound, second child and second son of
Willis Pound and Emily Barnard, born 27 Jan 1863
in Missouri and died in Arkansas. Married Louisa
---.

B41493.	Lucy	Alice
Pound, third child and and first daughter of
Willis Pound and Emily Barnard, born 16 Oct 1868
in Missouri and died about 1884.

B41494.	William Marion
Pound, fourth child and third son of Willis Pound
and Emily Barnard, born 28 Dec 1873 in Texas and
died 1917 in Oklahoma.	Married Alice Unger.

B41495.	Manda Arminda
Pound, fifth child and second daughter of Willis
Pound and Emily Barnard, born 8 Dec 1877 in
Arkansas and died 14 Apr 1962 in Arkansas.
Married Bishop Riddle.

B4149. Willis Bradshaw Pound,
ninth child and seventh son of Newman Pound, Sr.,
and Margaret ---, married fourthly to Mrs. Jennie
Ashe.	Willis Pound and Jennie Ashe had issue,
which was the eighth generation in America:

B41491.	Wylie	Boyd
Pound, first child and first son of Willis Pound
and Jennie Ashe, born 1902 in Arkansas and died
1974 in Arkansas.	Married Carrie Wentz.

B415.	Sarah (Sallie) Pound, fifth
child and second daughter of Reuben Pound and
Frances Merriman, born about 1770 in Virginia and
died in North Carolina.	Married 22 Sep 1781 in
Orange County, North Carolina to John Chisholm
(Chism), date and place of birth unknown, but he
died in Columbia County, Georgia.

B416.	Merriman Richard (Old Dicky)
Pounds, sixth child and fourth son of Reuben Pound
and Frances Merriman, born about 1770 in Virginia
and died about Mar 1843 in Putnam County, Georgia.
Buried Pound family cemetery, Jasper County,
Georgia.	Merriman married 1790 in Jasper County,
Georgia to Clarissa Ladufsia Herndon, daughter of
George Herndon and Elizabeth ---, born about 1770
in North Carolina, died 1843 in Putnam County,
Georgia. Buried in Pound family cemetery, Jasper
County, Georgia.	They settled in Putnam County,
Georgia when it was formed in 1807, and where

Merriman was one of the original settlers, becoming a wealthy planter there. Military records of the Washington County, Georgia muster rolls, dated 1779-1839, show that Private Merriman Pounds from Rabon's District had one horse and served in Captain Joseph Carson's Troop of Militia as a cavalryman. He served two terms of duty at Rock Landing Fort while Colonel John McKenzie served as fort commandant. A sworn statement from John McKenzie given 14 May 1833, stated that said military service was around 1793-1795. Because of old age, McKenzie could not recall the exact year. Merriman Pounds gave a sworn oath to the same service on 10 Aug 1833. Merriman is also listed as Corporal in Thomas' 2nd Regiment, Georgia Militia, serving during the War of 1812. His name is also registered on a list of those filing claims with the State of Georgia for property losses resulting from actions taken by the Creek Indians in 1799.

So, there are several references to the military involvement of this Putnam County pioneer. His story is an interesting one that relates how a native Virginian came to live in the southwest corner of a Georgia county, carving for himself and his family a home on the banks of Murder Creek. His Devil's Halfacre Plantation was on the edge of white settlement, and was probably viewed as an encroachment onto land what rightly had belonged to the Creek Indians. Merriman was the son of Reuben Pound, who served in the Revolutionary War with the Georgia Continental Line. The family lived in Orangé County, North Carolina and in South Carolina before moving to Georgia. Clarissa Ladufsia Herndon descended from William Herndon and Catherine Digges of Virginia. Both the Herndon and Digges families were among Virginia's most prosperous settlers prior to 1700. In late 1797, Merriman's father Reuben died and his heirs came into possession of his 230 acres in Green County, Georgia. Reuben's heirs sold this land to Stephen Bishop for $1000.00 and this was only ten years after the Creek Indians crossed the Oconee on its' west bank, murdering many Greene County residents. Such was the time in which this Pounds family lived. The Pound family cemetery is

located about 14 miles from Monticello, on Highway
212, going toward Milledgeville, near old
Stanfordville, on the old Merriman Pound place.
It can be seen on the left side of Highway 212.
This cemetery is in Putnam County. Many of the
descendants live in Jasper County and it is
fitting that this record be included here.
Merriman and Ladufsia had issue, which was the
seventh generation in America:
  B4161. Clarissa Pound, first
child and first daughter of Merriman Pound and
Clarissa Herndon, born at Devil's Half Acre,
Putnam County, Georgia. Married John Morgan.
  B4162. Merriman Pound, Jr.,
second child and first son of Merriman Pound and
Clarissa Herndon, born in Greene County, Georgia
and died in Georgia. Married Mary A. ---, born
about 1800 in Georgia. Merriman, Jr. and Mary A.
had issue, which was the eighth generation in
America:
  B41621. Alva P. Pounds,
first child and first daughter of Merriman Pound,
Jr. and Mary A. ---, born 1836 in Alabama.
  B41622. Victoria Pounds,
second child and second daughter of Merriman
Pound, Jr. and Mary A. ---, born 1841 in Alabama.
  B41623. Sarah A. Pounds,
third child and third daughter of Merriman Pound,
Jr. and Mary A. ---, born 1845 in Alabama.
  B4163. Sarah (Sally) Pound,
third child and second daughter of Merriman Pound
and Clarissa Herndon, born about 1795 in Green
County, Georgia. Married 6 May 1813 in Putnam
County, Georgia to Pelathia Whitehurst, born about
1790 at Tarboro, Edgecombe County, North Carolina
and died about 1836 in Leon County, Florida. No
children are known from this marriage and Sarah
married secondly a man whose first name is
unknown, but whose last name was Herley.
  B4164. Richard Pound, fourth
child and second son of Merriman Pound and
Clarissa Herndon, born 6 May 1796 in Greene
County, Georgia and died 11 Jun 1879 in
Mississippi. Richard married 30 Jun 1818 in
Putnam County, Georgia to Cynthia Harkness, date
and place of birth unknown, but she died after

103

1830 in Georgia. Richard married secondly to Elizabeth Watson and married thirdly 14 Dec 1859 in Harris County, Georgia to Elizabeth Austin. Richard Pound married fourthly to Nancy Thompson. Richard and Cynthia had issue, which was the eighth generation in America:

B41641. Newman Pound, first child and first son of Richard Pound and Cynthia Harkness. His date and place of birth are unknown and nothing is known about his subsequent life.

B41642. Richard Pound, Jr., second child and second son of Richard Pound and Cynthia Harkness, born in Georgia. Married 15 Apr 1832 in Harris County, Georgia to Elizabeth Watson, daughter of Isham Watson and Rhoda ---, born about 1813 in Georgia. Richard's brother Merriman married Elizabeth's sister Sarah.

B41643. Merriman Pound, third child and and third son of Richard Pound and Cynthia Harkness, born 30 Aug 1819 in Georgia and died 21 Jan 1891 in Lee County, Mississippi. Buried in Pounds cemetery, Lee County, Mississippi. Married 7 Apr 1840 in Harris County, Georgia to Sarah May Watson, daughter of Isham Watson and Rhoda ---, born 20 May 1825 in Georgia and died 26 Oct 1912. Buried in Pounds cemetery, Lee County, Mississippi. Merriman's brother Richard married Sarah's sister Elizabeth. Merriman Pound was a Civil War veteran. During the Civil War, in operations ranging through Kentucky, southwest Virginia, Tennessee, Mississippi, north Alabama and north Georgia, Merriman Pound distinguished himself as a commander of a sharpshooter unit. Early in 1863, in Tennessee, Captain M. Pound, Pound's (Mississippi) Battalion Sharpshooters, under Ector's Brigade, (Brigadier General Matthew D. Ector), under Walker's Division (Major General William H.T. Walker), Reserve Corps, performed prominently. Merriman and Sarah had issue, which was the ninth generation in America:

B416431. Sarah Jane Pound, first child and first daughter of Merriman Pound and Sarah Watson, born 17 Nov 1842 and died 20 Jul 1927 in Lee County, Mississippi. Married 9

Feb 1858 in Mississippi to Jesse Ivy Hunt, born 28 Dec 1831, died 7 Dec 1922 in Lee County, Mississippi.

B416432. Richard L. Pound, second child and first son of Merriman Pound and Sarah Watson, born 1845 in Harris County, Georgia.

B416433. Andrew J. Pound, third child and second son of Merriman Pound and Sarah Watson, born 1848 in Itawamba County, Mississippi.

B416434. Martha E. Pound, fourth child and second daughter of Merriman Pound and Sarah Watson, born 1 Aug 1851 and died 18 Jul 1866.

B416435. William T. Pound, fifth child and third son of Merriman Pound and Sarah Watson, born 1853 in Itawamba County, Mississippi.

B416436. Angelina Pound, sixth child and third daughter of Merriman Pound and Sarah Watson, date and place of birth unknown.

B41644. Caroline Pound, fourth child and first daughter of Richard Pound and Cynthia Harkness, born 7 Sep 1824 in Putnam County, Georgia, and died 1 Mar 1909 in Lee County, Mississippi. Buried in Andrews Chapel cemetery, south of Mooresville, Mississippi. Married 21 Oct 1841 to Mark Tally, born 16 Oct 1808 in Georgia, and died 15 Jan 1877 in Lee County, Mississippi. Buried at Andrews Chapel cemetery, south of Mooreville, Mississippi.

B416441. Sophia J. Tally, first child and first daughter of Caroline Pound and Mark Tally, born in Mississippi.

B416442. Marshall J. (twin) Tally, second child and first son of Caroline Pound and Mark Tally, born in Mississippi.

B416443. Merriman A. (twin) Tally, third child and second son of Caroline Pound and Mark Tally, born in Mississippi.

B416444. Emma A. Tally, fourth child and second daughter of

Caroline Pound and Mark Tally, born in Mississippi.

B41645. Martha Margaret Pound, fifth child and second daughter of Richard Pound and Cynthia Harkness, born 1 Aug 1826 in Harris County, Georgia and died 21 Jul 1889 in Mooreville, Lee County, Mississippi. Married 9 Aug 1843 in Harris County, Georgia to Eli C. Middlebrooks, son of Isaac Middlebrooks and Elizabeth Thompson, born 24 Aug 1817 in Harris County, Georgia and died 4 Oct 1875 in Mooreville, Lee County, Mississippi. Buried Boguefala cemetery, Mooreville, Mississippi. They had issue, which was the ninth generation in America:

B416451. George Wilkerson Middlebrooks, first child and first son of Martha Pound and Eli Middlebrooks, born 11 Dec 1846 in Harris County, Georgia and died 18 Sep 1924 in Ladonia, Fannin County, Texas. Married 7 Nov 1867 in Lee County, Mississippi to Mary Ann Elizabeth (Betty) Garner, born 7 Dec 1848 in Moore County, North Carolina and died 20 Jun 1922 in Ladonia, Fannin County, Texas.

B4164511. Claude Finis Middlebrooks, seventh child and fifth son of George Middlebrooks and Mary Garner, born 7 Jan 1884 in Tupelo, Lee County, Mississippi and died 16 Jun 1970 at Houston, Harris County, Texas. Married 10 Dec 1908 at Ladonia, Fannin County, Texas to Eva Atma (Mae) Jernigan, daughter of William Henry Jernigan and Amanda Elizabeth Southerland, born 25 Jun 1891 at Bangs, Brown County, Texas and died 10 Dec 1977 at Alice, Jim Wells County, Texas. Buried at Houston, Harris County, Texas.

B41645111. Juedon (Don) Dale Middlebrooks, fourth child and second son of Claude Middlebrooks and Eva Jernigan, born 7 Feb 1923 at Ladonia, Fannin County, Texas and died 10 Mar 1978 at Dallas, Dallas County, Texas. Married 24 Dec 1942 at Alamogordo, Otero County, New Mexico to Tex Yuma Heinrich, daughter of Steven August Heinrich and Elsie Louise Hildebrand, born 17 Feb 1926 at Yuma, Yuma County, Arizona.

B416451111. Carol Jean Middlebrooks, first child and first daughter of Juedon Middlebrooks and Tex Heinrich, born 26 Sep 1945 at Texarkana, Miller County, Arkansas. Married 17 Apr 1965 at Austin, Travis County, Texas to Leslie (Les) Dee Shroyer, born 3 Jun 1944 at Alexandria, Rapides Parish, Louisiana, son of Fred Alvin Shroyer and D'Alva Glenn.

B4164511111. Susan Kay Shroyer, first child and first daughter of Carol Jean Middlebrooks and Leslie Shroyer, born 23 Feb 1974 in Princeton, Princeton County, New Jersey.

B4164511112. Margaret Elaine Shroyer, second child and second daughter of Carol Jean Middlebrooks and Leslie Shroyer, born 29 Jul 1976 in Dallas, Dallas County, Texas.

B416452. Cynthia Middlebrooks, second child and first daughter of Martha Pound and Eli Middlebrooks, born 1848 in Harris County, Georgia and died in 1922. Married Samuel Whitesides.

B416453. Isaac Richard Middlebrooks, third child and second son of Martha Pound and Eli Middlebrooks, born 1850 in Harris County, Georgia and died 1934. Married Mary (Molly) Eubanks.

B416454. Mary Bridges Middlebrooks, fourth child and second daughter of Martha Pound and Eli Middlebrooks, born 1853 in Harris County, Georgia and died 1948 in Falls County, Texas. Married Major Calvin Whitesides.

B416455. Caroline Clarissa Middlebrooks, fifth child and third daughter of Martha Pound and Eli Middlebrooks, born 1858. Married Lee Brown.

B416456. Eli Jefferson Davis Middlebrooks, sixth child and third son of Martha Pound and Eli Middlebrooks, born 1862. Married Margaret A. Bigerstaff.

B4165. John Bohannon Pound, fifth child and third son of Merriman Pound and Clarissa Herndon, born 4 May 1799 at Devil's Half Acre, Putnam County, Georgia and died 25 Apr 1876 in Putnam County, Georgia. Buried Pound family cemetery in Jasper County, Georgia. Married 30 Dec 1823 in Jones County, Georgia to Amelia Gay, daughter of John Gay and Amelia Castleberry, born

29 Nov 1806 in Jones County, Georgia and died 3
Aug 1841 in Putnam County, Georgia. Buried Pound
family cemetery in Jasper County, Georgia. John
married secondly 1 Aug 1843 in Baldwin County,
Georgia to her sister, Mary Gay Harris. John
Bohannon and Amelia had issue, which was the
eighth generation in America:

B41651. Henrietta Hill
Pound, first child and first daughter of John
Pound and Amelia Gay, born 10 Apr 1825 in
Standardville, Putnam County, Georgia and died 7
Oct 1901 in Hawthorne, Alachua County, Florida.
Buried in Rock Mills, Randolph County, Alabama.
Married 5 Nov 1840 in Putnam County, Georgia to M.
Wilkins Stevens, born 1 Sep 1802 in Georgia and
died 5 Apr 1873 in Rock Mills, Randolph County,
Alabama. They had issue, which was the ninth
generation in America:

B416511. Mary Maria
Stevens, first child and first daughter of
Henrietta Pound and Wilkins Stevens, born 3 May
1857 in Rock Mills, Randolph County, Alabama and
died 19 Apr 1939 in Hawthorne, Alachua County,
Florida. Married William Robert Sharman, born 8
Apr 1846 in Chambers County, Alabama, died 5 Apr
1918 in Hawthorne, Alachua County, Florida. They
had issue, which was the tenth generation in
America:

B4165111. Annie
Belle Sharman, first child and first daughter of
Mary Stevens and William Sharman, born 30 Aug 1875
in Rock Mills, Randolph County, Alabama. Married
William Edgar Brown, born 21 Nov 1872 in Perry,
Houston County, Georgia and died 8 Mar 1932 in
Jacksonville, Duval County, Florida. They had
issue, which was the eleventh generation in
America:

B41651111. Gladys
Brown, first child and first daughter of Annie
Sharman and William Brown, date and place of birth
unknown. Married Kenneth Rudolph Brand.

B41652. Andrew Jackson
Pound, second child and first son of John Pound
and Amelia Gay, born 24 Jun 1826 in Putnam County,
Georgia and died 5 Jun 1886. Married 29 Oct 1844
in Putnam County, Georgia to Susan Greene. Andrew

married secondly to Betty Dumas. Andrew and Susan had issue, which was the ninth generation in America:

B416521. Joseph Bohannon Pound, first child and first son of Andrew Pound and Susan Greene, born 10 Apr 1849 in Georgia and died 6 May 1910 at Albany, Dougherty County, Georgia. Buried Jacksonville, Evergreen cemetery, Duval County, Florida. Married 14 Jul 1870 in Dooly County, Georgia to Ida Irene Stubbs, daughter of Abner Palmer Stubbs and Martha Ann Woodward, born 7 Jun 1854 at Perry, Houston County, Georgia and died 29 Jan 1940 at Jacksonville, Duval County, Florida. Buried Jacksonville, Evergreen cemetery, Florida. Joseph Pound and Ida Stubbs had issue, which was the tenth generation in America:

B4165211. Lura Alice Pound, first child and first daughter of Joseph Pound and Ida Stubbs, born 16 Mar 1873 in Vienna, Dooly County, Georgia and died 14 Aug 1964. Married 17 Dec 1889 to Charles Warren Bartleson.

B4165212. Nora Pound, second child and second daughter of Joseph Pound and Ida Stubbs, born 19 Nov 1874. Married 28 Jun 1900 to Dr. Walter B. Holmes.

B4165213. Hannon J. Pound, third child and first son of Joseph Pound and Ida Stubbs, born 17 Sep 1876. Date of death unknown in Jacksonville, Duval County, Florida. Married 1900 to Katy Jansen.

B4165214. Susie Slater Pound, fourth child and third daughter of Joseph Pound and Ida Stubbs, born 15 Sep 1878 and died 1921. Married 1897 to John W. Price.

B4165215. Fleta Ellen Pound, fifth child and fourth daughter of Joseph Pound and Ida Stubbs, born 19 Jul 1881 and died 8 Mar 1956 at Dallas, Dallas County, Texas. Married 1898 to Charles Brown.

B4165216. May Ida Pound, sixth child and fifth daughter of Joseph Pound and Ida Stubbs, born 2 Aug 1884. Married J.W. Aldridge.

B4165217. Abner Joseph Pound, seventh child and second son of Joseph Pound and Ida Stubbs, born 6 Jan 1888.

B4165218. Irene Amelia Pound, eighth child and sixth daughter of Joseph Pound and Ida Stubbs, born 14 Jun 1890 and died 25 Oct 1955. Married Benjamin Schooler.

B4165219. Lurine B. Pound, ninth child and seventh daughter of Joseph Pound and Ida Stubbs, born 12 Jan 1894. Married 15 Nov 1911 to Troy Lee.

B416522. Richard Pound, second child and second son of Andrew Pound and Susan Greene, date and place of birth unknown.

B416523. Cicero Pound, third child and third son of Andrew Pound and Susan Greene, date and place of birth unknown.

B416524. Jack Pound, fourth child and fourth son of Andrew Pound and Susan Greene, date and place of birth unknown.

B416525. Bragg Pound, fifth child and fifth son of Andrew Pound and Susan Greene, date and place of birth unknown.

B416526. Della Pound, sixth child and first daughter of Andrew Pound and Susan Greene, date and place of birth unknown.

B416527. Eva Johannon Pound, seventh child and second daughter of Andrew Pound and Susan Greene, date and place of birth unknown.

B41653. John Gay (twin) Pound, third child and second son of John Pound and Amelia Gay, born 1 Nov 1827 in Putnam County, Georgia. Married 8 Jan 1850 in Macon, Bibb County, Georgia to Thurza Fleming. They had issue, which was the ninth generation in America:

B416531. John Pound, first child and first son of John Pound and Thurza Fleming, date and place of birth unknown.

B416532. Abel Pound, second child and second of John Pound and Thurza Fleming, date and place of birth unknown. Married --- ---. They had issue, which was the tenth generation in America:

B41655321. Linton Pounds, first child

and first son of Abel Pound and --- ---, date and place of birth unknown.

B4165322. Grace Pound, second child and first daughter of Abel Pound and --- --- , date and place of birth unknown.

B4165323. Thomas Pound, third child and second son of Abel Pound and --- ---, date and place of birth unknown.

B4165324. George Pound, fourth child and third son of Abel Pound and --- ---, date and place of birth unknown.

B416533. Thomas Pound, third child and third son of John Pound and Thurza Fleming, date and place of birth unknown.

B416534. George Pound, fourth child and fourth son of John Pound and Thurza Fleming, date and place of birth unknown.

B41654. Merriman (twin) Pound, fourth child and third son of John Pound and Amelia Gay, born 1 Nov 1827 in Putnam County, Georgia. Married 25 Jan 1848 in Jasper County, Georgia to Mary Jane Goolsby, sister of James Bird Goolsby, born 1830 in Georgia. Merriman married secondly to --- Gantt and married thirdly to --- Worman. Merriman and Mary Jane had issue, which was the ninth generation in America:

B416541. Senia M. Pound, first child and first daughter of Merriman Pound and Mary Goolsby, date and place of birth unknown. Married Monroe Walls.

B416542. John Pound, second child and first son of Merriman Pound and Mary Goolsby, date and place of birth unknown.

B416543. Jim Pound, third child and second son of Merriman Pound and Mary Goolsby, date and place of birth unknown.

B416544. Spafford Pound, fourth child and third son of Merriman Pound and Mary Goolsby, date and place of birth unknown.

B416545. Mary Pound, fifth child and and second daughter of Merriman Pound and Mary Goolsby, date and place of birth unknown.

B416546. Clara Pound, sixth child and third daughter of Merriman Pound and Mary Goolsby, date and place of birth unknown. Married --- Freeman.

B416547. Julia Pound, seventh child and fourth daughter of Merriman Pound and Mary Goolsby, date and place of birth unknown. Married Septimus Freeman.

B416548. --- Pound, eighth child, but not known if son or daughter of Merriman Pound and Mary Goolsby, date and place of birth unknown.

B41655. Sarah Whitehurst Pound, fifth child and second daughter of John Pound and Amelia Gay, born 13 Oct 1830 in Putnam County, Georgia and died 2 Dec 1880. Married 9 Jun 1849 in Putnam County, Georgia to Sanford Morgan Tufts, born in Jones County, Georgia. They had issue, which was the ninth generation in America:

B416551. John Tufts, first child and first son of Sarah Pound and Sanford Tufts, date and place of birth unknown.

B416552. Mary Tufts, second child and second son of Sarah Pound and Sanford Tufts, date and place of birth unknown. Married Lee Smith. They had issue, which was the tenth generation in America:

B4165521. Lula Smith, first child and first daughter of Mary Tufts and Lee Smith, date and place of birth unknown. Married Charlie Farrar. They had issue, which was the eleventh generation in America:

B41655211. Louis Farrar, first child and first son of Lula Smith and Charlie Farrar, date and place of birth unknown.

B41655212. Frances Farrar, second child and first daughter of Lula Smith and Charlie Farrar, date and place of birth unknown.

B41655213. John Farrar, third child and second son of Lula Smith and Charlie Farrar, date and place of birth unknown.

B41656. Sinah Robins Pound, sixth child and third daughter of John Pound and Amelia Gay, born 1 Apr 1832 in Putnam County, Georgia. Married 7 Dec 1852 in Putnam County, Georgia to John Dabney Farrar. John Farrar was killed in the War Between the States. Sinah married secondly to Frank Skinner. Sinah and Frank had issue, which was the ninth generation in America:

B416561. Ebb Skinner, first child and first son of Sinah Pound and Frank Skinner, date and place of birth unknown.

B41657. Clara Jane Pound, seventh child and fourth daughter of John Pound and Amelia Gay, born 10 May 1833 in Putnam County, Georgia. Married 23 Mar 1858 in Putnam County, Georgia to David Lane, born Monticello, Jasper County, Georgia. They had issue, which was the ninth generation in America:

B416571. John Lane, first child and first son of Clara Pound and David Lane, date and place of birth unknown.

B416572. Dodie Lane, second child and first daughter of Clara Pound and David Lane, date and place of birth unknown.

B416573. Fannie Lane, third child and second daughter of Clara Pound and David Lane, date and place of birth unknown. Married --- Millen.

B41658. Richard Pound, eighth child and fourth son of John Pound and Amelia Gay, born 26 Dec 1834 at Devil's Half Acre, Putnam County, Georgia. Married --- Amos. Richard married secondly about 1863 to Mary J. Amos, his first wife's sister. Richard and --- Amos had issue, which was the ninth generation in America:

B416581. Bo Pound, first child and first son of Richard Pound and --- Amos, date and place of birth unknown.

B41658. Richard Pound, eighth child and fourth son of John Pound and Amelia Gay, born 26 Dec 1834 at Devil's Half Acre, Putnam County, Georgia. Married secondly about

1863 in Georgia to Mary J. Amos, born 1835 in Georgia. They had issue, which was the ninth generation in America:

B416581. John D. Pound, first child and first son of Richard Pound and Mary Amos, born 1864 in Georgia.

B416582. Richard A. Pound, second child and second son of Richard Pound and Mary Amos, born 1867 in Georgia and died 1893.

B41659. Boey Hannon Pound, ninth child and fifth son of John Pound and Amelia Gay, born 31 Mar 1836 at Devil's Half Acre, Putnam County, Georgia and died 7 Jul 1900 at Monticello, Jasper County, Georgia. Buried Pound family cemetery, Jasper County, Georgia. Married 9 Dec 1858 in Jones County, Georgia to Jane Adam Carey, daughter of Job Carey and Tabitha Mercer, born 6 Feb 1848 in Jones County, Georgia and died 18 Jul 1927 at Monticello, Jasper County, Georgia. Buried Pound family cemetery in Jasper County, Georgia. They had issue, which was the ninth generation in America:

B416591. John Bohannon Pound, first child and first son of Boey Pound and Jane Carey, born 1860 and died in 1866.

B416592. Sinah Georgia Pound, second child and first daughter of Boey Pound and Jane Carey, born 1861 in Putnam County, Georgia and died 1866 in Putnam County, Georgia.

B416593. Thomas Gay Pound, third child and second son of Boey Pound and Jane Carey, born 17 Oct 1866 in Jones County, Georgia and died 4 Jul 1931 at Monticello, Jasper County, Georgia. Married 23 Nov 1892 at Hillsboro Methodist Church in Jasper County, Georgia to Cora Eliza Goolsby, born 29 Dec 1865 and died 23 Jan 1954 at Monticello, Jasper County, Georgia. Buried Westview cemetery, Jasper County, Georgia. Thomas Gay was Clerk of Jasper County Superior Court from 1920 until his death, July 3, 1931. He was succeeded in office by his son, Clarence Braxton Pound, and then by his daughter-in-law Sara (Brown) Pound. His granddaughter Jane (Holland) Parrott was elected to the office in

1969.   Thomas Gay and Cora had issue, which was the tenth generation in America:

B4165931.   Emmie Eugenia Pound, first child and first daughter of Thomas Pound and Cora Goolsby, born 21 Nov 1894 and died 10 Jun 1971.   Married 20 Nov 1920 at Monticello, Jasper County, Georgia to Oscar Frank Holland, born 2 Feb 1894 and died 26 Jul 1969.

B4165932.   Cora Gay Pound, second child and second daughter of Thomas Pound and Cora Goolsby, born 26 Dec 1896 in Jasper County, Georgia.   Married Henry Hunter Jordan.

B4165933.   James Hannon Pound, Sr., third child and first son of Thomas Pound and Cora Goolsby, born 7 Sep 1899 in Jasper County, Georgia.   Married Heloise Boudreau Howard.   They had issue, which was the eleventh generation in America:

B41659331.   James Hannon Pound, Jr., first child and first son of James Hannon Pound, Sr. and Heloise Howard, born 9 Sep 1932 at Chattahoochee, Gadsden County, Florida.   Married Barbara Ann Fitchner.   They had issue, which was the twelfth generation in America:

B416593311.   James Hannon Pound III, first child and first son of James Hannon Pound, Jr. and Barbara Fitchner, born 31 May 1957 at Emory University, DeKalb County, Georgia.

B4165934.   Thomas Lee Pound, fourth child and second son of Thomas Pound and Cora Goolsby, born 1 Apr 1903 in Jasper County, Georgia and died 16 Jun 1940 at Monticello, Jasper County, Georgia.   Buried at Westview cemetery, Jasper County, Georgia.

B4165935.   Clarence Braxton Pound, fifth child and third son of Thomas Pound and Cora Goolsby, born 31 Oct 1906 at Monticello, Jasper County, Georgia and died 7 Jan 1979.   Married 18 Oct 1931 in Brunswick, Glynn County, Georgia to Sara Brown.   They had issue, which was the eleventh generation in America:

B41659351.   Clarence Braxton Pound, Jr., first child and first son of Clarence Pound and Sara Brown, born 1934.

B41659352.   Thomas
Gay Pound, second child and second son of Clarence
Pound and Sara Brown, born 1938.

B416594.   Eugenia
Henrietta Pound, fourth child and and second
daughter of Boey Pound and Jane Carey, born 1868
in Putnam County, Georgia and died 1919 at
Roanoke, Randolph County, Alabama. Married Jim A.
Wilson.

B416595.   Clarence
Elmo Pound, fifth child and third son of Boey
Pound and Jane Carey, born 24 Aug 1870 in Putnam
County, Georgia and died 19 Jun 1915 at
Monticello, Jasper County, Georgia. Buried Pound
family cemetery in Jasper County, Georgia.

B416596.   Eli
Ezekiel Pound, sixth child and fourth son of Boey
Pound and Jane Carey, born 1872 in Putnam County,
Georgia.

B416597.   E.V.
Pound, seventh child and third daughter of Boey
Pound and Jane Carey, born 1874 in Putnam County,
Georgia. Married 1894 to Charles Wesley Moran.

B416598.   William
Carey Pound, eighth child and fifth son of Boey
Pound and Jane Carey, born 1877 in Putnam County,
Georgia and died 1950 in Birmingham, Jefferson
County, Alabama.

B416599.   Richard
Francis Pound, ninth child and sixth son of Boey
Pound and Jane Carey, born 19 Sep 1879 in Putnam
County, Georgia and died 21 Oct 1934 at Atlanta,
Fulton County, Georgia. Buried Pound family
cemetery in Jasper County, Georgia.

B4165910.   Myrtle
Olive Pound, tenth child and fourth daughter of
Boey Pound and Jane Carey, born 1882 in Putnam
County, Georgia and died 1953. Married J.A.
Carlisle.

B41650.   Horatio Gay
Spafford Pound, tenth child and sixth son of John
Pound and Amelia Gay, born 22 Nov 1837 at Devil's
Half Acre, Putnam County, Georgia. Married 2 Feb
1864 in Putnam County, Georgia to Sarah A.
Bowdoin. Married secondly Mary Greene. Horatio

116

and Sarah had issue, which was the ninth generation in America:

B416501. John Pound, first child and first son of Horatio Pound and Sarah Bowdoin, date and place of birth unknown. Married Dodie Lane, his cousin, daughter of David Lane and Clara Jane Pounds.

B416502. Ludie Pound, second child and first daughter of Horatio Pound and Sarah Bowdoin, date and place of birth unknown. Married John Amos. They had issue, which was the tenth generation in America:

B4165021. Kate Arthur Amos, first child and first daughter of Ludie Pound and John Amos, date and place of birth unknown. Married --- Thornton, born Jackson, Butts County, Georgia.

B4165022. India Amos, second child and second daughter of Ludie Pound and John Amos, date and place of birth unknown.

B4165023. Sarah Amos, third child and third daughter of Ludie Pound and John Amos, date and place of birth unknown.

B4165024. Olive Amos, fourth child and fourth daughter of Ludie Pound and John Amos, date and place of birth unknown.

B4165025. Sidney Amos, fifth child and first son of Ludie Pound and John Amos, date and place of birth unknown.

B4165026. J.W. Amos, sixth child and second son of Ludie Pound and John Amos, date and place of birth unknown.

B4165027. Grace Amos, seventh child and fifth daughter of Ludie Pound and John Amos, date and place of birth unknown.

B41651. Eli Ezekiel (twin) Pound, eleventh child and seventh son of John Pound and Amelia Gay, born 9 Jan 1841 in Putnam County, Georgia and died 21 Dec 1895. Married 4 Oct 1859 at the Leverett residence, Jasper County, Georgia to Sallie A. Leverett, born

9 May 1838 in Putnam County, Georgia and died 24 Oct 1910 in Jackson County, Georgia. She was the daughter of William C. Leverett of Shady Dale, Georgia. Eli Ezekiel Pound must have been the most prominent of this family of that generation. He became County School Superintendent of Butts County and served for a number of years. He also served as Mayor of Jackson, Georgia. Eli Ezekiel attended college at Emory University at Oxford, Georgia. Boey Hannon Pound and his siste, Clara, were on their way to Oxford to see Eli graduate. They traveled by horse and carriage in the grand style of the day. They stopped in Monticello to spend the night at the Inn. As Clara alighted from the carriage, her daintly little foot and leg was glimpsed by a young gentleman who stood nearby, Mr. Davis Lane. On the way back from Oxford, Boey and his sister again stopped at the Inn. Mr. Lane sought an introduction. He courted Clara and they married some time later. After Mr. Land and Clara married, they lived in the hotel for a time. Clara brought her personal maid with her. She noticed the girl seemed unhappy and asked her what her trouble was. The girl replied, "They give me plenty of chicken, ham and cheese, but I'm hongry for turnip greens and pot likker, and cracklin bread". Eli and Sally had issue, which was the ninth generation in America:

B416511. Florence V. Pound, first child and first daughter of Eli Pound and Sally Leverett, date and place of birth unknown.

B416512. Augusta C. Pound, second child and second daughter of Eli Pound and Sally Leverett, date and place of birth unknown. Married J.T. Harris.

B416513. Osceola Pound, third child and third daughter of Eli Pound and Sally Leverett, date and place of birth unknown.

B416514. Lamar Pound, fourth child and first son of Eli Pound and Sally Leverett, born 21 Nov 1870 at Indian Springs, Butts County, Georgia and died at Nashville, Davidson County, Tennessee on 11 Nov 1949. Married 23 Jul 1896 at Atlanta, Fulton

County, Georgia to Elizabeth Katherine Allen, born 4 Feb 1877 at Newman, Coweta County, Georgia and died 15 Feb 1926 at Nashville, Davidson County, Tennessee. They had issue, which was the tenth generation in America:

B4165141. Katherine Elizabeth Pound, first child and first daughter of Lamar Pound and Elizabeth Allen, born 3 Apr 1904 at Richmond, Richmond County, Virginia and died 14 Oct 1978 at Nashville, Davidson County, Tennessee. Married 14 Jul 1923 at Nashville, Davidson County, Tennessee to Harry Boush Speier, born 17 May 1901 at Nashville, Davidson County, Tennessee and died 22 Aug 1989 at Hermitage, Davidson County, Tennessee. Katherine Pound and Harry Speier had issue, which was the eleventh generation in America:

B41651411. Mary Patricia Speier, first child and first daughter of Katherine Pound and Harry Speier, born 20 Nov 1930 at Bridgeport, Fairfield County, Connecticutt. Married 20 Nov 1954 at Nashville, Davidson County, Tennessee to Donald Carl Steiger, born 27 Oct 1924 at Oshkosh, Winnebago County, Wisconsin.

B416515. Eli Pound, fifth child and second son of Eli Pound and Sally Leverett, born 1875 in Butts County, Georgia.

B416516. Lilla Myrtle Pound, sixth child and fourth daughter of Eli Pound and Sally Leverett, born 1877 in Butts County, Georgia.

B416517. Ella Pound, seventh child and fifth daughter of Eli Pound and Sally Leverett, born 1878 in Butts County, Georgia.

B41652. Mary Frances (twin) Pound, twelfth child and fifth daughter of John Pound and Amelia Gay, born 9 Jan 1841 in Putnam County, Georgia. Married first Jack Barron (killed in The War between the States). Married secondly Jackie Sid Baynes. Mary Frances and Jackie had issue, which was the ninth generation in America:

B416521. Mamie Jack (Jackie) Baynes, first child and first daughter of Mary Frances Pound and Jackie Baynes, date and place of birth unknown. Mamie married --

119

- McDowell, they had issue, which was the tenth
generation in America:

B4165211. Lucille
McDowell, first child and first daughter of Mamie
Baynes and --- McDowell, date and place of birth
unknown.

B4166. Ladufsia Pound, sixth
child and third daughter of Merriman Pound and
Clarissa Herndon, born 4 Apr 1800 in Putnam
County, Georgia, died after 1870 in Dooly County,
Georgia. Married 29 Aug 1816 in Putnam County,
Georgia to Irwin Bullock, son of Daniel Bullock
and Mary Whitehurst, born 14 Nov 1793 in North
Carolina, died Sep 1864 in Dooly County, Georgia.
Her father, Merriman Pound was a veteran of the
Indian Wars and the War of 1812. Her mother,
Clarissa Ladufsia Herndon was descended from the
landed aristocratic Digges and Herndon families of
Virginia. Her brothers and sisters numbered more
than a dozen. Their descendants are scattered all
over the United States. Surely the children from
Irwin and Ladufsia's union would have patriotic
pride instilled in them. After all, both Great-
grandfather Reuben Pound and Grandfather Daniel
Bullock had paid a fair share during the American
Revolution. By 1850 the fifty-year old Ladufsia
would have only eight of her thirteen children
living at home. Charles I., George C., Daniel
Merryman, James R., Florida L., Victoria F.,
Joseph A., and Uriah B. must have been a great
help on the family farm located in the 24th
District of Dooly County. The issue of Ladufsia
and Irwin Bullock were the eighth generation in
America:

B41661. Sarah Ann
Catherine Bullock, first child and first daughter
of Ladufsia Pound and Irwin Bullock, born about
1817 in Georgia. Married 25 Apr 1833 in Bibb
County, Georgia to William B.F. Oliver, born about
1812 in North Carolina. They had issue, which was
the ninth generation in America:

B416611. John L.
Oliver, first child and first son of Sarah Bullock
and William Oliver, born about 1838 in Georgia.

B416612. William F.
Oliver, second child and second son of Sarah

Bullock and William Oliver, born about 1841 in Georgia.

B416613. Victoria L. Oliver, third child and first daughter of Sarah Bullock and William Oliver, born about 1843 in Georgia.

B416614. Henry G. Oliver, fourth child and third son of Sarah Bullock and William Oliver, born about 1846 in Georgia.

B416615. Alice T. Oliver, fifth child and second daughter of Sarah Bullock and William Oliver, born about 1848 in Georgia.

B41662. Eleanor C. Bullock, second child and second daughter of Ladufsia Pound and Irwin Bullock, born about 1821 in Georgia and died about 1890 in Dooly County, Georgia. Married 15 Nov 1838 in Bibb County, Georgia to William Blackstone Johnston, son of William Johnston and Millison S. Hogan, born about 1816 in Baldwin County, Georgia and died 20 Jul 1868 in Dooly County, Georgia. William Johnston had married previously 10 Oct 1833 in Bibb County, Georgia to Caroline B. Bailey. Eleanor Bullock and William Johnston had issue, which was the ninth generation in America:

B416621. Vastile Virginia Johnston, first child and first daughter of Eleanor Bullock and William Johnston, born about 1840 in Bibb County, Georgia. Married 10 Jul 1862 in Dooly County, Georgia to Charles R. Brown, born 11 Apr 1836 in Houston County, Georgia. They had issue, which was the tenth generation in America:

B4166211. Anna Brown, first child and first daughter of Vastile Johnston and Charles Brown, born about 1863 in Dooly County, Georgia.

B4166212. Augustus Brown, second child and first son of Vastile Johnston and Charles BRown, born about 1866 in Dooly County, Georgia.

B4166213. Eugenia Brown, third child and second daughter of Vastile

Johnston and Charles Brown, born about 1868 in Dooly County, Georgia.

B4166214. Lucy Brown, fourth child and third daughter of Vastile Johnston and Charles Brown, born Dec 1869 in Dooly County, Georgia.

B416622. Georgia M. Johnston, second child and second daughter of Eleanor Bullock and William Johnston, born about 1842 in Bibb County, Georgia.

B416623. Miriam L. Johnston, third child and third daughter of Eleanor Bullock and William Johnston, born about 1844 in Bibb County, Georgia. Married 3 Jun 1862 in Dooly County, Georgia to John I. Brown, born 3 Jun 1834 in Houston County, Georgia. They had issue, which was the tenth generation in America:

B4166231. Howard Brown, first child and first son of Miriam Johnston and John Brown, born about 1865 in Dooly County, Georgia.

B4166232. Julia Brown, second child and first daughter of Miriam Johnston and John Brown, born about 1867 in Dooly County, Georgia.

B4166233. Susan Brown, third child and second daughter of Miriam Johnston and John Brown, born about 1869 in Dooly County, Georgia.

B416624. Martha L. Johnston, fourth child and fourth daughter of Eleanor Bullock and William Johnston, born about 1846 in Bibb County, Georgia.

B416625. Luther J. Johnston, fifth child and first son of Eleanor Bullock and William Johnston, born about 1849 in Bibb County, Georgia and died 1889 in Dooly County, Georgia. Married about 1880 to Elizabeth ---, born about 1859 in Georgia. They had issue, which was the tenth generation in America:

B4166251. Morgan Johnston, first child and first son of Luther Johnston and Elizabeth ---, born 1881 in Dooly County, Georgia.

B4166252. Mildred Johnson, second child and first daughter of Luther

Johnston and Elizabeth ---, born about 1883 in Dooly County, Georgia.

B4166253. Arthur Johnston, third child and second son of Luther Johnston and Elizabeth ---, born about 1885 in Dooly County, Georgia.

B4166254. John Fielder Johnston, fourth child and third son of Luther Johnston and Elizabeth ---, born about 1887 in Dooly County, Georgia.

B416626. George B. Johnston, sixth child and second son of Eleanor Bullock and William Johnston, born about 1851 in Dooly County, Georgia. Married 31 Dec 1874 in Dooly County, Georgia to Emma Bullock, daughter of Daniel Merriman Bullock and Missouri H. Pitts, born about 1857 in Dooly County, Georgia. They had issue, which was the tenth generation in America:

B4166261. Maud Johnston, first child and first daughter of George Johnston and Emma Bullock, born about 1876 in Dooly County, Georgia.

B4166262. Joseph Johnston, second child and first son of George Johnston and Emma Bullock, born about 1878 in Dooly County, Georgia.

B4166263. Croel Johnston, third child and second son of George Johnston and Emma Bullock, born Jul 1879 in Dooly County, Georgia.

B416627. Morgan B. Johnston, seventh child and third son of Eleanor Bullock and William Johnston, born Oct 1853 in Dooly County, Georgia. Married 15 Mar 1887 in Pulaski County, Georgia to Annie Matenza Wood, born Mar 1852 in Georgia. They had issue, which was the tenth generation in America:

B4166271. Theodore C. Johnston, first child and first son of Morgan Johnston and Annie Wood, born Nov 1887 in Pulaski County, Georgia.

B4166272. Eleonore F. Johnston, second child and first daughter of Morgan Johnston and Annie Wood, born Feb 1890 in Pulaski County, Georgia.

123

B416628. Uriah Bell Johnston, eighth child and fourth son of Eleanor Bullock and William Johnston, born about 1856 in Dooly County, Georgia.

B416629. Florida Rebecca (Beck) Johnston, ninth child and fifth daughter of Eleanor Bullock and William Johnston, born Sep 1857 in Dooly County, Georgia and died after Mar 1919 in Crisp County, Georgia. Buried in Ward cemetery, Dooly County, Georgia. Married 26 Jun 1881 in Dooly County, Georgia to William (Will) Ward, son of David T. Ward and Sarah Ann Gamble, born Mar 1856 in Dooly County, Georgia and died about 1918 in Dooly County, Georgia. Buried in Gamble/Ward cemetery, Dooly County, Georgia. Beck and Will had issue, which was the tenth generation in America:

B4166291. David Patrick (Pat) Ward, first child and first son of Rebecca Johnston and William Ward, born Jun 1885 in Dooly County, Georgia and died in Florida. Married 7 Sep 1902 in Dooly County, Georgia to Ruby Lewicey Schofill, daughter of Phillip Harrison Schofill and Delilah Pink Grace, born 15 Nov 1885 in Pulaski County, Georgia. David and Ruby had issue, which was the eleventh generation in America:

B41662911. Lloyd Ward, first child and first son of David Ward and Ruby Schofill, born about 1904 in Dooly County, Georgia.

B41662912. John B. Ward, second child and second son of David Ward and Ruby Schofill, born about 1906 in Dooly County, Georgia.

B41662913. Walter Ward, third child and third son of David Ward and Ruby Schofill, born about 1908 in Dooly County, Georgia.

B4166292. William Emmett (Emp) Ward, second child and second son Rebecca Johnston and William Ward, born 28 Apr 1888 in Dooly County, Georgia and died 16 Jun 1962 in Dooly County, Georgia. Married 26 Dec 1909 in Dooly County, Georgia to Clara Christmas.

B4166293. Frances (Fannie) Elizabeth Ward, third child and and first daughter of Rebecca Johnston and William Ward, born 4 Sep 1890 in Dooly County, Georgia and died 21 Oct 1927 in Florida. Married 21 Oct 1927 in Florida to Virgil Leonidas Schofill, son of Phillip Harrison Schofill and Delilah Pink Grace, born 6 Feb 1881 in Pulaski County, Georgia and died 4 Apr 1937 at Adel, Cook County, Georgia. Buried at Crossroads cemetery, Cook County, Georgia. Frances and Virgil had issue, which was the eleventh generation in America:

B41662931. Wilbur Blackston Schofill, first child and first son of Frances Ward and Virgil Schofill, born 20 Nov 1904 in Crisp County, Georgia and died 24 Oct 1970. Married Alma ---.

B41662932. Ellen Thelma Schofill, second child and first daughter of Frances Ward and Virgil Schofill, born 19 Jan 1907 in Crisp County, Georgia and died 5 Mar 1989 at Gainesville, Alachua County, Florida. Married Tommy Davis. Ellen and Tommy had issue, which was the twelth generation in America:

B41669321. Frances Davis, first child and first daughter of Ellen Schofill and Tommy Davis, date and place of birth unknown.

B41662933. Veron Jerome Schofill, third child and second son of Frances Ward and Virgil Schofill, born 19 Nov 1909 in Crisp County, Georgia and died Feb 1989 in Gainesville, Alachua County, Florida. Married Gertrude Eva Byrd. Veron and Gertrude had issue, which was the twelth generation in America:

B416629331. Frances Elizabeth (Bibby) Schofill, first child and first daughter of Veron Schofill and Gertrude Byrd, date and place of birth unknown.

B416629332. Lonny Milton Schofill, second child and first son of Veron Schofill and Gertrude Byrd, date and place of birth unknown.

B41662934. Lillian Pauline Schofill, fourth child and second daughter of Frances Ward and Virgil Schofill, born 5 Sep 1920 in Crisp County, Georgia and died 18 Oct 1978 in Sumter County, Georgia. Married Mitchell Churchill Hall.

B41662935. Mildred Delilah Schofill, fifth child and third daughter of Frances Ward and Virgil Schofill, born 15 Dec 1924 in Crisp County, Georgia. Married 15 May 1945 in Crisp County, Georgia to Gerald Lawrence Nobles, son of Lewis Bryant Nobles and Essiemay Mason Varnadoe, born 2 Mar 1924 in Crisp County, Georgia and died 19 Nov 1973 at Cordele, Crisp County, Georgia. Buried in Sunnyside cemetery, Crisp County, Georgia. Mildred and Gerald had issue, which was the twelth generation in America:

B416629351. Lonnie Gerald Nobles, first child and first son of Mildred Schofill and Gerald Nobles, born 23 Dec 1946 at Cordele, Crisp County, Georgia. Married 18 May 1968 in Alabama to Murlene Ramer, born 26 Apr 1948 in Alabama. Lonnie and Murlene had issue, which was the thirteenth generation in America:

B4166293511. Allen Lee Nobles, first child and first son of Lonnie Nobles and Murlene Ramer, born 17 Jan 1970 at Florence, Florence County, South Carolina.

B4166293512. David Scott Nobles, second child and second son of Lonnie Nobles and Murlene Ramer, born 31 Jan 1972 at Florence, Florence County, South Carolina.

B416629352. L. Annette Nobles, second child and first daughter of Mildred Schofill and Gerald Nobles, born 8 Feb 1948 at Cordele, Crisp County, Georgia. Married 18 Oct 1969 at Wenona, Crisp County, Georgia to James Russell Strietelmeier, born 30 Mar 1947 in Columbus, Bartholomew County, Indiana. Annette and James had issue, which was the thirteenth generation in America:

B4166293521. Raymond Kyle Strietelmeier, first child and first son of Annette Nobles and James Strietelmeier, born 20 Dec 1977 in Decatur, Dekalb County, Georgia.

B4166293522. Troy James Strietelmeier, second child and second son of Annette Nobles and James Strietelmeier, born 8 Jan 1985 in Decatur, DeKalb County, Georgia.

B4166293523. Abby Lauren Strietelmeier, third child and first daughter of Annette Nobles and James Strietelmeier, born 28 Aug 1987 in Decatur, DeKalb County, Georgia.

B416629353. David Lawrence Nobles, third child and second son of Mildred Schofill and Gerald Nobles, born 1 Dec 1954 in Cordele, Crisp County, Georgia. Married 1978 to Debbie Brown, born about 1955 at Sandersville, Washington County, Georgia. Married secondly 1981 to Donna Archer, born about 1955 in Sandersville, Washington County, Georgia. David and Debbie had issue, which was the thirteenth generation in America:

B4166293531. Katie Elizabeth Nobles, first child and first daughter of David Nobles and Donna Archer, born 22 Aug 1982 in Nashville, Berrien County, Georgia.

B416629353. David Lawrence Nobles, third child and second son of Mildred Schofill and Gerald Nobles, married thirdly about 1986 to Jan Mixon, born about 1954 in Cordele, Crisp County, Georgia. David and Jan had issue, which was the thirteenth generation in America:

B4166293531. David Bryant Nobles, first child and first son of David Nobles and Jan Mixon, born 5 Mar 1977 in Georgia.

B416629353. David Lawrence Nobles, third child and second son of Mildred Schofill and Gerald Nobles married fourthly in 1987 to Tracy ---; married fifthly in 1989 to Jill ---. No children are known from these two marriages. David married sixthly in 1990 to Sandy Powell. No children are known from this marriage.

B416629354. Delia Lavon Nobles, fourth child and second daughter of Mildred Schofill and Gerald Nobles, born 10 Dec 1959 in Cordele, Crisp County, Georgia. Married 8 Jul 1978 at Wenona, Crisp County, Georgia to Phillip McCollum, born 7 Sep 1959 in Macon, Bibb County, Georgia. Delia and Phillip had issue, which was the thirteenth generation in America:

B4166293541. Jennifer Marie McCollum, first child and first daughter of Delia Nobles and Phillip McCollum, born 6 Feb 1992 in Macon, Bibb County, Georgia.

B416629355. Lewis Steven Nobles, fifth child and third son of Mildred Schofill and Gerald Nobles born 31 Mar 1965 in Cordele, Crisp County, Georgia. Married 15 Apr 1989 at Wenona, Crisp County, Georgia to Terri McGlamery.

B4166294. Julius Bell Ward, fourth child and third son of Rebecca Johnston and William Ward, born 11 Jan 1892 in Dooly County, Georgia and died 8 Feb 1968 in Micanopy, Alachua County, Florida. Married 17 Dec 1911 in Crisp County, Georgia to Maggie Sargent.

B4166295. George Leon Ward, fifth child and fourth son of Rebecca Johnston and William Ward, born 8 Sep 1894 in Dooly County, Georgia and died 11 May 1939 at Sparks, Cook County, Georgia. Married 9 Feb 1913 in Crisp County, Georgia to Susan Hall. George and Susan had issue, which was the eleventh generation in America:

B41662951. Sallie Estelle Ward, first child and first daughter of George Ward and Susan Hall, born 2 Mar 1916 in Georgia. Sallie married Hiram A. Sharpe.

B41662952. Susie Mae Ward, second child and second daughter of George Ward and Susan Hall, born about 1918 in Georgia.

B4166295. George Leon Ward, fifth child and fourth son of Rebecca Johnston and William Ward, married secondly 30 Mar 1919 in Dooly County, Georgia to Hallie Delma Bryant, daughter of Labon (Manny) Bryant and Lula Estelle Joyner, born about 1900 in Roberta, Crawford County, Georgia and died 28 May 1985 in Adel, Cook County, Georgia. Buried in Brushy Creek Baptist cemetery, Cook County, Georgia. George and Hallie had issue, which was the eleventh generation in America:

B41662951. William STI Ward, first child and first son of George Ward and Hallie Bryant, born and died in 1920 in Dooly County, Georgia.

B41662952. Thomas Preston Ward, second child and second son of George Ward and Hallie Bryant, born 25 Nov 1921 in Dooly County, Georgia and died 13 Sep 1974 in Tifton,

Tift County, Georgia. Buried Brushy Creek Baptist cemetery, Cook County, Georgia. Married 10 Aug 1941 in Berrien County, Georgia to Lois Lona Smith, daughter of Harmon Augustus Smith and Laura Belle Cook, born 8 Apr 1924 in Berrien County, Georgia and died 26 Nov 1989 at Nashville, Berrien County, Georgia. Buried Brushy Creek Baptist cemetery, Cook County, Georgia. Thomas and Lois had issue, which was the twelth generation in America:

B416629521. Bettie Jean Ward, first child and first daughter of Thomas Ward and Lois Smith, born 29 Jul 1943 at Sparks, Cook County, Georgia. Married Willie Eugene Baldree, Sr. Married secondly to Carlton Tyson. Bettie and Willie had issue, which was the thirteenth generation in America:

B4166295211. Willie Eugene Baldree, Jr., first child and first son of Bettie Ward and Willie Baldree, date and place of birth unknown. Married Sherry ---. Willie, Jr. and Sherry --- had issue, which was the fourteenth generation in America:

B41662952111. Willie Eugene Baldree III, first child and first son of Bettie Ward and Willie, Jr., date and place of birth unknown.

B41662952. Aubrey Thomas Ward, second child and first son of Thomas Ward and Lois Smith, born 11 Dec 1944 at Sparks, Cook County, Georgia. Married 23 May 1964 in Cook County, Georgia to Betty Jean Watson. Aubrey and Betty Jean had issue, which was the thirteenth generation in America:

B416629521. Chadwick Aubrey Ward, first child and first son of Aubrey Ward and Betty Watson, born 3 Nov 1971 in Adel, Cook County, Georgia.

B416629522. Pamela Dawn Ward, second child and first daughter of Aubrey Ward and Betty Watson, born 17 Jan 1974 in Adel, Cook County, Georgia.

B41662953. Linda Faye Ward, third child and second daughter of Thomas Ward and Lois Smith, born 30 Aug 1951 at Adel, Cook County, Georgia. Married 25 Sep 1971 in Cook County, Georgia to Russell Floyd Meadows. Linda and Russell had issue, which was the thirteenth generation in America:

B416629531. Allison Faye Meadows, first child and first daughter of Linda Ward and Russell Meadows, born 1 Feb 1970 in Berrien County, Georgia.

B416629532. Russell Bryan Meadows, second child and first son of Linda Ward and Russell Meadows, born 17 Nov 1976 in Tifton, Tift County, Georgia.

B41662954. Janice May (twin) Ward, fourth child and third daughter of Thomas Ward and Lois Smith, born 23 May 1954 at Adel, Cook County, Georgia. Married in Berrien County, Georgia to Lamar Grimsley. Janice and Lamar had issue, which was the thirteenth generation in America:

B416629541. Leigh Grimsley, first child and first daughter of Janice Ward and Lamar Grimsley, date and place of birth unknown.

B41662955. Jerry William (twin) Ward, fifth child and second son of Thomas Ward and Lois Smith, born 23 May 1954 in Adel, Cook County, Georgia and died 2 Feb 1987 in Tift County, Georgia. Married Sonja ---. Jerry and Sonja had issue, which was the thirteenth generation in America:

B416629551. Bryan Ward, first child and first son of Jerry Ward and Sonja ---, date and place of birth unknown.

B4166293. George Bivinnes Ward, third child and third son of George L. Ward and Hallie Bryant, born 11 Nov 1923 in Crisp County, Georgia and died 6 Jul 1964 in Adel, Cook County, Georgia. Married 14 Nov 1947 in Georgia to Merle Rowan. George B. and Merle had issue, which was the twelth generation in America:

B41662931. Shirley Nadine Ward, first child and first daughter of George B. Ward and Merle Rowan, born 29 Oct 1949 in Cook County, Georgia.

B41662932. Bobby Joe Ward, second child and first son of George B. Ward and Merle Rowan, born 31 Dec 1951 in Cook County, Georgia.

B41662933. Charles Wayne Ward, third child and second son of George B. Ward and Merle Rowan, born 23 Feb 1958 in Cook County, Georgia.

B4166294. James Louis Ward, fourth child and fourth son of George L. Ward and Hallie Bryant, born 3 Jan 1926 in Cook County, Georgia and died 3 Aug 1961 in Augusta, Richmond County, Georgia. Married Eloise Spires.

B4166295. Alonzo Buford Ward, fifth child and fifth son of George L. Ward and Hallie Bryant, born 15 May 1930 in Cook County, Georgia and died 7 Jan 1978 in Gainesville, Alachua County, Florida. Married Juanita Folsom.

B4166296. --- Ward, sixth child and not known whether male or female of George L. Ward and Hallie Bryant, born and died in 1931 in Sparks, Cook County, Georgia.

B4166296. James Gamble Ward, sixth child and fifth son of Rebecca Johnston and William Ward, born Feb 1897 in Dooly County, Georgia and died about 1913 in Crisp County, Georgia.

B416630. Susan E. Johnston, ninth child and sixth daughter of Eleanor Bullock and William Johnston, born about 1858 in Bibb County, Georgia.

B415631. Julia F. Johnston, tenth child and seventh daughter of Eleanor Bullock and William Johnston, born Aug 1860 in Bibb County, Georgia.

B41663. Amarilla L. Bullock, third child and third daughter of Ladufsia Pound and Irwin Bullock, born 15 Aug 1823 in Bibb County, Georgia and died 1 Sep 1895 in Dooly County, Georgia. Married 28 Jan 1841 in Bibb County, Georgia to Isaac J. Newberry, born about 1812 in North Carolina. Amarilla and Isaac had issue, which was the ninth generation in America:

B416631. Mary L. Newberry, first child and first daughter of Amarilla Bullock and Isaac Newberry, born about 1842 in Georgia.

B416632. John B. Newberry, second child and first son of Amarilla Bullock and Isaac Newberry, born about 1843 in Georgia.

B416633. Martha C. Newberry, third child and second daughter of Amarilla Bullock and Isaac Newberry, born about 1847 in Georgia.

B41664. Virginia E. (twin) Bullock, fourth child and fourth daughter of Ladufsia Pound and Irwin Bullock, born 1828 in Bibb County, Georgia. Married 16 Dec 1845 in Bibb County, Georgia to John G. Waller, born about 1812 in Georgia. Virginia and John had issue, which was the ninth generation in America:

B416641. Irwin C. Waller, first child and first son of Virginia Bullock and John Waller, born about 1847 in Georgia.

B416642. Charles J. Waller, second child and second son of Virginia Bullock and John Waller, born about 1849 in Georgia.

B41665. Mary Jane (twin) Bullock, fifth child and fifth daughter of Ladufsia Pound and Irwin Bullock, born 1828 in Bibb County, Georgia and died before 1864 in Georgia. Married 2 Nov 1848 in Dooly County, Georgia to Allen Waters, born about 1800 in South Carolina and died 1856 in Dooly County, Georgia. Mary and Allen had issue, which was the ninth generation in America:

B416651. Ladufsia P. Waters, first child and first daughter of Mary Bullock and Allen Waters, born about 1849 in Dooly County, Georgia.

B416652. Daniel M. Waters, second child and first son of Mary Bullock and Allen Waters, born about 1855 in Dooly County, Georgia.

B41666. Charles J. Bullock, sixth child and first son of Ladufsia Pound and Irwin Bullock, born 1829 in Bibb County, Georgia.

B41667. George C. Bullock, seventh child and second son of Ladufsia Pound and Irwin Bullock, born 1832 in Bibb County, Georgia and died 14 Nov 1853 in Dooly County, Georgia.

B41668. Daniel Merriman Bullock, eighth child and third son of Ladufsia Pound and Irwin Bullock, born about 1833 in Bibb County, Georgia. Married 1 May 1856 in Dooly County, Georgia to Missouri H. Pitts, daughter of Isaac Pitts and Martha D. Pitts, born about 1841 in Georgia. Daniel and Missouri had issue, which was the ninth generation in America:

B416681. Emma Bullock, first child and first daughter of Daniel Bullock and Missouri Pitts, born about 1857 in Dooly County, Georgia. Married 31 Dec 1874 in Dooly County, Georgia to George B. Johnston, son of William Blackstone Johnston and Eleanor C. Bullock, born about 1851 in Dooly County, Georgia. Emma and George had issue, which was the tenth generation in America:

B4166811. Maud Johnston, first child and first daughter of Emma Bullock and George Johnston, born about 1876 in Dooly County, Georgia.

B4166812. Joseph Johnston, second child and first son of Emma Bullock and George Johnston, born about 1878 in Dooly County, Georgia.

B4166813. Croel Johnston, third child and second son of Emma Bullock and George Johnston, born Jul 1879 in Dooly County, Georgia.

B416682. Eugenia Bullock, second child and second daughter of Daniel Bullock and Missouri Pitts, born about 1859 in Dooly County, Georgia.

B416683. Daniel Bullock, third child and first son of Daniel Bullock and Missouri Pitts, born about 1860 in Dooly County, Georgia.

B416684. Julia Bullock, fourth child and third daughter of Daniel Bullock and Missouri Pitts, born about 1860 in Dooly County, Georgia.

B416685. Milly Bullock, fifth child and fourth daughter of Daniel Bullock and Missouri Pitts, born about 1864 in Dooly County, Georgia.

B416686. Otta L. Bullock, sixth child and fifth daughter of Daniel Bullock and Missouri Pitts, born about 1867 in Dooly County, Georgia.

B416687. Minnie Bullock, seventh child and sixth daughter of Daniel Bullock and

Missouri Pitts, born Nov 1869 in Dooly County, Georgia.

B41669. James R. Bullock, ninth child and fourth son of Ladufsia Pound and Irwin Bullock, born 1835 in Bibb County, Georgia. Married 14 Jan 1866 in Dooly County, Georgia to Nancy Sentell.

B416610. Florida L. Bullock, tenth child and sixth daughter of Ladufsia Pound and Irwin Bullock, born about 1836 in Bibb County, Georgia. Married 23 Nov 1862 in Dooly County, Georgia to Charles R. Blalock.

B416611. Victoria Frances Bullock, eleventh child and seventh daughter of Ladufsia Pound and Irwin Bullock, born about 1838 in Bibb County, Georgia. Married 2 May 1861 in Dooly County, Georgia to John M. Baskin.

B416612. Joseph A. Bullock, twelth child and fifth son of Ladufsia Pound and Irwin Bullock, born about 1839 in Bibb County, Georgia and died 25 Jul 1874 in Dooly County, Georgia.

B416613. Uriah B. Bullock, thirteenth child and sixth son of Ladufsia Pound and Irwin Bullock, born May 1841 in Bibb County, Georgia and died 28 Dec 1853 in Dooly County, Georgia.

B4167. Frances Pound, seventh child and fourth daughter of Merriman Pound and Clarissa Herndon, born about 1802 in Putnam County, Georgia. Married about 1810 to Abner Champion, born about 1789 at Eatonton, Putnam County, Georgia and died 6 May 1836 in Fayette County, Georgia. Frances Pound and Abner Champion had issue, which was the eighth generation in America:

B41671. Will C. Champion, first child and first son of Frances Pound and Abner Champion, born 1811 and died 1883. Married 1834 to Harriet Belcher, date and place of birth unknown, but she died in 1854. Married secondly in 1854 to Eliza Bridges. Will Champion and Harriet Belcher had issue, which the ninth generation in America:

B416711. Willy B. Champion, first child and first son of Will Champion and Harriet Belcher, born 1836.

B416712. Mary Frances Champion, second child and first daughter of Will Champion and Harriet Belcher, born 9 Apr 1837. Married 22 Nov 1856 to Joshua P. Ogletree, born 1835 and died 1907. Mary Champion and Joshua Ogletree had issue, which was the tenth generation in America:

B4167121. John William Ogletree, first child and first son of Mary Champion and Joshua Ogletree, born 1857 and died 1926. Married 1880 to Tululah Kemp, born 1859 and died 1924. John Ogletree and Tululah Kemp had issue, which was the eleventh generation in America:

B41671211. John Pierce Ogletree, first child and first son of John Ogletree and Tululah Kemp, born 1890 and died 1952. Married 1923 to Geraldine Hodges, born 1897 and died 1953. John Ogletree and Geraldine Hodges had issue, which was the twelth generation in America:

B416712111. John Pierce Ogletree, Jr., first child and first son of John Ogletree and Geraldine Hodges, born 1927. Married 1950 to Arline Curry, born 1924.

B416713. Jackson N. Champion, third child and second son of Will Champion and Harriet Belcher, born 1839.

B416714. Martha A. Champion, fourth child and second daughter of Will Champion and Harriet Belcher, born 1842. Married 8 Dec 1859 to John W. Malear.

B416715. Francis D. Champion, fifth child and third son of Will Champion and Harriet Belcher, born 1843.

B416716. George W. Champion, sixth child and fourth son of Will Champion and Harriet Belcher, born 1845.

B416717. Isabella M. Champion, seventh child and third daughter of Will Champion and Harriet Belcher, born 1852.

B41671. Will Champion, first child and first son of Frances Pound and Abner Champion, married secondly in 1854 to Eliza Bridges. Will Champion and Eliza Bridges had issue, which was the ninth generation in America:

B416711. Ida Champion, first child and first daughter of Will Champion and Eliza Bridges, born 1856.

B416712. John Champion, second child and first son of Will Champion and Eliza Bridges, born 1859.

B416713. Rebecca E. Champion, third child and second daughter of Will Champion and Eliza Bridges, born 1859.

B41672. Willis Champion, second child and second son of Frances Pound and Abner Champion, born 1812. Married Jane ---. Willis Champion and Jane --- had issue, which was the ninth generation in America:

B416721. Margaret Frances Champion, first child and first daughter of Willis Champion and Jane ---, born about 1842.

B416722. Andrew J. Champion, second child and first son of Willis Champion and Jane ---, born about 1845.

B416723. Nancy J. Champion, third child and second daughter of Willis Champion and Jane ---, born about 1846.

B416724. James Champion, fourth child and second son of Willis Champion and Jane ---, born about 1847.

B416725. John Champion, fifth child and third son of Willis Champion and Jane ---, born about 1850,

B416726. Lucinda Champion, sixth child and third daughter of Willis Champion and Jane ---, born about 1852.

B416727. Clara Champion, seventh child and fourth daughter of Willis Champion and Jane ---, born about 1854.

B416728. Mary Champion, eighth child and fifth daughter of Willis Champion and Jane ---, born about 1860.

B4168. Caroline Pound, eighth child and fifth daughter of Merriman Pound and Clarissa Herndon, born about 1804 in Putnam County, Georgia. Married 12 Dec 1822 in Putnam County, Georgia to John Butler.

B4169. Catherine Pound, ninth child and sixth daughter of Merriman Pound and Clarissa Herndon, born about 1806 in Putnam County,

136

Georgia. Married 24 Mar 1825 in Putnam County, Georgia to William L. Worrell.

B41610. Newman Pound, tenth child and fourth son of Merriman Pound and Clarissa Herndon, born 1808 in Putnam County, Georgia and died in Georgia. Married 26 Oct 1831 in Wilkinson County, Georgia to Martha Clara Murphey, daughter of Ambrose Murphey and Sarah Horne, born 18 Apr 1811 in Georgia. Newman and Martha had issue, which was the eighth generation in America:

B416101. John H. Pound, first child and first son of Newman Pound and Martha Murphey, born 1838 in Monroe County, Georgia and died about 1882 in Pike County, Georgia. Married Sallie Johnson, born 1840 in Georgia. John and Sallie had issue, which was the ninth generation in America:

B4161011. Mattie Pound, first child and first daughter of John Pound and Sallie Johnson, born 1860 in Pike County, Georgia.

B4161012. George Holder Pound, second child and first son of John Pound and Sallie Johnson, born 1862 in Pike County, Georgia.

B4161013. John Pound, third child and second son of John Pound and Sallie Johnson, born 1866 in Pike County, Georgia.

B4161014. Ernest Pound, fourth child and third son of John Pound and Sallie Johnson, born 1868 in Pike County, Georgia.

B4161015. George Harry Pound, fifth child and third son of John Pound and Sallie Johnson, born 1871 in Pike County, Georgia.

B4161016. Florence Pound, sixth child and second daughter of John Pound and Sallie Johnson, born 1874 in Pike County, Georgia.

B4161017. Paul Pound, seventh child and foutth son of John Pound and Sallie Johnson, born 1877 in Pike County, Georgia.

B416102. Clara (Clarcy) Pound, second child and first daughter of Newman Pound and Martha Murphey, born 1842 in Monroe County, Georgia. Married John Ross.

B416103. Newman Pound, Jr., third child and second son of Newman Pound and Martha Murphey, born 1843 in Monroe County, Georgia and died 1860. Married Beatrice Lausia Pitts, daughter of Isaac Pitts and Martha D. Pitts, born 29 Mar 1845 in Georgia and died 22 Jul 1886 in Macon, Bibb County, Georgia. Newman married secondly 15 Aug 1833 in Jefferson County, Missouri to Lucinda Graham. Newman and Beatrice had issue, which was the ninth generation in America:

B4161031. Jerome Balaam Pound, first child and first son of Newman Pound, Jr. and Beatrice Pitts, born 1866 in Dooly County, Georgia and died in Macon, Bibb County, Georgia. Buried Rose Hill cemetery, Bibb County, Georgia. Jerome was a newspaper publisher, eventually owning five newspapers and a hotelier, owning several hotels. Jerome married 1885 in Macon, Bibb County, Georgia, to Madeline Palmer, daughter of Dr. John Turner Palmer and Virginia Buckmaster, born 16 Jan 1866 at Green's Cut, Burke County, Georgia and died 24 Jan 1897 at Knoxville, Knox County, Tennessee. Buried at Rose Hill cemetery, Macon, Bibb County, Georia. Jerome married secondly 5 Jan 1898 to Caroline Willingham, daughter of Winborn Joseph Willingham and Florence Margaret Baynard. Jerome and Madeline had issue, which was the tenth generation in America:

B41610311. Jerome Gordon Pound, first child and first son of Jerome B. Pound and Madeline Palmer, born 6 Oct 1886 at Macon, Bibb County, Georgia and died 2 Jul 1901 in Georgia.

B41610312. Aloysius Ferdnand Pound, second child and second son of Jerome B. Pound and Madeline Palmer, born 11 Jan 1889 at Chattanooga, Hamilton County, Tennessee and died 10 Oct 1889 at Chattanooga, Hamilton County, Tennessee.

B41610313. Kathleen Madeline Pound, third child and first daughter of Jerome B. Pound and Madeline Palmer, date and place of birth unknown. Married Joseph Hardwick Caldwell, son of James Leonidas Caldwell and Margaret Hardwick. Kathleen married secondly to Stanley Morton Robertson, son of Albert A. Robertson and Susan Horton. Kathleen and Joseph had issue, which was the eleventh generation in America:

B416103131. Joseph Hardwick Caldwell, Jr., first child and first son of Kathleen Pound and Joseph Caldwell, date and place of birth unknown.

B416103132. James Leonidas Caldwell, second child and second son of Kathleen Pound and Joseph Caldwell, date and place of birth unknown. Married Marjorie Henry, daughter of William Blodgett Henry and Freda Weber. James and Marjorie had issue, which was the twelfth generation in America:

B4161031321. Kathleen Pound Caldwell, first child and first daughter of James Caldwell and Marjorie Henry, date and place of birth unknown.

B4161031322. Marjorie Henry Caldwell, second child and second daughter of James Caldwell and Marjorie Henry, date and place of birth unknown.

B41610314. Carmelite Mercedes Pound, fourth child and second daughter of Jerome B. Pound and Madeline Palmer, date and place of birth unknown. Married Joseph Page Temple, son of Levi Wake Temple and Alice Page. Carmelite and Joseph had issue, which was the eleventh generation in America:

B416103141. Joseph Page Temple, Jr., first child and first son of Carmelite Pound and Joseph Temple, date and place of birth unknown. Married Martha Hopkins Lamoreaux, daughter of William Frances Lamoreaux and Maude Elma Hopkins. Joseph, Jr. and Martha had issue, which was the twelfth generation in America:

B4161031411. Virginia Page Temple, first child and first daughter of Joseph Temple, Jr. and Martha Lamoreaux, date and place of birth unknown.

B4161031412. Martha Pound Temple, second child and second daughter of Joseph Temple, Jr. and Martha Lamoreaux, date and place of birth unknown.

B416103142. Jerome Balaam Pound Temple, second child and second son of Carmelite Pound and Joseph Temple, date and place of birth unknown. Married Ann Glascock, daughter of James

Arthur Glascock and Lucille Carter. Jerome and
Ann had issue, which was the twelth generation in
America:
        B4161031421. Jerome Balaam
Pound Temple, Jr., first child and first son of
Jerome Temple and Ann Glascock, date and place of
birth unknown.
        B4161031422.   James
Glascock Temple, second child and second son of
Jerome Temple and Ann Glascock, date and place of
birth unknown.
        B41610315. Virginia Palmer Pound,
fifth child and third daughter of Jerome B. Pound
and Madeline Palmer, date and place of birth
unknown. Married Henry Harding Tift, Jr., son of
Captain Henry Harding Tift and Bessie Willingham.
Virginia and Henry had issue, which was the
eleventh generation in America:
        B416103151.   Virginia Pound
Tift, first child and first daughter of Virginia
Pound and Henry Tift, date and place of birth
unknown. Married Richard Gray Brumby, son of
Thomas Micajah Brumby, Jr. and Cordelia Gray.
Virginia Tift and Richard Brumby had isue, which
was the twelth generation in America:
        B4161031511. Richard Gray
Brumby, Jr., first child and first son of Virginia
Tift and Richard Brumby, date and place of birth
unknown.
        B4161031512.   Thomas
Micajah Brumby, second child and second son of
Virginia Tift and Richard Brumby, date and place
of birth unknown.
        B4161031513. Virginia Tift
Brumby, third child and first daughter of Virginia
Tift and Richard Brumby, date and place of birth
unknown.
        B4161031514. Jerome Pound
Brumby, fourth child and third son of Virginia
Tift and Richard Brumby, date and place of birth
unknown.
        B416103152. Henry Harding Tift
III, second child and first son of Virginia Pound
and Richard Brumby, date and place of birth
unknown. Married Christine Cole Lee, daughter of
Dr. William Green Lee and Christine Cole. Henry

and Christine had issue, which was the twelth generation in America:

B4161031521. Henry Harding Tift IV, first child and first son of Henry Tift and Christine Lee, date and place of birth unknown.

B4161031522. William Lee Tift, second child and second son of Henry Tift and Christine Lee, date and place of birth unknown.

B4161031523. Jerome Pound Tift, third child and third son of Henry Tift and Christine Lee, date and place of birth unknown.

B4161031. Jerome Balaam Pound, first child and first son of Newman Pound Jr. and Beatrice Pitts, born 1866 Dooly County, Georgia and died at Macon, Bibb County, Georgia. Buried at Rose Hill cemetery, Macon, Bibb County, Georgia; married secondly 5 Jan 1898 at Chattanooga, Hamilton County, Tennessee to Caroline Willingham, daughter of Winborn Joseph Willingham and Florence Margaret Baynard. Jerome and Caroline had issue, which was the tenth generation in America:

B41610311. Margaret Beatrice Pound, first child and first daughter of Jerome B. Pound and Caroline Willingham, born 13 Dec 1901 in Tennessee and died 12 Jun 1903 in Tennessee.

B41610312. Caroline Drucilla Pound, second child and second daughter of Jerome B. Pound and Caroline Willingham, date and place of birth unknown. Married John Garnett Andrews, son of Daniel Marshall Andrews and Adeline Van Court. Caroline and John had issue, which was the eleventh generation in America:

B416103121. Caroline Willingham Andrews, first child and first daughter of Caroline Pound and John Andrews, date and place of birth unknown.

B416103122. Adeline Van Court Andrews, second child and second daughter of Caroline Pound and John Andrews, date and place of birth unknown.

B4161032. Eugene Lee Pound, second child and second of Newman Pound, Jr. and Beatrice Pitts, born 27 Mar 1866 in Dooly County, Georgia and died 19 Sep 1887 in Macon, Bibb County, Georgia.

B4161033. Martha Drucilla Pound, third child and first daughter of Newman Pound, Jr. and Beatrice Pitts, born about 1864 in Dooly County, Georgia and died 1 Dec 1943 at Macon, Bibb County, Georgia. Buried at Riverside cemetery, Macon, Bibb County, Georgia. Martha was baptized in the Catholic Church as Martha Aloysius Pound and became a nun.

B416104. Ambrose Murphey Pound, fourth child and third son of Newman Pound and Martha Murphey, born 1846 in Monroe County, Georgia and died in Jasper County, Georgia. Married 2 Jan 1861 to Martha Frances Carey, daughter of John Carey and Tabitha Mercer. Ambrose and Martha had issue, which was the ninth generation in America:

B4161041. Butos Pound, first child and first daughter of Ambrose Pound and Martha Carey, born 5 Apr 1869 in Georgia and died in Jasper County, Georgia. Married Jarrett Carter Purcell, born 1862 at Stone Mountain, Gwinnett County, Georgia.

B4161042. Annie Reed Pound, second child and second daughter of Ambrose Pound and Martha Carey, born 27 May 1877 in Georgia and died in Jasper County, Georgia.

B4161043. Ralston Murphey Pound, third child and second son of Ambrose Pound and Martha Carey, born 28 Feb 1876 in Macon, Bibb County, Georgia and died in Jasper County, Georgia. Married 1919 in North Carolina to Frances Egerton Smoot, daughter of James Clinton Smoot and Frances Elizabeth Wood, born in Wilkesboro, Wilkes County, North Carolina. Ralston and Frances had issue, which was the tenth generation in America:

B41610431. Ralston Murphey Pound, Jr., first child and and first son of Ralston Pound and Frances Smoot, date and place of birth unknown. Married Billie Claudine Shaw, daughter of William Shaw and Mary Isabel Duckworth. Ralston Jr. and Claudine had issue, which was the eleventh generation in America:

B416104311. Ralston Murphey Pound III, first child and first son of Ralston

Pound Jr. and Claudine Shaw, date and place of birth unknown.

B41610432. Frances Smoot Pound, second child and first daughter of Ralston Pound and Frances Smoot, date and place of birth unknown. Married Charles Edward Fancher, son of Charles Henry Fancher and Christine Crites.

B41610433. Carey Pound, third child and second daughter of Ralston Pound and Frances Smoot, date and place of birth unknown.

B41610434. James Egerton Pound, fourth child and and second son of Ralston Pound and Frances Smoot, date and place of birth unknown.

B41611. James Jackson Pound, eleventh child and fifth son of Merriman Pound and Clarissa Herndon, born 1810 at Devil's HalfAcre, Putnam County, Georgia and died in Terrell, Terrell County, Texas. Married 3 Dec 1835 in Baldwin County, Georgia to Eppsy Ann Veazey, date and place of birth unknown, but she died in Texas. James and Eppsy had issue, which was the eighth generation in America:

B416111. Thomas Jackson Pound, first child and first son of James Pound and Eppsy Veazey, born 18 Apr 1837 in Putnam County, Georgia and died 22 Jul 1916 in Rains County, Texas. Buried in Symrna cemetery, Texas. Married 15 Nov 1866 in Van Zandt County, Texas to Nancy Raines Dubose, daughter of Willis Vernon Dubose and Anna Raines, born 11 Jan 1841 in Alabama and died 26 Dec 1889 in Rains County, Texas. Buried at Smyrna cemetery, Texas. Thomas J. Pound, familiarly known as "Uncle Tom" died at the home of his son, Willis Pound, in the Prospect community, near Emory, Texas on Saturday, Jul 22, 1916 and was interred in the Smyrna cemetery Sunday afternoon, with the funeral services being conducted under the auspices of the I.O.O.F. lodge, of which the deceased was an honored member, being a charter member of the first organization of that order in Rains County. Uncle Tom was born in Georgia and 81 years of age. He settled in Rains County in the early days and served as a Texas Ranger before the Civil War, being one of the last rangers that served in those days. He was a member of

Forrest's Cavalry during the War between the States and made an excellent record as a Confederate soldier. He helped survey and organize Rains County and served on the first grand jury in that county. He helped to survey the Texas and Pacific Railroad when the road was constructed through this county. He lived at Myrtle Springs with his family for several years and has many friends and acquaintances in this county who will regret his demise. The deceased is survived by four children as follows: Frank Pound of Henrietta, Mrs. W.O. Buttram of Oak Grove, Mrs. J.B. Box of Wills Point and W.W. Pound of Emory. All of the children were with him during his last illness. Thomas and Nancy's issue were the ninth generation in America:

B4161111. Frank Pound, first child and first son of Thomas Pound and Nancy Dubose, born 24 Feb 1869 and died 1 Jun 1958 in Kaufman, Kaufman County, Texas. Buried at Wills Point, White Rose cemetery, Van Zandt County, Texas. Married 13 Nov 1898 in Rains County, Texas to Lee Bird Buttram, born 31 Jul 1875 in Joplin, Jasper County, Missouri and died 25 Jul 1956 in Wills Point, Van Zandt County, Texas. Buried at Wills Point, White Rose cemetery, Van Zandt County, Texas. Frank and Lee had issue, which was the tenth generation in America:

B41611111. Josephine Pound, first child and first daughter of Frank Pound and Lee Buttram, born 5 Apr 1904 and died 28 Sep 1936. Buried at Wills Point, White Rose cemetery, Van Zandt County, Texas. Married Sam Rogers.

B4161112. Thomas J. Pound, second child and second son of Thomas Pound and Nancy Dubose, born 19 May 1870 in Texas and died 23 Aug 1894 in Rains County, Texas. Buried Smyrna cemetery, Texas. Married Rhonda V. ---, born Dec 1876 in Georgia. Thomas Pound and Rhonda --- had issue, which was the tenth generation in America:

B41611121. Sarah C. Pound, first child and first daughter of Thomas Pound and Rhonda ---, born Jan 1896 in Texas.

B41611122. Arthur T. Pound, second child and first son of Thomas Pound and Rhonda ---, born May 1897 in Texas.

B41611123. Ada E. Pound, third child and second daughter of Thomas Pound and Rhonda ---, born in Texas.

B41611124. Claud W. Pound, fourth child and second son of Thomas Pound and Rhonda ---, born May 1900 in Texas.

B4161113. Lula Eugenia (Jennie) Pound, third child and first daughter of Thomas Pound and Nancy Dubose, born 4 Dec 1872 in Texas and died 7 Jun 1917 in Van Zandt County, Texas. Buried at Myrtle Springs cemetery. Married 19 Nov 1891 in Rains County, Texas to William Orville (Bert) Buttram. Lula and William had issue, which was the tenth generation in America:

B41611131. Thomas Dotry (Dot) Buttram, first child and first son of Lula Pound and William Buttram, born 20 Jun 1893 and died 16 Dec 1949 in Van Zandt County, Texas. Buried in Myrtle Springs cemetery. Married Lillie Holloway.

B41611132. Leonara B. Buttram, second child and first daughter of Lula Pound and William Buttram, born 10 May 1896 and died 5 Oct 1990.

B41611133. Worthy Eugenia (Kitty) Buttram, third child and second daughter of Lula Pound and William Buttram, born 5 Oct 1898 and died 31 Jan 1974. Married Dan Henry Lee.

B41611134. Orville Rice Buttram, fourth child and second son of Lula Pound and William Buttram, born 24 Sep 1900 and died 6 May 1983. Married Zula Wylie.

B41611135. Jack Pound Buttram, fifth child and third son of Lula Pound and William Buttram, born 3 Oct 1902 and died 10 Apr 1988. Married Lillian Fay Price. Jack and Lillian had issue, which was the eleventh generation in America:

B416111351. Jack Rhea Buttram, first child and first son of Jack Pound Buttram and Lillian Price, born 8 Aug 1930 at DeKalb, Bowie County, Texas. Married 6 Sep 1953 at Decatur, Wise County, Texas to Cynthia Janice Kearby, daughter of Jerome Peyton Kearby and Ruby Anna

145

Ella Menkei, born 31 Oct 1932 at Hamilton, Hamilton County, Texas, daughter of Jerome Peyton Kearby and Ruby Anna Ella Menke. Jack and Cynthia had issue, which was the twelth generation in America:

B4161113511. Jack Kearby Buttram, first child and first son of Jack R. Buttram and Cynthia Kearby, born 26 Oct 1954 at Orange, Orange County, Texas.

B4161113512. Carolyn Janice Buttram, second child and first daughter of Jack Buttram and Cynthia Kearby, born 24 Oct 1956 at Orange, Orange County, Texas. Married 30 Jan 1982 at Victoria, Victoria County, Texas to John David Kanewske.

B4161113513. Mary Jennifer Buttram, third child and second daughter of Jack Buttram and Cynthia Kearby, born 22 Jun 1962 at Victoria, Victoria County, Texas. Married 4 Aug 1984 at Victoria, Victoria County, Texas to Paul Bruner Fisher.

B41611136. Veasy C. Buttram (twin), sixth child and fourth son of Lula Pound and William Buttram, born 7 Nov 1903 and died 19 Dec 1983. Married Anna May Lyall.

B41611137. Jarmon B. Buttram (twin), seventh child and fifth son of Lula Pound and William Buttram, born 7 Nov 1903. Married Lorene Lipe.

B4151114. Ida Pound, fourth child and second daughter of Thomas Pound and Nancy Dubose, born 24 Dec 1874 in Texas and died 2 Mar 1906. Married 21 Apr 1898 in Rains County, Texas to John J. Goode. Ida Pound was effectively disowned by her father, Thomas Jackson Pound, following her marriage, according to Wilbur Willis Pound. Ida and John had children, but the families did not communicate.

B4161115. Willis Walter Pound, fifth child and third son of Thomas Pound and Nancy Dubose, born 23 Oct 1876 in Texas and died 23 Nov 1954 in Emory, Rains County, Texas. Buried at City cemetery in Emory, Texas. Married first to Ethel Hodges, date and place of birth unknown, but she died in Rains County, Texas; but no children are known from this marriage. Married secondly 14 Jul

1904 to Mabel Grayson, born 5 Mar 1879 in Rains County, Texas and died 8 Jul 1970 at Mineola, Wood County, Texas. Buried at City cemetery in Emory, Texas. Willis and Mabel had issue, which was the tenth generation in America:

B41611151. Thomas Jackson Pound, first child and first son of Willis Pound and Mabel Grayson, born 6 Oct 1905 in Emory, Rains County, Texas and died 26 Jul 1991 at Tyler, Tyler County, Texas. Buried at City cemetery, Emory, Texas. Married 17 Jun 1949 to Dorothy Del Willis, born 13 Jan 1918 in Emory, Rains County, Texas and died 18 Aug 1988 in Emory, Rains County, Texas. Buried in City Cemetery at Emory, Texas. Thomas and Dorothy had issue, which was the eleventh generation in America:

B416111511. Nelda Jean Pound, first child and first daughter of Thomas Pound and Dorothy Willis, born 7 Mar 1951 in Emory, Rains County, Texas. Married Raymond Slatter, born in Emory, Van Zandt County, Texas. Nelda Pound and Raymond Slatter had issue, which was the twelth generation in America:

B4161115111. Erin Slatter, first child and first daughter of Nelda Pound and Raymond Slatter, born 3 Oct 1980 at Emory, Van Zandt County, Texas.

B4161115112. Landon Slatter, second child and first son of Nelda Pound and Raymond Slatter, born 19 Jan 1983 at Emory, Van Zandt County, Texas.

B4161115113. Reagan Slatter, third child and second son of Nelda Pound and Raymond Slatter, born 29 Oct 1989 at Emory, Van Zandt County, Texas.

B416111512. Lisa Ann Pound, second child and second daughter of Thomas Pound and Dorothy Willis, born 22 Jul 1956. Married 14 Feb 1987 to Jerald Peddy, born 10 Aug 1959. Lisa Pound and Jerald Peddy had issue, which was the twelth generation in America:

B4161115121. Cassandra Leeann Peddy, first child and first daughter of Lisa Pound and Jerald Peddy, born 19 Mar 1991.

B416111513. Alan Thomas Pound, third child and first son of Thomas Pound and Dorothy

Willis, born 18 Dec 1961. Married 21 Sep 1991 in Rains County, Texas to Charity Gore, born 26 Jul 1972.

B41611152. Gladys Alta Pound, second child and first daughter of Willis Pound and Mabel Grayson, born 21 Dec 1906 in Rains County, Texas. Married 2 Jun 1934 in Greenville, Hunt County, Texas to Harmon Durward Ivie, Sr., son of Dock Calloway Ivie and Kate Ryan, born 13 Nov 1902 in Rains County, Texas and died 20 Mar 1957 at Emory, Rains County, Texas. Buried at Emory, City cemetery. Texas. Gladys Pound and Harmon Ivie had issue, which was the eleventh generation in America:

B416111521. Suzanne Ivie, first child and first daughter of Gladys Pound and Harmon Ivie, born 17 Jun 1944 in Greenville, Hunt County, Texas. Married 2 Jun 1967 in Paris, Lamar County, Texas to Tracy Wayne Holmes, born 14 Oct 1943 in Tyler, Tyler County, Texas. Suzanne and Tracy had issue, which was the twelth generation in America:

B4161115211. Robin Holmes, first child and first daughter of Suzanne Ivie and Tracy Holmes, born 1 Feb 1973 in Greenville, Hunt County, Texas. Married 14 Jun 1991 to Paul Ryan Strait.

B4161115212. Courtney Holmes, second child and second daughter of Suzanne Ivie and Tracy Holmes, born 14 Dec 1977 in Tyler, Tyler County, Texas.

B416111522. Harmond Durward Ivie, Jr., second child and first son of Gladys Pound and Harmon D. Ivie, Sr., born 5 Feb 1947 in Greenville, Hunt County, Texas. Married 22 Mar 1969 in Winfield, Titus County, Texas to Wanda Ruth McCool, born 17 May 1948 in Mt. Pleasant, Titus County, Texas. Harmon Jr. and Wanda had issue, which was the twelth generation in America:

B4161115221. David Harmon Ivie, first child and first son of Harmon D. Ivie, Jr., and Wanda McCool, born 11 Aug 1977 in Dallas, Dallas County, Texas.

B41611153. Baby Pound, third child and second daughter of Willis Pound and Mabel Grayson, born 10 May 1913 in Rains County, Texas and died in Rains County, Texas.

B41611154. Veda Grace Pound, fourth child and third daughter of Willis Pound and Mabel Grayson, born 30 Sep 1917. Married 10 Sep 1942 to Olen Gilley, born 25 Dec 1904. Veda and Olen had issue, which was the eleventh generation in America:

B416111541. Lana Gilley, first child and first daughter of Veda Pound and Olen Gilley, born 3 Mar 1947 in Greenville, Hunt County, Texas. Married 4 Apr 1969 to Thomas Herman Waters, Jr., born 4 Oct 1946. Lana Gilley and Thomas Waters had issue, which was the twelth generation in America:

B4161115411. Bryan Thomas Waters, first child and first son of Lana Gilley and Thomas Waters, born 3 May 1975.

B4161115412. Jeremy Scott Waters, second child and second son of Lana Gilley and Thomas Waters, born 25 Jun 1978.

B41611142. DaLee Gilley, second child and second daughter of Veda Pound and Olen Gilley, born 16 Jul 1951. Married 3 Mar 1976 to Alan Howard Little. Dalee Gilley and Alan Little had issue, which was the twelth generation in America:

B416111421. Dana Lee Little, first child and first daughter of Dalee Gilley and Alan Little, born 12 Feb 1979.

B416111422. Rod Alan Little, second child and first son of Dalee Gilley and Alan Little, born 30 Jan 1981.

B41611155. Wilbur Willis Pound, fifth child and second son of Willis Pound and Mabel Grayson, born 22 Jun 1919 in Rains County, Texas. Married 9 Apr 1944 to Tommie Lou Putnam. Wilbur and Tommie had issue, which was the eleventh generation in America:

B416111551. Wilbur Wayne Pound, first child and first son of Wilbur Willis Pound and Tommie Putnam, born about 1945 in Ft. Worth, Tarrant County, Texas. Married Rebecca Humphries. Wilbur Wayne Pound and Rebecca Humphries had issue, which was the twelth generation in America:

B4161115511. Aaron Wayne Pound, first child and first son of Wilbur Wayne Pound and Rebecca Humphries, date and place of birth unknown.

B4161115512. Kelly Kathleen Pound, second child and first daughter of Wilbur Wayne Pound and Rebecca Humphries, born 15 Jun 1974.

B416111552. Thomas Kent Pound, second child and second son of Wilbur Willis Pound and Tommie Putnam, born about 1947 in Ft. Worth, Tarrant County, Texas. Married Barbara Ann Ashwood. Thomas and Barbara had issue, which was the twelth generation in America:

B4161115521. Gregory Thomas Pound, first child and first son of Thomas Pound and Barbara Ashwood, born 22 Mar 1974.

B4161115522. Karen Louise Pound, second child and first daughter of Thomas Pound and Barbara Ashwood, born 1 Aug 1975.

B4161115523. Laura Ann Pound, third child and second daughter of Thomas Pound and Barbara Ashwood, born 4 Jul 1979.

B4161115524. Neal Gordon Pound, fourth child and second son of Thomas Pound and Barbara Ashwood, born 24 Mar 1981.

B416111553. Barry Pound, third child and third son of Wilbur Willis Pound and Tommie Putnam, born in Ft. Worth, Tarrant County, Texas.

B41511116. Pat P. Pound, sixth child and fourth son of Thomas Pound and Nancy Dubose, born 4 Nov 1878 and died 16 Mar 1900 in Rains County, Texas. Buried Smyrna cemetery, Texas.

B41511117. Nora (Norine) Alta Pound, seventh child and third daughter of Thomas Pound and Nancy Dubose, born 24 Feb 1881 and died 31 Dec 1974 in Dallas, Dallas County, Texas. Buried in Restland cemetery, Dallas, Texas. Married 6 Aug 1905 to James Burnett Box. Nora Pound and James Box had issue, which was the tenth generation in America:

B416111171. Florence Box, first child and first daughter of Nora Pound and James Box, date and place of birth unknown.

B4161112. Annie Elizabeth Pound, second child and first daughter of James Pound and Eppsy Veazey, born 27 Aug 1839 in Alabama and died 16 Nov 1911 in Tennessee. Married W.E. Lenord.

B416113. Callie Adonia Pound, third child and second daughter of James Pound and Eppsy Veazey, born 5 Oct 1841 in Alabama and died 9 Apr 1912. Married 23 Apr 1867 to Joseph Glawson.

B416114. Bettie Pound, fourth child and third daughter of James Pound and Eppsy Veazey, born 1843 in Alabama and died 29 Dec 1935. Married Tom Presley.

B416115. John Bohannon Pound, fifth child and second son of James Pound and Eppsy Veazey, born 1845 in Alabama and died in California.

B41512. Mary Ann Pound, twelth child and seventh daughter of Merriman Pound and Clarissa Herndon, born 1821 at Devil's Half Acre, Putnam County, Georgia and died in Texas. Married 3 Feb 1839 in Georgia to Andrew Jackson Bridges.

B41613. Clarissa Pound, thirteenth child and eighth daughter of Merriman Pound and Clarissa Herndon, born in Putnam County, Georgia. Married John Morgan.

B417. Frances (Franky) Pound, seventh child and third daughter of Reuben Pound and Frances Merriman, born 1779 in Virginia and died after 1850 in Missouri. Franky married 26 Oct 1831 in Clarke County, Georgia to James M. Britton, Sr., born 1769 in Georgia and died about 1840 in Missouri. They had issue, which was the seventh generation in America:

B4171. William Britton, first child and first son of Franky Pound and James Britton, born about 1804 in Clarke County, Georgia and died 1865 in Crawford County, Missouri. Buried in Missouri. Married 6 Nov 1841 at Steelville, Crawford County, Missouri to Hannah Ramsey, daughter of Delefait Ramsey and Mary ---, born 1836 in Crawford County, Missouri. William Britton and Hannah Ramsey had issue, which was the eighth generation in America:

B41711. Mary Britton, first child and first daughter of William Britton and Hannah Ramsey, born 1836 in Crawford County, Missouri.

B41712. William R. Britton, second child and first son of William Britton and Hannah Ramsey, born 1840 in Crawford County, Missouri.

B41713. Ginna Britton, third child and second daughter of William Britton and Hannah Ramsey, born 1842 in Crawford County, Missouri.

151

B41714. Melinda C. Britton, fourth child and third daughter of William Britton and Hannah Ramsey, born 1845 in Crawford County, Missouri.

B41715. Arcipey Britton, fifth child and fourth daughter of William Britton and Hannah Ramsey, born 1848 in Crawford County, Missouri.

B41716. Delefaet Britton, sixth child and second son of William Britton and Hannah Ramsey, born 1853 in Crawford County, Missouri.

B4172. James M. Britton, Jr., second child and second son of Franky Pound and James M. Britton, Sr., born about 1800 in Clarke County, Georgia and died in Crawford County, Missouri. Married about 1835 in Benton (now Crawford) County, Missouri Susan ---, born about 1820 in Kentucky. James Jr. and Susan --- had issue, which was the eighth generation in America:

B41721. Mary Frances (Franky) Britton, first child and first daughter of James Britton Jr. and Susan ---, born 1836 in Crawford County, Missouri. Married Peter Huskey.

B41722. Vienna Britton, second child and second daughter of James Britton Jr. and Susan ---, born 1838 in Crawford County, Missouri.

B41723. James W. Britton, third child and first son of James Britton Jr. and Susan ---, born about 1840 in Crawford County, Missouri. Married about 1865 in Crawford County, Missouri to A. Emily ---, born 1851 in Missouri. James Britton and Emily --- had issue, which was the ninth generation in America:

B417231. W. James Britton, first child and first son of James Britton and Emily ---, born 1866 in Crawford County, Missouri.

B417232. J. John Britton, second child and second son of James Britton and Emily ---, born 1872 in Crawford County, Missouri.

B417233. B. William Britton, third child and third son of James Britton and Emily ---, born 1874 in Crawford County, Missouri.

B417234. M. Mary Britton, fourth child and first daughter of James Britton and Emily ---, born 1878 in Crawford County, Missouri.

B41724. N.B. Britton, fourth child and second son of James Britton Jr. and Susan ---, born 1840 in Crawford County, Missouri.

B41725. B. Bedford Britton, fifth child and third son of James Britton Jr. and Susan ---, born 1842 in Crawford County, Missouri.

B41726. Wilburn James Britton, sixth child and fourth son of James Britton Jr. and Susan ---, born 1849 in Crawford County, Missouri.

B41727. Green Britton, seventh child and fifth son of James Britton Jr. and Susan ---, born about 1850 in Crawford County, Missouri.

B41728. Lonzo Britton, eighth child and sixth son of James Britton Jr. and Susan ---, born 1851 in Crawford County, Missouri.

B41729. Solomon Britton, ninth child and seventh son of James Britton Jr. and Susan ---, born 1853 in Crawford County, Missouri.

B417210. W.S. Britton, tenth child and eighth son of James Britton Jr. and Susan ---, born 1855 in Crawford County, Missouri.

B417211. Clementine Britton, eleventh child and third daughter of James Britton Jr. and Susan ---, born 1857 in Crawford County, Missouri.

B417212. John Britton, twelth child and ninth son of James Britton Jr. and Susan ---, born 1859 in Crawford County, Missouri.

B4173. Wilburn Jones Britton, third child and third son of Franky Pound and James Britton, born about 1802 in Clarke County, Georgia. Married 21 Oct 1847 at Steelville, Crawford County, Missouri to Susan Turner.

B4174. Bedford S. Britton, fourth child and fourth son of Franky Pound and James Britton, born about 1804 in Crawford County, Missouri.

B4175. Nathaniel Britton, fifth child and fifth son of Franky Pound and James Britton, born about 1806 in Missouri.

B4176. Richard Britton, sixth child and sixth son of Franky Pound and James Britton, born about 1808 at Meremac, Crawford

County, Missouri and died about 1860 in Crawford County, Missouri. Married 21 Feb 1833 in Crawford County, Missouri to Elizabeth (Lizzy) Couch, born 1818 in Missouri. Richard Britton and Lizzy Couch had issue, which was the eighth generation in America:

B41761. Caroline Britton, first child and first daughter of Richard Britton and Lizzy Couch, born 1836 in Crawford County, Missouri.

B41762. Catherine Britton, second child and second daughter of Richard Britton and Lizzy Couch, born 1838 in Crawford County, Missouri. Married William Walls.

B41763. child Britton, third child and third daughter of Richard Britton and Lizzy Couch, born about 1835 in Crawford County, Missouri.

B41764. Valentine Britton, fourth child and fourth daughter of Richard Britton and Lizzy Couch, born 1841 in Crawford County, Missouri.

B41765. Frances Britton, fifth vhild and fifth daughter of Richard Britton and Lizzy Couch, born 1844 in Crawford County, Missouri.

B41766. Hannah Britton, sixth child and sixth daughter of Richard Britton and Lizzy Couch, born 1849 in Crawford County, Missouri.

B41767. Anderson Britton, seventh child and first son of Richard Britton and Lizzy Couch, born 1851 in Crawford County, Missouri.

B4177. Elizabeth Britton, seventh child and first daughter of Franky Pound and James Britton, born about 1810 in Crawford County, Missouri. Married about 1837 in Crawford County, Missouri to Thompson Benton, born 1813 in Missouri. Elizabeth Britton and Thompson Benton had issue, which was the eighth generation in America:

B41771. William Benton, first child and first son of Elizabeth Britton and Thompson Benton, born 1837 in Crawford County, Missouri.

B41772. Catherine Benton, second child and first daughter of Elizabeth Britton and Thompson Benton, born 1839 in Crawford County, Missouri.

B41773. Mary Benton, third child and second daughter of Elizabeth Britton and Thompson Benton, born 1842 in Crawford County, Missouri.

B41774. Margaret Benton, fourth child and third daughter of Elizabeth Britton and Thompson Benton, born 1843 in Crawford County, Missouri.

B41775. Isham (twin) Benton, fifth child and second son of Elizabeth Britton and Thompson Benton, born 1844 in Crawford County, Missouri.

B41776. Newman (twin) Benton, sixth child and third son of Elizabeth Britton and Thompson Benton, born 1844 in Crawford County, Missouri.

B41777. Samuel Benton, seventh child and fourth son of Elizabeth Britton and Thompson Benton, born 1845 in Crawford County, Missouri.

B41778. Elisha Benton, eighth child and fifth son of Elizabeth Britton and Thompson Benton, born 1846 in Crawford County, Missouri.

B4178. Riley Britton, eighth child and seventh son of Franky Pound and James Britton, born about 1814 in Crawford County, Missouri and died 8 Feb 1873 at Hartville, Wright County, Missouri. Buried at Hartville, Wright County, Missouri. Married 8 Oct 1840 at Steelville, Crawford County, Missouri to Julia Ann Strong, born 1824 in Tennessee. Riley Britton and Julia Strong had issue, which was the eighth generation in America:

B41781. Vienna Britton, first child and first daughter of Riley Britton and Julia Strong, born 1841 in Crawford County, Missouri.

B41782. Frances Britton, second child and second daughter of Riley Britton and Julia Strong, born 1843 in Crawford County, Missouri.

B41783.   L.A.   Britton, third child and third daughter of Riley Britton and Julia Strong, born 1846 in Crawford County, Missouri.

B41784.   G.O.   Britton, fourth child and first son of Riley Britton and Julia Strong, born 1848 in Crawford County, Missouri.

B4179.   Mahala Britton, ninth child and second daughter of Franky Pound and James Britton, born about 1816 in Crawford County, Missouri.   Married 1835 in Crawford County, Missouri to Harvey Cane.

B41710.   Roy Newman Britton, tenth child and eighth son of Franky Pound and James Britton, born about 1817 in Crawford County, Missouri and died 20 Apr 1869 in Crawford County, Missouri.   Buried at Hibbler cemetery, Crawford County, Missouri. Married 28 Dec 1837 in Crawford County, Missouri to Sarah Jane Cox, born 1822 in Illinois.   Roy Britton and Sarah Cox had issue, which was the eighth generation in America:

B417101.   William   R. Britton, first child and first son of Roy Britton and Sarah Cox, born 1840 in Crawford County, Missouri.

B417102.   Samuel   J. Britton, second child and second son of Roy Britton and Sarah Cox, born 1842 in Crawford County, Missouri.

B417103.   Andrew Britton, third child and third son of Roy Britton and Sarah Cox, born 1844 in Crawford County, Missouri.

B417104.   Catherine Britton, fourth child and fourth son of Roy Britton and Sarah Cox, born 1847 in Crawford County, Missouri.

B417105.   J.C.   Britton, fifth child and fifth son of Roy Britton and Sarah Cox, born 1849 in Crawford County, Missouri.

B417106.   Elizabeth Britton, sixth child and first daughter of Roy Britton and Sarah Cox, born 1851 in Crawford County, Missouri.

B417107.   Sarah Britton, seventh child and second daughter of Roy Britton and Sarah Cox, born 1852 in Crawford County, Missouri.

B417108. Amanda E. Britton, eighth child and third daughter of Roy Britton and Sarah Cox, born 1854 in Crawford County, Missouri.

B417109. Mary J. Britton, ninth child and fourth daughter of Roy Britton and Sarah Cox, born 1854 in Crawford County, Missouri.

B417110. Victoria Britton, tenth child and fifth daughter of Roy Britton and Sarah Cox, born about 1856 in Crawford County, Missouri.

B417111. Missouri Britton, eleventh child and sixth daughter of Roy Britton and Sarah Cox, born 1858 in Crawford County, Missouri.

B417112. Joseph Britton, twelth child and sixth son of Roy Britton and Sarah Cox, born 1862 in Crawford County, Missouri.

B417113. Rebecca Britton, thirteenth child and seventh daughter of Roy Britton and Sarah Cox, born 1865 in Crawford County, Missouri.

B42. John (V) Samuel Pound, second child and second son of John Pound and his Indian wife, born 1743 in Orange County, Virginia and died about 1816 in Georgia. Married Mary Walker, daughter of David Walker, Sr., and Sarah Slayden, born about 1764 and died 3 Dec 1819 in Hancock County, Georgia. John Pound (V) had land between Turkey Creek and Savannah River in Ninety Six District, South Carolina. He then moved into Hancock County, Georgia. In October 1796 he sold the farmland where he lived to David Walker. But he never moved from this land. Where he got title to the land is unknown as records of Washington County, Georgia were burned in 1855. On 12 May 1806, David Walker made a deed to his grandchildren: Joel, David, Martha Hall, Elizabeth and Mary Pound, two slaves saving and reserving for his daughter Mary Pound the benefit arising from their labor. Joel Pound was appointed sole trustee. On Feb 1807 David Walker deeded to his grandchildren (named above) the property (farm consisting of 150 acres) that he had previously purchased from his son-in-law John Pound. Again he reserved the use and benefit for the maintenance of his daughter Mary Pound during her natural life and for the maintenance of her husband John Pound during his natural life. Joel Pound was appointed trustee. Shortly after buying this property from John Pound, David Walker placed a notice in the Augusta Georgia Chronicle; warning persons not to trade with John Pound for the farm, equipment, livestock, et cetera, in that he had purchased same and that it was recorded in the court records of Hancock County, Georgia and Edgefield County, South Carolina. It seems that something was wrong, either physically or mentally with John Pound (perhaps he was a spendthrift or had a stroke), in any case, it is evident from the abovementioned deeds that David Walker was trying to protect and care for his daughter Mary Pound. Remember, that in those days if a woman owned property, it was under the control of her husband, or, David Walker gave this property to his grandchildren for the use and maintenance of his daughter, thereby taking it out of the control of John Pound. On 20 Apr 1816, John Pound and Mary made a will, leaving their estate to their 5 children. Their will does not appear to have been probated. Wills did not have to be probated provided all heirs agreed. John Pound and Mary Walker had issue, which was the sixth generation in America:

B421. John Pound, first child and first son of John (V) Pound and Mary Walker, born about 1776 in Anson County, North Carolina and died about 1852 in Bedford County, Tennessee. Married about 1783 to Lavinia Rorie, daughter of Reuben Rorie, born about 1790 in Anson County, North Carolina. John Pound and Lavinia Rorie had issue, which was the seventh generation in America:

B4211. David Thomas Pound, first child and first son of John Pound and Lavinia Rorie, born Perry County, Alabama.

B4212. William Marion Pounds, second child and second son of John Pound and Lavinia Rorie, born 4 Sep 1810 in Maury County, Tennessee and died 3 Jul 1851. Buried at Buena Vista, Shelby County, Texas. Married 14 Apr 1836 in Bedford County, Tennessee to Nancy Jane Hairgrove, daughter of Stephen Marion Hairgrove and Nancy Mary Brown, born 31 May 1816 in Bedford County, Tennessee and died 29 Sep 1896 at Marysville, Cooke County, Texas. [Stephen Marion Hairgrove and Nancy Mary Brown moved by ox wagon in the spring of 1806 from G uilford County, North Carolina to the Duck River Purchase, Bedford County, Tennessee, where they reared a large family. In 1853 they moved with a part of their family by ox wagon to Shelby County, in east Texas. Some of their family located in Alabama, Georgia, Louisiana and Mississippi. Stephen Marion Hairgrove served as a Captain under General Jackson in the War of 1812. This information was obtained from "Our Family Record," by Silas Brown Wright]. William Pounds and Nancy Hairgrove had issue, which was the eighth generation in America:

B42121. Mary L. Pounds, first child and first daughter of William Pounds and Nancy Hairgrove, born 17 Jan 1835 in

Bedford County, Tennessee, and died 21 May 1924. Buried Buena Vista, Texas. Married 9 Apr 1856 to John S. Foster, born 22 May 1830 and died 15 Sep 1860. Buried at Buena Vista, Texas. Mary Pounds and John Foster had issue, which was the ninth generation in America:

B421211. John Ragan Foster, first child and first son of Mary Pounds and John S. Foster, born 17 May 1857 at Teneha, Shelby County, Texas and died 27 Nov 1939. Buried at Teneha, Teneha cemetery, Texas. Married Artelia Henkie, born 26 Nov 1854 at Mansfield, Desoto Parish, Louisiana and died 7 Sep 1899. Buried at Teneha, Teneha cemetery, Texas. John Foster and Artelia Henkie had issue, which was the tenth generation in America:

B4212111. Joel M. Foster, first child and first son of John Foster and Artelia Henkie, born 5 Oct 1882 and died 5 Oct 1882.

B4212112. John Foster, second child and second son of John Foster and Artelia Henkie, born 12 Sep 1883 in Teneha, Shelby County, Texas. Married Annie D. Morris. John Foster and Annie Morris had issue, which was the eleventh generation in America:

B42121121. Henry Foster, first child and first son of John Foster and Annie Morris, date and place of birth unknown.

B42121122. Vida Foster, second child and first daughter of John Foster and Annie Morris, date and place of birth unknown.

B42121123. Emmitt Foster, third child and second son of John Foster and Annie Morris, date and place of birth unknown.

B42121124. Cleburn Foster, fourth child and third son of John Foster and Annie Morris, date and place of birth unknown.

B42121125. Grace Foster, fifth child and second daughter of John Foster and Annie Morris, date and place of birth unknown.

B42121126.
Gertie Foster, sixth child and third daughter of John Foster and Annie Morris, date and place of birth unknown.

B4212113. Ethel Foster, third child and first daughter of John Foster and Artelia Henkie, born 27 Apr 1884 in Teneha, Shelby County, Texas and died 10 Sep 1926. Married Duffy Paramore, date and place of birth unknown but died 1875. Ethel Foster and Duffy Paramore had issue, which was the eleventh generation in America:

B42121131. Gladys Paramore, first child and first daughter of Ethel Foster and Duffy Paramore, born 1 May 1904. Married Robert Tippett, born 20 Dec 1887.

B42121132. Raglan Paramore, second child and first son of Ethel Foster and Duffy Paramore, born 22 Jul 1905 in Teneha, Shelby County, Texas. Married Willie May Marshall. Raglan Paramore and Willie Marshall had issue, which was the twelth generation in America:

B421211321. Murline Paramore, first child and first daughter of Raglan Paramore and Willie Marshall, born 26 Dec 1928 in Timpson, Shelby County, Texas. Married John Lee Moore.

B421211322. Marline Paramore, second child and second daughter of Raglan Paramore and Willie Marshall, born 17 Aug 1936.

B42121133. Myra Paramore, third child and second daughter of Ethel Foster and Duffy Paramore, born 15 May 1907 in Teneha, Shelby County, Texas. Married Will Crawford. Myra Paramore and Will Crawford had issue, which was the twelth generation in America:

B421211331. Billy Gene Crawford, first child and first son of Myra Paramore and Will Crawford, date and place of birth unknown.

B421211332. Tubby Crawford, second child and second son of Myra Paramore and Will Crawford, date and place of birth unknown.

B42121134. Laverna Paramore, fourth child and third daughter of Ethel

Foster and Duffy Paramore, born 3 Mar 1908 in Teneha, Shelby County, Texas. Married Lyle Hillen, born 10 Jun 1910 Teneha, Shelby County, Texas.

B42121135. Lera Paramore, fifth child and fourth daughter of Ethel Foster and Duffy Paramore, born 10 Jun 1910 in Teneha, Shelby County, Texas. Married Orb Crawford.

B42121136. Afton Paramore, sixth child and second son of Ethel Foster and Duffy Paramore, born 4 Feb 1917. Married Eva Roberts, born 9 Nov 1920. Afton Paramore and Eva Roberts had issue, which was the twelth generation in America:

B421211361. Ronnie Paramore, first child and first son of Afton Paramore and Eva Roberts, date and place of birth unknown.

B421211362. Bennie Paramore, second child and second son of Afton Paramore and Eva Roberts, date and place of birth unknown.

B421211363. Annie Marie Paramore, third child and first daughter of Afton Paramore and Eva Roberts, date and place of birth unknown.

B421211364. Larry Paramore, fourth child and third son of Afton Paramore and Eva Roberts, date and place of birth unknown.

B421211365. Jerry Paramore, fifth child and fourth son of Afton Paramore and Eva Roberts, date and place of birth unknown.

B421211366. Jimmy Paramore, sixth child and fifth son of Afton Paramore and Eva Roberts, date and place of birth unknown.

B42121137. Bennie Paramore, seventh child and third son of Ethel Foster and Duffy Paramore, born 20 Oct 1920 in Teneha, Shelby County, Texas. Married Anne Marie ---, born 12 Sep 1919.

B4212114. Floyd Foster, fourth child and third son of John Foster and Artelia Henkie, born 14 Jun 1886 and died 14 Jun 1886.

B4212115. Ottis Foster, fifth child and fourth son of John Foster and Artelia Henkie,

date and place of birth unknown. Married Julia
Woodfin.

B4212116. Giles Foster, sixth child
and fifth son of John Foster and Artelia Henkie,
born 20 Mar 1891.

B4212117. Fred Foster, seventh child
and sixth son of John Foster and Artelia Henkie,
date and place of birth unknown. Married Inez
Bridges. Fred Foster and Inez Bridges had issue,
which was the eleventh generation in America:

B42121171. Orene Foster, first
child and first daughter of Fred Foster and Inez
Bridges, date and place of birth unknown.

B42121172. Thyra Foster, second
child and second daughter of Fred Foster and Inez
Bridges, date and place of birth unknown.

B42121173. Forest Foster, third
child and first son of Fred Foster and Inez
Bridges, date and place of birth unknown.

B42121174. Martell Foster,
fourth child and third daughter of Fred Foster and
Inez Bridges, date and place of birth unknown.

B42121175. Martha Nell Foster,
fifth child and fourth daughter of Fred Foster and
Inez Bridges, date and place of birth unknown.

B42121176. Gladys Foster, sixth
child and fifth daughter of Fred Foster and Inez
Bridges, date and place of birth unknown.

B4212118. Pearly Foster, eighth child
and second daughter of John Foster and Artelia
Henkie, date and place of birth unknown. Married
John Kyle. Pearly Foster and John Kyle had issue,
which was the eleventh generation in America:

B42121181. Byron Kyle, first
child and first son of Pearly Foster and John
Kyle, date and place of birth unknown.

B42121182. Curtis Kyle, second
child and second son of Pearly Foster and John
Kyle, date and place of birth unknown.

B42121183. Allie Kyle, third
child and first daughter of Pearly Foster and John
Kyle, date and place of birth unknown.

B42121184. Maurine Kyle, fourth
child and second daughter of Pearly Foster and
John Kyle, date and place of birth unknown.

B42121185. Agnes Kyle, fifth

child and third daughter of Pearly Foster and John Kyle, date and place of birth unknown.

B42121186. Evyone Kyle, sixth child and fourth daughter of Pearly Foster and John Kyle, date and place of birth unknown.

B4212119. Mary Foster, ninth child and third daughter of John Foster and Artelia Henkie, date and place of birth unknown. Married Cole Billingsly. Mary Foster and Cole Billingsly had issue, which was the eleventh generation in America:

B42121191. Jessie Billingsly, first child and first daughter of Mary Foster and Cole Billingsly, date and place of birth unknown.

B42121192. Ruby Billingsly, second child and second daughter of Mary Foster and Cole Billingsly, date and place of birth unknown.

B42121193. Velma Billingsly, third child and third daughter of Mary Foster and Cole Billingsly, date and place of birth unknown.

B42121194. Myra Billingsly, fourth child and fourth daughter of Mary Foster and Cole Billingsly, date and place of birth unknown.

B42121195. Henry Billingsly, fifth child and first son of Mary Foster and Cole Billingsly, date and place of birth unknown.

B421211. John Ragan Foster, first child and first son of John S. Foster and Mary L. Pounds, born 17 May 1857 at Teneha, Texas and died 27 Nov 1939. Buried Teneha, Teneha cemetery, Texas. Married secondly to Carrie McKay-Burgess, born 6 Nov 1871 and died 17 Aug 1909. John Foster married thirdly to Ellen Henry Witsley, but no children are known from this marriage. John Foster and Carrie McKay-Burgess had issue, which was the tenth generation in America:

B4212111. Bailey Foster, first child and first son of John Foster and Carrie McKay-Burgess, born 12 Jul 1905. Married Pauline Carnes. Bailey Foster and Pauline Carnes had issue, which was the eleventh generation in America:

B42121111. Sharon Foster, first child and first daughter of Bailey

Foster and Pauline Carnes, date and place of birth unknown.

B4212112. Normis Foster, second child and first daughter of John Foster and Carrie McKay-Burgess, born 11 Sep 1906.

B421212. Willie Foster, second child and second son of Mary Pounds and John Foster, born 19 Apr 1859 at Teneha, Shelby County, Texas and died 5 May 1926. Buried at Teneha, Teneha cemetery, Texas. Married Sarah Miller, born 9 Aug 1861 and died 3 Jun 1925. Buried at Teneha, Teneha cemetery, Texas. Willie Foster and Sarah Miller had issue, which was the tenth generation in America:

B4212121. Ernest Foster, first child and first son of Willie Foster and Sarah Miller, born 13 Nov 1879 in Teneha, Shelby County, Texas and died 28 Jun 1935. Married Nora Avery.

B4212122. Lonie Foster, second child and first daughter of Willie Foster and Sarah Miller, born 25 Jul 1880 in Teneha, Shelby County, Texas. Married John McDaniel.

B4212123. Ernest Foster, third child and second son of Willie Foster and Sarah Miller, born 5 Jan 1883 in Teneha, Shelby County, Texas. Married Anna Green.

B4212124. Oscar Foster, fourth child and third son of Willie Foster and Sarah Miller, born 3 Feb 1885.

B4212125. Iler Foster, fifth child and fourth son of Willie Foster and Sarah Miller, born 24 Aug 1887 in Teneha, Shelby County, Texas. Married Loraine Braly.

B4212126. Ola Foster, sixth child and second daughter of Willie Foster and Sarah Miller, born 25 Feb 1889 in Teneha, Shelby County, Texas. Married Ben Wilkinson.

B4212127. Riley Foster, seventh child and fifth son of Willie Foster and Sarah Miller, born 12 Feb 1891.

B4212128. Herman Foster, eighth child and sixth son of Willie Foster and Sarah Miller, born 27 Oct 1893 in

Teneha, Shelby County, Texas. Married Alma Antley.

B4212129. Henry Foster, ninth child and seventh son of Willie Foster and Sarah Miller, born and died 14 Aug 1895.

B4212130. Claude Foster, tenth child and eighth son of Willie Foster and Sarah Miller, born 18 Feb 1897 in Teneha, Shelby County, Texas. Married Betty ---.

B4212131. Myrtle Foster, eleventh child and third daughter of Willie Foster and Sarah Miller, born 19 Mar 1899 in Teneha, Shelby County, Texas. Married James Whiteworth.

B4212132. Annie Vera Foster, twelth child and fourth daughter of Willie Foster and Sarah Miller, born 31 Aug 1901 in Teneha, Shelby County, Texas. Married 20 Oct 1923 in Timpson, Shelby County, Texas to Belton Billingsly, born 20 Oct 1902 in Shelby County, Texas. Annie Foster and Belton Billingsly had issue, which was the eleventh generation in America:

B42121321. Leonard M. Billingsly, first child and first son of Annie Foster and Belton Billingsly, born 11 Jul 1927 in Teneha, Shelby County, Texas. Married 25 Mar 1950 to Vera Moore, born 22 Sep 1933 Shelby County, Texas. Leonard Billingsly and Vera Moore had issue, which was the twelth generation in America:
B421213211. Mary Jane Billingsly, first child and first daughter of Leonard Billingsly and Vera Moore, born 27 Sep 1951.

B421213. Roxannah Foster, third child and first daughter of Mary Pounds and John Foster, born 14 Sep 1860 in Teneha, Shelby County, Texas and died 27 Jan 1927. Buried at Sasakwa, Oklahoma. Married John Moody, born 12 Feb 1854 and died 27 Nov 1927. Roxannah Foster and John Moody had issue, which was the tenth generation in America:

B4212131. Willie M. Moody, first child and first son of Roxannah Foster and John Moody, born 14 Apr 1874. Married

Maggie Vineyard, born 25 Sep 1880. Willie Moody and Maggie Vineyward had issue, which was the eleventh generation in America:

B42121311. Ethel Moody, first child and first daughter of Willie Moody and Maggie Vineyard, born 22 Jun 1895 at Stratford, Garvin County, Oklahoma. Married 25 Sep 1915 to William Bynum, born 18 May 1897 Allen, Hughes County, Oklahoma.

B42121312. Walter Moody, second child and first son of Willie Moody and Maggie Vineyard, born 1 Mar 1896. Married Florida ---, born 15 May 1898. Walter Moody and Florida --- had issue, which was the twelth generation in America:

B421213121. L.W. Moody, first child and first son of Walter Moody and Florida ---, born 9 Feb 1920.

B421213122. Alva Moody, second child and first daughter of Walter Moody and Florida ---, born 2 Jan 1922.

B421213123. Doyle Moody, third child and second son of Walter Moody and Florida ---, born 14 Feb 1924.

B42121313. Willie Moody, third child and second daughter of Willie Moody and Maggie Vineyard, born 28 Nov 1898. Married James Uriel Fleming, born 23 Feb 1908 at Geary, Canadian County, Oklahoma. Willie Moody and James Fleming had issue, which was the twelth generation in America:

B421213131. Jerald Fleming, first child and first son of Willie Moody and James Fleming, born 26 Dec 1934.

B421213132. Donna Lee Fleming, second child and first daughter of Willie Moody and james Fleming, born 14 Feb 1938.

B42121314. Effie Moody, fourth child and third daughter of Willie Moody and Maggie Vineyard, born 25 Sep 1902 at Stratford, Garvin County, Oklahoma. Married James Uriel Fleming, who had previously married Effie's sister, Willie Moody. Effie Moody and James Fleming had issue, which was the twelth generation in America:

B421213141. Fern

167

Fleming, first child and first daughter of Effie Moody and James Fleming, born 15 Mar 1930. Married James Lee. Fern Fleming and James Lee had issue, which was the thirteenth generation in America:

B4212131411. Ronnie Lee, first child and first son of Fern Fleming and James Lee, born 26 Dec 1946.

B4212131412. David Wayne Lee, second child and second son of Fern Fleming and James Lee, born 14 May 1953.

B42121315. Elmer Moody, fifth child and second son of Willie Moody and Maggie Vineyard, born 31 Oct 1904. Married Lucille Johnson, born 11 Jun 1914.

B42121316. Homer Moody, sixth child and third son of Willie Moody and Maggie Vineyard, born 22 Aug 1909. Married Dovie Gore, born 13 Jun 1909. Homer Moody and Dovie Gore had issue, which was the twelth generation in America:

B421213161. Elna Faye Moody, first child and first daughter of Homer Moody and Dovie Gore, born 14 Mar 1930.

B421213162. Wayne Osell Moody, second child and first son of Homer Moody and Dovie Gore, born 13 Aug 1931.

B421213163. Harold Lee Moody, third child and second son of Homer Moody and Dovie Gore, born and died 3 Jun 1935.

B421213164. Donald Ray Moody, fourth child and third son of Homer Moody and Dovie Gore, born 26 Apr 1942.

B421213165. James Warren Moody, fifth child and fourth son of Homer Moody and Dovie Gore, born 22 Dec 1946.

B421213166. Edwin Keith Moody, sixth child and fifth son of Homer Moody and Dovie Gore, born 10 Nov 1951.

B42121317. Luther Moody, seventh child and fourth son of Willie Moody and Maggie Vineyard, born 5 Oct 1914. Married 27 Jul 1939 to Beatrice Jones, born 30 Apr 1921. Luther Moody and Beatrice Jones had issue, which was the twelth generation in America:

B421213171. Wanda

Lee Moody, first child and first daughter of Luther Moody and Beatrice Jones, born 15 Jan 1940.

B421213172. Leland Moody, second child and first son of Luther Moody and Beatrice Jones, born 11 Jul 1941.

B421213173. Billy Jean Moody, third child and second daughter of Luther Moody and Beatrice Jones, born 9 Jul 1942.

B421213174. Dale Keith Moody, fourth child and second son of Luther Moody and Beatrice Jones, born 9 Jun 1945.

B421213175. Bobby Glenn Moody, fifth child and third son of Luther Moody and Beatrice Jones, born 5 May 1951.

B42121318. Leonard Moody, eighth child and fifth son of Willie Moody and Maggie Vineyard, date and place of birth unknown.

B42121319. Ottis Moody, ninth child and sixth son of Willie Moody and Maggie Vineyard, date and place of birth unknown.

B42121320. Vernon Moody, tenth child and seventh son of Willie Moody and Maggie Vineyard, date and place of birth unknown.

B4212132. Eli Moody, second child and second son of Roxannah Foster and John Moody, date and place of birth unknown. Married Martha Barley. Eli Moody and Martha Barley had issue, which was the eleventh generation in America:

B42121321. Leonard Moody, first child and first son of Eli Moody and Martha Barley, date and place of birth unknown.

B42121322. Orbie Moody, second child and first daughter of Eli Moody and Martha Barley, date and place of birth unknown.

B42121323. May Moody, third child and second daughter of Eli Moody and Martha Barley, date and place of birth unknown.

B42121324. Ida Bell Moody, fourth child and third daughter of Eli Moody and Martha Barley, date and place of birth unknown.

B42121325. Earl Moody, fifth child and second son of Eli Moody and Martha Barley, date and place of birth unknown.

B42121326. Arnold Moody,

sixth child and third son of Eli Moody and Martha Barley, date and place of birth unknown.

B42121327. Hubert Moody, seventh child and fourth son of Eli Moody and Martha Barley, born 20 Aug 1915. Married Jessie Mae Hensley, born 4 Jun 1921. Hubert Moody and Jessie Hensley had issue, which was the twelth generation in America:

B421213271. Martha Sue Moody, first child and first daughter of Hubert Moody and Jessie Hensley, born 23 Nov 1946.

B421213272. Janice Louise Moody, second child and second daughter of Hubert Moody and Jessie Hensley, born 27 May 1949.

B421213273. Charles Eugene Moody, third child and first son of Hubert Moody and Jessie Hensley, born 25 Feb 1954.

B4212133. Robert Lee Moody, third child and third son of Roxannah Foster and John Moody, born 28 Jul 1878. Married Mary Ann Hall, born 27 Jan 1874. Robert Moody and Mary Hall had issue, which was the eleventh generation in America:

B42121331. Bertha Moody, first child and first daughter of Robert Moody and Mary Hall, born 23 Dec 1902. Married Jesse Provine. Bertha Moody and Jesse Provine had issue, which was the twelth generation in America:

B421213311. Oather Doyle Provine, first child and first son of Bertha Moody and Jesse Provine, born 12 Sep 1924.

B42121332. Dovie Moody, second child and second daughter of Robert Moody and Mary Hall, born 11 Dec 1909. Married Leonard A. Epperly, born 24 Dec 1908. Dovie Moody and Leonard Epperly had issue, which was the twelth generation in America:

B421213321. Leonard Epperly, Jr., first child and first son of Dovie Moody and Leonard Epperly, born 6 Nov 1926.

B421213322. Naoma Joan Epperly, second child and first daughter of Dovie Moody and Leonard Epperly, born 15 Apr 1936.

B421213323. Leona Faye Epperly, third child and second daughter of Dovie Moody and Leonard Epperly, born 6 Nov 1937.

B4212134. Albert Moody, fourth child and fourth son of Roxannah Foster and John Moody, date and place of birth unknown.

B4212135. Byron Ragan Moody, fifth child and fifth son of Roxannah Foster and John Moody, born 31 Jan 1885 in Marysville, Cooke County, Texas. Married Maggie Lou Rogers, born 26 Jul 1888 in Ft. Smith, Sebastian County, Arkansas. Byron Moody and Maggie Rogers had issue, which was the eleventh generation in America:

B42121351. Alma Juanita Moody, first child and first daughter of Byron Moody and Maggie Rogers, born and died 15 Mar 1907.

B42121352. Sylvia Lorene Moody, second child and second daughter of Byron Moody and Maggie Rogers, born 7 Mar 1908. Married John Joseph Kempf, born 28 Nov 1904. John Kempf and Sylvia Moody had issue, which was the twelth generation in America:

B421213521. Cecil Joe Kempf, first child and first son of John Kempf and Sylvia Moody, born 20 Nov 1927. Married Thea Ann Suman, born 5 Aug 1928. Cecil Kempf and Thea Suman had issue, which was the thirteenth generation in America:

B4212135211. Charles John Kempf, first child and first son of Cecil Kempf and Thea Suman, born 5 May 1950.

B421213522. Glenda Jean Kempf, second child and first daughter of John Kempf and Sylvia Moody, born 20 Jan 1934.

B42121353. Felix Carrol Moody, third child and first son of Byron Moody and Maggie Rogers, born 9 Jul 1909. Married Myrtle Depue, born 2 Dec 1915.

B42121354. Arthur Hershal Moody, fourth child and second son of Byron Moody and Maggie Rogers, born 19 Oct 1910. Married Katherine Louise Jones, born 14 Jan 1913. Arthur Moody and Katherine Jones had issue, which was the twelth generation in America:

B421213541. Robert Arthur Moody, first child and first son of

Arthur Moody and Katherine Jones, born 10 Jan 1934.

B421213542. Joe Bill Moody, second child and second son of Arthur Moody and Katherine Jones, born 11 Sep 1935.

B421213543. Jim Ed Moody, third child and third son of Arthur Moody and Katherine Jones, born 31 Jan 1941.

B421213544. Don Mike Moody, fourth child and fourth son of Arthur Moody and Katherine Jones, born 11 Oct 1944.

B421213545. Ki Lee Moody, fifth child and fifth son of Arthur Moody and Katherine Jones, born 20 Jul 1948.

B42121355. Jewell Corene Moody, fifth child and third daughter of Byron Moody and Maggie Rogers, born 10 Jan 1912. Married John William Warren, born 16 May 1917. Jewell Moody and John Warren had issue, which was the twelth generation in America:

B421213551. William Stephen Warren, first child and first son of Jewell Moody and John Warren, born 28 Jan 1953.

B42121356. Newell Carrie Moody, sixth child and third son of Byron Moody and Maggie Rogers, born 1 Feb 1913. Married Hazel Norris, born 11 Oct 1915. Newell Moody and Hazel Norris had issue, which was the twelth generation in America:

B421213561. John Reagan Moody, first child and first son of Newell Moody and Hazel Norris, born 29 Dec 1939.

B421213562. Kay Frances Moody, second child and first daughter of Newell Moody and Hazel Norris, born 14 Dec 1948.

B421213563. Joe Bob Moody, third child and second son of Newell Moody and Hazel Norris, born 25 Aug 1952.

B42121357. Beauford Reagan Moody, seventh child and fourth son of Byron Moody and Maggie Rogers, born 18 Mar 1914. Married Corene Remeninshneider, born 19 Jul 1919. Beauford Moody and Corene Remeninshneider had issue, which was the twelfth generation in America:

B421213571. La Tuend Fay Moody, first child and first daughter of

Beauford Moody and Corene Remeninshneider, born 13 Sep 1940.

B421213572. Beauford Charlie Moody, second child and first son of Beauford Moody and Corene Remeninshneider, born 13 Sep 1949.

B42121358. Herbert Eugene Moody, eighth child and fifth son of Byron Moody and Maggie Rogers, born 20 Aug 1915.

B42121359. Gladys Opal Moody, ninth child and fourth daughter of Byron Moody and Maggie Rogers, born 20 Mar 1917. Married Joseph Franklin McLendon, born 24 Feb 1914. Gladys Moody and Joseph McLendon had issue, which was the twelth generation in America:

B421213591. Judith Ann McLendon, first child and first daughter of Gladys Moody and Joseph McLendon, born 29 Jul 1944.

B421213592. Jo Carol McLendon, second child and second daughter of Gladys Moody and Joseph McLendon, born 10 Oct 1946.

B42121360. Ruby Otha Moody, tenth child and fifth daughter of Byron Moody and Maggie Rogers, born 23 Jul 1918. Married Winston A. Reynolds, born 23 Jan 1919.

B42121361. Edgar Clarence Moody, eleventh child and sixth son of Byron Moody and Maggie Rogers, born 30 Jul 1919. Married Maxine Palmer, born 7 Dec 1924. Edgar Moody and Maxine Palmer had issue, which was the twelth generation in America:

B421213611. John Donald Moody, first child and first son of Edgar Moody and Maxine Palmer, born 8 Mar 1954.

B42121362. Doy Alfred Moody, twelth child and seventh son of Byron Moody and Maggie Rogers, born 24 May 1921. Married Peggy Marie James, born 29 Apr 1925. Doy Moody and Peggy James had issue, which was the twelth generation in America:

B421213621. William Doy Moody, first child and first son of Doy Moody and Peggy James, born 12 Aug 1949.

B42121363. Virginia

Mildred Moody, thirteenth child and sixth daughter of Byron Moody and Maggie Rogers, born 20 Jun 1922. Married Herman Chris Piepke, born 14 Oct 1921. Virginia Moody and Herman Piepke had issue, which was the twelth generation in America:

B421213631. Linda Faye Piepke, first child and first daughter of Virginia Moody and Herman Piepke, born 20 May 1946.

B421213632. John Chris Piepke, second child and first son of Virginia Moody and Herman Piepke, born 15 Dec 1947.

B421213633. David Alan Piepke, third child and second son of Virginia Moody and Herman Peipke, born 13 Dec 1952.

B42121364. Jowe Calvin Moody, fourteenth child and eighth son of Byron Moody and Maggie Rogers, born 6 Aug 1923. Married Louise Imogene Mahnke, born 12 May 1927. Jowe Moody and Louise Mahnke had issue, which was the twelth generation in America:

B421213641. Russell Don Mahnke Moody, first child and first son of Jowe Moody and Louise Mahnke, born 1 Oct 1950.

B421213642. Caroleen Moody, second child and first daughter of Jowe Moody and Louise Mahnke, born 15 Feb 1952.

B42121365. Bobby Dale Moody, fifteenth child and ninth son of Byron Moody and Maggie Rogers, born and died 6 Apr 1925.

B42121366. Paul Moody, sixteenth child and tenth son of Byron Moody and Maggie Rogers, born 2 Feb 1927. Married Betty Joe Hall, born 22 Nov 1932.

B42121. Mary L. Pounds, first child and first daughter of William Pounds and Nancy Hairgrove, born 17 Jan 1835 in Bedford County, Tennessee and died 21 May 1924. Buried at Buena Vista, Texas. Married secondly 9 Jul 1862 to Frank Alexander, born 14 Aug 1832 in Shelbyville, Shelby County, Texas and died 6 Sep 1863. Buried at Shelbyville, Shelby County, Texas. Mary Pounds and Frank Alexander had issue, which was the ninth generation in America:

B421211. Nancy Letitia Alexander, first child and first daughter of Mary Pounds and Frank Alexander, born 7 May 1863 in Keatchie, Louisiana and died 19 Jun 1936 at Okmulgee, Okmulgee County, Oklahoma. Buried at Mineral Wells, Parker County, Texas. Married Fred Aaron Hall, born Bordeaux, France, died 19 Jun 1936. Buried Ofuskee, Oklahoma. Nancy Alexander and Fred Hall had issue, which was the tenth generation in America:

B4212111. Lorraine Hall, first child and first daughter of Nancy Alexander and Fred Hall, born 4 Jan 1893 Ardmore, Carter County, Oklahoma and died 1932.

B42121. Mary L. Pounds, born 17 Jan 1835 in Bedford County, Tennessee and died 21 May 1924. Buried at Buena Vista, Texas. Married thirdly 8 Feb 1865 to Thomas McCarthy, date and place of birth unknown, but died 6 Sep 1895. Mary Pounds married fourthly to James Scott, but no children are known from this marriage. Mary Pounds and Thomas McCarthy had issue, which was the ninth generation in America:

B421211. Mattie McCarthy, first child and first daughter of Mary Pounds and Thomas McCarthy, born 4 Jul 1866 in Logansport, Desoto Parish, Louisiana. Married 20 Sep 1885 to Charles John Doughty, born 15 Nov 1864 in Tuscaloosa, Louisiana and died 3 Jul 1948. Buried at Marysville, Cooke County, Texas. Mattie McCarthy and Charles Doughty had issue, which was the tenth generation in America:

B4212111. Minnie Ophelia Doughty, first child and first daughter of Mattie McCarthy and Charles Doughty, born 10 Sep 1886 at Marysville, Cooke County, Texas and died 14 Jun 1946. Buried at Marysville, Cooke County, Texas. Married 12 Apr 1904 at Marysville, Texas to Bernard M. Guthrie, born 1904 in Shelby County, Texas. Minnie Doughty and Bernard Guthrie had issue, which was the eleventh generation in America:

B42121111. Clarie Mart Guthrie, first child and first son of Minnie Doughty and Bernard Guthrie, born 21 Jan 1916 at Marysville, Cooke County, Texas. Married 5 Aug

1946 at Pilot Point, Denton County, Texas to
Frances Fisher, born 14 Dec 1922 at Pilot Point,
Denton County, Texas. Clarie Guthrie and Frances
Fisher had issue, which was the twelth generation
in America:

B421211111. Celia
Ophelia Guthrie, first child and first daughter of
Clarie Guthrie and Frances Fisher, born 11 Oct
1947.

B421211112. Carl
Bernard Guthrie, second child and first son of
Clarie Guthrie and Frances Fisher, born 25 Sep
1949.

B42121113. Brian
Claire Guthrie, third child and second daughter of
Clarie Guthrie and Frances Fisher, born 22 Sep
1951.

B4212112. Edward James
Doughty, second child and first son of Mattie
McCarthy and Charles Doughty, born 20 Feb 1888 at
Marysville, Cooke County, Texas. Married Della
Erwin, born 21 Jun 1891 at Marysville, Cooke
County, Texas. Edward Doughty and Della Erwin had
issue, which was the eleventh generation in
America:

B42121121. Carol Edward
Doughty, first child and first daughter of Edward
Doughty and Della Erwin, born and died 18 Sep
1917.

B42121122. Erwin Grady
Doughty, second child and first son of Edward
Dougnty and Della Erwin, born 4 Jun 1919 at
Marysville, Cooke County, Texas. Married 4 Dec
1949 to Eunice May Martin, born 20 Sep 1918.
Erwin Doughty and Eunice Martin had issue, which
was the twelth generation in America:

B421211221. Dennis
Erwin Doughty, first child and first son of Erwin
Doughty and Eunice Martin, born 15 Apr 1953.

B42121123. William Allen
Doughty, third child and second son of Edward
Doughty and Della Erwin, born 22 Nov 1924.
Married Ola Shepherd. Married secondly to Margie
Bell Beckman, born 10 Sep 1934. William Doughty
and Ola Shepherd had issue, which was the twelth
generation in America:

B421211231.
William Frederick Doughty, first child and first son of William Doughty and Ola Shepherd, born 2 Oct 1916. Married 28 Dec 1940 to Hazel Bernice Powell. William Doughty and Bernice Powell had issue, which was the thirteenth generation in America:

B4212112311.
Freddie Ronald Doughty, first child and first son of William Doughty and Bernice Powell, born 20 Dec 1941.

B4212112312.
Jackie Aaron Doughty, second child and second son of William Doughty and Bernice Powell, born 24 Apr 1945.

B4212112313.
Carlene Bernice Doughty, third child and first daughter of William Doughty and Bernice Powell, born 28 Jul 1948.

B421211232. Harold Leon Doughty, second child and second son of William Doughty and Ola Shepherd, born 29 Jun 1918. Married 16 Feb 1939 to Florine Boling. Harold Doughty and Florine Boling had issue, which was the thirteenth generation in America:

B4212112321.
Kenneth Leon Doughty, first child and first son of Harold Doughty and Florine Boling, born 9 Feb 1940.

B4212112322.
Glen Doyl Doughty, second child and second son of Harold Doughty and Florine Boling, born 13 Mar 1943.

B4212112323. Anita Fay Doughty, third child and first daughter of Harold Doughty and Florine Boling, born 18 Oct 1946.

B4212112324.
Sheron Jewell Doughty, fourth child and second daughter of Harold Doughty and Florine Boling, born 5 Dec 1947.

B4212112325.
Randall Goodle Doughty, fifth child and third son of Harold Doughty and Florine Boling, born 30 Oct 1950.

B421211233. Dorothy May

Doughty, third child and first daughter of William Doughty and Ola Shepherd, born 31 May 1920 and died 21 May 1946. Married in 1942 to Edd Rozell. Dorothy Doughty and Edd Rozell had issue, which was the thirteenth generation in America:

B4212112331. David Russell Rozell, first child and first son of Dorothy Doughty and Edd Rozell, born 26 Jul 1943.

B4212112332. Michael Paul Rozell, second child and second of Dorothy Doughty and Edd Rozell, born 29 Jun 1944.

B421211234. Thelma Lee Doughty, fourth child and second daughter of William Doughty and Ola Shepherd, born 2 Sep 1922. Married to Albert Byfield. Thelma Doughty and Albert Byfield had issue, which was the thirteenth generation in America:

B4212112341. Lionel Leroy Byfield, first child and first son of Thelma Doughty and Albert Byfield, born 27 Jan 1942.

B421211235. Minnie Pearl Doughty, fifth child and third daughter of William Doughty and Ola Shepherd, born 14 Aug 1924.

B421211236. Melba Jeacl Doughty, sixth child and fourth daughter of William Doughty and Ola Shepherd, born 17 Mar 1926. Married in 1942 to Hubert Leon Parker. Melba Doughty and Hubert Parker had issue, which was the thirteenth generation in America:

B4212112361. Landa Lawone Parker, first child and first daughter of Melba Doughty and Hubert Parker, born 18 Jun 1944.

B4212112362. Judith Ann Parker, second child and second daughter of Melba Doughty and Hubert Parker, born 22 Jul 1946.

B4212112363. Tommie Leon Parker, third child and first son of Melba Doughty and Hubert Parker, born 28 Jul 1948.

B421211237. Alva Mearl Doughty, seventh child and fifth daughter of William Doughty and Ola Shepherd, born 3 May 1929. Married 24 Sep 1946 to Ulis Morrow Duncan. Alva

Doughty and Ulis Duncan had issue, which was the thirteenth generation in America:

B4212112371. Wilma Sue Duncan, first child and first daughter of Alva Doughty and Ulis Duncan, born 25 Sep 1947.

B421211238. Alma Olive Doughty, eighth child and sixth daughter of William Doughty and Ola Shepherd, born 18 Feb 1934. Married 23 Nov 1949 to Bill Cooper.

B421211239. Jiles Geniva Doughty, ninth child and seventh daughter of William Doughty and Ola Shepherd, born 15 Oct 1936. Married in 1948 to Lowell Ramsey. Jiles Doughty and Lowell Ramsey had issue, which was the thirteenth generation in America:

B4212112391. Koron Fay Ramsey, first child and first daughter of Jiles Doughty and Lowell Ramsey, born 24 Oct 1948.

B4212112392. Vera Christine Ramsey, second child and second daughter of Jiles Doughty and Lowell Ramsey, born about 1951.

B421211240. Elsie Anna Doughty, tenth child and eighth daughter of William Doughty and Ola Shepherd, born 10 Jul 1936.

B42121123. William Allen Doughty, third child and third son of Edward Doughty and Della Erwin, born 22 Nov 1924. Married secondly to Margie Bell Beckman, born 10 Sep 1934. William Doughty and Margie Beckman had issue, which was the twelth generation in America:

B421211231. Patricia Ann Doughty, first child and first daughter of William Doughty and Margie Beckman, born 22 Dec 1950.

B421211232. Kathy Lee Doughty, second child and second daughter of William Doughty and Margie Beckman, born 18 Oct 1952.

B4212113. Wilma Doughty, third child and second daughter of Mattie McCarthy and Charles Doughty, date and place of birth unknown.

B4212114. Mary Elizabeth Doughty, fourth child and third daughter of Mattie

McCarthy and Charles Doughty, born 15 Apr 1891 at Marysville, Cooke County, Texas and died 9 Sep 1912. Married 19 Aug 1909 to Wilson Camp. Mary Doughty and Wilson Camp had issue, which was the eleventh generation in America:

B42121141. Wilma Ophelia Camp, first child and first daughter of Mary Doughty and Wilson Camp, born 26 May 1911. Married Arthur Paul Reeves. Wilma Camp and Arthur Reeves had issue, which was the twelth generation in America:

B421211411. Arthur Paul Reeves, first child and first son of Wilma Camp and Arthur Reeves, born 30 Jun 1929. Married 1 Dec 1947 Marjory Pearl Brayton. Arthur Reeves and Marjory Brayton had issue, which was the thirteenth generation in America:

B4212114111. Charyl Andrew Reeves, first child and first daughter of Arthur Reeves and Marjory Brayton, born 12 Oct 1948.

B421211412. Bobby Jean Reeves, second child and first daughter of Wilma Camp and Arthur Reeves, born 9 Sep 1934.

B421211413. Doris Jane Reeves, third child and second daughter of Wilma Camp and Arthur Reeves, born 15 Jul 1940.

B421211414. Patricia May Reeves, fourth child and third daughter of Wilma Camp and Arthur Reeves, born 24 Jul 1941.

B421211415. Linda Carol Reeves, fifth child and fourth daughter of Wilma Camp and Arthur Reeves, born 1 Aug 1948.

B4212115. Herbert Marvin Doughty, fifth child and second son of Mattie McCarthy and Charles Doughty, born 4 Jan 1893 at Marysville, Cooke County, Texas. Married 23 Aug 1916 to Lydia Bell Clifton, born 20 Aug 1898. Herbert Doughty and Lydia Clifton had issue, which was the eleventh generation in America:

B42121151. Lora Dale Doughty, first child and first daughter of Herbert Doughty and Lydia Clifton, born 13 Aug 1917. Married 9 Jun 1934 to Frank Mosley. Lora Doughty and Frank Mosley had issue, which was the twelth

generation in America:

B421211511. Maudine Mosley, first child and first daughter of Lora Doughty and Frank Mosley, born 3 Aug 1936.

B421211512. Yolunda Mosley, second child and second daughter of Lora Doughty and Frank Mosley, born 29 Dec 1946.

B42121152. Charles Jasper Doughty, second child and first son of Herbert Doughty and Lydia Clifton, born 14 Dec 1919.

B42121153. Andrew Carrol Doughty, third child and second son of Herbert Doughty and Lydia Clifton, born 9 Mar 1922.

B42121154. Lucile Doughty, fourth child and second daughter of Herbert Doughty and Lydia Clifton, born 30 May 1923. Married 1 Oct 1938 to Ira Mosley. Lucile Doughty and Ira Mosley had issue, which was the twelth generation in America:

B421211541. Wallace Jackson Mosley, first child and first son of Lucile Doughty and Ira Mosley, born 27 Oct 1939.

B421211542. Neva Lois Mosley, second child and first daughter of Lucile Doughty and Ira Mosley, born 14 Oct 1941.

B421211543. Kenneth Ray Mosley, third child and second son of Lucile Doughty and Ira Mosley, born 13 Nov 1943.

B421211544. Glen Edward Mosley, fourth child and third son of Lucile Doughty and Ira Mosley, born 22 Aug 1945.

B421211545. Michael Benson Doughty, fifth child and fourth son of Lucile Doughty and Ira Mosley, born 9 Jan 1948.

B42121155. Herbert Jesse Doughty, fifth child and third son of Herbert Doughty and Lydia Clifton, born 10 Sep 1925.

B42121156. Russell Bennett Doughty, sixth child and fourth son of Herbert Doughty and Lydia Clifton, born 23 Jun 1928.

B42121157. Vida May Doughty, seventh child and third daughter of Herbert Doughty and Lydia Clifton, born 3 Feb 1931. Married 10 Aug 1947 to Lonnie Fite. Vida

Doughty and Lonnie Fite had issue, which was the twelth generation in America:

B421211571. Jerry Harline Fite, first child and first son of Vida Doughty and Lonnie Fite, born 13 Oct 1948.

B42121158. Boyd Franklin Doughty, eighth child and fifth son of Herbert Doughty and Lydia Clifton, born 26 Sep 1933.

B42121159. Lydia Wanda Doughty, ninth child and fourth daughter of Herbert Doughty and Lydia Clifton, born 26 Sep 1939.

B42121160. Kenneth Ray Doughty, tenth child and sixth son of Herbert Doughty and Lydia Clifton, born 3 Jun 1941.

B4212116. William Allen Doughty, sixth child and third son of Mattie McCarthy and Charles Doughty, born 3 Jul 1895.

B4212117. Charles Maurice Doughty, seventh child and fourth son of Mattie McCarthy and Charles Doughty, born 24 May 1897 at Marysville, Cooke County, Texas. Married 26 Sep 1920 to Maggie Ramsey. Charles Doughty and Maggie Ramsey had issue, which was the eleventh generation in America:

B42121171. Raymond Leon Doughty, first child and first son of Charles Doughty and Maggie Ramsey, born 29 Sep 1921. Married 9 Oct 1945 to Ellen Fergerson. Raymond Doughty and Ellen Fergerson had issue, which was the twelth generation in America:

B421211711. Sharon Kay Doughty, first child and first daughter of Raymond Doughty and Ellen Fergerson, born 26 Jan 1947.

B421211712. Linda Ray Doughty, second child and second daughter of Raymond Doughty and Ellen Fergerson, born 24 Dec 1948.

B421211713. Charles Leon Doughty, third child and first son of Raymond Doughty and Ellen Fergerson, born 29 Jun 1950.

B42121172. Andrew Eugene Doughty, second child and second son of Charles Doughty and Maggie Ramsey, born 4 May 1923. Married 30 Nov 1942 to Frances Byfield. Andrew

Doughty and Frances Byfield had issue, which was the twelth generation in America:

B421211721. Jo Ann Doughty, first child and first daughter of Andrew Doughty and Frances Byfield, born 27 May 1944.

B421211722. Patsey Jean Doughty, second child and second daughter of Andrew Doughty and Frances Byfield, born 5 Jun 1947.

B421211723. Kathie Marie Doughty, third child and third daughter of Andrew Doughty and Frances Byfield, born 19 Jun 1951.

B42121173. Troy Franklin Doughty, third child and third son of Charles Doughty and Maggie Ramsey, born 5 Jan 1925. Married 26 Jan 1948 to Lola Adams. Troy Doughty and Lola Adams had issue, which was the twelth generation in America:

B421211731. Peggy Jo Doughty, first child and first daughter of Troy Doughty and Lola Adams, born 18 Apr 1949.

B421211732. Michael Troy Doughty, second child and first son of Troy Doughty and Lola Adams, born 13 Dec 1951.

B421211733. Debra Ann Doughty, third child and second daughter of Troy Doughty and Lola Adams, born 26 May 1952.

B42121174. Opal Marie Doughty, fourth child and first daughter of Charles Doughty and Maggie Ramsey, born 14 Jun 1927. Married 26 Dec 1944 to Ben Garner. Opal Doughty and Ben Garner had issue, which was the twelth generation in America:

B421211741. Glen Darrel Garner, first child and first son of Opal Doughty and Ben Garner, born 13 Jan 1946.

B421211742. Judy Diann Garner, second child and first daughter of Opal Doughty and Ben Garner, born 27 Feb 1948.

B421211743. Carol Elaine Garner, third child and second daughter of Opal Doughty and Ben Garner, born 27 Feb 1948.

B421211744. Richey Vaughn Garner, fourth child and second son

of Opal Doughty and Ben Garner, born 14 Apr 1951.
B42121175. Mildred
Inez Doughty, fifth child and second daughter of
Charles Doughty and Maggie Ramsey, born 8 Nov
1928. Married 6 Nov 1945 to Robert Adams.
Mildred Doughty and Robert Adams had issue, which
was the twelth generation in America:
B421211751.
Donna Jean Adams, first child and first daughter
of Mildred Doughty and Robert Adams, born 4 May
1946.
B421211752.
Garry Lee Adams, second child and first son of
Mildred Doughty and Robert Adams, born 7 Jan 1948.
B421211753.
Janis Fay Adams, third child and second daughter
of Mildred Doughty and Robert Adams, born 18 Oct
1949.
B42121176. Cecil
Glen Doughty, sixth child and fourth son of
Charles Doughty and Maggie Ramsey, born 24 Dec
1930.
B42121177. Jackie
Dale Doughty, seventh child and third daughter of
Charles Doughty and Maggie Ramsey, born 2 Feb
1934.
B4212118. Martha Lorene
Doughty, eighth child and fourth daughter of
Mattie McCarthy and Charles Doughty, born 26 Aug
1899 at Marysville, Cooke County, Texas. Married
23 Sep 1933 to William Henry Sloan, born 28 Jul
1888. Martha Doughty and William Sloan had issue,
which was the eleventh generation in America:
B42121181. Sara
Celia Sloan, first child and first daughter of
Martha Doughty and William Sloan, born 1 Aug 1934.
Married 17 May 1952 to Darrel Wright. Sara Sloan
and Darrel Wright had issue, which was the twelth
generation in America:
B421211811.
Darilyn Jayne Wright, first child and first
daughter of Sara Sloan and Darrel Wright, born 18
Oct 1953.
B42121182. William
Carter Sloan, second child and first son of Martha
Doughty and William Sloan, born 14 Feb 1940.

B4212119. Alice Vera Doughty, ninth child and fifth daughter of Mattie McCarthy and Charles Doughty, born 30 Nov 1900 at Marysville, Cooke County, Texas. Married to Jack Parker. Alice Doughty and Jack Parker had issue, which was the eleventh generation in America:

B42121191. Arthur Leo Parker, first child and first son of Alice Doughty and Jack Parker, born 6 Dec 1926.

B42121192. Virginia Pearl Parker, second child and first daughter of Alice Doughty and Jack Parker, born 8 May 1929. Married Buddy Grace.

B42121193. Laquita Fay Parker, third child and second daughter of Alice Doughty and Jack Parker, born 26 Jan 1932. Married 6 Jul 1947 to Billy Lambert.

B42121194. Baby Parker, fourth child of unknown sex of Alice Doughty and Jack Parker, born 8 Apr 1938.

B4212120. Vina Alulu Doughty, tenth child and sixth daughter of Mattie McCarthy and Charles Doughty, born 26 Aug 1902 at Marysville, Cooke County, Texas. Married 11 Apr 1925 to Earl Ritcherson, born 23 Jan 1903 in Marysville, Cooke County, Texas. Vina Doughty and Earl Ritcherson had issue, which was the eleventh generation in America:

B42121201. Richard Earl Ritcherson, first child and first son of Vina Doughty and Earl Ritcherson, born 31 Jan 1926. Married Helen Taft, born 18 Sep 1936 at Thackerville, Oklahoma. Richard Ritcherson and Helen Taft had issue, which was the twelth generation in America:

B421212011. Jessie Earl Ritcherson, first child and first daughter of Richard Ritcherson and Helen Taft, born 5 Feb 1949.

B421212012. Carl Leo Ritcherson, second child and first son of Richard Ritcherson and Helen Taft, born 2 Aug 1952.

B421212013. Bobby Glenn Ritcherson, third child and second son of Richard Ritcherson and Helen Taft, born 4 Jul 1954.

B42121202. Nina Joyce

Ritcherson, second child and first daughter of Vina Doughty and Earl Ritcherson, born 5 Jan 1929. Married 24 Aug 1945 to Clarence Fenton Bellar. Nina Ritcherson and Clarence Bellar had issue, which was the twelth generation in America:

B421212021. Carroll Ann Bellar, first child and first daughter of Nina Ritcherson and Clarence Bellar, born 13 Jan 1946.

B421212022. Michael Fenton Bellar, second child and first son of Nina Ritcherson and Clarence Bellar, born 14 Dec 1948.

B421212023. Jerry Clarence Bellar, third child and second son of Nina Ritcherson and Clarence Bellar, born 18 Sep 1950.

B421212024. Ronald Wayne Bellar, fourth child and third son of Nina Ritcherson and Clarence Bellar, born 2 Sep 1951.

B421212025. Benny Max Bellar, fifth child and fourth son of Nina Ritcherson and Clarence Bellar, born 17 Nov 1953.

B42121203. Edith Louise Ritcherson, third child and second daughter of Vina Doughty and Earl Ritcherson, born 16 Oct 1931. Married 28 Oct 1947 to Garven Oneal, born 22 May 1929. Edith Ritcherson and Garven Oneal had issue, which was the twelth generation in America:

B421212031. Catherine Louise Oneal, first child and first daughter of Edith Ritcherson and Garven Oneal, born 2 Feb 1951.

B421212032. Glynn Alex Oneal, second child and first son of Edith Ritcherson and Garven Oneal, born 30 Jan 1952.

B42121204. Wilma Lee Ritcherson, fourth child and third daughter of Vina Doughty and Earl Ritcherson, born 8 Feb 1933. Married 17 Feb 1948 to Cecil H. Stubblefield. Wilma Ritcherson and Cecil Stubblefield had issue, which was the twelth generation in America:

B421212041. Charles R. Stubblefield, first child and first son of Wilma Ritcherson and Cecil Stubblefield, born 28 Aug 1949.

B421212042. Donald Wayne

Stubblefield, second child and second son of Wilma Ritcherson and Cecil Stubblefield, born 24 Sep 1950.

B421212043. Billie Dean Stubblefield, third child and first daughter of Wilma Ritcherson and Cecil Stubblefield, born 30 Sep 1951.

B421212044. Stanley Glenn Stubblefield, fourth child and third son of Wilma Ritcherson and Cecil Stubblefield, born 30 Nov 1953.

B42121205. Betty Glee Ritcherson, fifth child and fourth daughter of Vina Doughty and Earl Ritcherson, born 18 Dec 1935.

B42121206. Marice Charline Ritcherson, sixth child and fifth daughter of Vina Doughty and Earl Ritcherson, born 8 Feb 1938. Married 13 Nov 1953 to Milton Parr Coffer. Marice Ritcherson and Milton Coffer had issue, which was the twelth generation in America:

B421212061. Ruth Lynn Coffer, first child and first daughter of Marice Ritcherson and Milton Coffer, born 6 Aug 1954.

B42121207. Donald Ray Ritcherson, seventh child and second son of Vina Doughty and Earl Ritcherson, born 7 Feb 1940.

B4212121. Carl Ezra Doughty, eleventh child and fifth son of Mattie McCarthy and Charles Doughty, born 3 Apr 1904 at Marysville, Cooke County, Texas. Married 28 Dec 1930 to Nettie Hyman, born 17 Oct 1906. Carl Doughty and Nettie Hyman had issue, which was the eleventh generation in America:

B42121211. Howard Dale Doughty, first child and first son of Carl Doughty and Nettie Hyman, born 11 Apr 1933.

B42121212. Wanda Maxine Doughty, second child and first daughter of Carl Doughty and Nettie Hyman, born 3 Feb 1937. Married 22 Dec 1952 to William Calvin Cash. Wanda Doughty and William Cash had issue, which was the twelth generation in America:

B421212121. Carl Hershel Cash, first child and first son of Wanda Doughty and William Cash, born 31 Jul 1953.

B421212122.   Bertie Virginia
Cash, second child and first daughter of Wanda
Doughty and William Cash, born 21 Jul 1954.
B42121213.   Mary Helen Doughty,
third child and second daughter of Carl Doughty
and Nettie Hyman, born 9 Jan 1939.
B42121214.   Linda Fay Doughty,
fourth child and third daughter of Carl Doughty
and Nettie Hyman, born 11 Feb 1950.
B4212122.   Loy Franklin Doughty, twelth
child and sixth son of Mattie McCarthy and Charles
Doughty, born 4 Feb 1906 at Marysville, Cooke
County, Texas.   Married 8 Oct 1927 to Orbie Anna
Shepherd, born 26 Dec 1910.   Loy Doughty and Orbie
Shepherd had issue, which was the eleventh
generation in America:
B42121221.   Floy Pauline Doughty,
first child and first daughter of Loy Doughty and
Orbie Shepherd, born 29 Oct 1928.   Married 12 Oct
1946 to Lewis Kindle.   Floy Doughty and Lewis
Kindle had issue, which was the twelth generation
in America:
B421212211.   Dorothy Marie
Kindle, first child and first daughter of Floy
Doughty and Lewis Kindle, born 3 Feb 1946.
B421212212.   Brenda Carol
Kindle, second child and second daughter of Floy
Doughty and Lewis Kindle, born 4 Apr 1948.
B421212213. David Leon Kindle,
third child and first son of Floy Doughty and
Lewis Kindle, born 26 May 1949.
B421212214.   Bobby Lewis
Kindle, fourth child and second son of Floy
Doughty and Lewis Kindle, born 21 Aug 1950.
B42121222.   Margie Nell Doughty,
second child and second daughter of Loy Doughty
and Orbie Shepherd, born 26 May 1930.   Married 5
Sep 1946 to Bud Silcox.   Margie Doughty and Bud
Silcox had issue, which was the twelth issue of
America:
B421212221.   Margaret Ann
Silcox, first child and first daughter of Margie
Doughty and Bud Silcox, born 14 Jul 1947.
B421212222. Edna Ruth Silcox,
second child and second daughter of Margie Doughty
and Bud Silcox, born 25 Sep 1948.

B421212223. Marilyn Jean Silcox, third child and third daughter of Margie Doughty and Bud Silcox, born 24 Aug 1950.

B42121223. Hazel Lorene Doughty, third child and third daughter of Loy Doughty and Orbie Shepherd, born 8 May 1933.

B42121224. Lois Frances Doughty, fourth child and fourth daughter of Loy Doughty and Orbie Shepherd, born 5 Feb 1936.

B42121225. Bobbie Wayne Doughty, fifth child and fifth daughter of Loy Doughty and Orbie Shepherd, born 15 Jul 1939.

B4212123. Joseph Richard Doughty, thirteenth child and seventh son of Mattie McCarthy and Charles Doughty, born 25 Jan 1912 at Marysville, Cooke County, Texas. Married 10 Aug 1930 to Verna Hodges, born 27 Aug 1912 in Leon, Oklahoma. Joseph Doughty and Verna Hodges had issue, which was the eleventh generation in America:

B42121231. Joe Sheldon (twin) Doughty, first child and first son of Joseph Doughty and Verna Hodges, born 2 Aug 1931. Married May 1952 to Texoma Sparkman. Joe Doughty and Texoma Sparkman had issue, which was the twelth generation in America:

B421212311. Kan Ellen Doughty, first child and first daughter of Joe Doughty and Texoma Sparkman, born Feb 1953.

B42121232. John Weldon (twin) Doughty, second child and second son of Joseph Doughty and Verna Hodges, born 2 Aug 1931. Married Apr 1952 to Louise Huggins. John Doughty and Louise Huggins had issue, which was the twelth generation in America:

B421212321. Gary Gene (twin) Doughty, first child and first son of John Doughty and Louise Huggins, born Mar 1953.

B421212322. Jerry Dean (twin) Doughty, second child and second son of John Doughty and Louise Huggins, born Mar 1953.

B42121233. Eugene Glen Doughty, third child and third son of Joseph Doughty and Verna Hodges, born 22 Apr 1933.

B42121234. Douglas Edward Doughty, fourth child and fourth son of Joseph Doughty and

Verna Hodges, born 18 Mar 1938.

B42121235. Jemmie Derriel Doughty, fifth child and fifth son of Joseph Doughty and Verna Hodges, born 4 Oct 1940.

B42121236. Cecil Wayne Doughty, sixth child and sixth son of Joseph Doughty and Verna Hodges, born 28 Dec 1945.

B421212. Sashie McCarthy, second child and second daughter of Mary Pounds and Thomas McCarthy, born 4 Sep 1869.

B421213. Lovina McCarthy, third child and third daughter of Mary Pounds and Thomas McCarthy, born 12 Aug 1874 at Logansport, Desoto Parish, Louisiana and died 30 May 1947 at Denver, Denver County, Colorado. Buried at Fair Memorial cemetery, Denver, Colorado.

B42122. Joel (Joseph) Marion David Pounds, second child and first son of William Pounds and Nancy Hairgrove, born 5 Dec 1836 in Bedford County, Tennessee and died 7 Mar 1921. Buried Marysville, Cooke County, Texas. Joel (Joseph) Marion Pounds fought in the Civil War, 2 Co D 15th Texas Infantry and 1 Co F 13th Texas Volunteers as a private. He was granted a pension from the State of Texas in June 1914, which he received until his death in 1921 in Cooke County, Texas. Married Roxanne Shelton. Joel Pounds and Roxanne Shelton had issue, which was the ninth generation in America:

B421221. Manda Pounds, first child and first daughter of Joel Pounds and Roxanne Shelton, born 27 Mar 1863 in Henderson County, Texas and died at Marysville, Cooke County, Texas. Buried Marysville, Cooke County, Texas. Married Johnny Arnold. Manda Pounds and Johnny Arnold had issue, which was the tenth generation in America:

B4212211. Milay Arnold, first child and first son of Manda Pounds and Johnny Arnold, date and place of birth unknown.

B4212212. Frank Arnold, second child and second son of Manda Pounds and Johnny Arnold, date and place of birth unknown.

B4212213. Jose Arnold, third child and third son of Manda Pounds and Johnny Arnold, date and place of birth unknown.

B4212214. Johnny Arnold, Jr., fourth

child and fourth son of Manda Pounds and Johnny Arnold, date and place of birth unknown.

B42122. Joel (Joseph) Marion David Pounds, second child and first son of William Pounds and Nancy Hairgrove, born 5 Dec 1836 in Bedford County, Tennessee and died 7 Mar 1921. Buried at Marysville, Cooke County, Texas. Married secondly 27 Aug 1864 to Eliza Wyatt, born 19 Aug 1942 at Talladega, Talladega County, Alabama and died 10 Feb 1932. Buried at Marysville, Cooke County, Texas. Joel Marion David Pounds filed a "Soldiers Application for a Pension" with the State of Texas from his home at Route 2, Gainesville, Cooke County, Texas in May 1914. It was granted as of June 1914, and he continued to receive the pension until his death in 1921 in Cooke County, Texas. The pension application is in his own handwriting and indicates that he served about three years, enlisting in 1861 at Tyler, Texas and paroled in 1865 at Marshall, Texas. Joel Pounds and Eliza Wyatt had issue, which was the ninth generation in America:

B421221. Julius Alex Robison Pounds, first child and first son of Joel Pounds and Eliza Wyatt, born and died 12 Feb 1866.

B421222. Cynthia Ann Medford Pounds, second child and first daughter of Joel Pounds and Eliza Wyatt, born 8 Mar 1867 at Marysville, Cooke County, Texas and died 11 Sep 1907 at Marysville, Cooke County, Texas. Buried at Marysville, Cooke County, Texas. Married 16 Jan 1885 at Marysville, Texas to William Sylvester Gilley. Married secondly to Thomas Jefferson Smith. Cynthia Pounds and William Gilley had issue, which was the tenth generation in America:

B4212221. Vernon Macon Moore Gilley, first child and first son of Cynthia Pounds and William Gilley, born 1 Jan 1886 at Marysville, Cooke County, Texas and died 10 Feb 1956. Married 12 Aug 1908 at Marietta, Love County, Oklahoma to Lovina McCarthy-Waddell, daughter of Thomas McCarthy and Mary L. Pounds, born 12 Aug 1874 at Logansport, Desoto Parish, Louisiana and died 30 May 1947 at Denver, Denver County, Colorado. Buried at Fair cemetery, Denver, Colorado. Married secondly 8 May 1948 to Effie Eldorado

Carpenter-Shegog, born 11 Apr 1889. Vernon Gilley and Lovina McCarthy-Waddell had issue, which was the twelth generation in America:

B42122211. Lloyd Vernon Gilley, first child and first son of Vernon Gilley and Lovina McCarthy-Waddell, born 26 Nov 1909 at Lawton, Comanche County, Oklahoma. Married 23 Jan 1932 at Denver, Denver County, Colorado to Virginia Maron Bush, born 28 Mar 1911. Lloyd Gilley and Virginia Bush had issue, which was the twelth generation in America:

B421222111. Dwight Richard Gilley, first child and first son of Lloyd Gilley and Virginia Bush, born 7 Apr 1937.

B421222112. Vernon Thomas (adopted) Gilley, second child and second son of Lloyd Gilley and Virginia Bush, born 5 Jan 1943.

B42122212. Wilma Marie Gilley, second child and first daughter of Vernon Gilley and Lovina McCarthy-Waddell, born 18 May 1915 at Las Animas, Las Animas County, Colorado. Married 18 Feb 1936 at Englewood, Arapahoe County, Colorado to Chester Thomas Wilson, born 15 Feb 1906.

B4212222. William Gilley, second child and second son of Cynthia Pounds and William Gilley, born 29 Oct 1898.

B4212223. Amy Gilley, third child and first daughter of Cynthia Pounds and William Gilley, born 21 Nov 1902.

B4212224. Margaret Gilley, fourth child and second daughter of Cynthia Pounds and William Gilley, born 1 Jun 1904.

B421222. Cynthia Ann Medford Pounds, second child and first daughter of Joel Pounds and Eliza Wyatt, born 8 Mar 1867 at Marysville, Cooke County, Texas and died 11 Sep 1907 at Marysville, Cooke County, Texas. Married secondly to Thomas Jefferson Smith, born 26 May 1861 at Atlanta, Fulton County, Georgia and died 20 Feb 1935 at Jimtown, Love County, Oklahoma. Cynthia Pounds and Thomas Smith had issue, which was the tenth generation in America:

B4212221. William Jennings Bryan Smith, first child and first son of Cynthia Pounds and Thomas Smith, born 29 Oct 1898 at Marysville,

Cooke County, Texas and died 26 Oct 1932 at Marietta, Love County, Oklahoma. Buried at Marietta, Love County, Oklahoma. Married Ida Mabry. William Smith and Ida Mabry had issue, which was the eleventh generation in America:

B42122211. Harry Maruis Smith, first child and first son of William Smith and Ida Mabry, date and place of birth unknown.

B4212222. Amy Smith, second child and first daughter of Cynthia Pounds and Thomas Smith, born 21 Nov 1902 at Marysville, Cooke County, Texas and died 21 Jan 1969. Married John Smith. Married secondly Harold Underwood. Amy Smith and John Smith had issue, which was the eleventh generation in America:

B42122221. Viola Smith, first child and first daughter of Amy Smith and John Smith, born 18 Sep 1925. Married Clarence Grimes.

B42122222. Earl Smith, second child and first son of Amy Smith and John Smith, born 8 Oct 1926. Married Patricia Mitchell. Earl Smith and Patricia Mitchell had issue, which was the twelth generation in America:

B421222221. Patricia Karon Smith, first child and first daughter of Earl Smith and Patricia Mitchell, born 15 Sep 1953.

B42122223. Pearl Smith, third child and second daughter of Amy Smith and John Smith, born 29 Oct 1928. Married Charles Jeffers, born 27 Oct 1928. Married secondly Raymond Joels. Pearl Smith and Charles Jeffers had issue, which was the twelth generation in America:

B421222231. Mary Jeffers, first child and first daughter of Pearl Smith and Charles Jeffers, born 27 Nov 1944.

B421222232. Louise Jeffers, second child and second daughter of Pearl Smith and Charles Jeffers, born 7 Dec 1946.

B4212222. Amy Smith, second child and first daughter of Cynthia Pounds and Thomas Smith, born 21 Nov 1902 at Marysville, Cooke County, Texas and died 21 Jan 1969. Married secondly Harold Underwood, born 15 May 1905. Amy Smith and Harold Underwood had issue, which was the eleventh generation in America:

B42122221. Harold Underwood, Jr.,

first child and first son of Amy Smith and Harold Underwood, born 30 Jul 1935.

B42122222.   Charles   Underwood, second child and second son of Amy Smith and Harold Underwood, born 6 Feb 1937.

B42122223.   Orville   Underwood, third child and third son of Amy Smith and Harold Underwood, born 12 Sep 1938.

B42122224.   Bessie May Underwood, fourth child and first daughter of Amy Smith and Harold Underwood, born 18 Jan 1941.

B4212223.   Margaret Irene Smith, third child and second daughter of Cynthia Pounds and Thomas Smith, born 1 Jun 1904 at Marysville, Cooke County, Texas and died 28 Mar 1990 at Spokane, Spokane County, Washington.   Married 12 Jan 1925 to James Cullen Hanna, Sr.   Margaret Smith and James Hanna had issue, which was the eleventh generation in America:

B42122231.   James   Cullen   Hanna, Jr., first child and first son of Margaret Smith and James Hanna, born 16 Dec 1925.   Married 19 Nov 1951 to Lois Marie Payne.   James Hanna and Lois Payne had issue, which was the twelth generation in America:

B421222311.   Fred   Theodore Hanna, first child and first son of James Hanna and Lois Payne, born 11 Aug 1952.

B421222312.   Thomas   Hanna, second child and second son of James Hanna and Lois Payne, date and place of birth unknown.

B4212224.   Vivian   Ona   Smith, fourth child and third daughter of Cynthia Pounds and Thomas Smith, born 4 Feb 1906 at Marysville, Cooke County, Texas and died 22 Aug 1931 at Oklahoma City, Oklahoma County, Oklahoma.   Buried at Hollis, Harmon County, Oklahoma.   Married John Martin.   Married secondly 26 Jul 1926 to William Otto Burgett.   Vivian Smith and John Martin had issue, which was the eleventh generation in America:

B42122241.   Lucretia Aslee Martin, first child and first daughter of Vivian Smith and John Martin, born 28 Jul 1923 at Oklahoma City, Oklahoma County, Oklahoma.   Married 3 Nov 1940 at Harmon County, Oklahoma to James R.G. Pierce, born

12 Nov 1920 at Hollis, Harmon County, Oklahoma. Lucretia Martin and James Pierce had issue, which was the twelth generation in America:

B421222411. Larry Martin Pierce, first child and first son of Lucretia Martin and James Pierce, born 30 Sep 1942 at Hollis, Harmon County, Oklahoma. Married Mary Frances Waddell. Married secondly Terry Kithcart. Larry Pierce and Terry Kithcart had issue, which was the thirteenth generation in America:

B4212224111. James Matthew Pierce, first child and first son of Larry Pierce and Terry Kithcart, born 17 Dec 1968 at Tucumcari, Quay County, New Mexico.

B4212224112. Michael Alan Pierce, second child and second son of Larry Pierce and Terry Kithcart, born 17 Dec 1970 at Tucumcari, Quay County, New Mexico.

B4212224113. Timothy Martin Pierce, third child and third son of Larry Pierce and Terry Kithcart, born 13 Jan 1973 at Tucumcari, Quay County, New Mexico.

B421222412. Alan Dale Pierce, second child and second son of Lucretia Martin and James Pierce, born 19 Dec 1944 at Clovis, Curry County, New Mexico.

B4212224. Vivian Ona Smith, fourth child and third daughter of Cynthia Pounds and Thomas Smith, born 4 Feb 1906 at Marysville, Cooke County, Texas and died 22 Aug 1931 at Oklahoma City, Oklahoma County, Oklahoma. Buried at Hollis, Harmon County, Oklahoma. Married firstly John Martin. Married secondly 26 Jul 1926 at Wellington, Collingsworth County, Texas to William Otto Burgett, son of John Samuel Burgett and Lillie Evalee Wray, born 31 Mar 1890 at Yukon, Canadian County, Oklahoma and died 7 May 1964 at Waterloo, Black Hawk County, Iowa. Buried at Mt. Hope cemetery, Buchanan County, Iowa. William Otto Burgett had married firstly to Villa Myrtle Hartin, daughter of Curtis B. Hartin, Sr. and Laura O. Jones. Vivian Smith and William Burgett had issue, which was the eleventh generation in America:

B42122241. Milbrey Otto Burgett, first child and first son of Vivian Smith and William

Burgett, born 4 Jan 1928 at Hollis, Harmon County, Oklahoma.   Married 10 Mar 1951 at Clovis, Curry County, New Mexico to La Juan Dunlap, daughter of T.L. Dunlap and Beaulah Ida Hanks, born 16 Oct 1929 at Chillicothe, Hardeman County, Texas. "Otto" was born and raised in Hollis, Harmon County, Oklahoma and entered the Marine Corps at age 18 for 2 years.   Then he entered the College of Engineering at the University of Oklahoma, where he was recalled to active duty in the Korean conflict and served in the Naval Communications Station unit at Washington, DC; which had become famous during WWII for "breaking" the Japanese code before their attack on Pearl Harbor, making possible a dramatic American victory at the Battle of Midway in 1942.   After his completion of his engineering studies with a Bachelor of Science degree in Industrial Management Engineering in 1954, he enjoyed a varied and interesting professional career working both for himself and others, highlighted by associations with the manufacture of nuclear material; fabrication of nuclear propulsion reactors for US Navy Polaris submarines; high-temperature non-metallic moldings and laminates for aerospace industry and airport runway lighting systems in the Saudi Arabian peninsula which were used extremely sucessfully during "Desert Storm."   Having been politically and community active, Otto now enjoys leisure activities together with genealogical research.

B42122242.   Ruby Dell (twin) Burgett, second child and first daughter of Vivian Smith and William Burgett, born 31 Jul 1930 at Hollis, Harmon County, New Mexico and died 14 Nov 1989 at Lubbock, Lubbock County, Texas.   Buried at Lubbock, Lubbock County, Texas.   Married 20 Sep 1947 at Yuma, Yuma County, Arizona to Tommie Gene Sirmons, born 22 Dec 1921 at Berrien County, Georgia.   Ruby Burgett and Tommie Sirmons had issue, which was the twelth generation in America:

B421222421.   Michael Gene Sirmons, first child and first son of Ruby Burgett and Tommie Sirmons, born 20 Dec 1950 at Inglewood, Los Angeles County, California.

B421222422.   Marla Gene Sirmons, second child and first daughter of Ruby Burgett and Tommie Sirmons, born 27 Apr 1952 at Hawthorne, Los Angeles County, California. Married 16 Dec 1972 at Lubbock, Lubbock County, Texas to Edward John Quirsfeld II, born 13 Jun 1945 at Chicago, Cook County, Illinois. Marla Sirmons and Edward Quirsfeld had issue, which was the thirteenth generation in America:

B4212224221. Edward John Quirsfeld III, first child and first son of Marla Sirmons and Edward Quirsfeld, born 19 Feb 1975 at Lubbock, Lubbock County, Texas.

B4212224222. Brent Alan Quirsfeld, second child and second son of Marla Sirmons and Edward Quirsfeld, born 27 Jun 1977 at Houston, Harris County, Texas.

B42122243. Ruth Nell (twin) Burgett, third child and second daughter of Vivian Smith and William Burgett, born 31 Jul 1930 at Hollis, Harmon County, New Mexico. Married 5 Jul 1947 at Los Angeles, Los Angeles County, California to Arthur Peter Scott, born 1 Jan 1928 at Independence, Buchanan County, Iowa. Ruth Burgett and Arthur Scott had issue, which was the twelth generation in America:

B421222431. Linda Cheryl Scott, first child and first daughter of Ruth Burgett and Arthur Scott, born 13 Feb 1948 at Hawthorne, Los Angeles County, California. Married 27 May 1967 at Waterloo, Black Hawk County, Iowa to Larry James Niedert, born 23 Oct 1946 at Waterloo, Black Hawk County, Iowa. Married 17 Mar 1989 to Phillip Jay Stover. Linda Scott and Larry Niedert had issue, which was the thirteenth generation in America:

B4212224311. Douglas Troy Niedert, first child and first son of Linda Scott and Larry Niedert, born 2 Feb 1968 at Cedar Rapids, Linn County, Iowa.

B4212224312. Michael James Niedert, second child and second son of Linda Scott and Larry Niedert, born 26 Jan 1970 at Waterloo, Black Hawk County, Iowa.

B4212224313. David Wayne Niedert, third child and third son of Linda Scott and Larry Niedert, born 24 Dec 1970 at Waterloo, Black Hawk County, Iowa and died 9 May 1971 at

Waterloo, Black Hawk County, Iowa.

B4212224314. Jeffrey Allen Niedert, fourth child and fourth son of Linda Scott and Larry Niedert, born 15 Aug 1972 at Waterloo, Black Hawk County, Iowa.

B421222432. Janice Elaine Scott, second chid and second daughter of Ruth Burgett and Arthur Scott, born 25 Sep 1952 at Independence, Buchanan County, Iowa. Married 25 Jun 1971 at Union City, Missouri to Ronald Burdette Voshell, born 20 Jan 1954 at Mancheste, Delaware County, Iowa. Married 18 Sep 1976 to John Richard Larsen, born 11 Nov 1952 at Waterloo, Black Hawk County, Iowa.

B421222433. Donna Lee Scott, third child and third daughter of Ruth Burgett and Arthur Scott, born 14 Dec 1955 at Independence, Buchanan County, Iowa. Married 1 Sep 1973 at Waterloo, Black Hawk County, Iowa to Scott Hubert White, born 28 Sep 1952 at Waterloo, Black Hawk County, Iowa. Donna Scott and Scott White had issue, which was the thirteenth generation in America:

B4212224331. Angela Lynn White, first child and first daughter of Donna Scott and Scott White, born 1 Mar 1974 at Cedar Falls, Black Hawk County, Iowa.

B4212224332. Rachel Dawn White, second child and second daughter of Donna Scott and Scott White, born 13 Jan 1978 at Cedar Falls, Black Hawk County, Iowa.

B421222434. Robert Wayne Scott, fourth child and first son of Ruth Burgett and Arthur Scott, born 19 Oct 1959 at Waterloo, Black Hawk County, Iowa. Married 20 Jan 1978 at Waterloo, Black Hawk County, Iowa to Janette Michelle Johnson, born 30 Aug 1961 at Waterloo, Black Hawk County, Iowa. Robert Scott and Janette Johnson had issue, which was the thirteenth generation in America:

B4212224341. Staci Michelle Scott, first child and first daughter of Robert Scott and Janette Johnson, born 25 Jun 1978 at Waterloo, Black Hawk County, Iowa.

B4212224342. Barbara Ann Scott, second child and second

daughter of Robert Scott and Janette Johnson, born 15 Apr 1982 at Cedar Falls, Black Hawk County, Iowa.

B4212225. Cynthia Weyland Smith, fifth child and fourth daughter of Cynthia Pounds and Thomas Smith, born 11 Sep 1907 at Marysville, Cooke County, Texas. Married Isom Edwards. Cynthia Smith and Isom Edwards had issue, which was the eleventh generation in America:

B42122251. Dorothy Edwards, first child and first daughter of Cynthia Smith and Isom Edwards, born 27 Feb 1924. Married Lyndell Davis. Dorothy Edwards and Lyndell Davis had issue, which was the twelth generation in America:

B421222511. Sandy Davis, first child and first daughter of Dorothy Edwards and Lyndell Davis, date and place of birth unknown.

B42122252. Isom Edwards, Jr., second child and first son of Cynthia Smith and Isom Edwards, born 10 Jul 1925.

B42122253. Billy Jean Edwards, third child and second daughter of Cynthia Smith and Isom Edwards, date and place of birth unknown.

B42122254. Carl Edwards, fourth child and second son of Cynthia Smith and Isom Edwards, date and place of birth unknown.

B42122255. Jack Edwards, fifth child and third son of Cynthia Smith and Isom Edwards, date and place of birth unknown.

B42122256. Pauline Edwards, sixth child and third daughter of Cynthia Smith and Isom Edwards, born and died 17 Jul 1930.

B42122257. Jimmie Edwards, seventh child and fourth son of Cynthia Smith and Isom Edwards, date and place of birth unknown.

B42122258. Maude Edwards, eighth child and fourth daughter of Cynthia Smith and Isom Edwards, date and place of birth unknown.

B42122259. Lou Edwards, ninth child and fifth daughter of Cynthia Smith and Isom Edwards, date and place of birth unknown.

B42122260. Tough Edwards, tenth child and fifth son of Cynthia Smith and Isom Edwards, date and place of birth unknown.

B42122261. Jackie Edwards, eleventh child and sixth daughter of Cynthia Smith and Isom

Edwards, date and place of birth unknown.
B42122262. Ruby Edwards, twelfth child and seventh daughter of Cynthia Smith and Isom Edwards, date and place of birth unknown.
B42122263. Roy Edwards, thirteenth child and sixth son of Cynthia Smith and Isom Edwards, date and place of birth unknown.
B4212223. Flemon Wyatt (Clem) Pounds, third child and second son of Joel Pounds and Eliza Wyatt, born 18 Jun 1868 at Marysville, Cooke County, Texas and died 6 Jun 1904 at Gate, Oklahoma. Buried at Gate, Oklahoma. Married Lillie Young, born 4 Mar 1872 and died 25 May 1943 at Pretty Prairie, Reno County, Kansas. Buried at Pretty Prairie, Reno County, Kansas. Flemon Pounds and Lillie Young had issue, which was the tenth generation in America:
B42122231. Fairy Sybil Pounds, first child and first daughter of Flemon Pounds and Lillie Young, born 25 Sep 1894. Married 10 Feb 1913 to Tola T. Smith, born 15 Dec 1889. Fairy Pounds and Tola Smith had issue, which was the eleventh generation in America:
B421222311. Glenn Eugene Smith, first child and first son of Fairy Pounds and Tola Smith, born 8 Jul 1914 at Gate, Oklahoma. Married Virginia Gustafsn. Glenn Smith and Virginia Gustafsn had issue, which was the twelth generation in America:
B4212223111. Donna Anne Smith, first child and first daughter of Glenn Smith and Virginia Gustafsn, born 13 May 1940.
B4212223112. Lorna Dee Smith, second child and second daughter of Glenn Smith and Virginia Gustafsn, born 18 Jun 1945.
B421222312. Claude Tola Smith, second child and second son of Fairy Pounds and Tola Smith, born 9 Nov 1916. Married Genivive Petermalo. Claude Smith and Genivive Petermalo had issue, which was the twelth generation in America:
B4212223121. David Lee Smith, first child and first son of Claude Smith and Genivive Petermalo, born 18 Nov 1936.

B4212223122. Nancy Anne Smith, second child and first daughter of Claude Smith and Genivive Petermalo, born 8 May 1942.

B4212223123. Linda Claudine Smith, third child and second daughter of Claude Smith and Genivive Petermalo, born 17 Nov 1950.

B421222313. Margaret Isabel Smith, third child and first daughter of Fairy Pounds and Tola Smith, born 28 Feb 1916 at Lamar, Prowers County, Colorado. Married Raymond Wills. Margaret Smith and Raymond Wills had issue, which was the twelth generation in America:

B4212223131. Brenda Jo Wills, first child and first daughter of Margaret Smith and Raymond Wills, born 21 Aug 1940.

B421222314. Cecil Herbert Smith, fourth child and third son of Fairy Pounds and Tola Smith, born 19 Sep 1919.

B421222315. Oren Lee Smith, fifth child and fourth son of Fairy Pounds and Tola Smith, born and died 8 Jul 1921.

B421222316. Mary Aileen Smith, sixth child and second daughter of Fairy Pounds and Tola Smith, born 11 Sep 1922 at Havana, Kansas. Married Floyd Riggsby.

B421222317. Agnes Wilma Smith, seventh child and third daughter of Fairy Pounds and Tola Smith, born 29 Oct 1924 at Havana, Kansas. Married William S. Fox. Agnes Smith and William Fox had issue, which was the twelth generation in America:

B4212223171. William Fox, first child and first son of Agnes Smith and William Fox, born 27 Nov 1940.

B4212223172. Michael Fox, second child and second son of Agnes Smith and William Fox, born 12 Sep 1942.

B4212223173. Larry Fox, third child and third son of Agnes Smith and William Fox, born 8 Jun 1944.

B4212223174. Yolanda Fox, fourth child and first daughter of Agnes Smith and William Fox, born 22 Jul 1946.

B421222318. Ernest Francis Smith, eighth child and fifth son of Fairy Pounds and Tola Smith, born 7 Dec 1928 at Havana, Kansas. Married Jolene Simmons. Married secondly Donie Lou Arpaka. Ernest Smith and Jolene Simmons had issue, which was the twelth generation in America:

B4212223181. Paula Jean Smith, first child and first daughter of Ernest Smith and Jolene Simmons, born 22 Nov 1948.

B421222318. Ernest Francis Smith, eighth child and fifth son of Fairy Pounds and Tola Smith, born 7 Dec 1928 at Havana, Kansas. Married secondly to Donie Lou Arpaka. Ernest Smith and Donie Arpaka had issue, which was the twelth generation in America:

B4212223181. Margaret Anne Smith, first child and first daughter of Ernest Smith and Donie Arpaka, born 18 Aug 1951.

B42122232. Joseph Eugene Pounds, second child and first son of Flemon Pounds and Lillie Young, born 12 Apr 1896. Married Kathryn Killian. Joseph Pounds and Kathryn Killian had issue, which was the eleventh generation in America:

B421222321. Claude T. Pounds, first child and first son of Joseph Pounds and Kathryn Killian, date and place of birth unknown.

B421222322. Marvin D. Pounds, second child and second son of Joseph Pounds and Kathryn Killian, date and place of birth unknown.

B42122233. Agnes Beatrice Pounds, third child and second daughter of Flemon Pounds and Lillie Young, born 28 Oct 1900. Married George A. Crider, born 23 Apr 1900.

B4212224. Cordelia Pounds, fourth child and second daughter of Joel Pounds and Eliza Wyatt, born 17 Jan 1869 and died 18 Jan 1869.

B4212225. Louvenia V. Pounds, fifth child and third daughter of Joel Pounds and Eliza Wyatt, born 30 Mar 1872 at Marysville, Cooke County, Texas. Married John Browder, born 7 Apr

202

1867 and died 10 Jan 1953 at Portales, Roosevelt County, New Mexico. Buried at Portales, Roosevelt County, New Mexico. Louvenia Pounds and John Browder had issue, which was the tenth generation in America:

B42122251. Lennah Browder, first child and first daughter of Louvenia Pounds and John Browder, born 27 Oct 1892. Married Robert Samuel Tucker, born 6 Feb 1881. Lennah Browder and Robert Tucker had issue, which was the eleventh generation in America:

B421222511. Hugh Tucker, first child and first son of Lennah Browder and Robert Tucker, born 15 Jul 1908. Married Ruby Beatrice Donaldson, born 28 Jun 1913. Hugh Tucker and Ruby Donaldson had issue, which was the twelth generation in America:

B4212225111. Wayne Tucker, first child and first son of Hugh Tucker and Ruby Donaldson, born 5 Mar 1933.

B4212225112. Robert Tucker, second child and second son of Hugh Tucker and Ruby Donaldson, born 12 Jun 1935.

B4212225113. Phyllis Tucker, third child and first daughter of Hugh Tucker and Ruby Donaldson, born 31 Jul 1936.

B4212225114. Barbara Tucker, fourth child and second daughter of Hugh Tucker and Ruby Donaldson, born 19 May 1945.

B421222512. Hershel Tucker, second child and second son of Lennah Browder and Robert Tucker, born 3 Nov 1909. Married Helen Faye Rigney, born 22 May 1912.

B42122252. Lon Browder, second child and first son of Louvenia Pounds and John Browder, born 13 Feb 1894 at Mira, Texas. Married Imogene Norwood. Lon Browder and Imogene Norwood had issue, which was the eleventh generation in America:

B421222521. Vernon Joe (adopted) Browder, first child and first son of Lon Browder and Imogene Norwood, date and place of birth unknown.

B421222522. Vincent Perry (adopted) Browder, second child and second son of Lon Browder and Imogene Norwood, date and place of birth unknown.

B42122253. Hazel Browder, third child and first daughter of Louvenia Pounds and John Browder, born 26 May 1911 at Mira, Texas. Married Tom Saxton. Hazel Browder and Tom Saxton had issue, which was the eleventh generation in America:

B421222531. Betty Saxton, first child and first daughter of Hazel Browder and Tom Saxton, born 31 Jan 1931. Married Kenneth Bryant. Betty Saxton and Kenneth Bryant had issue, which was the twelth generation in America:

B4212225311. Deena Lynn Bryant, first child and first daughter of Betty Saxton and Kenneth Bryant, born 17 May 1951.

B4212225312. Michael Paul Bryant, second child and first son of Betty Saxton and Kenneth Bryant, born 28 Feb 1954.

B421222532. Maxie Saxton, second child and second daughter of Hazel Browder and Tom Saxton, born 24 Sep 1935. Married Pat Grant.

B421222533. Harold Saxton, third child and first son of Hazel Browder and Tom Saxton, born 25 Feb 1938.

B4212226. Zoa Sagine Pounds, sixth child and fourth daughter of Joel Pounds and Eliza Wyatt, born 29 Oct 1874 at Marysville, Cooke County, Texas, and died 11 Feb 1942 at Marysville, Cooke County, Texas. Buried at Marysville, Cooke County, Texas. Married 29 Jul 1903 at Marysville, Cooke County, Texas to Elijah Hice Wadlington, born 10 Nov 1859 at Princeton, Caldwell County, Kentucky and died 21 Dec 1936 at Marysville, Cooke County, Texas. Buried at Marysville, Cooke County, Texas. Zoa Pounds and Elijah Wadlington had issue, which was the tenth generation in America:

B42122261. Pearl Wadlington, first child and first daughter of Zoa Pounds and Elijah Wadlington, born 23 May 1904 at Marysville, Cooke County, Texas and died 30 Jun 1965. Married 3 Jun 1920 at Gainesville, Cooke County, Texas to

Charles C. Lewis, born 27 Dec 1893 and died 23 Feb 1923 at Gainesville, Cooke County, Texas. Buried at Gainesville, Cooke County, Texas. Married secondly 4 Dec 1926 to William Smith. Pearl Wadlington and Charles Lewis had issue, which was the eleventh generation in America:

B421222611. Billie Lewis, first child and first daughter of Pearl Wadlington and Charles Lewis, born 29 Apr 1921 at Gainesville, Cooke County, Texas. Married 9 Oct 1951 to Edward L. Burow, born 19 Apr 1918 at Table Rock, Nebraska. Billie Lewis and Edward Burow had issue, which was the twelth generation in America:

B4212226111. Zoe Ann Burow, first child and first daughter of Billie Lewis and Edward Burow, born 5 May 1953.

B4212227. Edward Pounds, seventh child and third son of Joel Pounds and Eliza Wyatt, born and died 3 Jul 1875.

B4212228. Mamie Barkley Pounds, eighth child and fifth daughter of Joel Pounds and Eliza Wyatt, born 20 Nov 1878 at Marysville, Cooke County, Texas. Died 24 Jan 1967. Married John Eph Siebman, born 18 Feb 1884 at Collin County, Texas and died 17 Jan 1950. Buried Nelson cemetery. Mamie Pounds and John Siebman had issue, which was the tenth generation in America:

B42122281. Oneta Siebman, first child and first daughter of Mamie Pounds and John Siebman, born 1 Dec 1908. Married William C. Robinson, born 8 Jun 1901. Oneta Siebman and William Robinson had issue, which was the eleventh generation in America:

B421222811. Joy Lynne Robinson, first child and first daughter of Oneta Siebman and William Robinson, born 29 Nov 1935.

B4212229. Sudie Irene Pounds, ninth child and sixth daughter of Joel Pounds and Eliza Wyatt, born 4 Mar 1885 at Marysville, Cooke County, Texas. Died 16 Jul 1978 at Portales, Roosevelt County, New Mexico. Buried at Portales, Roosevelt County, New Mexico. Sudie Irene Pounds passed the "Family History" book by Silas Brown on to her granddaughter Marilyn Moon, who passed it on to her niece, Catherine Anne Moon in 1990. Sudie died at the age of 93 and she remained alert and interested in current events throughout her life. Married 29 Jun 1904 at Marysville, Cooke County, Texas to Elmer Lustus Moon, born 9 May 1880 and died 4 Mar 1944 at Portales, Roosevelt County, New Mexico. Sudie married secondly William H. Machen, born 5 Mar 1883 and married thirdly 11 Jul 1961 to Sam Brown. Sudie Pounds and Elmer Moon had issue, which was the tenth generation in America:

B42122291. Nita Beatrice Moon, first child and first daughter of Sudie Pounds and Elmer Moon, born 13 Jul 1905 at Marysville, Cooke County, Texas and died 27 Jul 1989 at Portales, Roosevelt County, New Mexico. Buried at Portales, Roosevelt County, New Mexico. Married 5 Oct 1921 to Norman L. Passmore, born 24 Oct 1894. Married secondly 3 Apr 1943 to Joseph H. Friend. Nita Moon and Norman Passmore had issue, which was the eleventh generation in America:

B421222911. Duward Norman Passmore, first child and first son of Nita Moon and Norman Passmore, born 26 Mar 1923 and died 20 Jul 1944 while in the military in World War II.

B42122292. Richard Durward Moon, second child and first son of Sudie Pounds and Elmer Moon, born 13 Mar 1910 at Marysville, Cooke County, Texas and died 6 May 1980 at San Bernardino, San Bernadino County, California. Buried at Hemet, San Bernadino County, Hemet Valley cemetery, California. Married 2 Jul 1929 at Portales, Roosevelt County, New Mexico to Janice Myrtle Parkins, born 2 Mar 1911 at Oklahoma City, Oklahoma County, Oklahoma. Richard Moon and Janice Parkins had issue, which was the eleventh generation in America:

B421222921. Marilyn Louise Moon, first child and first daughter of Richard Moon and Janice Parkins, born 21 Feb 1935 at Albuquerque, Bernalillo County, New Mexico. Married 5 Jun 1976 at Sydney, Australia to Chandru Kanyalal Tolani, born 8 Dec 1951 at Bombay, India. Married secondly 12 Jun 1985 at Sydney, Australia to Georges Jean Jacques Dehut, born 10 Jul 1957 at Rheims, Champagne Province, France.

B421222922. Gerald Lee Moon, second child and first son of Richard Moon and Janice Parkins, born 2 May 1938 at Albuquerque, Bernalillo County, New Mexico. Married about 1956 at Los Angeles County, California to Patricia ---. Married secondly 27 Dec 1959 to Christie Thatcher Marsh. Married thirdly about 1978 to Wendy Pole. Married fourthly about 1982 to Jennifer Wilcox. Married fifthly to Claudia Shakleford. Gerald Moon and Patricia --- had issue, which was the twelfth generation in America:

B4212229221. Catherine Anne Moon, first child and first daughter of Gerald Moon and Patricia ---, born 13 May 1966 at Hemet, San Bernadino County, California. Married Stephen J. Haight. Married 21 Nov 1989 at Las Vegas, Clark County, Nevada to Stephen R. Vowell, born 22 Feb 1955 at San Diego, San Diego County, California.

B4212229222. Jason Richard Moon, second child and first son of Gerald Moon and Patricia ---, born 11 Oct 1969 at Hemet, San Bernadino County, California.

B4212229223. Larry Shakleford, adopted son of Gerald Moon and Claudia Shakleford, date and place of birth unknown.

B4212229224. Andra Shakleford, adopted daughter of Gerald Moon and Claudia Shakleford, date and place of birth unknown.

B42122293. Lotus Geraldine Moon, third child and second daughter of Sudie Pounds and Elmer Moon, born 24 Mar 1917 at Marysville, Cooke County, Texas. Married Richard F. Anderson. Married secondly to Sylvano Stefani.

B42122294. Jack Edward Moon, fourth child and second son of Sudie Pounds and Elmer Moon, born 20 Apr 1925. Married 2 Mar 1946 at Portales, Roosevelt County, New Mexico to Ethel Elizabeth Bolejack, born 21 Nov 1925. Died about 1986 at Portales, New Mexico. Buried at Portales, New Mexico. Jack Moon and Ethel Bolejack had issue, which was the eleventh generation in America:

B421222941. Durward Lee

Moon, first child and first son of Jack Moon and Ethel Bolejack, born 15 Jan 1947 at Portales, Roosevelt County, New Mexico. Married to a spouse whose name is unknown.

B421222942. David Allen Moon, second child and second son of Jack Moon and Ethel Bolejack, born 18 Jun 1949 at Portales, Roosevelt County, New Mexico.

B421222943. Clifford Moon, third child and third son of Jack Moon and Ethel Bolejack, date and place of birth unknown.

B421222944. Travis Moon, fourth child and fourth son of Jack Moon and Ethel Bolejack, date and place of birth unknown.

B42122230. Nylethia Zuvendia Pounds, tenth child and seventh daughter of Joel Pounds and Eliza Wyatt, born 25 May 1887 at Marysville, Cooke County, Texas. Married 16 Aug 1903 at Marysville, Cooke County, Texas to Charlie Ward, born 13 Nov 1882 at Gainesville, Cooke County, Texas and died 16 Jan 1964. Nylethia Pounds and Charlie Ward had issue, which was the tenth generation in America:

B421222301. Orville H. Ward, first child and first son of Nylethia Pounds and Charlie Ward, born 12 Jun 1904 at Gainesville, Cooke County, Texas. Married 30 Apr 1929 at San Antonio, Bexar County, Texas to Ella F. Bradford, born 24 Jan 1907 at San Antonio, Bexar County, Texas.

B421222302. Buford Jose Ward, second child and second son of Nylethia Pounds and Charlie Ward, born and died 17 Sep 1905.

B42123. Lavina P. Pounds, third child and second daughter of William Pounds and Nancy Hairgrove, born 14 Aug 1837 in Bedford County, Tennessee. Married Marion Scott. Married secondly Capp Insmeinger. Lavina Pounds and Marion Scott had issue, which was the ninth generation in America:

B421231. Freeman Scott, first child and first son of Lavina Pounds and Marion Scott, date and place of birth unknown.

B421232. Andy Scott, second child and second son of Lavina Pounds and Marion Scott, date and place of birth unknown.

B421233. Archie Scott, third child and third son of Lavina Pounds and Marion Scott, date and place of birth unknown.

B42124. Amanda Palestine Pounds, fourth child and third daughter of William Pounds and Nancy Hairgrove, born 4 Jun 1840 in Bedford County, Tennessee and died 4 Aug 1875. Buried Saint Jo, Cooke County, Texas. Married Byron Ballard Lee, born 13 Sep 1826 at Mobile, Mobile County, Alabama and died 4 Jan 1910 at Bowie, Bowie County, Texas. Amanda Pounds and Byron Lee had issue, which was the ninth generation in America:

B421241. Armintie Lusatia Lee, first child and first daughter of Amanda Pounds and Byron Lee, born 12 Apr 1864 at Marysville, Cooke County, Texas and died 26 Aug 1914. Buried in Motley County, Texas. Married Minton Elmo Stewart, born 30 Jan 1862 and died 20 Jan 1926. Buried at Saint Jo, Cooke County, Texas. Armintie Lee and Minton Stewart had issue, which was the tenth generation in America:

B4212411. Byron Elmo Stewart, first child and first son of Armintie Lee and Minton Stewart, born 30 Jan 1882 and died 3 Oct 1934. Buried at Saint Jo, Cooke County, Texas.

B4212412. Inez Stewart, second child and first daughter of Armintie Lee and Minton Stewart, born 5 Aug 1883 at Marysville, Cooke County, Texas. Married at Saint Jo, Cooke County, Texas to Henry Orchard Prideaux, born 5 Aug 1883 and died 21 Sep 1950. Buried at Saint Jo, Cooke County, Texas. Inez Stewart and Henry Prideaux had issue, which was the eleventh generation in America:

B42124121. Richard Orchard Prideaux, first child and first son of Inez Stewart and Henry Prideaux, born 20 May 1911. Married Aubrey Felton.

B42124122. Larue Prideaux, second child and first daughter of Inez Stewart and Henry Prideaux, born 20 Jul 1913. Married Walter Robert Hall. Larue Prideaux and Walter Hall had issue, which was the twelfth generation in America:

B421241221. Michael

Harry Hall, first child and first son of Larue Prideaux and Walter Hall, born 4 Jul 1939.

B421241222. Sue Ellen Hall, second child and first daughter of Larue Prideaux and Walter Hall, born 14 Nov 1941.

B421241223. John Patrick Hall, third child and second son of Larue Prideaux and Walter Hall, born 14 Feb 1945.

B421241224. David Hall, fourth child and third son of Larue Prideaux and Walter Hall, born 15 Apr 1946.

B421241225. James Prideaux Hall, fifth child and fourth son of Larue Prideaux and Walter Hall, born 26 Aug 1950.

B42124123. Sadie Prideaux, third child and second daughter of Inez Stewart and Henry Prideaux, born 30 Jun 1916. Married Richard Baxter Greer. Sadie Prideaux and Richard Greer had issue, which was the twelth generation in America:

B421241231. Anita Louise Greer, first child and first daughter of Sadie Prideaux and Richard Greer, born 9 May 1942.

B421241232. Richard Byron Greer, second child and first son of Sadie Prideaux and Richard Greer, born 4 Dec 1943.

B42124124. Minton Albert Prideaux, fourth child and second son of Inez Stewart and Henry Prideaux, born 9 Aug 1918. Married Suzette Paull. Minton Prideaux and Suzette Paull had issue, which was the twelth generation in America:

B421241241. Pamela Prideaux, first child and first daughter of Minton Prideaux and Suzette Paull, born 16 Oct 1942.

B421241242. Minton Albert Prideaux, second child and first son of Minton Prideaux and Suzette Paull, born 6 Dec 1946.

B42124125. Nadine Prideaux, fifth child and third daughter of Inez Stewart and Henry Prideaux, born 25 Oct 1920. Married Charles Coe Loveless. Nadine Prideaux and Charles Loveless had issue, which was the twelth generation in America:

B421241251. Lucy

Loveless, first child and first daughter of Nadine
Prideaux and Charles Loveless, born 3 Jul 1945.
B421241252. Carolyn
Loveless, second child and second daughter of
Nadine Prideaux and Charles Loveless, born 22 Sep
1948.
B421242. Ottis Lee, second child
and first son of Amanda Pounds and Byron Lee, born
17 Dec 1870 at Marysville, Cooke County, Texas and
died 8 Sep 1948. Buried at Mountain View, Kiowa
County, Oklahoma. Married Annie Lee Jewell, born
26 Aug 1871 and died 28 Jun 1933. Ottis Lee and
Annie Jewell had issue, which was the tenth
generation in America:
B4212421. Clyde Lee, first
child and first son of Ottis Lee and Annie Jewell,
born 30 Dec 1892. Married Bessie Belle Rushton,
born 25 Dec 1895. Clyde Lee and Bessie Rushton
had issue, which was the eleventh generation in
America:
B42124211. Larry
McLintic Lee, first child and first son of Clyde
Lee and Bessie Rushton, born 9 Mar 1918 at Lone
Wolf, Greer County, Oklahoma. Married 28 Sep 1940
to Irene Bowlin, 5 Feb 1921 at Fort Cobb, Caddo
County, Oklahoma. Larry Lee and Irene Bowlin had
issue, which was the twelth generation in America:
B421242111.
Catherine Irene Lee, first child and first
daughter of Larry Lee and Irene Bowlin, born 7 Jan
1943.
B421242112. Larry
Finis Lee, second child and first son of Larry Lee
and Irene Bowlin, born 6 Feb 1949.
B421242113. Clyde
Lynden Lee, third child and second son of Larry
Lee and Irene Bowlin, born 25 Jul 1951.
B42124212. Edith Phoebe
Lee, second child and first daughter of Clyde Lee
and Bessie Rushton, born 12 Feb 1920 at Vancouver,
Clark County, Washington. Married Hugh Bowlin,
born 5 Oct 1918 at Boynton, Muscogee County,
Oklahoma. Edith Lee and Hugh Bowlin had issue,
which was the twelth generation in America:
B421242121. Loretta
Gayle Bowlin, first child and first daughter of

211

Edith Lee and Hugh Bowlin, born 18 Apr 1943.

B421242122. Lois Oleta Bowlin, second child and second daughter of Edith Lee and Hugh Bowlin, born 29 Jun 1950.

B4212413. Sidney Theodore Lee, third child and second son of Clyde Lee and Bessie Rushton, born 25 Jul 1922. Married 26 Jul 1946 to Nina Mae Langston, born 20 Nov 1923 at Wynnewood, Garvin County, Oklahoma. Sidney Lee and Nina Langston had issue, which was the twelth generation in America:

B42124131. Bobby Wayne Lee, first child and first son of Sidney Lee and Nina Langston, born 26 Nov 1947.

B42124132. Billy Ray Lee, second child and second son of Sidney Lee and Nina Langston, born 18 Oct 1950.

B42124133. Sharon Darline Lee, third child and first daughter of Sidney Lee and Nina Langston, born 19 Feb 1953.

B4212414. Clyde Bessie Lee, fourth child and second daughter of Clyde Lee and Bessie Rushton, born 7 Oct 1925. Married Jesse Lewis Teer.

B4212415. Elma Jerry Lee, fifth child and third daughter of Clyde Lee and Bessie Rushton, born 19 Sep 1928.

B4212416. Flossie Patricia Lee, sixth child and fourth daughter of Clyde Lee and Bessie Rushton, born 10 Dec 1933. Married Jim D. Sawyers. Flossie Lee and Jim Sawyers had issue, which was the twelfth generation in America:

B42124161. Robbin Ray Sawyers, first child and first son of Flossie Lee and Jim Sawyers, born 20 Apr 1954.

B4212422. Orville Lee, second child and second son of Ottis Lee and Annie Jewell, born 12 Nov 1895 at Mountain View, Kiowa County, Oklahoma. Married Thula Bush, born 13 May 1897. Orville Lee and Thula Bush had issue, which was the eleventh generation in America:

B42124221. Victor Lee, first child and first son of Orville Lee and Thula Bush, born 17 Aug 1917. Married 15 Sep 1942 to Evelyn Farris, born 28 Jun 1915. Victor Lee and

Evelyn Farris had issue, which was the twelth generation in America:

B421242211. Pamela Lee, first child and first daughter of Victor Lee and Evelyn Farris, born 14 Dec 1943.

B421242212. Rodger Lee, second child and first son of Victor Lee and Evelyn Farris, born 3 Mar 1945.

B421242213. Geraldine Lee, third child and second daughter of Victor Lee and Evelyn Farris, born 20 Oct 1949.

B42124222. Oran Robert Lee, second child and second son of Orville Lee and Thula Bush, born 13 Jun 1919.

B42124223. Joe Dean Lee, third child and third son of Orville Lee and Thula Bush, born 25 Aug 1927. Married 12 Mar 1949 to Barbara Ammerman, born 20 Nov 1930. Joe Lee and Barbara Ammerman had issue, which was the twelth generation in America:

B421242231. Melessa Dean Lee, first child and first daughter of Joe Lee and Barbara Ammerman, born 6 Feb 1950.

B42124224. Virginia Lee, fourth child and first daughter of Orville Lee and Thula Bush, born 29 Dec 1929. Married Dess Cowherd, Jr., born 19 Sep 1925. Virginia Lee and Dess Cowherd had issue, which was the twelth generation in America:

B421242241. James Lee Cowherd, first child and first son of Virginia Lee and Dess Cowherd, born 28 May 1950.

B421242242. Carole Ann Cowherd, second child and first daughter of Virginia Lee and Dess Cowherd, born 20 Aug 1952.

B42124225. Elmo Lee, fifth child and fourth son of Orville Lee and Thula Bush, born 25 Feb 1930.

B42125. Columbus Socite Pounds, fifth child and second son of William Pounds and Nancy Hairgrove, born 30 Jun 1845 in Bedford County, Tennessee and died 2 Jul 1921. Buried at Marlow, Stephens County, Oklahoma. Married Mary Ellen Cox, born 31 Jan 1862 at Marysville, Cooke County, Texas and died 28 Jul 1924. Buried at Mountain View, Kiowa County, Oklahoma. Columbus Pounds and

Mary Cox had issue, which was the ninth generation in America:

B421251. Metta Marina Pounds, first child and first daughter of Columbus Pounds and Mary Cox, born 8 Mar 1881 at Marlow, Stephens County, Oklahoma and died 15 Jul 1942. Buried at Marlow, Stephens County, Oklahoma. Married William Grubb, born 9 Mar 1860 and died 8 Aug 1909. Buried at Waldron, Scott County, Arkansas. Married secondly to Doctor Andrew A. Robertson, born 24 Jul 1862 and died 11 Sep 1940. Buried Marlow, Stephens County, Oklahoma. Metta Pounds and William Grubb had issue, which was the tenth generation in America:

B4212511. Bonnie Grubb, first child and first daughter of Metta Pounds and William Grubb, born 20 Dec 1897 at Marlow, Stephens County, Oklahoma. Married Guy Thompson. Bonnie Grubb and Guy Thompson had issue, which was the eleventh generation in America:

B42125111. Andrew Carroll Thompson, first child and first son of Bonnie Grubb and Guy Thompson, born 17 Mar 1923. Married 21 Jan 1942 to Lucille Roberts, born 27 Nov 1920. Andrew Thompson and Lucille Roberts had issue, which was the twelth generation in America:

B421251111. Camille Karen Thompson, first child and first daughter of Andrew Thompson and Lucille Roberts, born 11 Mar 1946.

B421251112. Jill Kathy Thompson, second child and second daughter of Andrew Thompson and Lucille Roberts, born 3 Dec 1947.

B421251113. Christy Ann Thompson, third child and third daughter of Andrew Thompson and Lucille Roberts, born 17 Sep 1953.

B42125112. Billy Guy Thompson, second child and second son of Bonnie Grubb and Guy Thompson, born 22 Sep 1924. Married 23 Nov 1950 to Louise Scott, born 13 Jan 1932. Billy Thompson and Louise Scott had issue, which was the twelth generation in America:

B421251121. Billy Ray Thompson, first child and first son of Billy

Thompson and Louise Scott, born 27 Apr 1952.
B42125113. Peggy Thompson, third child and first daughter of Bonnie Grubb and Guy Thompson, born 7 May 1926. Married 15 Dec 1945 to Homer Ward Palmore, born Jul 1916. Peggy Thompson and Homer Palmore had issue, which was the twelth generation in America:
B421251131. Verna Ruth Palmore, first child and first daughter of Peggy Thompson and Homer Palmore, born 25 Jan 1947.
B421251132. Glynna Lee Palmore, second child and second daughter of Peggy Thompson and Homer Palmore, born 23 Aug 1948.
B42125114. Metta Ann Thompson, fourth child and second daughter of Bonnie Grubb and Guy Thompson, born 19 Nov 1927.
B42125115. Nora Lee Thompson, fifth child and third daughter of Bonnie Grubb and Guy Thompson, born 28 Mar 1934. Married 25 Dec 1952 to J.B. Brown, born Sep 1934.
B4212512. Joseph (Joe) Grubb, second child and first son of Metta Pounds and William Grubb, born 20 Jan 1900. Married Beedie Hill. Married secondly to Faith Moore. Joseph Grubb and Beedie Hill had issue, which was the eleventh generation in America:
B42125121. Martha Grubb, first child and first daughter of Joseph Grubb and Beedie Hill, born in 1932. Married --- Keller. Martha Grubb and --- Keller had issue, which was the twelth generation in America:
B421251211. Kenneth D. Keller, first child and first son of Martha Grubb and --- Keller, born in 1953.
B4212513. Naomi Grubb, third child and second daughter of Metta Pounds and William Grubb, born 18 Sep 1902. Married Chester Lemon. Naomi Grubb and Chester Lemon had issue, which was the eleventh generation in America:
B42125131. Chester Andrew Lemon, first child and first son of Naoma Grubb and Chester Lemon, born 16 Nov 1924. Married Norma Pender. Chester Lemon and Norma Pender had issue, which was the twelth generation in America:
B421251311. Dewenel Lemon, first child and first son of Chester Lemon

and Norma Pender, born 11 Jan 1947.

B421251312. Richard Lemon, second child and second son of Chester Lemon and Norma Pender, born 18 Nov 1949.

B42125132. Gene Lemon, second child and second son of Naoma Grubb and Chester Lemon, born 6 Sep 1926. Married Evelyn Chaflin.

B42125133. Dewenel Lemon, third child and first daughter of Naoma Grubb and Chester Lemon, born 5 Jul 1928. Married R.M. John. Dewenel Lemon and R.M. John had issue, which was the twelth generation in America:

B421251331. Charles John, first child and first son of Dewenel Lemon and R.M. John, born 10 Mar 1951.

B42125134. Dick Lemon fourth child and third son of Naoma Grubb and Chester Lemon, born 18 Nov 1933.

B42125135. Mary Jane Lemon, fifth child and second daughter of Naoma Grubb and Chester Lemon, born 26 Dec 1935. Married Berrie Hatfield. Mary Lemon and Berrie Hatfield had issue, which was the twelth generation in America:

B421251351. Mike Hatfield, first child and first son of Mary Lemon and Berrie Hatfield, born 12 Jan 1953.

B42125136. Linda June Lemon, sixth child and third daughter of Naomi Grubb and Chester Lemon, born 6 Nov 1940.

B4212514. Rachael Grubb, fourth child and third daughter of Metta Pounds and William Grubb, born 23 Jan 1904. Married Deewitt Chetwood. Rachael Grubb and Deewitt Chetwood had issue, which was the eleventh generation in America:

B42125141. Judy Chetwood, first child and first daughter of Rachael Gubb and Deewitt Chetwood, born 19 Dec 1936.

B4212515. June Grubb, fifth child and fourth daughter of Matta Pounds and William Grubb, born 4 Jun 1906. Married Archie Cecil Waggoner, born 15 Nov 1902. June Grubb and Archie Waggoner had issue, which was the eleventh generation in America:

B42125151. Jerry Cecil Waggoner, first child and first son of June Grubb and Archie Waggoner, born 18 Sep 1928. Married Thelma Louise Cargill, born 19 Sep 1932.

B42125152. Tommy Richard Waggoner, second child and second son of June Grubb and Archie Waggoner, born 7 Jan 1932.

B421252. Walter C. Pounds, second child and first son of Columbus Pounds and Mary Cox, born 22 May 1883. Married 24 Dec 1905 at Marlow, Stephens County, Oklahoma to Susie A. Cobb. Walter Pounds and Susie Cobb had issue, which was the tenth generation in America:

B4212521. Albert A. Pounds, first child and first son of Walter Pounds and Susie Cobb, born 13 Jul 1908 at Marlow, Stephens County, Oklahoma. Married Frances Hardwick, born 20 Aug 1910. Albert Pounds and Frances Hardwick had issue, which was the eleventh generation in America:

B42125211. Walter Hardwick Pounds, first child and first son of Albert Pounds and Frances Hardwick, born 2 Feb 1932.

B42125212. Barbara Pounds, second child and first daughter of Albert Pounds and Frances Hardwick, born 6 Jan 1934.

B42125213. Allen H. Pounds, third child and second son of Albert Pounds and Frances Hardwick, born 27 Jul 1940.

B4212514. Pamela Pounds, fourth child and second daughter of Albert Pounds and Frances Hardwick, born 11 Jul 1942.

B4212515. Michael A. Pounds, fifth child and third son of Albert Pounds and Frances Hardwick, born 11 Oct 1944.

B4212516. Sara Beth Pounds, sixth child and third daughter of Albert Pounds and Frances Hardwick, born 6 Mar 1947.

B4212522. Walter C. Pounds, Jr., second child and second son of Walter Pounds and Susie Cobb, born 18 Oct 1913 at Marlow, Stephens County, Oklahoma. Married Mary Frances Tyler, born 20 Mar 1912. Walter Pounds and Mary Tyler had issue, which was the eleventh generation in America:

B42125221. Deborah Ann Pounds, first child and first daughter of Walter Pounds and Mary Tyler, born 28 Jun 1947.

B4212523. Aleta M. Pounds, third child and first daughter of Walter Pounds and Susie Cobb, born 11 Sep 1918 at Marlow, Stephens County, Oklahoma. Married Eugene Martin, born 14 Mar 1916. Aleta Pounds and Eugene Martin had issue, which was the eleventh generation in America:

B42125231. Larry Glenn Martin, first child and first son of Aleta Pounds and Eugene Martin, born 6 Jun 1947.

B4212524. Flora I. Pounds, fourth child and second daughter of Walter Pounds and Susie Cobb, born 2 Mar 1924 at Marlow, Stephens County, Oklahoma. Married Burl Gordon, born 17 Jan 1922. Flora Pounds and Burl Gordon had issue, which was the eleventh generation in America:

B42125241. Ray Lynn Gordon, first child and first son of Flora Pounds and Burl Gordon, born 14 Sep 1947.

B421253. Sophie Mary Pounds, third child and second daughter of Columbus Pounds and Mary Cox, born 16 Jul 1886. Married 22 Dec 1901 at Marlow, Stephens County, Oklahoma to Samuel Dwyer, born 18 Sep 1882. Sophie Pounds and Samuel Dwyer had issue, which was the tenth generation in America:

B4212531. Charlie Columbus Dwyer, first child and first son of Sophie Pounds and Samuel Dwyer, born 4 Oct 1902. Married Bell Compton, born 18 Nov 1908.

B4212532. Cecil (twin) Dwyer, second child and second son of Sophie Pounds and Samuel Dwyer, born 2 Jul 1903.

B4212533. Edward (twin) Dwyer, third child and third son of Sophie Pounds and Samuel Dwyer, born 2 Jul 1903.

B4212534. Walter Dwyer, fourth child and fourth son of Sophie Pounds and Samuel Dwyer, born 14 Jan 1907.

B42126. Elizabeth Acenith Pounds, sixth child and fourth daughter of William Pounds and Nancy Hairgrove, born 12 Mar 1848 in Bedford County, Tennessee and died 18 Feb 1925. Buried Marysville, Cooke County, Texas. Married 23 Feb 1871 at Marysville, Cooke County, Texas to Will D. (W.D.) Wyatt, born 13 Nov 1847 at Mobile, Mobile

County, Alabama and died 24 Apr 1922. Buried at Marysville, Cooke County, Texas. Elizabeth Pounds and Will Wyatt had issue, which was the ninth generation in America:

B421261. Nellie Wyatt, first child and first daughter of Elizabeth Pounds and Will Wyatt, born 19 Dec 1871 at Marysville, Cooke County, Texas and died 22 Jun 1903. Buried at Plainview, Hale County, Texas. Nellie Wyatt married 2 Apr 1895 at Marysville, Cooke County, Texas to James Davis (Jim) Ewing, born 18 Sep 1863 at Jacksonville, Anderson County, Texas and died 16 Sep 1945. Buried at Walters, Cotton County, Oklahoma. Nellie Wyatt and James Ewing had issue, which was the tenth generation in America:

B4212611. Lillie Ewing, first child and first daughter of Nellie Wyatt and James Ewing, born 25 Apr 1898 at Haskell, Haskell County, Texas. Married Daniel Forest Phelps. Lillie Ewing and Daniel Phelps had issue, which was the eleventh generation in America:

B42126111. Glendolyn Phelps, first child and first daughter of Lillie Ewing and Daniel Phelps, born 13 May 1920 at Ranger, Eastland County, Texas. Married 23 Sep 1939 to Jack Wright Gardner, born 13 Jun 1918 at Weatherford, Parker County, Texas. Glendolyn Phelps and Jack Gardner had issue, which was the twelth generation in America:

B421261111. Linda Louise Gardner, first child and first daughter of Glendolyn Phelps and Jack Gardner, born 4 Dec 1940.

B42126112. Warren Donald Phelps, second child and first son of Lillie Ewing and Daniel Phelps, born 25 Sep 1923 at Weatherford, Parker County, Texas. Married 4 Apr 1946 at Dallas, Dallas County, Texas to Margaret Bernice Templeton, born 16 Aug 1923 at Cleburne, Johnson County, Texas.

B42126113. Evelyn Joyce Phelps, third child and second daughter of Lillie Ewing and Daniel Phelps, born 5 Jun 1925 at Weatherford, Parker County, Texas. Married 10 Oct 1942 at Decatur, Wise County, Texas to Donald Sanford Howard, born 3 Aug 1922 at Frederick, Tillman

County, Oklahoma. Evelyn Phelps and Donald Howard had issue, which was the twelth generation in America:

B421261131. Janice Erroll Howard, first child and first daughter of Evelyn Phelps and Donald Howard, born 10 Dec 1944.

B421261132. Donna Joyce Howard, second child and second daughter of Evelyn Phelps and Donald Howard, born 7 Aug 1947.

B421261133. Valerie Howard, third child and third daughter of Evelyn Phelps and Donald Howard, born 30 Jun 1951.

B42126114. Nellie Ruth Phelps, fourth child and third daughter of Lillie Ewing and Daniel Phelps, born 1 Nov 1929 at Weatherford, Parker County, Texas. Married 18 Nov 1948 to Truman Quinton Olds, born 10 Jul 1928 at Breckenridge, Shackleford County, Texas. Nellie Phelps and Truman Olds had issue, which was the twelth generation in America:

B421261141. Michael Phelps Olds, first child and first son of Nellie Phelps and Truman Olds, born 18 Nov 1951.

B4212612. Robert S. Ewing, second child and first son of Nellie Wyatt and James Ewing, born 3 Oct 1899. Married Bessie B. Cox, born 16 Aug 1899. Robert Ewing and Bessie Cox had issue, which was the eleventh generation in America:

B42126121. Bettie Ruth Ewing, first child and first daughter of Robert Ewing and Bessie Cox, born 21 Dec 1924. Married 16 Sep 1943 to Arnold L. Wood, Jr. Bettie Ruth Ewing and Arnold Wood had issue, which was the twelth generation in America:

B421261211. Arnold L. Wood III, first child and first son of Ruth Ewing and Arnold Wood, born 19 Sep 1944.

B421261212. Constance Y. Wood, second child and first daughter of Ruth Ewing and Arnold Wood, born 4 Jun 1949.

B421261213. Donna K. Wood, third child and second daughter of Ruth Ewing and Arnold Wood, born 6 Jul 1951.

B42126122. Robert D. Ewing, second child and first son of Robert S. Ewing and Bessie Cox, born 30 Nov 1933.

B4212613. Verna Ewing, third child and second daughter of Nellie Wyatt and James Ewing, born 29 Sep 1901 at Haskell, Haskell County, Texas. Married at Walters, Cotton County, Oklahoma to John T. Conn, born 5 Feb 1893 at Henrietta, Clay County, Texas. Verna Ewing and John Conn had issue, which was the eleventh generation in America:

B42126131. Patricia Nell Conn, first child and first daughter of Verna Ewing and John Conn, born 2 May 1929 at San Benito, Cameron County, Texas and died 23 Aug 1954. Married Dell Oliver Palmer, born 17 Dec 1925 at Tankawa, Oklahoma. Patricia Conn and Dell Palmer had issue, which was the twelth generation in America:

B421261311. Viron Jean Palmer, first child and first daughter of Patricia Conn and Dell Palmer, born 24 Jun 1946.

B421261312. Dell Ange Palmer, second child and second daughter of Patricia Conn and Dell Palmer, born 25 Feb 1951.

B4212614. Ross Ewing, fourth child and second son of Nellie Wyatt and James Ewing, born 11 Jun 1903 at Running Water, Texas. Married 23 Nov 1926 at Wichita Falls, Wichita County, Texas to Daisy Krisher, born 7 Feb 1906 at Walters, Cotton County, Oklahoma. Ross Ewing and Daisy Krisher had issue, which was the eleventh generation in America:

B42126141. Jeannine Ewing, first child and first daughter of Ross Ewing and Daisy Krisher, born 4 Feb 1929 at Lawton, Comanche County, Oklahoma. Married John D. Aust.

B42126142. Gail Ewing, second child and second daughter of Ross Ewing and Daisy Krisher, born 5 Oct 1936.

B42126143. David Ewing, third child and first son of Ross Ewing and Daisy Krisher, born 6 Jun 1944.

B421262. Joseph Hodges Wyatt, second child and first son of Elizabeth Pounds and Will Wyatt, born 22 Jan 1873.

B421263. Willie A. Wyatt, third child and second son of Elizabeth Pounds and Will Wyatt, born 2 Oct 1874 at Marysville, Cooke County, Texas and died 21 Apr 1947. Buried at Marysville, Cooke

County, Texas. Married 5 Nov 1899 at Haskell, Haskell County, Texas to Rilla Couch, born 27 Nov 1880 at Munday, Knox County, Texas. Willie Wyatt and Rilla Couch had issue, which was the tenth generation in America:

B4212631. Joe Wyatt, first child and first son of Willie Wyatt and Rilla Couch, born 10 Oct 1900 at Marysville, Cooke County, Texas. Married Minnie Wilson.

B4212632. Everett Wyatt, second child and second son of Willie Wyatt and Rilla Couch, born 2 Mar 1902 at Marysville, Cooke County, Texas and died 13 Nov 1953. Married Lela Miller. Everett Wyatt and Lela Miller had issue, which was the eleventh generation in America:

B42126321. Helen Wyatt, first child and first daughter of Everett Wyatt and Lela Miller, born 4 Apr 1923. Married Albert Coe. Helen Wyatt and Albert Coe had issue, which was the twelth generation in America:

B421263211. Harvey Lee Coe, first child and first son of Helen Wyatt and Albert Coe, born 4 Apr 1943.

B421263212. Condyce Coe, second child and first daughter of Helen Wyatt and Albert Coe, born 3 Mar 1953.

B42126322. Marie Wyatt, second child and second daughter of Everett Wyatt and Lela Miller, born 7 Oct 1925. Married Hugh Lee. Marie Wyatt and Hugh Lee had issue, which was the twelth generation in America:

B421263221. Sandra Lee, first child and first daughter of Marie Wyatt and Hugh Lee, born 6 Jun 1945.

B421263222. Pamela Lee, second child and second daughter of Marie Wyatt and Hugh Lee, born 12 Dec 1950.

B42126323. Billie Jo Wyatt, third child and third daughter of Everett Wyatt and Lela Miller, born 14 Dec 1927. Married Preston Nokes. Billie Wyatt and Preston Nokes had issue, which was the twelth generation in America:

B421263231. Preston Nokes, Jr., first child and first son of Billie Wyatt and Preston Nokes, born 6 Jun 1947.

B421263232. Raymond Farris

Nokes, second child and second son of Billie Wyatt and Preston Nokes, born 4 Apr 1949.

B4212633. Loraine (twin) Wyatt, third child and first daughter of Willie Wyatt and Rilla Couch, born 13 Jan 1906 at Marysville, Cooke County, Texas. Married Earl Cochran, Loraine Wyatt and Earl Cochran had issue, which was the eleventh generation in America:

B42126331. Earl Wayne Cochran, first child and first son of Loraine Wyatt and Earl Cochran, born 9 Feb 1930. Married Darnell -- -. Earl Cochran and Darnell --- had issue, which was the twelth generation in America:

B421263311. Anna Lois Cochran, first child and first daughter of Earl Cochran and Darnell ---, born 7 Jul 1950.

B421263312. Earl Cochran III, second child and first son of Earl Cochran and Darnell ---, born 11 Nov 1952.

B42126332. Rheba Nell Cochran, second child and first daughter of Loraine Wyatt and Earl Cochran, born 10 Jan 1932. Married J.C. Thomas. Rheba Cochran and J.C. Thomas had issue, which was the twelth generation in America:

B421263321. Billie Lee Thomas, first child and first daughter of Rheba Cochran and J.C. Thomas, born 11 Nov 1952.

B4212634. Irene (twin) Wyatt, fourth child and second daughter of Willie Wyatt and Rilla Couch, born 13 Jan 1906 at Marysville, Cooke County, Texas. Married John Richey.

B4212635. Dorothy Wyatt, fifth child and third daughter of Willie Wyatt and Rilla Couch, born 23 Jun 1908. Married Fred Richey. Dorothy Wyatt and Fred Richey had issue, which was the eleventh generation in America:

B42126351. Robert Allen Richey, first child and first son of Dorothy Wyatt and Fred Richey, born 7 Nov 1929. Married Bettie Lemons, born 7 Jan 1930. Robert Richey and Bettie Lemons had issue, which was the twelth generation in America:

B421263511. Robert Ernest Richey, first child and first son of Robert Richey and Bettie Lemons, born 7 Jul 1951.

B421263512. Billie Richey,

second child and first daughter of Robert Richey and Bettie Lemons, born 4 Apr 1953.

B42126352. Nelda Richey, second child and first daughter of Dorothy Wyatt and Fred Richey, born 4 Jan 1935. Married John Barnes, born 12 Jul 1931. Nelda Richey and John Barnes had issue, which was the twelth generation in America:

B421263521. Donna Joyce Barnes, first child and first daughter of Nelda Richey and John Barnes, born 7 Jul 1953.

B42126353. Margaret Richey, third child and second daughter of Dorothy Wyatt and Fred Richey, born 3 May 1939.

B42126354. Larry Richey, fourth child and second son of Dorothy Wyatt and Fred Richey, born 6 Feb 1950.

B4212636. Thomas C. Wyatt, sixth child and third son of Willie Wyatt and Rilla Couch, born 16 Oct 1912 at Marysville, Cooke County, Texas. Married Marie McDaniel. Thomas Wyatt and Marie McDaniel had no issue, but had adopted a son, considered to be in the eleventh generation in America:

B42126361. Richard Mitchel (adopted) Wyatt, born 4 Nov 1941, first child and first (adopted) son of Thomas Wyatt and Marie McDaniel.

B4212637. Nellie Wyatt, seventh child and fourth daughter of Willie Wyatt and Rilla Couch, born 14 Nov 1914.

B421264. Manning E. Wyatt, fourth child and third son of Elizabeth Pounds and Will Wyatt, born 1 Oct 1876 at Marysville, Cooke County, Texas and died 14 Mar 1954. Buried at Valley View, Cooke County, Texas. Married 15 Nov 1892 at Marysville, Cooke County, Texas to Attie Roberts, born 18 Aug 1875 at Marysville, Cooke County, Texas. Manning Wyatt and Attie Roberts had issue, which was the tenth generation in America:

B4212641. Lowell R. Wyatt, first child and first son of Manning Wyatt and Attie Roberts, born 18 Aug 1900 at Marysville, Cooke County, Texas. Married 30 Jun 1922 at Fort Worth, Parker County, Texas to Charlice Ribble, born 28 Apr 1900 at Crowell, Foard County, Texas. Lowell Wyatt and

Charlice Ribble had issue, which was the eleventh generation in America:

B42126411. Robert Milton Wyatt, first child and first son of Lowell Wyatt and Charlice Ribble, born 14 Oct 1926. Married 30 Oct 1948 at Oklahoma City, Oklahoma County, Oklahoma to Patricia Emanuel, born 29 Dec 1925. Robert Wyatt and Patricia Emanuel had issue, which was the twelth generation in America:

B421264111. Frank Lowell Wyatt, first child and first son of Robert Wyatt and Patricia Emanuel, born 27 Sep 1949.

B421264112. Shirley Katherine Wyatt, second child and first daughter of Robert Wyatt and Patricia Emanuel, born 20 May 1953.

B4212642. Leonard D. Wyatt, second child and second son of Manning Wyatt and Attie Roberts, born 3 Jan 1903 at Marysville, Cooke County, Texas. Married 20 Feb 1948 at Chicago, Cook County, Illinois to Grace Donahue-Donovan, born 26 Sep 1901 at Chicago, Cook County, Illinois.

B4212643. Delbert C. Wyatt, third child and third son of Manning Wyatt and Attie Roberts, born 14 Nov 1904 at Marysville, Cooke County, Texas. Married 13 Jun 1932 at Marietta, Love County, Oklahoma to Ruby Lee Moon, born 6 Jun 1914 at Marysville, Cooke County, Texas. Delbert Wyatt and Ruby Moon had issue, which was the eleventh generation in America:

B42126431. Jean Frances Wyatt, first child and first daughter of Delbert Wyatt and Ruby Moon, born 28 Jul 1933.

B4212644. Magenta Lee Wyatt, fourth child and first daughter of Manning Wyatt and Attie Roberts, born 11 Dec 1909 at Marysville, Cooke County, Texas. Married 15 Nov 1930 at Gainesville, Cooke County, Texas to Earl Redell, born 27 Apr 1909. Magenta Wyatt and Earl Redell had issue, which was the eleventh generation in America:

B42126441. Lavonne Redell, first child and first daughter of Magenta Wyatt and Earl Redell, born 14 Aug 1932. Married 1 Sep 1951 to Gordon Cullum, born 1 Sep 1931.

B421265. Nola Brown Wyatt, fifth child and

second daughter of Elizabeth Pounds and Will
Wyatt, born 13 Feb 1879 at Marysville, Cooke
County, Texas and died 19 Mar 1918. Buried at
Marysville, Cooke County, Texas. Married 7 Sep
1898 to V. Marrow Ramsey, born 23 May 1877 at
Marysville, Cooke County, Texas. V. Marrow Ramsey
married secondly to Pearl Reeves. Nola Wyatt and
V. Ramsey had issue, which was the tenth
generation in America:

B4212651. Mabel Ramsey, first child and
first daughter of Nola Wyatt and V. Ramsey, born
14 Aug 1899 at Marysville, Cooke County, Texas.
Married J. Hershel Coffman, born 1 Jan 1897 at
Hillham, Tennessee. Mabel Ramsey and J. Coffman
had issue, which was the eleventh generation in
America:

B42126511. Nola Coffman, first
child and first daughter of Mabel Ramsey and J.
Coffman, born 26 Feb 1921.

B42126512. Willie (Billie)
Coffman, second child and second daughter of Mabel
Ramsey and J. Coffman, born 2 Jan 1923 at
Marysville, Cooke County, Texas. Married 9 Oct
1947 at Gainesville, Cooke County, Texas to Weldon
Gipson, born 15 Oct 1917 at Bowie, Bowie County,
Texas. Willie Coffman and Weldon Gipson had
issue, which was the twelth generation in America:

B421265121. Gary Weldon
Gipson, first child and first son of Willie
Coffman and Weldon Gipson, born 17 Jul 1954.

B42126513. Ralph Coffman, third
child and first son of Mabel Ramsey and J.
Coffman, born 17 Dec 1924 at Marysville, Cooke
County, Texas. Married 30 Nov 1947 to Jeanice
Stevens, born 26 Aug 1930 at Gainesville, Cooke
County, Texas. Ralph Coffman and Jeanice Stevens
had issue, which was the twelth generation in
America:

B421265131. Jerry Ralph
Coffman, first child and first son of Ralph
Coffman and Jeanice Stevens, born 23 Apr 1950.

B421265132. Janice Coffman,
second child and first daughter of Ralph Coffman
and Jeanice Stevens, born 28 Aug 1952.

B42126514. Rufus (twin) Coffman,
fourth child and second son of Mabel Ramsey and J.

226

Coffman, born 5 Oct 1926.

B42126515.   R.   Poston   (twin)
Coffman, fifth child and third son of Mabel Ramsey
and J. Coffman, born 5 Oct 1926.

B4212652.   Jewel Ramsey, second child
and second daughter of Nola Wyatt and V. Ramsey,
born 1 Feb 1907.

B4212653.   Ruth Ramsey, third child and
third daughter of Nola Wyatt and V. Ramsey, born 3
Oct 1911 at Marysville, Cooke County, Texas.
Married Willis Robson.   Ruth Ramsey and Willis
Robson   had   issue,   which   was   the   eleventh
generation in America:

B42126531. Ray David Robson, first
child and first son of Ruth Ramsey and Willis
Robson, born 28 Oct 1938.

B4212654.   Raymond Ramsey, fourth child
and first son of Nola Wyatt and V. Ramsey, born 15
Jul 1915.

B421266.   Mary Ann Wyatt, sixth child and
third daughter of Elizabeth Pounds and Will Wyatt,
born 15 Mar 1879.

B421267.   Inez Elizabeth Wyatt, seventh child
and fourth daughter of Elizabeth Pounds and Will
Wyatt, born 23 Aug 1880 at Marysville, Cooke
County, Texas.   Married Oscar Ballinger, born 10
Dec 1874 at Marysville, Cooke County, Texas.   Inez
Wyatt and Oscar Ballinger had issue, which was the
tenth generation in America:

B4212671.   Jean Ballinger, first child
and   first   daughter   of   Inez   Wyatt   and   Oscar
Ballinger, born 11 Nov 1899 at Marysville, Cooke
County, Texas.   Married Jimmie Hughes, born 6 Jun
1902 at Austin, Travis County, Texas.

B4212672.   Harry T. Ballinger, second
child and first son of Inez Wyatt and Oscar
Ballinger, born 29 Dec 1900 at Marysville, Cooke
County, Texas.   Married 7 Jun 1926 at Salem,
Marion County, Illinois to Juanita Massey.   Harry
Ballinger and Juanita Massey had issue, which was
the eleventh generation in America:

B42126721. Thomas Irwin Ballinger,
first child and first son of Harry Ballinger and
Juanita Massey, born 30 May 1927.

B42126722.   Fred D. Ballinger,
second child and second son of Harry Ballinger and

Juanita Massey, born 16 Sep 1930.

B4212673.   Halbert C. Ballinger, third child and second son of Inez Wyatt and Oscar Ballinger, born 22 May 1902 at Marysville, Cooke County, Texas.   Married 12 Oct 1930 at Marietta, Love County, Oklahoma to Leota Pitcher, born 22 Nov 1907 at Collinsville, Cooke County, Texas. Halbert Ballinger and Leota Ptcher had issue, which was the eleventh generation in America:

B42126731.   Jerry   Halbert Ballinger, first child and first son of Halbert Ballingr and Leota Pitcher, born 15 Apr 1934.

B42126732. Amanda Cecil Ballinger, second   child   and   first   daughter   of   Halbert Ballinger and Leota Pitcher, born 10 Sep 1938.

B42126733. Jo Ann Ballinger, third child and and second daughter of Halbert Ballinger and Leota Pitcher, born 1 Oct 1940.

B4212674.   Edward   Ballinger,   fourth child and third son of Inez Wyatt and Oscar Ballinger, born 17 Jan 1904 at Marysville, Cooke County, Texas.   Married 9 Aug 1927 to Gladys Johnson.   Edward Ballinger and Gladys Johnson had issue, which was eleventh generation in America:

B42126741.   Betty Jane Ballinger, first child and first daughter of Edward Ballinger and Gladys Johnson, born 18 Mar 1931.

B42126742.   Bobbie   Ballinger, second   child   and   second   daughter   of   Edward Ballinger and Gladys Johnson, born 10 Feb 1937.

B4212675. Ethel Ballinger, fifth child and second daughter of Inez Wyatt and Oscar Ballinger, born 19 Mar 1907 at Marysville, Cooke County, Illinois.   Married 7 Jun 1927 to Denton Floyd.   Ethel Ballinger and Denton Floyd had issue, which was the eleventh generation in America:

B42126751. Mary Floyd, first child and first daughter of Ethel Ballinger and Denton Floyd, born 6 Aug 1934.

B42126752.   Nancy Floyd, second child and second daughter of Ethel Ballinger and Denton Floyd, born 9 Dec 1939.

B4212676. Edith Ballinger, sixth child and third daughter of Inez Wyatt and Oscar Ballinger, born 10 Feb 1909 at Marysville, Cooke

County, Texas. Married 24 Dec 1930 to Tony Floyd. Edith Ballinger and Tony Floyd had issue, which was the eleventh generation in America:

B42126761. Betty Floyd, first child and first daughter of Edith Ballinger and Tony Floyd, born 4 Oct 1939.

B42126762. Tony Floyd, second child and first son of Edith Ballinger and Tony Floyd, date and place of birth unknown.

B421268. Alden Wyatt, eighth child and fourth son of Elizabeth Pounds and Will Wyatt, born 1 Dec 1882 at Marysville, Cooke County, Texas. Married 19 Nov 1919 at Lawton, Comanche County, Oklahoma to Sallie Bently, born 16 Apr 1885 at Pattonsburg, Davess County, Missouri. Alden Wyatt and Sallie Bently had issue, which was the tenth generation in America:

B4212681. Mary Francis Wyatt, first child and first daughter of Alden Wyatt and Sallie Bently, born 22 Dec 1920 at Fletcher, Comanche County, Oklahoma. Married Lewis McAdoo, born 30 Sep 1920 at Fletcher, Comanche County, Oklahoma. Mary Wyatt and Lewis McAdoo had issue, which was the eleventh generation in America;

B42126811. Robert David McAdoo, first child and first son of Mary Wyatt and Lewis McAdoo, born 5 Jul 1952.

B4212682. David Bently Wyatt, second child and first son of Alden Wyatt and Sallie Bently, born 9 Apr 1922 at Lawton, Comanche County, Oklahoma. Married 22 Jul 1943 at Lawton, Comanche County, Oklahoma to Gladys Brown, born 7 Jul 1924 at Checotah, McIntosh County, Oklahoma. David Wyatt and Gladys Brown had issue, which was the eleventh generation in America:

B42126821. Alden Ray Wyatt, first child and first son of David Wyatt and Gladys Brown, born 11 Oct 1944.

B42126822. Linda Ruth Wyatt, second child and first daughter of David Wyatt and Gladys Brown, born 22 May 1950.

B42126823. Charles Wesley Wyatt, third child and second son of David Wyatt and Gladys Brown, born 24 Aug 1953.

B421269. Floyd Wyatt, ninth child and fifth son of Elizabeth Pounds and Will Wyatt, born 9 Oct

1884 at Marysville, Cooke County, Texas. Married 1 Jan 1905 to Georgia Hedges, born 2 Feb 1886 at Marysville, Cooke County, Texas. Floyd Wyatt and Georgia Hedges had issue, which was the tenth generation in America:

B4212691. Bailey Addison Wyatt, first child and first son of Floyd Wyatt and Georgia Hedges, born 29 Jan 1906 at Marysville, Cooke County, Texas. Married 22 May 1933 at Clinton, Henry County, Missouri to Evelyn Lyon, born 5 May 1908 at Clinton, Henry County, Missouri. Bailey Wyatt and Evelyn Lyon had issue, which was the eleventh generation in America:

B42126911. Shirley May Wyatt, first child and first daughter of Bailey Wyatt and Evelyn Lyon, born 11 Feb 1934.

B42126912. Bailey Addison Wyatt, Jr., second child and first son of Bailey Wyatt and Evelyn Lyon, born 31 Jul 1935.

B42126913. Sandra Wyatt, third child and second daughter of Bailey Wyatt and Evelyn Lyon, born 3 Nov 1937.

B4212692. Chester Coleman Wyatt, second child and second son of Floyd Wyatt and Georgia Hedges, born 3 Feb 1908 at Marysville, Cooke County, Texas. Married Winna Barrett, born 22 Mar 1910. Chester Wyatt and Winna Barrett had issue, which was the eleventh generation in America:

B42126921. John Coleman Wyatt, first child and first son of Chester Wyatt and Winna Barrett, born 21 Sep 1930.

B42126922. Floyd Coleman Wyatt, second child and second son of Chester Wyatt and Winna Barrett, born 26 Nov 1933.

B42126923. Patricia Wyatt, third child and first daughter of Chester Wyatt and Winna Barrett, born 22 Mar 1939.

B42126924. Linda Lee Wyatt, fourth child and second daughter of Chester Wyatt and Winna Barrett, born 2 Feb 1943.

B4212693. Una Wyatt, third child and first daughter of Floyd Wyatt and Georgia Hedges, born 28 Apr 1910 at Marysville, Cooke County, Texas. Married 16 Oct 1933 at Ardmore, Carter County, Oklahoma to George Lewis, born 29 Apr 1909 at Gainesville, Cooke County, Texas. Una Wyatt and George Lewis had issue, which was the eleventh generation in America:

B42126931. George Phillip Lewis, first child and first son of Una Wyatt and George Lewis, born 6 Feb 1936.

B4212694. Ora Pauline Wyatt, fourth child and second daughter of Floyd Wyatt and Georgia Hedges, born 9 Apr 1914 at Marysville, Cooke County, Texas. Married 23 Jun 1933 at Marietta, Love County, Oklahoma to Raymond Lyons, born 21 Sep 1913 at Gainesville, Cooke County, Texas. Ora Wyatt and Raymond Lyons had issue, which was the eleventh generation in America:

B42126941. Ray Lyons, first child and first son of Ora Wyatt and Raymond Lyons, born 15 Jan 1935.

B42126942. Judith E. Lyons, second child and first daughter of Ora Wyatt and Raymond Lyons, born 1 Sep 1936.

B42126943. Beverly Sue Lyons, third child and second daughter of Ora Wyatt and Raymond Lyons, born 6 Sep 1938.

B42126944. Neil Lyons, fourth child and second son of Ora Wyatt and Raymond Lyons, born 21 Sep 1940.

B4212695. Rachael Elaine Wyatt, fifth child and third daughter of Floyd Wyatt and Georgia Hedges, born 10 Apr 1915 at Marysville, Cooke County, Texas. Married 19 Dec 1935 to John Tuggle. Rachael Wyatt and John Tuggle had issue, which was the eleventh generation in America:

B42126951. John David Tuggle, first child and first son of Rachael Wyatt and John Tuggle, born 31 Oct 1938.

B42126952. Deloris Tuggle, second child and first daughter of Rachael Wyatt and John Tuggle, born 9 Feb 1947.

B4212696. Jennie Lind Wyatt, sixth child and fourth daughter of Floyd Wyatt and Georgia Hedges, born 7 Dec 1917 at Gainesville, Cooke County, Texas. Married 15 Sep 1934 at Marietta, Love County, Oklahoma to Orville Branch, born 14 Jun 1914 at Gainesville, Cooke County, Texas. Jennie Wyatt and Orville Branch had issue, which was the eleventh generation in America:

B42126961. Shirley Ann Branch,

first child and first daughter of Jennie Wyatt and Orville Branch, born 19 Jun 1938.

B42126962. Linda Carroll Branch, second child and second daughter of Jennie Wyatt and Orville Branch, born 12 Jul 1944.

B42126963. Michael Branch, third child and first son of Jennie Wyatt and Orville Branch, born 26 Jul 1947.

B421270. Leonard M. Wyatt, tenth child and sixth son of Elizabeth Pounds and Will Wyatt, born 7 Apr 1887 at Marysville, Cooke County, Texas. Married 30 Dec 1917 at Gainesville, Cooke County, Texas to Mabel Beckelman, born 7 Jul 1897 at Gainesville, Texas. Leonard Wyatt and Mabel Beckelman had issue, which was the tenth generation in America;

B4212701. Tarence Emerson Wyatt, first child and first son of Leonard Wyatt and Mabel Beckelman, born 9 Oct 1922 at Gainesville, Cooke County, Texas. Married Doris Bomer, born 10 Jul 1927 at Gainesville, Cooke County, Texas. Tarence Wyatt and Doris Bomer had issue, which was the eleventh generation in America:

B42127011. Paul Wyatt, first child and first son of Tarence Wyatt and Doris Bomer, born 5 Mar 1948.

B42127012. Keith Wyatt, second child and second son of Tarence Wyatt and Doris Bomer, born 24 Jan 1951.

B42127013. Charles Kent Wyatt, third child and third son of Tarence Wyatt and Doris Bomer, born 24 Mar 1953.

B4212702. David F. (twin) Wyatt, second child and second son of Leonard Wyatt and Mabel Beckelman, born 19 Nov 1924 at Gainesville, Cooke County, Texas. Married Mary V. Meine, born 20 Apr 1925 at Gainesville, Cooke County, Texas. David Wyatt and Mary Meine had issue, which was the eleventh generation in America:

B42127021. Gregory D. Wyatt, first child and first son of David Wyatt and Mary Meine, born 17 Jun 1947.

B42127022. Anthony Wyatt, second child and second son of David Wyatt and Mary Meine, born 12 May 1950.

B42127023. Margaret Wyatt, third

child and first daughter of David Wyatt and Mary Meine, born 31 Oct 1951.

B4212703. Dale E. (twin) Wyatt, third child and third son of Leonard Wyatt and Mabel Beckelman, born 19 Nov 1924 at Gainesville, Cooke County, Texas. Married Eloise Kellner, born 29 Nov 1923 at Fort Worth, Parker County, Texas. Dale Wyatt and Eloise Kellner had issue, which was the eleventh generation in America:

B42127031. David B. Wyatt, first child and first son of Dale Wyatt and Eloise Kellner, born 9 Dec 1946.

B421271. John Wyatt, eleventh child and seventh son of Elizabeth Pounds and Will Wyatt, born 27 Mar 1889 at Marysville, Cooke County, Texas. Married 13 Dec 1913 at Marysville, Cooke County, Texas to Julia Owens, born 13 Nov 1895 at Marysville, Cooke County, Texas. John Wyatt and Julia Owens had issue, which was the tenth generation in America:

B4212711. Curtis W. Wyatt, first child and first son of John Wyatt and Julia Owens, born 4 Oct 1914 at Marysville, Cooke County, Texas. Married Oma Brewer. Curtis Wyatt and Oma Brewer had issue, which was the eleventh generation in America:

B42127111. Gary Donald Wyatt, first child and first son of Curtis Wyatt and Oma Brewer, born 22 May 1939.

B42127112. John Daniel Wyatt, second child and second son of Curtis Wyatt and Oma Brewer, born 10 Apr 1944.

B42127113. Katherine Lynn Wyatt, third child and first daughter of Curtis Wyatt and Oma Brewer, born 23 Aug 1951.

B4212712. Evelyn M. Wyatt, second child and first daughter of John Wyatt and Julia Owens, born 13 Nov 1919 at Marysville, Cooke County, Texas. Married Glenn E. Sills, born at Pawhuska, Sage County, Oklahoma. Evelyn Wyatt and Glenn Sills had issue, which was the eleventh generation in America:

B42127121. Denton Earl Sills, first child and first son of Evelyn Wyatt and Glenn Sills, born 13 Aug 1952.

B4212713. Daryl G. Wyatt, third child

and second son of John Wyatt and Julia Owens, born 6 Mar 1922 at Marysville, Cooke County, Texas. Married Leta Murl Chism.
B4212714. Fairy J. Wyatt, fourth child and second daughter of John Wyatt and Julia Owens, born 7 Jul 1927 at Marysville, Cooke County, Texas. Married William K. Harris, Jr. Fairy Wyatt and William Harris had issue, which was the eleventh generation in America:
B42127141. John Keith Harris, first child and first son of Fairy Wyatt and William Harris, born 10 Aug 1952.
B421272. Grace Wyatt, twelfth child and fifth daughter of Elizabeth Pounds and Will Wyatt, born 11 Dec 1893 at Marysville, Cooke County, Texas. Married Everett Ballinger, born 23 Aug 1883 at Marysville, Cooke County, Texas. Grace Wyatt and Everett Ballinger had issue, which was the tenth generation in America:
B4212721. Hazel Ballinger, first child and first daughter of Grace Wyatt and Everett Ballinger, born 25 Jun 1914.
B4212722. Verna Gean Ballinger, second child and second daughter of Grace Wyatt and Everett Ballinger, born 11 Dec 1927 at Marysville, Cooke County, Texas. Married 21 Aug 1948 to Robert Pait, born 23 Apr 1921. Verna Ballinger and Robert Pait had issue, which was the eleventh generation in America:
B4212723. Deanna Pait, first child and first daughter of Verna Ballinger and Robert Pait, born 8 Nov 1951.
B42127. Nancy Jane Pounds, seventh child and fifth daughter of William Pounds and Nancy Hairgrove, born 22 Nov 1850 at Shelbyville, Shelby County, Texas and died 28 Apr 1917. Buried Gainesville, Cooke County, Texas. Married 30 Oct 1882 at Gainesville, Cooke County, Texas to Augustus S. Wright, born 13 Nov 1852 at Tonti, Illinois and died 31 Jan 1930. Buried at Gainesville, Cooke County, Texas. Augustus Wright had married firstly 5 Oct 1874 to Josephina French. Nancy Pounds and Augustus Wright had issue, which was the ninth generation in America:
B421271. Silas Brown Wright, first child and first son of Nancy Pounds and Augustus Wright,

born 9 Nov 1883 at Jimtown, Oklahoma and died 17 Sep 1957. Married 28 Nov 1906 at Columbus, Franklin County, Ohio to Agnes Cerena Thompson, born 11 Apr 1875 at Logan, Logan County, Ohio and died 5 Feb 1921. Silas Brown Wright wrote the family record which preserved much of the family data for history. He was named for his great-great-grandmother Nancy Mary Brown.

B421272. Lillian Augustus Wright, second child and first daughter of Nancy Pounds and Augustus Wright, born 8 Jan 1885 at Leon, Oklahoma. Married 27 Jan 1902 at Shreveport, Boosier Parish, Louisiana to John R. Johnson. Married secondly 27 Sep 1912 to Sevrin Larson. Married thirdly 3 Sep 1919 to Charles Campbell. Lilliam Wright and John Johnson had issue, which was the tenth generation in America:

B4212721. Edgar Johnson, first child and first son of Lillian Wright and John Johnson, born 4 Jul 1905.

B4212722. William J. Johnson, second child and second son of Lillian Wright and John Johnson, born 11 Nov 1907.

B4212723. Lee E. Johnson, third child and third son of Lillian Wright and John Johnson, born 11 Nov 1910.

B4212724. Pearl E. Johnson, fourth child and first daughter of Lillian Wright and John Johnson, born 12 Jul 1912.

B421272. Lillian Augustus Wright, second child and first daughter of Nancy Pounds and Augustus Wright, born 8 Jan 1885 at Leon, Oklahoma. Married secondly 27 Sep 1912 at Brookings, Brookings County, South Dakota to Sevrin Larson. Lillian and Sevrin Larson had issue, which was the tenth generation in America:

B4212721. Raymond Larson, first child and first son of Lillian Wright and Sevrin Larson, born 4 Oct 1914.

B4212722. Alma Larson, second child and first daughter of Lillian Wright and Sevrin Larson, born 3 Sep 1920.

B4212723. Helen Larson, third child and second daughter of Lillian Wright and Sevrin Larson, born 30 Apr 1923.

B421272. Lillian Augustus Wright, second

child and first daughter of Nancy Pounds and Augustus Wright, born 8 Jan 1885 at Leon, Oklahoma. Married thirdly 3 Sep 1919 at Globe, Gila County, Arizona to Charles Campbell, born 5 May 1885 at Cordova, Walker County, Alabama. Lillian Wright and Charles Campbell had issue, which was the tenth generation in America:

B4212721. Alma Campbell, first child and first daughter of Lillian Wright and Charles Campbell, born 3 Sep 1920 at Bisbee, Cochise County, Arizona. Married James Sadik. Alma Campbell and James Sadik had issue, which was the eleventh generation in America:

B42127211. James Sadik, Jr., first child and first son of Alma Campbell and James Sadik, born 23 Mar 1939.

B4212722. Helen May Campbell, second child and second daughter of Lillian Wright and Charles Campbell, born 30 Apr 1923 at Bisbee, Chocise County, Arizona. Married 28 Feb 1939 at Claypool, Gila County, Arizona to Travis Brown, born 30 Apr 1923. Helen Campbell and Travis Brown had issue, which was the eleventh generation in America:

B42127221. Barbara Ann Brown, first child and first daughter of Helen Campbell and Travis Brown, born 5 Apr 1940.

B42127222. Norma Mae Brown, second child and second daughter of Helen Campbell and Travis Brown, born 23 Jun 1942.

B42127223. Walter Henry Brown, third child and first son of Helen Campbell and Travis Brown, born 8 Dec 1943.

B42127224. Charline Brown, fourth child and third daughter of Helen Campbell and Travis Brown, born 4 Jul 1944.

B42127225. Marie Brown, fifth child and fourth daughter of Helen Campbell and Travis Brown, born 18 dec 1951.

B4212723. Baryam Campbell, third child and first son of Lillian Wright and Charles Campbell, born 3 Nov 1925 at Claypool, Gila County, Arizona. Married Lula May Brock-Smith. Married secondly to Roberta Brudnell. Married thirdly 27 Jan 1952 to Marie Doyle, born 12 Apr 1925 at Flemingsburg, Fleming County, Kentucky.

B421273. James Benton Wright, third child and second son of Nancy Pounds and Augustus Wright, born 10 Non 1886 at Leon, Oklahoma. Married Myrtle Chaney, born 27 Aug 1896. James Wright and Myrtle Chaney had issue, which was the tenth generation in America:

B4212731. William Henry Wright, first child and first son of James Wright and Myrtle Chaney, born 27 Mar 1917. Married Mary Jean Hart, born 4 Jan 1919 at Flagstaff, Arizona. William Henry Wright married secondly to Hariett Margaret Truelsen-Hozarth, born 3 Apr 1919. William Wright and Margaret Truelsen-Hozarth had issue, which was the eleventh generation in America:

B42127311. James Benton Wright, first child and first son of William Wright and Mary Hart, born 6 Jul 1949.

B42127312. Janice Wright, second child and first daughter of William Wright and Mary Hart, born 15 Nov 1950.

B4212732. Harold Benton Wright, second child and second son of James Wright and Myrtle Chaney, born 30 Dec 1922. Married 21 Nov 1953 to Barbara Joan Jones.

B4212733. Helen Marjorie Wright, third child and first daughter of James Wright and Myrtle Chaney, born 18 May 1926. Married 24 Sep 1944 at Flagstaff, Arizona to George Walter Kovick, born 18 Feb 1910 at Van Hauten, New Mexico. Helen Wright and George Kovick had issue, which was the eleventh generation in America:

B42127331. Dorothy Ann Kovick, first child and first daughter of Helen Wright and George Kovick, born 8 Jul 1947.

B42127332. James Steven Kovick, second child and first son of Helen Wright and George Kovick, born 1 Feb 1949.

B42127333. Kristin Kovick, third child and second daughter of Helen Wright and George Kovick, born 10 Sep 1951.

B4212734. James R. Wright, fourth child and third son of James Wright and Myrtle Chaney, born 22 Nov 1930.

B4212735. Barbara Jean Wright, fifth child and second daughter of James Wright and Myrtle Chaney, born 9 Aug 1933 at Flagstaff,

Arizona. Married 19 Jun 1953 at Fresno, Fresno County, California to William George Meyer, born 2 Feb 1931. Barbara Wright and William Meyer had issue, which was the eleventh generation in America:

B42127351. William Lawrence Meyer, first child and first son of Barbara Wright and William Meyer, born 20 Aug 1954.

B421274. Nellie Alcenie Wright, fourth child and second daughter of Nancy Pounds and Augustus Wright, born 15 Jun 1890 at Lisbon, Texas and died 29 Dec 1918. Married 4 Jan 1907 to Neugent Edgar Little, born 11 Nov 1880 at Marysville, Cooke County, Texas and died 7 Aug 1948. Buried at Gainesville, Cooke County, Texas. Nellie Wright and Neugent Little had issue, which was the tenth generation in America:

B4212741. Cleo Little, first child and first daughter of Nellie Wright and Neugent Little, born 4 Dec 1907 at Marysville, Cooke County, Texa. Married at Waurika, Jefferson County, Oklahoma to R.W. Mercer. Married secondly to Harry Henson, born 12 Sep 1890.

B4212742. Erma Lee Little, second child and second daughter of Nellie Wright and Neugent Little, born 29 Aug 1909 at Gainesville, Cooke County, Texas. Married 23 Jun 1929 at Rankin, Oklahoma to Jack McDaniel, born 25 Dec 1904 at Walters, Cotton County, Oklahoma. Married secondly 25 Dec 1934 to Willie B. Crawford. Erma Little and Jack McDaniel had issue, which was the eleventh generation in America:

B42127421. Edgar Lee McDaniel, first child and first son of Erma Little and Jack McDaniel, born 4 May 1930.

B42127422. Janelle Crawford McDaniel, second child and first daughter of Erma Little and Jack McDaniel, born 18 May 1932 at Wichita Falls, Wichita County, Texas. Married 2 Oct 1950 to Tommy Disheroon, born 25 Sep 1932 at Fort Worth, Parker County, Texas. Janelle McDaniel and Tommy Disheroon had issue, which was the twelth generation in America:

B421274221. Thomas David Disheroon, first child and first son of Janelle McDaniel and Tommy Disheroon, born 27 Aug 1953.

B421274222. Kathy Dell Disheroon, second child and first daughter of Janelle McDaniel and Tommy Disheroon, born 26 Aug 1954.

B4212742. Erma Lee Little, second child and second daughter of Nellie Wright and Neugent Little, born 29 Aug 1909 at Gainesville, Cooke County, Texas. Married secondly 25 Dec 1934 at Walters, Cotton County, Oklahoma to Willie B. Crawford, born 2 Jul 1905 at San Saba, San Saba County, Texas. Erma Little and Willie Crawford had issue, which was the eleventh generation in America:

B42127421. Wesley Byron Crawford, first child and first son of Erma Little and Willie Crawford, born 30 Oct 1935.

B42127422. Deanna Dell Crawford, second child and first daughter of Erma Little and Willie Crawford, born 14 Jan 1938.

B4212743. Ruth Little, third child and third daughter of Nellie Wright and Neugent Little, born 10 Aug 1911 at Gainesville, Cooke County, Texas. Married Eldred Roach. Ruth Little and Eldred Roach had issue, which was the eleventh generation in America:

B42127431. Marinelle Roach, first child and first daughter of Ruth Little and Eldred Roach, born 28 Jun 1933.

B42127432. Eddie Gail Roach, second child and second daughter of Ruth Little and Eldred Roach, born 24 Dec 1934.

B4212744. Neugent Edgar Little, Jr., fourth child and first son of Nellie Wright and Neugent Little, born 8 Nov 1913 at Gainesville, Cooke County, Texas. Married 19 Jul 1941 to Helen Floy Drake, born 12 May 1914 at Fort Worth, Parker County, Texas.

B4212745. Jane Little, fifth child and second daughter of Nellie Wright and Neugent Little, born 8 Aug 1916 at Gainesville, Cooke County, Texas. Married 14 Jul 1938 at Walters, Cotton County, Oklahoma to Robert Carson, born 28 Jan 1916 at Holliday, Wichita County, Texas. Jane Little and Robert Carson had issue, which was the eleventh generation in America:

B42127451. Sandra Sue Carson,

first child and first daughter of Jane Little and Robert Carson, born 8 Aug 1940.

B421275. Mary Elizabeth Wright, fifth child and third daughter of Nancy Pounds and Augustus Wright, born 28 Nov 1894 at Lewisville, Denton County, Texas. Married 14 Apr 1911 to John D. McChesney, born 28 Nov 1894 at Gainesville, Cooke County, Texas and died 30 Apr 1940. Buried at Pauls Valley, Garvin County, Oklahoma. Mary Wright and John McChesney had issue, which was the tenth generation in America:

B4212751. Walter McChesney, first child and first son of Mary Wright and John McChesney, born 28 Mar 1912.

B4212752. Earl McChesney, second child and second son of Mary Wright and John McChesney, born 12 Jun 1913 at Pauls Valley, Garvin County, Oklahoma. Married 29 Oct 1933 at Pauls Valley, Garvin County, Oklahoma to Juanita (Neta) Harmon, born 9 Sep 1915 at Pauls Valley, Garvin County, Oklahoma. Earl McChesney and Juanita Harmon had issue, which was the eleventh generation in America:

B42127521. Ronald Douglas McChesney, first child and first son of Earl McChesney and Juanita Harmon, born 28 Oct 1934.

B4212753. Elaine McChesney, third child and first daughter of Earl McChesney and Juanita Harmon, born 31 May 1916 at Pauls Valley, Garvin County, Oklahoma. Married 24 Dec 1933 at Pauls Valley, Garvin County, Oklahoma to Odell Brotherton, born 14 Nov 1914. Elaine McChesney married secondly 14 May 1948 to Robert D. Hartcastle, born 23 Nov 1908 at Houston, Houston County, Texas. Elaine McChesney and Odell Brotherton had issue, which was the eleventh generation in America:

B42127531. Barbara Neil Brotherton, first child and first daughter of Elaine McChesney and Odell Brotherton, born 10 Sep 1936.

B42128. Amanda Pounds, eighth child and sixth daughter of William Pounds and Nancy Hairgrove, born about 1858 in Shelby County, Texas.

B42129. Joseph Pounds, ninth child and third son of William Pounds and Nancy Hairgrove, born about

1862 in Shelby County, Texas.

B4213. Reuben Pounds, third child and third son of John Pound and Lavinia Rorie, born 4 Aug 1812 in Bedford County, Tennessee and died 17 Dec 1849. Buried at Shreveport, Bossier Parish, Louisiana. Reuben Pounds was a farmer by occupation and he died on the way to Shelby County, Texas and was buried on the banks of the Red River in Shreveport, Bossier Parish, Louisiana. The cause of his death was cholera. Married 14 Apr 1836 in Perry County, Alabama to Elizabeth Catherine Smith, daughter of D. Harris Smith, born about 1815 in Perry County, Alabama and died 21 Jan 1891 in Shelby County, Texas. Reuben Pounds and Elizabeth Smith had issue, which was the eighth generation in America:

B42131. Joel Pounds, first child and first son of Reuben Pounds and Elizabeth Smith, born 9 Mar 1837 in Perry County, Alabama.

B42132. William S. Pounds, second child and second son of Reuben Pounds and Elizabeth Smith, born 7 Feb 1838 in Perry County, Alabama.

B42133. John Jackson Pounds, third child and third son of Reuben Pounds and Elizabeth Smith, born 25 Feb 1839 in Perry County, Alabama.

B42134. Mary L. Pounds, fourth child and first daughter of Reuben Pounds and Elizabeth Smith, born 17 Apr 1840 in Perry County, Alabama. Married James Scott.

B42135. Mary Levinia Pounds, fifth child and second daughter of Reuben Pounds and Elizabeth Smith, born 23 Feb 1841 in Perry County, Alabama and died 4 Nov 1909. Married William Emmett Lemons, born 1 Mar 1824 in Mason, Tipton County, Tennessee and died 11 Apr 1889 at Center, Shelby County, Texas. Mary Pounds and William Lemons had issue, which was the ninth generation in America:

B421351. Ann E. Lemons, first child and first daughter of Mary Pounds and William Lemons, born 4 Aug 1868 at Center, Shelby County, Texas and died 14 Feb 1902.

B42136. David Thomas Pounds, sixth child and fourth son of Reuben Pounds and Elizabeth Smith, born 18 Dec 1842 in Perry County, Alabama. Married Elizabeth Catherine Mise. David

Pounds and Elizabeth Mise had issue, which was the ninth generation in America:

B421361. Della Deborah Pounds, first child and first daughter of David Pounds and Elizabeth Mise, born 27 Feb 1872 at Garrison, Nacogdoches County, Texas. Married 31 Aug 1892 at Garrison, Nacogdoches County, Texas to J.R. Lewis.

B42137. Benjamin Bryan Pounds, seventh child and fifth son of Reuben Pounds and Elizabeth Smith, born 4 Nov 1847 in Perry County, Alabama.

B42138. Nancy Elizabeth Pounds, eight child and third daughter of Reuben Pounds and Elizabeth Smith, born 20 Sep 1848 in Perry County, Alabama. Married 5 Mar 1866 at Abbeville, Henry County, Alabama to David D. Melvin.

B4214. Isham Zachariah Pounds, fourth child and fourth son of John Pound and Lavinia Rorie, born 1820 in Bedford County, Tennessee and died 1893 at Randolph, Perry County, Alabama. Married 15 Jul 1839 in Perry County, Alabama to Harriett Elizabeth Barnett, daughter of Thomas Barnett and Pheraby Bishop, born 24 Jan 1823 in Perry County, Alabama and died 12 Jul 1878 at Lawley, Perry County, Alabama. Buried at Rehoboth Church cemetery, Perry County, Alabama. Isham Pounds was a school teacher and a soldier. It is said that Isham came from Bedford County, Tennessee to Perry County, Alabama with his father and three brothers when he was a young man. His father, John Pounds, was traveling through Perry County with a load of apples and they stopped overnight with a family by the name of Barnett. Mr. Barnett was impressed with young Isham and offered him a job as a farm hand, which he accepted. We don't know how many years he worked here, but we know that he married Mr. Barnett's daughter Harriett Elizabeth Barnett. They were married and continued to live in Perry County until 1845, then moved to Mississippi where he farmed and taught school. After about five years residence in Mississippi, they returned to Alabama and settled on the upper reaches of Oakmulgee Creek in Perry County, near Lawley in the Hurricane Community. Isham in addition to being a school teacher, was a blacksmith and skilled in the art of tool making and the working

242

of iron and from his forge came many of the tools that were used in the surrounding area. The Oakmulgee Creek flowed through his lands and he built a dam and formed a lake to provide power for a grist mill, sawmill and forge. Today his old home place still stands along a new asphalt road about one mile north of Lawley, Alabama. The dam has long since washed away but the stones that formed the foundation of the old millhouse can still be seen. Isham fought in the Civil War as a private in K Company, 11th Alabama Infantry in the Confederate Army. When Isham saw that the South had lost the war, he got on his horse and started back home to Perry County, Alabama. It took him six weeks to go from Mobile to Perry County because he had to dodge the Yankees on the way back home. After the war, he moved to Marion County, Alabama and was there when the 1870 census was taken, teaching school. Most likely they went to Marion County because Harriett's children were there along with her Thomas Barnett's widow, Elizabeth L. (Lewis) Barnett and several of their children. Several of Isham's children came to Marion County, including William Thomas, Martha and Henry Cash and Sara A.E. and John Bailus Barnett. Jo Royal Barnett, son of John and Margaret L. was in Marion County before the war, and his daughter Adaline married Wyatt N. Dodd. Isham Pounds married secondly 28 Jan 1879 to Lucinda Lawrence. Isham Pounds and Harriett Barnett had issue, which was the eighth generation in America:

B42141. William Thomas Pounds, first child and first son of Isham Pounds and Harriett Barnett, born 20 Apr 1840 in Perry County, Alabama and died 8 Jan 1912 at Escatawpa, Jackson County, Mississippi. Married 15 Oct 1857 in Bibb County, Alabama to Mary J. Langford, born about 1841 in North Carolina. Married secondly Elizabeth (Betty) Smith. William Pounds is believed to have fought in the Civil War in C 1 Battery Alabama Artillery as a private. William Pounds and Mary Langford had issue, which was the ninth generation in America:

B421411. Sarah Pounds, first child and first daughter of William Pounds and Mary

Langford, born about 1859 in Perry County, Alabama.

B421412. Mary H. Pounds, second child and second daughter of William Pounds and Mary Langford, born about 1860 in Perry County, Alabama.

B421413. Amanda J. Pounds, third child and third daughter of William Pounds and Mary Langford, born about 1866 in Perry County, Alabama.

B421414. Julia (Julie) L. Pounds, fourth child and fourth daughter of William Pounds and Mary Langford, born about 1868 in Marion County, Alabama. Married John Cromer.

B421415. Joseph David Pounds, fifth child and first son of William Pounds and Mary Langford, born 21 Jan 1871 in Chilton County, Alabama and died 9 Apr 1953 in Pascagoula, Jackson County, Mississippi. Buried at Escatawpa, Ferrel cemetery, Mississippi. Married 28 Apr 1896 in Perry County, Alabama to Lucinda Catherine (Katie) Pounds, his first cousin, daughter of Joseph Warren Pounds and Amanda F. Henderson, born 28 Apr 1881 in Perry County, Alabama and died 24 Feb 1965 in Pascagoula, Jackson County, Mississippi. Buried at Escatawpa, Ferrel cemetery, Mississippi. Joseph Pounds and Lucinda Pounds had issue, which was the tenth generation in America:

B4214151. Clara Arminta Pounds, first child and first daughter of Joseph Pounds and Lucinda Pounds, born 1 Apr 1900 at Hattiewburg, Perry County, Mississippi and died 27 Mar 1925. Married 10 Feb 1921 at Jackson County, Mississippi to Jack C. Ware, born in Vancleve, Jackson County, Mississippi.

B4214152. May Pounds, second child and second daughter of Joseph Pounds and Lucinda Pounds, date of birth unknown at Gulfport, Harrison County, Mississippi.

B4214153. Nannie Ruth Pounds, third child and third daughter of Joseph Pounds and Lucinda Pounds, born 1 Nov 1904 at Hattiesburg, Perry County, Mississippi and died at San Diego, San Diego County, California. Married 21 Mar 1922 at Jackson County, Mississippi to William H. Whittle. Married secondly to Anton P.

Koval. Married thirdly to Ray Walker. Married fourthly to Louis Davis. Nannie Pounds and William Whittle had issue, which was the eleventh generation in America:

B42141531. Winona Henrietta Whittle, first child and first daughter of Nannie Pounds and William Whittle, born 1923 at Gulfport, Harrison County, Mississippi.

B4214153. Nannie Ruth Pounds, third child and third daughter of Joseph Pounds and Lucinda Pounds, born 1 Nov 1904 at Hattiesburg, Perry County, Mississippi and died at San Diego, San Diego County, California. Married secondly to Anton P. Koval. Nannie Pounds and Anton Koval had issue, which was the eleventh generation in America:

B42141531. Robert Stewart Koval, first child and first son of Nannie Pounds and Anton Koval, born 12 Jul 1920 at Mobile, Mobile County, Alabama.

B4214154. Roy Pounds, fourth child and first son of Joseph Pounds and Lucinda Pounds, date of birth unknown at Long Beach, Harrison County, Mississippi.

B4214155. James Hewlet Pounds, fifth child and second son of Joseph Pounds and Lucinda Pounds, born 12 Jul 1909 at Hattiesburg, Perry County, Mississippi and died 24 Mar 1943 at Mobile, Mobile County, Alabama. Buried at Arlington National cemetery, Alabama. Married Rose Poulos, born 1911 at Mobile, Mobile County, Alabama. Rose Poulos married secondly Evander Gill. James Pounds and Rose Poulos had issue, which was the eleventh generation in America:

B42141551. Patricia Ann Pounds, first child and first daughter of James Pounds and Rose Poulos, born 12 Jul 1932 at Biloxi, Harrison County, Mississippi. Married James Ross. Married secondly Gilbert Dennis.

B42141552. Peggy Elaine Pounds, second child and second daughter of James Pounds and Rose Poulos, born 30 Aug 1933 at Biloxi, Harrison County, Mississippi. Married Idest J. Leblanc.

B4214156. Agnes Audrey

Pounds, sixth child and fourth daughter of Joseph Pounds and Lucinda Pounds, born 14 Feb 1912 at Hattiesburg, Perry County, Mississippi. Married 31 Oct 1931 at Pascagoula, Jackson County, Mississippi to Foster Barrow, son of Joseph Milton Barrow and Odelia Ladnier, born 23 Feb 1911 at Escatawpa, Jackson County, Mississippi. Agnes Pounds and Foster Barrow had issue, which was the eleventh generation in America:

B42141561. Gerald Foster Barrow, first child and first son of Agnes Pounds and Foster Barrow, born 25 Aug 1932 at Pascagoula, Jackson County, Mississippi. Married Barbara Jean Cotten.

B4214157. David Warren Pounds, seventh child and third son of Joseph Pounds and Lucinda Pounds, born 11 Feb 1913 at Pascagoula, Jackson County, Mississippi and died 24 Mar 1967 in Mississippi. Married Thelma ---.

B4214158. Gladys Marie Pounds, eighth child and fifth daughter of Joseph Pounds and Lucinda Pounds, born 5 Dec 1916 at Pascagoula, Jackson County, Mississippi. Married 4 Feb 1940 to Charles Arthur Purdy. Married secondly to Robert Patterson.

B4214159. William Edward Pounds, ninth child and fourth son of Joseph Pounds and Lucinda Pounds, born 3 Aug 1919 at Pascagoula, Jackson County, Mississippi. Married 12 Sep 1947 at Jackson County, Mississippi to Louise Simmons, daughter of Joseph Belton Simmons, born 6 May 1924 in Alabama. Louise Simmons married secondly to Colon Kittrel. William Pounds and Louise Simmons had issue, which was the eleventh generation in America:

B42141591. William Edward Pounds, Jr., first child and first son of William Pounds and Louise Simmons, born 26 Jul 1948.

B42141592. Cathy Jo Pounds, second child and first daughter of William Pounds and Louise Simmons, born 30 Oct 1950 at Pascagoula, Jackson County, Mississippi. Married Leon Forehand. Cathy Jo Pounds married secondly to James Johnson.

B42141510. Daisy Dean Pounds,

tenth child and sixth daughter of Joseph Pounds and Lucinda Pounds, born 29 Apr 1922 at Pascagoula, Jackson County, Mississippi. Married 23 Feb 1939 at Pascagoula, Jackson County, Mississippi to Lacy Edward Green, son of Tracy Edward Green and Mary Crespo, born 27 Jul 1920 at New Orleans, Orleans Parish, Louisiana. Daisy Pounds and Lacy Green had issue, which was the eleventh generation in America:

B421415101. James Lacy Green, first child and first son of Daisy Pounds and Lacy Green, born 6 Dec 1939 at Pascagoula, Jackson County, Mississippi. Married Nov 1960 to Barbra Ann Martin.

B421415102. Tracy Edward Green, second child and second son of Daisy Pounds and Lacy Green, born 14 Jul 1947 at Pascagoula, Jackson County, Mississippi. Married Mary Alice Stewart.

B421415103. Evelyn Marie Green, third child and first daughter of Daisy Pounds and Lacy Green, born 20 Aug 1955 at Pascagoula, Jackson County, Mississippi.

B421415104. William Ray Green, fourth child and third son of Daisy Pounds and Lacy Green, born 13 Dec 1956 at Pascagoula, Jackson County, Mississippi.

B421416. Emily F. Pounds, sixth child and fifth daughter of William Pounds and Mary Langford, born about 1874 in Chilton County, Alabama.

B421417. Benjamin D. Pounds, seventh child and second son of William Pounds and Mary Langford, born about 1875 in Chilton County, Alabama.

B421418. William B. Pounds, eighth child and third son of William Pounds and Mary Langford, born about 1877 in Chilton County, Alabama.

B421419. Harriette L. Pounds, ninth child and sixth daughter of William Pounds and Mary Langford, born about 1878 in Chilton County, Alabama.

B421420. Daniel C. Pounds, tenth child and fourth son of William Pounds and Mary Langford, born about 1880 in Chilton County, Alabama.

B421421. Agnes Pounds, eleventh child and

seventh daughter of William Pounds and Mary Langford, date and place of birth unknown. Married Abe Broom.

B4214. Isham Zachariah Pounds, fourth child and fourth son of John Pound and Lavinia Rorie, born 1820 in Bedford County, Tennessee and died 1893 in Randolph, Perry County, Alabama. Married secondly 28 Jan 1879 in Chilton County, Alabama to Lucinda Lawrence, born 1849 and died about 1912. Buried at New Salem Church cemetery, Chilton County, Alabama. Isham Pounds and Lucinda Lawrence had issue, which was the eighth generation in America:

B42141. John Marion Pounds, first child and first son of Isham Pounds and Lucinda Lawrence, born 1841 in Perry County, Alabama and died in the Civil War at Mobile, Mobile County, Alabama.

B42142. Sarah A.E. Pounds, second child and first daughter of Isham Pounds and Lucinda Lawrence, born about 1844 in Perry County, Alabama. Married 24 Aug 1867 in Perry County, Alabama to John Bailus Barnett, son of John Barnett and Elizabeth L. Lewis, born in Spartanburg, Spartanburg County, South Carolina. John Barnett was the brother of Thomas Barnett who married Pheraby Bishop, parents of Harriett Elizabeth Barnett Pounds. Sarah Pounds and John Barnett had issue, which was the ninth generation in America:

B421421. Harriett Elizabeth Barnett, first child and first daughter of Sarah Pounds and John Barnett, born in Perry County, Alabama.

B421422. Susan Barnett, second child and second daughter of Sarah Pounds and John Barnett, born in Marion County, Alabama.

B421423. E. Doria Barnett, third child and third daughter of Sarah Pounds and John Barnett, born in Marion County, Alabama.

B421424. Michael Barnett, fourth child and first son of Sarah Pounds and John Barnett, born in Marion County, Alabama.

B421425. Joseph Barnett, fifth child and second son of Sarah Pounds and John Barnett, born in Walker County, Alabama.

B421426. Liddy Barnett, sixth child and fourth daughter of Sarah Pounds and John Barnett, born in Walker County, Alabama.

B42143. Martha A. Pounds, third child and second daughter of Isham Pounds and Lucinda Lawrence, born 6 Apr 1846 in Marshall County, Mississippi and died 28 Dec 1908 in Perry County, Alabama. Buried at Lawtey, Rehoboth cemetery, Alabama. Married 31 Dec 1861 in Perry County, Alabama to Henry (Doc) Cash, born in Alabama. Martha Pounds and Henry Cash had issue, which was the ninth generation in America:

B421431. Mary H. Cash, first child and first daughter of Martha Pounds and Henry Cash, born 11 Nov 1862 in Perry County, Alabama and died 23 Jul 1928. Married Calhoun Wallace.

B421432. John Cash, second child and first son of Martha Pounds and Henry Cash, date and place of birth unknown.

B421433. Eva (Evie) J. Cash, third child and second daughter of Martha Pounds and Henry Cash, date and place of birth unknown.

B421434. Sara Ruth Cash, fourth child and third daughter of Martha Pounds and Henry Cash, born in Perry County, Alabama.

B421435. Helen Cash, fifth child and fourth daughter of Martha Pounds and Henry Cash, born in Perry County, Alabama.

B421436. Martha A. Cash, sixth child and fifth daughter of Martha Pounds and Henry Cash, born in Perry County, Alabama.

B421437. Henry Huff Cash, seventh child and second son of Martha Pounds and Henry Cash, born in Perry County, Alabama.

B421438. James Cash, eighth child and third son of Martha Pounds and Henry Cash, born in Perry County, Alabama.

B421439. Walter Cash, ninth child and fourth son of Martha Pounds and Henry Cash, born in Perry County, Alabama.

B421440. Lillie Cash, tenth child and sixth daughter of Martha Pounds and Henry Cash, born in Perry County, Alabama.

B42144. Araminta Jane Pounds, fourth child and third daughter of Isham Pounds and Lucinda Lawrence, born 1847 in Marshall County, Mississippi and died at Clanton, Chilton County, Alabama. Married Martin Holt.

B42145. Nancy M. Pounds, fifth child and fourth

daughter of Isham Pounds and Lucinda Lawrence, born 1849 in Marshall County, Mississippi and died before 1860.

B42146. Joseph Warren Pounds, sixth child and second son of Isham Pounds and Lucinda Lawrence, born 21 Jul 1852 in Perry County, Alabama and died in Mobile, Mobile County, Alabama. Married 21 Jul 1874 in Bibb County, Alabama to Amanda F. Henderson, daughter of Wallace Henderson, born 17 Sep 1852 at Mariana, Marshall County, Mississippi. Joseph Pounds and Amanda Henderson had issue, which was the ninth generation in America:

B421461. John Henry Pounds, first child and first son of Joseph Pounds and Amanda Henderson, born 4 Aug 1875 in Perry County, Alabama and died Apr 1931. Married Ellen Margaret Nelson, born 5 Sep 1900 and died 19 Sep 1991. John Pounds and Ellen Nelson had issue, which was the tenth generation in America:

B4214611. Amanda Frances Pounds, first child and first daughter of John Pounds and Ellen Nelson, born and died in 1920.

B4214612. Frances Marie Pounds, second child and second daughter of John Pounds and Ellen Nelson, born 10 Feb 1921. Married Adolph Van Schouwen.

B4214613. Emma Elizabeth Pounds, third child and third daughter of John Pounds and Ellen Nelson, born 19 Jan 1922. Married Jesse Kuhn.

B4214614. Sara Patricia Pounds, fourth child and fourth daughter of John Pounds and Ellen Nelson, born 10 Apr 1924. Married Elbert Mowery.

B4214615. Joseph Richard Pounds, fifth child and first son of John Pounds and Ellen Nelson, born 3 Mar 1926. Married Doris Lucille Woodstock.

B4214616. James Albert Pounds, sixth child and second son of John Pounds and Ellen Nelson, born 12 Oct 1928.

B421462. William Lewis Pounds, second child and second son of Joseph Pounds and Amanda Henderson, born 5 Aug 1878 in Perry County, Alabama and died 10 Mar 1965 in Mobile, Mobile County, Alabama. Married 17 Jun 1897 in Pike County, Mississippi to Beaulah Elizabeth Rushing, born 21 Mar 1880 in Pike County, Mississippi.

B4214621. William Frank Pounds, first child and first son of William Pounds and Beaulah Rushing, date and place of birth unknown, and died 10 Mar 1965 in Mobile, Mobile County, Alabama.

B4214622. Joseph B. Pounds, second child and second son of William Pounds and Beaulah Rushing, date and place of birth unknown.

B4214623. Annie Mae Pounds, third child and first daughter of William Pounds and Beaulah Rushing, date and place of birth unknown. Married Mann Siegler.

B4214624. Wilbur Pounds, fourth child and third son of William Pounds and Beaulah Rushing, date and place of birth unknown.

B4214625. Victor Pounds, fifth child and fourth son of William Pounds and Beaulah Rushing, date and place of birth unknown.

B421463. Thomas J. Pounds, third child and third son of Joseph Pounds and Amanda Henderson, born in Perry County, Alabama.

B421464. Lucinda Catherine (Katie) Pounds, fourth child and first daughter of Joseph Pounds and Amanda Henderson, born 28 Apr 1881 in Perry County, Alabama and died 24 Feb 1965 in Pascagoula, Jackson County, Mississippi. Buried at Escatawpa, Ferrel cemetery, Mississippi. Married 28 Apr 1896 in Perry County, Alabama to Joseph David Pounds, son of William Thomas Pounds and Mary Langford, her first cousin, born 21 Jan 1871 in Chilton County, Alabama.

B421465. Ellen Pounds, fifth child and second daughter of Joseph Pounds and Amanda Henderson, born in Perry County, Alabama. Married Edward Spicer.

B421466. Elizabeth Pounds, sixth child and third daughter of Joseph Pounds and Amanda Henderson, born in Perry County, Alabama. Married Clayborn Cook.

B421467. Nancy Caroline Pounds, seventh child and fourth daughter of Joseph Pounds and Amanda Henderson, born 15 Nov 1888 in Perry County, Alabama and died 10 Nov 1938 at Tylertown, Walthall County, Mississippi. Married Clark Dillon, born 12 Jul 1881 in Tylertown, Pike County, Mississippi. Nancy Pounds and Clark Dillon had issue, which was the tenth generation

251

in America:

B4214671. Mamie Ellen Dillon, first child and first daughter of Nancy Pounds and Clark Dillon, born 5 Mar 1910 in Walthall County, Mississippi. Married Jesse Graves.

B4214672. Ollie Eugene Dillon, second child and first son of Nancy Pounds and Clark Dillon, born 1 Nov 1911 in Walthall County, Mississippi and died about 1976. Married Myrtle Johnson.

B4214673. James Cullen Dillon, third child and second son of Nancy Pounds and Clark Dillon, born 26 Apr 1913 in Walthall County, Mississippi. Married Lizzie Jelks.

B4214674. John Erastus Dillon, fourth child and third son of Nancy Pounds and Clark Dillon, born 23 Apr 1916 in Walthall County, Mississippi. Married Barbara Marie Egan. John Dillon and Barbara Egan had issue, which was the eleventh generation in America:

B42146741. Patricia Anne Dillon, first child and first daughter of John Dillon and Barbara Egan, date and place of birth unknown.

B42146742. Anna Maria Dillon, second child and second daughter of John Dillon and Barbara Egan, date and place of birth unknown.

B42146743. Michael Jude Thaddeus Dillon, third child and first son of John Dillon and Barbara Egan, date and place of birth unknown.

B4214675. Jim General Dillon, fifth child and fourth son of Nancy Pounds and Clark Dillon, born 1 Jul 1917 in Walthall County, Mississippi. Married Ruth Petrentoni. Jim Dillon and Ruth Petrentoni had issue, which was the eleventh generation in America:

B42146751. Jimmy Dillon, first child and first son of Jim Dillon and Ruth Petrentoni, date and place of birth unknown.

B42146752. Ronnie Dillon, second child and second son of Jim Dillon and Ruth Petrentoni, date and place of birth unknown.

B42146753. Ernest Dillon, third child and third son of Jim Dillon and Ruth Petrentoni, date and place of birth unknown.

B4214676. Betty Jane Dillon, sixth child and second daughter of Nancy Pounds and

Clark Dillon, born 24 Jan 1919 in Walthall County, Mississippi. Married J.W. Lee, born 4 Nov 1913. Betty Dillon and J.W. Lee had issue, which was the eleventh generation in America:

B42146761. Bettie Marie Lee, first child and first daughter of Betty Dillon and J.W. Lee, date and place of birth unknown.

B42146762. Sybil Lee, second child and second daughter of Betty Dillon and J.W. Lee, date and place of birth unknown.

B42146763. Bobby Lee, third child and first son of Betty Dillon and J.W. Lee, date and place of birth unknown.

B4214677. Nellie Dillon, seventh child and third daughter of Nancy Pounds and Clark Dillon, born in Walthall County, Mississippi.

B4214678. Jewel Dillon, eighth child and fifth son of Nancy Pounds and Clark Dillon, born 22 Nov 1924 in Walthall County, Mississippi. Married Juanita Smith. Jewel Dillon and Juanita Smith had issue, which was the eleventh generation in America:

B42146781. John Neil Dillon, first child and first son of Jewel Dillon and Juanita Smith, date and place of birth unknown.

B42146782. Karen Dillon, second child and first daughter of Jewel Dillon and Juanita Smith, date and place of birth unknown.

B4214679. Hettie Dillon, ninth child and fourth daughter of Nancy Pounds and Clark Dillon, born in Walthall County, Mississippi.

B4214680. Earnest Howard Dillon, tenth child and sixth son of Nancy Pounds and Clark Dillon, born 22 Jun 1927 in Walthall County, Mississippi and died about 1975.

B4214681. Elisha David Dillon, eleventh child and seventh son of Nancy Pounds and Clark Dillon, born 9 May 1929 at Tylertown, Walthall County, Mississippi. Married Kathryn Virginia Laminack. Elisha Dillon and Kathryn Laminack had issue, which was the eleventh generation in America:

B42146811. Donald Dillon, first child and first son of Elisha Dillon and Kathryn Laminack, date and place of birth unknown.

B42146812. Karol Dianne Dillon,

second child and first daughter of Elisha Dillon
and Kathryn Laminack, date and place of birth
unknown.
B42146813. David Cullen Dillon,
third child and second son of Elisha Dillon and
Kathryn Laminack, date and place of birth unknown.
B42147. Benjamin Franklin Pounds, seventh child
and third son of Isham Pounds and Lucinda
Lawrence, born 29 Sep 1854 in Perry County,
Alabama and died 7 Mar 1924 at Corinth, Alcorn
County, Mississippi. Buried at Corinth, Henry
cemetery, Mississippi. Married 25 Dec 1873 at
Pikeville, Marion County, Alabama to Mary Ann
Dodd, daughter of Franklin Dodd and Elizabeth
Tucker, born 23 Sep 1859 in Marion County, Alabama
and died 10 Mar 1930 at Memphis, Shelby County,
Tennessee. Benjamin Franklin Pounds was a Justice
of the Peace and a Deputy Sheriff for many years
in Tishomingo County, Mississippi; and it was said
that if there was an especially dangerous man to
be arrested, the Sheriff would send Ben Pounds to
serve the warrant. He had a reputation of always
getting his man, not for the boldness or use of
guns, but because everybody knew him, and trusted
him for his sense of justice and fair play. He
made friends with people, and his word was as good
as his bond, and when he told a person he had been
sent to arrest that he would get a fair trial,
they usually submitted without resistance. In
addition to being a peace officer, he was a farmer
and a merchant; operating a general store in
Paden, Mississippi; a new railroad town for
several years. Benjamin Pounds and Mary Dodd had
issue, which was the ninth generation in America:
B421471. Mary Elizabeth Pounds, first child
and first daughter of Benjamin Pounds and Mary
Dodd, born 12 Mar 1875 at Pikeville, Marion
County, Alabama and died 27 Aug 1919. Married 24
Sep 1896 to Joseph Douglas Bonds.
B421472. Jane Priscilla Pounds, second child
and second daughter of Benjamin Pounds and Mary
Dodd, born 4 Mar 1879 in Marion County, Alabama
and died 25 Dec 1960 in Tishomingo County,
Mississippi. Married 2 Feb 1902 to Tillman
Clayton Medley.
B421473. Martha Ann Pounds, third child and

third daughter of Benjamin Pounds and Mary Dodd, born 9 Apr 1881 at Iuka, Tishomingo County, Mississippi and died 17 Mar 1943 in Lafayette County, Mississippi. Married Luther Paul Donaldson.

B421474. Araminta Agnus Pounds, fourth child and fourth daughter of Benjamin Pounds and Mary Dodd, born 12 May 1883 at Iuka, Tishomingo County, Mississippi and died 11 Jan 1958 in Tishomingo County, Mississippi. Married 29 Jan 1905 at Iuka, Tishomingo County, Mississippi to Walter Gipson Kennedy.

B421475. Emma Alice Pounds, fifth child and fifth daughter of Benjamin Pounds and Mary Dodd, born 23 Oct 1885 in Tishomingo County, Mississippi and died 1905 at Texas City, Galveston County, Texas. Married 12 Mar 1903 to Thomas H. Parker.

B421476. Ida Pounds, sixth child and sixth daughter of Benjamin Pounds and Mary Dodd, born 23 Jan 1889 at Iuka, Tishomingo County, Mississippi and died 17 Oct 1928 at Tupelo, Lee County, Mississippi. Buried at Palestine Church cemetery, Tishomingo County, Mississippi. Married 1 Apr 1906 at Iuka, Tishomingo County, Mississippi to Joseph Henry Kennedy, son of Daniel Pinkton Kennedy and Amanda Eliza McAnally, born 6 Apr 1883 at Iuka, Tishomingo County, Mississippi and died 24 Nov 1969 at Fulton, Itawamba County, Mississippi. Joseph Kennedy married secondly Mossie May (Henderson) Cagle. Ida Pounds and Joseph Kennedy had issue, which was the tenth generation in America:

B4214761. Clarence Odell Kennedy, first child and first son of Ida Pounds and Joseph Kennedy, born 28 Jun 1907 at Paden, Tishomingo County, Mississippi and died 1992. Married 3 Nov 1933 at Tupelo, Lee County, Mississippi to Mary Lillian McMurray, daughter of Thomas Lillian McMurray and Clara Elizabeth Yarbrough, born 15 Mar 1913 at Houlke, Chickasaw County, Mississippi. Clarence Kennedy and Mary McMurry had issue, which was the eleventh generation in America:

B42147611. Maurene Elizabeth Kennedy, first child and first daughter of Clarence Kennedy, and Mary McMurry, born 2 Feb 1935 at Tupelo, Lee County, Mississippi. Married

16 Mar 1954 to Mark Leroy Wahlquist.

B42147612. Mary Louise Kennedy, second child and second daughter of Clarence Kennedy and Mary McMurry, born 26 Jan 1937 at Tupelo, Lee County, Mississippi. Married 9 Apr 1956 to Ronald Dean Cupp.

B42147613. Tommi Jo Kennedy, third child and third daughter of Clarence Kennedy and Mary McMurry, born 4 Aug 1940 at Tupelo, Lee County, Mississippi. Married 29 Oct 1963 to David Gene Denton.

B42147614. Ida Delores Kennedy, fourth child and fourth daughter of Clarence Kennedy and Mary McMurry, born 25 Jan 1942 at Memphis, Shelby County, Tennessee. Married 23 Jul 1964 to Russell Winslow Jensen.

B42147615. William Grant Kennedy, fifth child and first son of Clarence Kennedy and Mary McMurry, born 9 Mar 1944 at Memphis, Shelby County, Tennessee. Married 23 Jul 1964 to Regenia Warren.

B42147616. Clara Faye Kennedy, sixth child and fifth daughter of Clarence Kennedy and Mary McMurry, born 27 May 1945 at Memphis, Shelby County, Tennessee. Married 14 Oct 1965 to William Arthur Rushing.

B42147617. Judith Ann Kennedy, seventh child and sixth daughter of Clarence Kennedy and Mary McMurry, born and died 27 Mar 1947 at Memphis, Shelby County, Tennessee.

B42147618. Jenny Ruth Kennedy, eighth child and seventh daughter of Clarence Kennedy and Mary McMurry, born 12 Jun 1949 at Memphis, Shelby County, Tennessee.

B42147619. Rebecca Jean Kennedy, ninth child and eighth daughter of Clarence Kennedy and Mary McMurry, born 18 Nov 1951 at Memphis, Shelby County, Tennessee.

B42147620. Joseph Michael Kennedy, tenth child and second son of Clarence Kennedy and Mary McMurry, born 18 Dec 1953 at Memphis, Shelby County, Tennessee.

B42147621. Stephen McKay Kennedy, eleventh child and third son of Clarence Kennedy and Mary McMurry, born 14 Mar 1959 at Memphis, Shelby County, Tennessee.

B4214762. Myrtle Gertrude Kennedy, second child and first daughter of Ida Pounds and Joseph Kennedy, born 29 Mar 1910 at Booneville, Prentiss County, Mississippi. Married Charley Powell. Married secondly 27 Oct 1927 to R.K. Houston.

B4214763. Cletus Faye Kennedy, third child and second daughter of Ida Pounds and Joseph Kennedy, born 29 Aug 1914 at Holcutt, Tishomingo County, Mississippi and died 3 Jul 1937 at Prentiss County, Mississippi. Married R.C. Jones.

B4214764. Noonan Golden Kennedy, fourth child and second son of Ida Pounds and Joseph Kennedy, born 27 Jun 1919 at Paden, Tishomingo County, Mississippi and died 7 Jul 1935.

B4214765. Ernestine Kennedy, fifth child and third daughter of Ida Pounds and Joseph Kennedy, born 1922 at Paden, Tishomingo County, Mississippi and died 1924.

B421477. Thomas Benjamin Pounds, seventh child and first son of Benjamin Pounds and Mary Dodd, born 15 Mar 1890 at Iuka, Tishomingo County, Mississippi and died 21 Mar 1932 at Memphis, Shelby County, Tennessee. Married Louve Wiley.

B421478. Leona Pounds, eighth child and seventh daughter of Benjamin Pounds and Mary Dodd, born 26 Jun 1892 at Iuka, Tishomingo County, Mississippi and died 18 May 1963 in Illinois. Married Ozy Butler Winningham. Married secondly Thomas Harris. Married thirdly John Miller. Married fourthly George Bozovich.

B421479. Maude Belle Pounds, ninth child and eighth daughter of Benjamin Pounds and Mary Dodd, born 6 Feb 1896 in Paden, Tishomingo County, Mississippi. Married 9 Oct 1919 to Millard Winningham.

B421480, Dewey Clayton Pounds, tenth child and second son of Benjamin Pounds and Mary Dodd, born 23 Oct 1897 at Paden, Tishomingo County, Mississippi and died 27 Feb 1898 in Tishomingo County, Mississippi.

B421481. Willie Blanche Pounds, eleventh child and ninth daughter of Benjamin Pounds and Mary Dodd, born 23 Mar 1900 at Iuka, Tishomingo County, Mississippi and died 15 Jan 1965 in Florida. Married Odell Meddows. Married secondly

Robert Broadfield Sullivan.

B42148. Lewis Barnett Pounds, eighth child and fourth son of Isham Pounds and Harriett Barnett born 2 Nov 1859 at Randolph, Perry County, Alabama and died about 1928 at Auburn, Lee County, Alabama. Buried at New Salem Church cemetery, Chilton County, Alabama. Married 1884 in Maplesville, Chilton County, Alabama to Leanna Lawrence, daughter of Benjamin Tucker Lawrence and Mary Ann ---, born 26 Jan 1869 at Maplesville, Chilton County, Alabama and died 19 Mar 1894 at Jemison, Chilton County, Alabama. Buried at Macedonia cemetery, Chilton County, Alabama. Married secondly 6 Aug 1896 at Chilton County, Alabama to Lutie Riggins, daughter of William Gant Riggins and Lucinda Childers. Lewis Pounds and Leanna Lawrence had issue, which was the ninth generation in America:

B421481. James (Jim) Johnson Pounds, first child and first son of Lewis Pounds and Leanna Lawrence, born 1885 at Maplesville, Chilton County, Alabama and died 24 Jul 1929 at Ft. Stanton, Lincoln County, New Mexico.

B421482. Isham Frank Pounds, second child and second son of Lewis Pounds and Leanna Lawrence, born 9 Jul 1887 at Randolph, Perry County, Alabama and died 24 Dec 1972 at Saraland, Mobile County, Alabama. Buried at Saraland, Memorial cemetery, Alabama. Married 24 Dec 1914 in Chilton County, Alabama to Minnie Jeanette Crane, daughter of James Bartley Crane and Ada Maxa Robinson, born 5 Dec 1894 at Pletcher, Chilton County, Alabama and died 1982 at Saraland, Mobile County, Alabama. Buried at Saraland, Memorial cemetery, Alabama. Isham Pounds married secondly Loucinda Lawrence. Isham Pounds and Minnie Crane had issue, which was the tenth generation in America:

B4214821. Ruth Kate Pounds, first child and first daughter of Isham Pounds and Minnie Crane, born 15 Nov 1915 at Pletcher, Chilton County, Alabama. Married Louis O. Bamberg, born 11 Feb 1939. Married secondly 14 Nov 1979 to Roger Barnhill.

B4214822. James Arthur Pounds, second child and first son of Isham Pounds and Minnie

258

Crane, born 1920. Married 9 Feb 1950 to Angela D. Rossetti, daughter of Joseph A. Rossetti and Benedetta A. DiCarlo, born 25 Nov 1920. James Pounds and Angela Rosetti had issue, which was the eleventh generation in America:

B42148221. Jeanette Angela Pounds, first child and first daughter of James Pounds and Angela Rossetti, date and place of birth unknown.

B4214823. Isham Frank Pounds, Jr., third child and second son of Isham Pounds and Minnie Crane, born 9 Feb 1923 at Pletcher, Chilton County, Alabama. Married Eugenia Dodson. Married secondly Carolyn Ann Hill.

B4214824. Rena Maxine Pounds, fourth child and second daughter of Isham Pounds and Minnie Crane, born 24 Jan 1928 at Mobile, Mobile County, Alabama. Married Andrew E. Scheurmann, Jr.

B421483. Arthur Knight (A.K.) Pounds, third child and third son of Lewis Pounds and Leanna Lawrence, born 15 Apr 1889 at Maplesville, Chilton County, Alabama and died 13 Jan 1953 at Pensacola, Escambia County, Florida. Married 20 Feb 1919 to Edna V. Riedel.

B421484. Mary Estelle Pounds, fourth child and first daughter of Lewis Pounds and Leanna Lawrence, born 1891 at Maplesville, Chilton County, Alabama and died 1921 at Clanton, Chilton County, Alabama. Married Jul 1911 to James Henry Tippett, date and place of birth unknown, but he died in 1921.

B421485. Marshall Bronson Pounds, fifth child and fourth son of Lewis Pounds and Leanna Lawrence, born 19 Feb 1893 at Jemison, Chilton County, Alabama and died 2 Aug 1925 at Pletcher, Chilton County, Alabama. Buried in Chilton County, Alabama. Married 1916 to Gertrude (Gertie) Klinner, born 10 Aug 1889 in Chilton County, Alabama and died 18 Jun 1971 at Gadsden, Etowah County, Alabama. Marshall Pounds and Gertrude Klinner had issue, which was the tenth generation in America:

B4214851. Orchid Pounds, first child and first daughter of Marshall Pounds and Gertrude Klinner, born 19 Jan 1920 at Elrod, Tuscaloosa County, Alabama and died 18 Jun 1962 in Detroit,

Wayne County, Michigan. Married Dewey Tuggle Marlow. Married secondly about 1944 at Gadsden, Etowah County, Alabama to Jack Davidson. Orchid Pounds and Dewey Marlow had issue, which was the eleventh generation in America. This issue was adopted by her second husband, Jack Davidson

B42148511. Elaine Marlow Davidson, first child and first daughter of Orchid Pounds and Jack Davidson, born 15 May 1950 at Tampa, Hillsborough County, Florida.

B42148512. Wesley Raymond Davidson, second child and first son of Orchid Pounds and Jack Davidson, born 15 May 1941 at Gadsden, Etowah County, Alabama and died 20 Jul 1941.

B42148513. Pete Jack Davidson, third child and second son of Orchid Pounds and Jack Davidson, born 22 Feb 1945 at Gadsden, Etowah County, Alabama.

B42148514. Freida Janice Davidson, fourth child and second daughter of Orchid Pounds and Jack Davidson, born 20 Apr 1946 at Gadsden, Etowah County, Alabama and died Jun 1983.

B4214852. Carl Raymond Pounds, second child and first son of Marshall Pounds and Gertrude Klinner, born 27 Sep 1921 at Elrod, Tuscaloosa County, Alabama and died 22 Jun 1961 at Gadsden, Alabama. Married about 1949 at Gadsden, Etowah County, Alabama to Jeanne Roden, born 15 Aug 1924 in Alabama. Carl Pounds and Jeanne Roden had issue, which was the eleventh generation in America:

B42148521. Carol Jeanne Pounds, first child and first daughter of Carl Pounds and Jeanne Roden, born 4 Jul 1955 at Gadsden, Etowah County, Alabama.

B42148522. Carl Raymond Pounds II, second child and first son of Carl Pounds and Jeanne Roden, born 24 Feb 1958 at Gadsden, Etowah County, Alabama.

B4214853. Marshall Dean Pounds, third child and second daughter of Marshall Pounds and Gertrude Klinner, born 19 Jan 1924 at McShan, Alabama. Married 7 Oct 1944 at Gadsden, Etowah County, Alabama to William Lon Barrett, Jr., son of William Lon Barrett and Mary Ellen Marshall, born 16 Oct 1921 at Surgoinsville, Hawkins County, Tennessee. Marshall Pounds and William Barrett had issue, which was the eleventh generation in America:

B42148531. Constance Lee Barrett, first child and first daughter of Marshall Pounds and William Barrett, born 20 Mar 1948 at Kingsport, Sullivan County, Tennessee. Married Larry Smith.

B42148532. William Lon Barrett III, second child and first son of Marshall Pounds and William Barrett, born 29 Aug 1952 at Kingsport, Sullivan County, Tennessee.

B42148533. Marsha Luella Barrett, third child and second daughter of Marshall Pounds and William Barrett, born 12 Oct 1959 at Kingsport, Sullivan County, Tennessee. Married Johnny McFall.

B42148. Lewis Barnett Pounds, eighth child and fourth son of Isham Pounds and Loucinda Lawrence, born 2 Nov 1859 at Randolph, Perry County, Alabama and died about 1928 at Auburn, Lee County, Alabama. Buried at New Salem Church cemetery, Chilton County, Alabama. Married secondly 6 Aug 1896 at Chilton County, Alabama to Lutie Riggins, daughter of William Gant Riggins and Lucinda Childers, born 1871 in Talladega County, Alabama, but she died after 1928 in Chilton County, Alabama. Buried in New Salem cemetery, Chilton County, Alabama. Lewis Barnett Pounds was a teacher, a preacher, an active farmer, a storekeeper and a general merchant, a tax assessor, a politician, a newspaper owner and editor, a member of the state legislature, a postmaster and a strong prohibitionist. Lewis Pounds and Lutie Riggins had issue, which was the ninth generation in America:

B421481. Grady Pounds, first child and first son of Lewis Pounds and Lutie Riggins, born in 1896 and died in 1898.

B421482. Lewis Barnett Pounds, Jr., second child and second son of Lewis Pounds and Lutie Riggins, born 1899 and died 1971 in Tuscaloosa, Tuscaloosa County, Alabama.

B421483. Moody Lyman Pounds, third child and third son of Lewis Pounds and Lutie Riggins, born

25 Apr 1901 and died 4 Oct 1957 in Tuscaloosa, Tuscaloosa County, Alabama. Buried at Thorsby, New Salem Baptist cemetery, Alabama. Married Margaret Ewen.

B421484. Mattie Gertrude Pounds, fourth child and first daughter of Lewis Pounds and Lutie Riggins, born 30 May 1904 and died 1970 in Tuscaloosa, Tuscaloosa County, Alabama. Married 1 Jul 1922 in Alabama to Fred William Golson, born 1902.

B421485. Ralph Pounds, fifth child and fourth son of Lewis Pounds and Lutie Riggins, born 1906.

B421486. Leroy Pounds, sixth child and fifth son of Lewis Pounds and Lutie Riggins, born 1908 and died 1980.

B42149. Lucinda Paralee Pounds, ninth child and fifth daughter of Isham Pounds and Lucinda Lawrence, born 1861 in Perry County, Alabama and died 17 Sep 1879. Married 17 Sep 1879 in Chilton County, Alabama to Walter M. Lawrence.

B422. Joel Pound, second child and second son of John (V) Pound and Mary Walker, born 26 Oct 1777 in Edgefield County, South Carolina and died 2 Aug 1842 in Hancock County, Georgia. Buried in Hancock County, Georgia. Married 17 Jan 1810 in Hancock County, Georgia to Elvah (Nelvy) Blount, daughter of Isaac Blount and Sallie ---. born 13 Aug 1792 in Hancock County, Georgia, and died 19 Aug 1871 in Hancock County, Georgia. Buried in Hancock County, Georgia. Joel Pound and Elvah Blount had issue, which was the seventh generation in America:

B4221. James William Pound, first child and first son of Joel Pound and Elvah Blount, born 3 May 1811 in Hancock County, Georgia and died 25 Sep 1889 at Shiloh, Talbot County, Georgia. Buried in Valley Grove Church cemetery, Talbot County, Georgia. Married 17 Jan 1832 in Talbot County, Georgia to Nancy Jestice Pickard, daughter of Micajah Pickard and Sarah Barksdale born 12 Nov 1812 in Hancock County, Georgia and died 25 Sep 1889 at Shiloh, Talbot County, Georgia. James Pound and Nancy Pickard had issue, which was the eighth generation in America:

B42211. Edwin Theophilus

Pound, first child and first son of James Pound and Nancy Pickard, born 2 Feb 1833 at Big Bethel Church, Hancock County, Georgia and died 24 Jun 1919 at Shellman, Randolph County, Georgia. Married 19 Apr 1855 in Pike County, Georgia to Elizabeth T. Bloodworth, daughter of Thomas Stokeley Bloodworth and Frances Caroline Maxey, born about 1839 at Unionville, Pike (now Lamar) County, Georgia. Edwin Pound and Elizabeth Bloodworth had issue, which was the ninth generation in America:

B422111. Isabella (Bell) Pound, first child and first daughter of Edwin Pound and Elizabeth Bloodworth, born 1857 in Pike County, Georgia. Married R.B. Goodwyn.

B422112. James Emmette Pound, second child and first son of Edwin Pound and Elizabeth Bloodworth, born about 1861 in Pike County, Georgia.

B422113. Jere Madison Pound, third child and second son of Edwin Pound and Elizabeth Bloodworth, born 23 Mar 1864 at Liberty Hill, Pike (now Lamar) County, Georgia and died 8 Feb 1935. In 1884 Jere Madison Pound of Barnesville was a second-honor graduate of the University of Georgia. The next year he came to Fort Valley to be principal of the Male and Female Institute. He married (1) Willie Ingram, the daughter of Dr. William Ingram Greene and the former Emily Plant. After the death of his wife, Professor Pound returned to Barnesville, where he became President of Gordon Institute, a position he held for many years. Professor Pound married secondly 12 Jul 1889 at Barnesville, Lamar County, Georgia to Ada Murphey, daughter of Erastus Jabes Murphey and Lavia Iva Merritt, born 12 Mar 1868 at Griffin, Spalding County, Georgia. She was one of the teachers at Gordon Institute, who graduated from Wesleyan College with second honor. Her parents were Erastus Jabes Murphey and his wife, Laura Ida, the daughter of Mickleberry and Jane (Brown) Merritt of Monroe County. Erastus J. Murphey left the senior class at Mercer to join the Confederate Army. He was a member of the Barnesville Blues, a local military company, and was wounded in the Battle of Murfreesboro. After the war was over, Mercer conferred an AB degree upon him. His wife, Laura Ida (Merritt) Murphey, attended Monroe Female College (later Tift College). The Congregational Methodist Church was organized in the parlor of the Mickleberry Merritt's home before the War Between the States. This house was still standing in 1972. After leaving Gordon, Professor Pound served as superintendent of the Bibb County Schools, President of East Florida Seminary, head of the department of psychology at Georgia College, State School Superintendent, president of Georgia State Teacher's College, and president of Valdosta State College until his resignation because of illness. In recognition of his prominence in the field of education, the University of Georgia in 1915 conferred on Dr. Pound the LLD Degree. Jere Pound and Ada Murphey had issue, which was the tenth generation in America:

B4221131. Willie Green Pound, first child and first daughter of Jere Pound and Ada Murphey, born at Barnesville, Lamar County, Georgia. Married William Russell Edwards, son of William Edwards and Maggie Houser. Willie Pound and William Edwards had issue, which was the eleventh generation in America:

B42211311. Maude Brown Edwards, first child and first daughter of Willie Pound and William Edwards, date and place of birth unknown. Married Rev. Robert Milton Green. Maude Edwards and Robert Green had issue, which was the twelth generation in America:

B422113111. Margaret Edwards Green, first child and first daughter of Maude Edwards and Robert Green, date and place of birth unknown.

B422113112. Laura Merritt Green, second child and second daughter of Maude Edwards and Robert Green, date and place of birth unknown.

B42211312. Ada Margaret Edwards, second child and second daughter of Willie Pound and William Edwards, date and place of birth unknown. Married Larry Colquitt Sweat. Ada Edwards and Larry Sweat had issue, which was the twelth generation in America:

B422113121. Larry Colquitt Sweat, Jr., first child and first son of Ada Edwards and Larry Sweat, date and place of birth unknown.

B422113122. Russell Edwards Sweat, second child and second son of Ada Edwards and Larry Sweat, date and place of birth unknown.

B42211313. William Russell Edwards, Jr., third child and first son of Willie Pound and William Edwards, date and place of birth unknown. Married Kathleen Crenshaw, born at Owensboro, Daviess County, Kentucky. William Edwards and Kathleen Crenshaw had issue, which was the twelth generation in America:

B422113131. Marianne Edwards, first child and first daughter of William Edwards and Kathleen Crenshaw, date and place of birth unknown.

B422113132. Patti Edwards, second child and second daughter of William Edwards and Kathleen Crenshaw, date and place of birth unknown.

B42211314. Patricia Edwards, fourth child and third daughter of Willie Pound and William Edwards, date and place of birth unknown.

B42211315. Jere Pound Edwards, fifth child and second son of Willie Pound and William Edwards, date and place of birth unknown.

B4221132. Murphey Pound, second child and first son of Jere Pound and Ada Murphey, born at Barnesville, Lamar County, Georgia and died in 1942. Married Eva Garrett Murphey. Murphey Pound and Eva Murphey had issue, which was the eleventh generation in America:

B42211321. Murphey Pound, Jr., first child and first son of Murphey Pound and Eva Murphey, date and place of birth unknown.

B42211322. Jere Madison Pound III, second child and second son of Murphey Pound and Eva Murphey, date and place of birth unknown.

B42211323. Eva Garrett Pound, third child and first daughter of Murphey Pound and Eva Murphey, date and place of birth unknown.

B4221133. Jere Madison Pound, Jr., third child and second son of Jere Pound and Ada Murphey, born 1895 at Barnesville, Lamar County, Georgia and died 7 May 1910 at Milledgeville, Baldwin County, Georgia. He was accidentally killed by a playmate at age 15 on Doctor Allen's plantation near Milledgeville.

B4221134. Merritt Bloodworth Pound, fourth child and third son of Jere Pound and Ada Murphey, born at Barnesville, Lamar County, Georgia. Married Marjory Carroll. Merritt Pound and Marjory Carroll had issue, which was the eleventh generation in America:

B42211341. Merritt Bloodworth Pound, Jr., first child and first son of Merritt Pound and Marjory Carroll, date and place of birth unknown. Married Lexie Withers.

B42211342. Marjorie Pound, second child and first daughter of Merritt Pound and Marjory Carroll, date and place of birth unknown.

B4221135. Ida Elizabeth Pound, fifth child and second daughter of Jere Pound and Ada Murphey, born at Macon, Bibb County, Georgia.

B4221136. Edwin Aldine Pound, sixth child and fourth son of Jere Pound and Ada Murphey, born at Milledgeville, Baldwin County, Georgia. Married Nan Garrett. Edwin Pound and Nan Garrett had issue, which was the eleventh generation in America:

B42211361. Edwin Aldine Pound III, first child and first son of Edwin Pound and Nan Garrett, date and place of birth unknown.

B42211362. Ida Elizabeth Pound, second child and first daughter of Edwin Pound and Nan Garrett, date and place of birth unknown. Married Hugh Paige.

B4221137. Lucy Floyd Pound, seventh child and third daughter of Jere Pound and Ada Murphey, born at Barnesville, Lamar County,

Georgia. Married Tryon K. Huggins. Lucy Pound and Tryon Huggins had issue, which was the eleventh generation in America:

B42211371. Tryon K. Huggins, Jr., first child and first son of Lucy Pound and Tryon Huggins, date and place of birth unknown.

B42211372. Jere Pound Huggins, second child and second son of Lucy Pound and Tryon Huggins, date and place of birth unknown.

B42211373. William Stokely Huggins, third child and third son of Lucy Pound and Tryon Huggins, date and place of birth unknown.

B4221138. William Stokely Pound, eighth child and fifth son of Jere Pound and Ada Murphey, born at Athens, Clarke County, Georgia. Married Jane Ellis. William Pound and Jane Ellis had issue, which was the eleventh generation in America:

B42211381. William Stokely Pound, Jr., first child and first son of William Pound and Jane Ellis, date and place of birth unknown.

B42211382. John (twin) Pound, second child and second son of William Pound and Jane Ellis, date and place of birth unknown.

B42211383. Edwin (twin) Pound, third child and third son of William Pound and Jane Ellis, date and place of birth unknown.

B422114. John Walter Pound, fourth child and third son of Edwin Pound and Elizabeth Bloodworth, born 26 Jul 1867 in Pike County, Georgia. Married Mary Lou Hodges.

B422115. Edwin Aldine Pound, fifth child and fourth son of Edwin Pound and Elizabeth Bloodworth, born 11 Sep 1870 in Pike County, Georgia. Married 26 Oct 1893 to Lucy Murphey. Married 14 Dec 1927 to Alma Norris.

B422116. Annie Pound, sixth child and second daughter of Edwin Pound and Elizabeth Bloodworth, born about 1876 in Pike County, Georgia. Married T.E. Arthur.

B42212. James Madison Pound, second

child and second son of James Pound and Nancy Pickard, born 10 Apr 1835 in Georgia. Married 27 Nov 1852 in Talbot County, Georgia to Mary Sarah Elizabeth Green. Married secondly 1 Jul 1858 in Upson County, Georgia to Mary Ann Ivey, born 1833 in Georgia. Married thirdly to Hortense Sherman. James Pound and Mary Green had issue, which was the ninth generation in America:

B422121. Emma J. Pound, first child and first daughter of James Pound and Mary Green, born 1854 in Upson County, Georgia.

B42212. James Madison Pound, second child and second son of James Pound and Nancy Pickard, born 10 Apr 1835 in Georgia. Married secondly 1 Jul 1858 in Upson County, Georgia to Mary Ann Ivey, born 1833 in Georgia. James Pound and Mary Ivey had issue, which was the ninth generation in America;

B422121. William L. Pound, first child and first son of James Pound and Mary Ivey, born about 1867 in Upson County, Georgia. Married Julia C. Atwater.

B422122. Virginia E. Pound, second child and first daughter of James Pound and Mary Ivey, born about 1870 in Upson County, Georgia.

B422123. Fannie E. Pound, third child and second daughter of James Pound and Mary Ivey, born about 1871 in Upson County, Georgia.

B422124. Emma J. Pound, fourth child and third daughter of James Pound and Mary Ivey, born about 1872 in Upson County, Georgia.

B422125. James E. Pound, fifth child and second son of James Pound and Mary Ivey, born about 1876 in Upson County, Georgia.

B42213. John Thomas Pound, third child and third son of James Pound and Nancy Pickard, born 26 Jul 1838 in Talbot County, Georgia and died 2 Jul 1862 at Richmond, Richmond County, Virginia. Buried at Richmond, National Cemetery, Virginia. John enlisted in the Confederate Army on 10 Sep 1861 and served as a private in Company K of the Georgia Infantry. He died at Chimborozo Hospital. Married 24 Dec 1857 in Meriwether County, Georgia to Rebecca H. Brown. Married 8 Nov 1860 to Louisa Maria Ellison, born 21 Oct 1839 in Talbot County, Georgia and died 10 Apr 1926 at

Woodland, Talbot County, Georgia. Buried at Sardis Methodist Church Cemetery, Talbot County, Georgia. John Pound and Louisa Ellison had issue, which was the ninth generation in America:

B422131. John James Pound, first child and first son of John Pound and Louisa Ellison, born 14 Aug 1861 at Woodland, Talbot County, Georgia and died 28 Dec 1920 at Woodland, Talbot County, Georgia. Buried at Woodland cemetery, Talbot County, Georgia. John Pound was a member of the Board of Education 1908-1918; Sunday school superintendent for 20 years; steward of Methodist Church 40 years, and a farmer. John James Pound was named John Ellison Pound at birth. His name was changed after the death of his father, John Thomas Pound. According to "The Offspring of John Pound", John James purchased the land from the estate of his grandfather, James Pound, and was a prosperous farmer in Talbot County. Married 10 Dec 1884 at Woodland, Talbot County, Georgia to Mary Alice Crawford, daughter of James Jefferson Crawford and Martha King, born 27 May 1866 in Harris County, Georgia and died 13 Jun 1938 at Woodland, Talbot County, Georgia. Buried at Woodland cemetery, Talbot County, Georgia. John Pound and Mary Crawford had issue, which was the tenth generation in America:

B4221311. James Jefferson Pound, first child and first son of John Pound and Mary Crawford, date and place of birth unknown. Married to Martha King.

B4221312. William Marvin Pound, second child and second son of John Pound and Mary Crawford, born 24 Sep 1885 in Talbot County, Georgia and died 23 Feb 1963 at Tallahassee, Leon County, Florida. Married 15 Feb 1902 in Talbot County, Georgia to Jennie Electra Allen, born 9 Oct 1887. William Pound and Jennie Allen had issue, which was the eleventh generation in America:

B42213121. James Aldene Pound, first child and first son of William Pound and Jennie Allen, born 8 Jan 1905. Married 16 Jul 1924 to Louise Henson. Married 5 Dec 1936 to Arlene Octmeyer. James Pound and Arlene Octmeyer had issue, which was the twelth generation in

America:

B422131211.
Patricia Ann Pound, first child and first daughter
of James Pound and Arlene Octmeyer, born 13 Jun
1941. Married 15 Jun 1963 at Washington, D.C. to
David Marshall Barry.

B4221313. Olin Crawford Pound,
Sr., third child and third son of John Pound and
Mary Crawford, born 29 Dec 1886 and died 22 Jun
1951. Olin Crawford Pound, Sr. was Vice-President
and Secretary-Treasurer of Eastman Cotton Mills in
Eastman, Georgia. Married 6 Feb 1913 to Lilly
Downs. Married 10 Sep 1927 to Lillian Sinclair
Bass, born 20 Dec 1907 and died 12 Oct 1938 at
Eastman, Dodge County, Georgia. Olin Pound and
Lilly Downs had issue, which was the eleventh
generation in America:

B42213131. Marion Crawford
Pound, first child and first son of Olin Pound and
Lilly Downs, born 19 Oct 1939 and died 5 Aug 1915.

B42213132. Josephine Leigh
Pound, second child and first daughter of Olin
Pound and Lilly Downs, born 16 Jun 1919. Married
Dec 1943 to E.F. O'Neill. Josephine Pound and
E.F. O'Neill had issue, which was the twelth
generation in America:

B422131321. Eddie O'Neill,
first child and first son of Josephine Pound and
E. F. O'Neill, born 23 Jan 1945.

B422131322. Debbie O'Neill,
second child and first daughter of Josephine Pound
and E.F. O'Neill, born 24 Nov 1948.

B4221313. Olin Crawford Pound,
Sr., third child and third son of John Pound and
Mary Crawford, born 29 Dec 1886 and died 22 Jun
1951. Married secondly 10 Sep 1927 to Lillian
Sinclair Bass, born 20 Dec 1907 and died 12 Oct
1938 in Eastman, Dodge County, Georgia. Olin
Pound and Lillian Bass had issue, which was the
eleventh generation in America:

B42213131. Olin Crawford
Pound, Jr., first child and and first son of Olin
Pound and Lillian Bass, born 10 Jan 1929. Married
15 Feb 1943 to Laura Jean Dillard. Olin Pound,
Jr. and Jean Dillard had issue, which was the
twelth generation in America:

B422131311. Mildred Sinclair Pound, first child and first daughter of Olin Pound, Jr. and Jean Dillard, born 31 Mar 1954.

B422131312. Olin Crawford Pound III, second child and first son of Olin Pound, Jr. and Jean Dillard, born 12 Jan 1956.

B422131313. Lawrence Dillard Pound, third child and second son of Olin Pound, Jr. and Jean Dillard, born 13 Aug 1960.

B4221314. Annie Lou Pound, fourth child and first daughter of John Pound and Mary Crawford, born 6 Oct 1888 in Georgia. Annie Lou Pound never married, and was a music teacher and Postmaster at Woodland, Talbot County, Georgia.

B4221315. Robert Ellison Pound, fifth child and fourth son of John Pound and Mary Crawford, born 4 Apr 1892. Married 24 Apr 1917 to Ruth Eunice Hilton, born at Charlotte, Mecklenburg County, North Carolina.

B4221316. Byron Griffith Pound, sixth child and fifth son of John Pound and Mary Crawford, born 1 Nov 1895 in Georgia. Married 28 Aug 1927 to Catherine Stewart, born at Carrollton, Carroll County, Georgia. Byron Pound and Catherine Stewart had issue, which was the eleventh generation in America:

B42213161. Mary Alice Pound, first child and first daughter of Byron Pound and Catherine Stewart, born 25 May 1928. Married 5 Jun 1955 to Walter R. McCannon. Mary Pound and Walter McCannon had issue, which was the twelth generation in America:

B422131611. Walter R. McCannon, Jr., first child and first son of Mary Pound and Walter McCannon, born 29 May 1956.

B42213162. Byron Griffith Pound, Jr., second child and first son of Byron Pound and Catherine Stewart, born 6 May 1934. Married Lois Landford.

B42213163. Montie Jane Pound, third child and second daughter of Byron Pound and Catherine Stewart, born 20 Aug 1936. Married 19 Nov 1956 to Robert Griffin. Montie Pound and Robert Griffin had issue, which was the

twelth generation in America:

B422131631. Catherine Elizabeth Griffin, first child and first daughter of Montie Pound and Robert Griffin, born 29 Jul 1957.

B422131632. Barbara Jane Griffin, second child and second daughter of Montie Pound and Robert Griffin, born 10 Sep 1961.

B4221317. Martha Thomas Pound, seventh child and second daughter of John Pound and Mary Crawford, born 7 Aug 1889 in Georgia and died 21 Jan 1902.

B4221318. James Alwin Pound, eighth child and sixth son of John Pound and Mary Crawford, born 19 Aug 1902 in The Valley, Talbot County, Georgia. Married 27 Jan 1927 at Woodland, Talbot County, Georgia to Annie Mildred Woodall. Married 16 Dec 1979 to Venice Langston Paschal. James Pound and Annie Woodall had issue, which was the eleventh generation in America:

B42213181. Martha Ann Pound, first child and first daughter of James Pound and Annie Woodall, born 20 Jan 1931. Married 19 Aug 1950 at Danville, Vermilion County, Illinois to William Marcus Nolan. Martha Pound and William Nolan had issue, which was the twelth generation in America:

B422131811. Anne Elizabeth Nolan, first child and first daughter of Martha Pound and William Nolan, born 31 Aug 1953 at Birmingham, Jefferson County, Alabama. Married 3 Aug 1975 at Findlay, Hancock County, Ohio to Roscoe E. Schlacter. Married 9 Jun 1984 to James Richard Michael.

B422131812. Marcia Pound Nolan, second child and second daughter of Martha Pound and William Nolan, born 23 Dec 1956 at Philadelphia, Philadelphia County, Pennsylvania.

B422131813. Carol Lynn Nolan, third child and third daughter of Martha Pound and William Nolan, born 21 Jun 1960 at Philadelphia, Philadelphia County, Pennsylvania. Married 4 Apr 1962 at Findlay, Ohio to William R. Perry. Married 17 Feb 1990 to Frederick William Drale.

B422131814. Mary Martha

Nolan, fourth child and fourth daughter of Martha Pound and William Nolan, born 4 Aug 1963 at Findlay, Ohio.

B4221382. Carolyn Woodall Pound, second child and second daughter of James Pound and Annie Woodall, born 4 Jan 1935. Married 25 Aug 1956 at Traverse City, Benzie County, Michigan to David Fletcher Gray. Carolyn Pound and David Gray had issue, which was the twelth generation in America:

B42213821. Lynn Anne Gray, first child and first daughter of Carolyn Pound and David Gray, born 29 May 1959 at Grand Rapids, Kent County, Michigan. Married 23 May 1987 at Grand Rapids, Kent County, Michigan to John Maclear Dorman.

B42213822. David James Gray, second child and first son of Carolyn Pound and David Gray, born 23 Aug 1962 at Grand Rapids, Michigan.

B42214. Joseph Gilbert Pound, fourth child and fourth son of James Pound and Nancy Pickard, born 7 Jan 1842 in Georgia and died 14 Jun 1925 at Molena, Georgia. Joseph served as a private in Company K, 27th Georgia Regiment, C.S.A; wounded at Fort Sumter, South Carolina November 13, 1863. Buried in Pike County, Georgia. Married Lourena W. Fox, born 31 Dec 1846 in Georgia and died 10 Jul 1938 at Molena, Pike County, Georgia. Buried in Pike County, Georgia. Joseph Pound and Lourena Fox had issue, which was the ninth generation in America:

B422141. Charles James Pound, first child and first son of Joseph Pound and Lourena Fox, born 7 Sep 1867 in Monroe County, Georgia and died 1931. Married Dec 1890 in Talbot County, Georgia to Gressie Baldwin, date and place of birth unknown, but she died in 1931.

B422142. Loula Lee Pound, second child and first daughter of Joseph Pound and Lourena Fox, born 7 Sep 1867 in Monroe County, Georgia and died 10 Nov 1929. Married 22 May 1890 in Georgia to Sutton Laben Hardy, born about 1863. Loula Pound and Sutton Hardy had issue, which was the tenth generation in America:

B4221421. Annie Ruth (twin)

Hardy, first child and first daughter of Loula Pound and Sutton Hardy, born and died 1895.

B4221422. Ruby Lou (twin), second child and second daughter of Loula Pound and Sutton Hardy, born and died 1895.

B4221423. Kathleen Hardy, third child and third daughter of Loula Pound and Sutton Hardy, date and place of birth unknown.

B4221424. Jannie Lee Hardy, fourth child and fourth daughter of Loula Pound and Sutton Hardy, born 24 Jan 1905.

B422143. Usula Bell Pound, third child and second daughter of Joseph Pound and Lourena Fox, born 22 May 1873 in Monroe County, Georgia and died 16 Jun 1914. Married Jun 1906 at Woodbury, Meriwether County, Georgia to Virgil B. Lovett. Usula Pound and Virgil Lovett had issue, which was the tenth generation in America:

B4221431. Marguarite Lovett, first child and first daughter of Usula Pound and Virgil Lovett, date and place of birth unknown. Married Harvey Portwood.

B4221432. Virgil B. Lovett, Jr., second child and first son of Usula Pound and Virgil Lovett, date and place of birth unknown.

B4221433. Warren Pound Lovett, third child and second son of Usula Pound and Virgil Lovett, date and place of birth unknown. Married Ethel Carpenter.

B422144. Mary Elizabeth Pound, fourth child and third daughter of Joseph Pound and Lourena Fox, born 15 Oct 1875 in Monroe County, Georgia and died Oct 1943 in Georgia. Married Apr 1900 to Andrew Burton Johnson, born about 1871. Mary Pound and Andrew Johnson had issue, which was the tenth generation in America:

B4221441. May Bell Johnson, first child and first daughter of Mary Pound and Andrew Johnson, date and place of birth unknown.

B4221442. Sarah Johnson, second child and second daughter of Mary Pound and Andrew Johnson, date and place of birth unknown.

B4221443. Mary Willie Johnson, third child and third daughter of Mary Pound and Andrew Johnson, date and place of birth unknown.

B4221444. Andrew Burton Johnson, Jr., fourth child and first son of Mary Pound and Andrew Johnson, date and place of birth unknown.

B4221445. Elizabeth Johnson, fifth child and fourth daughter of Mary Pound and Andrew Johnson, date and place of birth unknown.

B4221446. Jesse Lee Johnson, sixth child and second son of Mary Pound and Andrew Johnson, date and place of birth unknown.

B4221447. Margarite Johnson, seventh child and fifth daughter of Mary Pound and Andrew Johnson, date and place of birth unknown.

B4221448. Lena Johnson, eighth child and sixth daughter of Mary Pound and Andrew Johnson, date and place of birth unknown.

B422145. Maggie Mae Pound, fifth child and fourth daughter of Joseph Pound and Lourena Fox, born 26 Apr 1877 in Monroe County, Georgia and died 12 Jan 1943. Married George Pinkston Foreman. Maggie Pound and George Foreman had issue, which was the tenth generation in America:

B4221451. Madge Foreman, first child and first daughter of Maggie Pound and George Foreman, date and place of birth unknown. Married George Whitman.

B4221452. Martha Foreman, second child and second daughter of Maggie Pound and George Foreman, date and place of birth unknown. Married in Winston-Salem, Forsyth County, North Carolina to J.T. Joiner, Jr.

B4221453. George Pinkston Foreman, Jr., third child and first son of Maggie Pound and George Foreman, date and place of birth unknown. Married in Monroe, Ouachita Parish, Louisiana to Unice Dawson.

B422146. Jesse Robert Cureton Pound, sixth child and second son of Joseph Pound and Lourena Fox, born 12 Aug 1878 in Monroe County, Georgia and died 10 Mar 1927 in Taylor County, Georgia. Married Oct 1909 in Taylor County, Georgia to Frances Heath. Jesse Pound and Frances Heath had issue, which was the tenth generation in America:

B4221461. John Heath Pound, first child and first son of Jesse Pound and Frances

Heath, date and place of birth unknown.

B4221462. Charles Robert Pound, second child and second son of Jesse Pound and Frances Heath, date and place of birth unknown. Married in Statesboro, Bullock County, Georgia to Evalyn Matthews.

B4221463. Annie Ruth Pound, third child and first daughter of Jesse Pound and Frances Heath, date and place of birth unknown. Married at Swainsboro, Emanuel County, Georgia to David Bailey.

B422147. William Carrosee Pound, seventh child and third son of Joseph Pound and Lourena Fox, born 15 Apr 1880 in Monroe County, Georgia. Married Dec 1902 to Essie Powell, born about 1881. William Pound and Essie Powell had issue, which was the tenth generation in America:

B4221471. Eloise Pound, first child and first daughter of William Pound and Essie Powell, date and place of birth unknown.

B4221472. Elizabeth Pound, second child and second daughter of William Pound and Essie Powell, date and place of birth unknown.

B4221473. Robert Tooms Pound, third child and first son of William Pound and Essie Powell, date and place of birth unknown.

B4221474. Emmie Pound, fourth child and third daughter of William Pound and Essie Powell, date and place of birth unknown.

B4221475. Edwina Pound, fifth child and fourth daughter of William Pound and Essie Powell, date and place of birth unknown.

B4221476. Joseph Pound, sixth child and second son of William Pound and Essie Powell, date and place of birth unknown.

B422148. Janie Octavia Pound, eighth child and fifth daughter of Joseph Pound and Lourena Fox, born 24 May 1887 at Thomaston, Upson County, Georgia. Married 27 Dec 1912 at Molena, Pike County, Georgia to Frank Lester Adams, son of Lafayette Alonzo Adams and Mary Catherine Payne, born 1 Nov 1879 at Cleveland, White County, Georgia and died in 1950 at Zebulon, Pike County, Georgia. Janie Pound and Frank Adams had issue, which was the tenth generation in America:

B4221481. Frank Lester Adams, Jr.,

first child and first son of Janie Pound and Frank Adams, born 23 Apr 1914, born at Zebulon, Pike County, Georgia. Married 19 Apr 1941 to Esther Fernandez, born at Tampa, Hillsborough County, Florida. Frank Adams and Esther Fernandez had issue, which was the eleventh generation in America:

B42214811. Frank Lester Adams III, first child and first son of Frank Adams and Esther Fernandez, born 23 Oct 1945.

B42214812. Barbara Leigh Adams, second child and first daughter of Frank Adams and Esther Fernandez, born 19 May 1951, at Orlando, Orange County, Florida. Married Jerry Nickerson Barbara Adams and Jerry Nickerson had issue, which was the twelth generation in America:

B422148121. Jennifer Leigh, first child and first daughter of Barbara Adams and Jerry Nickerson, born 24 Jan 1960 at Tampa, Hillsborough County, Florida. Jennifer Leigh was raised by Frank & Esther Adams, and her last name was changed to Adams.

B4221482. Charles Lee Adams, second child and second son of Janie Pound and Frank Adams, born 25 Aug 1918 and died 7 Aug 1943. Married 2 Aug 1941 to Hazel Perkins. Charles Adams died in the U.S. Air Force and this marriage had no children.

B4221483. Mary Lou Adams, third child and first daughter of Janie Pound and Frank Adams, born 19 Jan 1920. Married 7 Jun 1940 to Linton Franklin Lee. Mary Adams and Linton Lee has issue, which was the tenth generation in America:

B42214831. Charles Adams Lee, first child and first son of Mary Adams and Linton Lee, born 1944.

B42214832. Brownie Elizabeth Lee, second child and first daughter of Mary Adams and Linton Lee, born 1945.

B42215. Sarah Frances Pound, fifth child and first daughter of James Pound and Nancy Pickard, born 1845 in Georgia.

B42216. Robert Barksdale Pound, sixth child and fifth son of James Pound and Nancy Pickard, born 19 Aug 1847 in Georgia.

B42217. William Matthew Pound, seventh child and sixth son of James Pound and Nancy Pickard, born 26 Feb 1849 in Georgia and died 1 Jun 1919. Married Susan Scott, born 26 Dec 1849 and died 1 Jun 1918. William Pound and Susan Scott had issue, which was the ninth generation in America:

B422171. James Scott Pound, first child and first son of William Pound and Susan Scott, born 18 Feb 1875 in Georgia. Married about 1898 to Agnes Moore. James Pound and Agnes Moore had issue, which was the tenth generation in America:

B4221711. Fred Pound, first child and first son of James Pound and Agnes Moore, born 4 May 1899.

B4221712. Jack Pound, second child and second son of James Pound and Agnes Moore, born 4 Jul 1901.

B4221713. Nell Pound, third child and first daughter of James Pound and Agnes Moore, date and place of birth unknown.

B4221714. Emily Pound, fourth child and second daughter of James Pound and Agnes Moore, date and place of birth unknown.

B4221715. Florence Pound, fifth child and third daughter of James Pound and Agnes Moore, date and place of birth unknown.

B422172. Lila Kate Pound, second child and first daughter of William Pound and Susan Scott, born 10 Aug 1877 in Georgia. Married 19 Jun 1895 in Georgia to Homer Jesse Benson. Lila Pound and Homer Benson had issue, which was the tenth generation in America:

B4221721. Mabel Claire Benson, first child and first daughter of Lila Pound and Homer Benson, born and died 30 May 1896.

B4221722. Homer Stanley Benson, second child and first son of Lila Pound and Homer Benson, born 26 Jun 1897. Married 26 Feb 1923 to Lou Ellen Bragg. Homer Benson and Lou Bragg had issue, which was the eleventh generation in America:

B42217221. Betty Fay Benson, first child and first daughter of Homer Benson and Lou Bragg, born 19 Jun 1924.

B42217222. Homer Stanley Benson, Jr., second child and first son of Homer

Benson and Lou Bragg, born 29 Dec 1925.

B42217223. Marion Garland Benson, third child and second son of Homer Benson and Lou Bragg, born 30 Apr 1906. Married 1 Aug 1926 to Delouise Shealey.

B4221723. Susie Myrtice Benson, third child and second daughter of Lila Pound and Homer Benson, born 18 Mar 1900.

B4221724. Eugene Adolphis Benson, fourth child and second son of Lila Pound and Homer Benson, born 21 Nov 1903.

B4221725. Joseph Paul Benson, fifth child and third son of Lila Pound and Homer Benson, born 19 Nov 1912.

B422173. Albert Marvin Pound, third child and second son of William Pound and Susan Scott, born about 1879 in Georgia. Married 8 Aug 1908 to Emma Mae Galagher. Albert Pound and Emma Galagher had issue, which was the tenth generation in America:

B4221731. Geraldine Pound, first child and first daughter of Albert Pound and Emma Galagher, born Oct 1910.

B4221732. Albert Marvin Pound, Jr., second child and first son of Albert Pound and Emma Galagher, born 30 Oct 1912.

B422174. Alice Susie Pound, fourth child and second daughter of William Pound and Susan Scott, born about 1881 in Georgia. Married 24 Dec 1898 in Georgia to Wade Hampton Graves, born about 1877. Alice Pound and Wade Graves had issue, which was the tenth generation in America:

B4221741. Jannie Graves, first child and first daughter of Alice Pound and Wade Graves, born 26 Feb 1900.

B4221742. Doris Graves (twin), second child and second daughter of Alice Pound and Wade Graves, born Aug 1903.

B4221743. Joe Bailey Graves (twin), third child and first son of Alice Pound and Wade Graves, born Aug 1903.

B4221744. Gladys Graves, fourth child and third daughter of Alice Pound and Wade Graves, date and place of birth unknown.

B422175. Clira Mae Pound, fifth child and third daughter of William Pound and Susan

Scott, born 17 Apr 1884 in Georgia. Married 1900 in Georgia to Rell Jackson Spiller, born about 1880. Clira Pound and Rell Spiller had issue, which was the tenth generation in America:

B4221751. Marguarette Spiller, first child and first daughter of Clira Pound and Rell Spiller, born 18 Nov 1903. Married 20 Sep 1922 to Johnny Suggs. Marguarette Spiller and Johnny Suggs had issue, which was the eleventh generation in America:

B42217511. Louise Mae Suggs, first child and first daughter of Marguarette Spiller and Johnny Suggs, born 7 Sep 1923.

B42217512. Rell Jackson Suggs, second child and first son of Marguarette Spiller and Johnny Suggs, born 29 Dec 1925.

B422176. William Fred Pound, sixth child and third son of William Pound and Susan Scott, born 21 Oct 1887 in Georgia and died 9 Oct 1888 in Georgia.

B422177. Gail Pound, seventh child and fourth daughter of William Pound and Susan Scott, born and died 22 Jan 1902 in Georgia.

B42218. Mary Ann Missouri Pound, eighth child and second daughter of James Pound and Nancy Pickard, date and birth place unknown, but she died in infancy.

B42219. Mary Elva Pound, ninth child and third daughter of James Pound and Nancy Pickard, born 1857 in Georgia. Married Jonathan Rouse, born 1854 in Georgia. Mary Pound and Jonathan Rouse had issue, which was the ninth generation in America:

B422191. Claude Rouse, first child and first son of Mary Pound and Jonathan Rouse, born about 1877 in Georgia.

B422192. Jimmie Rouse, second child and second son of Mary Pound and Jonathan Rouse, born about 1878 in Georgia.

B422193. Eva Rouse, third child and first daughter of Mary Pound and Jonathan Rouse, born about 1880 in Georgia.

B4222. Elijah Pound, second child and second son of Joel Pound and Elvah Blount, born 14 Oct 1812 in Hancock County, Georgia, and died 25 Nov 1812.

B4223. Sarah (Sallie) Pound, third child and

first daughter of Joel Pound and Elvah Blount, born 10 Oct 1813 in Hancock County, Georgia. Married 6 Dec 1838 in Hancock County, Georgia to John Reynolds, born about 1804 and died 20 Dec 1860. Sarah Pound and John Reynolds are mentioned several times in the history of Hancock County, Georgia. They were members of Hored Church near Mayfield. Sarah Pound and John Reynolds had issue, which was the eighth generation in America:

B42231. Joel Pound Reynolds, first child and first son of Sarah Pound and John Reynolds, born 1 Nov 1846 and died 28 Sep 1928. Joel was in the War Between the States and was a much respected citizen of Hancock County, Georgia. Buried at Hored Church cemetery, Hancock County, Georgia. Married Amanda Elizabeth Allen.

B42232. Jesse Mercer Reynolds, second child and and second son of Sarah Pound and John Reynolds, born 18 May 1848 and died 28 Apr 1903. Married Martha Cassandra Allen, born 23 Feb 1854 and died 19 May 1903. Jesse Reynolds and Martha Allen had issue, which was the ninth generation in America:

B422321. Henry Cooper Reynolds, first child and first son of Jesse Reynolds and Martha Allen, date and place of birth unknown. Married Carrie Humphreys.

B422322. Arthur Lester Reynolds, second child and second son of Jesse Reynolds and Martha Allen, date and place of birth unknown. Married Mattilu Yarbrough.

B422323. Herbert Ivey Reynolds, third child and third son of Jesse Reynolds and Martha Allen, date and place of birth unknown.

B422324. Cecil Wesley Reynolds, fourth child and fourth son of Jesse Reynolds and Martha Allen, date and place of birth unknown.

B422325. Elizabeth Gurtrude Reynolds, fifth child and first daughter of Jesse Reynolds and Martha Allen, date and place of birth unknown. Married Thomas M. Cheatham.

B422326. Clarence Franklin Reynolds, sixth child and fifth son of Jesse Reynolds and Martha Allen, date and place of birth unknown. Married Lillie Louise Kendrick.

B422327. Pearl Mable Reynolds, seventh

child and second daughter of Jesse Reynolds and Martha Allen, date and place of birth unknown. Married Milton Hudson.

B422328. Ruth Mae Reynolds, eighth child and third daughter of Jesse Reynolds and Martha Allen, date and place of birth unknown. Married Benjamin H. Clark.

B422329. Ralph Waldo Reynolds, ninth child and sixth son of Jesse Reynolds and Martha Allen, date and place of birth unknown. Married Katherine Meighari.

B42233. Sarah Frances Reynolds, third child and first daughter of Sarah Pound and John Reynolds, date and place of birth unknown. Married William James Brantley.

B42234. Martha Reynolds, fourth child and second daughter of Sarah Pound and John Reynolds, date and place of birth unknown. Married Julius Jackson.

B42235. William Reynolds, fifth child and third son of Sarah Pound and John Reynolds, date and place of birth unknown. Married Emily Howell.

B42236. Elizabeth Reynolds, sixth child and third daughter of Sarah Pound and John Reynolds, date and place of birth unknown. Married Billie Brantly.

B42237. David Daniel Reynolds, seventh child and fourth son of Sarah Pound and John Reynolds, date and place of birth unknown.

B42238. Henry Burt Reynolds, eighth child and fifth son of Sarah Pound and John Reynolds, date and place of birth unknown.

B4224. Mathew Pound, fourth child and third son of Joel Pound and Elvah Blount, born 11 Feb 1816 in Hancock County, Georgia. Married 30 Nov 1837 in Hancock County, Georgia to Sarah Reeves. Mathew Pound and Sarah Reeves had issue, which was the eighth generation in America:

B42241. James Thomas Pound, first child and first son of Mathew Pound and Sarah Reeves, born 1838 in Georgia. Married Nan ---. James Pound and Nan --- had issue, which was the ninth generation in America:

B422411. Frank M. Pound, first child and first son of James Pound and Nan ---, date and place of birth unknown. Married Lee ---.

B422412. Thomas J. Pound, second child and second son of James Pound and Nan ---, born Jul 1875 in Texas. Married Rhonda V. ---, born Dec 1876 in Georgia. Thomas Pound and Rhonda --- had issue, which was the tenth generation in America:

B4224121. Sarah C. Pound, first child and first daughter of Thomas Pound and Rhonda ---, born Jan 1896 in Texas.

B4224122. Arthur T. Pound, second child and first son of Thomas Pound and Rhonda -, born May 1897 in Texas.

B4224123. Ada E. Pound, third child and second daughter of Thomas Pound and Rhonda ---, born Nov 1898 in Texas.

B4224124. Claud W. Pound, fourth child and second son of Thomas Pound and Rhonda ---, born May 1900 in Texas.

B422413. Jennie Pound, third child and first daughter of James Pound and Nan ---, born 1872 in Texas.

B422414. Ida Pound, fourth child and second daughter of James Pound and Nan ---, born 1874 in Texas.

B422415. Willis W. Pound, fifth child and third son of James Pound and Nan ---, born Oct 1876 in Texas. Married Nora A. Butram.

B422416. Nora Pound, sixth child and third daughter of James Pound and Nan ---, born Feb 1881 in Texas.

B42242. Eliza Pound, second child and first daughter of Mathew Pound and Sarah Reeves, born 1840 in Georgia.

B42243. Sidney P. Pound, third child and second son of Mathew Pound and Sarah Reeves, born 1842 in Georgia.

B42244. Ellen Pound, fourth child and second daughter of Mathew Pound and Sarah Reeves, born 1844 in Georgia.

B42245. Julia Pound, fifth child and third daughter of Mathew Pound and Sarah Reeves, born 1846 in Georgia.

B42246. John J. Pound, sixth child and third son of Mathew Pound and Sarah Reeves, born 1848 in Georgia. Married Mary Alice Crawford, born 1848 in Georgia. John Pound and Mary Crawford had issue, which was the ninth generation in America:

B422461. Thomas J. Pound, first child and first son of John Pound and Mary Crawford, born 1873 in Texas.

B422462. Mary L. Pound, second child and first daughter of John Pound and Mary Crawford, born 1874 in Texas.

B422463. Dick J. Pound, third child and second son of John Pound and Mary Crawford, born Feb 1878 in Texas.

B422464. Sallie B. Pound, fourth child and second daughter of John Pound and Mary Crawford, born Jan 1880 in Texas.

B422465. James Pound, fifth child and third son of John Pound and Mary Crawford, born Mar 1882 in Texas.

B422466. Vallie Pound, sixth child and third daughter of John Pound and Mary Crawford, born Jun 1884 in Texas.

B422467. Nannie (twin) Pound, seventh child and fourth daughter of John Pound and Mary Crawford, born Jul 1886 in Texas.

B422468. Annie (twin) Pound, eighth child and fifth daughter of John Pound and Mary Crawford, born Jul 1886 in Texas.

B422469. Alma Pound, ninth child and sixth daughter of John Pound and Mary Crawford, born Sep 1888 in Texas.

B4224610. Robert Ellison Pound, tenth child and fourth son of James Pound and Mary Crawford, born Apr 1891 in Texas. Married 24 Apr 1917 to Ruth Eunice Hilton, born Charlotte, Mecklenburg County, North Carolina. Married secondly 7 Jul 1921 to Marie Blandford Cook.

B4225. David Pound, fifth child and fourth son of Joel Pound and Elvah Blount, born 9 May 1818 in Hancock County, Georgia and died 9 May 1880. Buried in Union Church cemetery, Washington County, Georgia. Married 30 May 1839 in Hancock County, Georgia to Mary A.L. Culver, born 1820 in Georgia. David Pound and Mary Culver had issue, which was the eighth generation in America:

B42251. Joel Augustus Pound, first child and first son of David Pound and Mary Culver, born about 1840 in Hancock County, Georgia and died 20 Jun 1864 at Fort Delaware, Delaware. Joel was in

Mississippi on 10 May 1861, where he enlisted in Company E 11th Regular Mississippi Infantry. He was in Richmond, Virginia when his enlistment expired. He had met up with "home town boys" so transferred to Company B 59th Regular Georgia Volunteer Infantry 22 Jan 1864. He died of inflammation of the lungs at Ft. Delaware, Delaware 20 Jun 1864. He is buried on the Jersey shore.

B42252. Edwin Franklin Pound, second child and second son of David Pound and Mary Culver, born 2 Jul 1845 in Hancock County, Georgia and died 18 Oct 1906. Buried at Union Church cemetery, Washington County, Georgia. Married about 1863 in Georgia to Mary Elizabeth Cook, born 22 Dec 1845 and died 21 Jan 1930. Buried at Union Church cemetery, Washington County, Georgia. Edwin Pound and Mary Cook had issue, which was the ninth generation in America:

B422521. Mary Pound, first child and first daughter of Edwin Pound and Mary Cook, born 1864 in Hancock County, Georgia.

B422522. Abbie Pound, second child and second daughter of Edwin Pound and Mary Cook, born 1867 in Hancock County, Georgia. Married William Jordan.

B422523. Frank Pound, third child and first son of Edwin Pound and Mary Cook, born 13 May 1869 in Hancock County, Georgia and died 14 Feb 1897 at Warthen, Washington County, Georgia. Buried at Union Church cemetery, Washington County, Georgia. Married Mary (Mollie) Etta Mayo, born 11 Apr 1871 and died 10 Feb 1892. Frank Pound and Mary Mayo had issue, which was the tenth generation in America:

B4225231. Eddie Mae Pound, first child and first daughter of Frank Pound and Mary Mayo, born 15 Mar 1892. Married 26 Jul 1908 to Charles G. Claxton. Married secondly to Henry J. Claxton.

B422524. Varilla Pound, fourth child and third daughter of Edwin Pound and Mary Cook, born 1872 in Hancock County, Georgia. Married --- Jordan. Married secondly --- Jackson.

B422525. Lula Pound, fifth child and fourth daughter of Edwin Pound and Mary Cook, born 20 Nov 1874 in Hancock County, Georgia and died 24 Nov

1874. Buried at Union Church cemetery, Washington County, Georgia.

B422526. Doria Pound, sixth child and fifth daughter of Edwin Pound and Mary Cook, born 1875 in Hancock County, Georgia.

B422527. Maude Pound, seventh child and fifth daughter of Edwin Pound and Mary Cook, born 1878 in Hancock County, Georgia. Married --- Hitchcock.

B422528. Rosa Lee Pound, eighth child and sixth daughter of Edwin Pound and Mary Cook, born 4 Nov 1884 in Hancock County, Georgia and died 1885.

B422529. Docia Pound, ninth child and seventh daughter of Edwin Pound and Mary Cook, born 12 Jul 1887 in Hancock County, Georgia and died 15 Aug 1942. Married J. Bennett Davis.

B42253. Eliza Pounds, third child and first daughter of David Pound and Mary Culver, born 1847 in Hancock County, Georgia.

B42254. Emiline Pound, fourth child and second daughter of David Pound and Mary Culver, born 1849 in Hancock County, Georgia and died 1920. Married Jacob J. Garner.

B42255. Catherine L. Pound, fifth child and third daughter of David Pound and Mary Culver, born 1850 in Hancock County, Georgia. Married 4 Apr 1872 to John (Jonathan) Smith.

B42256. Mary Susan (Susie) Pound, sixth child and fourth daughter of David Pound and Mary Culver, born 1854 in Hancock County, Georgia. Married J.G. Morris.

B42257. James Madison (Mat) Pound, seventh child and third son of David Pound and Mary Culver, born 11 Jan 1852 in Hancock County, Georgia and died 8 Oct 1920. Married Ella F. Hood, born 4 Mar 1858 and died 21 Jan 1884. Buried at Union Church cemetery, Washington County, Georgia. Married secondly to Mary Ruskin. Married thirdly to Julia Elizabeth Hood, born 1856 and died 1917. James Pound and Ella Hood had issue, which was the ninth generation in America:

B422571. Oscar H. Pound, first child and first son of James Pound and Ella Hood, born 6 Nov 1880 and died 26 Nov 1880.

B422572. Annie Lillian Pound, second

child and first daughter of James Pound and Ella Hood, born 2 Jan 1882 and died 24 Jun 1897.

B422573. Joel Fernanda Francis Pound, third child and second son of James Pound and Ella Hood, born 2 Jan 1884 and died 7 May 1884. Buried at Union Church cemetery, Washington County, Georgia.

B422574. Linsey Simon David Pound, fourth child and third son of James Pound and Ella Hood, born 24 Jan 1886 and died 6 Jul 1886. Buried at Union Church cemetery, Washington County, Georgia.

B422575. Eva Estella Pound, fifth child and second daughter of James Pound and Ella Hood, born 5 Oct 1889 and died 13 Dec 1972.

B422576. Marvin Gilbert Pound, sixth child and fourth son of James Pound and Ella Hood, born 17 Feb 1892. Married Camille Berry.

B42258. Charles D. Pound, eighth child and fourth son of David Pound and Mary Culver, born about 1858.

B42259. Susie Pound, ninth child and third daughter of David Pound and Mary Culver, date and place of birth unknown. Married J.G. Morris.

B4226. Jesse Pound, sixth child and fifth son of Joel Pound and Elvah Blount, born 7 Sep 1820 in Hancock County, Georgia. Married 1842 in Washington County, Georgia to Mary Tennille, born 1825 in Georgia. Jesse Pound was Sheriff of Washington County for a time about 1870 and owned land there, but left no will when he died. Jesse Pound and Mary Tennille had issue, which was the seventh generation in America:

B42261. Robert Thomas Pound, first child and first son of Jesse Pound and Mary Tennille, born 1 May 1844 in Washington County, Georgia and died 8 Oct 1889 at Sandersville, Washington County, Georgia. Buried at Warthen, Sisters Church cemetery, Georgia. Robert enlisted in the Civil War and became a 1st Corp. Captain at age of 18 in Company H, 49th Georgia Regiment at Sandersville, Washington County for 3 years. He was discharged at Camp Grigg, Fredericksburg, Virginia 31 Mar 1863. His physical description said his eyes were hazel, hair black, complexion fair, 6 feet tall. Married Fannie V. Sheppard, born 30 May 1844 in

287

Georgia and died 21 Apr 1908 in Washington County, Georgia. Buried at Warthen, Sisters Church cemetery, Georgia. Robert Pound and Fannie Sheppard had issue, which was the ninth generation in America:

B422611. Mattie Pound, first child and first daughter of Robert Pound and Fannie Sheppard, born 29 Jan 1869 in Washington County, Georgia and died 27 Jul 1923 at Sandersville, Washington County, Georgia. Married --- Peterson.

B422612. Roger E. Pound, second child and first son of Robert Pound and Fannie Sheppard, born 28 May 1871 in Washington County, Georgia and died 20 Aug 1892 in Washington County, Georgia.

B422613. Laura Pound, third child and second daughter of Robert Pound and Fannie Sheppard, date and place of birth unknown. Married --- Walden

B422614. Earnest T. Pound, fourth child and second son of Robert Pound and Fannie Sheppard, born 30 Nov 1876 in Georgia and died 27 Aug 1911 in Georgia. Buried at Sandersville, Sisters Church cemetery, Georgia. Married Bulah Trice, born Dec 1881. Earnest Pound and Bulah Trice had issue, which was the tenth generation in America:

B4226141. Louise Pound, first child and first daughter of Earnest Pound and Bulah Trice, born and died 22 Aug 1906 in Washington County, Georgia. Buried at Sandersville, Sisters Church cemetery, Georgia.

B4226142. Annie Bell Pound, second child and second daughter of Earnest Pound and Bulah Trice, born 8 Oct 1907 and died 5 Jan 1908. Buried at Sandersville, Sisters Church cemetery, Georgia.

B422615. Annie Belle Pound, fifth child and third daughter of Robert Pound and Fannie Sheppard, born 14 Nov 1877 in Washington County, Georgia and died 26 Sep 1905 in Washington County, Georgia. Buried at Warthen, Sisters Church cemetery, Georgia. Married Gordon T. Knight.

B422616. Albert S. Pound, sixth child and third son of Robert Pound and Fannie Sheppard, born Oct 1881 in Georgia.

B42262. Elizabeth G. Pound, second child and

first daughter of Jesse Pound and Mary Tennille, born about 1845 in Washington County, Georgia.

B42263. Harris B. Pound, third child and second son of Jesse Pound and Mary Tennille, born about 1848 in Washington County, Georgia. Married about 1870 in Georgia to Elizabeth S. ---, born 1849 in Georgia.

B422631. Balu Pound, first child and first daughter of Harris Pound and Elizabeth ---, born 1871 in Washington County, Georgia.

B422632. Mary L. Pound, second child and second daughter of Harris Pound and Elizabeth ---, born 1879 in Washington County, Georgia.

B42264. Martha R. Pound, fourth child and second daughter of Jesse Pound and Mary Tennille, born about 1850 in Georgia. Married --- Massey. Martha Pound and --- Massey had issue, which was the ninth generation in America:

B422641. Jesse P. Massey, first child and first son of Martha Pound and --- Massey, born about 1862.

B422642. John R. Massey, second child and second son of Martha Pound and --- Massey, date and place of birth unknown.

B42265. John R. Pound, fifth child and third son of Jesse Pound and Mary Tennille, born about 1860 in Georgia.

B42266. Jesse P. Pound, sixth child and fourth son of Jesse Pound and Mary Tennille, born about 1862 in Georgia. Married Minerva ---, born about 1860 in Georgia.

B422661. Tella Pound, first child and first daughter of Jesse Pound and Minerva ---, born 1876 in Hancock County, Georgia.

B42267. Martha (Mattie) Pound, seventh child and third daughter of Jesse Pound and Mary Tennille, born 29 Jan 1869 in Georgia and died 27 Jul 1923 in Washington County, Georgia. Buried at Sandersville, Sisters Church cemetery, Georgia. Married Lorenzo Dow Peterson, born 28 Sep 1865 and died 15 Mar 1935 in Washington County, Georgia. Buried at Sandersville, Sisters Church cemetery, Georgia. Martha Pound and Lorenzo Peterson had issue, which was the ninth generation in America:

B422671. Warren Wallace Peterson, first child and first son of Martha Pound and Lorenzo

Peterson, born 9 Sep 1895 and died 2 Nov 1895.

B422672. Nettie Mae Peterson, second child and first daughter of Martha Pound and Lorenzo Peterson, born 29 Sep 1897 in Georgia and died 5 Jun 1950 in Washington County, Georgia. Buried at Sandersville, Sisters Church cemetery, Georgia. Married Earnest Henderson, date and place of birth unknown, but died in Washington County, Georgia. Buried at Sandersville, Sisters Church cemetery, Georgia.

B422673. Maud Lena Peterson, third child and second daughter of Martha Pound and Lorenzo Peterson, born 16 Jan 1899 and died 16 Aug 1899.

B422674. Rubie Salome Peterson, fourth child and third daughter of Martha Pound and Lorenzo Peterson, born 26 May 1900 and died 16 Dec 1904.

B422675. Leslie Edward (twin) Peterson, fifth child and second son of Martha Pound and Lorenzo Peterson, born 16 Jan 1904 and died 16 Dec 1904.

B422676. Lester Dow (twin) Peterson, sixth child and third son of Martha Pound and Lorenzo Peterson, born 16 Jan 1904 and died 15 Aug 1909.

B42268. STI Pound, eighth child and fifth son of Jesse Pound and Mary Tennille, stillborn and date of birth or death unknown.

B4227. Mary Pound, seventh child and second daughter of Joel Pound and Elvah Blount, born 2 Jun 1822 in Hancock County, Georgia and died 15 Jun 1822 in Hancock County, Georgia.

B4228. John Pound, eighth child and sixth son of Joel Pound and Elvah Blount, born 7 Jul 1823 in Hancock County, Georgia. Married Mar 1846 in Hancock County, Georgia to Mary Ann (Millie) Ellis, daughter of --- Ellis and --- Ransom, born 1828 in Georgia. John Pound and Mary Ellis had issue, which was the eighth generation in America:

B42281. Martha J. (Mary) Pound, first child and first daughter of John Pound and Mary Ellis, born about 1848 in Georgia.

B42282. Julie Pound, second child and second daughter of John Pound and Mary Ellis, born about 1854.

B42283. John Thomas Pound, third child and first son of John Pound and Mary Ellis, born 31 Aug 1862 in Hancock County, Georgia and died 5 Apr 1943 in Georgia. Buried at Union Church cemetery, Washington County, Georgia. Married Mary Frances Reynolds, born 24 Jun 1866 and died 10 Feb 1938 in Georgia. Buried at Union Church cemetery, Washington County, Georgia. John Pound and Mary Reynolds had issue, which was the ninth generation in America:

B422831. Thomas Watson Pound, first child and first son of John Pound and Mary Reynolds, born 1882 and died 22 Apr 1900.

B422832. Lora Pound, second child and first daughter of John Pound and Mary Reynolds, born 22 Apr 1886 and died Oct 1886.

B422833. Jesse Burt Pound, third child and second son of John Pound and Mary Reynolds, born 25 Mar 1887 and died 10 Feb 1974. Married Sallie Mae Smith, born 27 Sep 1890 and died 11 Jun 1914. Married secondly Edna Miller.

B422834. Eddie James Pound, fourth child and third son of John Pound and Mary Reynolds, born 27 Jun 1888 and died 16 Oct 1946 at Warthen, Washington County, Georgia. Buried Union Church cemetery, Washington County, Georgia. Married Kate Osborne. Married secondly Annie McNeil.

B422835. Robert Lee Pound, fifth child and fourth son of John Pound and Mary Reynolds, born 1889 and died 21 May 1892.

B422836. Spurgeon Franklin Pound, sixth child and fifth son of John Pound and Mary Reynolds, born 13 Aug 1894. Married Vinna Mae Maddox. Married secondly 1 Jan 1912 at Sandersville, Washington County, Georgia to Willie Pearl Smith. Spurgeon Pound and Willie Smith had issue, which was the tenth generation in America:

B4228361. Willie Louise Pound, first child and first daughter of Spurgeon Pound and Willie Smith, born 21 Dec 1912 at Tennille, Washington County, Georgia.

B4228362. Vera Pound, second child and second daughter of Spurgeon Pound and Willie Smith, born 14 Nov 1929 at Milledgeville, Baldwin County, Georgia.

B422837. Annie Mae Pound, seventh child and second daughter of John Pound and Mary Reynolds, born 1896. Married Thomas Lane.

B422838. Rose Lee Pound, eighth child and third daughter of John Pound and Mary Reynolds, date and place of birth unknown.

B422839. Lena Bell Pound, ninth child and fourth daughter of John Pound and Mary Reynolds, date and place of birth unknown. Married J.B. Hughes.

B422840. Callie Laura Pound, tenth child and fifth daughter of John Pound and Mary Reynolds, born 1902. Married Lo Ennis.

B422841. Ernest Ellis Pound, eleventh child and sixth son of John Pound and Mary Reynolds, born 30 Mar 1905. Married Zimma Stevens.

B422842. Clarence Ennis Pounds, twelfth child and seventh son of John Pound and Mary Reynolds, born 9 Aug 1907 in Georgia and died 12 Sep 1943 at Warthen, Washington County, Georgia. Buried at Union Church cemetery, Washington County, Georgia. Married Louise Prince.

B42284. Jacob Pound, fourth child and second son of John Pound and Martha Ellis, date and place of birth unknown.

B42285. Joel Levin Pound, fifth child and third son of John Pound and Martha Ellis, born about 1860 in Hancock County, Georgia and died about 1936. Married 31 Dec 1875 at Devereux, Hancock County, Georgia to Martha (Mattie) Elizabeth Blount, born 1862 in Georgia. Joel Pound and Martha Blount had issue, which was the ninth generation in America:

B422851. Willie Dallas Pound, first child and first son of Joel Pound and Martha Blount, born 21 Aug 1879 and died 27 Jan 1930. Married Callie Morris. Willie Pound and Callie Morris had issue, which was the tenth generation in America:

B4228511. Ras Berry Pound, first child and first son of Willie Pound and Callie Morris, born 28 Dec 1903 at Carrs Station, Hancock County, Georgia.

B4228512. Carlos Chancey Pound, second child and second son of Willie Pound and

Callie Morris, born 19 Oct 1905 in Hancock County, Georgia. Married Lora Lee A. Quinn. Carlos Pound and Lora Quinn had issue, which was the eleventh generation in America:

B42285121. Carlos Chancey Pound, first child and first son of Carlos Pound and Lora Quinn, born 11 Dec 1937 in Hancock County, Georgia.

B422852. Charlie Green Pound, second child and second son of Joel Pound and Martha Blount, born 26 Aug 1886 in Hancock County, Georgia.

B422853. Algie Pound, third child and first daughter of Joel Pound and Martha Blount, date and place of birth unknown.

B422854. Bell Pound, fourth child and second daughter of Joel Pound and Martha Blount, date and place of birth unknown.

B422855. Sallie Lee Pound, fifth child and third daughter of Joel Pound and Martha Blount, date and place of birth unknown.

B422856. Lillie Memphis Pound, sixth child and fourth daughter of Joel Pound and Martha Blount, born in 1850 in Gwinnett County, Georgia. Married 1850 in Gwinnett County, Georgia to Jesse James Hammond.

B42286. Jesse Pound, sixth child and fourth son of John Pound and Martha Ellis, born about 1858 and died 1893.

B42287. Mattie Pound, seventh child and third daughter of John Pound and Martha Ellis, date and place of birth unknown.

B42288. Lucy Pound, eighth child and fourth daughter of John Pound and Martha Ellis, date and place of birth unknown.

B4229. Isaac Newton Pound, ninth child and seventh son of Joel Pound and Elvah Blount, born 9 Mar 1826 in Hancock County, Georgia. Married 24 Jan 1847 in Hancock County, Georgia to Julia Frances Ellis, born about 1830. Isaac Pound and Julia Ellis had issue, which was the eighth generation in America:

B42291. Joel Ransom Pound, first child and first son of Isaac Pound and Julia Ellis, born 7 Oct 1848 in Hancock County, Georgia and died 1 Jun 1927. Buried at Union Church cemetery, Washington

County, Georgia. Married Nancy Jane Turner, born 6 May 1855 and died 12 Jun 1924 at Warthen, Washington County, Georgia. Buried at Union Church cemetery, Washington County, Georgia. Joel Pound and Nancy Turner had issue, which was the ninth generation in America:

B422911. Buena B. Pound, first child and first daughter of Joel Pound and Nancy Turner, born about 1874.

B422912. Alexandra Pound, second child and second daughter of Joel Poumd and Nancy Turner, born about 1876.

B422913. Lula E. Pound, third child and third daughter of Joel Pound and Nancy Turner, born about 1879. Married --- Taylor.

B422914. Millard Ransom Pound, fourth child and first son of Joel Pound and Nancy Turner, born 30 Dec 1884 in Georgia and died 28 Dec 1912 at Warthen, Washington County, Georgia. Buried at Warthen, Union Church cemetery, Georgia.

B422915. Stephen B. Pound, fifth child and second son of Joel Pound and Nancy Turner, born Jan 1886 in Georgia.

B422916. Nannie Lou Pound, sixth child and fourth daughter of Joel Pound and Nancy Turner, born 6 Feb 1888 and died 24 Apr 1916 at Warthen, Washington County, Georgia. Buried at Union Church cemetery, Washington County, Georgia. Married Lonnie L. Garner.

B422917. Willie G. Pound, seventh child and third son of Joel Pound and Nancy Turner, born 1890 in Georgia.

B422918. Roger Lawson Pound, eighth child and fourth son of Joel Pound and Nancy Turner, born 25 Jul 1893 in Georgia and died 18 Oct 1921 at Warthen, Washington County, Georgia. Buried at Union Church cemetery, Washington County, Georgia.

B422919. Julian Pound, ninth child and fifth son of Joel Pound and Nancy Turner, born Feb 1898 in Georgia.

B42292. John Pound, second child and second son of Isaac Pound and Julia Ellis, born about 1848 in Hancock County, Georgia.

B42293. Julia Louise Pound, third child and first daughter of Isaac Pound and Julia Ellis, born 29 Aug 1850 in Hancock County, Georgia and died 14 Nov 1906 in Georgia. Married George M. Garner. Julia Pound and George Garner had issue, which was the ninth generation in America:

B422931. Memphis Viola Garner, first child and first daughter of Julia Pound and George Garner, date and place of birth unknown. Married John Marion Salter.

B422932. Eppy Leona Garner, second child and second daughter of Julia Pound and George Garner, date and place of birth unknown.

B422933. Donnie (Roughton) Garner, third child and first son of Julia Pound and George Garner, date and place of birth unknown.

B422934. Macon W. Garner, fourth child and second son of Julia Pound and George Garner, date and place of birth unknown.

B422935. Irene Garner, fifth child and third daughter of Julia Pound and George Garner, date and place of birth unknown.

B422936. Arthur Garner, sixth child and third son of Julia Pound and George Garner, date and place of birth unknown.

B422937. Grady Garner, seventh child and fourth son of Julia Pound and George Garner, date and place of birth unknown.

B42294. James Pound, fourth child and third son of Isaac Pound and Julia Ellis, born 1853 in Hancock County, Georgia. Married 1879 in Hancock County, Georgia to Mary ---, born about 1860 in Georgia.

B422941. Ellis Pound, first child and first son of James Pound and Mary ---, born 1879 in Hancock County, Georgia.

B42295. Mary Pound, fifth child and second daughter of Isaac Pound and Julia Ellis, born about 1856 in Hancock County, Georgia.

B42296. Millie Pound, sixth child and third daughter of Isaac Pound and Julia Ellis, born about 1858 in Hancock County, Georgia.

B42297. Evy Etta Pound, seventh child and fourth daughter of Isaac Pound and Julia Ellis, born about 1858 in Hancock County, Georgia.

B42298. Martha Pound, eighth child and fifth daughter of Isaac Pound and Julia Ellis, born about 1859 in Hancock County, Georgia.

B42299. Albert Pound, ninth child and fourth son of Isaac Pound and Julia Ellis, born about 1870 in Hancock County, Georgia. Albert Pound married, but the name of his first and second spouse is unknown. He married a third time to Ariel Hannah Register.

B42210. Martha Hall Pound, tenth child and third daughter of Joel Pound and Elvah Blount, born 6 Sep 1828 in Hancock County, Georgia and died 7 Jul 1855. Married 14 Jun 1843 in Hancock County, Georgia to William R. Gladin, born about 1823 in Hancock County, Georgia and died 29 Jul 1864 at Bunkwiller Hospital, Virginia. Martha Pound and William Gladin had issue, which was the eighth generation in America:

B422101. Grant Gladin, first child and first son of Martha Pound and William Gladin, born 18 May 1844 and died 27 May 1844.

B422102. Mary Elizabeth Gladin, second child and first daughter of Martha Pound and William Gladin, born 1845.

B422103. A. Mandy Jane Gladin, third child and second daughter of Martha Pound and William Gladin, born 10 Jul 1847.

B422104. Joseph Holmes Gladin, fourth child and second son of Martha Pound and William Gladin, born 4 Jul 1849.

B422105. STI (twin) Gladin, fifth child and third son of Martha Pound and William Gladin, born and died 8 Mar 1851.

B422106. Benjamin Franklin (twin) Gladin, sixth child and fourth son of Martha Pound and William Gladin, born 8 Mar 1851 and died 4 Apr 1851.

B422107. Lydia Ann Frances Gladin, seventh child and third daughter of Martha Pound and William Gladin, born 4 Apr 1852 and died 20 May 1853.

B42211. STI Pound, eleventh child and fourth daughter of Joel Pound and Elvah Blount, stillborn 9 Nov 1830 in Hancock County, Georgia.

B42212. Elizabeth Gilbert Pound, twelfth child and fifth daughter of Joel Pound and Elvah Blount, born 8 Apr 1832 in Hancock County, Georgia and died 10 Apr 1878 at Warthen, Washington County, Georgia. Buried at Union Church cemetery,

Washington County, Georgia. Married 25 Oct 1849 in Hancock County, Georgia to Ransom B. Frazier, born 25 Apr 1866 in Virginia. Elizabeth Pound and Ransom Frazier had issue, which was the eighth generation in America:

B422121. Antemedia Hazeltine Frazier, first child and first daughter of Elizabeth Pound and Ransom Frazier, born 10 Aug 1850 in Hancock County, Georgia and died Feb 1937 at Warthen, Washington County, Georgia. Buried at Union Church cemetery, Washington County, Georgia. Married S. Washington Garner, born 26 Nov 1848 and died 18 Dec 1928 at Warthen, Washington County, Georgia. Buried at Union Church cemetery, Washington County, Georgia. Antemedia Frazier and Washington Garner had issue, which was the ninth generation in America:

B4221211. Solomon Garner, first child and first son of Antemedia Frazier and Washington Garner, date and place of birth unknown. Married Sallie B. Tiespen.

B4221212. Betty Garner, second child and first daughter of Antemedia Frazier and Washington Garner, born 1872 and died 1945. Married Dallas Brown.

B4221213. Harper Moses Garner, third child and second son of Antemedia Frazier and Washington Garner, born 6 Aug 1880. Married Evie Turner.

B4221214. Clinton Garner, fourth child and third son of Antemedia Frazier and Washington Garner, born 23 Nov 1890. Married Nancy Turner.

B4221215. Tillie Garner, fifth child and second daughter of Antemedia Frazier and Washington Garner, date and place of birth unknown. Married Morgan Mills.

B422122. Trezine C. Frazier, second child and second daughter of Elizabeth Pound and Ransom Frazier, born 30 Oct 1851 in Hancock County, Georgia and died 28 May 1853.

B422123. Mary F. Frazier, third child and third daughter of Elizabeth Pound and Ransom Frazier, born 29 Apr 1853 in Hancock County, Georgia.

B422124. Sarah E. Frazier, fourth child and fourth daughter of Elizabeth Pound and Ransom

Frazier, date and place of birth unknown. Married William Aaron Garner.

B422125. Martha A. Frazier, fifth child and fifth daughter of Elizabeth Pound and Ransom Frazier, born 13 Apr 1857 in Hancock County, Georgia and died 3 Jul 1857.

B422126. Alafare Q. Frazier, sixth child and sixth daughter of Elizabeth Pound and Ransom Frazier, born 19 Oct 1858 in Hancock County, Georgia and died 20 Nov 1862.

B422127. Vindinissie Josephine Frazier, seventh child and seventh daughter of Elizabeth Pound and Ransom Frazier, born 17 Mar 1861 in Hancock County, Georgia and died 15 Feb 1949 at Warthen, Washington County, Georgia. Married 6 Aug 1876 to Charles Hamilton Womble, born 15 Nov 1859 at Keg Creek, Washington County, Georgia and died 3 Sep 1944. Vindinissie Frazier and Charles Womble had issue, which was the ninth generation in America:

B4221271. Joseph Clarence Womble, first child and first son of Vindinissie Frazier and Charles Womble, born 7 Jul 1877 at Keg Creek, Washington County, Georgia and died 3 Sep 1938. Married Nola (Nolie) Gadin, date and place of birth unknown, but she died in Washington County, Georgia.

B4221272. Ethel Chevette Womble, second child and first daughter of Vindinissie Frazier and Charles Womble, born 9 Sep 1879 at Keg Creek, Washington County, Georgia and died Jul 1943 at Warthen, Washington County, Georgia. Buried at Union Church cemetery, Washington County, Georgia. Married Lee Lewis. Ethel Womble and Lee Lewis had issue, which was the tenth generation in America:

B42212721. Newman Lewis, first child and first son of Ethel Womble and Lee Lewis, born 10 Feb 1905 in Georgia.

B4221273. Thomas Reid Womble, third child and second son of Vindinissie Frazier and Charles Womble, born 5 Apr 1881 at Keg Creek, Washington County, Georgia and died 1950 at Dublin, Laurens County, Georgia. Buried at Dublin, Laurens County, Georgia. Married Mamie Gadin.

B4221274. Herman Gembetti Womble,

fourth child and third son of Vindinissie Frazier and Charles Womble, born 20 Mar 1883 at Keg Creek, Washington County, Georgia and died 6 Jun 1884.

B4221275. Evelyn Lillian Womble, fifth child and second daughter of Vindinissie Frazier and Charles Womble, born 13 Oct 1884 at Keg Creek, Washington County, Georgia and died 4 Jul 1950. Buried at Milledgeville, Baldwin County, Georgia. Married Wyatt E. Baugh, date and place of birth unknown, but died 31 Dec 1939. Buried at Milledgeville, Baldwin County, Georgia.

B4221276. Jessie Golian Womble, sixth child and third daughter of Vindinissie Frazier and Charles Womble, born 10 Jun 1886 at Keg Creek, Washington County, Georgia and died 1919. Married Gordon Frazier, born 4 Jun 1882 in Hancock County, Georgia and died 26 Jun 1954 at Warthen, Washington County, Georgia. Buried at Union Church cemetery, Washington County, Georgia.

B4221277. Flossie V.F. Womble, seventh child and fourth daughter of Vindinissie Frazier and Charles Womble, born 28 Mar 1888 at Keg Creek, Washington County, Georgia and died 1960. Buried at Claxton, Evans County, Georgia. Married Luther Ross.

B4221278. German Fields Womble, eighth child and fourth son of Vindinissie Frazier and Charles Womble, born 5 May 1890 at Keg Creek, Washington County, Georgia and died 30 Aug 1969 at Sandersville Hospital, Washington County, Georgia. Married Zannie Peavy, date and place of birth unknown, but died Sep 1969 at Sandersville, Washington County, Georgia.

B4221279. Theo Noel Womble, ninth child and fifth son of Vindinissie Frazier and Charles Womble, born 12 Dec 1891 at Keg Creek, Washington County, Georgia and died 27 Mar 1905.

B4221280. Forest Leo Womble, tenth child and sixth son of Vindinissie Frazier and Charles Womble, born 30 Oct 1893 at Keg Creek, Washington County, Georgia and died 23 Dec 1963 at Milledgeville, Baldwin County, Georgia. Buried at Union Church cemetery, Washington County, Georgia. Married Nannie Lou Smith, born 26 Dec 1892 in Hancock County, Georgia and died Aug 1980 at Sandersville, Washington County, Georgia. Buried at Union Church cemetery, Washington County, Georgia.

B4221281. Infant Womble, eleventh child and fifth daughter of Vindinissie Frazier and Charles Womble, born 14 May 1895 at Keg Creek, Washington County, Georgia and died 6 Sep 1895.

B423. David Pound, third child and third son of John (V) Pound and Mary Walker, born about 1784 in Edgefield County, South Carolina. Married 24 Jan 1805 in Columbia County, Georgia to Caroline Gordon. David Pound and Caroline Gordon had issue, which was the seventh generation in America:

B4231. David M. Pound, first child and first son of David Pound and Caroline Gordon, born 1823 in Tennessee. Married Mary Ann Jones. David Pound and Mary Jones had issue, which was the eighth generation in America:

B42311. William Taylor Pound, first child and first son of David Pound and Mary Jones, born 1848 in Mississippi.

B42312. George Walker Pound, second child and second son of David Pound and Mary Jones, born 1850 in Mississippi.

B42313. Thomas Pound, third child and third son of David Pound and Mary Jones, date and place of birth unknown.

B42314. Sally Pound, fourth child and first daughter of David Pound and Mary Jones, date and place of birth unknown.

B42315. Alice Pound, fifth child and second daughter of David Pound and Mary Jones, date and place of birth unknown.

B4232. George Hardy Gordon Pound, second child and second son of David Pound and Caroline Gordon, born Apr 1826 in Tennessee. Married Eleanor Neely. George Pound and Eleanor Neely had issue, which was the eighth generation in America:

B42321. Frances Marion Pound, first child and first son of George Pound and Eleanor Neely, born 1852 in Mississippi and died 1884 in Texas. Married Bettie C. Reader. Married secondly --- Magnen. Frances Pound and Bettie Reader had issue, which was the ninth generation in America:

B423211. Claud Pound, first child

and first son of Frances Pound and Bettie Reader, born Mar 1878 in Texas.

B423212. Douglas Pound, second child and second son of Frances Pound and Bettie Reader, born Feb 1881 in Texas.

B423213. Myrtle Pound, third child and first daughter of Frances Pound and Bettie Reader, born Dec 1882 in Texas.

B423214. Ollie Pound, fourth child and second daughter of Frances Pound and Bettie Reader, born Oct 1813 in Texas.

B4233. James Pound, third child and third son of David Pound and Caroline Gordon, born 1813 in Georgia. Married Celia ---, born 1816 in North Carolina. James Pound and Celia --- had issue, which was the eighth generation in America:

B42331. Columbus C. Pound, first child and first son of James Pound and Celia ---, born 1838 in Georgia.

B42332. William H. Pound, second child and second son of James Pound and Celia ---, born 1840 in Georgia.

B42333. David A. Pound, third child and third son of James Pound and Celia ---, born 1846 in Georgia.

B42334. Sarah B. Pound, fourth child and first daughter of James Pound and Celia ---, born 1847 in Georgia.

B424. William Pound, fourth child and fourth son of John (V) Pound and Mary Walker, born 1785 in Edgefield County, South Carolina.

B425. Martha Pound, fifth child and first daughter of John (V) Pound and Mary Walker, born 1786 in Edgefield County, South Carolina and died 15 May 1882 in Washington County, Georgia. Married about 1805 in Hancock County, Georgia to John Hall, born about 1782 and died 1840 at Sandy Run Creek, Hancock County, Georgia. Martha Pound and John Hall had issue, which was the seventh generation in America:

B4251. David W. Hall, first child and first son of Martha Pound and John Hall, born 1804 in Hancock County, Georgia and died in Washington County, Georgia. Married 11 Ded 1828 in Hancock County, Georgia to Elizabeth Clayborne, born 1807.

B4252. William Bennett Hall, second child

301

and second son of Martha Pound and John Hall, born 19 Nov 1806 in Hancock County, Georgia and died 22 Feb 1893 in Hancock County, Georgia. Buried at Long family cemetery, Hancock County, Georgia. Married 2 Oct 1834 in Washington County, Georgia to Alafair D. Shehee, daughter of Daniel Shehee and Alafair Green, born 8 Jan 1817 in Georgia and died 12 Oct 1889 in Washington County, Georgia. Buried at White Oake cemetery, Washington County, Georgia. William Hall and Alafair Shehee had issue, which was the eighth generation in America:

B42521. Martha Hall, first child and first daughter of William Hall and Alafair Shehee, born about 1835 in Washington County, Georgia. Married Alexander Gavin Carswell.

B42522. Matilda Hall, second child and second daughter of William Hall and Alafair Shehee, born about 1837 in Washington County, Georgia. Married Robert Holly Wicker.

B42523. Augusta Hall, third child and third daughter of William Hall and Alafair Shehee, born about 1839 in Washington County, Georgia. Married John C. Williams.

B42524. John D. Hall, fourth child and first son of William Hall and Alafair Shehee, born 1841 in Washington County, Georgia and died 2 Nov 1892 in Washington County, Georgia. Married Elizabeth J. Warthen.

B42525. Sherrod Thomas Hall, fifth child and second son of William Hall and Alafair Shehee, born 1843 in Washington County, Georgia. Married Mary Louise Inman. Married secondly Belle ---.

B42526. Julian S. Hall, sixth child and third son of William Hall and Alafair Shehee, born 1845 in Washington County, America and died 1858.

B42527. Memphis H. Hall, seventh child and fourth daughter of William Hall and Alafair Shehee, born 1847 in Washington County, Georgia and died 1862.

B4253. Elizabeth Hall, third child and first daughter of Martha Pound and John Hall, born 1807 in Hancock County, Georgia and died 23 Aug 1833 in Hancock County, Georgia. Married 5 Jan 1825 in Hancock County, Georgia to James Wilkins, son of James Wilkins and Catherine ---. born 1 Dec 1805 in Hancock County, Georgia and died 30 Nov 1888 in Gregg County, Texas. Buried Mt. Moriah cemetery, Gregg County, Texas. Elizabeth Hall and James Wilkins had issue, which was the eighth generation in America:

B42531. Catherine Wilkins, first child and first daughter of Elizabeth Hall and James Wilkins, born 1827 in Hancock County, Georgia. Married 9 Oct 1845 in Chambers County, Alabama to Jesse Wallace.

B42532. John Hall Wilkins, second child and first son of Elizabeth Hall and James Wilkins, born 15 Oct 1829 in Hancock County, Georgia and died 24 Apr 1899 in Gregg County, Texas. Buried at Mt. Moriah cemetery, Gregg County, Texas. Married 31 Jan 1867 in Rusk County, Texas to Tennessee Holt, daughter of Lewis F. Holt and Emily Cummins. Married secondly in Smith County, Texas to Rebecca Jefferies Reynolds.

B4254. Martha Hall, fourth child and second daughter of Martha Pound and John Hall, born 1814 in Hancock County, Georgia and died 25 Jul 1838 in Hall County, Georgia. Married 12 Apr 1838 in Hall County, Georgia to George W. Davis, born 1818 in South Carolina and died 25 Jul 1838 in Hall County, Georgia.

B4255. Ransom S. Hall, fifth child and third son of Martha Pound and John Hall, born 1826 in Hancock County, Georgia and died before Jan 1854 in Hancock County, Georgia. Married 2 Oct 1845 in Hancock County, Georgia to America Shivers, daughter of William Shivers and Frances B. Pitt, born 26 Apr 1827 and died 5 May 1883 at Sparta, Hancock County, Georgia. Ransom Hall and America Shivers had issue, which was the eighth generation in America:

B42551. William Frances Hall, first child and first son of Ransom Hall and America Shivers, born 1850 at Sparta, Hancock County, Georgia.

B42552. Martha Ann Hall, second child and first daughter of Ransom Hall and America Shivers, born at Sparta, Hancock County, Georgia.

B426. Mary (Polly) Pound, sixth child and second daughter of John (V) Pound and Mary Walker, born about 1789 in Hancock County, Georgia and died

1842. Married 4 Apr 1810 in Hancock County, Georgia to Silas Herrendine.

B427. Elizabeth Pound, seventh child and third daughter of John (V) Pound and Mary Walker, born about 1793 in Hancock County, Georgia. Married 8 Aug 1814 in Hancock County, Georgia to Joseph Garrett.

B43. Samuel Pound, third child and third son of John Pound and his Indian Wife, born about 1747 in Orange County, Virginia and died 1 Apr 1830 in Anson County, North Carolina. Married about 1767 to Sarah Walker, daughter of David Walker and Elizabeth Slayden, born about 1762 in North Carolina and died 21 Sep 1847 in Anson County, North Carolina. Samuel Pound was in the Revolutionary War, serving in Colonel Robert Middleton's Battalion, Richmond County Militia. He enlisted in North Carolina on 16 May 1777 for three years. He was attached to Macon's Company, and was discharged in August of 1777. He was a private in 1779, also 1782. Colonel Elijah Clarke lists him as a refugee soldier. He drew 287 1/2 acres, Warrant #1398, Washington County, Georgia. The Court Records of Anson County, North Carolina give us this statement from testator J. White: I do hereby certify that I was personally acquainted with Samuel Pounds and his wife Sarah from my earliest recollection until their death. I think Mr. Pounds died about the first of April 1830 and his wife about the 21st of September 1847. I was born and raised within about five miles of where they both lived and died. In the life-time of Mr. Samuel Pounds, I have heard him speak of his Revolutionary Service. I heard him speak of being at the siege of Augusta (I think). The date and officers names I do not recollect, but heard him say that during the siege for three days and nights when he and others slept with their horses bridles on their arms. He also said about that time the Americans had a kind of fort or battery which they could move at pleasure constructed of raw hides which and that it protected them from the balls of small arms shot at them by the British. I also heard Mr. Pounds say that about this time the Americans tried to arrange a plan by undermining to blow up the enemy. Mr. Pounds said that a large number of Indians had collected there or near there to join the British and Tories and that the Americans put pine and cedar boughs in their hats and caps and the Indians thinking them Tories came out joyfully to meet and join them, and when they came within a suitable distance, the

Americans suddenly fired on the Indians and killed a great number, so many that it took the rails of a fence more than a mile long to burn them up. I have heard Mr. Pounds speak of being in other battles and think he said he was in a battle at Briar Creek. I am inclined to the belief that he said he was in a fight in ninety six. I believe he was a dragoon and from his statements believe he served at least twelve months in South Carolina and Georgia and was called out by authority of the United States. I also think he previously served six months in North Carolina in behalf of the United States as a private. There is no doubt that Samuel Pounds and his wife Sarah were lawfully married and they lived together as man and wife to the day of his death, they were quite respectable old people and I should have no hesitation in believing any statement either one of them made. If their oldest children were living, one or two of them would be at least fifty five years of age. They had two children that survived them, Samuel and Elizabeth. The above statement is true to the best of my knowledge and belief. Sworn to subscribed this 13th day of Jany 1851. [sig] J. White. Samuel Pound married Sarah Walker, sister of Mary Walker, both daughters of David Walker. Samuel Pound and Sarah Walker had issue, which was the sixth generation in America:

B431. Samuel Pound, first child and first son of Samuel Pound and Sarah Walker, born about 1770 and died Apr 1830 in Anson County, North Carolina. The following appears to pertain to this Samuel Pound(s) in part, but part does not, so it is questionable as to whether this material and this specific identity mesh. [From: General Services Administration, National Archives and Record Service. Order for Photocopies concerning Veteran: File Description: Samuel Pounds, R 8389, State of North Carolina, Anson County, January Term 1851;]

Then appears Samuel Pounds aged fifty years, a son of Samuel Pound(s) and Sarah Pounds, deceased, and after being duly sworn in open court, doth on his oath make the following declaration in order to obtain the benefits of the Act of Congress passed the 17th day of July 1838, or Act 2nd of Feb 1848 in behalf of himself and his sister Elizabeth Pounds, the two surviving children of the aforesaid Samuel and Sarah Pounds, deceased (viz).

My father was reputed and believed to have been a soldier in the Revolutionary War, and had the scars on him received in battles as I have often heard him say. He was born in Halifax County, North Carolina (if so, we have the wrong Samuel) and when the war came on, my father turned out a volunteer and joined the American Army under General Green. He was at the battle of Guilford Court House and served six months as a private in North Carolina. He was at the battle of Cowpens and Brier Creek. I think it was there the Americans were defeated and in retreating, my father with many others, got their horses over some water course on a large log. Some fell in the water and liked to have got drowned. He was then a Dragoon. In the battle of ninety-six, he said soldiers underwent great hardships eating nothing for three or four days but parched corn. He has said much about the skirmishes with Indians and Tories in the state of Georgia; particularly in the battle at the siege of Augusta. I think it was there that my father got wounded in the shoulder and that their suffering was great. I believe it was at that siege that they did not sleep for three days and nights without their horses bridles over their arms. He has told that the Americans killed so many Indians tht it took the rails of a fence of more than a mile long to burn them up. I have also heard him speak of a fort made of rawhides they could move about, and of the Americans trying to undermine the town and blow up the British with powder. My father was taken prisoner in some battle in the state of Georgia and the British wanted him to promise never to serve anymore against them, but he either ran away from them or was exchanged and continued in the Army in the state of Georgia and South Carolina, or near or quite near the end of the war. He must have belonged to the Lighthorse under General Green or General Lincoln in most of these battles. I have heard him speak of other officers, but I do not recollect their names. I

307

believe he served one year and six months in the states of Georgia and South Carolina in actual service called out by the Authority of the United States. I have heard him say he had rather right on a horse than any other way and when a battle was coming on, he felt a little bad but after the fighting commenced, he did not mind it afterwards. I am the fourth child my mother had according to the record kept by my father of his children's ages, but the Bible kept for that purpose has been either destroyed, lost or mislaid so that it can not be found. I have kept my own age as it was recorded and was born the 15th day of October 1800. My father died the 1st day of April 1830 and my mother the 21st day of September 1847, leaving two children, myself and Elizabeth Pounds, my sister. s/Samuel Pounds.

B432. Elizabeth (Sarah) Pound, second child and first daughter of Samuel Pound and Sarah Walker, born about 1772 in Georgia. Married 28 May 1795 in Columbia County, Georgia to Francis Bealle, son of Mannum Bealle and Frances ---, date and place of birth unknown, but he died before 14 Feb 1822 in Columbia County, Georgia.

B433. William Pounds, third child and second son of Samuel Pound and Sarah Walker, born 1780 in Wilkes County, Georgia and died 5 Nov 1844 in Taliaferro County, Georgia. Buried at Taliaferro County, Georgia. Married 27 Dec 1808 in Wilkes County, Georgia to Nancy Slayden, daughter of Daniel J. Slayden and Sallie Isbell, thought to be born 1780 in Goochland County, Virginia, was listed as 64 years of age in the 1850 Census of Meriwether County, Georgia. IF this be true, she was born in 1786; and she died after 1850 in Meriwether County, Georgia. In the Georgia Department of Archives and History, Drawer 108, Box 42 under Taliaferro County, Georgia; Ordinary Wills Book A 1826-1866 pp 182-83 is listed the last will and testament of William Pounds: LAST WILL AND TESTAMENT: In the Name of God Amen; I, WILLIAM POUNDS of the County and State aforesaid being of sound mind, memory and body, but knowing the uncertainty of human life, do make and declare this as my last will and testament in manner and form following to wit;

In the first place, I hereby give and bequeath unto David C. Daniel of the County and State aforesaid and Robert C. Daniel of the County of Oglethorpe and State aforesaid all my Estate both Real and Personal In Trust For my wife Nancy Pounds for and during the term of her Natural Life (or in the case of my said wife Nancy shall be willing thereto) untill the youngest Child herein named shall become of age, at which time (If my said wife Nancy shall be willing and not otherwise) The said Trustees shall distribute my said Estate in manner and form hereinafter named, but if my said wife Nancy should not be willing then said Division shall not take place as hereinafter directed until the death of my said wife Nancy.

Now having given my wife Nancy the whole of my estate both Real and Personal for and during her natural life except as heretofore (except she being willing to said exception and not otherwise). In the second place I will that after the death of my said wife Nancy or as before stated if she be willing thereto when the youngest child shall become of age, my said wife Nancy being then alive an equal division of my estate both Real and Personal, between and among my Children herein named, to wit; Daniel S. Pounds, Isham J. Pounds, Jared Pounds, William D. Pounds, Zachariah B. Pounds, Martha A.S. Pounds, and Lucy I. Pounds. At the same time willing and declaring that my daughter, Sarah I. Bankston the wife of Wildon L. Bankston or the said Wildon L. Bankston or any of their children it is my Intention to give or bequeath nothing at my death having given her and them all that I ever intend them to have during my lifetime or do intend them to have any thing at my death.

Hereby constituting, declaring and appointing David C. Daniel and Robert Daniel named herein before as trustees, as my Executors likewise of this my said last will and testament at the same time willing that if the said beforenamed David C. Daniel and Robert Daniel should refuse or from any other cause should not act in either capacity, that Wildon L. Bankston may not be allowed to become Administrator or Trustee or even Guardian to any of my children in any event.

In witness thereof, I have hereunto set my hand and seal this twentieth day of August in the year of Our Lord Eighteen Hundred and Thirty Eight.

Signed, sealed and acknowledges in the presence of

William T. Fluker   /s/
William Pounds
Saml. Glenn
V.L. Mathews

Georgia, Taliaferro County, Court of Ordinary, November Term 1844.

The last will and testament of William Pounds having been duly proven at this term in open court upon the oath of William T. Fluker, one of the subscribing witness to the same.

The Court ordered that the will and proceedings be recorded.

Attest Quinea O'Neal Clk, C.O.
Recorded Nov 5th 1844
Quinea O'Neal C.C.O.

Information concerning William Pounds, Nancy Pounds, their children's names, birth dates, death dates, marriage dates and place of Jared Walker Pounds, Eugenia Ely, and their children's names, birthdates were copied from the Jared Walker Pounds-Eugenia Ely Family Bible in the home of Fay Carmin Pounds Weeks, granddaughter of Benjamin Idus Pounds, at Jacksonville, Florida on 28 Sep 1952 by Willie Sophia Pounds Cook, granddaughter of Jared Walker Pounds. Bible now in possession of Jared Walker Pounds' great-great-grandson Carl Robert Pounds of Miami, Florida. William Pounds was a participant in the War of 1812. He was described by Captain William Starn who commanded the 5th Company of Georgia Militia as age 26, 6 ft tall, fair complexion, light hair, blue eyes.

This data in Researcher's Library of Georgia History, Genealogy and Records Sources by; Robert Scott Davis, Jr. William Pounds and Nancy Slayden had issue, which was the seventh generation in America

B4331. Daniel Slaton Pounds, first child and first son of William Pounds and Nancy Slayden, born 6 Nov 1809 at Winston, Douglas County, Georgia and died 12 May 1874 in Pike County, Georgia. Married 18 Oct 1831 in Oglethorpe County, Georgia to Melissa Short, born about 1810 in Georgia who married secondly to T. Brown Sanders. Daniel Pounds married secondly 12 Jun 1843 in Pike County, Georgia to Julia Amanda Slaton, born 1807 in Pike County, Georgia. Daniel Pounds and Melissa Short had issue, which was the eighth generation in America:

B43311. Mary C. Pounds, first child and first daughter of Daniel Pounds and Melissa Short, born 20 Jan 1836 in Pike County, Georgia. Married 20 Jan 1836 in Pike County, Georgia to Columbus W. Phillips.

B4331. Daniel Slaton Pounds, first child and first son of William Pounds and Nancy Slayden, born 6 Nov 1809 at Winston, Douglas County, Georgia and died 12 May 1874 in Pike County, Georgia. Married secondly 12 Jun 1843 in Pike County, Georgia to Julia Amanda Slaton, born about 1817. Daniel Pounds and Julia Slaton had issue, which was the eighth generation in America:

B43311. Nancy Jane Pounds, first child and first daughter of Daniel Pounds and Julia Slaton, born about 1841 in Georgia. Married 3 Jun 1860 in Pike County, Georgia to James D. Dumas.

B43312. James D. Pounds, second child and first son of Daniel Pounds and Julia Slaton, born about 1841 in Oglethorpe County, Georgia and died 3 May 1863 at Chancellorville, Spotsylvania County, Virginia. James Pounds served as Sergeant Co I 53rd Georgia Infantry, Confederate States Army. Married 24 Oct 1858 in Pike County, Georgia to Malissa Antoinette Willis, date and place of birth unknown, but died at Wrightsville, Johnson County, Georgia. Buried in City Cemetery, Wrightsville, Johnson County,

Georgia. James Pounds and Malissa Willis had issue, which was the ninth generation in America:

B433121. James Eley Pounds, first child and first son of James Pounds and Malissa Willis, born 10 Dec 1861 in Pike County, Georgia and died 13 Feb 1907 at Milner, Pike County, Georgia. Buried at Baptist Church cemetery, Milner, Pike County, Georgia. Married Belle Fisher, date and place of birth unknown, but died 18 Sep 1896 at Milner, Pike County, Georgia. Buried at Baptist Church cemetery, Milner. Pike County, Georgia. Married secondly 7 Jun 1897 in Banks County, Georgia to Lousanna Gray White, born 10 Apr 1879 in Banks County, Georgia and died 13 Jan 1976 at Commerce, Jackson County, Georgia. Buried at Sunrise cemetery, Banks County, Georgia. James Pounds and Belle Fisher had issue, which was the tenth generation in America:

B4331211. Ruth Isabel Pounds, first child and first daughter of James Pounds and Belle Fisher, born 2 Sep 1896 at Milner, Pike County, Georgia and died 3 Feb 1960 at Anderson, Anderson County, South Carolina. Buried at Starr Baptist Church cemetery, Starr, Anderson County, South Carolina. Married 23 Jun 1915 at Maysville, Banks County, Georgia to Frank Harkness Pettigrew, born 12 Mar 1891 at Iva, Anderson County, South Carolina and died 13 Nov 1977 at Anderson, Anderson County, South Carolina. Buried at Starr Baptist Church cemetery, Starr, Anderson County, South Carolina. Ruth Pounds and Frank Pettigrew had issue, which was the eleventh generation in America:

B43312111. Frank Preston Pettigrew, first child and first son of Ruth Pounds and Frank Pettigrew, born 17 Feb 1917 at Starr, Anderson County, South Carolina. Married 30 Jan 1943 at Greenville, Greenville County, South Carolina to Mary Alice Bangle, daughter of Coit Watson Bangle and Blanche Alease Wright, born 23 Dec 1919 at Greenville, Greenville County, South Carolina.

B43312112. Jack Pounds Pettigrew, second child and second son of Ruth Pounds and Frank Pettigrew, born 12 Apr 1919 at Starr, Anderson County, South Carolina.

Married 10 Sep 1946 at Anderson, Anderson County, South Carolina to Esther Mahaffey, born 25 Aug 1923 at Anderson, Anderson County, South Carolina. Jack Pettigrew and Esther Mahaffey had issue, which was the twelth generation in America:

B433121121. Donna Alice Pettigrew, first child and first daughter of Jack Pettigrew and Esther Mahaffey, born 29 Jan 1955 at Anderson, Anderson County, South Carolina. Married 28 Dec 1976 at Anderson, Anderson County, South Carolina to Jerry Randall Sargent. Donna Pettigrew and Jerry Sargent had issue, which was the thirteenth generation in America

B4331211211. Jerry Randall Sargent, Jr., first child and first son of Donna Pettigrew and Jerry Sargent, born at Orangeburg, Orangeburg County, South Carolina.

B4331211212. Jessica Leigh Sargent, second child and first daughter of Donna Pettigrew and Jerry Sargent, born Jul 1980 at Orangeburg, Orangeburg County, South Carolina.

B4331211213. Ashley Brooke Sargent, third child and second daughter of Donna Pettigrew and Jerry Sargent, born Aug 1982 at Orangeburg, Orangeburg County, South Carolina.

B433121122. Nancy Jane Pettigrew, second child and second daughter of Jack Pettigrew and Esther Mahaffey, born 6 Nov 1958 at Anderson, Anderson County, South Carolina. Married 19 May 1979 at Anderson, Anderson County, South Carolina to Bonner Gentry Brown.

B43312113. James Everette Pettigrew, third child and third son of Ruth Pounds and Frank Pettigrew, born 9 Jul 1922 at Starr, Anderson County, South Carolina. Married 31 May 1943 at Anderson, Anderson County, South Carolina to Mary Elizabeth Glenn, born 4 Sep 1923 at Anderson, Anderson County, South Carolina. James Pettigrew and Mary Glenn had issue, which was the twelth generation in America:

B433121131. James Everette Pettigrew, Jr., first child and first son of James Pettigrew and Mary Glenn, born 18 Nov 1950 at Charlotte, Mecklenburg County, North Carolina.

B433121132. Teddi Elizabeth Pettigrew, second child and first daughter of James Pettigrew and

Mary Glenn, born 23 Apr 1953 at Charlotte, Mecklenburg County, North Carolina. Married 23 Jul 1972 to Eddie Wilson Hoyle, date and place of birth unknown, but died 12 Sep 1974. Married secondly 4 Oct 1980 at Greensboro, Guilford County, North Carolina to Mark Steven Miller.
B433121133. Frank Glenn Pettigrew, third child and second son of James Pettigrew and Mary Glenn, born 5 May 1963 at Orangeburg, Orangeburg County, South Carolina and died Jul 1981.
B43312114. Beatrice Elaine Pettigrew, fourth child and first daughter of Ruth Pounds and Frank Pettigrew, born 11 Sep 1924 at Starr, Anderson County, South Carolina. Married 9 Mar 1968 at Starr, Anderson County, South Carolina to Litchman Lee Junkins, born 25 Mar 1908 at Anderson, Anderson County, South Carolina and died 12 Jul 1983 at Anderson, Anderson County, South Carolina. Buried at Anderson, Forest Lawn cemetery, South Carolina.
B43312115. Phillip Pettigrew, fifth child and fourth son of Ruth Pounds and Frank Pettigrew, born 6 Sep 1927 at Starr, Anderson County, South Carolina and died 27 Jul 1983 at Anderson, Anderson County, South Carolina. Buried at Starr Baptist Church cemetery, Starr, Anderson County, South Carolina. Married 17 Feb 1947 at Hartwell, Hart County, Georgia to Mildred Linda Loftis, daughter of Julian Ellis Loftis and Lilian Lewis, born 5 Apr 1929 at Iva, Anderson County, South Carolina and died 28 Jun 1949 at Anderson, Anderson County, South Carolina. Married secondly 12 Apr 1952 Williamston, Anderson County, South Carolina to Jacquelyn Bell. Phillip Pettigrew and Mildred Loftis had issue, which was the twelth generation in America:
B433121151. Phillip Randolph Pettigrew, first child and first son of Phillip Pettigrew and Mildred Loftis, born 27 Jun 1949 at Anderson, Anderson County, South Carolina. Married 9 Mar 1968 at Hartwell, Hart County, Georgia to Frances Annette Holley, daughter of Benton Holley, Jr. and Bernice Annette Shaw, born 24 Nov 1951 at Anderson, Anderson County, South Carolina. Phillip Pettigrew and Frances Holley had issue, which was the thirteenth generation in America:

B4331211511. Phyllis Ann Pettigrew, first child and first daughter of Phillip Pettigrew and Frances Holley, born 23 Sep 1954 at Anderson, Anderson County, South Carolina. Married 30 Jul 1977 at Starr, Anderson County, South Carolina to George Carl Jehlen, Jr. Phyllis Pettigrew and George Jehlen had issue, which was the fourteenth generation in America:

B43312115111. Jeffrey Russell (Rusty) Jehlen, first child and first son of Phyllis Pettigrew and George Jehlen, born 14 Oct 1980 at Marietta, Cobb County, Georgia.

B43312115112. Phillip Carl Jehlen, second child and second son of Phyllis Pettigrew and George Jehlen, born 3 Apr 1984 at Marietta, Cobb County, Georgia.

B4331211512. Michael Preston Pettigrew, second child and first son of Phillip Pettigrew and Frances Holley, born 16 Sep 1956 at Anderson, Anderson County, South Carolina. Married 18 Aug 1979 at Honea Path, Anderson County, South Carolina to Reba Jean Martin. Michael Pettigrew and Reba Martin had issue, which was the fourteenth generation in America:

B43312115121. Phillip Jason Pettigrew, first child and first son of Michael Pettigrew and Reba Martin, born 15 May 1980.

B4331211513. Malinda Annette Pettigrew, third child and second daughter of Phillip Pettigrew and Frances Holley, born 9 Mar 1969 at Anderson, Anderson County, South Carolina.

B4331212. John Pollock Pounds, second child and first son of James Pounds and Belle Fisher, born 27 Jan 1899 at Flovilla, Jasper County, Georgia and died 9 Feb 1972 at Commerce, Jackson County, Georgia. Buried at Sunrise cemetery, Maysville, Banks County, Georgia. Married 16 Feb 1919 at Maysville, Banks County, Georgia to Ina Lucille Saville, born 28 Mar 1898 at Maysville, Banks County, Georgia and died 12 Nov 1959 at Commerce, Jackson County, Georgia. Buried at Sunrise cemetery, Maysville, Banks County, Georgia. Married secondly 12 May 1960 at Maysville, Banks County, Georgia to Blatz Ray Perkins, born 26 Jul 1902 at Maysville, Banks County, Georgia and died May 1986 at Maysville, Banks County, Georgia.

Buried at Maysville, Banks County, Georgia. John
Pounds and Ina Saville had issue, which was the
eleventh generation in America:

B43312121. Frances Jeannette Pounds, first
child and first daughter of John Pounds and Ina
Saville, born 24 Nov 1919 at Maysville, Banks
County, Georgia. Married 9 Apr 1938 at Atlanta,
Fulton County, Georgia to Oliver McNair Bell, born
29 Oct 1917 at Blakely, Early County, Georgia.
Frances Pounds and Oliver Bell had issue, which
was the twelth generation in America:

B433121211. Edward McNair Bell, first
child and first son of Frances Pounds and Oliver
Bell, born 12 Dec 1939 at Washington, D.C.
Married 25 Jul 1959 at San Marino, Los Angeles
County, California to Margaret Angeline Jones,
born 16 Jun 1939 at LaGrange, Troup County,
Georgia. Edward Bell and Margaret Jones had
issue, which was the thirteenth generation in
America:

B4331212111. Elizabeth Angeline
Bell, first child and first daughter of Edward
Bell and Margaret Jones, born 7 Feb 1960 at
Arcadia, Los Angeles County, California.

B4331212112. Laura Catherine Bell,
second child and second daughter of Edward Bell
and Margaret Jones, born 16 Sep 1961 at Arcadia,
Los Angeles County, California.

B4331212113. Jill Charlotte Bell, third
child and third daughter of Edward Bell and
Margaret Jones, born 26 Sep 1967 at Fullerton,
Orange County, California.

B433121212. Olivia Jean Bell, second child
and first daughter of Frances Pounds and Oliver
Bell, born 2 Jan 1941 at Washington, D.C. Married
29 Jan 1964 at Pasadena, Los Angeles County,
California to Lynn John Willhite, born 25 Jul 1941
at New Ulm, Brown County, Minnesota. Olivia Bell
and Lynn Willhite had issue, which was the
thirteenth generation in America:

B4331212121. John Martin Willhite,
first child and first son of Olivia Bell and Lynn
Willhite, born 9 Sep 1970 at Pasadena, Los Angeles
County, California.

B4331212122. Pollie McNair Willhite,
second child and first daughter of Olivia Bell and

Lynn Willhite, born 12 Jan 1979 at Pasadena, Los Angeles County, California.

B433121213. Barbara Bell, third child and second daughter of Frances Pounds and Oliver Bell, born 31 Jul 1953 at Pasadena, Los Angeles County, California.

B433121214. Stephen McNair Bell, fourth child and second son of Frances Pounds and Oliver Bell, born 29 Aug 1955 at Pasadena, Los Angeles County, California. Married 28 Jan 1983 at Issaquah, King County, Washington to Laura Keckler. Stephen Bell and Laura Keckler had issue, which was the thirteenth generation in America:

B4331212141. Alexandria Bell, first child and first daughter of Stephen Bell and Laura Keckler, born 1987 at Issaquah, King County, Washington.

B43312122. Jack Morgan Pounds, second child and first son of John Pounds and Ina Saville, born 24 Jun 1922 at Maysville, Banks County, Georgia. Married 7 Dec 1947 at Maysville, Banks County, Georgia to Mary Clayton Henderson, daughter of Albert Jefferson Henderson and Cliffie Cook, born 19 Aug 1925 at Canton, Cherokee County, Georgia. Jack Pounds and Mary Henderson had issue, which was the twelth generation in America:

B433121221. Jack Morgan Pounds, Jr., first child and first son of Jack Pounds and Mary Henderson, born 4 Jul 1949 at Athens, Clarke County, Georgia. Married 3 Oct 1981 at Nashville, Davidson County, Tennessee to Jennifer Ann Keller, daughter of Ollie Keller and Dorothy Gordon, born 27 Jan 1957 at Knoxville, Knox County, Tennessee. Jack Pounds and Jennifer Keller had issue, which was the thirteenth generation in America:

B4331212211. Emily Ann Pounds, first child and first daughter of Jack Pounds and Jennifer Keller, born 4 Jul 1983 at Marietta, Cobb County, Georgia.

B4331212212. Mary Morgan Pounds, second child and second daughter of Jack Pounds and Jennifer Keller, born 9 Jun 1985 at Marietta, Cobb County, Georgia.

B433121222. Mary Elizabeth Pounds, second child and first daughter of Jack Pounds and Mary

Henderson, born 16 Aug 1950 at Athens, Clarke County, Georgia. Married 1 Jul 1978 at Marietta, Cobb County, Georgia to Charles Atwell Shepard, son of Frederick Michael Shepard and Margaret McKown Phillips, born 16 Mar 1952 at Atlanta, Fulton County, Georgia. Mary Pounds and Charles Shepard had issue, which was the thirteenth generation in America:

B4331212221. Charles Frederick Shepard, first child and first son of Mary Pounds and Charles Shepard, born 26 Feb 1980 at Marietta, Cobb County, Georgia.

B4331212222. Albert Benjamin Shepard, second child and second son of Mary Pounds and Charles Shepard, born 16 Nov 1983 at Marietta, Cobb County, Georgia.

B4331212223. Jonathan Atwell Shepard, third child and third son of Mary Pounds and Charles Shepard, born 21 Sep 1985 at Marietta, Cobb County, Georgia.

B433121223. Nancy Henderson Pounds, third child and second daughter of Jack Pounds and Mary Henderson, born 13 Apr 1954 at Marietta, Cobb County, Georgia. Married 6 Feb 1977 at Valdosta, Lowndes County, Georgia to Daryl William Bradley, son of E. Rawdon Bradley and Helen Jewel Moon, born 10 May 1948 at Douglas, Coffee County, Georgia.

B433121224. Carol Lee Pounds, fourth child and third daughter of Jack Pounds and Mary Henderson, born 26 Sep 1955 at Marietta, Cobb County, Georgia. Married 30 Jun 1979 at Marietta, Cobb County, Georgia to Derek L. Bowen, son of Billy Leon Bowen and Martha Yarbrough, born 17 Nov 1954 at LaGrange, Troup County, Georgia.

B433121225. Andrew Jefferson Pounds, fifth child and second son of Jack Pounds and Mary Henderson, born 30 Dec 1965 at Marietta, Cobb County, Georgia. Married 21 Mar 1992 at Jackson, Butts County, Georgia to Laura Kaye Mangham, daughter of Marvin Brumby Mangham and Elaine Britton, born 10 Jun 1968.

B4331213. Minnie Irene Pounds, third child and second daughter of James Pounds and Belle Fisher, born 25 Jun 1900 at Flovilla, Jasper County, Georgia. Married 10 Mar 1928 at Jacksonville,

Duval County, Florida to Stanley Knight Carr, son of J. Robert Carr and Frances Evans, born 29 Jan 1899 at Maysville, Banks County, Georgia and died 6 Jan 1965 at Gainesville, Alachua County, Florida. Buried at Sunrise cemetery, Maysville, Banks County, Georgia.

B4331214. Robert Morgan Pounds, fourth child and second son of James Pounds and Belle Fisher, born 6 Jun 1902 at Locust Grove, Henry County, Georgia. Married 25 Dec 1925 at Rossville, Walker County, Georgia to Gerthry Eugenia Smith, daughter of William Cicero Smith and Georgia May Keown, born 6 Aug 1899 at Lafayette, Walker County, Georgia and died 10 Apr 1931 at Atlanta, Fulton County, Georgia. Buried at Lafayette, Walker County, Georgia. Married secondly 16 Jun 1932 at Macon, Bibb County, Georgia to Lillian Mae Jackson, daughter of William C. Jackson and Maggie Peace, born 20 May 1900 in Laurens County, Georgia and died 25 Jan 1971 at Athens, Clarke County, Georgia. Buried at Maysville, Sunrise cemetery, Banks County, Georgia. Married thirdly 18 Apr 1972 at Maysville, Banks County, Georgia to Pauline Wilbanks, daughter of Tipton Paschal Wilbanks and Lula Ann Cauthen, born 1 Fob 1908 in Banks County, Georgia. Robert Pounds and Gerthry Smith had issue, which was the eleventh generation in America:

B43312141. Robert Smith Pounds, first child and first son of Robert Pounds and Gerthry Smith, born 11 Dec 1926 at Atlanta, Fulton County, Georgia. Married 19 Jun 1953 at Morristown, Morris County, New Jersey to Christina Mitchell Wilkie, daughter of James Soutar Wilkie and Mary Russell MacIntyre, born 3 Jul 1918 at Morristown, Morris County, New Jersey and died 17 Feb 1984 at Glen Ellyn, Page County, Illinois. Robert Pounds and Christina Wilkie had issue, which was the twelth generation in America:

B433121411. James Robert Pounds, first child and first son of Robert Pounds and Christina Wilkie, born 9 Mar 1944 at Morristown, Morris County, New Jersey. Married 4 Dec 1964 to Bonita Reba Osborne. James Pounds and Bonita Osborne had issue, which was the thirteenth generation in America:

B4331214111. James Allan Pounds, first child and first son of James Pounds and Bonita Osborne, born at Winston-Salem, Forsyth County, North Carolina.

B4331214112. Mary Beth Pounds, second child and first daughter of James Pounds and Bonita Osborne, born at Winston-Salem, Forsyth County, North Carolina.

B4331214113. Roberta Glenn Pounds, third child and second daughter of James Pounds and Bonita Osborne, born at Winston-Salem, Forsyth County, North Carolina.

B433121412. Anita Elise Pounds, second child and first daughter of Robert Pounds and Christina Wilkie, born 11 Nov 1954 at Winston-Salem, Forsyth County, North Carolina.

B433121413. Benjamin Smith Pounds, third child and second son of Robert Pounds and Christina Wilkie, born 28 Dec 1960 at Winston-Salem, Forsyth County, North Carolina.

B43312142. Minnie Lou Pounds, second child and first daughter of Robert Pounds and Gerthry Smith, born 3 Dec 1933 at Whitesburg, Carroll County, Georgia. Married 16 Sep 1950 at Maysville, Banks County, Georgia to William M. Webb, son of Paul Webb and Wilda Wood, born 25 Jan 1932 at Maysville, Banks County, Georgia. Minnie Pounds and William Webb had issue, which was the twelth generation in America:

B433121421. Lindy Lou Webb, first child and first daughter of Minnie Pounds and William Webb, born 14 Sep 1951 at Commerce, Jackson County, Georgia. Married 7 Jun 1969 at Maysville, Banks County, Georgia to David Carl Loggins, son of Carl Elmer Loggins and Mariam Hortense Tench, born 31 Jul 1948 at Gainesville, Hall County, Georgia. Married secondly to Tim Finnell. Lindy Webb and David Loggins had issue, which was the thirteenth generation in America:

B4331214211. Christopher David Loggins, first child and first son of Lindy Webb and David Loggins, born 17 Dec 1971 at Houston, Harris County, Texas.

B433121421. Lindy Lou Webb, first child and first daughter of Minnie Pounds and William

Webb, born 14 Sep 1951 at Commerce, Jackson County, Georgia. Married secondly to Tim Finnell. Lindy Webb and Tim Finnell had issue, which was the thirteenth generation in America:

B4331214211. Holly Nicole Finnell, first child and first daughter of Lindy Webb and Tim Finnell, born 23 Dec 1977.

B433121422. William Terry Webb, second child and first son of Minnie Pounds and William Webb, born 18 Dec 1954 at Commerce, Jackson County, Georgia.

B433121423. Virginia Caroline Webb, third child and second daughter of Minnie Pounds and William Webb, born 24 Dec 1956 at Marietta, Cobb County, Georgia. Married 2 Jun 1972 at Humble, Harris County, Texas to Hector Cantu, son of Pablo M. Cantu and Clara Wells, born 24 Feb 1954 at Harlingen, Cameron County, Texas. Virginia Webb and Hector Cantu had issue, which was the thirteenth generation in America:

B4331214231. Hector Alexander Cantu, first child and first son of Virginia Webb and Hector Cantu, born 2 Oct 1976 at Houston, Harris County, Texas.

B4331214232. Joseph Xavier Cantu, second child and second son of Virginia Webb and Hector Cantu, born 19 Jan 1978 at Houston, Harris County, Texas.

B433121424. Jeffrey Taylor Webb, fourth child and second son of Minnie Pounds and William Webb, born 26 Mar 1966 at Gravette, Benton County, Arkansas.

B4331215. Jimmy Lou Pounds, fifth child and third daughter of James Pounds and Belle Fisher, born 24 Jun 1907 at Maysville, Banks County, Georgia. Married 4 Jun 1926 at Atlanta, Fulton County, Georgia to John Eugene Fuller, son of James Daughtry Fuller and Margaret Louise Gantt, born 20 Dec 1900 at Cobb County, Georgia and died 25 Oct 1986 at Gainesville, Hall County, Georgia. Jimmy Pounds and John Fuller had issue, which was the eleventh generation in America:

B43312151. John Eugene Fuller, Jr., first child and first son of Jimmy Pounds and John Fuller, born 21 Mar 1927 at Atlanta, Fulton County, Georgia. Married 17 Mar 1950 at Decatur,

DeKalb County, Georgia to Dorothy Ann Bedenbaugh, daughter of J.L. Bedenbaugh and Daisy Mildred Jones, born 14 Feb 1930 at Griffin, Spalding County, Georgia. John Fuller and Dorothy Bedenbaugh had issue, which was the twelfth generation in America:

B433121511. Gordon Leigh Fuller, first child and first son of John Fuller and Dorothy Bedenbaugh, born 21 Dec 1953 at Richmond, Virginia. Married 31 Jan 1976 at Decatur, DeKalb County, Georgia to Connie Joyce Moore, daughter of Howard Righter Moore and Joyce Elaine Walton, born 30 Sep 1953 at Atlanta, Fulton County, Georgia. Gordon Fuller and Connie Moore had issue, which was the thirteenth generation in America:

B4331215111. Christopher Branon Fuller, first child and first son of Gordon Fuller and Connie Moore, born 14 Sep 1983 at Houston, Harris County, Texas.

B4331215112. James (Jimmy) Edgar Fuller, second child and second son of Gordon Fuller and Connie Moore, born 6 Jun 1986 at New Orleans, Orleans Parish, Louisiana.

B433121512. Sharon Leigh Fuller, second child and first daughter of John Fuller and Dorothy Bedenbaugh, born 5 Jan 1959 at Gainesville, Alachua County, Florida. Married 3 May 1985 at Decatur, DeKalb County, Georgia to Behrooz Lessani Abdi. Sharon Fuller and Behrooz Abdi had issue, which was the thirteenth generation in America:

B4331215121. Shirin Nicole Abdi, first child and first daughter of Sharon Fuller and Behrooz Abdi, born 13 Jan 1988 at Phoenix, Maricopa County, Arizona.

B4331215122. Amanda Sarah Abdi, second child and second daughter of Sharon Fuller and Behrooz Abdi, born 24 Jan 1990 at Phoenix, Maricopa County, Arizona.

B43313. Lucy Ann Pound, third child and second daughter of Daniel Pounds and Julia Slaton, born about 1847 in Pike County, Georgia.

B43314. Zachariah B. Pounds, fourth child and second son of Daniel Pounds and Julia Slaton, born about 1854 in Pike County, Georgia. Married about 1872 in Pike County, Georgia to Catharine ---, born about 1852 in Georgia. Zachariah Pounds and Catharine --- had issue, which was the ninth generation in America:

B433141. Sarah E. Pounds, first child and first daughter of Zachariah Pounds and Catharine ---, born about 1873 in Pike County, Georgia.

B433142. Mary Pounds, second child and second daughter of Zachariah Pounds and Catharine ---, born about 1876 in Pike County, Georgia.

B433143. Sam Pounds, third child and first son of Zachariah Pounds and Catharine ---, born about 1878 in Pike County, Georgia.

B43315. Martha F. Pounds, fifth child and third daughter of Daniel Pounds and Julia Slaton, born about 1856 in Georgia.

B43316. Jarrett Walker Pounds, sixth child and third son of Daniel Pounds and Julia Slaton, born about 1857 in Pike County, Georgia and died 1924. Married Elizabeth Abbott, born about 1856 in Georgia and died 21 Sep 1961. Jarrett Pounds and Elizabeth Abbott had issue, which was the ninth generation in America:

B433161. John Henry Pounds, first child and first son of Jarrett Pounds and Elizabeth Abbott, born about 1877 in Pike County, Georgia and died 21 Nov 1939. Married 1900 in Georgia to Sarah Elizabeth Vickers, born 18 Mar 1882 and died 21 Sep 1961. John Pounds and Sarah Vickers had issue, which was the ninth generation in America:

B4331611. Daisy Pounds, first child and first daughter of John Pounds and Sarah Vickers, born 1901. Married J. Sam Rodgers, born 1896 and died 1957 at Griffin, Spalding County, Georgia. Daisy Pounds and J. Sam Rogers had issue, which was the eleventh generation in America:

B43316111. Roberta Rodgers, first child and first daughter of Daisy Pounds and J. Sam Rodgers, born 1921 at Griffin, Spalding County, Georgia. Married 1947 to Andrew Leon Hudgins, Sr., born 1922 at Griffin, Spalding County, Georgia. Roberta Rodgers and Andrew Hudgins had issue, which was the twelth generation in America:

B433161111. Andrea Roberta Hudgins, first child and first daughter of Roberta Rodgers and Andrew Hudgins, born 1947 at Griffin,

Spalding County, Georgia and died 1949.

B433161112. Andrew Leon Hudgins, Jr., second child and first son of Roberta Rodgers and Andrew Hudgins, born 1951 at Griffin, Spalding County, Georgia.

B433161113. Roger Hudgins, third child and second son of Roberta Rodgers and Andrew Hudgins, born 1953 at Griffin, Spalding County, Georgia.

B433161114. Michael Hudgins, fourth child and third son of Roberta Rodgers and Andrew Hudgins, born 1956 at Griffin, Spalding County, Georgia.

B43316112. John L. Rodgers, second child and first son of Daisy Pounds and J. Sam Rodgers, born 1925 at Griffin, Spalding County, Georgia. Married 1944 to Annie B. Cullpeper, born 1946 at Griffin, Spalding County, Georgia. John Rodgers and Annie Cullpeper had issue, which was the twelth generation in America:

B433161121. Steve Rodgers, first child and first son of John Rodgers and Annie Cullpeper, born 1954.

B43316113. Sammie Rodgers, third child and second son of Daisy Pounds and J. Sam Rodgers, born 1931 at Griffin, Spalding County, Georgia.

B43316114. Joyce Rodgers, fourth child and second daughter of Daisy Pounds and J. Sam Rodgers, born 1931 at Griffin, Spalding County, Georgia. Married 1954 to Harris Starr, born 1928. Joyce Rodgers and Harris Starr had issue, which was the twelth generation in America:

B433161141. Keith Starr, first child and first son of Joyce Rodgers and Harris Starr, born 1955.

B433161142. Sammie Starr, second child and second son of Joyce Rodgers and Harris Starr, born 1961.

B4331612. Minnie Pounds, second child and second daughter of John Pounds and Sarah Vickers, born 1902 in Georgia. Married Henry Timmons, born 1901. Minnie Pounds and Henry Timmons had issue, which was the eleventh generation in America:

B43316121. Ray Timmons, first child and first son of Minnie Pounds and Henry Timmons, born 1920.

B43316122. Velma Timmons, second child and first daughter of Minnie Pounds and Henry Timmons, born 1924. Married 1941 to Aubry Truitt.

B4331613. Ernest Talmage Pounds, third child and first son of John Pounds and Sarah Vickers, born 1906 in Georgia.

B4331614. Albert Clifton Pounds, fourth child and second son of John Pounds and Sarah Vickers, born 1908 in Georgia. Married Ethel Crawford.

B4331615. Jarrett Jefferson Pounds, fifth child and third son of John Pounds and Sarah Vickers, born 1910 in Georgia. Married Jonnie Mae Balsch, born 1911.

B4331616. William Fletcher Pounds, sixth child and fourth son of John Pounds and Sarah Vickers, born 1913 in Georgia and died 1953. Married Maggie Brown.

B4331617. Jewel Roberta Pounds, seventh child and third daughter of John Pounds and Sarah Vickers, born 1915 in Georgia. Married Paul Carr, born 1910.

B4331618. John Henry Pounds, Jr., eighth child and fifth son of John Pounds and Sarah Vickers, born 3 Mar 1917 in Georgia. Married Inez Bailey. Married secondly to Cathrine Sheffield. John Pounds and Inez Bailey had issue, which was the eleventh generation in America:

B43316181. Ray Pounds, first child and first son of John Pounds and Inez Bailey, date and place of birth unknown.

B43316182. Sherry Pounds, second child and first daughter of John Pounds and Inez Bailey, date and place of birth unknown.

B4331618. John Henry Pounds, Jr., eighth child and fifth son of John Pounds and Sarah Vickers, born 3 Mar 1917. Married secondly to Cathrine Sheffield. John Pounds and Cathrine Sheffield had issue, which was the eleventh generation in America:

B43316181. Henry Sheffield Pounds, first child and first son of John Pounds and

325

Cathrine Sheffield, date and place of birth unknown.

B43316182. Cathie Pounds, second child and first daughter of John Pounds and Cathrine Sheffield, date and place of birth unknown.

B4331619. James Alfonce Pounds, ninth child and sixth son of John Pounds and Sarah Vickers, born 9 Jan 1920 at Griffin, Spalding County, Georgia. Married 22 Jun 1938 to Mary Muriel Griggers, daughter of Robert Lee Griggers and Janie Victoria Edwards, born 25 Jul 1919 at Griffin, Spalding County, Georgia. James Pounds and Mary Griggers had issue, which was the eleventh generation in America:

B43316191. James Alfonce Pounds, Jr., first child and first son of James Pounds and Mary Griggers, born 9 Sep 1939 at Griffin, Spalding County, Georgia. Married 23 Aug 1959 to Jacquline Batchlor Moore, born 1940 in Georgia. Married secondly to Elaine Kay Johnson. James Pounds and Jacquline Moore had issue, which was the twelth generation in America:

B433161911. Patricia Michelle Pounds, first child and first daughter of James Pounds and Jacquline Moore, born 5 Dec 1960 at Griffin, Spalding County, Georgia.

B43316192. Michael Lewis Pounds, second child and second son of James Pounds and Mary Griggers, born 2 Aug 1943 at Griffin, Spalding County, Georgia. Married 6 Aug 1963 to Nancy Browder. Michael Pounds and Nancy Browder had issue, which was the twelth generation in America:

B433161921. Tamera Lea Pounds, first child and first daughter of Michael Pounds and Nancy Browder, born 25 May 1964 at Columbus, Muscogee County, Georgia.

B433161922. Michelle Pounds, second child and second daughter of Michael Pounds and Nancy Browder, born 30 May 1969 at Columbus, Muscogee County, Georgia.

B43316193. Janie Patricia Pounds, third child and first daughter of James Pounds and Mary Griggers, born 8 Nov 1946 at Griffin, Spalding County, Georgia. Married Michael Ray

Marshall. Janie Pounds and Michael Marshall had issue, which was the twelth generation in America:

B433161931. Michael Ray Marshall, Jr., first child and first son of Janie Pounds and Michael Marshall, born 6 Dec 1967 at Columbus, Muscogee County, Georgia.

B433161932. James Fred Marshall, second child and second son of Janie Pounds and Michael Marshall, born 30 Jan 1970 at Columbus, Muscogee County, Georgia.

B433162. Berry W. Pounds, second child and second son of Jared Pounds and Elizabeth Abbott, born about 1878 in Pike County, Georgia.

B433163. Charlie Pounds, third child and third son of Jared Pounds and Elizabeth Abbott, born about 1880 in Pike County, Georgia and died at Meansville, Pike County, Georgia.

B433164. Dan Pounds, fourth child and fourth son of Jared Pounds and Elizabeth Abbott, born about 1882 in Georgia.

B433165. Blumer Pounds, fifth child and fifth son of Jared Pounds and Elizabeth Abbott, born about 1884 in Georgia.

B43317. Ophelia Pounds, seventh child and fourth daughter of Daniel Pounds and Julia Slaton, born about 1859 in Georgia.

B43318. Daniel Slaton Pounds, eighth child and fourth son of Daniel Pounds and Julia Slaton, born 8 Jan 1862 at Winston, Douglas County, Georgia and died 20 Feb 1912. Married Judaar Minda. Married secondly 1 Dec 1881 at Douglas, Winston County, Georgia to Nancy Elizabeth West. Daniel Pounds and Judaar Minda had issue, which was the ninth generation in America:

B433181. Euna Estalla Pounds, first child and first daughter of Daniel Pounds and Judaar Minda, born 19 Apr 1890 at Haralson, Tallapoosa County, Alabama. Married 31 Oct 1912 at Douglasville, Douglas County, Georgia to Ernest Mancel Wade.

B4332. Isham James Pounds, second child and second son of William Pounds and Nancy Slayden, born 13 Mar 1813 in Wilkes County, Georgia and died 10 Feb 1864 in Berrien County, Georgia. Married 27 Nov 1833 in Oglethorpe County, Georgia to Martha W. Ogden, daughter of Elisha Ogden, born

1817 in Oglethorpe County, Georgia and died May 1874 in Lowndes County, Georgia. Isham Pounds and Martha Ogden had issue, which was the eighth generation in America:

B43321. Elisha E. Pounds, first child and first son of Isham Pounds and Martha Ogden, born about 1835 in Georgia and died at Gause, Milam County, Texas. Buried at Gause, Pineoak cemetery, Texas. Elisha Pounds served in the Civil War; Company F, 22nd Texas Infantry Branch, (Waul's Brigade, Walker's Division). His rank was private and he also served in Company F, Timmon's Regiment, Texas Infantry Branch. Married Elizabeth Adams, born about 1837 in Georgia. Elisha Pounds and Elizabeth Adams had issue, which was the ninth generation in America:

B433211. John Quincy Pounds, first child and first son of Elisha Pounds and Elizabeth Adams, born 22 Mar 1854 in Georgia and died 20 Dec 1929 in Texas. Buried at Cherokee, San Saba County, Mt. Hope cemetery, Texas. Married Ella Light.

B433212. Marilla Pounds, second child and first daughter of Elisha Pounds and Elizabeth Adams, born about 1860 in Texas.

B433213. Luella Pounds, third child and second daughter of Elisha Pounds and Elizabeth Adams, born 29 Mar 1866 in Texas and died 2 Feb 1950 in Texas. Buried at Cherokee, San Saba County, Mt. Hope cemetery, Texas. Married A.C. Chandler. Luella Pounds and A.C. Chandler had issue, which was the tenth generation in America:

B4332131. Edna L. Chandler, first child and first daughter of Luella Pounds and A.C. Chandler, born 17 Jan 1901 in Texas and died 1 Jan 1979 in Texas. Married James E. Hodges.

B433214. Ida Pounds, fourth child and third daughter of Elisha Pounds and Elizabeth Adams, born 7 Apr 1875 in Texas and died 3 Jul 1953 in Texas. Buried at Wells, Nacogdoches County, Shooks Bluff cemetery, Texas. Married W.L. Chandler.

B433215. William S. Pounds, fifth child and second son of Elisha Pounds and Elizabeth Adams, born 1 Apr 1876 in Texas and died 9 Jan 1959 in

Texas. Buried at Cherokee, San Saba County, Mt. Hope cemetery, Texas. Married Eliza Chandler, born Oct 1889 in Texas and died 1 May 1972 in Texas. Buried at Cherokee, San Saba County, Mt. Hope cemetery, Texas. William Pounds and Eliza Chandler had issue, which was the tenth generation in America:

B4332151. Jack Pounds, first child and first son of William Pounds and Eliza Chandler, born 1904 in Texas and died 1906 in Texas. Buried at Wells, Nacogdoches County, Shooks Bluff cemetery, Texas.

B4332152. Josie Pounds, second child and first daughter of William Pounds and Eliza Chandler, born 19 Oct 1907 in Texas and died 16 Oct 1967 in Texas. Married Clayton Grayson.

B4332153. Gertrude Pounds, third child and second daughter of William Pounds and Eliza Chandler, date and place of birth unknown. Married Earl Luce.

B4332154. William Acey Pounds, fourth child and second son of William Pounds and Eliza Chandler, born 19 Jan 1917 in Texas and died 28 Nov 1964 in Texas. Married Lucille Scott.

B433216. Edward Pounds, sixth child and third son of Elisha Pounds and Elizabeth Adams, born 26 Aug 1878 in Texas and died Feb 1925 at Wells, Nacogdoches County, Texas. Married about 1902 to Minnie Chandler, born Jan 1878 and died 1937 at Rusk, Cherokee County, Texas. Edward Pounds and Minnie Chandler had issue, which was the tenth generation in America:

B4332161. Theodore J. Pounds, first child and first son of Edward Pounds and Minnie Chandler, born Oct 1895 in Texas.

B4332162. Ethel Pounds, second child and first daughter of Edward Pounds and Minnie Chandler, born Jan 1900 in Texas. Buried at Wells, Nacogdoches County, Shooks Bluff cemetery, Texas. Married Rube Mettlin. date and place of birth unknown, but buried at Wells, Shooks Bluff cemetery, Texas. Ethel Pounds and Rube Mettlin had issue, which was the eleventh generation in America:

B43321621. Charlie Mettlin, first child and first son of Ethel Pounds and Rube

Mettlin, date and place of birth unknown.

B43321622. Benoni Mettlin, second child and first daughter of Ethel Pounds and Rube Mettlin, date and place of birth unknown.

B43321623. R.B. Mettlin, third child and second son of Ethel Pounds and Rube Mettlin, date and place of birth unknown.

B43321624. Rube Ray Mettlin, fourth child and third son of Ethel Pounds and Rube Mettlin, date and place of birth unknown.

B4332163. Julius Caesar Pounds, third child and second son of Edward Pounds and Minnie Chandler, born 1 Jan 1906 in Milam County, Texas and died 6 Nov 1976 at Brownwood, Comanche County, Texas. Married 24 Jul 1926 in Texas to Bonnie Rena Teague, daughter of Daniel Rufus Teague and Bonnie Luteen Handley, born 26 Nov 1911 at San Antonio, Bexar County, Texas. Julius Pounds went to west Texas in 1926 from Milam County. He was a farmer for many years. He and Bonnie owned a 7-11 grocery in Brownwood, Comanche County, Texas from 1956. Son Tommy Pounds states "Dad did not like kinfolks and that is an understatement", in a letter dated 18 Mar 1991. Julius Pounds and Bonnie Teague had issue, which was the eleventh generation in America:

B43321631. William Eldon Pounds, first child and first son of Julius Pounds and Bonnie Teague, born 15 Jul 1928 in Coke County, Texas. Married Marie Smith. William Pounds and Marie Smith had issue, which was the twelth generation in America:

B433216311. Janice Marie Pounds, first child and first daughter of William Pounds and Marie Smith, date and place of birth unknown. Married Gary Mayes. Janice Pounds and Gary Mayes had issue, which was the thirteenth generation in America:

B4332163111. Shelly Mayes, first child and first daughter of Janice Pounds and Gary Mayes, date and place of birth unknown.

B4332163112. David Mayes, second child and first son of Janice Pounds and Gary Mayes, date and place of birth unknown.

B433216312. William Lee Pounds, second child and first son of William Pounds and Marie Smith, born 1 Jan 1955 in Texas and died 24 Oct 1974 in Texas.

B433216313. Doug Pounds, third child and second son of William Pounds and Marie Smith, date and place of birth unknown. Married Mary C. ---.

B433216314. Twila Jo Pounds, fourth child and second daughter of William Pounds and Marie Smith, born 25 Dec 1973.

B43321632. Julius Caesar Pounds, Jr., second child and second son of Julius Pounds and Bonnie Teague, born 27 Jul 1930. Married Annie Clyde Leddy, born 1950. Julius Pounds and Annie Leddy had issue, which was the twelth generation in America:

B433216321. Brenda Ann Pounds, first child and first daughter of Julius Pounds and Annie Leddy, born 1951. Married Stan Dodd.

B433216322. Dana Jeanette Pounds, second child and second daughter of Julius Pounds and Annie Leddy, date and place of birth unknown. Married Harlan Trowbridge.

B433216323. Pamela Sue Pounds, third child and third daughter of Julius Pounds and Annie Leddy, date and place of birth unknown. Married Kenneth Smith.

B433216324. Donnie Dwain Pounds, fourth child and first son of Julius Pounds and Annie Leddy, born 1956 in Texas and died 22 Jul 1892 in Midland, Midland County, Texas. He and his brother, Kyle, were killed in an automobile accident at Midland, Texas.

B433216325. Kyle Pounds, fifth child and second son of Julius Pounds and Annie Leddy, born 1965 in Texas and died 22 Jul 1982 in Midland, Midland County, Texas. He and his brother, Donnie, were killed in an automobile accident at Midland, Texas.

B43321633. Bonnie Mozelle Pounds, third child and first daughter of Julius Pounds and Bonnie Teague, born 16 Sep 1932. Married Charles Andrew Murray, Sr. 1949 in Ackerly, Martin County, Texas. Bonnie Pounds and Charles Murray had

issue, which was the twelth generation in America:
B433216331. Charles Andrew Murray, Jr., first child and first son of Bonnie Pounds and Charles Murray, born 1950. Married Rolene ---. Charles Murray and Rolene --- had issue, which was the thirteenth generation in America:
B4332163311. Janie Murray, first child and first daughter of Charles Murray and Rolene ---, date and place of birth unknown.
B4332163312. Felitia Murray, second child and second daughter of Charles Murray and Rolene ---, date and place of birth unknown.
B433216332. Roger Lynn Murray, second child and second son of Bonnie Pounds and Charles Murray, date and place of birth unknown. Married Jolita ---. Roger Murray and Jolita --- had issue, which was the thirteenth generation in America:
B4332163321. Kelly Joe Murray, first child and first son of Roger Murray and Jolita ---, date and place of birth unknown.
B433216333. Kathy Murray, third child and first daughter of Bonnie Pounds and Charles Murray, date and place of birth unknown.
B43321634. Thomas (Tommy) Wayne Pounds, fourth child and third son of Julius Pounds and Bonnie Teague, born 24 Jul 1934 in Maverick, Runnels County, Texas. Married 18 Apr 1958 to Kathryn Elaine McDonald, daughter of Roy Alvin McDonald and Bessie Clara Story, born 21 Feb 1938 in Miles, Runnels County, Texas. Thomas Pounds and Kathryn McDonald had issue, which was the twelth generation in America:
B433216341. Darla Elaine Pounds, first child and first daughter of Thomas Pounds and Kathryn McDonald, born 9 Mar 1959 at San Angelo, Tom Green County, Texas. Married Mar 1981 to Jerry Minton. whom she later divorced. Darla Pounds and Jerry Minton had issue, which was the thirteenth generation in America:
B4332163411. Brandy Lynn Minton, first child and first daughter of Darla Pounds and Jerry Minton, born 4 May 1982 at San Angelo, Tom Green County, Texas.
B433216342. Tammy Marie Pounds, second child and second daughter of Thomas Pounds

and Kathryn McDonald, born 29 Aug 1962 at San Angelo, Tom Green County, Texas and died 23 Feb 1983 at San Angelo, Tom Green County, Texas.

B43322. William Daniel Pounds, second child and second son of Isham Pounds and Martha Ogden, born about 1837 in Georgia and died 15 Jan 1882 in Liberty County, Texas. Married Martha Barrow. William Pounds and Martha Barrow had issue, which was the ninth generation in America:

B433221. Amanda Pounds, first child and first daughter of William Pounds and Martha Barrow, date and place of birth unknown.

B433222. George Washington Pounds, second child and first son of William Pounds and Martha Barrow, date and place of birth unknown.

B43323. Harriett A.P. Pounds, third child and first daughter of Isham Pounds and Martha Ogden, born 3 Sep 1838 in Berrien County, Georgia and died 1 Dec 1927 at Pollock, Trinity County, Texas. Married Isham Adams. Harriett Pounds and Isham Adams had issue, which was the ninth generation in America:

B433231. James Adams, first child and first son of Harriett Pounds and Isham Adams, date and place of birth unknown. Married Emma Golden.

B433232. Julia Adams, second child and first daughter of Harriett Pounds and Isham Adams, date and place of birth unknown. Married John Robert Gray. Julia Adams and John Gray had issue, which was the tenth generation in America:

B4332321. Wilma Gray, first child and first daughter of Julia Adams and John Gray, date and place of birth unknown. Married --- Ogletree.

B433233. Emily Adams, third child and second daughter of Harriett Pounds and Isham Adams, date and place of birth unknown. Married Randall C. Griffin.

B433234. Henry Adams, fourth child and second son of Harriett Pounds and Isham Adams, date and place of birth unknown. Married Doll Mowlin.

B433235. Ellen Adams, fifth child and third daughter of Harriett Pounds and Isham Adams, date and place of birth unknown. Married Elizah Alexander.

B43324. Martha Susan Pounds, fourth child and second daughter of Isham Pounds and Martha Ogden, born 31 Oct 1840 in Meriwether County, Georgia and died 5 Nov 1903 at Catcreek Church, Lowndes County, Georgia. Married 16 Sep 1858 in Berrien County, Georgia to Elbert Mathis, born 4 Oct 1836 in Lowndes County, Georgia and died 11 Nov 1915 at Catcreek Church, Lowndes County, Georgia. Martha Pounds and Elbert Mathis had issue, which was the ninth generation in America:

B433241. Julia C. Mathis, first child and first daughter of Martha Pounds and Elbert Mathis, born 1859 in Lowndes County, Georgia. Married 20 Nov 1881 to Thomas M. Ray.

B433242. Winfred Isham Mathis, second child and first son of Martha Pounds and Elbert Mathis, born 1861 in Lowndes County, Georgia. Married 22 Feb 1882 to Martha Missouri Ray.

B433243. Sally (Sarah) Mathis, third child and second daughter of Martha Pounds and Elbert Mathis, born 1863 in Lowndes County, Georgia. Married William Randall Peters.

B433244. Alonzo David Mathis, fourth child and second son of Martha Pounds and Elbert Mathis, born 1866 in Lowndes County, Georgia. Married Frances Baton. Married secondly to Mildred Brogdon.

B433245. Frances Mathis, fifth child and third daughter of Martha Pounds and Elbert Mathis, born 1869 in Lowndes County, Georgia. Married Columbus Williams.

B433246. Charles Mathis, sixth child and third son of Martha Pounds and Elbert Mathis, born 1871 in Lowndes County, Georgia.

B433247. Elva Mathis, seventh child and fourth daughter of Martha Pounds and Elbert Mathis, born 1874 in Lowndes County, Georgia. Married William Williams.

B433248. Margaret Mathis, eighth child and fifth daughter of Martha Pounds and Elbert Mathis, born 1879 in Lowndes County, Georgia. Married William Overstreet. Married secondly O.A. Knight.

B433249. Mattie Mathis, ninth child and sixth daughter of Martha Pounds and Elbert Mathis, born 1881 in Lowndes County, Georgia. Married Robert Dean Hazelhurst.

B433250. Eugene Mathis, tenth child and fourth son of Martha Pounds and Elbert Mathis, born 1883 in Lowndes County, Georgia. Married Mattie DeLoach.

B43325. James Dix Pounds, fifth child and third son of Isham Pounds and Martha Ogden, born 9 Jul 1843 in Oglethorpe County, Georgia and died 23 Dec 1875 at Hahira, Lowndes County, Georgia. Buried at Salem Church cemetery, Lowndes County, Georgia. Married 1865 in Lowndes County, Georgia to Mary Ann Bradford, daughter of Shadrick Bradford and Catherine Johnson, born 7 Feb 1846 in Lowndes County, Georgia and died 23 Aug 1875 at Hahira, Lowndes County, Georgia. Buried at Salem Church cemetery, Lowndes County, Georgia. James Pounds and Mary Bradford had issue, which was the ninth generation in America:

B433251. Willis Byron Pounds, first child and first son of James Pounds and Mary Bradford, born May 1866 in Georgia and died 1914 at Midland, Midland County, Texas. Married Mattie ---, born Oct 1882 in Texas. Willis Pounds committed suicide in 1914 at Midland, Midland County, Texas. Willis Pounds and Mattie --- had issue, which was the tenth generation in America:

B4332511. May (twin) Pounds, first child and first daughter of Willis Pounds and Mattie ---, born Jul 1899 in Texas.

B4332512. Kay (twin) Pounds, second child and second daughter of Willis Pounds and Mattie ---, born Jul 1899 in Texas.

B4332513. Child Pounds, third child, sex unknown of Willis Pounds and Mattie -- date and place of birth unknown.

B4332514. Child Pounds, fourth child, sex unknown of Willis Pounds and Mattie -- date and place of birth unknown.

B4332515. Child Pounds, fifth child, sex unknown of Willis Pounds and Mattie -- date and place of birth unknown.

B4332516. Child Pounds, sixth child, sex unknown of Willis Pounds and Mattie -- date and place of birth unknown.

B4332517. Child Pounds, seventh

child, sex unknown of Willis Pounds and Mattie -- date and place of birth unknown.

B433252. Catherine Pounds, second child and first daughter of James Pounds and Mary Bradford, born 1868 in Georgia and died about 1950 at Richmond, Richmond County, Virginia. She married, but the spouse's name and particulars are unknown. She married secondly to a spouse whose name and particulars are unknown. Catherine Pounds married thirdly to E.N. Dillard, date and place of birth unknown. No known children from either of these marriages.

B433253. Martha (Mattie) Pounds, third child and second daughter of James Pounds and Mary Bradford, born 13 Nov 1870 in Lowndes County, Georgia and died about 1945 at Hahira, Lowndes County, Georgia. Married 12 Dec 1888 in Lowndes County, Georgia to John Morgan Folsom, born about 1866 in Georgia. Martha Pounds and John Folsom had issue, which was the tenth generation in America:

B4332531. Effie Folsom, first child and first daughter of Martha Pounds and John Folsom, born about 1890 at Hahira, Lowndes County, Georgia and died at Birmingham, Jefferson County, Alabama. Married Clifford Martin.

B4332532. Ernest Folsom, second child and first son of Martha Pounds and John Folsom, born about 1892 at Hahira, Lowndes County, Georgia.

B4332533. Ada Folsom, third child and second daughter of Martha Pounds and John Folsom, born about 1894 at Hahira, Lowndes County, Georgia and died about 1950 at Sebring, Highlands County, Florida. Married 1911 at Hahira, Lowndes County, Georgia to Hardy Ryall, born about 1890.

B4332534. Leo Folsom, fourth child and second son of Martha Pounds and John Folsom, born about 1898 at Hahira, Lowndes County, Georgia and died at Indianapolis, Marion County, Indiana.

B4332535. Myol Folsom, fifth child and third son of Martha Pounds and John Folsom, born about 1900 at Hahira, Lowndes County, Georgia.

B433254. Isham Jones Pounds, fourth child and second son of James Pounds and Mary

Bradford, born 28 Dec 1872 in Lowndes County, Georgia and died 22 Sep 1964 at St. Petersburg, Pinellas County, Florida. Buried at St. Petersburg, Pinellas County, Florida. Married 5 Mar 1895 at Lowndes County, Georgia to Cora Ella Rountree, daughter of James Westley Rountree and Anna Judson Webb, born 24 Apr 1874 in Lowndes County, Georgia and died 14 Apr 1910 at Valdosta, Lowndes County, Georgia. Buried at Hahira, Salem Church cemetery, Lowndes County, Georgia. Married secondly to Fannie Horton. Isham Pounds and Cora Rountree had issue, which was the tenth generation in America:

B4332541. Anna Estelle Pounds, first child and first daughter of Isham Pounds and Cora Rountree, born 30 May 1896 at Lenox, Cook County, Georgia. Married 27 Oct 1914 at Tampa, Hillsborough, Florida to Lloyd McDuffie Hicks, Sr., born 14 Mar 1891 at Montgomery, Montgomery County, Alabama and died 6 Oct 1960 at Bradenton, Manatee County, Florida. Anna Pounds and Lloyd Hicks had issue, which was the eleventh generation in America:

B43325411. Lloyd McDuffie Hicks, Jr., first child and first son of Anna Pounds and Lloyd Hicks, born 15 Apr 1918 at Bradenton, Manatee County, Florida and died Apr 1992 at Bradenton, Manatee County, Florida. Married 30 Dec 1940 at Princeton, Dade County, Florida to Marilyn Williams.

B43325412. Thomas Warren Hicks, second child and second son of Anna Pounds and Lloyd Hicks, born 17 Jul 1921 at Bradenton, Manatee County, Florida. Married 30 Dec 1946 at Dalton, Whitfield County, Georgia to Betty Ring.

B4332542. Carl Minor Pounds, second child and first son of Isham Pounds and Cora Rountree, born 4 Dec 1898 at Lenox, Cook County, Georgia and died 6 Aug 1970 in Manatee County, Florida. Buried Skyway cemetery, Manatee County, Florida. Married 8 Jan 1945 at Raleigh, Wake County, North Carolina to Madge Griffin.

B4332543. Nora Mae Pounds, third child and second daughter of Isham Pounds and Cora Rountree, born 25 Jul 1900 at Quitman, Brooks County, Georgia and died 18 May 1902 at Quitman,

Brooks County, Georgia.

B4332544. James Talmadge Pounds, fourth child and second son of Isham Pounds and Cora Rountree, born 15 Mar 1902 at Valdosta, Lowndes County, Georgia and died 28 Jul 1905 at Valdosta, Lowndes County, Georgia.

B4332545. Charlie Isham Pounds, fifth child and third son of Isham Pounds and Cora Rountree, born 5 Mar 1904 at Valdosta, Lowndes County, Georgia and died 21 Feb 1959 at Miami, Dade County, Florida. Married about 1935 at Bradenton, Manatee County, Florida to Willie Mae (Billie) King. Charlie Pounds and Willie King had issue, which was the eleventh generation in America:

B4332541. Charles Pounds, first child and first son of Charlie Pounds and Willie King, born about 1937 at Clearwater, Pinellas County, Florida.

B4332546. William Wadeford Pounds, sixth child and fourth son of Isham Pounds and Cora Rountree, born 11 Nov 1906 at Valdosta, Lowndes County, Georgia and died 1974. Married about 1934 at St. Petersburg, Pinellas County, Florida to Anna Morris Wright. William Pounds and Anna Wright had issue, which was the eleventh generation in America:

B43325461. Dorothy Ann Pounds, first child and first daughter of William Pounds and Anna Wright, born 24 Mar 1936 at St. Petersburg, Pinellas County, Florida. Married 1965 at St. Petersburg, Pinellas County, Florida to Merrill Moore.

B43325462. Jane Pounds, second child and second daughter of William Pounds and Anna Wright, born 7 Nov 1942 at St. Petersburg, Pinellas County, Florida. Married 15 Jun 1958 at Folkston, Charlton County, Georgia to Ronald Murphy.

B433254. Isham Jones Pounds, fourth child and second son of James Pounds and Mary Bradford, born 28 Dec 1872 in Lowndes County, Georgia and died 22 Sep 1964 at St. Petersburg, Pinellas County, Florida. Buried at St. Petersburg, Pinellas County, Florida. Married secondly 5 Aug 1911 at Valdosta, Lowndes County,

Georgia to Fannie Horton, born 10 Mar 1888 and died 1969. Isham Pounds and Fannie Horton had issue, which was the tenth generation in America:

B4332541. James Horton Pounds, first child and first son of Isham Pounds and Fannie Horton, born 10 May 1912 at Valdosta, Lowndes County, Georgia and died 1981. Married about 1932 at St. Petersburg, Pinellas County, Florida to Bessie Fontaine.

B4332542. Jones Laverne Pounds, second child and second son of Isham Pounds and Fannie Horton, born 29 Apr 1914 at Bradenton, Manatee County, Florida. Married Edith Skinner. Married secondly to Virginia Holiday.

B4332543. Francis Wilson Pounds, third child and third son of Isham Pounds and Fannie Horton, born 22 Oct 1918 at Nichols, Polk County, Florida. Married 27 Oct 1941 at St. Petersburg, Pinellas County, Florida to Margory Evelyn Peacock, born 25 May 1921 at Newton, Dale County, Alabama. Francis Pounds and Margory Peacock had issue, which was the eleventh generation in America:

B43325431. Francis Wilson Pounds, Jr., first child and first son of Francis Pounds and Margory Peacock, born 20 Mar 1944 at St. Petersburg, Pinellas County, Florida. Married 19 Dec 1965 at St. Petersburg, Pinellas County, Florida to Gail Vivian Gerritts, daughter of George Anthony Gerrits and Marjorie Meyers, born 27 Jan 1946 in the Bronx, Bronx County, New York. Francis Pounds and Gail Gerritts had issue, which was the twelth generation in America:

B433254311. Stacie Ann Pounds, first child and first daughter of Francis Pounds and Gail Gerritts, born 10 Feb 1969 at Winter Park, Orange County, Florida.

B433254312. Michael Wilson Pounds, second child and first son of Francis Pounds and Gail Gerritts, born 19 Aug 1970 at Winter Park, Orange County, Florida.

B433254313. Katie Margaret Pounds, third child and second daughter of Francis Pounds and Gail Gerritts, born 19 Dec 1978 at St. Petersburg, Pinellas County, Florida.

B43325432. Margaret Kay

Pounds, second child and first daughter of Francis Pounds and Margory Peacock, born 3 Apr 1946 at St. Petersburg, Pinellas County, Florida and died 2 Sep 1974 at St. Petersburg, Pinellas County, Florida. Buried at St. Petersburg, Woodlawn Memorial Gardens, Pinellas County, Florida.

B4332544. Wilbur Owen Pounds, fourth child and fourth son of Isham Pounds and Fannie Horton, born 3 Aug 1920 at Export, Florida. Married Florene Hendrix.

B4332545. Fred Lacoy Pounds, fifth child and fifth son of Isham Pounds and Fannie Horton, born 28 Sep 1923 at Homeland, Polk County, Florida. Married Nadine Reed.

B433255. Dalton Pounds, fifth child and third daughter of James Pounds and Mary Bradford, born 1874 in Georgia. Married John Ogletree. Dalton Pounds and John Ogletree had issue, which was the tenth generation in America:

B4332551. Dick Ogletree, first child and first son of Dalton Pounds and John Ogletree, date and place of birth unknown.

B4332552. Clarence Ogletree, second child and second son of Dalton Pounds and John Ogletree, date and place of birth unknown.

B4332553. Kathryn Ogletree, third child and first daughter of Dalton Pounds and John Ogletree, date and place of birth unknown.

B43326. Lucy Jane Pounds, sixth child and third daughter of Isham Pounds and Martha Ogden, born 7 Jul 1844 in Berrien County, Georgia and died 9 Nov 1929 in Texas. Married 21 Jul 1861 in Berrien County, Georgia to John Hardy King.

B43327. Catherine Pounds, seventh child and fourth daughter of Isham Pounds and Martha Ogden, born about 1848 in Berrien County, Georgia. Married 21 Jul 1861 to John Ward King.

B43328. Henrietta Duke Pounds, eighth child and fifth daughter of Isham Pounds and Martha Ogden, born 1850 in Berrien County, Georgia.

B4333. Sally Isbell Pounds, third child and first daughter of William Pounds and Nancy Slayden, born 30 May 1814 in Wilkes County, Georgia. Married 1832 in Georgia to Wildon L.

Bankston. In 1850 Census Meriwether County, Georgia, she was residing with her mother, Nancy and brother Jared. Wildon not with family. Sally Pounds and Wildon Bankston had issue, which was the eighth generation in America:

B43331. Hiram Bankston, first child and first son of Sally Pounds and Wildon Bankston, born 1832 in Meriwether County, Georgia.

B43332. William S. Bankston, second child and second son of Sally Pounds and Wildon Bankston, born 1834 in Meriwether County, Georgia.

B43333. Nancy J. Bankston, third child and first daughter of Sally Pounds and Wildon Bankston, born 1839 in Meriwether County, Georgia.

B43334. Mary A. Bankston, fourth child and second daughter of Sally Pounds and Wildon Bankston, born 1842 in Meriwether County, Georgia.

B43335. Sarah Bankston, fifth child and third daughter of Sally Pounds and Wildon Bankston, born 1844 in Meriwether County, Georgia.

B43336. Lucy J. Bankston, sixth child and fourth daughter of Sally Pounds and Wildon Bankston, born 1847 in Meriwether County, Georgia.

B4334. Jared Walker Pounds, fourth child and third son of William Pounds and Nancy Slayden, born 22 Mar 1820 in Oglethorpe County, Georgia and died 7 Feb 1887 in Pike County, Georgia. Buried at Mount Vernon Baptist Church cemetery, Clay County, Georgia. Married 2 Dec 1857 in Lee County, Georgia to Temperance Eugenia Ely, daughter of Seaborn Ely and Martha West, born 1838 in North Carolina and died 6 Aug 1909 at Fort Gaines in Clay County, Georgia. Buried at Mount Vernon Baptist Church cemetery, Clay County, Georgia. Jared Walker Pounds served as a private in Co. D 28th Bonaud's Battalion, Georgia Siege Artillery and Bonaud's Battalion, Georgia Volunteers. Enlisted 6 Aug 1863 in Macon, Georgia for period of War. Sent to hospital Lake City, Florida, Apr 14 1864 by order of Surgeon, then furloughed home from the Civil War. Jared Walker Pounds was a southern planter. He owned land and slaves in Georgia. Jared Pounds and Temperance Ely had issue, which was the eighth generation in America:

B43341. William Ely Pounds, first child and

first son of Jared Pounds and Temperance Ely, born 10 Nov 1858 in Pike County, Georgia and died 1938 at Bluffton, Clay County, Georgia. Buried at Bluffton, Clay County, Georgia. Married 1 Sep 1881 in Clay County, Georgia to Palistine Tulula Lands, born Dec 1858 in Georgia and died at Bluffton, Clay County, Georgia. William Pounds and Palistine Lands had issue, which was the ninth generation in America:

B433411. William Eugene Pounds, first child and first son of William Pounds and Palistine Lands, born Jul 1882 in Pike County, Georgia and died in Georgia. Buried at Bluffton, Clay County, Georgia. Married Ola Killingsworth, born 1884 at Bluffton, Clay County, Georgia and died 19 May 1967 at Bluffton, Clay County, Georgia. Buried at Bluffton City cemetery, Georgia. William Pounds and Ola Killingsworth had issue, which was the tenth generation in America:
B4334111. Emma Pounds, first child and first daughter of William Pounds and Ola Killingsworth, born about 1906.
B433412. Leila Valeria Pounds, second child and first daughter of William Pounds and Palistine Lands, born 31 Dec 1885 in Clay County, Georgia and died at Vada, Seminole County, Georgia. Married 1913 in Georgia to John William Sharp, born about 1881 at Hopeful, Mitchell County, Georgia. Leila Pounds and John Sharp had issue, which was the tenth generation in America:
B4334121. John Wendell Sharp, first child and first son of Leila Pounds and John Sharp, date and place of birth unknown. Married Virginia Hill. John Sharp and Virginia Hill had issue, which was the eleventh generation in America:
B43341211. Shirley Sharp, first child and first daughter of John Sharp and Virginia Hill, date and place of birth unknown.
B4334122. Vance Ealy Sharp, second child and second son of Leila Pounds and John Sharp, date and place of birth unknown. Married Edna Louise Goodson. Vance Sharp and Edna Goodson had issue, which was the eleventh

generation in America:

B43341221. Vicky Lynn Sharp, first child and first daughter of Vance Sharp and Edna Goodson, date and place of birth unknown.

B43341222. Michael Anthony Sharp, second child and first son of Vance Sharp and Edna Goodson, date and place of birth unknown.

B4334123. Emma Juanita Sharp, third child and first daughter of Leila Pounds and John Sharp, date and place of birth unknown. Married Marion M. Cooper. Emma Sharp and Marion Cooper had issue, which was the eleventh generation in America:

B43341231. Harry James Cooper, first child and first son of Emma Sharp and Marion Cooper, date and place of birth unknown.

B43341232. Gene Raymond Cooper, second child and second son of Emma Sharp and Marion Cooper, date and place of birth unknown.

B43341233. Leila Marilyn Cooper, third child and first daughter of Emma Sharp and Marion Cooper, date and place of birth unknown.

B433413. Edgar Pounds, third child and second son of William Pounds and Palistine Lands, was stillborn with date and place unknown.

B433414. Joseph A. Pounds, fourth child and third son of William Pounds and Palistine Lands, born Nov 1887 in Clay County, Georgia.

B433415. Julius Jared Pounds, fifth child and fourth son of William Pounds and Palistine Lands, born Feb 1890 in Clay County, Georgia. Married Louise Hutto Speaker. Julius Pounds and Louise Speaker did not have issue, but Julius adopted Louise's daughter by her first marriage. This child is in the eleventh generation in America:

B4334151. Tena Speaker, stepdaughter of Julius Pounds and Louise Speaker, date and place of birth unknown.

B433416. John Rufus Pounds, sixth

child and fifth son of William Pounds and Palistine Lands, born Mar 1893 in Clay County, Georgia. Married Jessie Powell.

B433417. Sarah Elizabeth Pounds, seventh child and second daughter of William Pounds and Palistine Lands, born Feb 1896 in Clay County, Georgia. Married William Calvin Taylor. Sarah Pounds and William Taylor had issue, which was the tenth generation in America:

B4334171. --- Taylor, first child and first son of Sarah Pounds and William Taylor, date and place of birth unknown.

B43342. Jared Walker Pounds, Jr., second child and second son of Jared Pounds and Temperance Ely, born 13 Aug 1860 in Pike County, Georgia and died 11 Feb 1938 in Lubbock, Lubbock County, Texas. Buried at Houston, Harris County, Texas. Married 22 Apr 1885 at San Marcos, Hays County, Texas to Mary Frances Jones, daughter of James T. Jones and Salina Knowell, born 11 Apr 1854 at Fort Gaines, Clay County, Georgia and died 23 Jan 1932 at Houston, Harris County, Texas. Jared Pounds and Mary Jones had issue, which was the ninth generation in America:

B433421. Annie Lee Pounds, first child and first daughter of Jared Pounds and Mary Jones, born 11 Dec 1887 at San Marcos, Hays County, Texas and died 29 Jun 1963 at Lubbock, Lubbock County, Texas. Buried at Resthaven cemetery, Lubbock, Texas. Married 7 Oct 1904 in Georgetown, Williamson County, Texas to Washington Lee Talley, son of William Ransom Talley and Lira Sarah Clyne. Married secondly Dec 1926 in Texas to John Hamilton (Johnny) Stalnaker. Annie Pounds and Washington Talley had issue, which was the tenth generation in America:

B4334211. Porter Lee Talley, first child and first son of Annie Pounds and Washington Talley, born 8 Aug 1905 at Taylor, Williamson County, Texas.

B4334212. Arthur Samuel Talley, second child and second son of Annie Pounds and Washington Talley, born Dec 1907 at Dumas, Moore County, Texas and died 1915 at Ralls, Crosby County, Texas.

B4334213. James Dodson Talley,

third child and third son of Annie Pounds and Washington Talley, born 14 Jul 1910 at Vernon, Wilbarger County, Texas and died 11 Nov 1985 at Lubbock, Lubbock County, Texas. Buried at Englewood cemetery, Lubbock, Texas. Married 2 Apr 1935 at Posey, Lubbock County, Texas to Alma Lillie Louise Meyer, born 4 Mar 1914 at Taylor, Williamson County, Texas and died 11 Aug 1964 at Lubbock, Lubbock County, Texas. Buried at Slaton, Englewood cemetery, Lubbock County, Texas. James Talley and Alma Meyer had issue, which was the eleventh generation in America:

B43342131. Margaret Louise Talley, first child and first daughter of James Talley and Alma Meyer, born 20 Sep 1936 at Slaton, Lubbock County, Texas. Married 10 Oct 1954 at Slaton, Lubbock County, Texas to W.J. Johnson, born 2 Jan 1932 at Tioga, Cooke County, Texas. Margaret Talley and W.J. Johnson had issue, which was the twelth generation in America:

B433421311. Rose Marie Johnson, first child and first daughter of Margaret Talley and W.J. Johnson, born 21 Jul 1955 at Plainview, Hale County, Texas. Married 27 Jul 1989 at Fort Worth, Tarrant County, Texas to Bobby Wayne Rogers, born 11 Feb 1966 at Dallas, Dallas County, Texas. Rose Johnson and Bobby Rogers had issue, which was the thirteenth generation in America:

B4334213111. Christina Marie Johnson, first child and first daughter of Rose Johnson and Bobby Rogers, born 1 Oct 1975 at Lubbock, Lubbock County, Texas.

B433421312. Lajuana June Johnson, second child and second daughter of Margaret Talley and W.J. Johnson, born 31 Oct 1958 at Slaton, Lubbock County, Texas and died 12 Dec 1958 at Slaton, Lubbock County, Texas. Buried at Englewood cemetery, Lubbock, Texas.

B433421313. Nita Louise Johnson, third child and third daughter of Margaret Talley and W.J. Johnson, born 26 Apr 1960 at Slaton, Lubbock County, Texas.

B433421314. William Jay Johnson, fourth child and first son of Margaret Talley and W.J. Johnson, born 7 Jun 1962 at

Slaton, Lubbock County, Texas. Married Jul 1987 at Corsicana, Navarro County, Texas to Judith Louise McCullough, born 21 Mar 1970. William Johnson and Judith McCullough had issue, which was the fourteenth generation in America:

B4334213141. Jennifer Louise Johnson, first child and first daughter of William Johnson and Judith McCullough, born 22 Jul 1987 at Forth Worth, Tarrant County, Texas.

B43342132. Shirley Ann Talley, second child and second daughter of James Talley and Alma Meyer, born Nov 1940 in Lubbock County, Texas.

B43342133. John Lawrence Talley, third child and first son of James Talley and Alma Meyer, born 6 Dec 1945 at Lubbock, Lubbock County, Texas. Married 27 Nov 1971 at Ropesville, Hockley County, Texas to Pamela Sue Ream, born 30 Apr 1952 at Lubbock County, Texas. John Talley and Pamela Ream had issue, which was the twelth generation in America:

B433421331. Justin Lee Talley, first child and first son of John Talley and Pamela Ream, born 24 Jan 1978 in Lubbock County, Texas.

B4334214. Woodrow Wilson Talley, fourth child and fourth son of Annie Pounds and Washington Talley, born 6 Apr 1913 at Electra, Wichita County, Texas and died 26 Mar 1956 at Lubbock, Lubbock County, Texas. Buried at Resthaven cemetery, Lubbock, Texas.

B4334215. Mary Margaret Talley, fifth child and first daughter of Annie Pounds and Washington Talley, born 13 Feb 1916 at Ralls, Crosby County, Texas.

B4334216. Ella Rhea Talley, sixth child and second daughter of Annie Pounds and Washington Talley, born 5 May 1919 at Ranger, Eastland County, Texas and died 7 Jun 1979 at Childress, Lubbock County, Texas. Buried Resthaven cemetery, Lubbock County, Texas. Married A.B. (Satch) Landrum.

B433421. Annie Lee Pounds, first child and first daughter of Jared Pounds and Mary Jones, born 11 Dec 1887 at San Marcos, Hays County, Texas and died 29 Jun 1963 at Lubbock, Lubbock County, Texas. Buried at Resthaven cemetery, Lubbock, Texas. Married secondly Dec 1926 to John Hamilton (Johnny) Stalnaker. Annie Pounds and John Stalnaker had issue, which was the tenth generation in America:

B4334211. Johnny Helen Stalnaker, first child and first daughter of Annie Pounds and John Stalnaker, born 18 Jan 1926 at Amarillo, Potter County, Texas.

B4334212. Jo Norvelle Stalnaker, second child and second daughter of Annie Pounds and John Stalnaker, born 11 May 1927 at Amarillo, Potter County, Texas and died 10 Aug 1959 at Santa Barbara, Santa Barbara County, California.

B433422. Jarred Lucius Pounds, second child and first son of Jared Pounds and Mary Jones, born 22 Apr 1889 in Hays County, Texas and died 3 Aug 1941 at Lubbock, Lubbock County, Texas. Married 2 Aug 1913 in Ralls, Crosby County, Texas to Olena Blanche Elmore, born 24 Jul 1897 at Ralls, Crosby County, Texas and died 28 Jan 1981 at Plainview, Hale County, Texas. Jarred Pounds and Olena Elmore had issue, which was the tenth generation in America:

B4434221. Frances Estelle Pounds, first child and first daughter of Jarred Pounds and Olena Elmore, born 16 Aug 1915 at Ralls, Crosby County, Texas. Married 1934 to James A. Odom, date and place of birth unknown, but he died in 1971. Frances Pounds and James Odom had issue, which was the eleventh generation in America:

B44342211. James R. Odom, first child and first son of Frances Pounds and James Odom, born 1935.

B44342212. Elnora Frances Odom, second child and first daughter of Frances Pounds and James Odom, born 1936.

B4434222. Chester Darwin Pounds, second child and first son of Jarred Pounds and Olena Elmore, born 28 Oct 1916 at Ralls, Crosby County, Texas and died 25 Sep 1991 at St. George, Washington County, Utah. Married 1956 at Las Vegas, Clark County, Nevada to Gladys Chadwick.

B4434223. Leon Travis Pounds, third

child and second son of Jarred Pounds and Olena Elmore, born 21 Jan 1918 at Ralls, Crosby County, Texas and died bout 1983 at Columbus, Chattahoochee County, Georgia. Married Rita Janette Register, born 22 Jun 1927 and died about 1982 at Columbus, Chattahoochee County, Georgia. Leon Pounds and Rita Register had issue, which was the eleventh generation in America:

B44342231. Rita Jane Pounds, first child and first daughter of Leon Pounds and Rita Register, born 11 Apr 1949 at Columbus, Chattahoochee County, Georgia.

B44342232. Jerry Leon Pounds, second child and first son of Leon Pounds and Rita Register, born 28 Jun 1955 at Columbus, Chattahoochee County, Georgia.

B4434224. Christine Pounds, fourth child and second daughter of Jarred Pounds and Olena Elmore, born about 1922 and died about 1980. Married at Inglewood, Los Angeles County, California to Bill Wilson.

B433423. John Ross Pounds, third child and second son of Jared Pounds and Mary Jones, born 20 Feb 1891 at San Marcos, Hays County, Texas and died 21 Oct 1957 at Lubbock, Lubbock County, Texas. Married 1 Jun 1913 in Crosby County, Texas to Nettie Lena Pierce, born 6 Dec 1894 at Dexter, Grayson County, Texas. Married secondly to Frances Owens. John Pounds and Nettie Pierce had issue, which was the tenth generation in America:

B4334231. Royce Alton Pounds, first child and first son of John Pounds and Nettie Pierce, born 16 Dec 1916 at Post, Garza County, Texas and died 31 May 1939 at Lubbock, Lubbock County, Texas. Married 14 Feb 1939 in Dickens County, Texas to May Gannon.

B4334232. Avis Clearissia Pounds, second child and first daughter of John Pounds and Nettie Pierce, born 31 Jul 1918 at Ralls, Crosby County, Texas. Married 7 Dec 1938 at Clovis, Curry County, New Mexico to Rex Daniel Williams, born 27 Dec 1911. Avis Pounds and Rex Williams had issue, which was the eleventh generation in America:

B43342321. James Daniel Williams, first child and first son of Avis Pounds and Rex

Williams, born 20 Oct 1940. Married 7 Jun 1960 at Clovis, Curry County, New Mexico to Delores Jane Waggon, born 18 Oct 1941 at Muleshoe, Bailey County, Texas. James Williams and Delores Waggon had issue, which was the twelth generation in America:

B433423211. James Rance Williams, first child and first son of James Williams and Delores Waggon, born 23 Feb 1961 at Lubbock, Lubbock County, Texas.

B433423212. Jennifer Jo Williams, second child and first daughter of James Williams and Delores Waggon, born 16 Oct 1964 at Lubbock, Lubbock County, Texas.

B4334233. Marvin Pierce Pounds, third child and second son of John Pounds and Nettie Pierce, born 12 Jan 1920 at Tahona, Lynn County, Texas. Married 2 Jul 1950 at Los Angeles, Los Angeles County, California to Mary Hindmarsh.
Marvin Pounds and Mary Hindmarsh had issue, which was the eleventh generation in America:

B4334331. William Ross Pounds, first child and first son of Marvin Pounds and Mary Hindmarsh, born 4 Feb 1951 at Los Angeles, Los Angeles County, California.

B4334332. Steven David Pounds, second child and second son of Marvin Pounds and Mary Hindmarsh, born 5 Aug 1952 at Huntington Park, Los Angeles County, California.

B4334234. Helen Imogene Pounds, fourth child and second daughter of John Pounds and Nettie Pierce, born 11 Nov 1928 at Lorenzo, Crosby County, Texas. Married 21 Mar 1947 at Inglewood, Los Angeles County, California to Charles Thomas Acres, born 12 Aug 1922 at El Paso, El Paso County, Texas. Helen Pounds and Charles Acres had issue, which was the eleventh generation in America:

B4334341. Michael Thomas Acres, first child and first son of Helen Pounds and Charles Acres, born 9 Aug 1948 at Inglewood, Los Angeles County, California.

B4334342. Gregory Ives Acres, second child and second son of Helen Pounds and Charles Acres, born 21 Mar 1955 at Lubbock, Lubbock County, Texas.

B4334343. Sandra Gale Acres, third child and first daughter of Helen Pounds and Charles Acres, born 6 Apr 1959 at Lubbock, Lubbock County, Texas.

B4334235. Lamona Louise Pounds, fifth child and third daughter of John Pounds and Nettie Pierce, born 9 Apr 1933 at Lubbock, Lubbock County, Texas. Married 8 Aug 1950 at Inglewood, Los Angeles County, California to Paul W. Jackson, born 8 Aug 1931 at Inglewood, Los Angeles County, California. Lamona Pounds and Paul Jackson had issue, which was the eleventh generation in America:

B4334351. Timothy Lee Jackson, first child and first son of Lamona Pounds and Paul Jackson, born 1 Oct 1952 at Los Angeles, Los Angeles County, California.

B4334352. Jody Lynn Jackson, second child and first daughter of Lamona Pounds and Paul Jackson, born 8 Sep 1955 at Inglewood, Los Angeles County, California.

B4334353. Paula Louise Jackson, third child and second daughter of Lamona Pounds and Paul Jackson, born 31 Oct 1962 at Redondo Beach, Los Angeles County, California.

B4334236. Carol Jean Pounds, sixth child and fourth daughter of John Pounds and Nettie Pierce, born 2 Jan 1935 at Lubbock, Lubbock County, Texas. Married 21 Aug 1957 at Inglewood, Los Angeles County, California to James Allen McDowell, born 8 Aug 1933 at Wilmerding, Allegheny County, Pennsylvania. Carol Pounds and James McDowell had issue, which was the eleventh generation in America:

B4334361. Colleen McDowell, first child and first daughter of Carol Pounds and James McDowell, born 2 Dec 1959 at Inglewood, Los Angeles County, California.

B4334362. Mark Allen McDowell, second child and first son of Carol Pounds and James McDowell, born 26 Jan 1963 at Inglewood, Los Angeles County, California.

B4334363. Kelly McDowell, third child and second son of Carol Pounds and James McDowell, born 2 Mar 1966 at Pico Rivera, Los Angeles County, California.

B433424. Bessie Ostelle Pounds, fourth child and second daughter of Jared Pounds and Mary Jones, born 18 Oct 1892 at San Marcos, Hays County, Texas and died 9 Mar 1952 at Breckenridge, Stephens County, Texas. Married 22 Dec 1912 in Crosby County, Texas to John March Taylor, son of Wyatt Andrew Taylor and Mahala Horton, born 17 Sep 1891 at San Angelo, Tom Green County, Texas and died 15 Dec 1974 at Breckenridge, Stephens County, Texas. Bessie Pounds and John Taylor had issue, which was the tenth generation in America:

B4434241. John March Taylor, Jr., first child and first son of Bessie Pounds and John Taylor, born 18 Oct 1913 in Dickens County, Texas and died 22 Oct 1977 at Breckenridge, Stephens County, Texas. Married 13 Mar 1937 to Ora May Stimson, born 2 Aug 1920. John Taylor, Jr. and Ora Stimson had issue, which was the eleventh generation in America:

B44342411. Connie Dee Taylor, first child and first daughter of John Taylor, Jr. and Ora Stimson, born 20 Jun 1942 at Brownwood, Brown County, Texas. Married 3 Jul 1964 to R.L. Bien, born 25 Nov 1942. Connie Taylor and R.L. Bien had issue, which was the twelth generation in America:

B443424111. Ryan Larson Bien, first child and first son of Connie Taylor and R.L. Bien, born 6 Sep 1966.

B443424112. James Gregory Bien, second child and second son of Connie Taylor and R.L. Bien, born 11 Feb 1973.

B44342412. John March Taylor III, second child and first son of John Taylor, Jr. and Ora Stimson, born 1 Nov 1945 at Brownwood, Brown County, Texas. Married 17 Jun 1966 to Barbara Lynette, born 26 Dec 1946. John Taylor and Barbara Lynette had issue, which was the twelth generation in America:

B443424121. John March Taylor IV, first child and first son of John Taylor III and Barbara Lynette, born 16 Sep 1972 at Brownwood, Brown County, Texas.

B443424122. Jenifer Lynette Taylor, second child and first daughter of John Taylor III and Barbara Lynette, born 24 Apr 1974 at Brownwood, Brown County, Texas.

B44342413. Donna Jo Taylor, third child and second daughter of John Taylor, Jr. and Ora Stimson, born 18 Oct 1949 at Brownwood, Brown County, Texas. Married 1 Jul 1967 to Paul Ellis Seward, born 27 Jun 1943. Donna Taylor and Paul Seward had issue, which was the twelth generation in America:

B443424131. Christi Lee Seward, first child and first daughter of Donna Taylor and Paul Seward, born 18 Sep 1969 at Brownwood, Brown County, Texas.

B443424132. Stacy Leigh Seward, second child and second daughter of Donna Taylor and Paul Seward, born 17 Aug 1971 at Brownwood, Brown County, Texas.

B4434242. Donleita Ross Taylor, second child and first daughter of Bessie Pounds and John Taylor, born 20 Feb 1917 at Ralls, Crosby County, Texas. Married 15 Sep 1936 to Elvan Horace (Jimmie) Thorp, born 25 Feb 1913 at Houston, Harris County, Texas. Donleita Taylor and Elvan Thorp had issue, which was the eleventh generation in America:

B44342421. Sharon Donleita Thorp, first child and first daughter of Donleita Taylor and Elvan Thorp, born 8 Apr 1940 at Big Spring, Howard County, Texas. Married 7 Jun 1963 to Robert Berkley Bernard, from whom she later divorced. Sharon Thorp and Robert Bernard had issue, which was the twelth generation in America:

B443424211. Deanna Lillian Bernard, first child and first daughter of Sharon Thorp and Robert Bernard, born 9 Jul 1967 at Decatur, Wise County, Texas.

B443424212. Bradley Harrison Bernard, second child and first son of Sharon Thorp and Robert Bernard, born 1 Nov 1968 at Oklahoma City, Oklahoma County, Oklahoma.

B4434243. Townes Horton (Bill) Taylor, third child and second son of Bessie Pounds and John Taylor, born 5 Mar 1919 at Ralls, Crosby County, Texas. Married 17 Jun 1945 to Edna Maxine Hays, born 9 Nov 1920.

B4434244. Richard Randolph Taylor, fourth child and third son of Bessie Pounds and

John Taylor, born 5 May 1921 at Breckenridge, Stephens County, Texas. Married in 1942 to Vida Ruth Thomas, born 15 Jan 1926 and died 7 Sep 1970. Richard Taylor married secondly 8 Jan 1972 in Midland, Midland County, Texas to Kathleen Walker Wolfenburger. Richard Taylor and Vida Thomas had issue, which was the eleventh generation in America:

B44342441. Richard Randolph Taylor, Jr., first child and first son of Richard Taylor and Vida Thomas, born 22 Dec 1942 at Breckenridge, Stephens County, Texas. Married 6 Aug 1962 to Barbara Ledbetter. Richard Taylor and Barbara Ledbetter had issue, which was the twelth generation in America:

B443424411. Leeann Taylor, first child and first daughter of Richard Taylor and Barbara Ledbetter, born 1 Jun 1966.

B443424412. Catherine (Cathy) Taylor, second child and second daughter of Richard Taylor and Barbara Ledbetter, born 1 Dec 1967.

B443424413. Matthew Bullock Taylor, third child and first son of Richard Taylor and Barbara Ledbetter, born 6 Jun 1980, adopted by Richard and Barbara.

B44342442. Patricia Jean Taylor, second child and first daughter of Richard Taylor and Vida Thomas, born 4 Jun 1949 at Levelland, Hockley County, Texas. Married Jun 1968 at Midland, Midland County, Texas to Johnny Wayne Holt. Patricia Taylor and Johnny Holt had issue, which was the twelth generaion in America:

B443424421. Johnny Wayne Holt, Jr., first child and first son of Patricia Taylor and Johnny Holt, born 11 Apr 1969.

B443424422. Thomas Taylor Holt, second child and second son of Patricia Taylor and Johnny Holt, born 12 Sep 1971.

B443424423. John Randolph Holt, third child and third son of Patricia Taylor and Johnny Holt, born 23 Nov 1975.

B443424424. Robbyn Melinda Holt, fourth child and first daughter of Patricia Taylor and Johnny Holt, born 15 Aug 1978.

B4434245. Lindsey Dan Taylor,

fifth child and fourth son of Bessie Pounds and John Taylor, born 7 Jun 1926 at Breckenridge, Stephens County, Texas and died 30 Jun 1977. Buried at Denver, Ft. Logan National Cemetery, Colorado. Married 16 Nov 1947 to Jo Rene Ferrill. Lindsey Taylor and Jo Ferrill had issue, which was the eleventh generation in America:

B44342451. Lindsey Dan Taylor, Jr., first child and first son of Lindsey Taylor and Jo Ferrill, born 5 Sep 1948 at Brownwood, Brown County, Texas. Married 18 Sep 1971 at Denver, Jefferson County, Colorado to June Ellen Marlen. Lindsey Taylor and June Marlen had issue, which was the twelth generation in America:

B443424511. Debra Taylor, first child and first daughter of Lindsey Taylor and June Marlen, born 1 Sep 1972 at Denver, Jefferson County, Colorado.

B443424512. Jennifer Jean Taylor, second child and second daughter of Lindsey Taylor and June Marlen, born 27 Apr 1974 at Denver, Jefferson County, Colorado.

B443424513. Natalie Ann Taylor, third child and third daughter of Lindsey Taylor and June Marlen, born 14 Sep 1978 at Littleton, Jefferson County, Colorado.

B44342452. William Randolph Taylor, second child and second son of Lindsey Taylor and Jo Ferrill, born 30 Apr 1955 at Wichita Falls, Wichita County, Texas. Married at Denver, Jefferson County, Colorado to Darlene Marie Garrimore. William Taylor and Darlene Garrimore had issue, which was the twelth generation in America:

B443424521. Nicole Taylor, first child and first daughter of William Taylor and Darlene Garrimore.

B443424522. Scott Taylor, second child and first son of William Taylor and Darlene Garrimore.

B443424523. William Randolph Taylor, Jr., third child and second son of William Taylor and Darlene Garrimore.

B4434246. Murray Freeman Taylor, sixth child and fifth son of Bessie Pounds and John Taylor, born 30 Sep 1929 at Breckenridge,

Stephens County, Texas. Married 30 Sep 1953 to Mary Beth Bates, from whom he later divorced. Murray Taylor married secondly Carol (Jeanie) Jean, date and place of birth unknown, but she died 22 Nov 1975. Murray Taylor married thirdly 1 Mar 1976 to Betty Louise Keck. Murray Taylor and Mary Bates had issue, which was the eleventh generation in America:

B44342461. Lee Ann Taylor, first child and first daughter of Murray Taylor and Mary Bates, born 4 Jun 1959 at Breckenridge, Stephens County, Texas.

B44342462. Wyatt Taylor, second child and first son of Murray Taylor and Mary Bates, born 6 Nov 1960 at Breckenridge, Stephens County, Texas.

B4434246. Murray Freeman Taylor, sixth child and fifth son of Bessie Pounds and John Taylor, born 30 Sep 1929 at Breckenridge, Stephens County, Texas. Married secondly Carol (Jeanie) Jean, date and place of birth unknown, but she died 22 Nov 1975. Murray Taylor and Carol Jean had issue, which was the eleventh generation in America:

B44342461. Mark Freeman Taylor, first child and first son of Murray Taylor and Carol Jean, born 14 Aug 1963 at Kermit, Winkler County, Texas.

B433425. Jones Walker Pounds, fifth child and third son of Jared Pounds and Mary Jones, born 15 Aug 1894 in Bastrop, Bastrop County, Texas and died 9 Mar 1961 at Lubbock, Lubbock County, Texas. Buried at City cemetery, Lubbock, Texas. Married 26 Dec 1925 to Lillie Mae Barker.

B433426. Eva May Pounds, sixth child and third daughter of Jared Pounds and Mary Jones, born 15 Feb 1897 at Lytton, Caldwell County, Texas and died 11 Dec 1988 at Bloomfield, San Juan County, New Mexico. Buried at Cortez, Montezuma County, Colorado. Married 7 Jun 1914 at Ralls, Crosby County, Texas to Herbert Lowima Rogers, Sr., born 16 Mar 1890 at Grapevine, Tarrant County, Texas and died 5 Apr 1959. Eva Pounds and Herbert Rogers had issue, which was the tenth generation in America:

B4334261. Mary Virginia Rogers, first child and first daughter of Eva Pounds and Herbert Rogers, born 2 Aug 1915. Married 20 May 1933 to Thurson Clement Hall. Mary Rogers and Thurson Hall had issue, which was the eleventh generation in America:

B43342611. Allie Jane Hall, first child and first daughter of Mary Rogers and Thurson Hall, born 2 May 1935. Married 14 Aug 1953 to Theodore Charles Hilder II, date and place of birth unknown and died May 1966 in California. Allie Hall and Theodore Hilder had issue, which was the twelth generation in America:

B433426111. Majorie Denise Hilder, first child and first daughter of Allie Hall and Theodore Hilder, born 31 Oct 1954.

B433426112. Theodore Charles Hilder III, second child and first son of Allie Hall and Theodore Hilder, born 27 May 1956.

B433426113. Julia Rebecca Hilder, third child and second daughter of Allie Hall and Theodore Hilder, born 25 Aug 1960.

B43342612. Richard Wayne Hall, second child and first son of Mary Rogers and Thurson Hall, born 29 Feb 1937. Married 6 Jul 1955 to Beverly Dee Wheeler. Richard Hall and Beverly Wheeler had issue, which was the twelth generation in America:

B433426121. Richard Hall, first child and first son of Richard Hall and Beverly Wheeler, born 28 Aug 1957.

B433426122. Wayne Hall, second child and second son of Richard Hall and Beverly Wheeler, born 16 Dec 1962.

B43342613. Robert Lynn Hall, third child and second son of Mary Rogers and Thurson Hall, born 12 Sep 1945.

B4334262. Winnifred Lorena Rogers, second child and second daughter of Eva Pounds and Herbert Rogers, born 11 Oct 1917. Married 11 Oct 1935 at Monticello, San Juan County, Utah to Carlos M. Hall, born 28 Sep 1909 at Couch, Oregon County, Missouri. Winnifred Rogers and Carlos Hall had issue, which was the eleventh generation in America:

B43342621. Virginia June Hall, first child and first daughter of Winnifred Rogers and Carlos Hall, born 20 Jun 1936 and died 11 Jul 1945.

B43342622. Theodore Carlos Hall, second child and first son of Winnifred Rogers and Carlos Hall, born 7 Apr 1938 and died 13 Nov 1962 at Dove Creek, Dolores County, Colorado. Married 17 Feb 1960 to Beverly Joyce Daniels, born 20 Dec 1943 at Louisville, Cass County, Nebraska. Theodore Hall and Beverly Daniels had issue, which was the twelth generation in America:

B433426221. Wendy Lee Hall, first child and first daughter of Theodore Hall and Beverly Daniels, born 2 Dec 1960 at Monticello, San Juan County, Utah. Married 21 Jun 1985 at Salt Lake City, Salt Lake County, Utah to Curtis Edward Walker, born 21 Aug 1956 in South Dakota. Wendy Hall and Curtis Walker had issue, which was the thirteenth generation in America:

B4334262211. Theodore Curtis Walker, first child and first son of Wendy Hall and Curtis Walker, born 27 Apr 1987 at Salt Lake City, Salt Lake County, Utah.

B4334262212. Grace Rosalie Walker, second child and first daughter of Wendy Hall and Curtis Walker, born 3 May 1989 at Elko, Elko County, Nevada.

B433426222. Thea Joy Hall, second child and second daughter of Theodore Hall and Beverly Daniels, born 4 Oct 1961 at Monticello, San Juan County, Utah.

B43342623. Roger Evan Hall, third child and second son of Winnifred Rogers and Carlos Hall, born 12 Dec 1939 at Dove Creek, Dolores County, Colorado. Married 13 Sep 1962 at Moab, Grand County, Utah to Sharon Haaland, born 5 Sep 1944 at Dove Creek, Dolores County, Colorado. Roger Hall and Sharon Haaland had issue, which was the twelth generation in America:

B433426231. Jeffery Evan Hall, first child and first son of Roger Hall and Sharon Haaland, born 20 Aug 1967 at Moab, Grand County, Utah. Married 24 Nov 1989 at Las Cruces, Dona Ana County, New Mexico to Melinda Janine Rogers, born 6 Feb 1968 at Albuquerque, Bernalillo

County, New Mexico. Jeffery Hall and Melinda Rogers had issue, which was the thirteenth generation in America:

B4334262311. Corrina Frances Hall, first child and first daughter of Jeffery Hall and Melinda Rogers, born 1 May 1990 at Las Cruces, Dona Ana County, New Mexico.

B433426232. David Theodore Hall, second child and second son of Roger Hall and Sharon Haaland, born 10 Feb 1971 at Tucson, Pima County, Arizona.

B43342624. Janet Arlene Hall, fourth child and second daughter of Winnifred Rogers and Carlos Hall, born 12 Dec 1941 at San Francisco, San Francisco County, California. Married 6 Apr 1963 at Monticello, San Juan County, Utah to John Washington Knuckles, born 31 Dec 1939 at Dove Creek, Dolores County, Colorado. Janet Hall and John Knuckles had issue, which was the twelth generation in America:

B433426241. Valeria June Knuckles, first child and first daughter of Janet Hall and John Knuckles, born 18 Jul 1964 at Salt Lake City, Salt Lake County, Utah. Married 30 May 1987 at Salt Lake City, Salt Lake County, Utah to Steven P. Simpson, born 11 Oct 1958 at Monticello,San Juan County, Utah. Valeria Knuckles and Steven Simpson had issue, which was the thirteenth generation in America:

B4334262411. Dacia Leigh Simpson, first child and first daughter of Valeria Knuckles and Steven Simpson, born 1 Oct 1990 at Salt Lake City, Salt Lake County, Utah.

B433426242. John Roger Knuckles, second child and first son of Janet Hall and John Knuckles, born 23 Dec 1968 at Las Cruces, Dona Ana County, New Mexico.

B43342625. Majorie Evelyn Hall, fifth child and third daughter of Winnifred Rogers and Carlos Hall, born 14 Jun 1943 at San Francisco, San Francisco County, California. Married 19 Aug 1961 at Grants, Cibola County, New Mexico to Floyd Johnson, born 9 Jan 1940 at Dove Creek, Dolores County, Colorado. Majorie Hall and Floyd Johnson had issue, which was the twelth generation in America:

B433426251. William Troy Johnson, first child and first son of Majorie Hall and Floyd Johnson, born 30 Jun 1962 at Monticello, San Juan County, Utah. Married in Italy to Patricia Ann Davis. Married secondly in New York to Diane Lucius. Married thirdly to Deborah Marie Major, born 21 Apr 1958 at Dallas, Dallas County, Texas. William Johnson and Deborah Major had issue, which was the thirteenth generation in America:

B4334262511. William Jacob (twin) Johnson, first child and first son of William Johnson and Deborah Major, born 25 Feb 1991 in New York.

B4334262512. Henry Gage (twin) Johnson, second child and second son of William Johnson and Deborah Major, born 25 Feb 1991 in New York.

B433426252. Raymond Kent Johnson, second child and second son of Majorie Hall and Floyd Johnson, born 28 Nov 1967 at Rock Springs, Sweetwater County, Wyoming.

B43342626. Winnifred Eileen Hall, sixth child and fourth daughter of Winnifred Rogers and Carlos Hall, born 17 Nov 1944 at Moab, Grand County, Utah. Married 30 Sep 1965 at Moab, Grand County, Utah to Danny Carlos Anderson, born 10 Jun 1947. Winnifred Hall and Danny Anderson had issue, which was the twelth generation in America:

B433426261. Danny Carlos Anderson, Jr., first child and first son of Winnifred Hall and Danny Anderson, born 3 Feb 1967 at Carlin, Elko County, Nevada. Married 1 Jan 1988 at Elko, Elko County, Nevada to Melissa Jean Simonson, born 2 Feb 1967 at Elko, Elko County, Nevada. Danny Anderson and Melissa Simonson had issue, which was the thirteenth generation in America:

B4334262611. Kassandra Danielle Anderson, first child and first daughter of Danny Anderson and Melissa Simonson, born 30 Jun 1988 at Elko, Elko County, Nevada.

B433426262. Steve Terry Anderson, second child and second son of Winnifred

Hall and Danny Anderson, born 14 Feb 1969 at Elko, Elko County, Nevada. Married Feb 1989 at Elko, Elko County, Nevada to Shirlene Nethery.

B433426263. Steven Terry Anderson, third child and third son of Winnifred Hall and Danny Anderson, born 21 Apr 1990 at Elko, Elko County, Nevada.

B43342627. Barbara Joy Hall, seventh child and fifth daughter of Winnifred Rogers and Carlos Hall, born 20 Feb 1945 at Albuquerque, Bernalillo County, New Mexico. Married 21 Sep 1963 at Bluff, San Juan County, Utah to Charles Bradley Pearson, born 16 Oct 1940 at Mancos, Montezuma County, Colorado. Barbara Hall and Charles Pearson had issue, which was the twelth generation in America:

B433426271. Pamela Ann Pearson, first child and first daughter of Barbara Hall and Charles Pearson, born 4 May 1964 at Monticello, San Juan County, Utah. Married 8 Oct 1988 at Elko, Elko County, Nevada to Jeffrey Royce Hanson, born 3 Sep 1964 at Pierre, Stanley County, South Dakota. Pamela Pierson and Jeffrey Hanson had issue, which was the thirteenth generation in America:

B4334262711. Emily Louise Hanson, first child and first daughter of Pamela Pearson and Jeffrey Hanson, born 11 Jun 1991 at Elko, Elko County, Nevada.

B433426272. Lorena Ruth Pearson, second child and second daughter of Barbara Hall and Charles Pearson, born 12 Oct 1966 at Monticello, San Juan County, Utah. Married 28 Feb 1981 at Monticello, San Juan County, Utah to Michael Royce Allred, born 23 Apr 1964 at Ganado, Navajo County, Arizona. Lorena Pearson and Michael Allred had issue, which was the thirteenth generation in America:

B4334262721. Tana Elaine Allred, first child and first daughter of Lorena Pearson and Michael Allred, born 21 Jun 1981 at Price, Carbon County, Utah.

B433426273. Charles Bradley Pearson, Jr., third child and first son of Barbara Hall and Charles Pearson, born 18 Feb 1969 at Moab, Grand County, Utah. Married 7 May 1990 at

Price, Carbon County, Utah to Judy Lynn Housekeeper, born 24 Apr 1970 at Price, Carbon County, Utah. Charles Pearson and Judy Housekeeper had issue, which was the thirteenth generation in America:

B4334262731. Charles Garret Pearson, first child and first son of Charles Pearson and Judy Housekeeper, born 13 Apr 1991 at Price, Carbon County, Utah.

B433426274. Rena Lyn Pearson, fourth child and first daughter of Barbara Hall and Charles Pearson, born 25 Mar 1970 at Monticello, San Juan County, Utah. Married 3 Dec 1988 at Monticello, San Juan County, Utah to Glenn Shane Prestwich, born at Provo, Lake County, Utah.

B433426275. Tricia Danette Pearson, fifth child and second daughter of Barbara Hall and Charles Pearson, born 10 Jun 1971 at Monticello, San Juan County, Utah. Married 18 May 1991 at Price, Carbon County, Utah to Richard Van Wagoner.

B43342628. Marilyn Kaye Hall, eighth child and sixth daughter of Winnifred Rogers and Carlos Hall, born 7 Jun 1949 at Monticello, San Juan County, Utah. Married 11 Jun 1974 at Oakland, Alameda County, California to Dennis Reid Hendricks, born 15 Nov 1946 at Logan, Cache County, Utah. Marilyn Hall and Dennis Hendricks had issue, which was the twelth generation in America:

B433426281. Austin Reid Hendricks, first child and first son of Marilyn Hall and Dennis Hendricks, born 17 Jun 1978 at Fremont, Alameda County, California.

B433426282. Erin Kelly Hendricks, second child and first daughter of Marilyn Hall and Dennis Hendricks, born 7 Apr 1981 at Fremont, Alameda County, California.

B4334263. Corrie Ann Rogers, third child and third daughter of Eva Pounds and Herbert Rogers, born 16 Nov 1919. Married 24 Nov 1942 to Carlton Mack Posey. Corrie Rogers and Carlton Posey had issue, which was the eleventh generation in America:

B43342631. Carol M. Posey, first

child and first daughter of Corrie Rogers and Carlton Posey, born 1 Apr 1947.

B4334264. Joyce Josephine Rogers, fourth child and fourth daughter of Eva Pounds and Herbert Rogers, born 22 Jul 1922 and died 28 Jun 1987 at Sacramento, Sacramento County, California.

B4334265. Herbert Lowima Rogers, Jr., fifth child and first son of Eva Pounds and Herbert Rogers, born 28 Jun 1924.

B4334266. John Judson Rogers, sixth child and second son of Eva Pounds and Herbert Rogers, born 1 Mar 1928. Married 22 Nov 1953 to Edna Mae Black. John Rogers and Edna Black had issue, which was the eleventh generation in America:

B43342661. Kelly Wayne Rogers, first child and first son of John Rogers and Edna Black, born 4 Dec 1954.

B43342662. Betty Lyn Rogers, second child and first daughter of John Rogers and Edna Black, born 7 Aug 1955.

B43342663. Brenda Kay Rogers, third child and second daughter of John Rogers and Edna Black, born 14 May 1959.

B4334267. Bessie May Rogers, seventh child and fifth daughter of Eva Pounds and Herbert Rogers, born 28 May 1929. Married 27 Aug 1947 to Robert Thayer Jordan. Bessie Rogers and Robert Jordan had issue, which was the eleventh generation in America:

B43342671. Ingrid Corrine Jordan, first child and first daughter of Bessie Rogers and Robert Jordan, born 6 Sep 1952.

B43342672. Vickie Marion Jordan, second child and second daughter of Bessie Rogers and Robert Jordan, born 12 Jun 1954.

B43342673. Eva Eleanore Jordan, third child and third daughter of Bessie Rogers and Robert Jordan, born 29 Sep 1959.

B43342674. Robert Thayer Jordan, Jr., fourth child and first son of Bessie Rogers and Robert Jordan, born 2 Jun 1962.

B4334268. Jarred William Rogers, eighth child and third son of Eva Pounds and Herbert

Rogers, born 27 Aug 1932. Married 18 Jan 1953 to Norma Lou Gilbreth. Jarred Rogers and Norma Gilbreth had issue, which was the eleventh generation in America:

B43342681. John Steven Rogers, first child and first son of Jarred Rogers and Norma Gilbreth, born 25 Jan 1954.

B43342682. Leslie William Rogers, second child and second son of Jarred Rogers and Norma Gilbreth, born 29 Apr 1955.

B43342683. Rhonda Darlene Rogers, third child and first daughter of Jarred Rogers and Norma Gilbreth, born 23 Oct 1957.

B43342684. Teresa Korrine Rogers, adopted as the fourth child and second daughter of Jarred Rogers and Norma Gilbreth, born 11 Dec 1967.

B4334269. Patricia Maxine Rogers, ninth child and sixth daughter of Eva Pounds and Herbert Rogers, born 1 Jun 1935. Married James Edwin Henderson. Patricia Rogers and James Henderson had issue, which was the eleventh generation in America:

B43342691. Deborah Jean Henderson, first child and first daughter of Patricia Rogers and James Henderson, born 18 May 1954.

B43342692. Patricia Joy Henderson, second child and second daughter of Patricia Rogers and James Henderson, born 6 Feb 1956.

B43342693. James Robert Henderson, third child and first son of Patricia Rogers and James Henderson, born 23 Mar 1958.

B43342694. Danny Leroy Henderson, fourth child and second son of Patricia Rogers and James Henderson, born 8 Aug 1960.

B433427. Ella Rhea Pounds, seventh child and fourth daughter of Jared Pounds and Mary Jones, born 17 Mar 1899 at Lubbock, Lubbock County, Texas and died 25 Dec 1924 at Lubbock, Lubbock County, Texas. Married 24 Mar 1924 at Lubbock, Lubbock County, Texas to Roy Jones.

B43343. Thomas Payton Pounds, third child and third son of Jared Pounds and Temperance Ely, born 8 Oct 1862 at Fort Gaines, Clay County, Georgia and died 27 Apr 1919 at Attapulgus, Decatur County, Georgia. Buried at Attapulgus,

Presbyterian cemetery, Georgia. Married 12 Feb 1888 in Clay County, Georgia to Jane Amanda Bell, daughter of James Thomas Bell and Jane Fuller, born 17 Apr 1864 in Clay County, Georgia and died 8 Jan 1951 at Daytona Beach, Volusia County, Florida. Buried at Attapulgus, Presbyterian cemetery, Georgia. Thomas Pounds and Jane Bell had issue, which was the ninth generation in America:

B433431. Cora Iva Pounds, first child and first daughter of Thomas Pounds and Jane Bell, born 24 Mar 1889 at Fort Gaines, Clay County, Georgia and died 12 Dec 1966 at Attapulgus, Decatur County, Georgia. Buried at Attapulgus, Presbyterian cemetery, Georgia. Married 26 Nov 1913 in Decatur County, Georgia to Robert Martin Darsey, son of Joseph Hutto Darsey and Sarah E. McNair, born 4 Aug 1879 at Concord, Gadsden County, Florida and died 27 Nov 1972 at Attapulgus, Decatur County, Georgia. Buried at Attapulgus, Presbyterian cemetery, Georgia. Cora Pounds and Robert Darsey had issue, which was the tenth generation in America:

B4334311. Jane Margaret Darsey, first child and first daughter of Cora Pounds and Robert Darsey, born 4 Apr 1917 at Calvary, Grady County, Georgia. Married 4 Aug 1943 at Jacksonville, Duval County, Florida to Spence Patrick Mitchell, son of William Green Mitchell and Sandra Caroline Spence, born 16 Jan 1920 at Quincy, Gadsden County, Florida and died 14 Feb 1945. Spence Mitchell was killed in World War II off the California coast in an aviation accident while flying a Navy Corsair enroute to a carrier in the Pacific. He flew into a storm and was never heard from. Jane Darsey and Spence Mitchell had issue, which was the eleventh generation in America:

B43343111. Janie Helen Mitchell, first child and first daughter of Jane Darsey and Spence Mitchell, born 17 Mar 1944 at Jacksonville, Duval County, Florida. Married 19 Jun 1956 at Bainbridge, Decatur County, Georgia to Wallace Bartosz, born 26 Sep 1923 and died 28 Jan 1990 at Bainbridge, Decatur County, Georgia. Janie Mitchell and Wallace Bartosz had issue, which was the twelth generation in America:

B433431111. Helen Margaret Bartosz, first child and first daughter of Janie Mitchell and Wallace Bartosz, born 21 Jul 1966 at Jacksonville, Duval County, Florida.

B433431112. Adam Francesca Bartosz, second child and second daughter of Janie Mitchell and Wallace Bartosz, born 10 Jan 1968 at Raleigh, Wake County, North Carolina.

B433431113. Elizabeth Evangeline Bartosz, third child and third daughter of Janie Mitchell and Wallace Bartosz, born 25 Feb 1970 at Fayette, Fayette County, Iowa.

B4334311. Jane Margaret Darsey, first child and first daughter of Cora Pounds and Robert Darsey, born 4 Apr 1917 at Calvary, Grady County, Georgia. Jane Darsey married secondly 18 Jun 1949 to Robert Donalson Humphrey, born 2 Oct 1918 in Decatur County, Georgia. Robert Humphrey was awarded the Pacific and Atlantic War Zone Bar confirming active service in the U.S. Merchant Marines in the war area. Robert was named 1968 Georgia Farmer of the Year by the Georgia Farmer Magazine. Robert was honored as the Baldwin Master Farmer, a selection made by the Abraham Baldwin Agricultural College Alumni group, from Tifton, Georgia. He was twice named the "Man of the Year" award in soil water conservation in the Flint River District.

B4334312. John Robert Darsey, second child and first son of Cora Pounds and Robert Darsey, born 22 Aug 1928 at Thomasville, Decatur County, Georgia. Married 20 Oct 1951 at Bradenton, Manatee County, Florida to Ann Wynn Sharp, born 7 May 1931 at Bradenton, Manatee County, Florida. John Darsey was a Sergeant in the U.S. Army; Co A, 21st Infantry Division and served from 25 Sep 1946 to 21 Feb 1948. He received the WWII Victory Medal and the Army of Occupation Medal-Japan. John Darsey and Ann Sharp had issue, which was the eleventh generation in America:

B43343121. David R. Darsey, first child and first son of John Darsey and Ann Sharp, born 21 Jan 1955 at Bradenton, Manatee County, Florida.

B43343122. Karen E. Darsey, second

child and first daughter of John Darsey and Ann Sharp, born 17 Feb 1957 at Bradenton, Manatee County, Florida.

B43343123. Anne Sinn Darsey, third child and third daughter of John Darsey and Ann Sharp, born 10 Sep 1959 at Bradenton, Manatee County, Florida.

B433432. Olivette (Ollie) Lucille Pounds, second child and second daughter of Thomas Pounds and Jane Bell, born 26 Sep 1890 at Fort Gaines, Clay County, Georgia and died 25 May 1964 at Sylvester, Worth County, Georgia. Buried at Hillcrest cemetery, Worth County, Georgia. Married 14 Nov 1909 at Mt. Pleasant, Gadsden County, Florida to James Clarence McCorkle, son of Montreal McCorkle and Louvenia Cooper, born 13 Jul 1889 in Clay County, Georgia and died 18 Oct 1953 at Sylvester, Worth County, Georgia. Buried at Hillcrest cemetery, Worth County, Georgia. Olivette Pounds and James McCorkle had issue, which was the tenth generation in America:

B4334321. Marvin Curtis McCorkle, first child and first son of Olivette Pounds and James McCorkle, born 21 Dec 1910 at Edison, Calhoun County, Georgia and died 8 Jun 1964 at Valdosta, Lowndes County, Georgia. Buried Riverview cemetery, Valdosta, Lowndes County, Georgia. Married 30 Oct 1937 at Sylvester, Worth County, Georgia to Anna Evylen Shiver, daughter of Orus Jacob Shiver and Lessie Tina Brady, born 12 Mar 1918, at Red Rock, Worth County, Georgia and died 3 Mar 1990. Buried at Riverview cemetery, Valdosta, Georgia. Marvin McCorkle and Anna Shiver had issue, which was the eleventh generation in America:

B43343211. Laura Lynn Shiver McCorkle, first child and first daughter of Marvin McCorkle and Anna Shiver, born 2 Nov 1949 at Walled Lake, Oakland County, Michigan. Married 6 Jun 1971 to Martin Jay Miller, son of Sol Miller and Lillian Krupnick, born 17 Jul 1943 in Brooklyn, Kings County, New York. Laura McCorkle and Martin Miller had issue, which was the twelth generation in America:

B433432111. Maura Anslie Miller, first child and first daughter of Laura

McCorkle and Martin Miller, born 16 Oct 1975 at Valdosta, Lowndes County, Georgia.

B4334322. Sara Maxine McCorkle, second child and first daughter of Olivette Pounds and James McCorkle, born 27 May 1915 in Calhoun County, Georgia and died 16 Sep 1974 at Columbus, Muscogee County, Georgia. Buried at Park Hill cemetery, Columbus, Muscogee County, Georgia. Married 10 Dec 1932 in Worth County, Georgia to Chesley H. McCrary, son of George Gaston McCrary and Angie F. McDonald, born 10 May 1910 in Worth County, Georgia and died 11 Mar 1963 at Columbus, Muscogee County, Georgia. Buried at Park Hill cemetery, Columbus, Muscogee County, Georgia. Sara McCorkle and Chesley McCrary had issue, which was the eleventh generation in America:

B43343221. Betty Jean McCrary, first child and first daughter of Sara McCorkle and Chesley McCrary, born 29 Jan 1935 at Sylvester, Worth County, Georgia and died 27 Jul 1989 at Columbus, Muscogee County, Georgia. Buried at Park Hill cemetery, Columbus, Muscogee County, Georgia. Married 10 Sep 1952 to Charles Howard Rinaldo. son of Pasquale Rinaldo and Katie Lamb, born 12 Feb 1928 at Columbus, Muscogee County, Georgia and died 1978. Buried at Park Hill cemetery, Columbus, Georgia. Betty McCrary and Charles Rinaldo had issue, which was the twelth generation in America:

B433432211. Rebecca Jean Rinaldo, first child and first daughter of Betty McCrary and Charles Rinaldo, born 27 Apr 1956 at Columbus, Muscogee County, Georgia. Married 20 May 1974 to Anthony Arthur Bartrug, born 29 Jan 1956 at Fort Sill, Oklahoma, son of Arthur Bartrug and Agnes Marie Wolcheski. Rebecca Rinaldo and Anthony Bartrug had issue, which was the thirteenth generation in America:

B4334322111. Tracy Lynn Bartrug, first child and first daughter of Rebecca Rinaldo and Anthony Bartrug, born 21 Jan 1975 at Columbus, Muscogee County, Georgia.

B433432212. Sara Cheslie Rinaldo, second child and second daughter of Betty McCrary and Charles Rinaldo, born 14 Jan

367

1959 at Columbus, Muscogee County, Georgia and died 10 Nov 1990. Buried Park Hill cemetery, Columbus, Muscogee County, Georgia. Married 10 Sep 1978 to Jay Edward Bartrug, born 19 Sep 1959, son of Arthur Bartrug and Agnes Marie Wolcheskie. Married secondly Stephen Paul Buschel. Sara Rinaldo and Jay Bartrug had issue, which was the thirteenth generation in America:

B4334322121. Damien Branden Bartrug, first child and first son of Sara Rinaldo and Jay Bartrug, born 29 Apr 1979 at Columbus, Muscogee County, Georgia.

B4334322122. Brandi Leigh Bartrug, second child and first daughter of Sara Rinaldo and Jay Bartrug, born 19 May 1984 at Columbus, Muscogee County, Georgia.

B433432213. Lori Ann Rinaldo, third child and third daughter of Betty McCrary and Charles Rinaldo, born 1 Jan 1964 at Columbus, Muscogee County, Georgia. Married 10 Mar 1981 to Jessie Vaughn Damren, born 15 Aug 1960. Married secondly 31 Mar 1989 to John Peter Foster, son of Aubrey Calvin Foster and Stilla Marie Margott, born 29 Mar 1955 at Augsburg, Germany.

B4334322. Sara Maxine McCorkle, second child and first daughter of Olivette Pounds and James McCorkle, born 27 May 1915 in Calhoun County, Georgia. Married secondly 8 May 1965 to Frank Edward Turner, son of Robert Lee Turner and Leola Ray, born 9 Jan 1901 in Heard County, Georgia and died 24 Jun 1987. Sara McCorkle and Frank Turner had issue, which was the eleventh generation in America:

B43343221. Frank Edward Turner, Jr., first child and first son of Sara McCorkle and Frank Turner, born 19 Jan 1946 in Muscogee County, Georgia. Married Linda Caldwell. Frank Turner and Linda Caldwell had issue, which was the twelth generation in America:

B433432211. Mellissa Lyn Turner, first child and first daughter of Frank Turner and Linda Caldwell, born 7 May 1968 at Kodiak, Kodiak County, Alaska.

B433432212. Kimberly Alyssa Turner, second child and second

daughter of Frank Turner and Linda Caldwell, born 7 Sep 1970 at Falls Church, Fairfax County, Virginia.

B43343222. William Douglas McCrary, second child and first son of Sara McCorkle and Chesley McCrary, born 1 Aug 1939 at Sylvester, Worth County, Georgia. Married 17 Jul 1959 at Smith, Lee County, Alabama to Shirley Ann Brown, daughter of Floyd Elmore Brown and Mary Frances Lee, born 25 Jul 1941 at Salem, Lee County, Alabama. William McCrary and Shirley Brown had issue, which was the twelth generation in America:

B433432221. Susan Frances McCrary, first child and first daughter of William McCrary and Shirley Brown, born 20 Oct 1960 at Columbus, Muscogee County, Georgia. Married 2 Jan 1982 to Richard Keith Vinyard, son of Robert Eugene Vinyard and Adaline Ann Tupa, born 2 Aug 1962 at Columbus, Muscogee County, Georgia.

B433432222. William Douglas McCrary, Jr., second child and first son of William McCrary and Shirley Brown, born 22 Apr 1962 at Columbus, Muscogee County, Georgia. Married 14 Sep 1991 to Mary Anne Musselman, born 25 Oct 1971 at Columbus, Muscogee County, Georgia, daughter of Charles Richard Musselman and Elizabeth Anne Hepburn. William McCrary and Mary Musselman had issue, which was the thirteenth generation in America:
B4334322221. Ashley Elizabeth McCrary, first child and first daughter of William McCrary and Mary Musselman, born 26 Jan 1993 at Columbus, Muscogee County, Georgia.

B433432223. Kathryn Anne McCrary, third child and second daughter of William McCrary and Shirley Brown, born 2 May 1965 at Columbus, Muscogee County, Georgia. Married 27 Oct 1984 to John Waylon Lindsey, son of John Waylon Lindsey and Margot Elisabeth Zingraff, born 25 Feb 1962 at Anchorage, Anchorage County, Alaska. Kathryn McCrary and John Lindsey had issue, which was the thirteenth generation in America:
B4334322231. Sara Ann Lindsey, first child and

first daughter of Kathryn McCrary and John Lindsey, born 22 Mar 1988 at Columbus, Muscogee County, Georgia.

B4334322232. Kathryn Elisabeth Lindsey, second child and second daughter of Kathryn McCrary and John Lindsey, born 14 Jun 1990 at Columbus, Muscogee County, Georgia.

B4334323. James Clarence McCorkle, Jr., third child and second son of Olivette Pounds and James McCorkle, born 22 Jan 1917 at Edison, Calhoun County, Georgia. Married 29 Aug 1937 at Waycross, Ware County, Georgia to Claudia Humphrey, daughter of Brantley Lewis Humphrey and Agnes Johnson, born 22 Dec 1919 in Worth County, Georgia. James McCorkle and Claudia Humphrey had issue, which was the eleventh generation in America:

B43343231. Claudia Lynette McCorkle, first child and first daughter of James McCorkle and Claudia Humphrey, born 29 Sep 1938 in Worth County, Georgia. Married 24 Nov 1957 at Albany, Dougherty County, Georgia to Robert Jackson Sizemore, born 9 Sep 1933 at Nashville, Berrien County, Georgia. Claudia McCorkle and Robert Sizemore had issue, which was the twelth generation in America:

B433432311. Cheryl Denise Sizemore, first child and first daughter of Claudia McCorkle and Robert Sizemore, born 14 Aug 1959 in Duval County, Florida.

B433432312. Melinda Joy Sizemore, second child and second daughter of Claudia McCorkle and Robert Sizemore, born 29 Dec 1963 in Duval County, Florida.

B43343232. James Clarence McCorkle III, second child and first son of James McCorkle and Claudia Humphrey, born 8 Nov 1942 at Albany, Dougherty County, Georgia. Married 14 Mar 1967 to Sandra Kay Pollack, born 2 Jul 1946 at Pelham, Mitchell County, Georgia. James McCorkle and Sandra Pollack had issue, which was the twelth generation in America:

B433432321. Alison Renee McCorkle, first child and first daughter of James McCorkle and Sandra Pollack, born 30 Jun 1969 at Albany, Dougherty County, Georgia.

B43343233. Norma Jean McCorkle, third child and second daughter of James McCorkle and Claudia Humphrey, born 4 Jun 1944. Married 20 Jun 1960 at Albany, Dougherty County, Georgia to Charles Wayne Smith, born 22 Mar 1945 at Albany, Dougherty County, Georgia. Married secondly 3 Feb 1963 to Phillip Michael Littlejohn, Sr. Norma McCorkle and Charles Smith did not have issue, but adopted a son, who was considered to be in the twelth generation in America:

B433432331. Phillip Michael Smith (adopted), born 15 Nov 1964.

B43343234. Deborah Kaye McCorkle, fourth child and third daughter of James McCorkle and Claudia Humphrey, born 18 Aug 1951 at Albany, Dougherty County, Georgia.

B43343235. Donna Ray McCorkle, fifth child and fourth daughter of James McCorkle and Claudia Humphrey, born 14 Dec 1952.

B4334324. Richard Murry McCorkle, fourth child and third son of Olivette Pounds and James McCorkle, born 3 Jun 1922 at Edison, Calhoun County, Georgia. Married 17 Mar 1945 at Tifton, Tift County, Georgia to Sue Elizabeth Kitchens, daughter of Walter Gaines Kitchens and Nellie Thompson, born 15 Nov 1923 at Oglethorpe, Macon County, Georgia. Richard McCorkle and Sue Kitchens had issue, which was the eleventh generation in America:

B43343241. Pamela Jean McCorkle, first child and first daughter of Richard McCorkle and Sue Kitchens, born 11 Apr 1946 at Columbus, Muscogee County, Georgia and died 8 Oct 1985 at Hogstown, Walton County, Florida. Buried at Elizabeth Chapel cemetery, Chumuckla, Santa Rosa County, Florida. Married 21 Jun 1969 at Jacksonville, Duval County, Florida to Charles Ray Niemann, born 13 Oct 1946 at Milton, Santa Rosa County, Florida. Married secondly 30 Sep 1973 at Milton, Santa Rosa County, Florida to Clayton Webb Mapoles, Jr., son of Clayton Webb Mapoles and Hazel Carolyn Byrd, born 26 Nov 1944 at Milton, Santa Rosa County, Florida and died 8 Oct 1985 at Hogstown, Walton County, Florida. Buried at Milton, Santa Rosa County, Florida. Pamela McCorkle and Clayton Mapoles had issue, which was the twelth generation in America:

B433432411. Richard Murry Mapoles, first child and first son of Pamela McCorkle and Clayton Mapoles, born 23 Jan 1977 at Milton, Santa Rosa County, Florida.

B433432412. James Matthew Mapoles, second child and second son of Pamela McCorkle and Clayton Mapoles, born 18 May 1981 at Panama City, Bay County, Florida.

B43343242. Sandra Ann McCorkle, second child and second daughter of Richard McCorkle and Sue Kitchens, born 2 Jun 1947 at Albany, Dougherty County, Georgia and died 10 Jul 1948 at Key West, Monroe County, Florida. Buried at Key West, Monroe County, Florida.

B4334325. Thomas William McCorkle, fifth child and fourth son of Olivette Pounds and James McCorkle, born 19 Nov 1923 at Leary, Dougherty County, Georgia and died 15 Oct 1987. Buried at Crown Hill cemetery, Albany, Dougherty County, Georgia. Married 22 Jul 1941 at Ashburn, Turner County, Georgia to Mae Shirley Dobbs, daughter of William Alton Dobbs and Mary Mable Sosebee, born 29 Apr 1926 at Marietta, Cobb County, Georgia. Thomas McCorkle and Mae Dobbs had issue, which was the eleventh generation in America:

B43343251. Patricia (Patsy) Lynn McCorkle, first child and first daughter of Thomas McCorkle and Mae Dobbs, born 1 Jul 1945 at Albany, Dougherty County, Georgia. Married 30 Jun 1963 at Albany, Dougherty County, Georgia to Roger Lanis Hatcher, son of James Arthur Hatcher and Naomi Cato, born 16 Dec 1943 in Worth County, Georgia. Patricia McCorkle and Roger Hatcher had issue, which was the twelth generation in America:

B433432511. Roger William Hatcher, first child and first son of Patricia McCorkle and Roger Hatcher, born 16 Dec 1964 at Albany, Dougherty County, Georgia. Married 14 Nov 1987 in Worth County, Georgia to Katherine Ann Olson. Married secondly 29 Nov 1991 at Sylvester, Worth County, Georgia to Debbie Lynn Griffin McDowell, born 27 Nov 1970. Roger Hatcher and Debbie McDowell had issue, which was the thirteenth generation in America:

B4334325111. Jeremy Kyle

Hatcher, first child and first son of Roger Hatcher and Debbie McDowell, born 18 May 1993 at Albany, Dougherty County, Georgia.

B433432512. Christopher Heath Hatcher, second child and second son of Patricia McCorkle and Roger Hatcher, born 27 Jul 1974 at Albany, Dougherty County, Georgia.

B43343252. Cynthia Joy McCorkle, second child and second daughter of Thomas McCorkle and Mae Dobbs, born 21 Apr 1950 at Albany, Dougherty County, Georgia. Married Aug 1976 at Albany, Dougherty County, Georgia to Carroll Jay Freeman.

B43343253. Larry Keith McCorkle, third child and first son of Thomas McCorkle and Mae Dobbs, born 16 Oct 1969 at Albany, Dougherty County, Georgia.

B4334326. Harry Arthur McCorkle, sixth child and fifth son of Olivette Pounds and James McCorkle, born 18 Jun 1925 at Sumner, Worth County, Georgia. Married 6 Jun 1946 at Albany, Dougherty County, Georgia to Nell I. Carlton. Married secondly 27 Nov 1954 at Warner Robins, Houston County, Georgia to Claudine Peacock, daughter of Crawley M. Peacock and Frances Ollie Waters, born 8 Apr 1932 at Screven, Wayne County, Georgia. Harry McCorkle and Claudine Peacock did not have issue, but adopted a son, who was considered to be in the eleventh generation in America:

B43343261. Harry Stephen (adopted) McCorkle, born 8 Jul 1963 at Warner Robins, Houston County, Georgia. Married 8 Jun 1985 at Warner Robins, Houston County, Georgia to Sonya Michelle Grice, daughter of Robert B. Grice and Barbara Ann Radford, born 16 Dec 1963 in Houston County, Georgia. Harry McCorkle and Sonya Grice had issue, which was the twelth generation in America:

B433432611. Ashley Brooke McCorkle, first child and first daughter of Harry McCorkle and Sonya Grice, born 10 Jun 1990 at Columbus, Muscogee County, Georgia.

B4334327. Julian Robert McCorkle, seventh child and sixth son of Olivette Pounds and James McCorkle, born 27 Jun 1928 in Tift County, Georgia. Married 6 Sep 1946 to Emma Mildred

Farmer, born 30 Oct 1928 in Worth County, Georgia. Julian McCorkle and Emma Farmer had issue, which was the eleventh generation in America:

B43343271. Diane Julia McCorkle, first child and first daughter of Julian McCorkle and Emma Farmer, born 30 Jun 1947 in Volusia County, Florida. Married 15 Dec 1968 at Moultrie, Colquitt County, Georgia to Bernard Wallace Bridges, Jr., son of Bernard Wallace Bridges and Peggy Geraldine Cooksey. Diane McCorkle and Bernard Bridges had issue, which was the twelfth generation in America:

B433432711. Dana Lynn Bridges, first child and first daughter of Diane McCorkle and Bernard Bridges, born 3 May 1970.

B43343272. Julian Robert McCorkle, Jr., second child and first son of Julian McCorkle and Emma Farmer, born 31 Jul 1948 in Volusia County, Florida.

B43343273. Mildred Gail McCorkle, third child and second daughter of Julian McCorkle and Emma Farmer, born 6 Dec 1949 in Colquitt County, Georgia. Married Doyle Allen Smith, son of Silas Edward Smith and Bonnie Elizabeth Butler, born 1 Dec 1947. Mildred McCorkle and Doyle Smith had issue, which was the twelfth generation in America:

B433432731. Robbie Allen Smith, first child and first son of Mildred McCorkle and Doyle Smith, born 9 Jul 1970 at Great Falls, Cascade County, Montana.

B43343274. Allen Kenneth McCorkle, fourth child and second son of Julian McCorkle and Emma Farmer, born 25 Jul 1951 in Colquitt County, Georgia. Married 5 Jan 1971 in Ware County, Georgia to Tiny Herlong, born 1950 in Ware County, Georgia. Allen McCorkle and Tiny Herlong had issue, which was the twelfth generation in America:

B433432741. Allen Kenneth McCorkle, Jr., first child and first son of Allen McCorkle and Tiny Herlong, date and place of birth unknown.

B43343275. Lynda McCorkle, fifth child and third daughter of Julian McCorkle and Emma Farmer, born 10 Jul 1953 in Colquitt County, Georgia.

B433433. Willie Sophia Pounds, third child

and third daughter of Thomas Pounds and Jane Bell, born 30 May 1892 at Fort Gaines, Clay County, Georgia. Married James Arthur Robinson, born 1892 and died 1951 at Bascom, Jackson County, Florida. Married secondly 20 Nov 1912 to Carl Robert Cook, son of Airel Cook, Sr., and Elizabeth Gibson, born 22 Aug 1888 in Georgia and died 23 Aug 1932 at Attapulgus, Decatur County, Georgia. Buried at Attapulgus, Presbyterian cemetery, Georgia. "Aunt Willie" had an abiding interest in genealogy and it is due to her extensive work that much of the foundation of the family history of her branch of the Pounds tree has been developed.

B433434. Eula Payton Pounds, fourth child and fourth daughter of Thomas Pounds and Jane Bell, born 7 Feb 1894 at Fort Gaines, Clay County, Georgia and died 21 Dec 1964 at Daytona Beach, Volusia County, Florida. Buried at Daytona Beach, Bellevue Gardens, Florida. Married 24 May 1919 to Marion Lee Holloway, son of Christopher Columbus Holloway and Sarah Cobb, born 27 Oct 1870 in Calhoun County, Georgia and died 21 Dec 1937 at Edison, Calhoun County, Georgia. Buried at Salem cemetery, Calhoun County, Georgia. Marion Holloway had been married previously 27 Nov 1892 to Sarah Alice Lewis. Eula Pounds and Marion Holloway had issue, which was the tenth generation in America:

B4334341. Virginia Lucille Holloway, first child and first daughter of Eula Pounds and Marion Holloway, born 21 Feb 1920 in Calhoun County, Georgia. Married Broward Crews. Married secondly 14 Feb 1948 in Georgia to Earl Dillard Horne, born 23 Mar 1924 in Wayne County, Georgia. Virginia Holloway and Earl Horne had issue, which was the eleventh generation in America:

B43343411. Sherry Darlene Horne, first child and first daughter of Virginia Holloway and Earl Horne, born 23 Oct 1951 in Volusia County, Florida. Married 7 Feb 1970 to Ray Alfred Miller Register, Jr., son of Ray Alfred Miller Register and Greta Schmidt. Sherry Horne and Ray Register had issue, which was the twelth generation in America:

B433434111. Stacy Ann Miller Register, first child and first daughter of Sherry

Horne and Ray Register, date and place of birth
unknown.
B4334342. Hansel Marion Holloway,
second child and first son of Eula Pounds and
Marion Holloway, born 20 Jun 1932 at Edison,
Calhoun County, Georgia and died 22 Mar 1963 at
Gainesville, Alachua County, Florida. Buried at
Gainesville, Sunland cemetery, Florida.
B433435. Thomas Homer Pounds, fifth child
and first son of Thomas Pounds and Jane Bell, born
5 Jun 1896 at Fort Gaines, Clay County, Georgia
and died 7 Jan 1958 at Waynesboro, Wayne County,
Mississippi. Buried at Waynesboro, Wayne County,
Mississippi. Married 27 Jun 1929 to Ruby
Dickerson, daughter of James Burg Dickerson and
Jessie McKay, born 28 Nov 1901 at Waynesboro,
Wayne County, Mississippi. Thomas Pounds and Ruby
Dickerson had issue, which was the tenth
generation in America:
B4334351. Dorothy V. Pounds, first
child and first daughter of Thomas Pounds and Ruby
Dickerson, date of birth unknown at Waynesboro,
Wayne County, Mississippi.
Married to Harold Kersh. Dorothy Pounds and
Harold Kersh had issue, which was the eleventh
generation in America:
B43343511. Robert Kersh, first
child and first son of Dorothy Pounds and Harold
Kersh, date and place of birth unknown.
B43343512. Janice Kersh, second
child and first daughter of Dorothy Pounds and
Harold Kersh, date and place of birth unknown.
B4334352. Ruby Fay Pounds, second child
and second daughter of Thomas Pounds and Ruby
Dickerson, date of birth unknown at Waynesboro,
Wayne County, Mississippi.
Married Norman D. Odum.
B4334353. Thomas Richard Pounds, third
child and first son of Thomas Pounds and Ruby
Dickerson, born 26 Mar 1932 at Waynesboro, Wayne
County, Mississippi. Married 7 Jul 1950 in
Mississippi to Esther Zellawaine Williams,
daughter of John Sharp Williams and Sally Esther
Cook, born 17 Dec 1933 at Hiwannee, Wayne County,
Mississippi. Thomas Pounds and Esther Williams
had issue, which was the eleventh generation in

America:

B43343531. Thomas Richard Pounds, Jr., first child and first son of Thomas Pounds and Esther Williams, born 18 Feb 1952 at Laurel, Jones County, Mississippi.

B43343532. Emily Sue Pounds, first child and first daughter of Thomas Pounds and Esther Williams, born 19 May 1953 at Laurel, Jones County, Mississippi.

B43343533. Esther Elizabeth Pounds, third child and second daughter of Thomas Pounds and Esther Williams, born 30 Aug 1954 at Laurel, Jones County, Mississippi.

B4334354. James Ray Pounds, fourth child and second son of Thomas Pounds and Ruby Dickerson, born 1 Nov 1933 at Waynesboro, Wayne County, Mississippi. Married 22 Sep 1957 at Meridian, Lauderdale County, Mississippi to Bonnie Jean Curtis, born 9 May 1931 at Meridian, Lauderdale County, Mississippi. James Pounds and Bonnie Curtis had issue, which was the eleventh generation in America:

B43343541. James Ray Pounds, Jr., first child and first son of James Pounds and Bonnie Curtis, born 16 Dec 1958 at Meridian, Lauderdale County, Mississippi.

B43343542. Jeffrey Peyton Pounds, second child and second son of James Pounds and Bonnie Curtis, born 15 Jul 1960 at El Campo, Wharton County, Texas.

B43343543. Troy Pounds, third child and third son of James Pounds and Bonnie Curtis, born 27 Oct 1969 at Laurel, Jones County, MIssissippi.

B4334355. Lowell Russell Pounds, fifth child and third son of Thomas Pounds and Ruby Dickerson, born 9 Mar 1936 at Waynesboro, Wayne County, Mississippi. Married 9 Mar 1955 at Hattiesburg, Forrest County, Mississippi to Carol Pinnix, daughter of James Leon Pinnix and Edith Thompson, born 26 Apr 1936 at Hamilton, Monroe County, Mississippi. Lowell Pounds and Carol Pinnix had issue, which was the eleventh generation in America:

B43343551. Lowell Russell Pounds, Jr., first child and first son of Lowell

Pounds and Carol Pinnix, born 21 Jan 1956 at Hattiesburg, Forrest County, Mississippi.

B43343552. Gary Dale Pounds, second child and second son of Lowell Pounds and Carol Pinnix, born 2 Nov 1957 at Lafayette, Lafayette Parish, Louisiana.

B43343553. Dawn Carole Pounds, third child and first daughter of Lowell Pounds and Carol Pinnix, born 12 Mar 1963 at Lafayette, Lafayette Parish, Louisiana.

B4334356. Jane Pounds, sixth child and third daughter of Thomas Pounds and Ruby Dickerson, born 28 Dec 1941 at Waynesboro, Wayne County, Mississippi and died 1950 at Waynesboro, Wayne County, Mississippi.

B433436. Roy Idus Pounds, sixth child and second son of Thomas Pounds and Jane Bell, born 3 Aug 1898 at Fort Gaines, Clay County, Georgia and died 7 Dec 1963 at Attapulgus, Decatur County, Georgia. Buried at Attapulgus, Presbyterian cemetery, Georgia. Roy never married.

B433437. Earl Jackson (twin) Pounds, Sr., seventh child and third son of Thomas Pounds and Jane Bell, born 17 Nov 1901 at Fort Gaines, Clay County, Georgia and died 14 May 1952 at Daytona Beach, Volusia County, Florida. Buried at Attapulgus, Presbyterian cemetery, Decatur County, Georgia. Married 3 May 1925 at Tampa, Hillsborough County, Florida to Marie (Martha Stutts) Jones, born 25 Apr 1908 at Hosford, Liberty County, Florida and died 14 Feb 1987 at Winter Haven, Polk County, Florida. Buried at Attapulgus, Presbyterian cemetery, Decatur County, Georgia. Martha Stutts adopted by William Everett Jones and Clara Estelle Wahl and her name was changed to Marie Jones upon adoption before Judge R.C. Warren at Bristol, Liberty County, Florida. Earl Pounds and Marie Jones had issue, which was the tenth generation in America:

B4334371. Earl Jackson Pounds, Jr., first child and first son of Earl Pounds and Marie Jones, born 22 Feb 1926 at Manatee County, Florida and died 1 Oct 1969 at Daytona Beach, Volusia County, Florida. Buried at Daytona Beach, Bellevue Gardens, Florida. Married 19 Nov 1943 in Volusia County, Florida to Gwendolyn Gray, daughter of Oscar Lee Gray and Ethlyn Marie Maley, born 14 Sep 1925 at Daytona Beach, Volusia County, Florida. Earl Pounds and Gwendolyn Gray had issue, which was the eleventh generation in America:

B43343711. Earl Jackson Pounds III, first child and first son of Earl Pounds and Gwendolyn Gray, born 23 Aug 1947 at Daytona Beach, Volusia County, Florida. Married 20 Aug 1976 at Valdosta, Lowndes County, Georgia to Julia Margaret Veatch, born 2 Aug 1950 at Valdosta, Lowndes County, Georgia. Married secondly 26 Aug 1991 to Carol Casada. Earl Pounds and Julia Veatch had issue, which was the twelth generation in America:

B433437111. Jamie Lynn Pounds, first child and first daughter of Earl Pounds and Julia Veatch, born 15 Jul 1980 at Fort Walton Beach, Okaloosa County, Florida.

B43343712. Carl Robert Pounds, second child and second son of Earl Pounds and Gwendolyn Gray, born 6 Sep 1952 at Hackensack, Bergen County, New Jersey and died 25 Dec 1993 at Miami, Dade County, Florida. Buried at Bellevue Gardens, Daytona Beach, Volusia County, Florida. A graduate of Mainland High School, DBCC and had a master's degree from Northwestern University. Carl never married. For more than a decade, he worked at FPL, first at its corporate headquarters and later at the utility's Turkey Point Nuclear Power Plant. He was an FPL spokesman, appearing before the media to answer questions ranging from power outages to surveys on electrical consumption. He also wrote manuals and edited the internal newsletter at Turkey Point. And even though his home was devastated by Hurricane Andrew, he still worked around the clock for FPL. Carl had a long-term interest in genealogy and made principal contributions of information to this book.

B43343713. Gregory Alan Pounds, third child and third son of Earl Pounds and Gwendolyn Gray, born 5 Feb 1954 at Hackensack, Bergen County, New Jersey. Married 12 Nov 1981 at Orlando, Orange County, Florida to Donna Woods, daughter of William Woods and Gloria ---. born 23

Mar 1955 at Miami, Dade County, Florida. Gregory Pounds and Donna Woods had issue, which was the twelth generation in America:

B433437131. Patrice Nichole Pounds, first child and first daughter of Gregory Pounds and Donna Woods, born 25 Nov 1982.

B433437132. Natalie Ann Pounds, second child and second daughter of Gregory Pounds and Donna Woods, born 14 Feb 1984.

B43343714. Jean Marie Pounds, fourth child and first daughter of Earl Pounds and Gwendolyn Gray, born 4 Nov 1956 at Daytona Beach, Volusia County, Florida.

B4334372. Clara Nell Pounds, second child and first daughter of Earl Pounds and Marie Jones, born 24 Oct 1927 at Attapulgus, Decatur County, Georgia. Married 7 Nov 1943 to John Jefferson Clark, Jr., son of John Jefferson Clark and Addie Jefferson, born 30 Dec 1922 at Shrewsburg, Worcester County, Massachusetts. Clara Pounds and John Clark had issue, which was the eleventh generation in America:

B43343721. John Jefferson Clark II, first child and first son of Clara Pounds and John Clark, born 25 Apr 1951 at Athens, Clarke County, Georgia. Married 6 Jun 1970 at Kalamazoo, Kalamazoo County, Michigan to Karen Louise Thas. John Clark and Karen Thas had issue, which was the twelth generation in America:

B433437211. John Jefferson Clark III, first child and first son of John Clark and Karen Thas, born 10 Nov 1976.

B43343722. Kimberly Clark, second child and first daughter of Clara Pounds and John Clark, born 24 Feb 1957 at St. Paul, Ramsey County, Minnesota.

B43343723. Jay Cameron Clark, third child and second son of Clara Pounds and John Clark, born 29 Aug 1964 at Kalamazoo, Kalamazoo County, Michigan. Married 24 Jul 1986 to Jan Speich, born 7 Dec 1963. Jay Clark and Jan Speich had issue, which was the twelth generation in America:

B433437231. Jared Clark, first child and first son of Jay Clark and Jan

Speich, born 1989.

B433437232. MItchell Cameron Clark, second child and second son of Jay Clark and Jan Speich, born May 1991.

B4334373. Thomas William Pounds, third child and second son of Earl Pounds and Marie Jones, born 27 Nov 1929 at Attapulgus, Decatur County, Georgia. Married 17 Jul 1950 at Yuma, Yuma County, Arizona to Wilma Bernice Richardson, daughter of Carl Clinton Richardson and Margaret Caroline Shannon, born 1 Feb 1929 at Bonne Terre, Washington County, Missouri. Thomas Pounds served in the military in both the US Navy and US Air Force, from which he retired 1 Aug 1972. Achieved a BS Degree from Metropolitan State College in Denver, Colorado in 1979. Subsequent employment in various management positions. Appointed to a Civil Service position with the Veterans Administration as a counselor in veterans affairs; later transferring to a computer specialist position, and retiring from the VA on 3 May 1986. Active in genealogy, giving major input to the family tree. Thomas Pounds and Wilma Richardson had issue, which was the eleventh generation in America:

B43343731. Gary Thomas Pounds, first child and first son of Thomas Pounds and Wilma Richardson, born 14 Mar 1952 at Bonne Terre, Washington County, Missouri.

B43343732. Rich William Pounds, second child and second son of Thomas Pounds and Wilma Richardson, born 4 May 1953 at Gainesville, Alachua County, Florida.

B43343733. Jeffrey Scott Pounds, third child and third son of Thomas Pounds and Wilma Richardson, born 16 Feb 1957 at Bonne Terre, Washington County, Missouri.

B4334374. Alice Marie Pounds, fourth child and second daughter of Earl Pounds and Marie Jones, born 2 Sep 1936 at Manatee County, Florida. Married Terrence Miles Meyerhoff, son of Walter Jennings Meyerhoff and Mary Anna Miller, born 17 Jan 1936 at Joliet, Will County, Illinois. Alice Pounds and Terrence Meyerhoff had issue, which was the eleventh generation in America:

B43343741. Michael Shawn Meyerhoff, first child and first son of Alice Pounds and Terrence Meyerhoff, born 12 Sep 1958 at Joliet, Will County, Illinois. Married Sandra Jean Holbrook, born 22 Jul 1957. Michael Meyerhoff and Sandra Holbrook had issue, which was the twelth generation in America:

B433437411. Ashley Margarite Meyerhoff, first child and first daughter of Michael Meyerhoff and Sandra Holbrook, born 10 Apr 1984 at Joliet, Will County, Illinois.

B433437412. Erin Michelle Meyerhoff, second child and second daughter of Michael Meyerhoff and Sandra Holbrook, born 11 Jun 1986 at Joliet, Will County, Illinois.

B433437413. Allison Ellyn Meyerhoff, third child and third daughter of Michael Meyerhoff and Sandra Holbrook, born 3 Oct 1988 at Joliet, Will County, Illinois.

B43343742. Marsha Lynn Meyerhoff, second child and first daughter of Alice Pounds and Terrence Meyerhoff, born 21 Nov 1959 at Joliet, Will County, Illinois. Married 3 Nov 1979 to Marc Leslie Cronkite, born 25 Apr 1960. Marsha Meyerhoff and Marc Cronkite had issue, which was the twelth generation in America:

B433437421. Cassandra Marie Cronkite, first child and first daughter of Marsha Meyerhoff and Marc Cronkite, born 16 Sep 1977 at Joliet, Will County, Illinois.

B433437422. Kariann Leslie Cronkite, second child and second daughter of Marsha Meyerhoff and Marc Cronkite, born 11 Jun 1981 at Joliet, Will County, Illinois.

B433437423. Kaitlyn Danae Cronkite, third child and third daughter of Marsha Meyerhoff and Marc Cronkite, born 18 Jan 1983 at Joliet, Will County, Illinois.

B43343743. Robert Miles Meyerhoff, third child and second son of Alice Pounds and Terrence Meyerhoff, born 31 Oct 1965.

B43343744. Mark Bradley Meyerhoff, fourth child and third son of Alice Pounds and Terrence Meyerhoff, born 4 Apr 1971.

B4334375. Guy Bruce Pounds, fifth child and third son of Earl Pounds and Marie Jones, born

12 Nov 1945 at Charleston, Charleston County, South Carolina. Married 29 Feb 1968 at St. Augustine, St. Johns County, Florida to Linda Diane Bergsten, daughter of Floyd Carl Arthur Bergsten and Virginia Ruth Davis, born 18 Feb 1948 at Melrose, Suffolk County, Massachusetts. Guy Pounds and Linda Bergsten had issue, which was the eleventh generation in America:

B43343751. Stephen Bruce Pounds, first child and first son of Guy Pounds and Linda Bergsten, born 8 Jan 1969 at Joliet, Will County, Illinois.

B43343752. Victoria Michel Pounds, second child and first daughter of Guy Pounds and Linda Bergsten, born 19 Jan 1972 at Daytona Beach, Volusia County, Florida.

B433438. Ernest Jared (twin) Pounds, eighth child and fourth son of Thomas Pounds and Jane Bell, born 17 Nov 1901 at Fort Gaines, Clay County, Georgia and died 9 Dec 1966. Buried at Attapulgus, Presbyterian cemetery, Decatur County, Georgia. Married 11 Sep 1929 to Ethel Renfrow, daughter of Oscar Bunyan Renfrow and Bethany Tenn Heath, born 2 Nov 1897 at Marietta, Love County, Oklahoma. Ernest Pounds and Ethel Renfrow had issue, which was the tenth generation in America:

B4334381. Wendell Duane Pounds, first child and first son of Ernest Pounds and Ethel Renfrow, born 10 Sep 1930 at Los Angeles, Los Angeles County, California. Married 29 Sep 1952 at El Monte, Los Angeles County, California to Marilyn Joyce Beasley. Wendell Pounds and Marilyn Beasley had issue, which was the eleventh generation in America:

B43343811. Cathlene Ann Pounds, first child and first daughter of Wendell Pounds and Marilyn Beasley, born 31 Jul 1953.

B43343812. Jeffery Duane Pounds, second child and first son of Wendell Pounds and Marilyn Beasley, born 30 Jan 1957.

B43343813. Cynthia Lou Pounds, third child and second daughter of Wendell Pounds and Marilyn Beasley, born 22 Jun 1961.

B4334382. Wanda Ethel Pounds, second child and first daughter of Ernest Pounds and Ethel Renfrow, born 17 Jan 1932 at Los Angeles,

Los Angeles County, California. Married 5 Feb 1955 at Los Angeles, Los Angeles County, California to Ronald D. Woofruff. Wanda Pounds and Ronald Woofruff had issue, which was the eleventh generation in America:

B43343821. Gerald Elliott Woofruff, first child and first son of Wanda Pounds and Ronald Woofruff, born 3 Mar 1956 at Inglewood, Los Angeles County, California and died 2 Aug 1956 at Inglewood, Los Angeles County, California.

B433439. Wallace Henry Pounds, ninth child and fifth son of Thomas Pounds and Jane Bell, born 23 Jul 1904 at Shellman, Randolph County, Georgia. Wallace never married.

B43344. James (Jim) Porter Pounds, fourth child and fourth son of Jared Pounds and Temperance Ely, born 26 Apr 1864 at Fort Gaines, Clay County, Georgia and died 16 Aug 1918 at Blakely, Early County, Georgia. Buried at Blakely, Centerville cemetery, Georgia. Married 1887 in Miller County, Georgia to Camilla Elizabeth (Mary) Jackson, daughter of William Miles Jackson and Nancy Elvira Souther, born 24 Dec 1873 in Union County, Georgia and died 1921 at Blakely, Early County, Georgia. Buried at Blakely, Bush cemetery, Georgia. The only personal data available about James Pounds is that he and his wife, Camilla Jackson, raised a family of five sons and four daughters. He was a third-generation Georgian and must have been a farmer, judging from the location where they lived, which was Blakely, Georgia; in Early County, which was predominantly agricultural in nature, with the main crops being cotton and peanuts. James Pounds and Camilla Jackson had issue, which was the ninth generation in America:

B433441. Leona Pounds, first child and first daughter of James Pounds and Camilla Jackson, born 15 Mar 1889 in Miller County, Georgia and died 17 Apr 1892 in Clay County, Georgia. Buried at Mount Vernon cemetery, Clay County, Georgia.

B433442. Jarrett (Jack) Wesley Pounds, second child and first son of James Pounds and Camilla Jackson, born 16 May 1890 at Colquitt,

Miller County, Georgia and died 22 May 1935 at
DeLeon Springs, Volusia County, Florida. Buried
at DeLand, Bethel cemetery, Volusia County,
Florida. Married 1913 at Blakely, Early County,
Georgia to Mattie Irene Parr, born 29 May 1896 at
Blakely, Early County, Georgia and died 22 Aug
1970 at DeLand, Volusia County, Florida. Buried
at Bethel cemetery, DeLand, Volusia County,
Florida. Jarrett Pounds and Mattie Parr had
issue, which was the tenth generation in America:

B4334421. William Walker Pounds,
first child and first son of Jarrett Pounds and
Mattie Parr, born 23 Dec 1917 at Blakely, Early
County, Georgia and died 19 Jun 1950 at DeLand,
Volusia County, Florida. Buried at DeLand,
Oakdale cemetery, Volusia County, Florida.
Married Emily (Loutrell) Clark, born 6 Feb 1914
and died 7 Mar 1991 at DeLand, Volusia County,
Florida. Buried at DeLand, Oakdale cemetery,
Volusia County, Florida. "Willie" was an employee
of the Florida State Department of Transportation,
and part of his duties was the restriping of the
centerline road stripe, which was what he was
doing the day he was killed by an inattentive
motorist. After William's death, his spouse
remarried, to --- Barker, but apparently she
wanted to be buried as Willie's wife, as the name
on her tombstone is Pounds.

B4334422. Emma Irene Pounds,
second child and first daughter of Jarrett Pounds
and Mattie Parr, born 27 Oct 1920 at Blakely,
Early County, Georgia, and died 7 May 1994 at
Altamonte Springs, Seminole County, Florida.
Buried at Bartow, Wildwood cemetery, Polk County,
Florida. Married 8 Dec 1935 at DeLand, Volusia
County, Florida to Reverend Leonard B. Branton,
son of John Wesley Branton and Henrietta Butler,
born 17 Jul 1915 at Union Hill, Morgan County,
Alabama. Irene Pounds and Leonard Branton had
issue, which was the eleventh generation in
America:

B43344221. Shirley Irene
Branton, first child and first daughter of Irene
Pounds and Leonard Branton, born 22 Jun 1939 at
Jacksonville, Duval County, Florida. Married 20
Dec 1957 at Highland City, Polk County, Florida to

James Howard Ellis, Sr., born 2 Apr 1935 at Lake Garfield, Florida. Shirley Branton and James Ellis had issue, which was the twelth generation in America:

B443442211. James (Jay) Howard Ellis, II, first child and first son of Shirley Branton and James Ellis, born 24 Nov 1961 at Lakeland, Polk County, Florida. Married 18 Dec 1984 at Bartow, Polk County, Florida to Cynthia (Cindy) Joan Manley, born 3 Jun 1961. James Ellis and Cynthia Manley had issue, which was the thirteenth generation in America:

B4334422111. Kara Suzanne Ellis, first child and first daughter of James Ellis and Cynthia Manley, born 18 Apr 1989 at Bradenton, Manatee County, Florida.

B4334422112. James (Jay) Howard Ellis III, second child and first son of James Ellis and Cynthia Manley, born 12 Jul 1992 at Bradenton, Manatee County, Florida.

B433442212. Julie Lyne Ellis, second child and first daughter of Shirley Branton and James Ellis, born 21 Mar 1965 at Lakeland, Polk County, Florida. Married 20 Mar 1987 in Bartow, Polk County, Florida to Lonzo Snow Pinkard, born 13 Feb 1958. Julie Ellis and Lonzo Pinkard had issue, which was the thirteenth generation in America:

B4334422121. William Ellis Pinkard, first child and first son of Julie Ellis and Lonzo Pinkard, born 15 May 1989 at Birmingham, Jefferson County, Alabama.

B43344222. Judy Ilene Branton, second child and second daughter of Irene Pounds and Leonard Branton, born 27 Oct 1943 at DeLeon Springs, Volusia County, Florida. Married 22 Aug 1964 at Bartow, Polk County, Florida to Frederick Richard Clark, born 14 Dec 1941 at Bartow, Polk County, Florida. Judy Branton and Frederick Clark had issue, which was the twelth generation in America:

B433442221. Frederick Richard (Ricky) Clark, first child and first son of Judy Branton and Frederick Clark, born 1 May 1966 at Lakeland, Polk County, Florida.

B433442222. Julie Lynne Clark, second child and first daughter of Judy Branton and Frederick Clark, born 25 Jan 1979 at Lakeland, Polk County, Florida.

B4334423. James Thomas (J.T.) Pounds, third child and second son of Jarrett Pounds and Mattie Parr, born 17 Aug 1922 at Blakely, Early County, Georgia and died 21 Oct 1983 at DeLand, Volusia County, Florida. Buried at DeLand, Bethel cemetery, Volusia County, Florida. Married in Florence, Italy to Maria Alberta Fossi, born 25 Apr 1917 at Florence, Italy and died 6 Aug 1991 at Waseca, Waseca County, Minnesota. Buried at DeLand, Bethel cemetery, Volusia County, Florida. James Pounds and Maria Fossi had issue, which was the eleventh generation in America:

B43344231. James Cesar (J.C.) Pounds, first child and first son of James Pounds and Maria Fossi, born 3 Feb 1955 at Fort Rucker, Alabama. Married 20 Aug 1978 at Gainesville, Alachua County, Florida to Janet Lee Pressler, daughter of William J. Pressler and Barbara A. Gunn, born 26 Nov 1956 at Honolulu, Honolulu County, Hawaii. J.C. and Janet later divorced in 1993.

B4334424. Jessie Mae Pounds, fourth child and second daughter of Jarrett Pounds and Mattie Parr, born 15 Dec 1925 at Blakely, Early County, Georgia and died 28 Sep 1993 at DeLand, Volusia County, Florida. Buried at DeLand Memorial Gardens, DeLand, Florida. Married 19 Jul 1941 in DeLand, Volusia County, Florida to Grady McMahon, son of W. Nelson McMahan and Lou ---, born 8 Jun 1915 at Asheville, Buncombe County, North Carolina and died Aug 1967 at DeLand, Volusia County, Florida. Married secondly James F. Hodson. Jessie Pounds and Grady McMahon had issue, which was the eleventh generation in America:

B43344241. Joyce Louise McMahon, first child and first daughter of Jessie Pounds and Grady McMahon, born 6 Mar 1943 at DeLand, Volusia County, Florida. Married 26 Nov 1965 at DeLand, Volusia County, Florida to Joseph Lonzo Abbott, son of Robert Leslie Abbott and

Thelma Morris, born 27 Nov 1938 at Seville, Volusia County, Florida. Joyce McMahon and Joseph Abbott had issue, which was the twelthth generation in America:

B433442411. Dorissa Gail Abbott, first child and first daughter of Joyce McMahon and Joseph Abbott, born 18 Dec 1967 at Orlando, Orange County, Florida. Married 10 Feb 1989 at DeLeon Springs, Volusia County, Florida to David Curtis Drury, son of Hansel Earl Drury and Jean Fegley, born 28 Mar 1964 at Charlotte, Mecklenburg, North Carolina.

B433442412. Joseph Lonzo (Jody) Abbott II, first child and first son of Joyce McMahon and Joseph Abbott, born 30 May 1974 at Orlando, Orange County, Florida.

B433442413. Jolie Renee Abbott, third child and second daughter of Joyce McMahon and Joseph Abbott, born 28 Sep 1976 at Orlando, Orange County, Florida.

B43344242. Arthur Grady McMahon, second child and first son of Jessie Pounds and Grady McMahon, born 22 Dec 1944 at DeLand, Volusia County, Florida.

B43344243. Jarrett Nelson McMahon, third child and second son of Jessie Pounds and Grady McMahon, born 29 Jul 1948 at DeLand, Volusia County, Florida.

B43344244. Katherine Sue McMahon, fourth child and second daughter of Jessie Pounds and Grady McMahon, born 19 Jun 1950 at DeLand, Volusia County, Florida.

B43344245. Leonard Byron (B.D.) McMahon, fifth child and third son of Jessie Pounds and Grady McMahon, born 31 Oct 1955 at DeLand, Volusia County, Florida.

B43344246. Donna Carole McMahon, sixth child and third daughter of Jessie Pounds and Grady McMahon, born 11 Mar 1959 at DeLand, Volusia County, Florida and died 11 Jan 1961 at DeLand, Volusia County, Florida.

B43344247. Deborah Lynn McMahon, seventh child and fourth daughter of Jessie Pounds and Grady McMahon, born 7 Feb 1960 at DeLand, Volusia County, Florida.

B433443. Mary Elizabeth Pounds, third

child and second daughter of James Pounds and Camilla Jackson, born 3 Sep 1891 in Clay County, Georgia and died 1 Jan 1948 at Daytona Beach, Volusia County, Florida. Buried at DeLand, Oakdale cemetery, Volusia County, Florida. Married 20 Mar 1909 at Blakely, Early County, Georgia to Joseph Alexander Young, born 23 Apr 1890 in Georgia and died 27 Dec 1968 at Leesburg, Lake County, Florida. Buried at Leesburg, Florida. Mary Pounds and Joseph Young had issue, which was the tenth generation in America:

B4334431. Jimmy Alexander Young, first child and first son of Mary Pounds and Joseph Young, born 19 Jan 1911 in Georgia and died 7 Oct 1912 in Georgia.

B4334432. Chester Lee Young, second child and second son of Mary Pounds and Joseph Young, born 17 Nov 1913 at Blakely, Early County, Georgia. Married 1 Jun 1941 at Berea College, Madison County, Kentucky to Ellen Darr Taylor, born 13 Nov 1915 at Sawyer, McCreary County, Kentucky. Chester Young and Ellen Taylor had issue, which was the eleventh generation in America:

B43344321. Thomas Lee Young, first child and first son of Chester Young and Ellen Taylor, born 29 Mar 1943 at Berea, Madison County, Kentucky. Married at Raleigh, Wake County, North Carolina to Alice Rumfelt. Thomas Young and Alice Rumfelt had issue, which was the twelth generation in America:

B433443211. Robert Chester Lee Young, first child and first son of Thomas Young and Alice Rumfelt, born 2 Sep 1965 at Fairborn, Greene County, Ohio.

B433443212. Alice Terresa Young, second child and first daughter of Thomas Young and Alice Rumfelt, born 1 May 1967 at Fairborn, Greene County, Ohio.

B43344322. Donald Chester Young, second child and second son of Chester Young and Ellen Taylor, born 9 Aug 1946 at Jacksonville, Duval County, Florida. Married 2 Jul 1965 at Springfield, Clark County, Ohio to Virginia Errett. Donald Young and Virginia Errett had issue, which was the twelth generation in

389

America:

B433443221. Donald Lee Young, first child and first son of Donald Young and Virginia Errett, born 20 May 1966 at Springfield, Clark County, Ohio.

B433443222. Jeffery Paul Young, second child and second son of Donald Young and Virginia Errett, born 11 Mar 1969 at Cincinnati, Hamilton County, Ohio.

B433443223. Kevin Michael Young, third child and third son of Donald Young and Virginia Errett, born 15 May 1970 at Cincinnati, Hamilton County, Ohio.

B4334323. Michael Taylor Young, third child and third son of Chester Young and Ellen Taylor, born 20 Jan 1948 at Perry, Taylor County, Florida. Married 8 Jun 1968 at Englewood, Montgomery County, Ohio to Susan ---.

B4334433. Nellie Young, third child and first daughter of Mary Pounds and Joseph Young, born 27 Jun 1915 at Blakely, Early County, Georgia and died 8 Aug 1985 at Jacksonville, Duval County, Florida. Buried at Jacksonville, Arlington Memorial Park, Florida. Married 4 Jun 1932 at DeLand, Volusia County, Florida to B. Nicholas Jones. Nellie Young and Nick Jones had issue, which was the eleventh generation in America:

B43344331. Juanita Marilyn Jones, first child and first daughter of Nellie Young and Nick Jones, born 22 Jan 1936 at DeLand, Volusia County, Florida. Married Robert Peter Lynch. Married secondly to James Pritchard. Juanita Jones and Robert Lynch had issue, which was the twelth generation in America:

B433443311. Robert Peter Lynch, Jr., first child and first son of Juanita Jones and Robert Lynch, date and place of birth unknown.

B433443312. Christy Diane Lynch, second child and first daughter of Juanita Jones and Robert Lynch, date and place of birth unknown.

B433443313. Kelly Suframe Lynch, third child and second daughter of Juanita Jones and Robert Lynch, date and place of birth unknown.

B43344332. Wilford Dean Jones, second child and first son of Nellie Young and Nick Jones, born 30 Dec 1938 at DeLand, Volusia County, Florida.

B43344333. Wanda Gayle Jones, third child and second daughter of Nellie Young and Nick Jones, born 30 Sep 1942 at DeLand, Volusia County, Florida. Married Franklin Monroe Harvey. Wanda Jones and Franklin Harvey had issue, which was the twelth generation in America:

B433443331. Franklin Monroe Harvey, Jr., first child and first son of Wanda Jones and Franklin Harvey, date of birth unknown at Jacksonville, Duval County, Florida.

B433443332. Mark Edward Harvey, second child and second son of Wanda Jones and Franklin Harvey, date of birth unknown at Detroit, Wayne County, Michigan.

B433443333. Matthew Lewis Harvey, third child and third son of Wanda Jones and Franklin Harvey, date of birth unknown at Detroit, Wayne County, Michigan.

B4334434. Ida Lee Young, fourth child and second daughter of Mary Pounds and Joseph Young, born 28 Mar 1917 at Blakely, Early County, Georgia. Married at DeLand, Volusia County, Florida to James A. Brinson, born at Glennville, Tattnall County, Georgia and died 21 Mar 1993 at Jacksonville, Duval County, Florida. Ida Young and James Brinson had issue, which was the eleventh generation in America:

B43344341. Joseph Hubert (Bud) Brinson, first child and first son of Ida Young and James Brinson, born 21 Nov 1935 at DeLand, Volusia County, Florida. Married at Leesburg, Lake County, Florida to Shelia A. Blount, born DeLand, Volusia County, Florida.

B43344342. Eula Jean Brinson, second child and first daughter of Ida Young and James Brinson, born 16 Feb 1939 at DeLand, Volusia County, Florida and died 28 May 1989 at Jacksonville, Duval County, Florida. Buried at Jacksonville, Arlington Memorial Park, Florida. Married at Jacksonville, Duval County, Florida to Robert Maurice Rigdon, born in Georgia. Eula

Brinson and Robert Rigdon had issue, which was the twelth generation in America:

B433443421. Robert Maurice Rigdon, Jr., first child and first son of Eula Brinson and Robert Rigdon, date of birth unknown at Charleston, Charleston County, South Carolina.

B433443422. Robin Michelle Rigdon, second child and first daughter of Eula Brinson and Robert Rigdon, born at Charleston, Charleston County, South Carolina.

B433443423. Holly Lynne Rigdon, third child and second daughter of Eula Brinson and Robert Rigdon, born at Jacksonville, Duval County, Florida.

B433443424. Lori Elizabeth Rigdon, fourth child and third daughter of Eula Brinson and Robert Rigdon, born at Jacksonville, Duval County, Florida.

B43344343. Jerald Alton Brinson, third child and second son of Ida Young and James Brinson, born 6 Aug 1940 at DeLand, Volusia County, Florida. Married at Jacksonville, Duval County, Florida to Mary Ann Kennedy, born at Jacksonville, Duval County, Florida. Married secondly at Jacksonville, Duval County, Florida to Barbara Ellen Smith. Jerald Brinson and Mary Kennedy had issue, which was the twelfth generation in America:

B433443431. Kimberly Ann Brinson, first child and first daughter of Jerald Brinson and Mary Kennedy, born at Miami, Dade County, Florida.

B433443432. Anna Louise Brinson, second child and second daughter of Jerald Brinson and Mary Kennedy, born at Colorado Springs, El Paso County, Colorado.

B4334435. Ruby Mae Young, fifth child and third daughter of Mary Pounds and Joseph Young, born 2 Mar 1919 at Blakely, Early County, Georgia. Married 31 Mar 1933 at DeLand, Volusia County, Florida to Richard Nelson Mellette, son of Richard Miller Mellette and Margaret Camilla Robeson, born 11 Aug 1906 at Turbeville, Clarendon County, South Carolina. Ruby Young and Nelson Mellette had issue, which was the eleventh

generation in America:

B43344351. Camilla Elizabeth Mellette, first child and first daughter of Ruby Young and Nelson Mellette, born 15 Sep 1934 at DeLand, Volusia County, Florida. Married Dick Holbrook. Married secondly to Herbert Young.

B43344352. R. Nelson Lavonne Mellette, second child and first son of Ruby Young and Nelson Mellette, born at Daytona Beach, Volusia County, Florida. Married Irma Mann.

B43344353. Doster Vernon Mellette, third child and second son of Ruby Young and Nelson Mellette, born 8 Aug 1939 at Ormond Beach, Volusia County, Florida. Married 23 Jan 1957 to Euie Earley.

B4334436. Robert Henry Young, sixth child and third son of Mary Pounds and Joseph Young, born 7 Jan 1922 at Blakely, Early County, Georgia. Married Sybel Christian.

B4334437. Lola Belle Young, seventh child and fourth daughter of Mary Pounds and Joseph Young, born 13 Oct 1924 at Madella, Florida. Married 1941 to Alven R. Tyre, born in Florida. Married secondly to Lester L. Blount. Lola Young and Alven Tyre had issue, which was the eleventh generation in America:

B43344371. Alan R. Tyre, first child and first son of Lola Young and Alven Tyre, born 4 Apr 1940 at DeLand, Volusia County, Florida. Married in Germany to Ingred Gardner. Alan Tyre and Ingred Gardner had issue, which was the twelth generation in America:

B433443711. Tammy Tyre, first child and first daughter of Alan Tyre and Ingred Gardner, born in Germany.

B433443712. Martell Marshall Tyre, second child and first son of Alan Tyre and Ingred Gardner, born in North Carolina.

B433443713. Michael A. Tyre, third child and second son of Alan Tyre and Ingred Gardner, born at Daytona Beach, Volusia County, Florida.

B43344372. Alfred Richard Tyre, second child and second son of Lola Young and Alven Tyre, born 30 Mar 1941 at DeLand, Volusia County, Florida and died 23 Apr 1971 at Jasper,

Hamilton County, Florida. Married in South Carolina to Carol Slick. Alfred Tyre and Carol Slick had issue, which was the twelth generation in America:

B433443721. Cheryl Lynn Tyre, first child and first daughter of Alfred Tyre and Carol Slick, born at Daytona Beach, Volusia County, Florida.

B433443722. Troy A. Tyre, second child and first son of Alfred Tyre and Carol Slick, born at Jacksonville, Duval County, Florida.

B433443723. Richard Randall Tyre, third child and second son of Alfred Tyre and Carol Slick, born at Jacksonville, Duval County, Florida.

B433443734. Cory Mathew Tyre, fourth child and third son of Alfred Tyre and Carol Slick, born at Jacksonville, Duval County, Florida.

B43344373. Roberta Pauline Tyre, third child and first daughter of Lola Young and Alven Tyre, born 28 Oct 1942 at Avon Park, Highlands County, Florida. Married Floyd Watts. Roberta Tyre and Floyd Watts had issue, which was the twelth generation in America:

B433443731. Shelia Ann Watts, first child and first daughter of Roberta Tyre and Floyd Watts, born in the Panama Canal Zone.

B4334437. Lola Belle Young, seventh child and fourth daughter of Joseph Young and Mary Pounds, born 13 Oct 1924 at Madella, Florida. Married secondly to Lester L. Blount. Lola Young and Lester Blount had issue, which was the eleventh generation in America:

B43344371. Lester L. Blount, Jr., first child and first son of Lola Young and Lester Blount, born at Starke, Bradford County, Florida.

B43344372. Wendell K. Blount, second child and second son of Lola Young and Lester Blount, born at Jacksonville, Duval County, Florida.

B43344373. JoAnn Blount, third child and first daughter of Lola Young and Lester Blount, born at Jacksonville, Duval County, Florida. Married at Jacksonville, Duval County,

Florida to Roger Dunn.

B433444. James Porter (J.P.) Pounds, Jr., fourth child and second son of James Pounds and Camilla Jackson, born 1895 at Coleman, Clay County, Georgia and died 7 May 1957 at DeLand, Volusia County, Florida. Buried at DeLand, Bethel cemetery, Volusia County, Florida. Married at Blakely, Early County, Georgia to Rossie Craft, born 1 Apr 1895 in Georgia and died 3 Apr 1969 at DeLand, Volusia County, Florida. Buried at DeLand, Oakdale cemetery, Volusia County, Florida. James Pounds and Rossie Craft had issue, which was the tenth generation in America:

B4334441. STI Pounds, first child of unknown sex of James Pounds and Rossie Craft, date and place of birth unknown.

B433445. Ethel Lee Pounds, fifth child and third daughter of James Pounds and Camilla Jackson, born 27 Jun 1896 in Early County, Georgia and died 26 Nov 1939 at Colquitt, Miller County, Georgia. Buried at Blakely, Centerville cemetery, Georgia. Married William Jackson Young, born 5 May 1888 at Colquitt, Miller County, Georgia and died 29 Nov 1939 at Blakely, Early County, Georgia. Buried at Blakely, Centerville cemetery, Early County, Georgia. William Jackson Young and Ethel Lee Pounds were maritally separated and she was staying about a mile from his house. On the evening of 29 Nov 1939, William Young walked over to her house and shot to death Ethel Pounds Young and their children; Max Lavon Young and Shirley Eugenia Young, and then committed suicide himself. Ethel Pounds and William Young had issue, which was the tenth generation in America:

B4334451. Willie Evelyn Young, first child and first daughter of Ethel Pounds and William Young, born 18 Jan 1915 at Blakely, Early County, Georgia and died 22 Sep 1957 at Middleboro, Bell County, Kentucky. Buried at Bush cemetery, Blakely, Early County, Georgia. Married Jan 1940 at DeLand, Volusia County, Florida to Alma (Al) B. Steele, born at Lakeland, Polk County, Florida and died 1969. Buried at Lakeland, Polk County, Florida. Evelyn Young and Al Steele had issue, which was the eleventh generation in America:

B43344511. Stanley Brian Steele, Sr., first child and first son of Evelyn Young and Al Steele, born 10 Nov 1942 at DeLand, Volusia County, Florida. Married 4 Sep 1966 to Janice Rebecca Smith, born at Manchester, Meriwether County, Georgia. Stanley Steele and Janice Smith had issue, which was the twelth generation in America:

B433445111. Stanley Brian Steele, Jr., first child and first son of Stanley Steele and Janice Smith, born 27 Jan 1968 at Athens, Clarke County, Georgia. Married 19 Sep 1987 to Andrew Louise Yarnell.

B433445112. Leslie Suzanne Steele, second child and first daughter of Stanley Steele and Janice Smith, born 7 Dec 1969 at Columbus, Muscogee County, Georgia. Married 9 Nov 1991 at Columbus, Muscogee County, Georgia to Steven Matthew Sikes.

B433445113. Stephanie Louise Steele, third child and second daughter of Stanley Steele and Janice Smith, born 9 May 1971 at Columbus, Muscogee County, Georgia. Married 22 Aug 1992 at Columbus, Muscogee County, Georgia to Earnest Miller Merritt.

B43344512. Beverly Dawn Steele, second child and first daughter of Evelyn Young and Al Steele, born 27 Mar 1944 at Blakely, Early County, Georgia. Married Frank Barron. Married secondly to Tommy Creel. Beverly Steele and Frank Barron had issue, which was the twelth generation in America:

B433445121. Donna Barron, first child and first daughter of Beverly Steele and Frank Barron, born 2 Apr 1961 at Blakely, Early County, Georgia. Married T.D. Sears, born 1965. Donna Barron and T.D. Sears had issue, which was the thirteenth generation in America:

B4334451211. John Michael Sears, first child and first son of Donna Barron and T.D. Sears, born 21 Jul 1988.

B4334451212. Jessica Dawn Sears, second child and first daughter of Donna Barron and T.D. Sears, born 21 Nov 1989.

B433445122. Lee Barron, second child and first son of Beverly Steele and Frank

Barron, born 20 Aug 1962 at Blakely, Early County, Georgia. Married Rhonda ---, born 1963. Lee Barron and Rhonda --- had issue, which was the thirteenth generation in America:

B4334451221. Christopher Lee Barron, first child and first son of Lee Barron and Rhonda ---, born 15 Nov 1985.

B433445123. Scott Barron, third child and second son of Beverly Steele and Frank Barron, born 22 Sep 1965 at Blakely, Early County, Georgia. Married 16 Jun 1990 at Columbus, Lowndes County, Mississippi to Tamera Faye (Tammy) Kain.

B43344512. Beverly Dawn Steele, second child and first daughter of Evelyn Young and Al Steele, born 27 Mar 1944 at Blakely, Early County, Georgia. Married secondly to Tommy Creel, born at Blakely, Early County, Georgia. Beverly Steele and Tommy Creel had issue, which was the twelth generation in America:

B43345121. Denice Creel, first child and first daughter of Beverly Steele and Tommy Creel, born 17 May 1969 at Blakely, Early County, Georgia. Married Rob McDowell.

B43344513. Robert Leslie Steele, Sr., third child and second son of Evelyn Young and Al Steele, born 6 May 1947 at Blakely, Early County, Georgia. Married Dolores Morales. Robert Steele and Dolores Morales had issue, which was the twelth generation in America:

B433445131. Robert Leslie (Robbie) Steele, Jr., first child and first son of Robert Steele and Dolores Morales, born 26 Oct 1974 at Jacksonville, Duval County, Florida.

B433445132. Randall Travis (Randy) Steele, second child and second son of Robert Steele and Dolores Morales, born 11 May 1979 at Tallahassee, Leon County, Florida.

B4334452. Odie Mae Young, second child and second daughter of Ethel Pounds and William Young, born 18 Mar 1917 at Blakely, Early County, Georgia. Married 22 Sep 1934 to Charles Tennant (Charlie) Moore, born 16 Feb 1906 in Early County, Georgia and died 21 Mar 1991 at Blakely, Early County, Georgia. Odie Mae Young and Charlie Moore had issue, which was the eleventh generation in

America:

B43344521. Hubert Phillip Moore, first child and first son of Odie Mae Young and Charlie Moore, born 6 Aug 1938 at Blakely, Early County, Georgia. Married 19 Mar 1958 at Blakely, Early County, Georgia to Martha Irene Pritchett, born 12 Aug 1940 at Blakely, Early County, Georgia. Phillip Moore and Martha Pritchett had issue, which was the twelth generation in America:

B433445211. Martha Phyllis Moore, first child and first daughter of Phillip Moore and Martha Pritchett, born 18 Mar 1959 at Blakely, Early County, Georgia. Married 1979 to John Fulton Moseley, Jr., born 1954. Martha Moore and John Moseley had issue, which was the thirteenth generation in America:

B4334452111. John Fulton (Trip) Moseley III, first child and first son of Martha Moore and John Moseley, born 19 Nov 1981.

B4334452112. William (Will) Matthew Moseley, second child and second son of Martha Moore and John Moseley, born 13 Jun 1983.

B4334452113. Joseph Dalton (Joey) Moseley, third child and third son of Martha Moore and John Moseley, born 3 Apr 1985.

B4334452114. Martha Manannah Moseley, fourth child and first daughter of Martha Moore and John Moseley, born 11 May 1987.

B433445212. Hubert Phillip (Judge) Moore, Jr., second child and first son of Phillip Moore and Martha Pritchett, born 28 Jun 1960 at Blakely, Early County, Georgia. Married 11 Jul 1987 to Cynthia Diane (Cindy) Bowen, born 1962 at Manchester, Meriwether County, Georgia.

B433445213. Joseph Clinton Moore, third child and second son of Phillip Moore and Martha Pritchett, born and died 17 Jul 1966 at Blakely, Early County, Georgia.

B433445214. Tony Allen Moore, fourth child and third son of Phillip Moore and Martha Pritchett, born 31 Jul 1967 at Blakely, Early County, Georgia and died 13 Oct 1967 at Blakely, Early County, Georgia.

B43344522. Kenneth Spencer Moore, second child and second son of Odie Mae Young and Charlie Moore, born 20 Mar 1940 in Cobb County, Georgia. Married 28 Jun 1963 at Bluffton, Clay County, Georgia to Regina Ann Williams, born Nov 1942 at Bluffton, Clay County, Georgia. Kenneth Moore and Regina Williams had issue, which was the twelth generation in America:

B433445221. Steven Kenneth Moore, first child and first son of Kenneth Moore and Regina Williams, born 13 Dec 1967 at Blakely, Early County, Georgia. Married 17 Aug 1991 to Michelle Lynn Avery, born 1967.

B4334453. Ira Glycern (Shorty) Young, third child and first son of Ethel Pounds and William Young, born 22 Aug 1919 at Blakely, Early County, Georgia and died 2 Jul 1991 at Monterey, Monterey County, California. Married 1940 to Grace Virginia (Gin) Posey, daughter of James Arthur Posey and Martha Grace Smith, date and place of birth unknown, but she died 6 Feb 1962. Married secondly to Sally Barnes. Married thirdly to Edna Monday. Married fourthly in 1964 to Clara Walls, born at Carmel, Monterey County, California. Ira Young and Grace Posey had issue, which was the eleventh generation in America:

B43344531. Martha Joyce Young, first child and first daughter of Ira Young and Grace Posey, born 30 Jul 1941 at Jacksonville, Duval County, Florida. Married 21 May 1956 to Richard Charles Bartell. Married secondly to Floyd Leroy Mood, Jr. Married thirdly to Rudy Mark Rubio. Married fourthly to Anthony Chiavaro. Married fifthly to Derrick Lamb. Married sixthly to James Clinton Godwin. Married seventhly to --- Owings. Martha Young and Floyd Mood had issue, which was the twelth generation in America:

B433445311. Floyd Leroy Mood III, first child and first son of Martha Young and Floyd Mood, born 24 Jan 1962 at Jacksonville, Duval County, Florida.

B43344531. Martha Joyce Young, first child and first daughter of Ira Young and Grace Posey, born 30 Jul 1941 at Jacksonville, Duval County, Florida. Married thirdly by commonlaw to Rudy Mark Rubio. Martha Young and Rudy Rubio had issue, which was the twelth generation in America:

B433445311. Stephan John (Buster) Young, first child and first son of Martha Young and Rudy Rubio, born 3 Sep 1963 at Las Vegas, Clark County, Nevada. Married Crystal ---. Stephan Young and Crystal --- had issue, which was the thirteenth generation in America:

B4334453111. Sean Young, first child and first son of Stephan Young and Crystal ---, date and place of birth unknown.

B4334453112. Nicholas Young, second child and second son of Stephan Young and Crystal ---, date and place of birth unknown.

B43344531. Martha Joyce Young, first child and first daughter of Ira Young and Grace Posey, born 30 Jul 1941 at Jacksonville, Duval County, Florida. Married seventhly to --- Owings. Martha Young and --- Owings had issue, which was the twelth generation in America:

B433445311. Brenda Ann Bartell Owings, first child and first daughter of Martha Young and --- Owings, born 23 Sep 1957 at Jacksonville, Duval County, Florida. Married Robert Middleton. Married secondly to Gary Charach. Brenda Owings and Robert Middleton had issue, which was the thirteenth generation in America:

B4334453111. Susan Marie Middleton, first child and first daughter of Brenda Owings and Robert Middleton, born 27 Aug 1975 at Las Vegas, Clark County, Nevada.

B433445312. Richard Charles Bartell Owings, Jr., second child and first son of Martha Young and --- Owings, born 5 Sep 1958 at Jacksonville, Duval County, Florida and died 17 Feb 1991. Married 8 Nov 1980 at Reno, Storey County, Nevada to Laura Wilcox. Richard Owings and Laura Wilcox had issue, which was the thirteenth generation in America:

B4334453121. Karen Michelle Owings, first child and first daughter of Richard Owings and Laura Wilcox, born 12 Sep 1981 at Salt Lake City, Salt Lake County, Utah.

B4334453122. Alicia Katherine Owings, second child and second daughter of Richard Owings and Laura Wilcox, born 3 May 1984 at Salt Lake City, Salt Lake County, Utah.

B4334453123. Thomas Gordon Owings, third child and first son of Richard Owings and Laura Wilcox, born 27 Aug 1987 at Oakland, Contra Costa County, California.

B4334453124. Julie Owings, fourth child and third daughter of Richard Owings and Laura Wilcox, born 1990.

B4334454. Ruth Roberta Young, fourth child and third daughter of Ethel Pounds and William Young, born 16 Jan 1922 at Blakely, Early County, Georgia. Married Lester Raymond Amos, Sr, born 7 Jan 1917 in Early County, Georgia and died 24 Dec 1987. They divorced in 1963. Lester Amos married secondly Janet ---, by whom he had a son Raymond Allen Amos, born 7 Jun 1978 at Jacksonville, Duval County, Florida. Roberta Young and Lester Amos had issue, which was the eleventh generation in America:

B43344541. Lester Raymond Amos, Jr., first child and first son of Roberta Young and Lester Amos, born 13 Dec 1938 at Cedar Springs, Early County, Georgia. Married 1961 to Eloise Kelly, born Wilmington, Brunswick County, North Carolina. Married secondly to Lori Campbell. Lester Amos and Eloise Kelly had issue, which was the twelth generation in America:

B433445411. Lester Raymond Amos III, first child and first son of Lester Amos and Eloise Kelly, born 30 Jul 1962 at Camp Lejeune, North Carolina.

B433445412. Stanley Frank Amos, second child and second son of Lester Amos and Eloise Kelly, born 15 Jun 1964 at Kahana, Hawaii. Married 5 Mar 1988 to Michelle ---. Stanley Amos and Michelle --- had issue, which was the twelth generation in America:

B4334454121. Rachel Amos, first child and first daughter of Stanley Amos and Michelle ---, date and place of birth unknown.

B4334454122. Aura Armos, second child and first son of Stanley Amos and Michelle ---, born 1992.

B433445413. Derek Lyle Amos, third child and third son of Lester Amos and

Eloise Kelly, born 30 Jun 1971 at Wilmington, Brunswick County, North Carolina.

B43344541. Lester Raymond Amos, Jr., first child and first son of Lester Amos and Roberta Young, born 13 Dec 1938 at Blakely, Early County, Georgia. Married secondly to Lori Campbell. Lester Amos and Lori Campbell did not have issue, but adopted two girls, which are considered to be in the twelth generation in America:

B433445411. Amy Amos, adopted daughter of Lester Amos and Lori ---, born 1973. Through petition to the court by her biological mother, Amy Amos was returned to the natural mother.

B433445412. Emily Joy Amos, adopted daughter of Lester Amos and Lori Campbell, born 1983. Emily was the natural daughter of Lester Amos and Eloise Kelly, his first wife, and was adopted by Lester after he and Eloise divorced.

B43344542. Mary Ruth Amos, second child and first daughter of Roberta Young and Lester Amos, born 4 Feb 1941 at Orlando, Orange County, Florida. Married 3 Nov 1959 at Blakely, Early County, Georgia to Ben Kemp. Divorced in 1960. Married secondly Aug 1962 to Richard Highsmith. Mary Amos and Richard Highsmith had issue, which was the twelth generation in America:

B433445421. Brian Alan Highsmith, first child and first son of Mary Amos and Richard Highsmith, born 17 Mar 1963 at Jacksonville, Duval County, Florida.

B433445422. Stacy Lee Highsmith, second child and first daughter of Mary Amos and Richard Highsmith, born 7 Feb 1967 at Jacksonville, Duval County, Florida. Married 1989 at Jacksonville, Duval County, Florida to James Truitt. Divorced 1990.

B43344543. Danny Franklin Amos, third child and second son of Roberta Young and Lester Amos, born 19 Jul 1943 at Blakely, Early County, Georgia and died 1 Aug 1951 at Detroit, Wayne County, Michigan. Buried at Blakely, Bush cemetery, Georgia.

B43344544. Barry Lynn Amos, fourth

child and third son of Roberta Young and Lester Amos, born 12 Mar 1949 at Highland Park, Wayne County, Michigan.

B4334455. Oscar Frank Young, fifth child and second son of Ethel Pounds and William Young, born 26 Oct 1924 at Lakeland, Polk County, Florida. Married 23 Sep 1946 at Blakely, Early County, Georgia to Nora Denmark, born 13 Apr 1930 in Early County, Georgia. Oscar Young and Nora Denmark had issue, which was the eleventh generation in America:

B43344551. Samuel Glycen Young, first child and first son of Oscar Young and Nora Denmark, born 23 Sep 1947 at Blakely, Early County, Georgia and died 3 Dec 1990 at Everett, Snohomish County, Washington. Buried at Everett, Evergreen cemetery, Washington. Married Sep 1969 to Charlene Hodges. Married secondly 24 Jun 1986 to VIcke Jo Alex. Samuel Young and Charlene Hodges had issue, which was the twelth generation in America:

B433445511. Tammie Elizabeth Young, first child and first daughter of Samuel Young and Charlene Hodges, born 14 Jun 1970 at Charleston, Charleston County, South Carolina.

B433445512. Bridget Gail Young, second child and second daughter of Samuel Young and Charlene Hodges, born 30 Jan 1973 at Meridian, Lauderdale County, Mississippi.

B43344551. Samuel Glycen Young, first child and first son of Oscar Young and Nora Denmark, born 23 Sep 1947 at Blakely, Early County, Georgia and died 3 Dec 1990 at Everett, Snohomish County, Washington. Buried at Everett, Everett cemetery, Washington. Married secondly 24 Jun 1986 to Vicke Jo Alex, born 25 Aug 1954 at Gold Beach, Curry County, Oregon. Samuel Young and Vicke Alex did not have issue, but Samuel Young adopted Vicke's children by her previous marriage, which were considered to be in the twelth generation in America:

B433445511. Charla Michell Alex (stepdaughter), born 8 Dec 1976 at Jacksonville, Anderson County, Texas.

B433445512. Alesha Nell Alex (stepdaughter), born 11 Dec 1979 at Rusk, Rusk

County, Texas.

B43344552. Mary Ethel Young, second child and first daughter of Oscar Young and Nora Denmark, born 10 Aug 1949 at Blakely, Early County, Georgia. Married 1971 to Gary Davis Cave. Mary Young and Gary Cave had issue, which was the twelth generation in America:

B433445521. Shane Cave Young, first child and first son of Mary Young and Gary Cave, born 26 Sep 1972 at Athens, Henderson County, Texas.

B43344553. Oscar Warren Young, third child and second son of Oscar Young and Nora Denmark, born 10 Jan 1951 at Blakely, Early County, Georgia. Married 3 Jul 1971 at Long Beach, Harrison County, Mississippi to Patricia Kay Allen, born 1953. Married secondly to Connie ---. Oscar Young and Patricia Allen had issue, which was the twelth generation in America:

B433445531. Susan Kaye Young, first child and first daughter of Oscar Young and Patricia Allen, born 29 Sep 1973 at Biloxi, Harrison County, Mississippi.

B433445532. Candace Lynn Young, second child and second daughter of Oscar Young and Patricia Allen, born 18 Nov 1977 at Pensacola, Escambia County, Florida.

B43344554. Margaret Roberta Young, fourth child and second daughter of Oscar Young and Nora Denmark, born 14 Nov 1962 at Athens, Clarke County, Georgia. Married 14 Aug 1986 to Gregory Allen Kientop, born 1962. Margaret Young and Gregory Kientop had issue, which was the twelth generation in America:

B433445541. Joshua Alexander Young Kientop, first child and first son of Margaret Young and Gregory Kientop, born 18 Dec 1990 at Paterson, Bergen County, New Jersey.

B4334456. Thomas Ellen Young, sixth child and fourth daughter of Ethel Pounds and William Young, born 16 May 1927 at Blakely, Early County, Georgia and died 15 Sep 1934 at Blakely, Early County, Georgia. Buried at Blakely, Centerville cemetery, Georgia.

B4334457. Max Lavon Young, seventh child and third son of Ethel Pounds and William

Young, born 6 Jun 1929 at Blakely, Early County, Georgia and died 29 Nov 1939 at Blakely, Early County, Georgia. Buried at Blakely, Centerville cemetery, Georgia.

B4334458. Shirley Eugenia Young, eighth child and fifth daughter of Ethel Pounds and William Young, born 29 Feb 1935 at Blakely, Early County, Georgia and died 29 Nov 1939 at Blakely, Early County, Georgia. Buried at Blakely, Centerville cemetery, Georgia.

B433446. Rufus Reuben Pounds, sixth child and third son of James Pounds and Camilla Jackson, born 30 Sep 1902 at Blakely, Early County, Georgia and died 3 Dec 1959 at DeLand, Volusia County, Florida. Buried at DeLand, Oakdale cemetery, Volusia County, Florida. Married at Blakely, Early County, Georgia to Vera Jessie Parr, daughter of Jesse Parr and Irene ---born 14 Sep 1902 at Blakely, Early County, Georgia and died 9 Apr 1953 at DeLand, Volusia County, Florida. Buried at Oakdale cemetery, DeLand, Volusia County, Florida. Rufus Pounds and Vera Parr had issue, which was the tenth generation in America:

B4334461. Dorothy (Dot) Lee Pounds, first child and first daughter of Rufus Pounds and Vera Parr, born 19 Jul 1924 at Blakely, Early County, Georgia. Married 18 Aug 1952 at DeLand, Volusia County, Florida to Palmer Bruce (Cullen) McCollum, son of Bruce Arthur McCollum and Lillie May Kennicott, born 27 Jun 1925 at Boulder, Boulder County, Colorado. Dorothy Pounds retired as Personnel Manager after 41 years sevice with Southern Bell Telephone Company.

B4334462. Annie Pearl Pounds, second child and second daughter of Rufus Pounds and Vera Parr, born 5 Sep 1925 at Blakely, Early County, Georgia. Married 10 May 1941 at DeLand, Volusia County, Florida to Walter White, son of Raymond White and Esther Farr, born 13 Sep 1922 at Blakely, Early County, Georgia. Annie Pounds and Walter White had issue, which was the eleventh generation in America:

B43344621. Edna Pearl White, first child and first daughter of Annie Pounds and Walter White, born 14 Nov 1941 at DeLand, Volusia

County, Florida. Married 25 Oct 1960 at Folkston, Charlton County, Georgia to William Austin McGhee, son of Jerry Fleetwood McGhee and Lizzie Viola Varnadoe, born 21 Jan 1939 at Alamo, Wheeler County, Georgia. William McGhee served over 24 years with the Florida Department of Transportation and Volusia County government in design engineering. Edna White McGhee served 24 years with Volusia County government, ending her career as a senior staff assistant with the County Property Appraiser. Edna White and William McGhee had issue, which was the twelth generation in America:

B433446211. William Austin McGhee II, first child and first son of Edna White and William McGhee, born 16 Aug 1961 at DeLand, Volusia County, Florida. Married Stacey Lee Davis. Married secondly to Robin Powers. William McGhee and Robin Powers had issue, which was the thirteenth generation in America:

B433462111. Catelyn McGhee, first child and first daughter of William McGhee and Robin Powers, born 13 Mar 1989 at DeLand, Volusia County, Florida.

B433446212. Deborah Diane McGhee, second child and first daughter of Edna White and William McGhee, born 26 Nov 1962 at DeLand, Volusia County, Florida. Married Thomas Chadwick McCray III. Married secondly to Percy Lee Martin. Deborah McGhee and Thomas McCray had issue, which was the thirteenth generation in America:

B4334462121. Thomas Chadwick McCray IV, first child and first son of Deborah McGhee and Thomas McCray, born 2 Jul 1981 at DeLand, Volusia County, Florida.

B4334462122. Melissa Sue McCray, second child and first daughter of Deborah McGhee and Thomas McCray, born 3 May 1984 at DeLand, Volusia County, Florida.

B43344622. Walter White, Jr., second child and first son of Annie Pounds and Walter White, born 12 Feb 1943 at DeLand, Volusia County, Florida. Married 15 Apr 1966 at DeLand, Volusia County, Florida to Brenda Georgine Finch, daughter of George Jacob Finch and Prudence Aletha Blount. Walter White, Jr. is a graduate of Massey Business College and has had a career in the banking business. Brenda Finch White has had over 28 years service with the Florida Department of Transportation. Walter White and Brenda Finch had issue, which was the twelth generation in America:

B433446221. Kimberly Colleen White, first child and first daughter of Walter White and Brenda Finch, born 29 Jun 1973 at DeLand, Volusia County, Florida.

B43344623. Linda Faye White, third child and second daughter of Annie Pounds and Walter White, born 30 May 1949 at DeLand, Volusia County, Florida. Married 7 Mar 1967 at Waycross, Charlton County, Georgia to Gary Winfred Miller, son of Winfred Miller and Bernice Vivian Brooks, born 18 Aug 1946 at Jacksonville, Duval County, Florida. Linda White and Gary Miller had issue, which was the twelth generation in America:

B433446231. Kristy Linn Miller, first child and first daughter of Linda White and Gary Miller, born 28 Jan 1977 at DeLand, Volusia County, Florida.

B43344624. Barbara Ann White, fourth child and third daughter of Annie Pounds and Walter White, born 31 Oct 1951 at DeLand, Volusia County, Florida. Married 29 Dec 1972 at DeLand, Volusia County, Florida to Frank Eubanks, son of Clarence Eubanks and Ruth Burkes, born 2 Feb 1942 at Amherst, Amherst County, Virginia. Married secondly 1993 to George Doyle.

B4334463. Thomas Eugene Pounds, third child and first son of Rufus Pounds and Vera Parr, born 16 Nov 1928 at DeLand, Volusia County, Florida and died 6 Jun 1993 at Portland, Washington County, Oregon. Married at DeLand, Volusia County, Florida to Miriam (Coke) Collins. Thomas Pounds and Miriam Collins had issue, which was the eleventh generation in America:

B43344631. Mary Elizabeth Pounds, first child and first daughter of Thomas Pounds and Miriam Collins, date and place of birth unknown. Married John Crea.

B4334464. William (Bill) Henry Pounds, fourth child and second son of Rufus Pounds and

Vera Parr, born 17 Mar 1929 at DeLand, Volusia County, Florida and died 6 Sep 1986 at DeLand, Volusia County, Florida. Buried at DeLand, Oakdale cemetery, Florida. Married 18 Dec 1964 at Augsburg, Germany to Annamarie (Marion) Englehardt Poepperl. William Pounds and Marion Peopperl did not have issue, but William adopted Marion's daughter by her previous marriage, considered to be in the eleventh generation in America:

B43344641. Alexandra (Sandy) Renati Poepperl Pounds (stepdaughter), born 9 Jun 1957 at Bonanwoerth, Germany. Married 24 Mar 1979 to Casey Dagenhardt. Sandy Pounds and Casey Dagenhardt had issue, which was the twelfth generation in America:

B433446411. Alexander Robert Dagenhardt, first child and first son of Sandy Pounds and Casey Dagenhardt, born 10 Jul 1985 at Dayton, Greene County, Ohio.

B433447. William Edgar (Doc) Pounds, seventh child and fourth son of James Pounds and Camilla Jackson, born 1905 at Cuba, Early County, Georgia and died at Blakely, Early County, Georgia. Buried at Blakely, Bush cemetery, Georgia.

B433448. Mattie Lou Pounds, eighth child and fourth daughter of James Pounds and Camilla Jackson, born 13 Mar 1908 at Blakely, Early County, Georgia and died 2 Apr 1948 at DeLand, Volusia County, Florida. Buried at DeLand, Oakdale cemetery, Florida. Married 9 Nov 1919 to Acy L. Floyd Beach, born 3 Apr 1887 and died 2 Oct 1932 at DeLand, Volusia County, Florida. Buried at DeLand, Bethel cemetery, Florida. Married secondly to Gerald Lee Padgett. Mattie Pounds and Acy Beach had issue, which was the tenth generation in America:

B4334481. Mary Elizabeth Beach, first child and first daughter of Mattie Pounds and Acy Beach, born 10 Sep 1925 at Blakely, Early County, Georgia. Married 20 Jul 1940 at Dothan, Houston County, Alabama to Woodrow Clark, born 11 Feb 1919 in Mitchell County, Georgia. Mary Beach and Woodrow Clark had issue, which was the eleventh generation in America:

B43344811. Hosea Ralph Clark, first child and first son of Mary Beach and

Woodrow Clark, born 3 May 1941 at Dothan, Houston County, Alabama. Married Carolyn King. Hosea Clark and Carolyn King had issue, which was the twelth generation in America:

B433448111. Kelly Charlene Clark, first child and first daughter of Hosea Clark and Carolyn King, born 20 Jan 1967 at Jacksonville, Duval County, Florida.

B433448112. Russell A. Clark, second child and first son of Hosea Clark and Carolyn King, born 8 Mar 1969 at Chandler/Phoenix, Maricopa County, Arizona.

B43344812. Wilmer Clyde Clark, second child and second son of Mary Beach and Woodrow Clark, born 12 Jun 1942 at Dothan, Houston County, Alabama. Married 21 Nov 1961 at Jacksonville, Duval County, Florida to Joyce Patricia Rowe. Wilmer Clark and Joyce Rowe had issue, which was the twelth generation in America:

B433448121. Jonathan Clark, first child and first son of Wilmer Clark and Joyce Rowe, born 14 Aug 1965 at Jacksonville, Duval County, Florida.

B43344813. Janice Patricia Clark, third child and first daughter of Mary Beach and Woodrow Clark, born 22 Jun 1946 at Dothan, Houston County, Alabama. Married Aug 1966 in Georgia to Robert C. Alig.

B43344814. Donald Ray Clark, fourth child and third son of Mary Beach and Woodrow Clark, born 20 Oct 1947 at Dothan, Houston County, Alabama. Married 17 Sep 1966 in Duval County, Florida to Paulette Eichenlaub. Donald Clark and Paulette Eichenlaub had issue, which was the twelth generation in America:

B433448141. Donald Ray Clark, Jr., first child and first son of Donald Clark and Paulette Eichenlaub, born 8 Jun 1968 at Jacksonville, Duval County, Florida.

B433448142. Ronald Clark, second child and second son of Donald Clark and Paulette Eichenlaub, born 30 Dec 1969 at Jacksonville, Duval County, Florida.

B433448. Mattie Lou Pounds, eighth child and fourth daughter of James Pounds and Camilla Jackson, born 13 Mar 1908 at Blakely, Early

County, Georgia. Married secondly in Emanuel County, Georgia to Gerald Lee Padgett, born 3 Jul 1888 at Swainsboro, Emanuel County, Georgia. Mattie Pounds and Gerald Padgett had issue, which was the tenth generation in America:

B4334481. Gracie Lou Padgett, first child and first daughter of Mattie Pounds and Gerald Padgett, date and place of birth unknown. Married about 1962 to David Dowling. Gracie Padgett and David Dowling had issue, which was the eleventh generation in America:

B43344811. Helen Dowling, first child and first daughter of Gracie Padgett and David Dowling, date and place of birth unknown.

B43344812. Mark Dowling, second child and first son of Gracie Padgett and David Dowling, date and place of birth unknown.

B4334482. Lois Ethel Padgett, second child and second daughter of Mattie Pounds and Gerald Padgett, date and place of birth unknown. Married about 1964 to David White. Lois Padgett and David White had issue, which was the eleventh generation in America:

B43344821. Hank White, first child and first son of Lois Padgett and David White, date and place of birth unknown.

B43344822. Carol White, second child and first daughter of Lois Padgett and David White, date and place of birth unknown.

B4334483. Annie Janet Padgett, third child and third daughter of Mattie Pounds and Gerald Padgett, born 30 Jan 1937 at DeLand, Volusia County, Florida. Married Kenneth Davis. Annie Padgett and Kenneth Davis had issue, which was the eleventh generation in America:

B43344831. Shelia Ann Davis, first child and first daughter of Annie Padgett and Kenneth Davis, date and place of birth unknown.

B43344832. Darin Davis, second child and first son of Annie Padgett and Kenneth Davis, date and place of birth unknown.

B4334484. Herman Lee Padgett, fourth child and first son of Mattie Pounds and Gerald Padgett, born 2 Jun 1938 at Ocala, Marion County, Florida. Married Carol ---.

B4334485. Sam Henry Padgett, fifth

child and second son of Mattie Pounds and Gerald Padgett, born 11 Jul 1940 at Ocala, Marion County, Florida. Married 19 Jul 1958 in Volusia County, Florida to Barbara Emmons, born 3 Aug 1940 at Webster, Worcester County, Massachusetts. Sam Padgett and Barbara Emmons had issue, which was the eleventh generation in America:

B43344851. Ronnie Lee Padgett, first child and first son of Sam Padgett and Barbara Emmons, born 14 Oct 1959 in Volusia County, Florida.

B43344852. Donnie Lee Padgett, second child and second son of Sam Padgett and Barbara Emmons, born 30 Mar 1961 in Volusia County, Florida.

B43344853. Johnson Richard Padgett, third child and third son of Sam Padgett and Barbara Emmons, born 10 Jun 1962 in Volusia County, Florida.

B43344854. Lesie Louise Padgett, fourth child and first daughter of Sam Padgett and Barbara Emmons, born 18 Sep 1966 in Volusia County, Florida.

B433449. Walter Carlton Pounds, ninth child and fifth son of James Pounds and Camilla Jackson, born 16 Aug 1909 at Blakely, Early County, Georgia and died 4 Apr 1956 at DeLand, Volusia County, Florida. Buried at DeLand, Oakdale cemetery, Volusia County, Florida. Married 21 Dec 1928 at DeLand, Volusia County, Florida to Lottie Leola Wiseman, daughter of Clinton Irvin Wiseman and Corrie Camilla Dalton, born 9 Sep 1914 at Americus, Sumter County, Georgia. Walter Pounds was a WWII veteran, serving in the U.S. Navy. Though he had only three years formal schooling, "Carlton" was possessed of a high degree of native intelligence. From an early childhood familiarity with farming and the attainment of practical experience with general knowledge in many fields he was able to find work that supported his large family (large by modern meaning), endind his work career as a fireman-custodian at the DeLand Post Office, due to a coronary thrombosis Apr 4, 1956. Among the many jobs he had to find to support his family were: fairgrounds gardener; packing house box-maker; sawmill operator; and his final job as fireman-custodian at the DeLand Post Office, where his duties included repairing bicycles, painting mail boxes, as well as interior and exterior maintenance of the building operations. At his funeral, it looked as if the whole town had turned out to pay their final respects, which was an indication of how much everyone thought of him who knew him. Walter Pounds and Lottie Wiseman had issue, which was the tenth generation in America:

B4334491. STI Pounds, first child and first daughter of Walter Pounds and Lottie Wiseman, stillborn 2 May 1930 at DeLand, Volusia County, Florida. Buried at DeLand, Florida.

B4334492. Walter Carlton Pounds, Jr., second child and first son of Walter Pounds and Lottie Wiseman, born 14 May 1931 at DeLand, Volusia County, Florida. Walter never married. Walter Pounds was a Korean War veteran; served 2 years in the U.S. Army where he was a personnel specialist and then served as a communications supervisor in the communications intelligence field doing classified work for 10 years in the U.S. Air Force. Upon return to civilian life, and several jobs later adjusting to that status, he then served 21 years in the U.S. Postal Service; progressing from clerk and carrier positions to Postmaster rank; first, as Postmaster at Cassadaga, Florida and then promoted to Postmaster at DeLeon Springs, Florida, from which he retired. Was moderator of a series of town meetings in DeLeon Springs and served as Vice President of the DeLeon Springs Merchants Association. Is active in genealogy, and served as Treasurer of the Roots and Branches Genealogical Society of West Volusia County and has served in every office of the DeLeon Springs Lions Club.

B4334493. STI Pounds, third child and second daughter of Walter Pounds and Lottie Wiseman, still born 1933 at DeLand, Volusia County, Florida.

B4334494. Frances Jeannette (Janet) Pounds, fourth child and third daughter of Walter Pounds and Lottie Wiseman, born 10 Dec 1934 at DeLand, Volusia County, Florida. Married 13 Jul 1958 at DeLand, Volusia County, Florida to Ronald

Leonard (Mike) Hamer, son of John Albert Hamer, Jr., and Edith P. Stimmel, born 11 Sep 1934 at Pittsburgh, Allegheny County, Pennsylvania. Janet Pounds and Ronald Hamer had issue, which was the eleventh generation in America:

B43344941. Susan Lynn Hamer, first child and first daughter of Janet Pounds and Ronald Hamer, born 12 Mar 1959 at Miami, Dade County, Florida. Married 21 Dec 1979 at DeLand, Volusia County, Florida to Kenneth Lee Halsey, born 17 May 1937. Susan Hamer and Kenneth Halsey had issue, which was the twelth generation in America:

B433449411. Betsy Ann Halsey, first child and first daughter of Susan Hamer and Kenneth Halsey, born 12 Jul 1980 at DeLand, Volusia County, Florida.

B433449412. Catherine Irene Halsey, second child and second daughter of Susan Hamer and Kenneth Halsey, born 31 Mar 1983 at DeLand, Volusia County, Florida.

B43344942. Patricia Ann Hamer, second child and second daughter of Janet Pounds and Ronald Hamer, born 7 Apr 1962 at Jacksonville, Duval County, Florida. Married 14 Feb 1982 at DeLand, Volusia County, Florida to Kurtis Lund Kennedy, son of Ernest Wayne Kennedy and Patricia JoAnn Gregory, born 19 Nov 1961 at DeLand, Volusia County, Florida. Patricia Hamer and Kurtis Kennedy had issue, which was the twelth generation in America:

B433449421. Kurtis Wayne Kennedy, first child and first son of Patricia Hamer and Kurtis Kennedy, born 11 Jan 1983 at DeLand, Volusia County, Florida.

B433449422. David Lee Kennedy, second child and second son of Patricia Hamer and Kurtis Kennedy, born 26 Sep 1989 at DeLand, Volusia County, Florida.

B4334495. Paul Wesley Pounds, fifth child and second son of Walter Pounds and Lottie Wiseman, born 27 Oct 1936 at DeLand, Volusia County, Florida and died 13 Aug 1983 at DeLand, Volusia County, Florida. Buried at DeLand, Oakdale cemetery, Florida. Schooled in DeLand, Florida where his early love was for the Future

Farmers of America, at which he became Chapter President, highlighted by a trip to the National FFA Headquarters in Kansas City, Missouri. In later work life he entered the police force of the City of DeLand; progressing from patrolman to sergeant; lieutenant; captain, and finally Chief of Police. He attained a Bachelor's Degree of Criminal Justice from Rollins College; and later a Master's Degree in Criminal Justice from Rollins. Through political maneuvering within the City of DeLand, his role as Chief of Police was terminated due to favortism for another employee; relegating him to the role of Major, second in command. He suffered a series of strokes, all within hours of each other, dying at the critical care unit of West Volusia Hospital in DeLand, Florida on 13 Aug 1983. Prior to his police career, Paul worked as a foreman for Farrens Tree Surgeons, maintaining clear cut rights of way for state roads and railroads. During this time, he had a short marriage to his first wife, Sally Teague, but was soon divorced due to incompatibility. Later, while he was in police work, he married again, to Rose Degruso Hennessy, daughter of Vito DeGruso and Rose Lomedico, by whom he had a daughter, Jennifer Carrie Pounds, and also raised a step-daughter (Joyce Hennessy) and step-son (Robert Hennessy). Source: Family Records of Paul Wesley Pounds. Married 28 Dec 1959 at DeLand, Volusia County, Florida to Sally Susan Teague. Married secondly 30 Apr 1970 to Rose Marie Degruso, born 21 Aug 1935 in Brooklyn, New York, who had been married previously 18 Sep 1955 to Francis Robert Hennessy, born 9 Jul 1935 in Brooklyn, Brooklyn County, New York. Paul Pounds and Rose Degruso had issue, which was the eleventh generation in America:

B43344951. Jennifer Carrie Pounds, first child and first daughter of Paul Pounds and Rose Degruso, born 13 Jul 1976 at DeLand, Volusia County, Florida.

B4334496. Myra Leola Pounds, sixth child and third daughter of Walter Pounds and Lottie Wiseman, born 2 Apr 1939 at DeLand, Volusia County, Florida. Married 4 Oct 1957 at Tifton, Tift County, Georgia to Bruce Lee Stone, son of

414

Samuel Judson Stone and Miriam Anna Stilton, born 9 Aug 1936 at DeLand, Volusia County, Florida. Myra Pounds and Bruce Stone had issue, which was the eleventh generation in America:

B43344961. Richard Lee Stone, first child and first son of Myra Pounds and Bruce Stone, born 13 Aug 1958 at Belle Glade, Palm Beach County, Florida.

B43344962. James Gregory Stone, second child and second son of Myra Pounds and Bruce Stone, born 29 Dec 1961 at DeLand, Volusia County, Florida. Married 18 Jan 1980 at DeLand, Volusia County, Florida to Nicki McCrea, daughter of Ralph Maurice McCrea and Meryl Imogene Wagner, born 31 Jan 1963 at DeLand, Volusia County, Florida. Married secondly 26 Jun 1993 at DeLand, Volusia County, Florida to Teri L. Dixon, daughter of Thomas Dixon, Jr., and Lavera Jean Carnathan. James Stone and Nicki McCrea had issue, which was the twelth generation in America:

B433449621. Benjamin James Stone, first child and first son of James Stone and Nicki McCrea, born 25 Mar 1981 at DeLand, Volusia County, Florida.

B433449622. Kristopor Malcolm Stone, second child and second son of James Stone and Nicki McCrea, born 1 May 1985 at DeLand, Volusia County, Florida.

B43344963. Jeffrey Lawrence Stone, third child and third son of Myra Pounds and Bruce Stone, born 25 Oct 1964 at DeLand, Volusia County, Florida. Married 24 Jun 1989 at DeLand, Volusia County, Florida to Rungnipa (Noke) Thuaimuen, daughter of James Neblett and On Thuaimuen, born 9 Apr 1968 in Udorn, Thailand.

B43344964. Eric Glenn Stone, fourth child and fourth son of Myra Pounds and Bruce Stone, born 23 Mar 1966 at Miami, Dade County, Florida. Married 23 May 1987 at DeLand, Volusia County, Florida to Melinda Jill Haynie, daughter of James Maurice Haynie and Gayla Jeannette Adams, born 16 May 1967 at Orlando, Orange County, Florida. Eric Stone and Melinda Haynie had issue, which was the twelth generation in America:

B433449641. Cody James Stone,

first child and first son of Eric Stone and Melinda Haynie, born 10 Jul 1991 at DeLand, Volusia County, Florida.

B4334497. John Edward Pounds, seventh child and third son of Walter Pounds and Lottie Wiseman, born 4 Aug 1941 at DeLand, Volusia County, Florida and died 10 Aug 1988 at Gainesville, Alachua County, Florida. Buried at Lake City, Forest Lawn Gardens, Florida. Married 15 Mar 1963 at Winter Haven, Polk County, Florida to Glennis Joan Hughes, daughter of John Harrison Hughes and Deen Conley, born 30 Dec 1943 at Winter Haven, Polk County, Florida. John Pounds and Glennis Hughes had issue, which was the eleventh generation in America:

B43344971. Kimberly Kae Pounds, first child and first daughter of John Pounds and Glennis Hughes, born 8 Nov 1965 at Titusville, Brevard County, Florida. Married 12 Apr 1986 at Lake City, Columbia County, Florida to Alan Blake Ross, son of Alfred Lee Ross and Mildred Thompson, born 30 Nov 1964 at South Miami, Dade County, Florida. Kim and Alan were divorced in 1993. Kimberly Pounds and Alan Ross had issue, which was the twelth generation in America:

B433449711. Alan John (A.J.) Ross, first child and first son of Kimberly Pounds and Alan Ross, born 4 Aug 1993 at Lake City, Columbia County, Florida.

B43344972. Lisa Dawn Pounds, second child and second daughter of John Pounds and Glennis Hughes, born 4 May 1971 at Leesburg, Lake County, Florida. Married 13 May 1991 at Lake City, Columbia County, Florida to Lance Michael Todd, son of Mike Todd and Debra Bell Phillips, born 12 Dec 1971 at Fort Campbell, Trigg County, Kentucky. Divorced 1993.

B4334498. Wayne Clinton Pounds, eighth child and fourth son of Walter Pounds and Lottie Wiseman, born 15 Aug 1942 at DeLand, Volusia County, Florida. Married 21 Jun 1968 at Berlin-Zehlendorf, Germany to Regina Dorothea Klein, daughter of Friedrick Klein and Herta Emma Olga Salinger, born 6 May 1944 at Herrnhut-Sachsen, Germany. Wayne Pounds and Regina Klein had issue, which was the eleventh generation in America:

B43344981. Louis Clinton Pounds, first child and first son of Wayne Pounds and Regina Klein, born 11 Apr 1969 at Tucson, Pinal County, Arizona.

B4334499. Douglas Michael Pounds, ninth child and fifth son of Walter Pounds and Lottie Wiseman, born 30 Nov 1943 at DeLand, Volusia County, Florida. Married 26 Dec 1965 at Pierson, Volusia County, Florida to Elizabeth Anne Rohrbach, daughter of Franklin W. Rohrbach and Florence M. Lesher, born 2 Jul 1944 at DeLand, Volusia County, Florida. Douglas Pounds and Elizabeth Rohrbach had issue, which was the eleventh generation in America:

B43344991. Sherelle Lenor Pounds, first child and first daughter of Douglas Pounds and Elizabeth Rohrbach, born 18 Jul 1970 at Dothan, Houston County, Alabama.

B43344992. Alicia Diane Pounds, second child and second daughter of Douglas Pounds and Elizabeth Rohrbach, born 6 Jul 1974 at Jacksonville, Duval County, Florida.

B43344910. Pearl Cauridel Pounds, tenth child and fifth daughter of Walter Pounds and Lottie Wiseman, born 29 Dec 1944 at DeLand, Volusia County, Florida, and died 10 Oct 1993 at DeLand, Volusia County, Florida. Buried at Oakdale cemetery, DeLand, Florida. Married 7 Feb 1970 at DeLand, Volusia County, Florida to Luke Breaux Guidry, Jr., son of Luke Breaux Guidry and Hilda Marie Walters, born 24 Nov 1937 at Lafayette, Lafayette Parish, Louisiana. Divorced 3 May 1988. Though not schooled formally in music, Pearl was well-known locally for her wonderful singing voice. Pearl Pounds and Luke Guidry had issue, which was the eleventh generation in America:

B433449101. Michele (Shelly) Dorne Guidry, first child and first daughter of Pearl Pounds and Luke Guidry, born 4 Mar 1971 at New Orleans, Orleans Parish, Louisiana. Married 16 Jul 1990 at Acworth, Cobb County, Georgia to John Robert Gookins, son of Larry Eugene Gookins and Richie Louise Garrison, born 10 Apr 1970 at Greensburg, Decatur County, Indiana. Married secondly 7 May 1993 in Georgia to Mark Rowell, son of Larry Dale Rowell and Brenda ---, born 5 Feb 1968 at Dallas, Paulding County, Georgia. Michele Guidry and John Gookins had issue, which was the twelth generation in America:

B4334491011.   Chad Michael Gookins, first child and first son of Michele Guidry and John Gookins, born 26 Sep 1989 at Marietta, Cobb County, Georgia.

B433449102.   Luke Breaux (Trey) Guidry III, second child and first son of Pearl Pounds and Luke Guidry, born 8 Dec 1973 at Nashville, Davidson County, Tennessee.

B43344911.   Sybil Christine Pounds, eleventh child and sixth daughter of Walter Pounds and Lottie Wiseman, born 6 Se; 1947 at DeLand, Volusia County, Florida. Sybil never married.

B43345. Charles Adolphus Pounds, fifth child and fifth son of Jared Pounds and Temperance Ely, born 30 Aug 1868 at Fort Gaines, Clay County, Georgia and died 14 Aug 1938 at Miami, Dade County, Florida. Buried at Miami, Graceland cemetery, Florida. Married about 1894 at Henry County, Alabama to Martha Susan (Susie Mae) Summerford, daughter of William Summerford and Martha J. Boone, born 1 Aug 1871 in Henry County, Alabama and died 1 Nov 1927 at Bibb City, Muscogee County, Georgia. Buried at Phenix City, Russell County, Alabama. Charles Pounds married secondly 1930 to Bertha Kemp, born about 1865. Charles Pounds and Martha Summerford had issue, which was the ninth generation in America:

B433451. Alto Leon Pounds, first child and first son of Charles Pounds and Martha Summerford, born 17 Nov 1894 at Columbia, Henry County, Alabama and died 19 Dec 1971 at Columbus, Muscogee County, Georgia. Buried at River View cemetery, Columbus, Muscogee County, Georgia. Married 25 Jun 1916 at Columbia, Henry County, Alabama to Emma Kate Walker, daughter of William Thomas Walker and Jessie Magnolia Blount, born 14 Feb 1894 at Opp, Covington County, Alabama and died 18 Apr 1980 at Jesup, Wayne County, Georgia. Buried at River View cemetery, Columbus, Muscogee County, Georgia. Alto Pounds and Emma Walker had issue, which was the tenth generation in America:

418

B4334511. Edna Eugenia Pounds, first child and first daughter of Alto Pounds and Emma Walker, born 3 Oct 1917 at Columbia, Houston County, Alabama. Married 24 Aug 1935 at Columbus, Muscogee County, Georgia to Wyatt Wilson Miles, son of John Henry Miles and Sarah Emma Jones, born 8 Jul 1911 at Franklin, Heard County, Georgia and died 26 Apr 1960 at Columbus, Muscogee County, Georgia. Buried at River View cemetery, Columbus, Muscogee County, Georgia. Edna Pounds and Wyatt Miles had issue, which was the eleventh generation in America:

B43345111. Wyatt Wilson Miles, Jr., first child and first son of Edna Pounds and Wyatt Miles, born 5 Nov 1937 at Columbus, Muscogee County, Georgia. Married 1958 at Jacksonville, Duval County, Florida to Terresa Ann Bocox, born 1936 in Illinois. Married secondly to June ---. Wyatt Miles and Terresa Bocox had issue, which was the twelth generation in America:

B433451111. Russell Scott Miles, first child and first son of Wyatt Miles and Terresa Bocox, born 29 Dec 1959 at Sanford, Seminole County, Florida.

B433451112. Holly Kaye Miles, second child and first daughter of Wyatt Miles and Terresa Bocox, born 3 Dec 1961 at Columbus, Muscogee County, Georgia.

B433451113. Susan Gail Miles, third child and second daughter of Wyatt Miles and Terresa Bocox, born Feb 1963 at Columbus, Muscogee County, Georgia.

B43345112. Edward Carroll Miles, second child and second son of Edna Pounds and Wyatt Miles, born 10 May 1939 at Columbus, Muscogee County, Georgia. Married 14 May 1960 at Sanford, Seminole County, Florida to Mary Elizabeth Adams, daughter of Warren Durfee Adams and Margaret Ransom Chapman, born 15 Apr 1941 at Olney, Montgomery County, Maryland. Edward Miles and Mary Adams had issue, which was the twelth generation in America:

B433451121. Elizabeth Anne Miles, first child and first daughter of

Edward Miles and Mary Adams, born 19 May 1962 at Sault St. Marie, Chippewa County, Michigan. Married 9 Jun 1984 at Sanford, Seminole County, Florida to Aaron James Merrick, son of Herbert Arnold Merrick, Jr., and Donna Annette Tibbetts, born 7 Jun 1966. Married secondly to Jack Ratley. Elizabeth Miles and Aaron Merrick had issue, which was the thirteenth generation in America:

B4334511211. Aaron James Merrick, Jr., first child and first son of Elizabeth Miles and Aaron Merrick, born 7 Sep 1985 at Sanford, Seminole County, Florida.

B433451121. Elizabeth Anne Miles, first child and first daughter of Edward Miles and Mary Adams, born 19 May 1962 at Sault St. Marie, Chippewa County, Michigan. Married secondly to Jack Ratley, born 5 Apr 1965 in Texas. Elizabeth Miles and Jack Ratley had issue, which was the thirteenth generation in America:

B4334511211. Charles Christopher Ratley, first child and first son of Elizabeth Miles and Jack Ratley, born 15 Mar 1990 at Tampa, Hillsborough County, Florida.

B4334511212. Tasha Renee Ratley, second child and first daughter of Elizabeth Miles and Jack Ratley, born 24 Jun 1991 at Baytown, Houston County, Texas.

B433451122. Margaret Crista Miles, second child and second daughter of Edward Miles and Mary Adams, born 30 Jul 1964 at Sault St. Marie, Chippewa County, Michigan. Married 19 Mar 1983 at Sanford, Seminole County, Florida to James Michael Novak, son of James Novak and Beverly ---, born 19 Sep 1965 at Orlando, Orange County, Florida. Margaret Miles and James Novak had issue, which was the thirteenth generation in America:

B4334511221. James Christopher Novak, first child and first son of Margaret Miles and James Novak, born 14 Jan 1984 at Orlando, Orange County, Florida.

B4334511222. Rachel Monique Novak, second child and first daughter of Margaret Miles and James Novak, born 4 Jul 1986 at

Anchorage, Anchorage County, Alaska.

B4334511223. Shawn Kevin Novak (twin), third child and second son of Margaret Miles and James Novak, born 21 Jun 1991 at Anchorage, Anchorage County, Alaska.

B4334511224. Matthew Lane Novak (twin), fourth child and third son of Margaret Miles and James Novak, born 21 Jun 1991 at Anchorage, Anchorage County, Alaska.

B433451123. Camille Lizette Miles, third child and third daughter of Edward Miles and Mary Adams, born 20 Jul 1971 at Laurium, Keweenaw County, Michigan. Married 5 Oct 1991 at Sanford, Seminole County, Florida to Shane Lawrence Fitzpatrick, son of Leo H. Fitzpatrick and Angela Lawrence Pool, born 10 Dec 1962 at St. Petersburg, Hillsborough County, Florida.

B43345113. Harold Eugene Miles, third child and third son of Edna Pounds and Wyatt Miles, born 29 Dec 1940 at Columbus, Muscogee County, Georgia. Married Oct 1960 at Columbus, Muscogee County, Georgia to Judy Ann Kernopt. Married secondly Linda ---. Harold Miles and Judy Kernopt had issue, which was the twelth generation in America:

B433451131. Remona Darnell Miles, first child and first daughter of Harold Miles and Judy Kernopt, born 18 Aug 1961 at Columbus, Muscogee County, Georgia. Married Joe Johnson. Married secondly --- Amberson. Remona Miles and Joe Johnson had issue, which was the thirteenth generation in America:

B4334511311. Brett Johnson, first child and first son of Remona Miles and Joe Johnson, born 7 Jan 1989 in Norfolk County, Virginia.

B433451131. Remona Darnell Miles, first child and first daughter of Harold Miles and Judy Kernopt, born 18 Aug 1961 at Columbus, Muscogee County, Georgia. Married secondly --- Amerson. Remona Miles and --- Amerson had issue, which was the thirteenth generation in America:

B4334511311. Jared Amerson, first child and first son of Remona Miles and --- Amerson, born 19 Jun 1979 at Phenix City,

Russell County, Alabama.

B433451132.   Mark   Alan
Miles, second child and first son of Harold Miles
and Judy Kernopt, born 18 Mar 1965 at Columbus,
Muscogee County, Georgia.

B433451133.   Danny   Keith
Miles, third child and second son of Harold Miles
and Judy Kernopt, born 19 Mar 1966 at Columbus,
Muscogee County, Georgia.

B43345113.   Harold   Eugene
Miles, third child and third son of Wyatt Miles
and Edna Pounds, born 29 Dec 1940 at Columbus,
Muscogee County, Georgia.   Married secondly to
Linda ---.   Harold Miles and Linda --- had issue,
which was the twelth generation in America:

B433451131.   Harold
Eugene Miles, Jr., first child and first son of
Harold Miles and Linda ---, born 24 Jul 1972 at
Florence, Florence County, North Carolina.

B43345114.   Perry   Julian
Miles, fourth child and fourth son of Edna Pounds
and Wyatt Miles, born 2 Aug 1942 at Columbus,
Muscogee County, Georgia.

B43345115.   Reuben Lee Miles,
fifth child and fifth son of Edna Pounds and Wyatt
Miles, born 13 Oct 1943 at Columbus, Muscogee
County, Georgia.   Married 1973 at Daytona Beach,
Volusia County, Florida to Nancy Davis, born in
MIssissippi.   Reuben Miles and Nancy Davis had
issue, which was the twelth generation in America:

B433451151.   Andrew
Miles, first child and first son of Reuben Miles
and Nancy Davis, born 12 Mar 1974 at Daytona
Beach, Volusia County, Florida.

B43345116.   Edna   Eugenia
Miles, sixth child and first daughter of Edna
Pounds and Wyatt Miles, born 9 Dec 1945 at
Columbus, Muscogee County, Georgia.   Married 14
Aug 1966 at Columbus, Muscogee County, Georgia to
Dennis L. Greene, born 11 Apr 1940 in North
Carolina. Edna Miles and Dennis Greene had issue,
which was the twelth generation in America:

B433451161.   Angelia
Denise Greene, first child and first daughter of
Edna Miles and Dennis Greene, born 19 Mar 1968 at
Greenville, Greenville County, South Carolina.

Married 5 Dec 1990 at Shelby, Cleveland County, North Carolina to Douglas Greene.

B43345117. Gerald Don (Dunn) Miles, seventh child and sixth son of Edna Pounds and Wyatt Miles, born 17 Feb 1947 at Columbus, Muscogee County, Georgia. Married 26 Apr 1969 at Columbus, Muscogee County, Georgia to Brenda Gail Harrelson, daughter of Kenneth Gray Harrelson and Geraldine Airona Sanders, born 11 Aug 1949 at Columbus, Muscogee County, Georgia. Gerald Miles and Brenda Harrelson had issue, which was the twelth generation in America:

B433451171. Tiffany Leigh Miles, first child and first daughter of Gerald Miles and Brenda Harrelson, born 4 Dec 1972 at Fort Rucker, Coffee County, Alabama.

B433451172. Gerald Dunn Miles, Jr., second child and first son of Gerald Miles and Brenda Harrelson, born 25 Nov 1979 at Fort Leavenworth, Leavenworth County, Kansas.

B43345118. Catherine Louise Miles, eighth child and second daughter of Edna Pounds and Wyatt Miles, born 12 Jun 1950 at Columbus, Muscogee County, Georgia. Married 21 Feb 1969 at Columbus, Muscogee County, Georgia to Ricky C. Barton, born 12 Feb 1950 at Columbus, Muscogee County, Georgia. Catherine Miles and Ricky Barton had issue, which was the twelth generation in America:

B433451181. Shannon Dawn Barton, first child and first daughter of Catherine Miles and Ricky Barton, born 26 Dec 1973 at Columbus, Muscogee County, Georgia.

B433451182. Brandi Summer Barton, second child and second daughter of Catherine Miles and Ricky Barton, born 24 Mar 1977 at Columbus, Muscogee County, Georgia.

B43345119. Sara Nadine Miles, ninth child and third daughter of Edna Pounds and Wyatt Miles, born 19 Sep 1952 at Columbus, Muscogee County, Georgia. Married 3 Oct 1970 to Patrick Todd Land, born at Salt Lake City, Salt Lake County, Utah. Married secondly 24 Jan 1974 at Columbus, Muscogee County, Georgia to Larry Floyd Minnick, son of Floyd Minnick and Averil Stripland, born 21 Sep 1948 at LaGrange, Troup

County, Georgia. They were later divorced. Sara Miles and Larry Minnick had issue, which was the twelth generation in America:

B433451191. Larry Christopher Minnick, first child and first son of Sara Miles and Larry Minnick, born 27 Aug 1970 at Columbus, Muscogee County, Georgia. Married 16 Aug 1990 to Sherry Gilliland, born 24 Aug 1971 at Columbus, Muscogee County, Georgia.

B433451192. Jared Michael (Land) Minnick, second child and second son of Sara Miles and Larry Minnick, born 29 Dec 1971 at Beaufort, Beaufort County, South Carolina. Married 22 Aug 1992 at Marietta, Cobb County, Georgia to Amy Michelle Lewler, born 23 Jul 1971 in Lemler, Rhode Island. Jared Minnick and Amy Lewler had issue, which was the thirteenth generation in America:

B4334511921. Tyler Christian Minnick, first child and first son of Jared Minnick and Amy Lewler, born 13 Mar 1992 at Newport, Newport County, Rhode Island.

B4334511922. Colby Logan Minnick, second child and second son of Jared Minnick and Amy Lewler, born 5 Jun 1993 at Middletown, Newport County, Rhode Island.

B433451193. Nan Michelle Minnick, third child and first daughter of Sara Miles and Larry Minnick, born 12 May 1976 at Columbus, Muscogee County, Georgia.

B4334512. Jewel Kate Pounds, second child and second daughter of Alto Pounds and Emma Walker, born 26 Jun 1920 at Columbus, Muscogee County, Georgia. Married 16 Dec 1943 at Miami, Dade County, Florida to Ralph T. Allen, born 20 May 1915 in Tennessee. Jewel Pounds and Ralph Allen had issue, which was the eleventh generation in America:

B43345121. Michael T. Allen, first child and first son of Jewel Pounds and Ralph Allen, born 15 Nov 1943 at Miami, Dade County, Florida. Married 27 Jul 1963 at Miami, Dade County, Florida to Barbara Flyne, born 17 Sep 1943 at Miami, Dade County, Florida. Michael Allen and Barbara Flyne had issue, which was the twelfth

generation in America:

B433451211. Lance Allen, first child and first son of Michael Allen and Barbara Flyne, date and place of birth unknown.

B43345121. Michael T. Allen, first child and first son of Jewel Pounds and Ralph Allen, born 15 Nov 1943 at Miami, Dade County, Florida. Married secondly to a spouse whose name is unknown. Michael Allen and this unknown spouse had issue, which was the twelfth generation in America:

B433451211. Jessica Allen, first child and first daughter of Michael Allen and his second wife with name unknown, date and place of birth unknown.

B43345121. Michael T. Allen, first child and first son of Jewel Pounds and Ralph Allen, born 15 Nov 1943 at Miami, Dade County, Florida. Married thirdly to Bonnie ---. Married fourthly to Dee ---, born at Indianapolis, Marion County, Indiana. Michael Allen and Dee --- had issue, which was the twelth generation in America:

B433451211. --- Allen, first child and first daughter of Michael Allen and Dee ---, born Jul 1991.

B433451212. --- Allen, second child and first son of Michael Allen and Dee ---, born 6 Aug 1992.

B43345122. Ronald William (Ronnie) Allen, second child and first son of Jewel Pounds and Ralph Allen, born 14 Jan 1946 at Miami, Dade County, Florida and died 1946.

B4334513. Ruby Louise Pounds, third child and third daughter of Alto Pounds and Emma Walker, born 24 Jun 1922 at Columbus, Muscogee County, Georgia and died 13 Oct 1940 at Miami, Dade County, Florida.

B4334514. Roy Leon Pounds, fourth child and first son of Alto Pounds and Emma Walker, born 21 Aug 1924 at Columbus, Muscogee County, Georgia. Married Edith L. Harris, born 18 Nov 1910 at Providence, Providence County, Rhode Island and died 17 Dec 1986 at Sanford, Seminole County, Florida. Buried at Lake Mary, Oaklawn cemetery, Seminole County, Florida. Married secondly Jul 1990 at Orlando, Orange County, Florida to

425

Elizabeth H. Bartlett.

B4334515. Jessie Mildred Pounds, fifth child and fourth daughter of Alto Pounds and Emma Walker, born 22 Sep 1927 at Omaha, Stewart County, Georgia. Married 16 Apr 1949 at Miami, Dade County, Florida to John E. Collins, born 28 Oct 1920 at Glenville, Tattnall County, Georgia and died 17 May 1974 at Jesup, Wayne County, Georgia. Jessie Pounds and John Collins had issue, which was the eleventh generation in America:

B43345151. Edmon Foster Collins, first child and first son of Jessie Pounds and John Collins, born 5 May 1950 at Miami, Dade County, Florida. Married Susan Marie Sowell. Edmon Foster and Susan Sowell had issue, which was the twelth generation in America:

B433451511. Kacey Marie Collins, first child and first daughter of Edmon Foster and Susan Sowell, date and place of birth unknown.

B43345152. David Allen Collins, second child and second son of Jessie Pounds and John Collins, born 20 Feb 1953 at Glenville, Tattnall County, Georgia and died 7 Nov 1976 at Jesup, Wayne County, Georgia.

B43345153. Fay Ellen Collins, third child and first daughter of Jessie Pounds and John Collins, born 21 Nov 1954 at Miami, Dade County, Florida. Married Stephen Robinson. Fay Collins and Stephen Robinson had issue, which was the twelth generation in America:

B433451531. David Bradley Robinson, first child and first son of Fay Collins and Stephen Robinson, born 1990.

B43345154. Catherine Louise Collins, fourth child and second daughter of Jessie Pounds and John Collins, born 18 Feb 1957 at Miami, Dade County, Florida. Married Stephen Hamilton, from whom she later divorced. Catherine Collins and Stephen Hamilton had issue, which was the twelth generation in America:

B433451541. Tara Marie Hamilton, first child and first daughter of Catherine Collins and Stephen Hamilton, date and place of birth unknown.

B43345155. Dennis Gregory Collins,

fifth child and third son of Jessie Pounds and John Collins, born 27 Oct 1959 at Savannah, Chatham County, Georgia.

B43345156. Gerald Lee Collins, sixth child and fourth son of Jessie Pounds and John Collins, born 27 Feb 1963 at Savannah, Chatham County, Georgia.

B4334516. Walter Carrol (Wally) Pounds, sixth child and second son of Alto Pounds and Emma Walker, born 30 Nov 1930 at Omaha, Stewart County, Georgia and died Oct 1967 in a plane crash in the Atlantic Ocean, in the area known as the Devil's Triangle. Married about 1959 in Florida to Margaret Ann (Peggy) Elder. Walter Pounds and Peggy Elder had issue, which was the eleventh generation in America:

B43345161. Jeffery Allen Pounds, first child and first son of Walter Pounds and Peggy Elder, born 9 Mar 1960 in Florida. Married 28 Apr 1984 at Enid, Garfield County, Oklahoma to Stephanie Lynn Dahlen, born 21 Feb 1961 at Enid, Garfield County, Oklahoma. Jeffery Pounds and Stephanie Dahlen had issue, which was the twelth generation in America:

B433451611. Alex Michael Pounds, first child and first son of Jeffery Pounds and Stephanie Dahlen, born 24 Sep 1985 at Tacoma, Pierce County, Washington.

B433451612. Brian Kyle Pounds, second child and second son of Jeffery Pounds and Stephanie Dahlen, born 14 Jun 1989 at Enid, Garfield County, Oklahoma.

B433452. Ruth Ely Pounds, second child and first daughter of Charles Pounds and Martha Summerford, born 17 Aug 1897 in Henry County, Alabama and died Jan 1992 at Auburndale, Polk County, Florida. Buried at Auburndale, Polk County, Florida. Married about 1927 at Auburndale, Polk County, Florida to John W. Bruner, born 12 Nov 1880 in Alabama and died 11 Feb 1959 in Florida. Buried at Auburndale, Polk County, Florida. Ruth Pounds and John Bruner had issue, which was the tenth generation in America:

B4334521. Ruby Louise Bruner, first child and first daughter of Ruth Pounds and John Bruner, born 24 Jun 1922 and died 13 Oct 1940 at Miami, Dade County, Florida. Buried at Miami, Memorial Park cemetery, Florida.

B4334522. Evelyn Bruner, second child and second daughter of Ruth Pounds and John Bruner, born 1 Jan 1928. Married Gilbert Galloway. Evelyn Bruner and Gilbert Galloway had issue, which was the eleventh generation in America:

B43345221. Shirlene Galloway, first child and first daughter of Evelyn Bruner and Gilbert Galloway, born 1943.

B4334523. John W. Bruner, Jr., third child and first son of Ruth Pounds and John Bruner, date and place of birth unknown.

B4334524. Cecil Bruner, fourth child and second son of Ruth Pounds and John Bruner, date and place of birth unknown.

B4334525. Sarah Bruner, fifth child and third daughter of Ruth Pounds and John Bruner, date and place of birth unknown. Married Reverend Otis Guy.

B433453. Robert Nathaniel Pounds, third child and second son of Charles Pounds and Martha Summerford, born 26 Nov 1899 in Henry County, Alabama and died Nov 1969 at Andalusia, Covington County, Alabama. Married 1921 in Alabama to Verbie Hawkins, born 1900.

B433454. Lola Eugenia Pounds, fourth child and second daughter of Charles Pounds and Martha Summerford, born 4 Apr 1905 in Henry County, Alabama and died 26 Dec 1938 at Miami, Dade County, Florida. Buried at Miami, Graceland cemetery, Florida.

B433455. Charlie Jared Pounds, fifth child and third son of Charles Pounds and Martha Summerford, born 19 Dec 1907 in Henry County, Alabama and died Apr 1981 in Dade County, Florida. Buried at Miami, Dade County, Florida. Married 30 Nov 1941 to Sarah Compton Robinson, born 1908. Charlie Pounds adopted Sarah's daughter from her first marriage and the child is considered to be in the tenth generation in America:

B4334551. Frances Robinson, adopted child and daughter of Charlie Pounds and Sarah Robinson, date and place of birth unknown.

B433456. Annie May Pounds, sixth child and third daughter of Charles Pounds and Martha Summerford, born 1 May 1910 in Henry County, Alabama and died Mar 1976. Married 1929 in Georgia to William M. Crawford, born 16 Feb 1917 and died Dec 1980 at Columbus, Muscogee County, Georgia. Annie Pounds and William Crawford had issue, which was the tenth generation in America:

B4334561. William Adolphus Crawford, first child and first son of Annie Pounds and William Crawford, born 14 Jan 1930. Married Betty Rozell. William Crawford and Betty Rozell had issue, which was the eleventh generation in America:
B43345611. Jeff Crawford, first child and first son of William Crawford and Betty Rozell, date and place of birth unknown.
B43345612. Kimberly Ann Crawford, second child and first daughter of William Crawford and Betty Rozell, date and place of birth unknown.
B4334562. Nona Sue Crawford, second child and first daughter of Annie Pounds and William Crawford, born 3 Jan 1932. Married Lenard Reese Perry. Married secondly to Eugene A. Tucker. Nona Crawford and Lenard Perry had issue, which was the eleventh generation in America:
B43345621. Felton Edward Perry, first child and first son of Nona Crawford and Lenard Perry, date and place of birth unknown.
B433456211. Nancy Ann Perry, second child and first daughter of Nona Crawford and Lenard Perry, date and place of birth unknown.
B4334563. Homer David Crawford, third child and second son of Annie Pounds and William Crawford, born 12 Dec 1934 at Columbus, Muscogee County, Georgia. Married 1958 in Georgia to Sylvia Booth. Homer Crawford and Sylvia Booth had issue, which was the eleventh generation in America:
B43345631. Mark Crawford, first child and first son of Homer Crawford and Sylvia Booth, date and place of birth unknown.
B43345632. Cecilia Crawford,

second child and first daughter of Homer Crawford
and Sylvia Booth, date and place of birth unknown.
Married McLendon Wash Jenkins.
B433457. John Darsey Pounds, seventh
child and fourth son of Charles Pounds and Martha
Summerford, born 16 Oct 1913 in Henry County,
Alabama and died Apr 1982 in Hollywood, Broward
County, Florida. Married 1934 to Lula Mae
Callopy. John Pounds and Lula Callopy had issue,
which was the tenth generation in America:
B4334571. Homer David Pounds,
first child and first son of John Pounds and Lula
Callopy, born 12 Dec 1934. Married 1958 to Sylvia
Booth.
B4334572. Gloria Ann Pounds,
second child and first daughter of John Pounds and
Lula Callopy, born 1936. Married Ray Maystone,
born 1935. Gloria Pounds and Ray Maystone had
issue, which was the eleventh generation in
America:
B43345721. Sherell Maystone,
first child and first daughter of Gloria Pounds
and Ray Maystone, born 1954.
B43345722. Karen Maystone,
second child and second daughter of Gloria Pounds
and Ray Maystone, born 1959.
B4334573. Charles H. Pounds, third
child and second son of John Pounds and Lula
Callopy, born 1940.
B43346. Jessie Emma Pounds, sixth child and first
daughter of Jared Pounds and Temperance Ely, born
13 Jan 1871 at Fort Gaines, Clay County, Georgia
and died 10 May 1938 at Blakely, Early County,
Georgia. Buried at Blakely, Early County,
Georgia. Married 22 Jan 1896 in Clay County,
Georgia to Rodger Monroe Duke, son of David Dewart
Duke and Mary Frances Albritton, born 21 Jan 1875
in Clay County, Georgia and died 13 Apr 1949 at
Blakely, Early County, Georgia. Jessie Pounds and
Rodger Duke had issue, which was the ninth
generation in America:
B433461. Jessie Clyde Duke, first child and
first daughter of Jessie Pounds and Rodger Duke,
born 6 Nov 1896 in Baker County, Georgia and died
15 Dec 1962 in Randolph County, Georgia. Married
5 Oct 1913 in Randolph County, Georgia to Charles

Lumpkin Whatley, born 1 Sep 1889 and died Mar 1968.

B433462. Julia Ely Duke, second child and second daughter of Jessie Pounds and Rodger Duke, born 26 Mar 1898 in Baker County, Georgia. Married 8 Oct 1916 at Cuthbert, Randolph County, Georgia to George Millard Gulledge, son of John Franklin Gulledge and Elizabeth Ellen Mann, born 20 Mar 1895. Julia Duke and George Gulledge had issue, which was the tenth generation in America:

B4334621. Mildred Louise Gulledge, first child and first daughter of Julia Duke and George Gulledge, born 20 Jan 1918 in Monroe County, Georgia. Married 16 Jun 1947 to William Andrew Simmons.

B4334622. Jessie Lillian Gulledge, second child and second daughter of Julia Duke and George Gulledge, born 2 Mar 1922 in Clay County, Georgia. Married 15 Mar 1941 to James Walter Bailey, born 27 Dec 1912 in Fayette County, Georgia. Jessie Gulledge and James Bailey had issue, which was the eleventh generation in America:

B43346221. Andrea Louise Bailey, first child and first daughter of Jessie Gulledge and James Bailey, born 17 Jan 1942 in Upson County, Georgia. Married 28 Aug 1962 to Paul Robert Fallin.

B43346222. Maxine Enita Bailey, second child and second daughter of Jessie Gulledge and James Bailey, born 6 Apr 1947 in Upson County, Georgia. Married 2 Dec 1966 to Clark Smith.

B43346223. Julia Elizabeth Bailey, third child and third daughter of Jessie Gulledge and James Bailey, born 18 Jun 1952 in Upson County, Georgia.

B4334623. John Felton Gulledge, third child and first son of Julia Duke and George Gulledge, born 5 May 1928 in Cochran County, Georgia and died 13 Jun 1928.

B433463. Maude Eugenia Duke (twin), third child and third daughter of Jessie Pounds and Rodger Duke, born 12 Dec 1902 in Baker County, Georgia. Married 27 Jul 1920 to George William Whatley, Sr., born 26 Apr 1887 in Lamar County,

Georgia. Maude Duke and George Whatley had issue,
which was the tenth generation in America:
B4334631. George William Whatley, Jr.,
first child and first son of Maude Duke and George
Whatley, born 4 May 1921 in Randolph County,
Georgia and died 31 Dec 1944.
B4334632. Emma Nelle Whatley, second
child and first daughter of Maude Duke and George
Whatley, born 18 Sep 1923 in Randolph County,
Georgia. Married 5 Dec 1944 to Charles Edward
Ashley, born 26 Mar 1926. Emma Whatley and
Charles Ashley had issue, which was the eleventh
generation in America:
B43346321. Charles William Ashley,
first child and first son of Emma Whatley and
Charles Ashley, born 3 Feb 1948.
B43346322. Debra Lynn Ashley,
second child and first daughter of Emma Whatley
and Charles Ashley, born 17 Aug 1954.
B43346323. Tony Edwin Ashley,
third child and second son of Emma Whatley and
Charles Ashley, born 6 Dec 1955.
B4334633. Carrie Christine Whatley,
third child and second daughter of Maude Duke and
George Whatley, born 11 Feb 1926 in Randolph
County, Georgia. Married Hiram A. Lofton.
B433464. Mary Eugenia Duke (twin), fourth
child and fourth daughter of Jessie Pounds and
Rodger Duke, born 12 Dec 1902 in Baker County,
Georgia. Married 6 Sep 1921 to Claude E. Jones,
born 1900 and died Jun 1971. Mary Duke and Claude
Jones had issue, which was the tenth generation in
America:
B4334641. Claude Edward Jones, Jr.,
first child and first son of Mary Duke and Claude
Jones, born 17 Oct 1922. Married Rose Hill.
B4334642. Mairee J. Jones, second child
and first daughter of Mary Duke and Claude Jones,
born 24 Jun 1927 and died 19 Feb 1947. Married
Duke Davis. Mairee Jones and Duke Davis had
issue, which was the eleventh generation in
America:
B43346421. Eugenia Davis, first
child and first daughter of Mairee Jones and Duke
Davis, born 19 Feb 1943.
B433465. Minnie Lee Duke, fifth child and

fifth daughter of Jessie Pounds and Rodger Duke, born 20 Aug 1904 in Randolph County, Georgia. Married 29 Aug 1920 to Thomas Floyd Whatley, son of Thomas Maron Whatley and Emma Sally Mann, born 31 Mar 1886 in Randolph County, Georgia. Minnie Duke and Thomas Whatley had issue, which was the tenth generation in America:

B4334651. Dorothy Whatley, first child and first daughter of Minnie Duke and Thomas Whatley, born 2 May 1924 in Randolph County, Georgia and died 6 Sep 1970. Married 23 Dec 1942 to William Thomas Nix, son of Levi Nix and Mattie Earnest, born 1 Jan 1902. Dorothy Whatley and William Nix had issue, which was the eleventh generation in America:
B43346511. Lois Elizabeth Nix, first child and first daughter of Dorothy Whatley and William Nix, born 22 Jun 1949 at Fort Belvoir, Virginia.
B43346512. Richard Thomas Nix, second child and first son of Dorothy Whatley and William Nix, born 16 Aug 1954 at Augsburg, Germany.
B4334652. Frances Whatley, second child and second daughter of Minnie Duke and Thomas Whatley, born 2 Jul 1926 at Blakely, Early County, Georgia. Married 26 Mar 1949 to William Clarence Adams, son of John Thomas Adams and Mary Maud Brown, born 16 Sep 1918 in Lamar County, Georgia. Frances Whatley and William Adams had issue, which was the eleventh generation in America:
B43346521. Brian Keith Adams, first child and first son of Frances Whatley and William Adams, born 24 Jul 1957 in Upson County, Georgia.
B43346522. William Clarence Adams, Jr., second child and second son of Frances Whatley and William Adams, born 26 May 1959 in Upson County, Georgia.
B4334653. Carolyn Merline Whatley, third child and third daughter of Minnie Duke and Thomas Whatley, born 2 Dec 1928 at Blakely, Early County, Georgia.
B4334654. Thomas Floyd Whatley, Jr., fourth child and first son of Minnie Duke and

Thomas Whatley, born 19 Nov 1933 at Blakely, Early County, Georgia. Married 21 Nov 1953 to Bonita Churchwell, daughter of Luther Churchwell, born 1 Jan 1934 at Norman, Cleveland County, Oklahoma. Thomas Whatley and Bonita Churchwell had issue, which was the eleventh generation in America:

B43346541.   Paula Faye Whatley, first child and first daughter of Thomas Whatley and Bonita Churchwell, born 3 Dec 1954 in Upson County, Georgia.

B43346542.   Thomas FLoyd Whatley III, second child and first son of Thomas Whatley and Bonita Churchwell, born 13 Dec 1955 in Upson County, Georgia.

B43346543.   William David Whatley, third child and second son of Thomas Whatley and Bonita Churchwell, born 11 Dec 1957 at Blakely, Early County, Georgia.

B43346544.   Matthew Wayne Whatley, fourth child and third son of Thomas Whatley and Bonita Churchwell, born 18 Feb 1960 at Sanford, Seminole County, Florida and died 30 Dec 1964 at Blakely, Early County, Georgia.

B43346545.   Cheryl Jean Whatley, fifth child and second daughter of Thomas Whatley and Bonita Churchwell, born 3 Oct 1961 at Sanford, Seminole County, Florida.

B43346546.   Tammy Darlene Whatley, sixth child and third daughter of Thomas Whatley and Bonita Churchwell, born 5 Aug 1965 at Beeville, Bee County, Texas.

B4334655.   Ruth Whatley, fifth child and fourth daughter of Minnie Duke and Thomas Whatley, born 7 May 1937 at Blakely, Early County, Georgia. Married 1 Jul 1956 to David Wallace Massengale, son of Frank Massengale and Mattie Threadgill, born 31 Aug 1933.   Ruth Whatley and David Massengale had issue, which was the eleventh generation in America:

B43346551.   David Wallace Massengale, Jr., first child and first son of Ruth Whatley and David Massengale, born 20 Dec 1958 in Upson County, Georgia.

B43346552.   Carolyn Wylene Massengale, second child and first daughter of

Ruth Whatley and David Massengale, born 21 Aug 1961 in Upson County, Georgia.

B4334656. Roger Maron Whatley, sixth child and second son of Minnie Duke and Thomas Whatley, born 24 Apr 1941 at Blakely, Early County, Georgia. Married 11 Oct 1959 to Judy Bean, daughter of James Wllace Bean and Virginia - --, born 24 Jul 1940 at Sturgis, Union County, Kentucky. Roger Whatley and Judy Bean had issue, which was the eleventh generation in America:

B43346561. William Scott Whatley, first child and first son of Roger Whatley and Judy Bean, born 15 Dec 1957 at Sturgis, Union County, Kentucky.

B43346562. Barbara Marylee Whatley, second child and first daughter of Roger Whatley and Judy Bean, born 17 Oct 1961 in Upson County, Georgia.

B43346563. Roger Maron Whatley, Jr., third child and second son of Roger Whatley and Judy Bean, born 7 Jan 1961 at Henderson, Henderson County, Kentucky.

B4334657. Peggy Ann Whatley, seventh child and fifth daughter of Minnie Duke and Thomas Whatley, born 9 Sep 1943 at Blakely, Early County, Georgia. Married 16 Aug 1959 to Archie Lee Jones, son of Otehl Jones and Lucy ---, born 31 Oct 1931 at Wallace, Pender County, North Carolina. Peggy Whatley and Archie Jones had issue, which was the eleventh generation in America:

B43346571. Susan Lucinda Jones, first child and first daughter of Peggy Whatley and Archie Jones, born 27 Nov 1960 in Suffolk County, Virginia.

B43346572. Lucy Lee Jones, second child and second daughter of Peggy Whatley and Archie Jones, born 3 Aug 1964 in Suffolk County, Virginia.

B433466. Cecil Wade Duke, sixth child and first son of Jessie Pounds and Rodger Duke, born 17 Jan 1906 in Randolph County, Georgia and died 6 Jun 1929 at Cartersville, Bartow County, Georgia. Married 27 Mar 1927 to Emma Eugene Ellwood.

B433467. Mamie Lois Duke, seventh child and sixth daughter of Jessie Pounds and Rodger Duke, born 6 Feb 1908 in Randolph County, Georgia.

Married Charlie Edgar Yelverton, born 13 Feb 1884. Mamie Duke and Charlie Yelverton had issue, which was the tenth generation in America:

B4334671. Curtis Odell Yelverton, first child and first son of Mamie Duke and Charlie Yelverton, born 1 Mar 1928. Married Virginia Hull, born 2 Oct 1927. Curtis Yelverton and Virginia Hull had issue, which was the eleventh generation in America:

B43346711. Bruce James Yelverton, first child and first son of Curtis Yelverton and Virginia Hull, born 6 Jul 1953.

B43346712. Robert Curtis Yelverton, second child and second son of Curtis Yelverton and Virginia Hull, born 6 Oct 1958.

B43346713. Cynthia Gail Yelverton, third child and first daughter of Curtis Yelverton and Virginia Hull, born 24 Apr 1960.

B43346714. Deborah Kay Yelverton, fourth child and second daughter of Curtis Yelverton and Virginia Hull, born 1 Jan 1963.

B4334672. Julian Edgar Yelverton, second child and second son of Mamie Duke and Charlie Yelverton, born 23 Nov 1930. Married Hazel Deal. Julian Yelverton and Hazel Deal had issue, which was the eleventh generation in America:

B43346721. Dennis Alva Yelverton, first child and first son of Julian Yelverton and Hazel Deal, born 7 Sep 1955.

B43346722. Arthur Wayne Yelverton, second child and second son of Julian Yelverton and Hazel Deal, born 23 May 1956.

B43346723. John Randolph Yelverton, third child and third son of Julian Yelverton and Hazel Deal, born 5 Sep 1957.

B43346724. Marcia Elaine Yelverton, fourth child and first daughter of Julian Yelverton and Hazel Deal, born 10 Jan 1959.

B43346725. Patricia Ruth Yelverton, fifth child and second daughter of Julian Yelverton and Hazel Deal, born 10 May 1961.

B4334673. Leona Yelverton, third child and first daughter of Mamie Duke and Charlie

Yelverton, born 21 Nov 1931. Married France Chambliss. Leona Yelverton and France Chambliss had issue, which was the eleventh generation in America:

B43346731. Loren France Chambliss, first child and first son of Leona Yelverton and France Chambliss, born 10 Jan 1961.

B4334674. Joseph Howard Yelverton, fourth child and third son of Mamie Duke and Charlie Yelverton, born 17 Apr 1933. Married Carol White, born 20 Nov 1937. Joseph Yelverton and Carol White had issue, which was the eleventh generation in America:

B43346741. Raymond Wade Yelverton, first child and first son of Joseph Yelverton and Carol White, born 18 Jul 1956.

B43346742. Pamela Fay Yelverton, second child and first daughter of Joseph Yelverton and Carol White, born 9 May 1962.

B4334675. Margie Wynette Yelverton, fifth child and second daughter of Mamie Duke and Charlie Yelverton, born 17 Feb 1937. Married Emory Lamb, born 1936. Margie Yelverton and Emory Lamb had issue, which was the eleventh generation in America:

B43346751. Kathryn Leona Lamb, first child and first daughter of Margie Yelverton and Emory Lamb, born 1 Jul 1958.

B43346752. Emory Powell Lamb, second child and first son of Margie Yelverton and Emory Lamb, born 29 Oct 1959.

B43346753. Daniel Reid Lamb, third child and second son of Margie Yelverton and Emory Lamb, born 9 Jul 1962.

B4334676. Charlie Duke Yelverton, sixth child and fourth son of Mamie Duke and Charlie Yelverton, born 13 Aug 1942. He married but his spouse's name is unknown. Charlie Yelverton and --- --- had issue, which was the eleventh generation in America:

B43346761. Lois Jewell Yelverton, first child and first daughter of Charlie Yelverton and --- ---, born 8 Jul 1961.

B43346762. Susan Yelverton, second child and second daughter of Charlie Yelverton and ---

---, born 4 Aug 1963.

B4334677. Cheryl Lynn Yelverton, seventh child and third daughter of Mamie Duke and Charlie Yelverton, born 8 Apr 1948.

B433468. Herbert Monroe Duke, eighth child and second son of Jessie Pounds and Rodger Duke, born 10 Jul 1910 in Randolph County, Georgia. Married 7 Aug 1942 at Jacksonville, Duval County, Florida to Mattie Odessa Carter, born 14 May 1918. Herbert Duke and Mattie Carter had issue, which was the tenth generation in America:

B4334681. Charles Herbert Duke, first child and first son of Herbert Duke and Mattie Carter, born 8 Jun 1944 at Jacksonville, Duval County, Florida. Married 15 Jun 1968 at Los Angeles, Los Angeles County, California to Barbara Sorenson, born 26 Apr 1948. Charles Duke and Barbara Sorenson had issue, which was the eleventh generation in America:

B43346811. Enoch Duke, first child and first son of Charles Duke and Barbara Sorenson, born and died 16 Apr 1970 at Provo, Wasatch County, Utah.

B43346812. Amy Elizabeth Duke, second child and first daughter of Charles Duke and Barbara Sorenson, born 23 Nov 1971 at Gainesville, Alachua County, Florida.

B4334682. Phillip Rodger Duke, second child and second son of Herbert Duke and Mattie Carter, born 11 Jun 1947 at Jacksonville, Duval County, Florida. Married 30 Jul 1969 at Salt Lake City, Salt Lake County, Utah to Amelia Ann Beasley, born 8 Jul 1949. Phillip Duke and Amelia Beasley had issue, which was the eleventh generation in America:

B43346821. Rodger Herbert Duke, first child and first son of Phillip Duke and Amelia Beasley, born 21 Mar 1970 at Provo, Wasatch County, Utah.

B433469. George Andrew Duke, ninth child and third son of Jessie Pounds and Rodger Duke, born 22 Feb 1912 and died 22 May 1930.

B43347. Benjamin Idus Pounds, seventh child and sixth son of Jared Pounds and Temperance Ely, born 30 Aug 1872 at Fort Gaines, Clay County, Georgia. Married 1898 in Henry County, Alabama to Olivia Jorden, born 1887 in Baker County, Georgia. Benjamin Pounds and Olivia Jorden had issue, which was the ninth generation in America:

B433471. Joe James Pounds, first child and first son of Benjamin Pounds and Olivia Jorden, born 9 Dec 1897 in Baker County, Georgia. Married 1 May 1921 in Georgia to Carmen Clifford Timmons, born 17 Nov 1902 in Georgia. Joe Pounds and Carmen Timmons had issue, which was the tenth generation in America:

B4334711. Fay Carmen Pounds, first child and first daughter of Joe Pounds and Carmen Timmons, born 24 Jan 1934 in Baker County, Georgia. Married Wallace Weeks. Fay Pounds and Wallace Weeks had issue, which was the eleventh generation in America:

B43347111. Lynda Lee Weeks, first child and first daughter of Fay Pounds and Wallace Weeks, born 2 Nov 1954 at Savannah, Chatham County, Georgia.

B43347112. Robert Douglas Weeks, second child and first son of Fay Pounds and Wallace Weeks, born 22 Jan 1959 in Georgia.

B43347113. Russell Keith Weeks, third child and second son of Fay Pounds and Wallace Weeks, born 4 Jan 1963 in Georgia.

B4334712. Jimmy Carl Pounds, second child and first son of Joe Pounds and Carmen Timmons, born 8 Aug 1936 in Baker County, Georgia. Married 17 Dec 1961 to Mary Jo Collier. Jimmy Pounds and Mary Collier had issue, which was the eleventh generation in America:

B43347121. Ginger Ruth Pounds, first child and first daughter of Jimmy Pounds and Mary Collier, born 24 Mar 1963 in Baker County, Georgia.

B43347122. Nancy Carmen Pounds, second child and second daughter of Jimmy Pounds and Mary Collier, born 22 Jul 1966 in Baker County, Georgia.

B433472. Mable Lee Pounds, second child and second daughter of Benjamin Pounds and Olivia Jorden, born 1901 in Baker County, Georgia.

B433473. Margaret Olivia Pounds, third

child and second daughter of Benjamin Pounds and Olivia Jorden, born 21 Sep 1904 and died 7 Oct 1958 at Orlando, Orange County, Florida. Buried in Atlanta, Fulton County, Georgia. Married 15 Oct 1920 to Edgar Lee Darsey, Jr., born 21 Nov 1904 at Atlanta, Fulton County, Georgia and died Nov 1960 at Orlando, Orange County, Florida. Buried at Atlanta, Westview cemetery, Fulton County, Georgia. Margaret Pounds and Edgar Darsey had issue, which was the tenth generation in America:

B4334731. Helen Elizabeth Darsey, first child and first daughter of Margaret Pounds and Edgar Darsey, born 13 Jan 1930. Married 18 Jun 1952 to James Spaldin Playter. Helen Darsey and James Playter had issue, which was the eleventh generation in America:

B43347311. Darryl A.J. Playter, first child and first son of Helen Darsey and James Playter, born 10 Aug 1954 at Austin, Austin County, Texas.

B43347312. Brian Darsey Playter, second child and second son of Helen Darsey and James Playter, born 21 Oct 1956.

B43347313. Patrice Olivia Playter, third child and first daughter of Helen Darsey and James Playter, born 29 Sep 1958.

B4334732. Hervery Lee Darsey, second child and first son of Margaret Pounds and Edgar Darsey, born 6 Feb 1932.

B433474. Earlene Pounds, fourth child and third daughter of Benjamin Pounds and Olivia Jorden, born 1905 in Baker County, Georgia.

B433475. Early Irene Pounds, fifth child and fourth daughter of Benjamin Pounds and Olivia Jorden, born 1908 in Baker County, Georgia.

B43348. Nancy Eugenia Pounds, eighth child and second daughter of Jared Pounds and Temperance Ely, born 9 Feb 1874 in Clay County, Georgia and died 6 Aug 1933 in Baker County, Georgia. Married 21 Sep 1898 in Baker County, Georgia to Ernest Edward Ivey, son of Robert Darsey Ivey, born 1856 in Baker County, Georgia and died 1943 in Baker County, Georgia. Buried Ivey cemetery, Baker County, Georgia. Nancy Pounds and Ernest Ivey had issue, which was the ninth generation in America:

B433481. John Miller Ivey, first child and first son of Nancy Pounds and Ernest Ivey, born 3 Oct 1899 and died 17 Sep 1900 in Baker County, Georgia. Buried Ivey cemetery, Baker County, Georgia. Married Ethel Cain.

B433482. Nancy Eugenia Ivey, second child and first daughter of Nancy Pounds and Ernest Ivey, born 6 Oct 1903 in Randolph County, Georgia. Married 6 Nov 1921 to D.L. Jones, son of John Thomas Jones and Lula Elizabeth Holland, born 31 Oct 1899 in Paulding County, Georgia. Nancy Ivey and D.L. Jones had issue, which was the tenth generation in America:

B4334821. Robert Marlin (twin) Jones, first child and first son of Nancy Ivey and D.L. Jones, born 22 Nov 1922 in Randolph County, Georgia. Married 17 Oct 1953 at Greenville, Greenville County, South Carolina to Doris C. Langley, born 25 Dec 1926 at Greenville, Greenville County, South Carolina. Robert Jones and Doris Langley had issue, which was the eleventh generation in America:

B43348211. Robert Marlin Jones, Jr., first child and first son of Robert Jones and Doris Langley, born 29 Nov 1954 at Atlanta, Fulton County, Georgia.

B43348212. Larry Edward Jones, second child and second son of Robert Jones and Doris Langley, born at Rome, Floyd County, Georgia. Buried at Atlanta, Westview cemetery, Georgia.

B43348213. David Allen Jones, third child and third son of Robert Jones and Doris Langley, born 5 May 1958 at Atlanta, Fulton County, Georgia.

B4334822. Ernest Merlin (twin) Jones, second child and second son of Nancy Ivey and D.L. Jones, born 22 Nov 1922 in Randolph County, Georgia. Married 11 Jun 1953 at Dallas, Paulding County, Georgia to Shirley Ann Wood, born 29 Nov 1931 at Rome, Floyd County, Georgia. Ernest Jones and Shirley Wood had issue, which was the eleventh generation in America:

B43348221. Sherry Teresa Jones, first child and first daughter of Ernest Jones and Shirley Wood, born 14 Sep 1954 at Rome,

Floyd County, Georgia.

B43348222. Ernest Merlin Jones, Jr., second child and first son of Ernest Jones and Shirley Wood, date and place of birth unknown.

B43348223. Melinda Luanne Jones, third child and second daughter of Ernest Jones and Shirley Wood, born 22 Oct 1958.

B43348224. Susan Lynn Jones, fourth child and third daughter of Ernest Jones and Shirley Wood, date and place of birth unknown.

B433484225. Jeffery Vernon Jones, fifth child and second son of Ernest Jones and Shirley Wood, born 1966 at Atlanta, Fulton County, Georgia.

B4334823. Mary Lucy Jones, third child and first daughter of Nancy Ivey and D.L. Jones, born 1 Aug 1925 in Alachua County, Florida. Married 23 Apr 1945 at Dallas, Paulding County, Georgia to Frank Dewey Mays, Jr., born 19 Sep 1919 at Atlanta, Fulton County, Georgia. Mary Jones and Frank Mays had issue, which was the eleventh generation in America:

B43348231. Frank Dewey Mays III, first child and first son of Mary Jones and Frank Mays, born 4 Aug 1947 at Pensacola, Santa Rosa County, Florida.

B43348232. Margaret Anne Mays, second child and first daughter of Mary Jones and Frank Mays, born 3 Aug 1951 at Pensacola, Santa Rosa County, Florida.

B4334824. Virgil Ivey Jones, fourth child and third son of Nancy Ivey and D.L. Jones, born 2 Sep 1928 in Bradford County, Florida and died May 1932 in Baker County, Georgia. Buried Ivey cemetery, Baker County, Georgia.

B4334825. D.L. Jones, Jr., fifth child and fourth son of Nancy Ivey and D.L. Jones, born 28 Aug 1931 in Baker County, Georgia. Married 19 Nov 1955 at Belleville, St. Clair County, Illinois to Caroline S. Hamilton, born 25 Dec 1936 at Belleville, St. Clair County, Illinois. D.L. Jones and Caroline Hamilton had issue, which was the eleventh generation in America:

B43348251. Linda Joe Jones,

first child and first daughter of D.L. Jones and Caroline Hamilton, born 12 Feb 1956 at Belleville, St. Clair County, Illinois.

B43348252. Nancy Elizabeth Jones, second child and second daughter of D.L. Jones and Caroline Hamilton, born 2 May 1957 in Okinawa.

B43348253. Barry Lee Jones, third child and first son of D.L. Jones and Caroline Hamilton, date and place of birth unknown.

B4334826. Clara Eugenia Jones, sixth child and second daughter of Nancy Ivey and D.L. Jones, born 9 Nov 1937 in Baker County, Georgia. Married 14 Mar 1958 in Mississippi to Edward L. Irby, born 18 May 1934 in South Carolina. Clara Jones and Edward Irby had issue, which was the eleventh generation in America:

B43348261. Michael Edward Irby, first child and first son of Clara Jones and Edward Irby, born 1 Jun 1959 at Atlanta, Fulton County, Georgia.

B43348262. Michelle Alayne Irby, second child and first daughter of Clara Jones and Edward Irby, born 21 Feb 1962 at Atlanta, Fulton County, Georgia.

B43348263. Melissa Rene Irby, third child and second daughter of Clara Jones and Edward Irby, born 2 Oct 1968 at Birmingham, Jefferson County, Alabama.

B433483. Robert Dorsey Ivey, third child and second son of Nancy Pounds and Ernest Ivey, born 30 Dec 1904 in Randolph County, Georgia. Married Catherine ---. Married secondly Mildred ---. Robert Ivey and Catherine --- had issue, which was the tenth generation in America:

B4334831. Laura Ann Ivey, first child and first daughter of Robert Ivey and Catherine ---, born Oct 1933 at Miami, Dade County, Florida.

B4334832. Robert Dorsey Ivey, Jr., second child and first son of Robert Ivey and Catherine ---, born at Miami, Dade County, Florida.

B433484. Charlie Estelle Ivey, fourth child and second daughter of Nancy Pounds and

443

Ernest Ivey, born 8 Oct 1908 in Randolph County, Georgia. Married 25 Dec 1927 at Shellman, Randolph County, Georgia to Royce Middleton Gainey, son of Leroy Gainey and Mary Jane Tempy Baxter, born 23 Aug 1907 in Bradford County, Florida. Charlie Ivey and Royce Gainey had issue, which was the tenth generation in America:

B4334841. Mildred Eloise Gainey, first child and first daughter of Charlie Ivey and Royce Gainey, born 15 Dec 1931 in Bradford County, Florida. Married 12 Sep 1954 at Folkston, Charlton County, Georgia to Alfred Wells Smith, son of John Hiram Smith and Sarah Jennie Davis, born 5 Dec 1912 in Screven County, Georgia. Mildred Gainey and Alfred Smith had issue, which was the eleventh generation in America:

B43348411. David Wells Smith, first child and first son of Mildred Gainey and Alfred Smith, born 10 Sep 1955 at Jacksonville, Duval County, Florida.

B4334842. Ronald Lee Gainey, second child and first son of Charlie Ivey and Royce Gainey, born 18 Nov 1940 in Bradford County, Florida. Married 13 Mar 1965 at Jacksonville, Duval County, Florida to Angela Carole Dill, daughter of Charles Edward Dill and Florida Mary Harrold, born 29 Jan 1946. Ronald Gainey and Angela Dill had issue, which was the eleventh generation in America:

B43348421. Ronald Lee Gainey, Jr., first child and first son of Ronald Gainey and Angela Dill, born 5 Jan 1970 at Jacksonville, Duval County, Florida.

B433485. Eloise Ivey, fifth child and third daughter of Nancy Pounds and Ernest Ivey, born 5 Jan 1911 in Randolph County, Georgia and died 5 Feb 1911 in Baker County, Georgia. Buried Ivey cemetery, Baker County, Georgia.

B43349. Mary E. Pounds, ninth child and third daughter of Jared Pounds and Temperance Ely, born 20 Mar 1880 in Clay County, Georgia and died 15 Aug 1885 in Clay County, Georgia.

B4335. William David Pounds, fifth child and fourth son of William Pounds and Nancy Slayden, born 13 Mar 1822 in Oglethorpe County, Georgia and died 27 Jun 1862 near Gaines Mill, at Hanover

County, Virginia in the Civil War, while serving as a private in Co. Alabama Troop, Yancy's Grays 14th Regiment. Buried at Chattanooga, Hamilton County, Tennessee. Married 29 Apr 1845 in Meriwether County, Georgia to Rebecca B. Mann, daughter of Baker Mann and Martha McCoy, born 6 Aug 1824 in Walton County, Georgia and died about 1912 at Ashdown, Little River County, Arkansas. Buried at Old Ashdown cemetery, Little River County, Arkansas. William Pounds and Rebecca Mann had issue, which was the eighth generation in America:

B43351. Martha A. Pounds, first child and first daughter of William Pounds and Rebecca Mann, born 1846 at Griffin, Pike County, Georgia and died 1932 at Ashdown, Little River County, Arkansas. Buried at Old Ashdown cemetery, Little River County, Arkansas. Married 7 Sep 1865 in Meriwether County, Georgia to William D. Dupree, born 1847 and died after Jul 1897. Buried at Old Ashdown cemetery, Little River County, Arkansas. Martha Pounds and William Dupree had issue, which was the ninth generation in America:

B433511. Sally B. Dupree, first child and first daughter of Martha Pounds and William Dupree, born 1867 in Georgia and died 1945. Buried at Old Ashdown cemetery, Little River County, Arkansas. Married John H. Coggins, born 1869 and died 1945. Sally Dupree and John Coggins had issue, which was the tenth generation in America:

B4335111. Queenie Coggins, first child and first daughter of Sally Dupree and John Coggins, date and place of birth unknown.

B4335112. Anna Bell C. Coggins, second child and second daughter of Sally Dupree and John Coggins, date and place of birth unknown.

B4335113. Homer Coggins, third child and first son of Sally Dupree and John Coggins, date and place of birth unknown.

B4335114. John Allen Coggins, fourth child and second son of Sally Dupree and John Coggins, date and place of birth unknown.

B433512. Martha R. Dupree, second child and second daughter of Martha Pounds and William Dupree, born 1868 in Georgia and died 1948.

Buried at Richmond cemetery, Little River County, Arkansas. Married about 1896 to William S. Crouch, born 1848 and died 1927. Martha Dupree and William Crouch had issue, which was the tenth generation in America:

B4335121. Addie Crouch, first child and first daughter of Martha Dupree and William Crouch, date and place of birth unknown.

B4335122. Lottie Crouch, second child and second daughter of Martha Dupree and William Crouch, date and place of birth unknown.

B4335123. Mattie Bell Crouch, third child and third daughter of Martha Dupree and William Crouch, date and place of birth unknown.

B4335124. Frank Crouch, fourth child and first son of Martha Dupree and William Crouch, date and place of birth unknown.

B433513. Mary L. (Babe) Dupree, third child and third daughter of Martha Pounds and William Dupree, born Oct 1869 in Georgia. Married 15 Dec 1886 in Little River County, Arkansas to W.H. Ward.

B433514. Annie N. Dupree, fourth child and fourth daughter of Martha Pounds and William Dupree, born 11 Apr 1872 and died 1 Jan 1964. Buried at Old Ashdown cemetery, Little River County, Arkansas. Married 22 Sep 1895 in Little River County, Arkansas to Robert Wright.

B433515. Allie Bell Dupree, fifth child and fifth daughter of Martha Pounds and William Dupree, born 18 Feb 1874 in Georgia and died 19 Jul 1956 in Little River County, Arkansas. Buried at Winthrop, Campground cemetery, Little River County, Arkansas. Married 6 Nov 1892 in Little River County, Arkansas to Dr. William M. Lambert, born 16 Dec 1858 and died 1929. Allie Dupree and William Lambert had issue, which was the tenth generation in America:

B4335151. Baby Lambert, first child and sex unknown but presumed to be the first daughter of Allie Dupree and William Lambert, date and place of birth unknown.

B4335152. George W. Lambert, second child and first son of Allie Dupree and William Lambert, born 1894 and died 1968.

B4335153. William D. Lambert, third child and second son of Allie Dupree and William Lambert, born 1896 and died 1898.

B4335154. Jessie D. Lambert, fourth child and second daughter of Allie Dupree and William Lambert, born and died 1906.

B4335155. Mattie B. Lambert, fifth child and third daughter of Allie Dupree and William Lambert, born 1907 and died 1908.

B4335156. Andrew Lambert, sixth child and third son of Allie Dupree and William Lambert, date and place of birth unknown.

B433516. John C. Dupree, sixth child and first son of Martha Pounds and William Dupree, born 30 Jun 1876 in Georgia and died 14 Jan 1919. Buried at Old Ashdown cemetery, Little River County, Arkansas. Married Mosella Dulaney. Married secondly Mary Caswell. John Dupree and Mosella Dulaney had issue, which was the tenth generation in America:

B4335161. Charlene Dupree, first child and first daughter of John Dupree and Mosella Dulaney, date and place of birth unknown.

B4335162. Paul Dupree, second child and first son of John Dupree and Mosella Dulaney, date and place of birth unknown.

B433517. Palmer Dupree, seventh child and second son of Martha Pounds and William Dupree, born about 1879 in Georgia.

B433518. Rosa (Rosie) L. Dupree, eighth child and sixth daughter of Martha Pounds and William Dupree, born 17 Feb 1881 in Arkansas and died 24 Jun 1965. Buried at Hopewell cemetery, Little River County, Arkansas. Married 5 Aug 1900 in Arkansas to Will Fountain. Married secondly 24 Nov 1915 to --- Bedwell. Married thirdly to Albert Hamilton. Married fourthly to William C. Duncan.

B433519. Minnie Dupree, ninth child and seventh daughter of Martha Pounds and William Dupree, born 16 Apr 1883 in Arkansas and died 14 Dec 1911. Buried at Old Ashdown cemetery, Little River County, Arkansas. Married 14 Mar 1901 in Little River County, Arkansas to Tom Sawyer.

B433520. Hymond Dupree, tenth child and third son of Martha Pounds and William Dupree, born 1887 in Arkansas. Married 5 Sep 1909 in Little River County, Arkansas to Winnie Chewing.

B433521. Hettie Dupree, eleventh child and eighth daughter of Martha Pounds and William Dupree, date of birth unknown but died 12 Jun 1897. Buried at Old Ashdown cemetery, Little River County, Arkansas.

B43352. Baker Mann Pounds, second child and first son of William Pounds and Rebecca Mann, born 8 Nov 1848 at Griffin, Pike County, Georgia and died 5 Dec 1929 at Ashdown, Little River County, Arkansas. Buried at Old Ashdown cemetery, Little River County, Arkansas. Married 21 Oct 1869 in Meriwether County, Georgia to Mary Ann Bowles, born 30 May 1844 in Georgia and died 28 Apr 1892 in Little River County, Arkansas. Buried at Old Ashdown cemetery, Little River County, Arkansas. Married secondly to Julia Savannah Ligon, born 1827 and died 1925. Baker Pounds and Mary Bowles had issue, which was the ninth generation in America:

B433521. Josephene A. (Josie) Pounds, first child and first daughter of Baker Pounds and Mary Bowles, born 4 Sep 1870 in Meriwether County, Georgia and died 11 Oct 1904 in Arkansas. Buried at Old Ashdown cemetery, Little River County, Arkansas. Married 14 Jun 1890 in Little River County, Arkansas to J.B. Jackson. Josephene Pounds and J.B. Jackson had issue, which was the tenth generation in America:

B4335211. Alvin Jackson, first child and first son of Josephene Pounds and J.B. Jackson, date and place of birth unknown.

B433522. Elizabeth R. (Bettie) Pounds, second child and second daughter of Baker Pounds and Mary Bowles, born Sep 1874 in Meriwether County, Georgia and died 16 Feb 1948 at Glenwood, Pike County, Arkansas. Married 14 Jan 1897 in Little River County, Arkansas to David C. Stough, born 20 Jan 1861 and died 5 Jul 1941. Elizabeth Pounds and David Stough had issue, which was the tenth generation in America:

B4335221. Maude I. Stough, first child and first daughter of Elizabeth Pounds and David Stough, date and place of birth unknown.

B4335222. Lillian D. Stough,

second child and second daughter of Elizabeth Pounds and David Stough, date and place of birth unknown.

B4335223 . Clarence Stough, third child and first son of Elizabeth Pounds and David Stough, date and place of birth unknown.

B4335224. Olar Pearl Stough, fourth child and third daughter of Elizabeth Pounds and David Stough, date and place of birth unknown.

B433523. Mary Lavada Pounds, third child and third daughter of Baker Pounds and Mary Bowles, born 23 Sep 1877 in Meriwether County, Georgia and died 3 Nov 1942 in Arkansas. Buried at Old Ashdown cemetery, Little River County, Arkansas. Married 19 Dec 1897 in Little River County, Arkansas to Jesse R. Cummings, born 1882 and died 1903. Mary Pounds and Jesse Cummings had issue, which was the tenth generation in America:

B4335231. Jessie Cummings, first child and first daughter of Mary Pounds and Jesse Cummings, date and place of birth unknown.

B433524. Georgia Pounds, fourth child and fourth daughter of Baker Pounds and Mary Bowles, born 2 Oct 1879 in Meriwether County, Georgia and died 8 Apr 1948 in Arkansas. Buried at Old Ashdown cemetery, Little River County, Arkansas. Married 13 Dec 1900 in Little River County, Arkansas to William B. Prewitt, born 28 Nov 1872 and died 19 Nov 1928. Georgia Pounds and William Prewitt did not have issue, but adopted a child, who was considered to be in the tenth generation in America:

B4335241. Charley (adopted) Prewitt, first child and first son of Georgia Pounds and William Prewitt, date and place of birth unknown.

B433525. Elisa E. Pounds, fifth child and fifth daughter of Baker Pounds and Mary Bowles, born 11 Dec 1881 in Meriwether County, Georgia and died 6 Dec 1955 in Arkansas. Buried at Old Ashdown cemetery, Little River County, Arkansas. Married John P. Keith, born 8 Jan 1879 and died 4 Aug 1960. Elisa Pounds and John Keith had issue, which was the tenth generation in America:

B4335251. Juliette Keith, first child and first daughter of Elisa Pounds and John Keith, date and place of birth unknown.

B4335252. Ethel Keith, second child and second daughter of Elisa Pounds and John Keith, date and place of birth unknown.

B4335253. Georgetta Keith, third child and third daughter of Elisa Pounds and John Keith, date and place of birth unknown.

B4335254. Ruby Keith, fourth child and fourth daughter of Elisa Pounds and John Keith, date and place of birth unknown.

B4335255. Perry Keith, fifth child and first son of Elisa Pounds and John Keith, date and place of birth unknown.

B4335256. Claude Keith, sixth child and second son of Elisa Pounds and John Keith, date and place of birth unknown.

B4335257. William Keith, seventh child and third son of Elisa Pounds and John Keith, date and place of birth unknown.

B433526. Harvey E. Pounds, sixth child and first son of Baker Pounds and Mary Bowles, born Jun 1884 in Meriwether County, Georgia. Married 2 Sep 1906 in Pike County, Arkansas to Artoe Babbitt. Married secondly 11 Feb 1923 in Pike County, Arkansas to Vadie Martin. Harvey Pounds and Artoe Babbitt had issue, which was the tenth generation in America:

B4335261. Jessie Pounds, first child and first daughter of Harvey Pounds and Artoe Babbitt, date and place of birth unknown.

B4335262. Mable Pounds, second child and second daughter of Harvey Pounds and Artoe Babbitt, date and place of birth unknown.

B43353. Jackson R. (Jack) Pounds, third child and second son of William Pounds and Rebecca Mann, born 24 Sep 1851 at Griffin, Pike County, Georgia and died 15 Jul 1925 at Salem, Pike County, Arkansas. Buried at Salem Church cemetery, Pike County, Arkansas. Married 12 Dec 1872 in Meriwether County, Georgia to Nancy Catherine Thrash, daughter of F.L. Thrash and Sarah ---, born 4 Oct 1851 in Meriwether County, Georgia and died 20 Feb 1939 in Glenwood, Pike County, Arkansas. Buried at Salem Church cemetery, Pike County, Arkansas. Jackson Pounds and Nancy Thrash had issue, which was the ninth generation in America:

B433531. William Isaac Pounds, first child and first son of Jackson Pounds and Nancy Thrash, born 24 Sep 1873 in Meriwether County, Georgia and died 11 Feb 1939 in Pike County, Arkansas. Buried at Salem Church cemetery, Pike County, Arkansas. Married Virginia N. Orrick, born 1875 and died 1901. Married secondly to Lou Emma Foshee, born 1870 and died 1912. Married thirdly to Callie Watson, born 1883 and died 1927. William Pounds and Virginia Orrick had issue, which was the tenth generation in America:

B4335311. Dewey H. Pounds, first child and first son of William Pounds and Virginia Orrick, born 1898.

B433531. William Isaac Pounds, first child and first son of Jackson Pounds and Nancy Thrash, born 24 Sep 1873 in Meriwether County, Georgia and died 11 Feb 1939 in Pike County, Arkansas. Married secondly to Lou Emma Foshee, born 1870 and died 1912. Married thirdly to Callie Watson. William Pounds and Lou Foshee had issue, which was the tenth generation in America:

B4335311. Junnie Lula Pounds, first child and first daughter of William Pounds and Lou Foshee, born 1902. Married William Gibbs.

B4335312. Bertie Pounds, second child and second daughter of William Pounds and Lou Foshee, born 1904. Married Thomas Black.

B4335313. Vilia Pounds, third child and first son of William Pounds and Lou Foshee, born 1905. Married Jewel Tackett.

B4335314. Alvin Pounds, fourth child and second son of William Pounds and Lou Foshee, born 1906. Married Ilene Copeland.

B4335315. Cleo Pounds, fifth child and third daughter of William Pounds and Lou Foshee, born 1908 and died 1952. Married A.L. Wyatt, born 1900 and died 1967.

B4335316. Joseph Robert Pounds, sixth child and third son of William Pounds and Lou Foshee, born 1910. Married Martha

Louise Williams, born 1910. Joseph Pounds and Martha Williams had issue, which was the eleventh generation in America:

B43353161. Bobbie Lou Pounds, first child and first daughter of Joseph Pounds and Martha Williams, born 1933. Married Mark Abington. Bobbie Pounds and Mark Abington had issue, which was the twelth generation in America:

B433531611. Mark Abington, first child and first son of Bobbie Pounds and Mark Abington, date and place of birth unknown.

B433531612. Lori Abington, second child and first daughter of Bobbie Pounds and Mark Abington, date and place of birth unknown.

B43353162. James William Pounds, second child and first son of Joseph Pounds and Martha Williams, born 1939. Married Evelyn Ann Allison, born 1940. James Pounds and Evelyn Allison had issue, which was the twelth generation in America:

B433531621. Allison Ann Pounds, first child and first daughter of James Pounds and Evelyn Allison, born 1963.

B433531622. Jami Louise Pounds, second child and second daughter of James Pounds and Evelyn Allison, born 1966.

B433531. William Isaac Pounds, first child and first son of Jackson Pounds and Nancy Thrash, born 24 Sep 1873 in Meriwether County, Georgia and died 11 Feb 1939 in Pike County, Arkansas. Buried at Salem Church cemetery, Pike County, Arkansas. Married thirdly to Callie Watson, born 1883 and died 1927. William Pounds and Callie Watson had issue, which was the tenth generation in America:

B4335311. Earl Pounds, first child and first son of William Pounds and Callie Watson, born 1912.

B4335312. Watson Pounds, second child and second son of William Pounds and Callie Watson, born 1914. Married Lillian Moran.

B4335313. Odessa Pounds, third child and first daughter of William Pounds and Callie Watson, born 1918. Married Russell Wilson.

B4335314. Ardue Pounds, fourth child and third son of William Pounds and Callie Watson, born 1920.

B4335315. Luese Pounds, fifth child and second daughter of William Pounds and Callie Watson, born 1924. Married --- Kern.

B433532. Christopher Columbus Pounds, second child and second son of Jackson Pounds and Nancy Thrash, born 26 Apr 1876 in Meriwether County, Georgia and died 1945 in Arkansas. Buried at Rock Creek Road cemetery, Pike County, Arkansas. Married 10 Dec 1895 in Pike County, Arkansas to Sallie S. Foshee, born 1880 and died 1971. Christopher Pounds and Sallie Foshee had issue, which was the tenth generation in America:

B4335321. William Felex Pounds, first child and first son of Christopher Pounds and Sallie Foshee, born 1897 and died 1924. Married Grace Bailey, born 1902.

B4335322. Essie L. Pounds, second child and first daughter of Christopher Pounds and Sallie Foshee, born 1899. Married Martin C. Howard, born 1895.

B4335323. Veda Pounds, third child and second daughter of Christopher Pounds and Sallie Foshee, born 1901. Married Earnie Bailey, born 1898.

B4335324. Leonard Pounds, fourth child and second son of Christopher Pounds and Sallie Foshee, born 1903. Married Mabel Gregory, born 1906.

B4335325. Kate Pounds, fifth child and third daughter of Christopher Pounds and Sallie Foshee, born 1907. Married E.V. Rose, born 1905.

B4335326. Elsie Pounds, sixth child and fourth daughter of Christopher Pounds and Sallie Foshee, born 1907 and died 1911.

B4335327. Bryant Pounds, seventh child and third son of Christopher Pounds and Sallie Foshee, date and place of birth unknown.

B433533. Amanda L. Pounds, third

child and first daughter of Jackson Pounds and Nancy Thrash, born 11 May 1882 at Kirby, Pike County, Arkansas and died after 1910 at Hot Springs, Hot Spring County, Arkansas. Married before 1900 in Arkansas to Lawrence Orrick.

B433534. Cosie Ann Pounds, fourth child and second daughter of Jackson Pounds and Nancy Thrash, born 8 Jan 1884 at Kirby, Pike County, Arkansas and died 26 Jan 1960 in Salem, Fulton County, Arkansas. Married 23 Oct 1902 in Pike County, Arkansas to William Riley Foshee, born 1881 and died 1961. Cosie Pounds and William Foshee had issue, which was the tenth generation in America:

B4335341. Ella Veola Foshee, first child and first daughter of Cosie Pounds and William Foshee, date and place of birth unknown.

B433535. Ella Pounds, fifth child and third daughter of Jackson Pounds and Nancy Thrash, born 1 Aug 1887 at Kirby, Pike County, Arkansas and died 1941 in Arkansas. Married 4 Oct 1908 in Pike County, Arkansas to J. Sam Odom, born 1873 and died 1944.

B433536. Grover Jackson Pounds, sixth child and third son of Jackson Pounds and Nancy Thrash, born 9 Sep 1892 at Kirby, Pike County, Arkansas and died 17 Apr 1953 in Salem, Pike County, Arkansas. Buried at Salem Church cemetery, Pike County, Arkansas. Married 19 Apr 1914 in Pike County, Arkansas to Mary Ruth Dingler, born 3 Feb 1893 and died 8 Oct 1939. Grover Pounds and Mary Dingler had issue, which was the tenth generation in America:

B4335361. Haze A. Pounds, first child and first son of Grover Pounds and Mary Dingler, born 1915 in Kirby, Pike County, Arkansas and died 9 Aug 1979 in Salem, Pike County, Arkansas. Buried at Salem cemetery, Arkansas. Married 7 Apr 1934 to Wilma Estelle Reid, born 5 Apr 1917 at Newhope, Howard County, Arkansas. Haze Pounds and Wilma Reid had issue, which was the eleventh generation in America:

B43353611. Louie Janiece Pounds, first child and first daughter of Haze Pounds and Wilma Reid, born 23 Nov 1934 at Newhope, Howard County, Arkansas. Married 22 Jul

1956 at Mountain Pine, Garland County, Arkansas to
William Butler Green, born 1933.

B43353612. Margaret Ann
Pounds, second child and second daughter of Haze
Pounds and Wilma Reid, born 18 Aug 1939 at
Blakely, Garland County, Arkansas. Married 25 Dec
1956 at Mountain Pine, Garland County, Arkansas to
John B. Wagner.

B43353613. Douglas Haze
Pounds, third child and first son of Haze Pounds
and Wilma Reid, born 6 Feb 1947 at Hot Spring, Hot
Spring County, Arkansas. Married first to Donna
Graves. Married secondly to Nancy ---.

B4335362. Wilson B. Pounds,
second child and second son of Grover Pounds and
Mary Dingler, born 30 Sep 1918 at Kirby, Pike
County, Arkansas. Married Leona Patton.

B433537. Robert Quinton Pounds,
seventh child and fourth son of Jackson Pounds and
Nancy Thrash, born 19 Mar 1896 at Kirby, Pike
County, Arkansas and died 1982 in Arkansas.
Buried at Salem Church cemetery, Pike County,
Arkansas. Married 2 May 1915 in Pike County,
Arkansas to Theolia Hubbert, born 1898 and died
1960. Married secondly to Zona Inez Tribble, born
1917.

B43354. Lucy E. Pounds, fourth child
and second daughter of William Pounds and Rebecca
Mann, born Aug 1854 in Chambers County, Alabama
and died 20 Feb 1906 in Ashdown, Little River
County, Arkansas. Buried at Old Ashdown cemetery,
Little River County, Arkansas. Married 28 Jan
1891 in Little River County, Arkansas to Philetus
Cincinattis (Deedle) Thrash, born 26 Feb 1846 in
Georgia and died 15 Mar 1925 in Arkansas. Buried
at Old Ashdown cemetery, Little River County,
Arkansas. Philetus Thrash married secondly to
Sarah A. Mann, by whom he had four children. The
first child was Lenora B. Thrash, born 9 Jun 1872
in Meriwether County, Georgia and died 17 Dec
1894. Buried at Old Ashdown cemetery, Little
River County, Arkansas. The second child was
Baker (Bob) Stell Thrash, born 17 Jun 1878 in
Meriwether County, Georgia and died 12 Sep 1861.
Buried at Old Ashdown cemetery, Little River
County, Arkansas. Married Lillie Essie Simmons.

Married secondly Cleora (Black) Scott. The third child was Neatie Pearl Thrash, born 17 Sep 1881 in Pike County, Arkansas and died 13 Oct 1899. Buried at Old Ashdown cemetery, Little River County, Arkansas. The fourth child was James Calhoun Thrash, born 8 Oct 1884 in Pike County, Arkansas and died 14 Nov 1964. Buried at Ashdown cemetery, Little River County, Arkansas. Married Tillie Brown.

B43355. Amanda J. Pounds, fifth child and third daughter of William Pounds and Rebecca Mann, born 4 Sep 1856 in Chambers County, Alabama and died 8 Jun 1915 at Powers Chapel, Pike County, Arkansas. Buried at Powers Chapel cemetery, Pike County, Arkansas. Married 4 Dec 1873 in Meriwether County, Georgia to John C. Liggin, born 28 Jun 1852 in Meriwether County, Georgia and died 22 Apr 1896 in Pike County, Arkansas. Buried at Powers Chapel cemetery, Pike County, Arkansas. Amanda Pounds and John Liggin had issue, which was the ninth generation in America:

B433551. Mattie Liggin, first child and first daughter of Amanda Pounds and John Liggin, born about 1875 in Meriwether County, Georgia. Married before 1895 in Pike County, Arkansas to C.H. Coker. Mattie Liggin and C.H. Coker had issue, which was the tenth generation in America:

B4335511. Lola Coker, first child and first daughter of Mattie Liggin and C.H. Coker, date and place of birth unknown.

B433552. Philetus T. Liggin, second child and first son of Amanda Pounds and John Liggin, born Jun 1877 in Meriwether County, Georgia. Married 15 Sep 1898 in Pike County, Arkansas to Lela Bell Watson, born 1879. Philetus Liggin and Lela Watson had issue, which was the tenth generation in America:

B4335521. John Clint Liggin, first child and first son of Philetus Liggin and Lela Watson, born 1900. Married Ruth Whitted, born 1905.

B4335522. Freeman Liggin, second child and second son of Philetus Liggin and Lela Watson, born 1905. Married Earnestine Thompson, born 1905.

456

B433553. Fred T. Liggin, third child and second son of Amanda Pounds and John Liggin, born Oct 1879 in Pike County, Arkansas. Married 10 Aug 1899 in Pike County, Arkansas to Acquiella Yarbrough, born 1884.

B433554. Alonzo J. Liggin, fourth child and third son of Amanda Pounds and John Liggin, born Feb 1882 in Pike County, Arkansas. Married Olla (Ora) ---, date of birth unknown but died in 1918. Married secondly 5 Sep 1920 in Pike County, Arkansas to Wonda Robertson, born 1899. Alonzo Liggin and Olla --- had issue, which was the tenth generation in America:

B4335541. Lois Liggin, first child and first daughter of Alonzo Liggin and Olla ---, dae and place of birth unknown.

B4335542. Opel Mae Liggin, second child and second daughter of Alonzo Liggin and Olla ---, date and place of birth unknown.

B433555. Caddie S. Liggin, fifth child and second daughter of Amanda Pounds and John Liggin, born Jun 1884 in Pike County, Arkansas. Married 27 Sep 1914 in Pike County, Arkansas to J.W. McWha, born 1881.

B433556. Charles (twin) Liggin, sixth child and fourth son of Amanda Pounds and John Liggin, born 21 Feb 1887 in Pike County, Arkansas and died 5 Sep 1933. Buried at Salem Church cemetery, Pike County, Arkansas. Married M.C. (Girtie) ---. Charles Liggin and Girtie --- had issue, which was the tenth generation in America:

B4335561. Girtie Lee Liggin, first child and first daughter of Charles Liggin and Girtie ---, date and place of birth unknown.

B433557. Ollie (twin) Liggin, seventh child and third daughter of Amanda Pounds and John Liggin, born 21 Feb 1887 in Pike County, Arkansas. Married --- Bridges.

B433558. Robert (twin) Liggin, eighth child and fifth son of Amanda Pounds and John Liggin, born Dec 1889 in Pike County, Arkansas. Married 19 Nov 1911 in Pike County, Arkansas to Vernola Jarrell, born 1891.

B433559. Rosa (twin) Liggin, ninth child and fourth daughter of Amanda Pounds and

John Liggin, born Dec 1889 in Pike County, Arkansas. Married Edd Malone, born 1889.

B4335510. Horace Liggin, tenth child and sixth son of Amanda Pounds and John Liggin, born Jan 1893 in Pike County, Arkansas. Married 27 Sep 1914 in Pike County, Arkansas to Samantha Jerrell.

B4335511. Homer Liggin, eleventh child and seventh son of Amanda Pounds and John Liggin, born Jan 1896 in Pike County, Arkansas. Married --- ---. Married secondly 18 Jan 1920 in Pike County, Arkansas to Pattie Garrett, born 1898. Homer Liggin and --- --- had issue, which was the tenth generation in America:

B43355111. Everett Liggin, first child and first son of Homer Liggin and --- ---, date and place of birth unknown.

B43356. William Franklin Pounds, sixth child and third son of William Pounds and Rebecca Mann, born 1859 in Chambers County, Alabama and died 25 Jan 1899 in Ashdown, Little River County, Arkansas. Buried at Old Ashdown cemetery, Little River County, Arkansas. Married 16 Jan 1881 in Pike County, Arkansas to Susan Emma Dreghorn, daughter of Adam Johnson Dreghorn and Susan Emma Ligon, born 27 Oct 1863 in Meriwether County, Georgia and died 1906 at Salem, Pike County, Arkansas. Buried at Powers Chapel cemetery, Pike County, Arkansas. William Pounds and Susan Dreghorn had issue, which was the ninth generation in America:

B433561. Lallie Mae Pounds, first child and first daughter of William Pounds and Susan Dreghorn, born 3 May 1882 in Pike County, Arkansas and died 29 Jan 1916 in Little River County, Arkansas. Buried at Ashdown, Hicks cemetery, Arkansas. Married 30 Jan 1899 in Little River County, Arkansas to Lucious Hardiman Simmons, born 22 Oct 1881 in Hempstead County, Arkansas and died 26 Jun 1929 in Little River County, Arkansas. Buried at Ashdown, Hicks cemetery, Arkansas. Lallie Pounds and Lucious Simmons had issue, which was the tenth generation in America:

B4335611. Gertrude Simmons, first child and first daughter of Lallie Pounds and Lucious Simmons, born Feb 1900 in Little River County, Arkansas and died 5 Jul 1911 in Little River County, Arkansas. Buried at Ashdown, Hicks cemetery, Arkansas.

B4335612. Viola Simmons, second child and second daughter of Lallie Pounds and Lucious Simmons, born 1 Dec 1901 in Little River County, Arkansas. Married 10 Apr 1919 in Little River County, Arkansas to Euclid Cooper, born 1899. Married secondly --- Scott. Viola Simmons and --- Scott had issue, which was the eleventh generation in America:

B43356121. Doris Ella Scott, first child and first daughter of Viola Simmons and --- Scott, date and place of birth unknown. Married Billy Hodges.

B4335613. Cleora Simmons, third child and third daughter of Lallie Pounds and Lucious Simmons, born 30 Nov 1903 in Little River County, Arkansas. Married 16 Jul 1920 in Little River County, Arkansas to E.B. Dulaney, born 1896. Cleora Simmons and E.B. Dulaney had issue, which was the eleventh generation in America:

B43356131. Bowen Dulaney, first child and first son of Cleora Simmons and E.B. Dulaney, date and place of birth unknown.

B43356132. Dale Dulaney, second child and first daughter of Cleora Simmons and E.B. Dulaney, date and place of birth unknown.

B4335614. Clara Frances Simmons, fourth child and fourth daughter of Lallie Pounds and Lucious Simmons, born 1 Nov 1905 in Little River County, Arkansas. Married 5 Dec 1922 in Miller County, Arkansas to Ernest Metcalf, born 1899. Clara Simmons married secondly to John Bevel. Clara Simmons and Ernest Metcalf had issue, which was the eleventh generation in America:

B43356141. Alice Maye Metcalf, first child and first daughter of Clara Simmons and Ernest Metcalf, date and place of birth unknown. Married --- Brown.

B4335615. Floyd Hardiman Simmons, fifth child and first son of Lallie

Pounds and Lucious Simmons, born 24 Oct 1908 in Little River County, Arkansas and died 26 Oct 1985 at Ashdown, Little River County, Arkansas. Buried at Ashdown, Hicks cemetery, Arkansas.

B4335616. Irene Simmons, sixth child and fifth daughter of Lallie Pounds and Lucious Simmons, born 23 Aug 1910 in Little River County, Arkansas and died Dec 1990. Married 28 Dec 1926 in Miller County, Arkansas to T.J. Clarke, born 1908. Irene Simmons and T.J. Clarke had issue, which was the eleventh generation in America:

B43356161. Tillman Clarke, first child and first son of Irene Simmons and T.J. Clarke, date and place of birth unknown.

B43356162. Jorene Clarke, second child and first daughter of Irene Simmons and T.J. Clarke, date and place of birth unknown.

B4335617. Nellie Blanche Simmons, seventh child and sixth daughter of Lallie Pounds and Lucious Simmons, born 4 Mar 1912 in Little River County, Arkansas and died 30 Sep 1912 in Little River County, Arkansas. Buried at Ashdown, Hicks cemetery, Arkansas.

B4335618. Woodrow David Simmons, eighth child and second son of Lallie Pounds and Lucious Simmons, born Aug 1914 in Little River County, Arkansas. Married --- ---. Woodrow Simmons and --- --- had issue, which was the eleventh generation in America:

B43356181. David Simmons, first child and first son of Woodrow Simmons and --- ---, date and place of birth unknown.

B43356182. Lurine Simmons, second child and first daughter of Woodrow Simmons and --- ---, date and place of birth unknown.

B43356183. Jeanie Simons, third child and second daughter of Woodrow Simmons and --- ---, date and place of birth unknown.

B433562. Hadris Pennon (Bud) Pounds, second child and first son of William Pounds and Susan Dreghorn, born Jan 1884 in Pike County,

460

Arkansas and died about Oct 1900 in Little River County, Arkansas. Buried at Old Ashdown cemetery, Little River County, Arkansas.

B433563. Exie Lee (Babe) Pounds, third child and second daughter of William Pounds and Susan Dreghorn, born Nov 1885 in Pike County, Arkansas and died after Jun 1900 in Little River County, Arkansas. Buried at Old Ashdown cemetery, Little River County, Arkansas.

B433564. William Franklin Pounds, fourth child and second son of William Pounds and Susan Dreghorn, born 24 Jun 1888 in Little River County, Arkansas and died 21 Feb 1957 in Little River County, Arkansas. Buried at Ashdown cemetery, Little River County, Arkansas. Married 7 Mar 1909 in Little River County, Arkansas to Lola Jane Hinton, born 27 Feb 1894 in Little River County, Arkansas and died 3 May 1976 in Little River County, Arkansas. Buried at Ashdown cemetery, Little River County, Arkansas. William Pounds and Lola Hinton had issue, which was the tenth generation in America:

B4335641. Monroe Franklin Pounds, first child and first son of William Pounds and Lola Hinton, born 6 Feb 1910 in Little River County, Arkansas. Married 10 Aug 1930 in Little River County, Arkansas to Jettie Waldo, born 1911. Monroe Pounds and Jettie Waldo had issue, which was the eleventh generation in America:

B43356411. Joe Bob Pounds, first child and first son of Monroe Pounds and Jettie Waldo, born 1931. Married Margie Faye Grose.

B43356412. William Edward Pounds, second child and second son of Monroe Pounds and Jettie Waldo, date and place of birth unknown. Married Andrea Lee Bass.

B4335642. Claudia Pennon (Buddy) Pounds, second child and second son of William Pounds and Lola Hinton, born 21 Oct 1911 in Little River County, Arkansas. Married 27 Dec 1935 to Willie (Billie) Morrison. Claudia Pounds and Willie Morrison had issue, which was the eleventh generation in America:

B43356421. Paul Edward Pounds, first child and first son of Claudia

461

Pounds and Willie Morrison, date and place of birth unknown.

B43356422. David Wayne Pounds, second child and second son of Claudia Pounds and Willie Morrison, date and place of birth unknown.

B43356423. Greta Jo Pounds, third child and first daughter of Claudia Pounds and Willie Morrison, date and place of birth unknown.

B4335643. Ninnie Autherine Pounds, third child and first daughter of William Pounds and Lola Hinton, born 17 May 1915 in Little River County, Arkansas. Married 31 Aug 1937 to Joseph Daniel Osborne. Ninnie Pounds and Joseph Osborne had issue, which was the eleventh generation in America:

B43356431. Mary Jane Osborne, first child and first daughter of Ninnie Pounds and Joseph Osborne, date and place of birth unknown. Married --- Hogard.

B43356432. Loretta A. Osborne, second child and second daughter of Ninnie Pounds and Joseph Osborne, date and place of birth unknown. Married David L. Brewer.

B43356433. Linda Sue Osborne, third child and third daughter of Ninnie Pounds and Joseph Osborne, date and place of birth unknown.

B4335644. Albert Britton Pounds, fourth child and third son of William Pounds and Lola Hinton, born 24 Jul 1917 in Little River County, Arkansas. Married 2 Oct 1943 to Sue Furgerson. Albert Pounds and Sue Furgerson had issue, which was the eleventh generation in America:

B43356441. Britton Pounds, first child and first son of Albert Pounds and Sue Furgerson, date and place of birth unknown.

B4335645. Isaac Minor Gipson Pounds, fifth child and fourth son of William Pounds and Lola Hinton, born 7 Jun 1919 in Little River County, Arkansas. Married 22 Apr 1939 in Little River County, Arkansas to Allie Mae Golden, born 1922. Isaac Pounds and Allie Golden had issue, which was the eleventh generation in

America:

B43356451. William (Billy) Pounds, first child and first son of Isaac Pounds and Allie Golden, date and place of birth unknown. Married Dorris Burns.

B4335646. Quillie Marie Pounds, sixth child and second daughter of William Pounds and Lola Hinton, born 22 Mar 1922 in Little River County, Arkansas. Married 28 Dec 1940 in Little River County, Arkansas to Autry Lee Hughes, born 1916. Quillie Pounds and Autry Hughes had issue, which was the eleventh generation in America:

B43356461. Patricia Ann Hughes, first child and first daughter of Quillie Pounds and Autry Hughes, date and place of birth unknown.

B4335647. Exie Lee Pounds, seventh child and third daughter of William Pounds and Lola Hinton, born 13 Jun 1924 in Little River County, Arkansas and died 12 Jun 1974 in Michigan. Buried at Ashdown, Hicks cemtery, Arkansas. Married 16 Feb 1948 in Little River County, Arkansas to Jesse Wise (Dub) Phillips, born 1922. Exie Pounds and Jesse Phillips had issue, which was the eleventh generation in America:

B43356471. Frank Leslie Phillips, first child and first son of Exie Pounds and Jesse Phillips, date and place of birth unknown.

B43356472. Ronald Phillips, second child and second son of Exie Pounds and Jesse Phillips, date and place of birth unknown.

B4335648. William Forrest Pounds, eighth child and fifth son of William Pounds and Lola Hinton, born 11 Dec 1926 in Little River County, Arkansas and died 21 Mar 1987. Buried at Ashdown, Hicks cemetery, Little River County, Arkansas. Married Emma Lea Jean Tucker. William Pounds and Emma Tucker had issue, which was the eleventh generation in America:

B43356481. William Pounds, first child and first son of William Pounds and Emma Tucker, date and place of birth unknown.

B43356482. Melba Pounds, second child and first daughter of William Pounds and Emma Tucker, date and place of birth unknown.

Married Ronnie T. Brazeal.

B43356483. William Robert Pounds, third child and second son of William Pounds and Emma Tucker, date and place of birth unknown. Married Suellen Fawcett.

B43356484. Mike Pounds, fourth child and third son of William Pounds and Emma Tucker, date and place of birth unknown.

B43356485. Barbara Lee Pounds, fifth child and second daughter of William Pounds and Emma Tucker, date and place of birth unknown. Married Paul Patrick Murphy.

B4335649. Charles Ray Pounds, ninth child and sixth son of William Pounds and Lola Hinton, born 17 Dec 1929 in Little River County, Arkansas. Married 17 Oct 1948 in Little River County, Arkansas to Annie Grace (Sally) Massey. Charles Pounds and Annie Massey had issue, which was the eleventh generation in America:

B43356491. Charlotte Pounds, first child and first daughter of Charles Pounds and Annie Massey, date and place of birth unknown. Married Ray Lee McCullough.

B43356492. Pamela Jane Pounds, second child and second daughter of Charles Pounds and Annie Massey, date and place of birth unknown. Married Larry Wayne Bennett.

B43356493. Roger Pounds, third child and first son of Charles Pounds and Annie Massey, date and place of birth unknown.

B43356494. Douglas Richard Pounds, fourth child and second son of Charles Pounds and Annie Massey, date and place of birth unknown. Married Debbie Lynn.

B43356495. Gary Pounds, fifth child and third son of Charles Pounds and Annie Massey, date and place of birth unknown.

B43356496. Lisa Pounds, sixth child and third daughter of Charles Pounds and Annie Massey, date and place of birth unknown.

B4335650. Jack Kenneth Pounds, tenth child and seventh son of William Pounds and Lola Hinton, born 4 Aug 1932 in Little River County, Arkansas and died 19 Dec 1932 in Little

River County, Arkansas. Buried at Old Ashdown
cemtery, Little River County, Arkansas.

B4335651. Horace Clifton (Nookie)
Pounds, eleventh child and eighth son of William
Pounds and Lola Hinton, born 26 Jul 1933 in Little
River County, Arkansas. Married 17 Feb 1953 in
Little River County, Arkansas to Berneice Eulon
Ford. Horace Pounds and Berneice Ford had issue,
which was the eleventh generation in America:

B43356511. Clifton Pounds,
first child and first son of Horace Pounds and
Berneice Ford, date and place of birth unknown.

B43356512. Donald Pounds,
second child and second son of Horace Pounds and
Berneice Ford, date and place of birth unknown.

B43356513. William Louis
Pounds, third child and third son of Horace Pounds
and Berneice Ford, date and place of birth
unknown.

B43356514. Curtis Pounds,
fourth child and fourth son of Horace Pounds and
Berneice Ford, date and place of birth unknown.
Married Carla O'Neal.

B43356515. Peggy Pounds,
fifth child and first daughter of Horace Pounds
and Berneice Ford, date and place of birth
unknown.

B43356516. Shari Pounds,
sixth child and second daughter of Horace Pounds
and Berneice Ford, date and place of birth
unknown.

B43356517. David Pounds,
seventh child and fifth son of Horace Pounds and
Berneice Ford, date and place of birth unknown.

B433565. Floyd Adam Pounds, fifth
child and third son of William Pounds and Susan
Dreghorn, born after 1890 in Little River County,
Arkansas and died after Oct 1899 in Little River
County, Arkansas. Buried at Old Ashdown cemetery,
Little River County, Arkansas.

B433566. Emma Myrtle Pounds, sixth
child and third daughter of William Pounds and
Susan Dreghorn, born 2 Sep 1892 in Little River
County, Arkansas and died 18 Dec 1987. Buried at
Ashdown cemetery, Little River County, Arkansas.
Married 2 Mar 1907 in Little River County,

Arkansas to David Franklin Hinton, son of Wiley
Bradford Hinton and Luna A. Simmons, born 7 Sep
1887 at Spring Hill, Hempstead County, Arkansas
and died 7 May 1979 at Ashdown, Little River
County, Arkansas. Buried at Ashdown cemetery,
Little River County, Arkansas. Emma Pounds and
David Hinton had issue, which was the tenth
generation in America:

B4335661. Alma Susan Hinton,
first child and first daughter of Emma Pounds and
David Hinton, born 17 Nov 1907 in Little River
County, Arkansas. Married 22 Nov 1924 in Little
River County, Arkansas to William Edgar Setliff,
born 1905 and died 1992. Alma Hinton and William
Setliff had issue, which was the eleventh
generation in America:

B43356611. William David
Setliff, first child and first son of Alma Hinton
and William Setliff, born 1925 and died 1945.

B43356612. Eloise
Setliff, second child and first daughter of Alma
Hinton and William Setliff, born 1933. Married
Roland Adair Copeland, born 1931 and died 1971.
Eloise Setliff and Roland Copeland had issue,
which was the twelth generation in America:

B433566121. Debora
Sue Copeland, first child and first daughter of
Eloise Setliff and Roland Copeland, born 1952.
Married Danny Hicks. Married secondly George
Morton. Debora Copeland and Danny Hicks had
issue, which was the thirteenth generation in
America:

B4335661211.
Tony Dale Hicks, first child and first son of
Debora Copeland Danny Hicks, date and place of
birth unknown.

B4335661212.
Shelie Denise Hicks, second child and first
daughter of Debora Copeland and Danny Hicks, date
and place of birth unknown. Married Steve Keyes.
Shelie Hicks and Steve Keyes had issue, which was
the fourteenth generation in America:
B43356612121. Travis Keyes, first child and first
son of Shelie Hicks and Steve Keyes, date and
place of birth unknown.
B43356612122. Tracy Keyes, second child and first

daughter of Shelie Hicks and Steve Keyes, date and place of birth unknown.

B433577121. Debora Sue Copeland, first child and first daughter of Eloise Setliff and Roland Copeland, born 1952. Married secondly to George Morton. Debora Copeland and George Morton had issue, which was the thirteenth generation in America:

B4335771211. Joshua Neil Morton, first child and first son of Debora Copeland and George Morton, born 1981.

B433566122. Pamela Ann Copeland, second child and second daughter of Eloise Setliff and Roland Copeland, born 1955. Married Rickey Charles Lindsey, born 1954. Pamela Copeland and Rickey Lindsey had issue, which was the thirteenth generation in America:

B4335661221. Jason Corey Lindsey, first child and first son of Pamela Copeland and Rickey Lindsey, born 1977.

B4335661222. Ashley Adair Lindsey, second child and first daughter of Pamela Copeland and Rickey Lindsey, born 1981.

B4335661223. Jenne Lindsey, third child and second daughter of Pamela Copeland and Rickey Lindsey, born 1985.

B433566123. Sheri Lynn Copeland, third child and third daughter of Eloise Setliff and Roland Copeland, born 1956. Married Stanley Madison McDaniel. Sheri Copeland and Stanley McDaniel had issue, which was the thirteenth generation in America:

B4335661231. Seth Madison McDaniel, first child and first son of Sheri Copeland and Stanley McDaniel, born 1980.

B4335661232. Sarah McDaniel, second child and first daughter of Sheri Copeland and Stanley McDaniel, born 1985.

B4335662. William Bradford Hinton, second child and first son of Emma Pounds and David Hinton, born 12 Dec 1909 in Little River County, Arkansas. Married 24 Dec 1930 in Little River County, Arkansas to Willie Bernice Foughtenburry, born 1911 and died 1991. William Hinton and Willie Foughtenburry had issue, which was the eleventh generation in America:

B43356621. Billy Joe Hinton, first child and first son of William Hinton and Willie Foughtenburry, born 1931. Married Jeanette Beeman, born 1933. Billy Hinton and Jeanette Beeman had issue, which was the twelth generation in America:

B433566211. Susan Kay Hinton, first child and first daughter of Billy Hinton and Jeanette Beeman, born 1959. Married Michael Allen Hickman. Susan Hinton and Michael Hickman had issue, which was the thirteenth generation in America:

B4335662111. Candice Hickman, first child and first daughter of Susan Hinton and Michael Hickman, born 1983.

B4335662112. Cathryn Hickman, second child and second daughter of Susan Hinton and Michael Hickman, born 1988.

B433566212. Karen Deneice Hinton, second child and second daughter of Billy Hinton and Jeanette Beeman, born 1963.

B433566213. Billy Keith Hinton, third child and first son of Billy Hinton and Jeanette Beeman, born 1963.

B43356622. Effie Jean Hinton, second child and first daughter of William Hinton and Willie Foughtenburry, born 1932. Married Thaddeus Irvin Jones, born 1930. Effie Hinton and Thaddeus Jones had issue, which was the twelth generation in America:

B433566221. Carolan Bernice Jones, first child and first daughter of Effie Hinton and Thaddeus Jones, born 1955. Married Dennis Kendrick Mahr.

B433566222. Amanda Gail Jones, second child and second daughter of Effie Hinton and Thaddeus Jones, born 1959. Married Keith Gralan Watkins, born 1960. Amanda Jones and Keith Watkins had issue, which was the thirteenth generation in America:

B4335662221. Joshua Watkins, first child and first son of Amanda Jones and Keith Watkins, born 1985.

B4335662222. Whitney Watkins, second child and second son of

Amanda Jones and Keith Watkins, born 1987.

B43356623. Margaret Ann Hinton, third child and second daughter of William Hinton and Willie Foughtenburry, born 1940. Married Donald Ray Cobb, born 1939. Margaret Hinton and Donald Cobb had issue, which was the twelth generation in America:

B433566231. Kenneth Ray Cobb, first child and first son of Margaret Hinton and Donald Cobb, born 1961. Married Gretchen Ann Thom, born 1962. Kenneth Cobb and Gretchen Thom had issue, which was the thirteenth generation in America:

B4335662311. Matthew Cobb, first child and first son of Kenneth Cobb and Gretchen Thom, born 1983.

B4335662312. Tye Cobb, second child and second son of Kenneth Cobb and Gretchen Thom, born 1987.

B433566232. Lisa Ann Cobb, second child and first daughter of Margaret Hinton and Donald Cobb, born 1967. Married Harris Hatchett. Lisa Cobb and Harris Hatchett had issue, which was the thirteenth generation in America:

B4335662321. Haley Alisa Hatchett, first child and first daughter of Lisa Cobb and Harris Hatchett, born 1991.

B433566233. Anthony Brian Cobb, third child and second son of Margaret Hinton and Donald Cobb, born and died 1977.

B43356624. Emma Carol Hinton, fourth child and third daughter of William Hinton and Willie Foughtenburry, born 1944. Married Harold Oden Warren, born 1939. Emma Hinton and Harold Warren had issue, which was the twelth generation in America:

B433566241. Jay Lynne Warren, first child and first daughter of Emma Hinton and Harold Warren, born 1962.

B4335663. Cecil Madella Hinton, third child and second daughter of Emma Pounds and David Hinton, born 4 Sep 1912 in Little River County, Arkansas. Married 7 Sep 1929 in Little River County, Arkansas to Thomas Earl

Willson, born 1909. Cecil Hinton and Thomas
Willson had issue, which was the eleventh
generation in America:
        B43356631. Thomas Odean
Willson, first child and first son of Cecil Hinton
and Thomas Willson, born 1931. Married Jimmie Lou
Taylor, born 1930. Thomas Willson and Jimmie
Taylor had issue, which was the twelth generation
in America:
        B433566311. Thomas
Randall Willson, first child and first son of
Thomas Willson and Jimmie Taylor, born 1954.
Married Brenda Tausworthe. Married secondly to
Deniese Eskau. Thomas Willson and Deniese Eskau
had issue, which was the thirteenth generation in
America:
        B4335663111.
Thomas Ryan Willson, first child and first son of
Thomas Willson and Deniese Eskau, born 1985.
        B4335663112.
Scott Anthony Willson, second child and second son
of Thomas Willson and Deniese Eskau, born 1989.
        B433566312. Kathy
Lou Willson, second child and first daughter of
Thomas Willson and Jimmie Taylor, born 1957.
Married Dennis Frank Hayes. Married secondly to
James Mullinex. Kathy Willson and Dennis Hayes
had issue, which was the thirteenth generation in
America:
        B4335663121.
Chrystal Jean Hayes, first child and first
daughter of Kathy Willson and Dennis Hayes, born
1982.
        B433566312. Kathy
Lou Willson, second child and first daughter of
Thomas Willson and Jimmie Taylor, born 1957.
Married secondly to James Mullinex. Kathy Willson
and James Mullinex had issue, which was the twelth
generation in America:
        B4335663121.
Kemberly Dian Mullinex, first child and first
daughter of Kathy Willson and James Mullinex, born
1991.
        B43356632. Derrell
Clifton Willson, second child and second son of
Cecil Hinton and Thomas Willson, born 1933.

Married Jeannette Moore.   Married secondly to
Darlene ---.   Married thirdly to Ann Allison.
Derrell Willson and Jeannette Moore had issue,
which was the twelth generation in America:
B433566321. Derrell
Clifton Willson II, first child and first son of
Derrell Willson and Jeannette Moore, born 1954.
Married Jackie Lumado, born 1954.   Married
secondly to Brenda Evans, born 1956.   Derrell
Willson and Jackie Lumado had issue, which was the
thirteenth generation in America:
B4335663211.
Derrell Clifton Willson III, first child and first
son of Derrell Willson and Jackie Lumado, born
1974.
B4335663212.
Jacob Chrisopher Willson, second child and second
son of Derrell Willson and Jackie Lumado, born
1977.
B433566322.   Lynda
Darleen Willson, second child and first daughter
of Derrell Willson and Jeannette Moore, born 1959.
Married Johnny Alm, born 1959.   Married secondly
to Larry Evans.   Lynda Willson and Johnny Alm had
issue, which was the thirteenth generation in
America:
B4335663221.
Summer Lyn Alm, first child and first daughter of
Lynda Willson and Johnny Alm, born 1978.
B433566322.   Lynda
Darleen Willson, second child and first daughter
of Derrell Willson and Jeannette Moore, born 1959.
Married secondly to Larry Evans.   Lynda Willson
and Larry Evans had issue, which was the
thirteenth generation in America:
B4335663221.
Fawn Ashley Evans, first child and first daughter
of Lynda Willson and Larry Evans, born 1986.
B43356633.   Robert Earl
Willson, third child and third son of Cecil Hinton
and Thomas Willson, born 1939.   Married Anna Mae
Hicks, born 1940.   Married secondly to Muriel
(Sam) Morrison.   Robert Willson and Anna Hicks had
issue, which was the twelfth generation in America:
B433566331. LaDonna
Gayle Willson, first child and first daughter of

Robert Willson and Anna Hicks, born 1959. Married Wendell Keith Shippey. LaDonna Willson and Wendell Shippey had issue, which was the thirteenth generation in America:

B4335663311. Bryan Keith Shippey, first child and first son of LaDonna Willson and Wendell Shippey, born 1980.

B4335663312. Christopher Michael Shippey, second child and second son of LaDonna Willson and Wendell Shippey, born 1984.

B4335663313. Matthew Robert Shippey, third child and third son of LaDonna Willson and Wendell Shippey, born 1988.

B433566332. Rosemary Willson, second child and second daughter of Robert Willson and Anna Hicks, born 1960. Married Wayne Hamilton. Rosemary Willson and Wayne Hamilton had issue, which was the thirteenth generation in America:

B4335663321. Joshua Wayne Hamilton, first child and first son of Rosemary Willson and Wayne Hamilton, born 1985.

B4335663322. Jessica Ann Hamilton, second child and first daughter of Rosemary Willson and Wayne Hamilton, born 1988.

B433566333. Lucretia Darlene Willson, third child and third daughter of Robert Willson and Anna Hicks, born 1961. Married Jimmy Smith. Lucretia Willson and Jimmy Smith had issue, which was the thirteenth generation in America:

B4335663331. Alishia Lynn Smith, first child and first daughter of Lucretia Willson and Jimmy Smith, born 1980.

B4335663332. Jeromy Ryan Smith, second child and first son of Lucretia Willson and Jimmy Smith, born 1985.

B43356634. Royce Dwayne Willson, fourth child and fourth son of Cecil Hinton and Thomas Willson, born 1943. Married Patricia Dingler, born 1945. Royce Willson and Patricia Dingler had issue, which was the twelth generation in America:

B433566341.

William Lewis Willson, first child and first son of Royce Willson and Patricia Dingler, born 1971.

B433566342. Michail Scott Willson, second child and second son of Royce Willson and Patricia Dingler, born 1974.

B4335664. Ruth Adelia Hinton, fourth child and third daughter of Emma Pounds and David Hinton, born 31 Aug 1916 in Little River County, Arkansas. Married 27 May 1935 in Miller County, Arkansas to John Thomas Cowling, born 1916 and died 1987. Ruth Hinton and John Cowling had issue, which was the eleventh generation in America:

B43356641. Emma Jo Cowling, first child and first daughter of Ruth Hinton and John Cowling, born 1938. Married Joe D. Allen, born 1937. Emma Cowling and Joe Allen had issue, which was the twelth generation in America:

B433566411. Gregory Joe Allen, first child and first son of Emma Cowling and Joe Allen, born 1960.

B433566412. Gary Dale Allen, second child and second son of Emma Cowling and Joe Allen, born 1961. Married Susan Amato. Married secondly to Kimberly Robeson Meeker.

B433566413. Glen Thomas Allen, third child and third son of Emma Cowling and Joe Allen, born 1963.

B433566414. Tammie Renee Allen, fourth child and first daughter of Emma Cowling and Joe Allen, born 1965. Married Larry Burnaman. Tammie Allen and Larry Burnaman had issue, which was the thirteenth generation in America:

B4335664141. Ashley Adelia Burnaman, first child and first daughter of Tammie Allen and Larry Burnaman, date and place of birth unknown.

B4335665. Gladys Jewell Hinton, fifth child and fourth daughter of Emma Pounds and David Hinton, born 7 Jun 1919 in Little River County, Arkansas and died 1 Mar 1969 at Ashdown, Little River County, Arkansas. Buried at Ashdown cemetery, Little River County, Arkansas.

Married 12 Jun 1937 in Little River County, Arkansas to T.C. Hughes, born 1915 and died 1977. Gladys Hinton and T.C. Hughes had issue, which was the eleventh generation in America:

B43356651. Rebecca Jane Hughes, first child and first daughter of Gladys Hinton and T.C. Hughes, born 1952. Married Jesse L. Clayton, born 1949. Rebecca Hughes and Jesse Clayton had issue, which was the twelth generation in America:

B433566511. Mark Anthony Clayton, first child and first son of Rebecca Hughes and Jesse Clayton, born 1971.

B433566512. Melinda Ann Clayton, second child and first daughter of Rebecca Hughes and Jesse Clayton, born 1973. Married Ronnie Belew. Melinda Clayton and Ronnie Belew had issue, which was the thirteenth generation in America:

B4335665121. Jimmy Dale Belew, first child and first son of Melinda Clayton and Ronnie Belew, born 1979.

B4335666. Robert Debrell Hinton, sixth child and second son of Emma Pounds and David Hinton, born 13 Nov 1921 in Little River County, Arkansas. Married 21 Apr 1945 in Logan County, Arkansas to Mable Ruth Hollis, born 1920 and died 1984. Married secondly V. Nadine Smith Aldrich, born 1920.

B4335667. David Wesley Hinton, seventh child and third son of Emma Pounds and David Hinton, born 23 Jan 1925 in Little River County, Arkansas and died 17 May 1990. Married 22 Jan 1949 in Little River County, Arkansas to Lelia Faye Waldrop, born 1931 and died 1980. David Hinton and Lelia Waldrop had issue, which was the eleventh generation in America:

B43356671. Sandra Faye Hinton, first child and first daughter of David Hinton and Lelia Waldrop, born 1949. Married James Alfred Hartline, born 1949. Sandra Hinton and James Hartline had issue, which was the twelth generation in America:

B433566711. Tammy Rene Hartline, first child and first daughter of Sandra Hinton and James Hartline, born 1970.

Married --- Whatley. Married secondly to Michael Van Antwerp. Tammy Hartline and --- Whatley had issue, which was the thirteenth generation in America:

B4335667111. Ashley Nicole Whatley, first child and first daughter of Tammy Hartline and --- Whatley, born 1989.

B433566711. Tammy Rene Hartline, first child and first daughter of Sandra Hinton and James Hartline, born 1970. Married secondly to Michael Van Antwerp. Tammy Hartline and Michael Van Antwerp had issue, which was the thirteenth generation in America:

B4335667111. Tonya Marie Van Antwerp, first child and first daughter of Tammy Hartline and Michael Van Antwerp, born 1978.

B4335667112. Terri Ann Van Antwerp, second child and second daughter of Tammy Hartline and Michael Van Antwerp, born 1980.

B43356672. Donna Sue Hinton, second child and second daughter of David Hinton and Lelia Waldrop, born 1951. Married Leroy Keopke. Donna HInton and Leroy Keopke had issue, which was the twelth generation in America:

B433566721. Christopher Lee Keopke, first child and first son of Donna Hinton and Leroy Keopke, born 1974.

B433566722. Christy Lynn Keopke, second child and first daughter of Donna Hinton and Leroy Keopke, born 1977.

B433566723. Michael Keopke, third child and second son of Donna Hinton and Leroy Keopke, date and place of birth unknown.

B43356673. Katherine Rene Hinton, third child and third daughter of David Hinton and Lelia Waldrop, born 1957. Married but the spouse's name is unknown. Married secondly to Watson Pinion. Katherine Hinton and her unnamed spouse had issue, which was the twelth generation in America:

B433566731. Brian Randall Hinton, first child and first son of Katherine Hinton and --- ---, born 1973.

B433566732. Brandi
Renee Hinton, second child and first daughter of
Katherine Hinton and --- ---, born 1975.
B43356673. Katherine
Rene Hinton, third child and third daughter of
David Hinton and Lelia Waldrop, born 1957.
Married secondly to Watson Pinion. Katherine
Hinton and Watson Pinion had issue, which was the
twelth generation in America:
B433566731. Jason
Pinion, first child and first son of Katherine
Hinton and Watson Pinion, date and place of birth
unknown.
B4335668. Howard Emanuel
Hinton, eighth child and fourth son of Emma Pounds
and David Hinton, born 26 Oct 1928 in Little River
County, Arkansas and died 16 May 1984 at Metairie,
Jefferson Parish, Louisiana. Married 29 Jan 1954
in Little River County, Arkansas to Phyllis Jean
Mabrey, born 1929. Howard Hinton and Phyllis
Mabrey had issue, which was the eleventh
generation in America:
B43356681. Cynthia Ann
Hinton, first child and first daughter of Howard
Hinton and Phyliss Mabrey, born 1956. Married
Kenneth Ray Guillory, born 1956. Cynthia Hinton
and Kenneth Guillory had issue, which was the
twelth generation in America:
B433566811. Melissa
Nicole Guillory, first child and first daughter of
Cynthia Hinton and Kenneth Guillory, born 1980.
B433566812. Michael
Howard Guillory, second child and first son of
Cynthia Hinton and Kenneth Guillory, born 1984.
B43356682. Julia Diane
Hinton, second child and second daughter of Howard
Hinton and Phyllis Mabrey, born 1960.
B4335669. Doyle Ray Hinton,
ninth child and fifth son of Emma Pounds and David
Hinton, born 30 Jun 1931 in Little River County,
Arkansas. Married 3 Sep 1950 in Little River
County, Arkansas to Betty Lou Maze, born 8 Mar
1932 in Kay County, Oklahoma. Doyle Hinton and
Betty Maze had issue, which was the twelth
generation in America:
B43356691. Doyle Ray

Hinton, Jr., first child and first son of Doyle Hinton and Betty Maze, born 1953. Married Mary Margaret (Peggy) Marshall, born 1960. Doyle Hinton and Mary Marshall had issue, which was the thirteenth generation in America:

B433566911. Doyle Ray (Sonny) Hinton III, first child and first son of Doyle Hinton and Mary Marshall, born 1976.

B433566912. Mark David Hinton, second child and second son of Doyle Hinton and Mary Marshall, born 1981.

B43356692. David Kevin Hinton, second child and second son of Doyle Hinton and Betty Maze, born 1954. Married Sharon Jo Williams, born 1954. David Hinton and Sharon Williams had issue, which was the twelfth generation in America:

B433566921. Dustin Paul Hinton, first child and first son of David Hinton and Sharon Williams, born 1981.

B433566922. Danielle Elizabeth Hinton, second child and first daughter of David Hinton and Sharon Williams, born 1982.

B433566923. Drew Alexandria Hinton, third child and second daughter of David Hinton and Sharon Williams, born 1984.

B43356693. Elizabeth Dianne Hinton, third child and first daughter of Doyle Hinton and Betty Maze, born 1956. Married Russell Allen Greenwood. Married secondly to Brian Whitley Davis, born 1954. Elizabeth Hinton and Russell Greenwood had issue, which was the twelfth generation in America:

B433566931. Mikeal Jared Greenwood, first child and first son of Elizabeth Hinton and Russell Greenwood, born 1977.

B43356693. Elizabeth Dianne Hinton, third child and first daughter of Doyle Hinton and Betty Maze, born 1956. Married secondly to Brian Whitley Davis, born 1954. Elizabeth Hinton and Brian Davis had issue, which was the twelfth generation in America:

B433566931. Naticia Dianne Davis, first child and first daughter of Elizabeth Hinton and Brian Davis, born 1986.

477

B433566932.　Megan Whitley Davis, second child and second daughter of Elizabeth Hinton and Brian Davis, born 1988.

B433567.　Eura Viola Pounds, seventh child and fourth daughter of William Pounds and Susan Dreghorn, born 18 Oct 1894 in Little River County, Arkansas and died 31 Aug 1978 in Little River County, Arkansas.　Buried at Ashdown, Hicks cemetery, Little River County, Arkansas.　Married Thomas William Gill, born 19 Jan 1888 in Arkansas and died 4 Apr 1964 in Little River County, Arkansas.　Buried at Ashdown, Hicks cemetery, Little River County, Arkansas.　Eura Pounds and Thomas Gill had issue, which was the tenth generation in America:

B4335671.　Thomas Roy Gill, first child and first son of Eura Pounds and Thomas Gill, born 31 Jul 1910 in Little River County, Arkansas and died 20 Dec 1940.　Buried at Ashdown, Hicks cemetery, Little River County, Arkansas.

B4335672.　Hubert Benjamin Gill, second child and second son of Eura Pounds and Thomas Gill, born 3 Oct 1912 in Little River County, Arkansas.　Married Lucille Jeffery.　Hubert Gill and Lucille Jeffery had issue, which was the eleventh generation in America:

B43356721.　Michael Gill, first child and first son of Hubert Gill and Lucille Jeffery, date and place of birth unknown.

B43356722.　David Gill, second child and second son of Hubert Gill and Lucille Jeffery, date and place of birth unknown.

B4335673.　Lallie Lois Gill, third child and first daughter of Eura Pounds and Thomas Gill, born 29 Aug 1914 in Little River County, Arkansas and died 25 Nov 1970 in Little River County, Arkansas.　Buried at Ashdown, Hicks cemetery, Little River County, Arkansas.　Married Herbert Musgrove.

B4335674.　Paul Britton Gill, fourth child and third son of Eura Pounds and Thomas Gill, born 15 Nov 1916 in Little River County, Arkansas and died 7 Jan 1976 at Cisco, Eastland County, Texas.　Married Gladys ---.

B4335675.　Watson Emanuel Gill, fifth child and fourth son of Eura Pounds and Thomas

Gill, born 22 Jul 1918 in Little River County, Arkansas and died 28 Dec 1987. Married Myrida Jester. Watson Gill and Myrida Jester had issue, which was the eleventh generation in America:

B43356751. Gayla Gill, first child and first daughter of Watson Gill and Myrida Jester, date and place of birth unknown.

B4335676. Edison Brooks Gill, sixth child and fifth son of Eura Pounds and Thomas Gill, born 22 Jul 1921 in Little River County, Arkansas.

B4335677. James Allen Gill, seventh child and sixth son of Eura Pounds and Thomas Gill, born 23 Aug 1928 in Little River County, Arkansas. Married Doris White. James Gill and Doris White had issue, which was the eleventh generation in America:

B43356771. Annette Gill, first child and first daughter of James Gill and Doris White, date and place of birth unknown.

B4335678. Lucy Gloria Gill, eighth child and second daughter of Eura Pounds and Thomas Gill, born 1 Dec 1931 in Little River County, Arkansas. Married 26 Dec 1951 in Little River County, Arkansas to William T. Davis, Jr. Lucy Gill and William Davis had issue, which was the eleventh generation in America:

B43356781. William T. Davis III, first child and first son of Lucy Gill and William Davis, date and place of birth unknown.

B4335679. Charlene Frances (twin) Gill, ninth child and third daughter of Eura Pounds and Thomas Gill, born 31 Aug 1933 in Little River County, Arkansas. Married 27 May 1951 in Little River County, Arkansas to Edward Hawkins. Charlene Gill and Edward Hawkins had issue, which was the eleventh generation in America:

B43356791. Elizabeth Hawkins, first child and first daughter of Charlene Gill and Edward Hawkins, date and place of birth unknown. Married --- Epps. Elizabeth Hawkins and --- Epps had issue, which was the twelfth generation in America:

B433567911. Edward Alan Epps, first child and first son of Elizabeth Hawkins and --- Epps, date and place of birth unknown.

B433567912. Dollie Epps, second child and first daughter of Elizabeth Hawkins and --- Epps, date and place of birth unknown.

B43356792. Terri Hawkins, second child and daughter of Charlene Gill and Edward Hawkins, date and place of birth unknown. Married --- Jeanes. Married secondly to Randy James. Terri Hawkins and --- Jeanes had issue, which was the twelth generation in America:

B433567921. Lucy Jeanes, first child and first daughter of Terri Hawkins and --- Jeanes, date and place of birth unknown.

B4335680. Charles Franklin (twin) Gill, tenth child and seventh son of Eura Pounds and Thomas Gill, born 31 Aug 1933 in Little River County, Arkansas.

B4335681. William (Billy) Glen Gill, eleventh child and eighth son of Eura Pounds and Thomas Gill, born 8 Nov 1938 in Little River County, Arkansas and died 14 Jan 1941 in Little River County, Arkansas. Buried at Ashdown, Hicks cemetery, Little River County, Arkansas.

B433568. Emmanuel Britton Pounds, eighth child and fourth son of William Pounds and Susan Dreghorn, born 29 Jan 1897 in Little River County, Arkansas and died 19 Apr 1974 at Adrian, Oldham County, Texas. Buried at Vega cemetery, Oldham County, Texas. Married 19 Jul 1919 in Little River County, Arkansas to Orange Bankston. Married secondly 19 Jan 1934 at Little Rock, Pulaski County, Arkansas to Betty Virginia Moran, born 16 Jun 1907 at Kirby, Pike County, Arkansas and died 7 Feb 1991 at Amarillo, Potter County, Texas. Buried at Vega cemetery, Oldham County, Texas. Emmanuel Pounds and Betty Moran had issue, which was the tenth generation in America:

B4335681. Minor Emmanuel Pounds, first child and first son of Emmanuel Pounds and Betty Moran, born 23 Dec 1934 at Little Rock, Pulaski County, Arkansas. Married Cecelia Kotara. Minor Pounds and Cecelia Kotara had issue, which was the eleventh generation in America:

B43356811. Sheryl Pounds, first child and first daughter of Minor Pounds and Cecelia Kotara, date and place of birth unknown.

B43356812. Shelly Pounds, second child and second daughter of Minor Pounds and Cecelia Kotara, date and place of birth unknown.

B43356813. Sheila Pounds, third child and third daughter of Minor Pounds and Cecelia Kotara, date and place of birth unknown.

B43356814. Sharon Pounds, fourth child and fourth daughter of Minor Pounds and Cecelia Kotara, date and place of birth unknown.

B4335682. John Moran Pounds, second child and second son of Emmanuel Pounds and Betty Moran, born 14 Nov 1936 at Little Rock, Pulaski County, Arkansas. Married Erma Lou Jordan. John Pounds and Erma Jordan had issue, which was the eleventh generation in America:

B43356821. Denny Moran Pounds, first child and first son of John Pounds and Erma Jordan, date and place of birth unknown.

B43356822. John David Pounds, second child and second son of John Pounds and Erma Jordan, date and place of birth unknown.

B43356823. Drew Arthur Pounds, third child and third son of John Pounds and Erma Jordan, date and place of birth unknown.

B4335683. Neil Alan Pounds, third child and third son of Emmanuel Pounds and Betty Moran, born 3 Dec 1937 at Little Rock, Pulaski County, Arkansas. Married Carol Blackburn. Neil Pounds and Carol Blackburn had issue, which was the eleventh generation in America:

B43356831. Elizabeth Pounds, first child and first daughter of Neil Pounds and Carol Blackburn, date and place of birth unknown.

B43356832. Brittalann Pounds, second child and second daughter of Neil Pounds and Carol Blackburn, date and place of birth unknown.

B4335684. Katie Ninnette Pounds, fourth child and first daughter of Emmanuel Pounds and Betty Moran, born 25 Aug 1942 at Little Rock, Pulaski County, Arkansas. Married Ted H. Boydstun. Katie Pounds and Ted Boydstun had issue, which was the eleventh generation in America:

B43356841. Renae Collete Boydstun, first child and first daughter of Katie Pounds and

481

Ted Boydstun, date and place of birth unknown.

B43356842. Kelli Dawn Boydstun, second child and second daughter of Katie Pounds and Ted Boydstun, date and place of birth unknown.

B43356843. Mitchell Britton Boydstun, third child and first son of Katie Pounds and Ted Boydstun, date and place of birth unknown.

B433569. Minor Paul Pounds, ninth child and fifth son of William Pounds and Susan Dreghorn, born 1 Oct 1899 in Little River County, Arkansas and died 22 Nov 1969 at El Paso, El Paso County, Texas. Married 24 Jun 1922 in Little River County, Arkansas to Evelena Martin, date and place of birth unknown, but died 31 Aug 1987 at El Paso, El Paso County, Texas. Minor Pounds and Evelena Martin had issue, which was the tenth generation in America:

B4335691. Peggy Pounds, first child and first daughter of Minor Pounds and Evelena Martin, date and place of birth unknown. Married Orba Lee Malone. Peggy Pounds and Orba Malone had issue, which was the eleventh generation in America:

B43356911. Paul Malone, first child and first son of Peggy Pounds and Orba Malone, date and place of birth unknown.

B43356912. John Malone, second child and second son of Peggy Pounds and Orba Malone, date and place of birth unknown.

B43356913. David Malone, third child and third son of Peggy Pounds and Orba Malone, date and place of birth unknown.

B43356914. Daniel Malone, fourth child and fourth son of Peggy Pounds and Orba Malone, date and place of birth unknown.

B43356915. Mary Carol Malone, fifth child and first daughter of Peggy Pounds and Orba Malone, date and place of birth unknown.

B4335692. Mary Paula Pounds, second child and second daughter of Minor Pounds and Evelena Martin, date and place of birth unknown. Married John D. Wallace. Mary Pounds and John Wallace had issue, which was the eleventh generation in America:

B43356921. Lisa Wallace, first child and first daughter of Mary Pounds and John

Wallace, date and place of birth unknown. Married Bill Trusler. Lisa Wallace and Bill Trusler had issue, which was the twelth generation in America:

B433569211. John Trusler, first child and first son of Lisa Wallace and Bill Trusler, date and place of birth unknown.

B433569212. Will Trusler, second child and second son of Lisa Wallace and Bill Trusler, date and place of birth unknown.

B433569213. Austin Trusler, third child and third son of Lisa Wallace and Bill Trusler, date and place of birth unknown.

B43356922. Robin Wallace, second child and second daughter of Mary Pounds and John Wallace, date and place of birth unknown. Married Lynn Dawson. Robin Wallace and Lynn Dawson had issue, which was the twelth generation in America:

B433569221. Rebecca Dawson, first child and first daughter of Robin Wallace and Lynn Dawson, date and place of birth unknown.

B433569222. Lindsey Dawson, second child and first son of Robin Wallace and Lynn Dawson, date and place of birth unknown.

B433569223. Drew Dawson, third child and second son of Robin Wallace and Lynn Dawson, date and place of birth unknown.

B43356923. Becky Wallace, third child and third daughter of Mary Pounds and John Wallace, date and place of birth unknown. Married Tim Harris. Becky Wallace and Tim Harris had issue, which was the twelth generation in America:

B433569231. Stephanie Harris, first child and first daughter of Becky Wallace and Tim Harris, date and place of birth unknown.

B433569232. Paul Harris, second child and first son of Becky Wallace and Tim Harris, date and place of birth unknown.

B43356924. Doyle Wallace, fourth child and first son of Mary Pounds and John Wallace, date and place of birth unknown. Married Deanna ---. Doyle Wallace and Deanna --- had issue, which was the twelth generation in America:

B433569241. Bonnie Wallace, first child and first daughter of Doyle Wallace and Deanna ---, date and place of birth unknown.

B433569242. John Doyle

Wallace, second child and first son of Doyle Wallace and Deanna ---, date and place of birth unknown.

B43357. Anna Melinda Pounds, seventh child and fourth daughter of William Pounds and Rebecca Mann, born 1862 in Chambers County, Alabama and died after 1928 in California. Married 31 Oct 1878 in Meriwether County, Georgia to John M. Cooper, born 1857 in Georgia and died after 1910. Anna Pounds and John Cooper had issue, which was the ninth generation in America:

B433571. William (Willie) J. Cooper, first child and first son of Anna Pounds and John Cooper, born Jul 1879 in Meriwether County, Georgia. Married 16 Mar 1902 in Pike County, Arkansas to Estell Trash. Married secondly 14 Apr 1904 in Little River County, Arkansas to Nellie Johnson. William Cooper and Nellie Johnson had issue, which was the tenth generation in America:

B4335711. Albert Cooper, first child and first son of William Cooper and Nellie Johnson, date and place of birth unknown. Married Irene ---.

B433572. Pearl Cooper, second child and first daughter of Anna Pounds and John Cooper, born Jul 1881 in Arkansas. Married 1 Aug 1895 in Little River County, Arkansas to J.R. Liverman. Pearl Cooper and J.R. Liverman had issue, which was the tenth generation in America:

B4335721. Abia Liverman, first child and first daughter of Pearl Cooper and J.R. Liverman, date and place of birth unknown.

B4335722. Debrell Liverman, second child and first son of Pearl Cooper and J.R. Liverman, date and place of birth unknown.

B433573. Alice Cooper, third child and second daughter of Anna Pounds and John Cooper, born 1884 in Arkansas. Married 30 Jun 1901 in Little River County, Arkansas to Joe Whitman.

B433574. Ollie Cooper, fourth child and third daughter of Anna Pounds and John Cooper, born 1888 in Arkansas. Married 6 Mar 1904 in Little River County, Arkansas to J.F. Jackson.

B433575. Julia Bay Cooper, fifth child and fourth daughter of Anna Pounds and John Cooper, born 1891 in Arkansas. Married 5 Sep 1907 in Little River County, Arkansas to J.M. Fuller.

B433576. Lucy Cooper, sixth child and fifth daughter of Anna Pounds and John Cooper, born 1893 in Arkansas. Married 4 Oct 1908 in Little River County, Arkansas to Frank Fuller.

B433577. Effie Cooper, seventh child and sixth daughter of Anna Pounds and John Cooper, born 1893.

B433578. Rufus A. Cooper, eighth child and second son of Anna Pounds and John Cooper, born 1897 in Arkansas.

B433579. Ernest O. Cooper, ninth child and third son of Anna Pounds and John Cooper, born 1902 in Arkansas.

B4336. Zachariah Benjamin Pounds, sixth child and fifth son of William Pounds and Nancy Slayden, born 17 Aug 1824 in Taliaferro County, Georgia and died 28 Apr 1863 at Chattanooga, Hamilton County, Tennessee. Buried at Confederate cemetery, Chattanooga, Tennessee. He served as a private in the Civil War in Company B. 8th (Wade's) Confederate Calvary. This was a cavalry unit supported by the Confederate government, not a state supported unit. Zachariah Pounds' will was recorded Vol 3 page 110 Chambers County, Alabama Feb 24, 1863.

THE STATE OF ALABAMA
CHAMBERS COUNTY   February 24, 1863

I, Zachariah B. Pounds of said County and State aforesaid considering the mortality of man and the uncertainty of life and particular in that of a soldier life and being desirous that my Estate should be kept together for the mutual benefit of my wife and children do make this my Last Will and Testament.

1st. At my death, I publish and constitute my wife Elizabeth A. Pounds to be sole Executrix of this my last will and testament directing my said Executrix to pay all my just debts and expenses and the remainder of my Estate I desire or will that it shall be kept together for the mutual benefit of my wife and children during her natural life or widowhood.

2nd. In the event that my wife should marry again it is my will that the whole of my Estate be sold and equally distributed between my wife and children.

3rd. If my wife should not marry again it is my will that she should keep my Estate together and raise and educate my children and give to each one of them when they become of age according to her ability.

4th. I give unto my Executrix the right to sell any property with which she may become dissatisfied with or that may prove to the interest of my Estate this February 28, 1863

/s/ Zachariah B. Pounds

Test:
L.S.
William A. Hunter
J. Hood

Elizabeth made a petition 13 May 1863 in Chambers County, Alabama (Probate Packet #1476) to John Appleby, Judge of Probate.

THE STATE OF ALABAMA
CHAMBERS COUNTY
February 24, 1863

PETITION OF ELIZABETH POUNDS

Chambers County, Alabama Probate Packet #1476

The State of Alabama, Chambers County

To the Hon. John Appleby, Judge of Probate in and for said county.

The petition of Elizabeth A. Pounds respectfully represents unto your honor that the late Zachariah B. Pounds, who was an inhabitant of the county, departed this life on the 28th of April 1863 at Chattanooga in the State of Tennessee leaving a last will and testament duly signed and published by him and attested by William A. Hunter, Jr., J.C. Hood who reside in the county in which your petitioner is named as executrix thereof, which said will is herewith produced to your Honor and propounded for probate and recor in the Court. Your petitioner further states that she is a widow of the said deceased and resides in this county, and that the next of the kin of said decedent are his children Mary A.S. Pounds, John W. Pounds, minors over the age of fourteen years. James Jarrett Pounds, Sarah Slayton Pounds, Henry David Pounds, Emma Lucy Pounds, Thomas Judge Pounds, Zachariah Benjamin Pounds, minors under the age of fourteen years all of whom reside with your petitioner in this county. In consideration of all which your petitioner prays that a day may be set for hearing the matter of the petition, that subpoenas may be issued to being in said subscribing witnesses to testify on such appointed day, that due notice of the application may be given to the said next of kin of said deceased and that such other proceedings, orders, and decrees may be had and made in the premises, as may be requisite and proper to affect the due probate and record of the said will according to law and as in duty bound your petitioner will not pray (again?).

s/s Elizabeth A. Pounds

Subscribed and sworn to before me the 13th day of
May 1863. John Appleby, Judge of Probate.

Zachariah Benjamin Pounds married 10 Apr 1845 in Meriwether County, Georgia to Elizabeth Agnes Sutton, born 13 Jan 1832 in Georgia and died 18 Jul 1896 at Sulphur Springs, Hopkins County, Texas. Buried at Martin Springs cemetery, Hopkins County, Texas. Zachariah Pounds and Elizabeth Sutton had issue, which was the eighth generation in America:
B43361. Mary Ann Susan Pounds, first child

and first daughter of Zachariah Pounds and Elizabeth Sutton, born 20 Apr 1847 in Chambers County, Alabama and died after 1900 in Texas. Married 25 Jan 1866 in Chambers County, Alabama to Judson Hunter, born 1844 in Alabama and died after 1910 in Texas. Mary Pounds and Judson Hunter had issue, which was the ninth generation in America:

B433611. Emma L. Hunter, first child and first daughter of Mary Pounds and Judson Hunter, born 1867 in Alabama.

B433612. John L. (T.) Hunter, second child and first son of Mary Pounds and Judson Hunter, born Oct 1871 in Hopkins County, Texas. Married Annie B. ---. John Hunter and Annie B. --- had issue, which was the tenth generation in America:

B4336121. William E. Hunter, first child and first son of John Hunter and Annie ---, born 1892 in Texas.

B4336122. Kate L. Hunter, second child and first daughter of John Hunter and Annie ---, born 1894 in Texas.

B4336123. Irene Hunter, third child and second daughter of John Hunter and Annie ---, born 1896 in Texas.

B4336124. John L. Hunter, fourth child and second son of John Hunter and Annie --- born 1901 in Texas.

B4336125. Emma R. Hunter, fifth child and third daughter of John Hunter and Annie ---, born 1906 in Texas.

B433613. Mineola O. Hunter, third child and second daughter of Mary Pounds and Judson Hunter, born 1874 in Hopkins County, Texas. Married --- Rictor. Married secondly to William Means. Mineola Hunter and --- Rictor had issue, which was the tenth generation in America:

B4336131. Mary V. Rictor, first child and first daughter of Mineola Hunter and --- Rictor, born 1897 in Texas.

B4336132. John M. Rictor, second child and first son of Mineola Hunter and --- Rictor, born 1900 in Texas.

B4336133. Minnie Rictor, third child and second daughter of Mineola Hunter and --- Rictor, born 1903 in Texas.

B4336134. Lena M. Rictor, fourth child and third daughter of Mineola Hunter and --- Rictor, born 1905 in Texas.

B433613. Mineola O. Hunter, third child and second daughter of Mary Pounds and Judson Hunter, born 1874 in Hopkins County, Texas. Married secondly to William Means, born 1874. Mineola Hunter and William Means had issue, which was the tenth generation in America:

B4336131. William L. Means, first child and first son of Mineola Hunter and William Means, born May 1909 in Texas.

B433614. Nora Hunter, fourth child and third daughter of Mary Pounds and Judson Hunter, born 1876 in Hopkins County, Texas.

B433615. Oscar Hunter, fifth child and second son of Mary Pounds and Judson Hunter, born Jan 1878 in Hopkins County, Texas. Married Mattie ---, born 1890. Oscar Hunter and Mattie --- had issue, which was the tenth generation in America:

B4336151. John C. Hunter, first child and first son of Oscar Hunter and Mattie -- born 1908 in Texas.

B433616. Joseph L. Hunter, sixth child and third son of Mary Pounds and Judson Hunter, born Apr 1880 in Hopkins County, Texas.

B433617. Maggie Hunter, seventh child and fourth daughter of Mary Pounds and Judson Hunter, born Sep 1882 in Hopkins County, Texas.

B433618. Willie Hunter, eighth child and fourth son of Mary Pounds and Judson Hunter, born Jan 1885 in Hopkins County, Texas. Married Dora ---, born 1891.

B43362. John William Zachariah Pounds, second child and first son of Zachariah Pounds and Elizabeth Sutton, born 24 Jan 1849 in Chambers County, Alabama and died 1924 at Sulphur Springs, Hopkins County, Texas. Married 29 Sep 1872 in Hopkins County, Texas to Fannie Werner, date of birth unknown, but death was before 1877 in Hopkins County, Texas. John Pounds and Fannie Werner had issue, which was the ninth generation in America:

B433621. John T. Pounds, first child and first son of John Pounds and Fannie Werner, born 13 Apr 1878 in Hopkins County, Texas and died

15 Jul 1916 in Hopkins County, Texas. Buried at Richland cemetery in Hopkins County, Texas. Married 6 Sep 1896 in Hopkins County, Texas to Ada O. Smith, born Dec 1878 in Texas. John Pounds and Ada Smith had issue, which was the tenth generation in America:

B4336211. Clovis Pounds, first child and first son of John Pounds and Ada Smith, born Aug 1899 in Hopkins County, Texas.

B4336212. Ben T. Pounds, second child and second son of John Pounds and Ada Smith, born 1904 in Hopkins County, Texas.

B4336213. Lola R. Pounds, third child and first daughter of John Pounds and Ada Smtih, born 1906 in Hopkins County, Texas.

B4336214. Clara L. Pounds, fourth child and second daughter of John Pounds and Ada Smith, born Feb 1910 in Hopkins County, Texas.

B43362. John William Zachariah Pounds, second child and first son of Zachariah Pounds and Elizabeth Sutton, born 24 Jan 1849 in Chambers County, Alabama and died 1924 at Sulphur Springs, Hopkins County, Texas. Married 29 Sep 1872 to Fannie Werner. Married secondly 18 Jan 1877 Mary E. McGinnis, born 1858 and died 1889 in Hopkins County, Texas. John Pounds and Mary McGinnis had issue, which was the ninth generation in America:

B433621. Lee Pounds, first child and first son of John Pounds and Mary McGinnis, born about 1878 in Hopkins County, Texas and died 1919.

B433622. Maude Pounds, second child and first daughter of John Pounds and Mary McGinnis, born about 1880 in Hopkins County, Texas. Married Ben Brooks.

B433623. Lennie Rufus Pounds, third child and second son of John Pounds and Mary McGinnis, born Oct 1883 in Hopkins County, Texas and died 29 Jul 1967 in Hopkins County, Texas. Married 11 Oct 1908 in Hopkins County, Texas to Irene Ray Curdeller. Lennie Pounds and Irene Curdeller had issue, which was the tenth generation in America:

B4336211. Mary Lois Pounds, first child and first daughter of Lennie Pounds and Irene Curdeller, born 16 Nov 1909 in Hopkins County, Texas. Married --- Kennedy.

B4336212. Royal Ray Pounds, second child and first son of Lennie Pounds and Irene Curdeller, born 7 Mar 1920 in Hopkins County, Texas.

B4336213. Dorothy Nell Pounds, third child and second daughter of Lennie Pounds and Irene Curdeller, born 3 Jul 1920 in Hopkins County, Texas and died 17 Oct 1934 in Hopkins County, Texas. Buried at Seymore cemetery, Hopkins County, Texas.

B4336214. Betty Jean Pounds, fourth child and third daughter of Lennie Pounds and Irene Curdeller, born 15 Oct 1919 in Hopkins County, Texas. Married --- Smith.

B433624. Katie (Susan K.) Pounds, fourth child and second daughter of John Pounds and Mary McGinnis, born Nov 1887 in Hopkins County, Texas.

B43362. John William Zachariah Pounds, second child and first son of Zachariah Pounds and Elizabeth Sutton, born 24 Jan 1849 in Chambers County, Alabama and died 1924 at Sulphur Springs, Hopkins County, Texas. Married 29 Sep 1872 to Fannie Werner. Married 18 Jan 1877 to Mary E. McGinnis. Married thirdly 14 Sep 1890 to Emma Weeks, born Sep 1868 in Alabama and died 11 Jul 1934 in Hopkins County, Texas. John Pounds and Emma Weeks had issue, which was the ninth generation in America:

B433621. William E.B. Pounds, first child and first son of John Pounds and Emma Weeks, born Jul 1891 in Hopkins County, Texas and died 1970. Married 20 Oct 1917 in Texas to Ethel O. ---, born 16 Sep 1895 and died 5 May 1971.

B433622. Henry James Pounds, second child and second son of John Pounds and Emma Weeks, born 25 Dec 1892 in Hopkins County, Texas and died Jan 1973 at Norman, Cleveland County, Oklahoma.

B43363. James Jarrett Pounds, third child and second son of Zachariah Pounds and Elizabeth Sutton, born 12 Jun 1851 in Chambers County, Alabama and died 1875 in Texas. Married 27 Feb 1876 in Hopkins County, Texas to Mary Ann Bradford, born 1846 and died 1880. Married secondly in Texas to Sallie Adeline Smith, born

Apr 1858 in Alabama and died 21 Mar 1950 in Dawson County, Texas. James Pounds and Mary Bradford had issue, which was the ninth generation in America:

B433631. L.R. Pounds, first child and first son of James Pounds and Mary Bradford, born Oct 1883 in Texas.

B433632. Natie Pounds, second child and first daughter of James Pounds and Mary Bradford, born Nov 1887 in Texas.

B433633. William Pounds, third child and second son of James Pounds and Mary Bradford, born Jul 1891 in Texas.

B433634. Henry J. Pounds, fourth child and third son of James Pounds and Mary Bradford, born Dec 1892 in Texas.

B43363. James Jarrett Pounds, third child and second son of Zachariah Pounds and Elizabeth Sutton, born 12 Jun 1851 in Chambers County, Alabama and died 1875 in Texas. Married secondly in Texas to Sallie Adeline Smith, born Apr 1858 in Alabama and died 21 Mar 1940 in Dawson County, Texas. James Pounds and Sallie Smith had issue, which was the ninth generation in America:

B433631. Ada Pounds, first child and first daughter of James Pounds and Sallie Smith, born 27 Dec 1878 in Texas and died 24 Apr 1963 in Hopkins County, Texas. Buried at Richland cemetery, Hopkins County, Texas.

B433632. John W. Pounds, second child and first son of James Pounds and Sallie Smith, born Jan 1880 in Hopkins County, Texas.

B433633. James Edward Pounds, third child and second son of James Pounds and Sallie Smith, born 14 Jul 1882 in Hopkins County, Texas and died 6 Sep 1960 in Falls County, Texas.

B433634. Henry F. Pounds, fourth child and third son of James Pounds and Sallie Smith, born Apr 1885 in Texas.

B433635. Mary A. Pounds, fifth child and second daughter of James Pounds and Sallie Smith, born Jan 1888 in Texas.

B433636. Robert A. Pounds, sixth child and fourth son of James Pounds and Sallie Smith, born Aug 1890 in Texas.

B433637. Chaple D. Pounds, seventh child and fifth son of James Pounds and Sallie

Smith, born Feb 1897 in Texas.

B433638. Otis Kidd Pounds, eighth child and sixth son of James Pounds and Sallie Smith, born Nov 1899 in Texas and died 20 Dec 1974 in El Paso County, Texas.

B43364. Sarah Slayton Pounds, fourth child and second daughter of Zachariah Pounds and Elizabeth Sutton, born 30 Apr 1853 in Chambers County, Alabama and died 8 Feb 1929 in Chambers County, Alabama. Buried at Center Baptist cemetery, Chambers County, Alabama. Married 12 Jan 1870 in Chambers County, Alabama to Robert G. Gilliland, born 7 Jun 1848 in Georgia and died 28 Mar 1924 in Chambers County, Alabama. Buried at Center Baptist cemetery, Chambers County, Alabama. Sarah Pounds and Robert Gilliland had issue, which was the ninth generation in America:

B433641. James William Gilliland, first child and first son of Sarah Pounds and Robert Gilliland, born 24 Aug 1871 in Chambers County, Alabama and died 11 Nov 1933. Married 25 Dec 1891 in Alabama to Addie Lee Rearden.

B433642. John Robert Gilliland, second child and second son of Sarah Pounds and Robert Gilliland, born 1876 in Chambers County, Alabama. Married 29 Dec 1904 in Alabama to Mattie Lou Tebow.

B433643. Mary Edna Gilliland, third child and first daughter of Sarah Pounds and Robert Gilliland, born Mar 1886 in Chambers County, Alabama. Married 16 Nov 1904 in Alabama to James Louis Rearden.

B433644. Janice Gilliland, fourth child and second daughter of Sarah Pounds and Robert Gilliland, born in Chambers County, Alabama. Married 21 Dec 1904 in Alabama to John A. Stewart.

B43365. Henry David Pounds, fifth child and third son of Zachariah Pounds and Elizabeth Sutton, born 11 Jun 1855 in Chambers County, Alabama and died 8 Aug 1887 in Hopkins County, Texas. Buried at Martin Springs cemetery, Hopkins County, Texas. Married 2 Mar 1878 in Hopkins County, Texas to Laura Jennie Brinker, born 1860 in Alabama and died 1889 in Hopkins County, Texas. Buried at Martin Springs cemetery, Hopkins County, Texas. Henry Pounds and Laura Brinker had issue, which was the tenth generation in America:

B433651. Benjamin Jasper Pounds, first child and first son of Henry Pounds and Laura Brinker, born 11 Jan 1880 in Hopkins County, Texas and died 13 Oct 1970 at Austin, Travis County, Texas. Buried at Austin, Travis County, Texas. Married Bella ---. Benjamin Pounds and Bella --- had issue, which was the eleventh generation in America:

B4336511. Benjamin Jasper Pounds, Jr., first child and first son of Benjamin Pounds and Bella ---, born 21 May 1922 at Austin, Travis County, Texas.

B43366. Emma Lucy Pounds, sixth child and third daughter of Zachariah Pounds and Elizabeth Sutton, born 1 Dec 1857 in Chambers County, Alabama and died 1 Jun 1918 at Sulphur Springs, Hopkins County, Texas. Buried at Martin Springs cemetery, Hopkins County, Texas. Married 25 Oct 1874 in Hopkins County, Texas to Jeremiah Hezekiah Zachariah Seale. Married secondly to Jeremiah Taylor Seale, born 26 Mar 1855 in Mississippi and died 26 Feb 1929 at Sulphur Springs, Hopkins County, Texas. Buried at Martin Springs cemetery, Hopkins County, Texas. Emma Pounds and Jeremiah H. Seale had issue, which was the ninth generation in America:

B433661. Zachariah A. Seale, first child and first son of Emma Pounds and Jeremiah Seale, born 4 Sep 1875 in Hopkins County, Texas and died 4 May 1934 in Tennessee.

B433662. Robert Lee Seale, second child and second son of Emma Pounds and Jeremiah Seale, born 25 Jun 1877 in Hopkins County, Texas and died 9 Jun 1936 in Texas. Married to Laura C. ---, born 1882 in Texas. Robert Seale and Laura --- had issue, which was the tenth generation in America:

B4336621. Beatrice A. Seale, first child and first daughter of Robert Seale and Laura ---, born 1903 in Hopkins County, Texas.

B4336622. Stella C. Seale, second child and second daughter of Robert Seale and Laura ---, born 1905 in Hopkins County, Texas.

B433663. Rosa L. Seale, third child and first daughter of Emma Pounds and Jeremiah Seale,

born Aug 1879 in Hopkins County, Texas. Married -
-- Green. Rosa Seale and --- Green had issue,
which was the tenth generation in America:

B4336631. Paul H. Green, first
child and first son of Rosa Seale and --- Green,
born 1901 in Texas.

B4336632. William J. Green, second
child and second son of Rosa Seale and --- Green,
born 1902 in Texas.

B433664. Thomas Seale, fourth child and
third son of Emma Pounds and Jeremiah Seale, born
Feb 1882 in Hopkins County, Texas. Married Alice
M. ---, born 1882. Thomas Seale and Alice --- had
issue, which was the tenth generation in America:

B4336641. Ralph E. Seale, first
child and first son of Thomas Seale and Alice ---
born 1905 in Hopkins County, Texas.

B4336642. Willie L. Seale, second
child and second son of Thomas Seale and Alice --
born 1909 in Hopkins County, Texas.

B433665. Linnie F. Seale, fifth child
and second daughter of Emma Pounds and Jeremiah
Seale, born Mar 1885 in Hopkins County, Texas.

B433666. Marion H. Seale, sixth child
and fourth son of Emma Pounds and Jeremiah Seale,
born Feb 1888 in Hopkins County, Texas. Married
Ruth M. ---, born 1890 in Texas. Marion Seale and
Ruth --- had issue, which was the tenth generation
in America:

B4336661. Marion F. Seale, first
child and first son of Marion Seale and Ruth ---,
born 1908 in Hopkins County, Texas.

B4336662. Alma C. Seale, second
child and first daughter of Marion Seale and Ruth
---, born 1909 in Hopkins County, Texas.

B433667. William J.B. Seale, seventh
child and fifth son of Emma Pounds and Jeremiah
Seale, born Aug 1891 in Hopkins County, Texas.

B433668. Ora Ollie Seale, eighth child
and third daughter of Emma Pounds and Jeremiah
Seale, born Aug 1894 in Hopkins County, Texas.

B433669. Gideon Seale, ninth child and
sixth son of Emma Pounds and Jeremiah Seale, born
Dec 1897 in Hopkins County, Texas and died 12 Sep
1898 in Hopkins County, Texas. Buried at Martin
Springs cemetery, Hopkins County, Texas.

B43367. Thomas Judge Pounds, seventh child and fourth son of Zachariah Pounds and Elizabeth Sutton, born 28 Sep 1859 in Chambers County, Alabama and died 2 Aug 1936 at Gilmer, Upshur County, Texas. Buried at Old Gilmer cemetery, Upshur County, Texas. Married 14 Mar 1880 in Hopkins County, Texas to Martha Jane Nolan, born 25 Dec 1865 in Alabama and died 7 Jun 1904 in Hopkins County, Texas. Buried at Martin Springs cemetery, Hopkins County, Texas. Married secondly about 1905 in Texas to Sallie Elizabeth Long, born 13 Jan 1875 in Alabama and died 16 Mar 1958 at Gilmore, Upshur County, Texas. Buried at Old Gilmore cemetery, Upshur County, Texas. Thomas Pounds and Martha Nolan had issue, which was the ninth generation in America:

B433671. Edna Elizabeth Pounds, first child and first daughter of Thomas Pounds and Martha Nolan, born 8 Sep 1881 at Sulphur Springs, Hopkins County, Texas and died 26 May 1967. Married about 1909 in Texas to Edward Huey Young, born 15 Jan 1872 in Texas and died 11 Aug 1914 in Hopkins County, Texas. Buried at Martin Springs cemetery, Hopkins County, Texas. Married secondly to Bob Blalock. Edna Pounds and Edward Young had issue, which was the tenth generation in America:

B4336711. Earl C. Young, first child and first son of Edna Pounds and Edward Young, born 1900 in Hopkins County, Texas.

B4336712. Steve Young, second child and second son of Edna Pounds and Edward Young, born 5 Sep 1903 in Hopkins County, Texas and died 11 Nov 1904 in Hopkins County, Texas. Buried at Martin Springs cemetery, Hopkins County, Texas.

B4336713. Jennette B. Young, third child and first daughter of Edna Pounds and Edward Young, born 1907 in Hopkins County, Texas.

B433672. Thomas Elmer Pounds, second child and first son of Thomas Pounds and Martha Nolan, born 2 Jul 1883 at Sulphur Springs, Hopkins County, Texas and died 17 Dec 1964. Married 16 Jun 1910 in Texas to Effie Dunn.

B433673. Oscar Dial Pounds, third child and second son of Thomas Pounds and Martha Nolan, born 28 Sep 1884 at Sulphur Springs, Hopkins

County, Texas and died 19 Nov 1949 in Hopkins County, Texas. Buried in Como cemetery, Hopkins County, Texas. Married 4 Jan 1911 in Texas to Jewel M. Addy, born 6 Jul 1888 and died 6 Aug 1975 in Dallas County, Texas. Buried at Como cemetery, Hopkins County, Texas.

B433674. Warren Vester Pounds, fourth child and third son of Thomas Pounds and Martha Nolan, born 17 Mar 1887 at Sulphur Springs, Hopkins County, Texas and died 29 Jan 1892 in Hopkins County, Texas.

B433675. James Roy Pounds, fifth child and fourth son of Thomas Pounds and Martha Nolan, born 5 Feb 1889 at Sulphur Springs, Hopkins County, Texas and died 18 Sep 1958 at Dallas, Dallas County, Texas. Buried at Reilly Springs cemetery, Hopkins County, Texas. Married 26 Dec 1911 in Texas to Bessie R. McKay, born 1889 and died 6 May 1936 in Texas. Buried at Reilly Springs cemetery, Hopkins County, Texas. James Pounds and Bessie Mckay had issue, which was the tenth generation in America:

B4336751. Annie Pounds, first child and first daughter of James Pounds and Bessie McKay, born 1913 and died 1987. Married Oscar Kerr, born 1911 and died 1952. Buried at Sulphur Springs, Hopkins County, Texas. Annie Pounds and Oscar Kerr had issue, which was the eleventh generation in America:

B43367511. Anita Kerr, first child and first daughter of Annie Pounds and Oscar Kerr, born 18 Dec 1937. Married Nolan Cason.

B433676. Granville Mann (twin) Pounds, sixth child and fifth son of Thomas Pounds and Martha Nolan, born 8 Aug 1891 at Sulphur Springs, Hopkins County, Texas and died 14 Sep 1948 at Dallas, Dallas County, Texas. Married 30 Jan 1916 in Texas to Nellie Williamson, date and place of birth unknown, and date of death unknown, but burial was at Martin Springs cemetery, Hopkins County, Texas. Granville Pounds and Nellie Williamson had issue, which was the tenth generation in America:

B4336761. Truman Pounds, first child and first son of Granville Pounds and Nellie Williamson, date and place of birth unknown.

B433677. Artella (twin) Pounds, seventh child and second daughter of Thomas Pounds and Martha Nolan, born 8 Aug 1891 at Sulphur Springs, Hopkins County, Texas and died in Hopkins County, Texas. Buried at Martin Springs cemetery, Hopkins County, Texas. Married 16 Jan 1910 in Texas to James Oliver Summerlin, born 14 Mar 1883 and died 3 Nov 1945. Buried at Martin Springs cemetery, Hopkins County, Texas.

B433678. Lillian Pounds, eighth child and third daughter of Thomas Pounds and Martha Nolan, born 3 Sep 1895 at Sulphur Springs, Hopkins County, Texas and died 26 May 1898 at Sulphur Springs, Hopkins County, Texas. Married Clyde Martin.

B433679. Clyde Pounds, ninth child and fourth daughter of Thomas Pounds and Martha Nolan, born Nov 1897 at Sulphur Springs, Hopkins County, Texas. Married 29 Jan 1914 in Texas to Gabe Martin.

B43368. Zachariah B. Price Pounds, eighth child and fifth son of Zachariah Pounds and Elizabeth Sutton, born 18 Jan 1862 in Chambers County, Alabama and died 14 Mar 1927 at Brownfield, Terry County, Texas. Buried at Brownfield cemetery, Terry County, Texas. Married 18 Sep 1884 in Hopkins County, Texas to Martha (Mattie) Malita Bethell, born 22 Nov 1867 in Claiborne Parish, Louisiana and died 30 Mar 1939 at Mobeetie, Wheeler County, Texas. Buried at Mobeetie cemetery, Wheeler County, Texas. Zachariah Pounds and Martha Bethell had issue, which was the ninth generation in America:

B433681. Maryetta Pounds, first child and first daughter of Zachariah Pounds and Martha Bethell, born 29 Jun 1885 in Hopkins County, Texas and died 26 Nov 1963 at Rochester, Haskell County, Texas. Buried at Haskell County, Texas. Married 17 Jan 1904 at Rochester, Haskell County, Texas to Jacob Dillard Speck, born 1 May 1881 at Albany, Clinton County, Kentucky and died 17 Nov 1961 at Rochester, Haskell County, Texas. Buried at Haskell County, Texas. Maryetta Pounds and Jacob Speck had issue, which was the tenth generation in America:

B4336811. Daisy Irene Speck, first

child and first daughter of Maryetta Pounds and Jacob Speck, born 7 Feb 1905 at Rochester, Haskell County, Texas and died Sep 1989 in California. Buried at Mundy, Knox County, Texas. Married John Keifor Beauchamp, born at Rochester, Haskell County, Texas and died Oct 1926 at Rochester, Haskell County, Texas. Married secondly 14 Oct 1929 to Wiley Johnson. Daisy Speck and John Beauchamp had issue, which was the eleventh generation in America:

B43368111. Sybil Fay Beauchamp, first child and first daughter of Daisy Speck and John Beauchamp, born 12 May 1924 at Rochester, Haskell County, Texas.
Married Braxton Chandler. Sybil Beauchamp and Braxton Chandler had issue, which was the twelfth generation in America:

B433681111. Betty Sue Chandler, first child and first daughter of Sybil Beauchamp and Braxton Chandler, date and place of birth unknown. Married to Garrett Fitzgibbon.

B433681112. Roy Dale Chandler, second child and first son of Sybil Beauchamp and Braxton Chandler, date and place of birth unknown. Married to Pamela ---. Roy Chandler and Pamela --- had issue, which was the thirteenth generation in America:

B4336811121. Brandon Ray Chandler, first child and first son of Roy Chandler and Pamela ---, date and place of birth unknown.

B43368112. Delbert Keifor Beauchamp, second child and first son of Daisy Speck and John Beauchamp, born 4 Jan 1925 at Rochester, Haskell County, Texas. Married Helen ---, date and place of birth unknown, but she died 25 Jun 1992 in Ripley, Tippah County, Mississippi. Buried in Greenwood cemetery, Fort Worth, Tarrant County, Texas. Delbert Beauchamp and Helen --- had issue, which was the twelfth generation in America:

B433681121. Rachel Sue Beauchamp, first child and first daughter of Delbert Beauchamp and Helen ---, date and place of birth unknown. Married Robert Green. Rachel Beauchamp and Robert Green had issue, which was the thirteenth generation in America:

B4336811211. Molly Susana Green, first child and first daughter of Rachel Beauchamp and Robert Green, date and place of birth unknown.

B4336811212. Laura Katherin Green, second child and second daughter of Rachel Beauchamp and Robert Green, date and place of birth unknown.

B4336811213. Logan Green, third child and first son of Rachel Beauchamp and Robert Green, date and place of birth unknown.

B433681122. Dennis Keifor Beauchamp, second child and first son of Delbert Beauchamp and Helen ---, date and place of birth unknown. Married Malissa ---. Dennis Beauchamp and Malissa --- had issue, which was the thirteenth generation in America:

B4336811221. Dan Keifor Beauchamp, first child and first son of Dennis Beauchamp and Malissa ---, date and place of birth unknown.

B4336811222. Andrew Price Beauchamp, second child and second son of Dennis Beauchamp and Malissa ---, date and place of birth unknown.

B4336811223. Roy Arlis Beauchamp, third child and third son of Dennis Beauchamp and Malissa ---, date and place of birth unknown.

B43368113. Bettie John Beauchamp, third child and second daughter of Daisy Speck and John Beauchamp, born 3 Feb 1927 at Rochester, Haskell County, Texas. Married Gene Chandler. Bettie Beauchamp and Gene Chandler had issue, which was the twelth generation in America:

B433681131. Ronald Gene Chandler, first child and first son of Bettie Beauchamp and Gene Chandler, date and place of birth unknown. Married Amy ---.
Ronald Chandler and Amy --- had issue, which was the thirteenth generation in America:

B4336811311. Kim Michelle Chandler, first child and first daughter of Ronald Chandler and Amy ---, date and place of birth unknown.

B4336811312. Kari Ann Chandler, second child and second daughter of Ronald Beauchamp and Amy ---, date and place of birth unknown.

B433681132. Carol Ann Chandler, second child and first daughter of Bettie Beauchamp and Gene Chandler, date and place of birth unknown. Married Dennis Evans. Carol Chandler and Dennis Evans had issue, which was the thirteenth generation in America:

B4336811321. Dennis Neil Evans, first child and first son of Carol Chandler and Dennis Evans, date and place of birth unknown.

B4336811322. Randell McCoy Evans, second child and second son of Carol Chandler and Dennis Evans, date and place of birth unknown.

B4336811. Daisy Irene Speck, first child and first daughter of Jacob Speck and Maryetta Pounds, born 7 Feb 1905 at Rochester, Haskell County, Texas and died Sep 1989 in California. Buried at Mundy, Knox County, Texas. Married secondly 14 Oct 1929 to Wiley Johnson. Daisy Speck and Wiley Johnson had issue, which was the eleventh generation in America:

B43368111. Don Johnson, first child and first son of Daisy Speck and Wiley Johnson, date and place of birth unknown. Married Gwen ---. Don Johnson and Gwen --- had issue, which was the twelth generation in America:

B433681111. Julie Irene Johnson, first child and first daughter of Don Johnson and Gwen ---, date and place of birth unknown. Married Jim Morse. Julie Johnson and Jim Morse had issue, which was the thirteenth generation in America:

B4336811111. Jausch Allen Morse, first child and first son of Julie Johnson and Jim Morse, date and place of birth unknown.

B4336811112. Israel Morse, second child and second son of Julie Johnson and Jim Morse, date and place of birth unknown.

B4336812. Myrtie Jane Speck, second child and second daughter of Maryetta Pounds and Jacob Speck, born 13 Nov 1906. Married 10 Feb 1925 to H.R. Beauchamp, date of birth unknown but died 9 Aug 1984. Myrtie Speck and H.R. Beauchamp had issue, which was the eleventh generation in America:

B43368121. Infant Beauchamp, first child and first daughter of Myrtie Speck and H.R. Beauchamp, born and died 18 Feb 1926.

B43368122. Janice Elrena Beauchamp, second child and second daughter of Myrtie Speck and H.R. Beauchamp, born 9 Apr 1927. Married 11 Jun 1945 to Phillip Bill Essary. Janice Beauchamp and Phillip Essary had issue, which was the twelth generation in America:

B43368123. Phillip Bill Essary, Jr., first child and first son of Janice Beauchamp and Phillip Essary, born 27 Aug 1946. Married 14 Sep 1974 to Vickie Turner. Phillip Essary and Vickie Turner had issue, which was the thirteenth generation in America:

B433681231. Scotty Wayne Essary, first child and first son of Phillip Essary and Vickie Turner, born 30 Aug 1976.

B433681232. Mathew Dean Essary, second child and second son of Phillip Essary and Vickie Turner, born 4 Jul 1990.

B43368124. Donna Gail Essary, second child and first daughter of Janice Beauchamp and Phillip Essary, born 19 Dec 1951. Married 8 Jun 1969 to Russell Good. Donna Essary and Russell Good had issue, which was the thirteenth generation in America:

B433681241. April Michelle Good, first child and first daughter of Donna Essary and Russell Good, born 30 Oct 1973.

B433681242. Heather Christen Good, second child and second daughter of Donna Essary and Russell Good, born 29 Oct 1981.

B433681243. Holly Nicole Good, third child and third daughter of Donna Essary and Russell Good, born 12 Dec 1985.

B43368125. Jimmy Lynn Essary, third child and second son of Janice Beauchamp and Phillip Essary, born 12 Oct 1953. Married Leda --

-. Jimmy Essary married secondly, but the spouse's name is unknown.
Jimmy Essary and Leda --- had issue, which was the thirteenth generation in America:

B433681251. Kristal Ann Essary, first child and first daughter of Jimmy Essary and Leda ---, born 29 Dec 1971. Married 4 Apr 1988 to Tim Lackey.

B43368125. Jimmy Lynn Essary, third child and second son of Janice Beauchamp and Phillip Essary, born 12 Oct 1953. Married secondly --- ---. Jimmy Essary and --- --- had issue, which was the thirteenth generation in America:

B433681251. Teddy L. Essary, first child and first son of Jimmy Essary and --- ---, born 30 Oct 1973.

B433681252. Andrew J. Essary, second child and second son of Jimmy Essary and --- ---, born 22 Jul 1976.

B43368123. Glen Dale Beauchamp, third child and first son of Myrtie Speck and H.R. Beauchamp, born 15 Nov 1930. Married 16 Aug 1952 to Carol LaVaughn Crockett. Glen Beauchamp and Carol Crockett had issue, which was the twelth generation in America:

B433681231. Stephen Dale Beauchamp, first child and first son of Glen Beauchamp and Carol Crockett, born 2 Dec 1954. Married 30 Jul 1976 to Linda Joyce Goff. Stephen Beauchamp and Linda Goff had issue, which was the thirteenth generation in America:

B4336812311. Jennifer Lynn Beauchamp, first child and first daughter of Stephen Beauchamp and Linda Goff, born 25 Feb 1978.

B4336812312. Michelle Ranae Beauchamp, second child and second daughter of Stephen Beauchamp and Linda Goff, born 1 Oct 1980.

B4336812313. Richard Adam Beauchamp, third child and first son of Stephen Beauchamp and Linda Goff, born 1 Jun 1983.

B433681232. David Ray (twin) Beauchamp, second child and second son of

Glen Beauchamp and Carol Crockett, born 22 Nov 1957. Married 21 Aug 1982 to Deborah Jean Wortzon. David Beauchamp and Deborah Wortzon had issue, which was the thirteenth generation in America:

B4336812321. John David Beauchamp, first child and first son of David Beauchamp and Deborah Wortzon, born 2 Dec 1983.

B4336812322. Sarah Elizabeth Beauchamp, second child and first daughter of David Beauchamp and Deborah Wortzon, born 15 Nov 1985.

B4336812323. Luke Andrew Beauchamp, third child and second son of David Beauchamp and Deborah Wortzon, born 27 Jul 1988.

B4336812324. Anna Beauchamp, fourth child and second daughter of David Beauchamp and Deborah Wortzon, born Aug 1992.

B433681233. Debbie Kay (twin) Beauchamp, third child and first daughter of Glen Beauchamp and Carol Crockett, born 22 Nov 1957. Married 14 Jun 1987 to Don Kirkland.

B43368124. Cecil Ray Beauchamp, fourth child and second son of Myrtie Speck and H.R. Beauchamp, born 28 Mar 1938. Married 2 Dec 1958 to Janet Wood. Cecil Beauchamp and Janet Wood had issue, which was the twelth generation in America:

B433681241. Tamera Lyn Beauchamp, first child and first daughter of Cecil Beauchamp and Janet Wood, born 5 Jan 1961. Married 10 Jun 1978 to Chad Arnold. Married secondly 28 Aug 1987 to Hershell Jones. Tamera Beauchamp and Chad Arnold had issue, which was the thirteenth generation in issue in America:

B4336812411. Barney Daniel Arnold, first child and first son of Tamera Beauchamp and Chad Arnold, date and place of birth unknown.

B433681241. Tamera Lyn Beauchamp, first child and first daughter of Cecil Beauchamp and Janet Wood, born 5 Jan 1961. Married secondly 28 Aug 1987 to Hershell Jones.

Tamera Beauchamp and Hershell Jones had issue, which was the thirteenth generation in America:
B4336812411. Rhet Lee Jones, first child and first son of Tamera Beauchamp and Hershell Jones, born 28 Sep 1988.

B433681242. Ray (Sonny) Gordon Beauchamp, second child and first son of Cecil Beauchamp and Janet Wood, born 27 May 1965. Married 1 Jul 1989 to Gayle Camille Buchenew.

B433681243. Lisa Beauchamp, third child and second daughter of Cecil Beauchamp and Janet Wood, born 14 Nov 1969. Married 22 Dec 1990 to Ryan Ashford.

B4336813. Fannie Molytie Speck, third child and third daughter of Maryetta Pounds and Jacob Speck, born 21 Dec 1908, died 13 Nov 1992 at Wichita Falls, Wichita County, Texas. Buried at Abilene, Taylor County, Texas Married 18 Dec 1932 to Lee Ballew.

B4336814. Walter Jacob Speck, fourth child and first son of Maryetta Pounds and Jacob Speck, born 15 Apr 1911 and died 13 Oct 1986. Married 18 Dec 1932 to Lois Brooks. Walter Speck and Lois Brooks had issue, which was the eleventh generation in America:
B43368141. Jerald Dee Speck, first child and first son of Walter Speck and Lois Brooks, born 3 Oct 1934.

B43368142. Sadie Sue Speck, second child and first daughter of Walter Speck and Lois Brooks, born 23 Feb 1937. Married 6 Dec 1957 to John Quinn. Sadie Speck and John Quinn had issue, which was the twelth generation in America:
B433681421. Deborah Jean Quinn, first child and first daughter of Sadie Speck and John Quinn, born 23 Nov 1958.

B433682. William David Pounds, second child and first son of Zachariah Pounds and Martha Bethell, born 21 Feb 1887 in Hopkins County, Texas and died 24 Oct 1889. Married 5 Dec 1860 in Nacogdoches County, Texas to Caroline F. Hutchison.

B433683. Lucy Agnes Pounds, third child and second daughter of Zachariah Pounds and Martha Bethell, born 31 Aug 1888 at Colbert, Bryan

County, Oklahoma and died 21 Dec 1964 at Mobeetie, Wheeler County, Texas. Married 31 Jul 1907 at Rochester, Haskell County, Texas to Alcuen Arnett Burch, born 27 Feb 1882 at Wallhill, Marshall County, Mississippi and died 10 Feb 1972 at Pampa, Gray County, Texas. Buried at Mobeetie, Wheeler County, Texas. Lucy Pounds and Alcuen Burch had issue, which was the eleventh generation in America:

B4336831. Lucy Arnett Burch, first child and first daughter of Lucy Pounds and Alcuen Burch, born 28 Oct 1908 at Rochester, Haskell County, Texas and died 20 Jun 1975 at Pampa, Gray County, Texas. Married 2 Oct 1932 at Sayre, Beckham County, Oklahoma to James D. Sackett, born 17 Feb 1897 and died 30 May 1981 at Pampa, Gray County, Texas. Lucy Burch and James Sackett had issue, which was the twelth generation in America:

B43368311. Floyd Ernest Sackett, first child and first son of Lucy Burch and James Sackett, born 17 Jun 1934 at Rochester, Haskell County, Texas. Married 15 Jun 1957 at Hale Center, Hale County, Texas to Janice Allman. Floyd Sackett and Janice Allman had issue, which was the thirteenth generation in America:

B433683111. Edmond Dawson Sackett, first child and first son of Floyd Sackett and Janice Allman, born 24 Oct 1960 at Pampa, Gray County, Texas. Married 29 Dec 1984 to Paula Kay Allison. Edmond Sackett and Paula Allison had issue, which was the fourteenth generation in America:

B4336831111. Lindsey Rebecca Sackett, first child and first daughter of Edmond Sackett and Paula Allison, born 18 Jul 1990 at Winter Haven, Polk County, Florida.

B43368312. Paul Clarence Sackett, second child and first son of Lucy Burch and James Sackett, born 9 Jan 1937 at Pampa, Gray County, Texas. Married 22 Nov 1963 to Martha ---.

B43368313. Daniel Cuen Sackett, third child and third son of Lucy Burch and James Sackett, born 7 Feb 1938 at Pampa, Gray County, Texas. Married 1 Jul 1959 at Albuquerque, Bernalillo County, New Mexico to Audrey Goodwin.

Daniel Sackett and Audrey Goodwin had issue, which was the twelth generation in America:

B433683131. Daniel Cuen Sackett, Jr., first child and first son of Daniel Sackett and Audrey Goodwin, born 8 Jun 1960 at Pampa, Gray County, Texas. Married 28 Jan 1989 at Amarillo, Potter County, Texas to Cinda Leigh Anderson. Daniel Sackett and Cinda Anderson had issue, which was the thirteenth generation in America:

B4336831311. Nicholas Alexander Sackett, first child and first son of Daniel Sackett and Cinda Anderson, born 22 Jun 1990 at Amarillo, Potter County, Texas.

B433683132. Tammy Fay Sackett, second child and first daughter of Daniel Sackett and Audrey Goodwin, born 5 Dec 1961 at Pampa, Gray County, Texas. Married 29 Jul 1979 at Amarillo, Potter County, Texas to Bobby Don Nokes. Tammy Sackett and Bobby Nokes had issue, which was the thirteenth generation in America:

B4336831321. Maria Fay Nokes, first child and first daughter of Tammy Sackett and Bobby Nokes, born 1 Dec 1980 at Plainview, Hale County, Texas.

B4336831322. Bobbie Dawn Nokes, second child and second daughter of Tammy Sackett and Bobby Nokes, born 17 Dec 1984 at Amarillo, Potter County, Texas.

B4336831323. Thomas Avery Nokes, third child and first son of Tammy Sackett and Bobby Nokes, born 1 Sep 1988 at Amarillo, Potter County, Texas.

B433683133. Lucy Janell Sackett, third child and second daughter of Daniel Sackett and Audrey Goodwin, born 25 Jan 1964 at Gillette, Campbell County, Wyoming. Married 14 Feb 1984 at Amarillo, Potter County, Texas to Jimmy Glynn Tuter. Married secondly 8 Sep 1989 at Amarillo, Potter County, Texas to Richard Mathew Holmes, born 9 Mar 1966 at Amarillo, Potter County, Texas. Lucy Sackett and Jimmy Tuter had issue, which was the thirteenth generation in America:

B4336831331. Julie Janell Tuter, first child and first daughter of Lucy Sackett and Jimmy Tuter, born 29 Aug 1984 at Amarillo, Potter County, Texas.

B433683133. Lucy Janell Sackett, third child and second daughter of Daniel Sackett and Audrey Goodwin, born 25 Jan 1964 at Gillette, Campbell County, Wyoming. Married secondly 8 Sep 1989 to Richard Mathew Holmes, born 9 Mar 1966 at Amarillo, Potter County, Texas. Lucy Sackett and Richard Holmes had issue, which was the thirteenth generation in America:

B4336831331. Heather Leah Holmes, first child and first daughter of Lucy Sackett and Richard Holmes, born 1 Aug 1991 at Amarillo, Potter County, Texas.

B43368314. Edna Agness Sackett, fourth child and first daughter of Lucy Burch and James Sackett, born 12 Jan 1940 at Pampa, Gray County, Texas. Married 2 Jun 1965 at Pampa, Gray County, Texas to Don Eugene Bryant. Edna Sackett and Don Bryant had issue, which was the twelth generation in America:

B433683141. Daniel Eugene Bryant, first child and first son of Edna Sackett and Don Bryant, born 19 Feb 1966 at Pampa, Gray County, Texas.

B433683142. Selina Carol Bryant, second child and first daughter of Edna Sackett and Don Bryant, born 12 Mar 1969 at Pampa, Gray County, Texas. Married 28 Jul 1989 to Ricky McMillon.

B43368315. Charlie Henry Sackett, fifth child and fourth son of Lucy Burch and James Sackett, born 11 Oct 1943 at Pampa, Gray County, Texas. Married 17 Apr 1964 at Pampa, Gray County, Texas to Barbara Jo Wakefield. Charlie Sackett and Barbara Wakefield had issue, which was the twelth generation in America:

B433683151. Charlie Henry Sackett, Jr., first child and first son of Charlie Sackett and Barbara Wakefield, born 14 Jan 1965 in Pampa, Gray County, Texas.

B433683152. James Clinton Sackett, second child and second son of Charlie Sackett and Barbara Wakefield, born 9 Mar 1968 at Pampa, Gray County, Texas.

B43368316. Jerry Richard Sackett, sixth child and fifth son of Lucy Burch and James Sackett, born 7 Aug 1945 at Pampa, Gray County, Texas.

B4336832. Mary Jane Katherine Burch, second child and second daughter of Lucy Pounds and Alcuen Burch, born 3 Apr 1910 at Rochester, Haskell County, Texas and died 3 May 1986 at Jacksonville, Cherokee County, Texas. Married 7 Mar 1933 at Sayre, Beckam County, Oklahoma to Thomas R. Cooper. Mary Burch and Thomas Cooper had issue, which was the eleventh generation in America:

B43368321. Tommie Rae Cooper, first child and first daughter of Mary Burch and Thomas Cooper, born 23 May 1935. Married --- Hunt.

B43368322. Billie Jane Cooper, second child and second daughter of Mary Burch and Thomas Cooper, born 14 Jul 1936 at Pampa, Gray County, Texas. Married 28 Jul 1953 at Yuma, Yuma County, Arizona to Charles Everett Cary, born 20 Nov 1930 in Texas. Billie Cooper and Charles Cary had issue, which was the twelth generation in America:

B433683221. Cynthia Diann Cary, first child and first daughter of Billie Cooper and Charles Cary, born 28 Apr 1954 at Whittier, Los Angeles County, California. Married 20 Sep 1974 to Robert Lee Ward, born 10 Apr 1955 at Jollyville, Travis County, Texas. Married secondly 31 Aug 1990 to Michael Caddell, born 6 Oct 1964 at Kaufman, Kaufman County, Texas. Cynthia Cary and Robert Ward had issue, which was the thirteenth generation in America:

B4336832211. Michelle Leann Ward, first child and first daughter of Cynthia Cary and Robert Ward, born 22 Aug 1979 at Garland, Dallas County, Texas.

B433683222. Charles Everett Cary, Jr., second child and first son of Billie Cooper and Charles Cary, born 23 Jul 1956 at Jacksonville, Cherokee County, Texas. Married 27 Jun 1978 at Houston, Harris County, Texas to Stephanie Jo Fellars, born 23 Dec 1958. Charles Cary and Stephanie Fellars had issue, which was the thirteenth generation in America:

B4336832221. Charles Everett Cary III, first child and first son of Charles Cary and Stephanie Fellars, born 28 Sep 1981 at Houston, Harris County, Texas.

B4336832222. Sean Eugene Cary, second child and second son of Charles Cary and Stephanie Fellars, born 9 Nov 1984 at Houston, Harris County, Texas.

B4336832223. Elizabeth Jo Cary, third child and first daughter of Charles Cary and Stephanie Fellars, born 28 Dec 1987 at Houston, Harris County, Texas.

B433683223. Clifford Arnet Cary, third child and second son of Billie Cooper and Charles Cary, born 6 Oct 1959 at Jacksonville, Cherokee County, Texas. Married 8 Aug 1982 to Deborah Lynn Persons. Clifford Cary and Deborah Persons had issue, which was the thirteenth generation in America:

B4336832231. Clifford Arnet Cary, Jr., first child and first son of Clifford Cary and Deborah Persons, born 9 Aug 1984 at Jacksonville, Cherokee County, Texas.

B4336832232. Kimberly Jo Cary, second child and first daughter of Clifford Cary and Deborah Persons, born 7 Jul 1988 at Tyler, Smith County, Texas.

B433683224. Cecile Delois Cary, fourth child and second daughter of Billie Cooper and Charles Cary, born 16 Jan 1962 at Jacksonville, Cherokee County, Texas. Married 1 Feb 1986 to Wade Burke.

B43368323. Gayla June Cooper, third child and third daughter of Mary Burch and Thomas Cooper, born 15 May 1938. Married --- Peftey.

B43368324. Bobbie Rae Cooper, fourth child and fourth daughter of Mary Burch and Thomas Cooper, born 29 Apr 1940. Married --- Quaglicta.

B4336833. Alice Mallie Burch, third child and third daughter of Lucy Pounds and Alcuen Burch, born 16 Jan 1912 at Matador, Motley County, Texas. Married 10 Dec 1938 at Sayre, Beckam County, Oklahoma to Frances B. Flaherty.

Alice Burch and Frances Flaherty had issue, which was the eleventh generation in America:

B43368331. Leo Henry Flaherty, first child and first son of Alice Burch and Frances Flaherty, born 7 Aug 1938 at Pampa, Gray County, Texas.

B43368332. Wanda Flaherty, second child and first daughter of Alice Burch and Frances Flaherty, born 22 Aug 1939 at Pampa, Gray County, Texas. Married --- Montgomery. Wanda Flaherty and --- Montgomery had issue, which was the twelth generation in America:

B433683321. Stanley Montgomery, first child and first son of Wanda Flaherty and --- Montgomery, date and place of birth unknown.

B433683322. Frances Kay Montgomery, second child and first daughter of Wanda Flaherty and --- Montgomery, date and place of birth unknown.

B43368333. Charles R. Flaherty, third child and second son of Alice Burch and Frances Flaherty, born 24 Sep 1943 at Pampa, Gray County, Texas. Married 13 Mar 1965 to --- ---. Charles Flaherty and his unnamed spouse had issue, which was the twelth generation in America:

B433683331. Steve Flaherty, first child and first son of Charles Flaherty and --- ---. born 29 Sep 1965 at Norwalk, Los Angeles County, California.

B433683332. Joanne Flaherty, second child and first daughter of Charles Flaherty and --- ---, born 8 Aug 1970 at Downey, Los Angeles County, California.

B4336834. Wilber Octavia Burch, fourth child and fourth daughter of Lucy Pounds and Alcuen Burch, born 3 Apr 1914 at Lovington, Lea County, New Mexico. Married 22 Dec 1934 at Wheeler, Wheeler County, Texas to Ottis G. Beck, born 15 Jan 1910. Wilber Burch and Ottis Beck had issue, which was the eleventh generation in America:

B43368341. Glynnda Gearldean Beck, first child and first daughter of Wilber Burch and Ottis Beck, born 1 May 1944 at

Wheeler, Wheeler County, Texas. Married 15 Jul 1966 to Wayne Allen Leatherman, Sr., born 2 Oct 1943 at Silver Springs, Montgomery County, Maryland. Glynnda Beck and Wayne Leatherman had issue, which was the twelth generation in America:

B433683411. Wayne Allen Leatherman, Jr., first child and first son of Glynnda Beck and Wayne Leatherman, born 14 Apr 1967 at Walker AFB, Chavez County, New Mexico. Married Shanna Etherdge.

B433683412. Kimberly Michelle Leatherman, second child and first daughter of Glynnda Beck and Wayne Leatherman, born and died 26 Dec 1968 at Culpeper, Culpeper County, Virginia.

B433683413. Christopher Nakoa Leatherman, third child and second son of Glynnda Beck and Wayne Leatherman, born 24 Aug 1980.

B4336835. Charles Price Burch, fifth child and first son of Lucy Pounds and Alcuen Burch, born 22 Mar 1916 at Lovington, Lea County, New Mexico and died 16 Nov 1968 at Bakersfield, Kerr County, California. Married 24 Dec 1939 to Tommie Owens.

B4336836. Ella Ruth Burch, sixth child and fifth daughter of Lucy Pounds and Alcuen Burch, born 8 Jul 1918 at Lovington, Lea County, New Mexico and died 23 Aug 1992 in Texas. Married 23 Jul 1938 to Louis Keith.

B4336837. Clarence William Burch, seventh child and second son of Lucy Pounds and Alcuen Burch, born 9 Feb 1928 at Quanah, Hardeman County, Texas. Married 8 Jun 1957 at Mobeetie, Wheeler County, Texas to Melba Corene Rector. Clarence Burch and Melba Rector had issue, which was the eleventh generation in America:

B43368371. Melody Carol Burch, first child and first daughter of Clarence Burch and Melba Rector, born 12 Dec 1959 at Pampa, Gray County, Texas. Married 24 May 1977 to Kenny Dewayne Sherrell. Melody Burch and Kenny Sherrell had issue, which was the twelth generation in America:

B433683711. Christy

Ann Sherell, first child and first daughter of Melody Burch and Kenny Sherell, born 28 Jun 1978 at Bartlesville, Washington County, Oklahoma.

B433683712. Anthony Michael Sherell, second child and first son of Melody Burch and Kenny Sherell, born 7 Sep 1979 at Bartlesville, Washington County, Oklahoma.

B433683713. Debra Leigh Sherell, third child and second daughter of Melody Burch and Kenny Sherell, born 5 Apr 1983 at Bartlesville, Washington County, Oklahoma.

B43368372. Clarence William Burch, Jr., second child and first son of Clarence Burch and Melba Rector, born 13 Oct 1961 at Pampa, Gray County, Texas. Married Nov 1980 to Darla Eliot. Married secondly 23 May 1987 to Patricia Lynn White. Clarence Burch and Patricia White had issue, which was the twelth generation in America:

B433683721. Tyler William Burch, first child and first son of Clarence Burch and Particia White, born 12 Jul 1991 at Amarillo, Potter County, Texas.

B433684. Benjamin Claude Pounds, fourth child and second son of Zachariah Pounds and Martha Bethell, born 31 Oct 1890 at Colbert, Bryan County, Oklahoma and died 6 Aug 1892.

B433685. Callie Octavie Pounds, fifth child and third daughter of Zachariah Pounds and Martha Bethell, born 15 Sep 1892 at Colbert, Bryan County, Oklahoma and died 9 May 1983. Married 20 Jan 1914 in Texas to Jesse Campbell Speck, born 14 Apr 1889 and died 24 Sep 1945. Callie Pounds and Jesse Speck had issue, which was the tenth generation in America:

B4336851. Granville Speck, first child and first son of Callie Pounds and Jesse Speck, born 8 Mar 1915 and died 31 Jul 1917.

B4336852. Gertie Speck, second child and first daughter of Callie Pounds and Jesse Speck, born 4 Jun 1916. Married Weldon J. Lewis. Married secondly to Cleatis L. Canary, date and place of birth unknown but he died 1976. Gertie Speck and Weldon Lewis has issue, which was the eleventh generation in America:

B43368521. Raymond Weldon Lewis,

first child and first son of Gertie Speck and Weldon Lewis, born 26 Oct 1942. Married Sharon Hamblin, born 19 Jul 1950. Raymond Lewis and Sharon Hamblin had issue, which was the twelth generation in America:

B433685211. Nicol R. Lewis, first child and first daughter of Raymond Lewis and Sharon Hamblin, born 10 Nov 1976.

B433685212. Brandon Weldon Lewis, second child and first son of Raymond Lewis and Sharon Hamblin, born 8 Nov 1981.

B43368522. Lloyd A. Lewis, second child and second son of Gertie Speck and Weldon Lewis, born 8 May 1947 and died 11 May 1947.

B4336853. Raymon F. Speck, third child and second daughter of Callie Pounds and Jesse Speck, born 7 Mar 1918 in Haskell County, Texas and died 30 Jan 1984. Married to --- Barrera. Married secondly to Johnnie Lewis, born 11 Jul 1926. Raymon Speck and --- Barrera had issue, which was the eleventh generation in America:

B43368531. Ronald Speck Barrera, first child and first son of Raymon Speck and --- Barrera, born 27 Sep 1943. Married --- ---. Ronald Barrera and --- --- had issue, which was the twelth generation in America:

B433685311. ·Tawny Barrera, first child and first daughter of Ronald Barrera and --- ---, born 17 Jul 1962.

B433685312. Boomer Barrera, second child and first son of Ronald Barrera and --- ---, born 28 Jun 1964.

B433685313. Debra Barrera, third child and second daughter of Ronald Barrerra and --- ---, born 3 Aug 1979.

B4336854. Opal B. Speck, fourth child and third daughter of Callie Pounds and Jesse Speck, born 25 Apr 1921 in Haskell County, Texas. Married Clint C. Roberts. Opal Speck and Clint Roberts had issue, which was the eleventh generation in America:

B43368541. Linda K. Roberts, first child and first daughter of Opal Speck and Clint Roberts, born 3 Jan 1942. Married Jerry Cates, born 27 Sep 1941. Linda Roberts and Jerry Cates had issue, which was the twelth generation in

America:
B433685411. Timothy D. Cates, first child and first son of Linda Roberts and Jerry Cates, born 23 Mar 1967.

B433685412. Terry B. Cates, second child and second son of Linda Roberts and Jerry Cates, born 27 Feb 1972.

B433686. Clarence Pounds, sixth child and third son of Zachariah Pounds and Martha Bethell, born 5 Nov 1894 at Colbert, Bryan County, Oklahoma and died 26 Aug 1926. Married 11 Mar 1917 to Florence Buckner.

B433687. Howard Adolphas Pounds, seventh child and fourth son of Zachariah Pounds and Martha Bethell, born 4 Dec 1896 at Greenville, Hunt County, Texas and died 2 Oct 1971 at Campbell, Santa Clara County, California. Buried at Campbell, California. Married 28 Apr 1918 at Weinert, Haskell County, Texas to Gertrude Velma Coffee, born 23 Sep 1899 in Texas and died 31 Mar 1971 at Campbell, Santa Clara County, California. Buried at Campbell, California. Howard Pounds and Gertrude Coffee had issue, which was the tenth generation in America:

B4336871. Buel Wendell Pounds, first child and first son of Howard Pounds and Gertrude Coffee, born 21 Dec 1919 in Haskell County, Texas. Married Mary Burchett Gibbs. Married secondly to Doris Ames.

B4336872. Bueford (Buck) Lowell Pounds, second child and second son of Howard Pounds and Gertrude Coffee, born 21 Sep 1921 in Haskell County, Texas. Married 5 Jul 1941 to Blance Lucille Smith. Bueford Pounds and Blance Smith had issue, which was the eleventh generation in America:

B43368721. Lowell Wendell Pounds, first child and first son of Bueford Pounds and Blance Smith, born 24 Feb 1943. Married Judy --- Married secondly to Sue Haag. Lowell Pounds and Judy --- had issue, which was the twelfth generation in America:

B433687211. Kathy Pounds, first child and first daughter of Lowell Pounds and Judy ---, born 6 May 1968.

B433687212. Robert Pounds,

second child and first son of Lowell Pounds and Judy ---, born 21 Sep 1971.

B43368721. Lowell Wendell Pounds, first child and first son of Bueford Pounds and Blance Smith, born 24 Feb 1943. Married secondly to Sue Haag. Lowell Pounds and Sue Haag had issue, which was the twelth generation in America:

B433687211. Lisa Marie Pounds, first child and first daughter of Lowell Pounds and Sue Haag, born 2 Jun 1990.

B43368722. Gerald Duane Pounds, second child and second son of Bueford Pounds and Blance Smith, born 21 Nov 1945. Married Lucille ---. Gerald Pounds and Lucille --- had issue, which was the twelth generation in America:

B433687221. Sandra Pounds, first child and first daughter of Gerald Pounds and Lucille ---, born 12 Feb 1973.

B43368723. Ronald Eugene Pounds, third child and third son of Bueford Pounds and Blance Smith, born 21 Aug 1949.

B4336873. Zada Ozell Pounds, third child and first daughter of Howard Pounds and Gertrude Coffee, born 9 Dec 1923 at Weinert, Haskell County, Texas. Married 1941 to James Edward Vestal. Zada Pounds and James Vestal had issue, which was the eleventh generation in America:

B43368731. Lora Carole Vestal, first child and first daughter of Zada Pounds and James Vestal, born 24 May 1942 at Ventura, Ventura County, California. Married 1961 to Troy Lee Boyd, Jr. Lora Vestal and Troy Boyd had issue, which was the twelth generation in America:

B433687311. Troy Lee Boyd III, first child and first son of Lora Vestal and Troy Boyd, born 24 Mar 1962 in California.

B433687312. Todd Michael Boyd, second child and second son of Lora Vestal and Troy Boyd, born 27 Jun 1965 in California and died 24 Jun 1985 in California.

B43368732. Richard Lyn Vestal, second child and first son of Zada Pounds and James Vestal, born 19 Mar 1948 at San Jose, Santa Clara County, California.

B4336874. Loye A.V. Pounds, fourth

child and third son of Howard Pounds and Gertrude Coffee, born 18 Mar 1926 in Haskell County, Texas. Married 1967 to Alice Varnadoe. Loye Pounds and Alice Varnadoe had issue, which was the eleventh generation in America:

B43368741. Allison Marye Pounds, first child and first daughter of Loye Pounds and Alice Varnadoe, born 2 Oct 1967 in California and died 8 Apr 1986 in California.

B43368742. Cynthia Pounds, second child and second daughter of Loye Pounds and Alice Varnadoe, born 6 Jun 1969.

B4336875. Marvin Lynn Pounds, fifth child and fourth son of Howard Pounds and Gertrude Coffee, born 5 Apr 1931 in New Mexico.

B4336876. Fern Lonelle Pounds, sixth child and second daughter of Howard Pounds and Gertrude Coffee, born 20 Dec 1933 in Texas. Married 1956 to Steve Stuart Allen. Married secondly 1972 to Jerry Sisson. Fern Pounds and Steve Allen had issue, which was the eleventh generation in America:

B43368761. Brian Allen, first child and first son of Fern Pounds and Steve Allen, born 29 Apr 1957. Married Jan 1991 at Reno, Washoe County, Nevada to Andrea Swan. Brian Allen and Andrea Swan had issue, which was the twelth generation in America:

B433687611. Chelsea Duane Allen, first child and first son of Brian Allen and Andrea Swan, born 7 Apr 1991 in California.

B43368762. Jeff Allen, second child and second son of Fern Pounds and Steve Allen, born 12 May 1959. Married 30 Aug 1986 to Jackee Ellis. Jeff Allen and Jackee Ellis had issue, which was the twelth generation in America:

B433687621. Adelaide Diane Allen, first child and first daughter of Jeff Allen and Jackee Ellis, born 5 Jan 1989 in California.

B433687622. Travis Jeffrey Allen, second child and first son of Jeff Allen and Jackee Ellis, born 8 Jan 1991 in California.

B43368763. Greg Allen, third child and third son of Fern Pounds and Steve Allen, born 3 Jan 1963. Married 30 May 1987 to Carolann

Tosoni. Greg Allen and Carolann Tosoni had issue, which was the twelth generation in America:

B433687631. Ashley Hannah Allen, first child and first daughter of Greg Allen and Carolann Tosoni, born 21 Jul 1990 in California.

B433688. Vera Pounds, eighth child and fourth daughter of Zachariah Pounds and Martha Bethell, born 3 Dec 1898 at Colbert, Bryan County, Oklahoma and died 23 Aug 1981 at Big Spring, Howard County, Texas. Buried at Snyder-Snyder cemetery, Scurry County, Texas. Married 23 Nov 1917 at Rochester, Haskell County, Texas to John Trousdale Gross, son of Charles Richard Gross and Elizabeth (Betty) Maroon, born 9 Oct 1896 at Jackson (Indian Territory), Bryan County, Oklahoma and died 30 Oct 1969 at Big Spring, Howard County, Texas. Buried at Snyder-Snyder cemetery, Scurry County, Texas. Vera Pounds and John Gross had issue, which was the tenth generation in America:

B4336881. Oleta Pauline Gross, first child and first daughter of Vera Pounds and John Gross, born 14 Sep 1919 at Lakecreek, Texas. Married 30 Jun 1940 to Hershel Johnson, born 18 May 1918. Oleta Gross and Hershel Johnson had issue, which was the eleventh generation in America:

B43368811. Caroll Annette Johnson, first child and first daughter of Oleta Gross and Hershel Johnson, born 5 Aug 1942. Married 6 Jul 1963 at Alamogordo, Otero County, New Mexico to John Gustin, born 16 Feb 1949. Carroll Johnson and John Gustin had issue, which was the twelth generation in America:

B433688111. Jamie Shawn Gustin, first child and first son of Carroll Johnson and John Gustin, born 27 Sep 1966. Married Sep 1990 to Kerri ---.

B433688112. John Eric Gustin, second child and second son of Carroll Johnson and John Gustin, date and place of birth unknown.

B43368812. Sheron Lee Johnson, second child and second daughter of Oleta Gross and Hershel Johnson, born 5 Mar 1947. Married 19 Jun 1965 at Alamogordo, Otero County,

New Mexico to Bruce Thomas Crosby, born 9 Jul 1945. Sheron Johnson and Bruce Crosby had issue, which was the twelth generation in America:

B433688121. Velvet Renee Crosby, first child and first daughter of Sheron Johnson and Bruce Crosby, born 30 Dec 1966.

B433688122. Kelly Shane Crosby, second child and second daughter of Sheron Johnson and Bruce Crosby, born 31 Oct 1968.

B4336882. Gaston T. Gross, second child and first son of Vera Pounds and John Gross, born 14 Nov 1921 at Hermleigh, Scurry County, Texas and died 10 Mar 1922 at Hermleigh, Scurry County, Texas. Buried at Snyder cemetery, Scurry County, Texas.

B4336883. A.J. Gross, third child and second son of Vera Pounds and John Gross, born 10 Feb 1923 at Hermleigh, Scurry County, Texas. Married 8 Sep 1945 to Lois Beverly Erickson, born 19 May 1926 at Noonan, Divide County, North Dakota. A.J. Gross and Lois Erickson had issue, which was the eleventh generation in America:

B43368831. Carla Jayne (twin) Gross, first child and first daughter of A.J. Gross and Lois Erickson, born 8 Jun 1946 at Big Spring, Howard County, Texas. Married 8 Sep 1967 at Brownwood, Brown County, Texas to Michael John Machate, born 27 Nov 1946 at Spokane, Spokane County, Washington. Carla Gross and Michael Machate had issue, which was the twelth generation in America:

B433688311. John Michael Machate, first child and first son of Carla Gross and Michael Machate, born 2 Mar 1970 at Bergstrom AFB, Texas. Married 19 Dec 1990 to Tandi O'Dine Tucker, born 19 Mar 1971 at Abilene, Taylor County, Texas.

B433688312. Kevin Jason Machate, second child and second son of Carla Gross and Michael Machate, born 19 Oct 1971 at Bergstrom AFB, Texas.

B43368832. Charles Wayne (twin) Gross, second child and first son of A.J. Gross and Lois Erickson, born 8 Jun 1946 at Big Spring, Howard County, Texas. Married 10 Nov 1972 to Bobbie Blankenship, born 13 Sep 1936.

B43368833. Terry Lynn Gross, third child and second daughter of A.J. Gross and Lois Erickson, born 15 Nov 1955 at Charleston, Charleston County, South Carolina. Married 21 Dec 1973 to Jeffery Gregory. Married secondly 16 Apr 1980 at Austin, Travis County, Texas to Stephen Anthony Sutton, born Jul 1957 at Five Points, Chambers County, Alabama. Terry Gross and Jeffery Gregory had issue, which was the twelth generation in America:

B433688331. Brittany Nicole Gregory, first child and first daughter of Terry Gross and Jeffery Gregory, born 25 Dec 1983 at Walter Reed Army Hospital, Washington, D.C.

B433688332. Anthony John Gregory, second child and first son of Terry Gross and Jeffery Gregory, born 21 Aug 1991 at Lackland AFB, Bexar County, Texas.

B4336884. Doris Evelyn Gross, fourth child and second daughter of Vera Pounds and John Gross, born 23 Nov 1924 at Hermleigh, Scurry County, Texas. Married 12 Jan 1944 to Percy Oscar Maneval, born 23 Dec 1923. Doris Gross and Percy Maneval had issue, which was the eleventh generation in America:

B43368841. Nancy Eugene Maneval, first child and first daughter of Doris Gross and Percy Maneval, born 18 Apr 1946 in Washington. Married 1 Oct 1965 to Paul Robert Baron, born 1 Aug 1946. Nancy Maneval and Paul Baron had issue, which was the twelth generation in America:

B433688411. Michelle Annette Baron, first child and first daughter of Nancy Maneval and Paul Baron, born 10 Jun 1966 in Washington. Married 1990 to Wes Pond.

B433688412. Jeffery Paul Baron, second child and first son of Nancy Maneval and Paul Baron, born 1 May 1970 in Washington.

B433688413. Jason Christopher Baron, third child and second son of Nancy Maneval and Paul Baron, born 5 Mar 1974 in Washington.

B433688414. Justin Eric Baron, fourth child and third son of Nancy Maneval and Paul Baron, born 28 Nov 1975 in Washington.

B433688415.　　　Jared Michael Baron, fifth child and fourth son of Nancy Maneval and Paul Baron, born 21 Jul 1978 in Washington.

B43368842.　　　Patricia Ann Maneval, second child and second daughter of Doris Gross and Percy Maneval, born 29 Mar 1949 in Washington. Married 5 Mar 1977 in Washington to John Fuller, born 9 Jan 1940. Patricia Maneval and John Fuller had issue, which was the twelth generation in America:

B433688421. Andrew John Fuller, first child and first son of Patricia Maneval and John Fuller, born 15 Dec 1977 in Washington.

B43368843.　　　Peggy Marie Maneval, third child and third daughter of Doris Gross and Percy Maneval, born 16 Jun 1951 in Washington. Married Dale Jacobsen, born 19 Mar 1946. Peggy Maneval and Dale Jacobsen had issue, which was the twelth generation in America:

B433688431. Kimberly Ann Jacobsen, first child and first daughter of Peggy Maneval and Dale Jacobsen, born 3 Jul 1972 in Washington.

B433688432.　　　Brenda Jacobsen, second child and second daughter of Peggy Maneval and Dale Jacobsen, born 4 Jan 1974 in Washington.

B433688433.　　　Ryan Jake Jacobsen, third child and first son of Peggy Maneval and Dale Jacobsen, born 17 Oct 1980 in Washington.

B43368844.　　　Richard John Maneval, fourth child and first son of Doris Gross and Percy Maneval, born 28 Jul 1953 in Washington. Married 1989 to Andre ---.

B43368845.　　　Barbara Kay Maneval, fifth child and fourth daughter of Doris Gross and Percy Maneval, born 16 Jun 1955 in Washington. Married Anthony Pezzullo. Married secondly to Jim Tobin. Barbara Maneval and Anthony Pezzullo had issue, which was the twelth generation in America:

B433688451. Joshua Lee Pezzullo, first child and first son of Barbara

Maneval and Anthony Pezzullo, born 19 Sep 1977 in Washington.

B4336885. Bettie Dean (twin) Gross, fifth child and third daughter of Vera Pounds and John Gross, born 18 Apr 1929 in Texas. Married 16 Jul 1950 to Loyd Barnett Crow, born 25 Feb 1919 and died 26 Jan 1993 at Jacksonville, Cherokee County, Texas. Bettie Gross and Loyd Crow had issue, which was the eleventh generation in America:

B43368851. Phillip Crow, first child and first son of Bettie Gross and Loyd Crow, born 11 Aug 1951. Married Patricia Copeland.

B43368852. Gayla Jean Crow, second child and first daughter of Bettie Gross and Loyd Crow, born 11 Feb 1953. Married 9 Sep 1972 to Barry Gene Campbell. Gayla Crow and Barry Campbell had issue, which was the twelth generation in America:

B433688521. Jennifer Gail Campbell, first child and first daughter of Gayla Crow and Barry Campbell, born 29 Jan 1974.

B433688522. Wendy Michelle Campbell, second child and second daughter of Gayla Crow and Barry Campbell, born 10 Feb 1978.

B43368853. Ottis Lynn Crow, third child and second son of Bettie Gross and Loyd Crow, born 11 Oct 1954. Married Virginia ---. Married secondly Jo Gayle ---. Married thirdly 1990 to --- ---. Ottis Crow and Virginia --- had issue, which was the twelth generation in America:

B433688531. Christie Lynn Crow, first child and first daughter of Ottis Crow and Virginia ---, date and place of birth unknown.

B433688532. April Dawn Crow, second child and second daughter of Ottis Crow and Virginia ---, date and place of birth unknown.

B433688533. Jeremiah Lloyd Crow, third child and first son of Ottis Crow and Virginia ---, date and place of birth unknown.

B433688534. Joshua

Thomas Crow, fourth child and second son of Ottis Crow and Virginia ---, date and place of birth unknown.

B433688535. Infant Crow, fifth child and whose sex was not defined, date and place of birth unknown.

B43368854. Valarie Dean Crow, fourth child and second daughter of Bettie Gross and Loyd Crow, born 23 Jun 1956. Married 1978 to John McMullen. Married 1989 in Texas to David Prather. Valarie Crow and John McMullen had issue, which was the twelth generation in America:

B433688541. Stephanie Ann McMullen, first child and first daughter of Valarie Crow and John McMullen, born 24 Apr 1979 in California.

B433688542. Sean Patrick McMullen, second child and first son of Valarie Crow and John McMullen, born 16 Apr 1981 in California.

B43368855. Beattie La Joan Crow, fifth child and third daughter of Bettie Gross and Loyd Crow, born 22 Nov 1959. Married Charles Ray Copeland. Beattie Crow and Charles Copeland had issue, which was the twelth generation in America:

B433688551. Cody Lane Copeland, first child and first son of Beattie Crow and Charles Copeland, born 7 Jan 1979 in Texas.

B433688552. Darrell Glen Copeland, second child and second son of Beattie Crow and Charles Copeland, born 29 Aug 1981 in Texas.

B43368856. Laura Denise Crow, sixth child and fourth daughter of Bettie Gross and Loyd Crow, born 15 Nov 1960. Married 1982 to Kirk Ellis. Laura Crow and Kirk Ellis had issue, which was the twelth generation in America:

B433688561. Adrian Scott Ellis, first child and first son of Laura Crow and Kirk Ellis, born 19 May 1982 in Texas.

B433688562. Amber Cherie Ellis, second child and first daughter of Laura Crow and Kirk Ellis, born 11 Aug 1983 in Texas.

B433688563. Abigail Joy

Ellis, third child and second daughter of Laura Crow and Kirk Ellis, born 12 Nov 1984 in Texas.

B4336886. Betty Jean (twin) Gross, sixth child and fourth daughter of Vera Pounds and John Gross, born 18 Apr 1929 in Texas. Married 26 Nov 1946 to Grady Max Walker, born 15 Jul 1927. Betty Gross and Grady Walker had issue, which was the eleventh generation in America:

B43368861. Arlis Lane Walker, first child and first son of Betty Gross and Grady Walker, born 2 Feb 1953 in Texas. Married 18 Dec 1981 in Texas to Sherry Holmes, born 6 Jan 1962. Arlis Walker and Sherry Holmes had issue, which was the twelth generation in America:

B433688611. Taggart Lane Walker, first child and first son of Arlis Walker and Sherry Holmes, born 27 May 1983 at Austin, Travis County, Texas.

B433688612. Danielle Nicole Walker, second child and first daughter of Arlis Walker and Sherry Holmes, born 3 Feb 1986 at Austin, Travis County, Texas.

B43368862. Ramona Dean Walker, second child and first daughter of Betty Gross and Grady Walker, born 23 Oct 1954 in Texas. Married 1980 to Gus Eckert.

B43368863. Twila Jean Walker, third child and second daughter of Betty Gross and Grady Walker, born 28 May 1958 in Texas. Married M. Townsend. Married secondly Kerry Denson. Twila Walker and M. Townsend had issue, a son, adopted by Kerry Denson, and the child was in the twelth generation in America:

B433688631. Charlie Wilfred (Townsend) Denson, first child and first son of Twila Walker and Kerry Denson, born 1979 in Texas.

B43368864. Timothy Allen Walker, fourth child and son of Betty Gross and Grady Walker, born 14 Apr 1960 in Texas. Married --- ---. Married secondly to Christi ---. Timothy Walker and --- --- had issue, which was the twelth generation in America:

B433688641. Tye Walker, first child and first son of Timothy Walker and --- ---, date and place of birth unknown.

B4336887. Easter Laverne Gross, seventh child and fifth daughter of Vera Pounds and John Gross, born 4 Apr 1931 in Texas. Married 16 Dec 1949 at Big Spring, Howard County, Texas to Claude Irvin Morris, born 24 Feb 1925 and died 16 Jul 1983 at Big Spring, Howard County, Texas. Easter Gross and Claude Morris had issue, which was the eleventh generation in America:

B43368871. Martha Ann Morris, first child and first daughter of Easter Gross and Claude Morris, born 19 Apr 1956 in Texas. Married 26 Feb 1976 in Texas to Bruce Myers, born 28 Nov 1954. Martha Morris and Bruce Myers had issue, which was the twelth generation in America:

B433688711. Jeremy Myers, first child and first son of Martha Morris and Bruce Myers, born 2 May 1980 in Texas.

B4336888. Donald Ray Gross, eighth child and third son of Vera Pounds and John Gross, born 25 Oct 1933 in Texas. Married 1954 to Irene Hood. Married secondly 8 Jun 1980 in California to Beverly Link. Donald Gross and Irene Hood had issue, which was the eleventh generation in America:

B43368881. Charles Ray Gross, first child and first son of Donald Gross and Irene Hood, born 27 Mar 1955 at Albuquerque, Bernalillo County, New Mexico. Married Terri Anderson. Married secondly 10 Mar 1984 to Tamara Goidzink. Charles Gross and Terri Anderson had issue, which was the twelth generation in America:

B433688811. Cheney Gross, first child and first son of Charles Gross and Terri Anderson, born 9 Jun 1976 in Texas.

B433688812. Charles Ray Gross, Jr., second child and second son of Charles Gross and Terri Anderson, born 2 Mar 1985 in California.

B433688813. Chad Randell Gross, third child and third son of Charles Gross and Terri Anderson, born 30 Dec 1986 in California.

B43368882. Katherin Ann Gross, second child and first daughter of Donald Gross and Irene Hood, born 17 Jan 1957 at Las Vegas, Clark County, Nevada. Married 2 Aug 1974 to Steven Ray. Katherin Gross and Steven Ray had issue, which was the twelth generation in America:

B433688821. Cody Shane Ray, first child and first son of Katherin Gross and Steven Ray, born 16 Feb 1975 in Texas.

B433688822. Wacy Monroe Ray, second child and second son of Katherin Gross and Steven Ray, born 12 Sep 1979 in Texas.

B43368883. James Edward Gross, third child and second son of Donald Gross and Irene Hood, born 10 Feb 1960 at Las Vegas, Clark County, Nevada. Married 16 Jun 1985 in Texas to Debbie Evans. James Gross and Debbie Evans had issue, which was the twelth generation in America:

B433688831. Brandon James Gross, first child and first son of James Gross and Debbie Evans, born 16 Jun 1986 in Texas.

B433688832. Lance Taylor Gross, second child and second son of James Gross and Debbie Evans, born 1989 in Abilene, Taylor County, Texas.

B433689. Sarah Dovie Pounds, ninth child and fifth daughter of Zachariah Pounds and Martha Bethell, born 21 Dec 1900 in Haskell County, Texas and died 7 Dec 1992 at Dublin, Comanche County, Texas. Buried Liveoak cemetery, Dublin, Texas. Married 29 Sep 1918 in Texas to Henry Mayberry. Married secondly in Texas 25 Sep 1921 to Albert Sidney Traweek, born 3 Mar 1894 and died 31 Jul 1984 at Dublin, Erath County, Texas. Buried at Dublin, Like Oak cemetery, Texas. Sarah Pounds and Albert Traweek had issue, which was the tenth generation in America:

B4336891. Leslie Albert Traweek, first child and first son of Sarah Pounds and Albert Traweek, born 23 Feb 1923 in Texas and died 18 Feb 1980 at Dallas, Dallas County, Texas. buried at Stevenville, Erath County, Texas. Married 23 Jul 1946 to Joyce Marie Hamilton, born 15 Oct 1927 in Motley County, Texas. Leslie Traweek and Joyce Hamilton had issue, which was the eleventh generation in America:

B43368911. Linda Joyce Traweek, first child and first daughter of Leslie Traweek and Joyce Hamilton, born 12 Dec 1947 at Odessa,

Ector County, Texas. Married 11 Aug 1967 to Eddie Gene Phillips, born 6 Aug 1944 at Weatherford, Parker County, Texas. Linda Traweek and Eddie Phillips had issue, which was the twelth generation in America:

B433689111. Wendy Renee Phillips, first child and first daughter of Linda Traweek and Eddie Phillips, born 27 Dec 1968 at Weatherford, Parker County, Texas.

B43368912. Andrew Lewis Traweek, second child and first son of Leslie Traweek and Joyce Hamilton, born 12 Nov 1956 at Fort Worth, Tarrant County, Texas. Married 10 Nov 1978 at Fort Worth, Tarrant County, Texas to Deborah Ann Liebig. Andrew Traweek and Deborah Liebig had issue, which was the twelth generation in America:

B433689121. Christopher Leslie Traweek, first child and first son of Andrew Traweek and Deborah Liebig, born 20 Mar 1980 at Fort Worth, Tarrant County, Texas.

B433689122. Jeremy Michael Traweek, second child and second son of Andrew Traweek and Deborah Liebig, born 30 Aug 1983 at Fort Worth, Tarrant County, Texas.

B433689123. Nicholas Albert Traweek, third child and third son of Andrew Traweek and Deborah Liebig, born 17 Jul 1990 at Fort Worth, Tarrant County, Texas.

B4336892. William Burrell Traweek, second child and second son of Sarah Pounds and Albert Traweek, born 23 Apr 1928 at Portales, Roosevelt County, New Mexico. Married Peggy June Hancock. Married 17 May 1963 to Jocelence Boase. William Traweek and Peggy Hancock had issue, which was the eleventh generation in America:

B43368921. Debra Ann Traweek, first child and first daughter of William Traweek and Peggy Hancock, born 16 Sep 1952. Married --- Durham. Debra Traweek and --- Durham had issue, which was the twelth generation in America:

B433689211. Kathryn Irene Durham, first child and first daughter of Debra Traweek and --- Durham, born 9 Jun 1986.

B43368922. William Alan Traweek, second child and first son of William Traweek and Peggy Hancock, born 25 Apr 1954. Married --- ---

William Traweek and --- --- had issue, which was the twelth generation in America:

B433689221. Michael Austin Traweek, first child and first son of William Traweek and --- ---, born 19 Jan 1984.

B433689222. Joseph Alan Traweek, second child and second son of William Traweek and --- ---, born 27 Jun 1989.

B43368923. Sheri Lynn Traweek, third child and second daughter of William Traweek and Peggy Hancock, born 30 Sep 1956. Married --- Lafabreque. Sheri Traweek and --- Lafabreque had issue, which was the twelth generation in America:

B433689231. Christopher Shane Lafabreque, first child and first son of Sheri Traweek and --- Lafabreque, born 21 Mar 1985.

B4336893. Bettie Traweek, third child and first daughter of Sarah Pounds and Albert Traweek, date and place of birth unknown. Married Don Harrison. Married secondly to --- Carter. Bettie Traweek and Don Harrison had issue, which was the eleventh generation in America:

B43368931. Gary Don Harrison, first child and first son of Bettie Traweek and Don Harrison, date and place of birth unknown.

B43368932. Pam Harrison, second child and first daughter of Bettie Traweek and Don Harrison, date and place of birth unknown.

B43368933. Brian Harrison, third child and second son of Bettie Traweek and Don Harrison, date and place of birth unknown.

B43368934. Curtis Harrison, fourth child and third son of Bettie Traweek and Don Harrison, date and place of birth unknown.

B4336894. Bobby Joe Traweek, fourth child and third son of Sarah Pounds and Albert Traweek, born 3 Feb 1935 at Hope, Eddy County, New Mexico. Married 29 Jan 1956 to Neva Louise Mote. Bobby Traweek and Neva Mote had issue, which was the eleventh generation in America:

B43368941. Brenda Traweek, first child and first daughter of Bobby Traweek and Neva Mote, born 24 Jan 1957. Married Ben Carroll. Brenda Traweek and Ben Carroll had issue, which was the twelth generation in America:

B433689411. Alecia Carroll,

first child and first daughter of Brenda Traweek and Ben Carroll, born 30 Aug 1985.

B433689412. Adam Carroll, second child and first son of Brenda Traweek and Ben Carroll, born 9 May 1989.

B43368942. Donna Traweek, second child and second daughter of Bobby Traweek and Neva Mote, born 26 Oct 1960. Married --- Watson. Married secondly to --- Moss. Donna Traweek and --- Watson had issue, which was the twelfth generation in America:

B433689421. Tommy Joe Watson, first child and first son of Donna Traweek and --- Watson, born 25 Oct 1981.

B43368942. Donna Traweek, second child and second daughter of Bobby Traweek and Neva Mote, born 26 Oct 1960. Married secondly to --- Moss. Donna Traweek and --- Moss had issue, which was the twelfth generation in America:

B433689421. Bradley David Moss, first child and first son of Donna Traweek and --- Moss, born 26 Jul 1988.

B4336895. James Thomas Traweek, fifth child and fourth son of Sarah Pounds and Albert Traweek, born 15 Jun 1936. Married 8 Feb 1958 to Dorothy Ann Bagwell, born 2 Sep 1937. James Traweek and Dorothy Bagwell had issue, which was the eleventh generation in America:

B43368951. Elizabeth Ann Traweek, first child and first daughter of James Traweek and Dorothy Bagwell, born 12 Nov 1958. Married 12 Jan 1980 to David Lynn Albrecht, born 26 Nov 1955. Elizabeth Traweek and David Albrecht had issue, which was the twelfth generation in America:

B433689511. Amanda Ann Albrecht, first child and first daughter of Elizabeth Traweek and David Albrecht, born 31 Dec 1980.

B433689512. Ashley Lynn Albrecht, second child and second daughter of Elizabeth Traweek and David Albrecht, born 26 Jul 1984.

B43368952. Cynthia Eileen Traweek, second child and second daughter of James Traweek and Dorothy Bagwell, born 4 Mar 1961. Married 20 Aug 1983 to Paul Phillip Grafe, born 12 Nov 1962.

Cynthia Traweek and Paul Grafe had issue, which was the twelth generation in America:

B433689521. Richard Thomas Grafe, first child and first son of Cynthia Traweek and Paul Grafe, born 15 Feb 1987.

B433689522. Stephanie Eileen Grafe, second child and first daughter of Cynthia Traweek and Paul Grafe, born 13 Jan 1989.

B43368953. James Richard Traweek, third child and first son of James Traweek and Dorothy Bagwell, born 12 Aug 1962. Married 20 Jul 1985 to Rebecca Dee Schindler, born 29 May 1965. James Traweek and Rebecca Schindler had issue, which was the twelth generation in America:

B433689531. Rachael Lauren Traweek, first child and first daughter of James Traweek and Rebecca Schindler, born 6 Dec 1989.

B43368954. John Randolph Traweek, fourth child and second son of James Traweek and Dorothy Bagwell, born 8 Apr 1964. Married 17 Jun 1986 to Donna Lynn Mast, born 3 Apr 1967. John Traweek and Donna Mast had issue, which was the twelth generation in America:

B433689541. Heather Lynn Traweek, first child and first daughter of John Traweek and Donna Mast, born 11 Jan 1987.

B433689542. Jordan LaNae Traweek, second child and second daughter of John Traweek and Donna Mast, born 20 Jul 1989.

B433690. Rosa Ella Pounds, tenth child and sixth daughter of Zachariah Pounds and Martha Bethell, born 23 Dec 1902 in Haskell County, Texas and died 26 Aug 1938 at Littlefield, Lamb County, Texas. Married 9 Oct 1919 in Delta County, Texas to John Calvin Beckham, born 31 Jul 1895 in Delta County, Texas and died 5 Mar 1973. Rosa Pounds and John Beckham had issue, which was the tenth generation in America:

B4336901. Hollis Beckham, first child and first son of Rosa Pounds and John Beckham, born 7 Feb 1921 and died 17 Mar 1929.

B4336902. Kenneth Doyle Beckham, second child and second son of Rosa Pounds and John Beckham, born 14 Oct 1922 and died 7 Oct 1979. Married 10 Aug 1947 to Molly Williams. Kenneth Beckham and Molly Williams had issue, which was the eleventh generation in America:

B43369021. Celeste Linell Beckham, first child and first daughter of Kenneth Beckham and Molly Williams, born 11 Jun 1948. Married Jim Mead. Celeste Beckham and Jim Mead had issue, which was the twelth generation in America:

B433690211. Angela Nicole Mead, first child and first daughter of Celeste Beckham and Jim Mead, born 2 May 1983.

B433690212. Troy Evan Mead, second child and first son of Celeste Beckham and Jim Mead, born 27 Feb 1987.

B43369022. Doyle Kenneth Beckham, third child and second son of Kenneth Beckham and Molly Williams, born 16 Aug 1950.

B43369023. Glen Dale Beckham, second child and first son of Kenneth Beckham and Molly Williams, born 26 Aug 1955.

B4336903. Geraldine Beckham, third child and first daughter of Rosa Pounds and John Beckham, born 19 Jul 1925. Married 19 Feb 1946 to J.B. Springer. Geraldine Beckham and J.B. Springer had issue, which was the eleventh generation in America:

B43369031. Sharon Joyce Springer, first child and first daughter of Geraldine Beckham and J.B. Springer, born 27 Jun 1951. Married 20 Feb 1971 to Gary Potter. Sharon Springer and Gary Potter had issue, which was the twelth generation in America:

B433690311. Jerry Glen Potter, first child and first son of Sharon Springer and Gary Potter, born 30 Jan 1972.

B43369032. J.B. Springer, Jr., second child and first son of Geraldine Beckham and J.B. Springer, born 6 Mar 1954. Married 21 Jan 1972 to Patricia Ann Graham. J.B. Springer and Patricia Graham had issue, which was the twelth generation in America:

B433690321. Sheri Ann Springer, first child and first daughter of J.B. Springer and Patricia Graham, born 17 Jun 1972.

B433690322. Rebecca Dawn Springer, second child and second daughter of J.B. Springer and Patricia Graham, born 23 May 1973.

B43369033. Glen Dale Springer,

third child and second son of Geraldine Beckham and J.B. Springer, born 4 Feb 1958. Married Sharon Kay Boswell. Married secondly 3 Oct 1985 to Teresa Ann Gowin. Glen Springer and Sharon Boswell had issue, which was the twelth generation in America:

B433690331. Glen Dale Springer, Jr., first child and first son of Glen Springer and Sharon Boswell, born 2 Apr 1976.

B4336904. Vonda Lee Beckham, fourth child and second daughter of Rosa Pounds and John Beckham, born 29 Mar 1927. Married James William Jones. Married secondly 21 Sep 1978 to Oscar Rex Baird. Vonda Beckham and James Jones had issue, which was the eleventh generation in America:

B43369041. Ladena Raye Jones, first child and first daughter of Vonda Beckham and James Jones, born 16 Aug 1952.

B43369042. James Darrell Jones, second child and first son of Vonda Beckham and James Jones, born 23 Feb 1955. Married Marla McAliley. Married secondly 6 Mar 1987 to Ranah Juanell Brooks. James Jones and Marla McAliley had issue, which was the twelth generation in America:

B433690421. James Damon Jones, first child and first son of James Jones and Marla McAliley, born 2 Feb 1973.

B433690422. Mark Lorne Jones, second child and second son of James Jones and Marla McAliley, born 4 Sep 1979.

B43369043. Renetta Sue Jones, third child and second daughter of Vonda Beckham and James Jones, born 20 Mar 1958. Married Charlie Joe Wheat. Married secondly Mar 1987 to William Neal. Renetta Jones and Charlie Wheat had issue, which was the twelth generation in America:

B433690431. Judy Marie Wheat, first child and first daughter of Renetta Jones and Charlie Wheat, born 7 Nov 1980.

B433690432. Jenifer Rose Wheat, second child and second daughter of Renetta Jones and Charlie Wheat, born 24 Feb 1983.

B4336905. Martha Alice Beckham, fifth child and third daughter of Rosa Pounds and John Beckham, born 29 Mar 1931. Married 16 Feb 1947 to

Harvey Hull. Martha Beckham and Harvey Hull had issue, which was the eleventh generation in America:

B43369051. Alice Elaine Hull, first child and first daughter of Martha Beckham and Harvey Hull, born 30 May 1950. Married 31 Jul 1973 to Nickolas Bukis. Alice Hull and Nickolas Bukis had issue, which was the twelth generation in America:

B433690511. Julie Elaine Bukis, first child and first daughter of Alice Hull and Nickolas Bukis, born 24 Sep 1975.

B433690512. Michelle Mari Bukis, second child and second daughter of Alice Hull and Nickolas Bukis, born 28 Mar 1979.

B43369052. Harvey Howard Hull, second child and first son of Martha Beckham and Harvey Hull, born 4 Sep 1952. Married 20 Oct 1975 to Kristi Linn Ollom. Harvey Hull and Kristi Ollom had issue, which was the twelth generation in America:

B433690521. Jim Taylor Hull, first child and first son of Harvey Hull and Kristi Ollom, born 9 Nov 1980.

B433690522. Adam Marchall Hull, second child and second son of Harvey Hull and Kristi Ollom, born 20 Nov 1983.

B433690523. Kyle Harvey Hull, third child and third son of Harvey Hull and Kristi Ollom, born 4 Aug 1987.

B43369053. Tammy Michelle Hull, third child and second daughter of Martha Beckham and Harvey Hull, born 9 Jun 1964. Married 17 Mar 1983 to Gary Bunkick.

B4336906. Joyce Beckham, sixth child and fourth daughter of Rosa Pounds and John Beckham, born 29 Apr 1933. Married 31 Jul 1954 to Homer Neal Burroughs. Joyce Beckham and Homer Burroughs had issue, which was the eleventh generation in America:

B43369061. William Lynn Burroughs, first child and first son of Joyce Beckham and Homer Burroughs, born 15 Mar 1956. Married 3 Apr 1982 to Linda Sue Watts. William Burroughs and Linda Watts had issue, which was the twelth generation in America:

B433690611. James Ashley Burroughs, first child and first son of William Burroughs and Linda Watts, born 30 Oct 1982.

B433690612. Jon Ross Burroughs, second child and second son of William Burroughs and Linda Watts, born 17 Oct 1986.

B43369062. Jill Ranae Burroughs, second child and first daughter of Joyce Beckham and Homer Burroughs, born 15 Mar 1959. Married 3 Mar 1978 to Damon Ray Andrews. Jill Burroughs and Damon Andrews had issue, which was the twelth generation in America:

B433690621. Damon Eric Andrews, first child and first son of Jill Burroughs and Damon Andrews, born 5 Aug 1982.

B433690622. Tiffany Dawn Andrews, second child and first daughter of Jill Burroughs and Damon Andrews, born 3 Feb 1986.

B4336907. John Keith Beckham Hewlett, seventh child and third son of Rosa Pounds and John Beckham, born 22 Jun 1935. John Keith Beckham was adopted by a family named Hewlett after the death of Rosa Ella Pounds Beckham. John Hewlett married Myrna Jean Kaatz. Married secondly 24 Apr 1982 to Sue Spain. John Hewlett and Myrna Kaatz had issue, which was the eleventh generation in America:

B43369071. John Keith Hewlett, Jr., first child and first son of John Hewlett and Myrna Kaatz, born 30 Oct 1956 at Lubbock, Lubbock County, Texas and died 19 May 1992 at Slaton, Lubbock County, Texas. Buried Green Memorial cemetery.

B43369072. Pamela Kay Hewlett, second child and first daughter of John Hewlett and Myrna Kaatz, born 20 Dec 1962.

B4336908. Glen Dale Beckham Boyett, eighth child and fourth son of Rosa Pounds and John Beckham, born 25 Aug 1938 at Littlefield, Lamb County, Texas. Glen Dale Beckham was adopted by a family named Boyett after the death of Rosa Ella Pounds Beckham. He married 8 Aug 1960 to Shirley Noren. Glen Boyett and Shirley Noren had issue, which was the eleventh generation in America:

B43369081. Kelly Lynn Boyett,

first child and first daughter of Glen Boyett and Shirley Noren, born 7 Dec 1961. Married 23 Jul 1988 to Brian Lane Welsh. Kelly Boyett and Brian Welsh had issue, which was the twelth generation in America:

B433690811. Joshua Lee Welsh, first child and first son of Kelly Boyett and Brian Welsh, born 26 Feb 1991.

B43369082. Kimberly Leigh Boyett, second child and second daughter of Glen Boyett and Shirley Noren, born 3 Mar 1963.

B43369083. Glen Dale Boyett, Jr., third child and first son of Glen Boyett and Shirley Noren, born 19 Apr 1965.

B433691. Farris Samuel Pounds, eleventh child and fifth son of Zachariah Pounds and Martha Bethell, born 18 May 1905 in Haskell County, Texas and died 2 Oct 1972 at Bovina, Parmer County, Texas. Married Mamie ---. Married secondly to Hazel Gilman. Farris Pounds and Mamie --- had issue, which was the tenth generation in America:

B4336911. John Robert Pounds, first child and first son of Farris Pounds and Mamie ---, born 11 Jul 1928 at Wayside, Armstrong County, Texas and died 15 Jun 1976 at Portales, Roosevelt County, New Mexico. Buried at Resthaven, Roosevelt County, New Mexico. Married 2 Jan 1954 to Dona Laura Carmicheal, born 31 Aug 1936 at Fort Wayne, Allen County, Indiana. John Pounds and Dona Carmicheal had issue, which was the eleventh generation in America:

B43369111. Estelle Kathleen Pounds, first child and first daughter of John Pounds and Dona Carmicheal, born 8 May 1955 at Brush, Morgan County, Colorado. Married 14 Jun 1981 to Jerry Robert Evans, Jr., born 26 Jul 1958 at Winfield, Cowley County, Kansas. Estelle Pounds and Jerry Evans had issue, which was the twelth generation in America:

B433691111. Michael Pounds Evans, first child and first son of Estelle Pounds and Jerry Evans, born 16 Mar 1978 at Portales, Roosevelt County, New Mexico.

B433691112. Amanda Tara Michelle Evans, second child and first daughter of Estelle Pounds and Jerry Evans, born 7 Mar 1982 at

Winfield, Cowley County, Kansas.

B433691113.   Nicole   Marie
Evans, third child and second daughter of Estelle
Pounds and Jerry Evans, born 20 Dec 1989 at
Winfield, Cowley County, Kansas.

B43369112.   Karen   Sue   Pounds,
second child and second daughter of John Pounds
and Dona Carmicheal, born 12 Aug 1957 at Brush,
Morgan County, Colorado.   Married George Glen
Wilson. Married secondly 4 Dec 1982 to Edgar Lynn
Dillard.   Karen Pounds and George Wilson had
issue, which was the twelth generation in America:

B433691121.   Deacon   George
Wilson, first child and first son of Karen Pounds
and George Wilson, born 14 Aug 1974 at Portales,
Roosevelt County, New Mexico.

B433691122.   Dereque   Lee
Wilson, second child and second son of Karen
Pounds and George Wilson, born 15 Nov 1976 at
Portales, Roosevelt County, New Mexico.   Dereque
Wilson was adopted by Edgar Lyn Dillard 26 Jul
1985.

B433691123.   Danny   William
Wilson, third child and third son of Karen Pounds
and George Wilson, born 9 Aug 1978 at Portales,
Roosevelt County, New Mexico.   Danny Wilson was
adopted by Edgar Lynn Dillard 27 Jul 1985.

B43369113.   Britton   Lee   Pounds,
third child and first son of John Pounds and Dona
Carmicheal, born 23 Nov 1958 at Brush, Morgan
County, Colorado.   Married Debi Reed.   Married
secondly to Rhonda ---.   Married thirdly to
Elenore Yanez.   Britton Pounds and Debi Reed had
issue, which was the twelth generation in America:

B433691131.   Britton   Don
Pounds, first child and first son of Britton
Pounds and Debi Reed, born 2 Jun 1979 at Norfolk,
Virginia.

B433691132.   Dusten Prentiss
Pounds, second child and second son of Britton
Pounds and Debi Reed, born 18 Oct 1982 at Norfolk,
Virginia and died 15 Jan 1983.

B433691133.   Shawn   Michael
(triplet) Pounds, third child and third son of
Britton Pounds and Debi Reed, born 18 Nov 1989 at
Burbank, Los Angeles County, California.

B433691134. Andrew Lee (triplet) Pounds, fourth child and fourth son of Britton Pounds and Debi Reed, born 18 Nov 1989 at Burbank, Los Angeles, California and died 4 Dec 1989.

B433691135. Jake Allen (triplet) Pouds, fifth child and fifth son of Britton Pounds and Debi Reed, born 18 Nov 1989 at Burbank, Los Angeles County, California and died 25 Dec 1989.

B43369114. Brenda Kay Pounds, fourth child and third daughter of John Pounds and Dona Carmicheal, born 17 Apr 1965. Married 27 Jan 1990 to Bobby Cook.

B43369115. Patricia Ann Pounds, fifth child and fourth daughter of John Pounds and Dona Carmicheal, born 6 Dec 1970 at Topeka, Shawnee County, Kansas. Married Donnie Charles Lee. Married secondly 19 Jul 1986 to Richard Dean Reynolds, born 9 Aug 1956 at Cleveland, Cuyahoga County, Ohio. Patricia Pounds and Donnie Lee had issue, which was the twelth generation in America:

B433691151. Anthony Blake Lee, first child and first son of Patricia Pounds and Donnie Lee, born 20 Nov 1978 at Portales, Roosevelt County, New Mexico.

B433691152. Carolyn Deann Lee, second child and first daughter of Patricia Pounds and Donnie Lee, born 21 Jun 1981 at Slaton, Lubbock County, Texas.

B4336912. Jerry Lou Pounds, second child and second daughter of Farris Pounds and Mamie ---, born 25 Jan 1930. Married --- Pate. Married secondly Ova Vestal Bennett, born 26 Apr 1922. Jerry Pounds and --- Pate had issue, which was the eleventh generation in America:

B43369121. Debra Sue Pate, first child and first daughter of Jerry Pounds and --- Pate, born 11 Jan 1951. Married --- Cox. Debra Pate and --- Cox had issue, which was the twelth generation in America:

B433691211. Saundra Lynn Cox, first child and first daughter of Debra Pate and --- Cox, born 8 Oct 1970.

B433691212. Tamera Louise Cox, second child and second daughter of Debra

Pate and --- Cox, born 10 Sep 1972.

B433691213. Jolyn Cox, third child and third daughter of Debra Pate and --- Cox, born 21 Jul 1974.

B43369122. Farris Lyn Pate, second child and first son of Jerry Pounds and --Pate, born 16 Jan 1953.

B4336913. Martha Lavell Pounds, third child and first daughter of Farris Pounds and Mamie ---, born 10 Feb 1933 at Jackboro, Jack County, Texas. Married Jack G. Crocker. Married secondly 13 Dec 1969 to Calby Brice Wilson. Martha Pounds and Jack Crocker had issue, which was the eleventh generation in America:

B43369131. William David Crocker, first child and first son of Martha Pounds and Jack Crocker, born 25 Jan 1953. Married 14 Jul 1978 to Cynthia J. Bennett. William Crocker and Cynthia Bennett had issue, which was the twelth generation in America:

B433691311. Candace Renea Crocker, first child and first daughter of William Crocker and Cynthia Bennett, born 30 Dec 1979.

B3369132. Donald Glenn Crocker, second child and second son of Martha Pounds and Jack Crocker, born 29 Apr 1956. Married 13 Dec 1979 to Bonnie Gonzalez. Donald Crocker and Bonnie Gonzalez had issue, which was the twelth generation in America:

B433691321. Calby Don Crocker, first child and first son of Donald Crocker and Bonnie Gonzalez, born 5 Oct 1982.

B433691322. Carissa Celeste Crocker, second child and first daughter of Donald Crocker and Bonnie Gonzalez, born 29 Jan 1984.

B433691323. Christa Coleen Crocker, third child and second daughter of Donald Crocker and Bonnie Gonzalez, born 6 Dec 1985.

B43369133. Patricia Marceia Crocker, third child and first daughter of Martha Pounds and Jack Crocker, born 27 Sep 1959. Married 24 Nov 1979 to James E. VanLandingham. Patricia Crocker and James VanLandingham had issue, which was the twelth generation in America:

B433691331. James E. VanLandingham, Jr., first child and first son of

Patricia Crocker and James VanLandingham, born 21 Apr 1981.

B433691332. Tabetha Machele VanLandingham, second child and first daughter of Patricia Crocker and James VanLandingham, born 15 Mar 1983.

B43369134. Tommy Gene Crocker, fourth child and third son of Martha Pounds and Jack Crocker, born 21 Nov 1961.

B4336914. Danny Cuen Pounds, fourth child and third son of Farris Pounds and Mamie --- born 29 May 1935 at Wayside, Armstrong County, Texas. Married 23 Dec 1956 at Bethel, New Mexico to Eva LaDene Gunn, born 30 Jan 1937 at Floyd, Roosevelt County, New Mexico. Danny Pounds and Eva Gunn had issue, which was the eleventh generation in America:

B43369141. Denise Darlene Pounds, first child and first daughter of Danny Pounds and Eva Gunn, born 14 Aug 1958 at Houston, Harris County, Texas.

B43369142. Dan Dwayne Pounds, second child and first son of Danny Pounds and Eva Gunn, born 5 May 1960 at Portales, Roosevelt County, New Mexico. Married 14 Apr 1981 at Woodroe, Lubbock County, Texas to Misti Ann Oats, born 7 Dec 1961. Dan Pounds and Misti Oats had issue, which was the twelth generation in America:

B433691421. Katy Brook Pounds, first child and first daughter of Dan Pounds and Misti Oats, born 17 May 1986.

B43369143. Dusty Deann Pounds, third child and second daughter of Danny Pounds and Eva Gunn, born 6 May 1969 at Lubbock, Lubbock County, Texas.

B4336915. Dee Pounds, fifth child and second daughter of Farris Pounds and Mamie ---, born 12 Mar 1939. Married 18 Feb 1956 to Billy Robert Jamison, born 15 Nov 1936. Dee Pounds and Billy Jamison had issue, which was the eleventh generation in America:

B43369151. Pamela Lee Jamison, first child and first daughter of Dee Pounds and Billy Jamison, born 24 Dec 1956. Married --- Broman. Married secondly Keith Kiser. Pamela Jamison and --- Broman had issue, which was the

539

twelth generation in America:

B433691511. Becky Lee Broman, first child and first daughter of Pamela Jamison and --- Broman, born 6 Mar 1975.

B433691512. James Robert Broman, second child and first son of Pamela Jamison and --- Broman, born 11 May 1981.

B433691513. David Paul Broman, third child and second son of Pamela Jamison and --- Broman, born 5 Jun 1983.

B43369152. Billy Douglas Jamison, second child and first son of Dee Pounds and Billy Jamison, born 12 Jan 1958. Married Tommy Lynn Martin, born 20 Mar 1961. Billy Jamison and Tommy Martin had issue, which was the twelth generation in America:

B433691521. Traci Lee Jamison, first child and first daughter of Billy Jamison and Tommy Martin, born 28 Jul 1976.

B433691522. Billy West (twin) Jamison, second child and first son of Billy Jamison and Tommy Martin, born 9 Aug 1980.

B433691523. Brandon Douglas (twin) Jamison, third child and second son of Billy Jamison and Tommy Martin, born 9 Aug 1980.

B43369153. Kathy Kaye Jamison, third child and second daughter of Dee Pounds and Billy Jamison, born 4 Apr 1962. Married Donald Ray Colls, born 1 Sep 1957. Kathy Jamison and Donald Colls had issue, which was the twelth generation in America:

B433691531. Wesley Chad Colls, first child and first son of Kathy Jamison and Donald Colls, born 10 Sep 1980.

B433691532. Heston Ross Colls, second child and second son of Kathy Jamison and Donald Colls, born 7 Apr 1987.

B43369154. Kevin Robert Jamison, fourth child and second son of Dee Pounds and Billy Jamison, born 28 Jul 1962. Married Tammy McDonald.

B4336916. Sammy Gene Pounds, sixth child and fourth son of Farris Pounds and Mamie -- -, born 3 Mar 1946 at Clovis, Curry County, New Mexico. Married Wanda Jean --. Sammy Pounds and Wanda --- had issue, which was the eleventh

540

generation in America:

B43369161. Tina Lynn Pounds, first child and first daughter of Sammy Pounds and Wanda ---, born at Lubbock, Lubbock County, Texas.

B4336917. Betty Ann Pounds, seventh child and third daughter of Farris Pounds and Mamie ---, born 26 Nov 1948 at Clovis, Curry County, New Mexico. Married --- ---.

B433692. Britton Pounds, twelfth child and seventh son of Zachariah Pounds and Martha Bethell, born 21 Feb 1907 in Haskell County, Texas and died 7 Apr 1986 in San Jose, Santa Clara County, California. Married 5 Jun 1927 at Lubbock, Lubbock County, Texas to Rita Conner. Britton Pounds and Rita Conner had issue, which was the tenth generation in America:

B4336921. --- Pounds, first child but not known if male or female but thought to be male, of Britton Pounds and Rita Conner, born 17 Dec 1929 in Texas.

B4336922. Jack Britton Pounds, second child and second son of Britton Pounds and Rita Conner, born 11 Jul 1931 at Hereford, Deaf Smith County, Texas. Married Elsie Marie Fugate, born 26 Feb 1934 in Oklahoma. Jack Pounds and Elsie Fugate had issue, which was the eleventh generation in America:

B43369221. Jack Dean Pounds, first child and first son of Jack Pounds and Elsie Fugate, born 22 May 1952 at Camp Roberts, California.

B43369222. Gary Wendell Pounds, second child and second son of Jack Pounds and Elsie Fugate, born 25 May 1955 at San Jose, Santa Clara County, California.

B4336923. Melvin Richard Pounds, third child and third son of Britton Pounds and Rita Conner, born 24 Jul 1934 at Slaton, Lubbock County, Texas. Married Frances Chaboya.

B4336924. Barbara Pounds, fourth child and first daughter of Britton Pounds and Rita Conner, born 27 Oct 1944 at Amherst, Lamb County, Texas. Married Steve Pryor.

B4337. Martha A.S. Pounds, seventh child and second daughter of William Pounds and Nancy Slayden, born 1829 at Chattooga, Taliaferro

County, Georgia. Married 30 Oct 1845 in Meriwether County, Georgia to John H. Hay, born 1819 in Carroll County, Georgia. Martha Pounds and John Hay had issue, which was the eighth generation in America:

B43371. Antinet Hay, first child and first daughter of Martha Pounds and John Hay, born 1849 in Meriwether County, Georgia.

B43372. James Hay, second child and first son of Martha Pounds and John Hay, born 1853 in Meriwether County, Georgia.

B43373. Sarah Hay, third child and second daughter of Martha Pounds and John Hay, born 1856 in Meriwether County, Georgia.

B43374. Eugenia Hay, fourth child and third daughter of Martha Pounds and John Hay, born Dec 1859 in Meriwether County, Georgia.

B43375. William House Hay, fifth child and second son of Martha Pounds and John Hay, born 12 Jan 1862 in Meriwether County, Georgia and died 18 Oct 1890 at Woodbury, Meriwether County, Georgia. Married Mollie Hay Marshall.

B43376. Louisa Hay, sixth child and fourth daughter of Martha Pounds and John Hay, born 1864 in Meriwether County, Georgia. Married George Magonisk.

B43377. Stephen Hay, seventh child and third son of Martha Pounds and John Hay, born 1870 in Meriwether County, Georgia.

B4338. Lucy J. Pounds, eighth child and third daughter of William Pounds and Nancy Slayden, born about 1833 in Meriwether County, Georgia. Married 20 Oct 1844 in Wilkes County, Georgia to William H. Coates, born 1820 in Georgia. Lucy Pounds and William Coates had issue, which was the eighth generation in America:

B43381. Nancy E. T. Coates, first child and first daughter of Lucy Pounds and William Coates, born 1847 in Meriwether County, Georgia.

B43382. Sarah A. Coates, second child and second daughter of Lucy Pounds and William Coates, born Apr 1850 in Meriwether County, Georgia.

B434. James Jared Pound, fourth child and third son of Samuel Pound and Sarah Walker, born about 1780 in Onslow County, North Carolina and died 6 Nov 1831 in Columbia County, Georgia. Married 29

Oct 1807 in Columbia County, Georgia to Keziah Jane Simms, daughter of James Simms and Christian Nature, born about 1786 in Georgia and she died 2 Jan 1832 in Columbia County, Georgia. Married secondly 18 Jan 1821 in Wilkes County, Georgia to Rachel Beall, daughter of John Beall and Mary ---, born about 1800.. James Pound and Keziah Simms had issue, which was the seventh generation in America:

B4341. Leroy Pounds, first child and first son of James Pound and Keziah Simms, born 1795 in North Carolina and thought to have died in Tennessee.

B4342. Robert Simms Pounds, second child and second son of James Pound and Keziah Simms, born 7 Nov 1808 in Columbia County, Georgia and died 10 Nov 1871 in Lincoln County, Georgia. Married 10 Jan 1828 in Columbia County, Georgia to Elizabeth (Ella) Fuller, date of birth unknown but she died 8 Nov 1868. Robert Pounds and Elizabeth Fuller had issue, which was the eighth generation in America:

B43421. William Pounds, first child and first son of Robert Pounds and Elizabeth Fuller, born 1829 in Columbia County, Georgia.

B43422. George Pounds, second child and second son of Robert Pounds and Elizabeth Fuller, born 1832 in Columbia County, Georgia.

B43423. Robert Pounds, third child and third son of Robert Pounds and Elizabeth Fuller, born 1837 in Columbia County, Georgia.

B43424. Mary Pounds, fourth child and first daughter of Robert Pounds and Elizabeth Fuller, born 1845 in Columbia County, Georgia.

B4343. Albert Walker Pounds, third child and third son of James Pound and Keziah Simms, born 9 Nov 1809 in Georgia and died 22 Sep 1812.

B4344. Hillard Pounds, fourth child and fourth son of James Pound and Keziah Simms, born 16 Sep 1810 in Georgia.

B4345. David Pounds, fifth child and fifth son of James Pound and Keziah Simms, born 25 Sep 1812 in Georgia and died 26 Sep 1812.

B4346. Jonathan Thomas Pounds, sixth child and sixth son of James Pound and Keziah Simms, born 19 Aug 1814 in Columbia County, Georgia and died 13 Dec 1895.

B4347.   James   Jared Pounds, Jr., seventh
child and seventh son of James Pound and Keziah
Simms, born 12 Aug 1819 in Columbia County,
Georgia and died 29 Jun 1905 at Lincolnton,
Lincoln County, Georgia.   Buried at Cordele,
Sunnyside   cemetery,   Crisp   County,   Georgia.
Married 25 Apr 1846 in Lincoln County, Georgia to
Elizabeth Johnston, daughter of Alexander Johnston
and Nancy Gullatt, born 17 Sep 1826 at Lincolnton,
Lincoln County, Georgia and died 17 Jan 1901 at
Lincolnton, Lincoln County, Georgia.   Buried at
Cordele,   Sunnyside   cemetery,   Crisp   County,
Georgia.   James Pounds and Elizabeth Johnston had
issue, which was the eighth generation in America:

B43471.   Mary Ann Pounds, first child
and first daughter of James Pounds and Elizabeth
Johnston, born 12 Mar 1849 at Lincolnton, Lincoln
County, Georgia and died 6 Sep 1914 at Lincolnton,
Lincoln County, Georgia.   Buried at Lincolnton,
City cemetery, Lincoln County, Georgia.

B43472. Eliza Jane Pounds, second child
and second daughter of James Pounds and Elizabeth
Johnston, born 21 Feb 1851 in Lincoln County,
Georgia and died 1923 at Augusta, Richmond County,
Georgia.   Buried at Lincolnton City cemetery,
Lincoln County, Georgia.   Married 14 Nov 1872 in
Lincoln County, Georgia to George Woods, date of
birth unknown but he died 14 Nov 1892.

B43473.   Elizabeth   Rebecca   (Becky)
Pounds, third child and third daughter of James
Pounds and Elizabeth Johnston, born 2 Apr 1853 in
Columbia County, Georgia and died 8 Jun 1948 at
Palatka, Putnam County, Florida.   Buried at
Palatka, Oak Hill cemetery, Florida. Married Dec
1881 in Lincoln County, Georgia to Thomas Edwin
Reid, son of Robert Raymond Reid and Rhenannah
Mosley, born 2 Apr 1853 in Columbia County,
Georgia and died 8 Jun 1948 at Palatka, Putnam
County, Florida.   Buried at Palatka, Oak Hill
cemetery, Putnam County, Florida.   Elizabeth
Pounds and Thomas Reid had issue, which was the
ninth generation in America:

B434731. Bessie Reid, first child
and first daughter of Elizabeth Pounds and Thomas
Reid, born about 1879 in Georgia.

B434732. Eva Mae Reid, second child and second daughter of Elizabeth Pounds and Thomas Reid, born 17 Sep 1882 in Lincoln County, Georgia. Married 1 Nov 1899 to Edward Jackson.

B434733. Marie Alice Reid, third child and third daughter of Elizabeth Pounds and Thomas Reid, born 22 Nov 1886 in Lincoln County, Georgia and died 26 Sep 1951 in Georgia. Married Sep 1907 to Holcombe T. Jackson.

B434734. James Edwin Reid, fourth child and first son of Elizabeth Pounds and Thomas Reid, born 23 Aug 1891 in Lincoln County, Georgia and died 29 Jan 1988 at Palatka, Putnam County, Florida. Buried at Palatka, Oak Hill cemetery, Putnam County, Florida. Married 18 Feb 1914 to Betty Elizabeth Dykes. Married secondly 1 Jun 1928 to Margaret Ellen Arnold, daughter of Orris Bertram Arnold and Emma Jane Lively, born 4 Aug 1901 at Byer, Jackson County, Ohio and died 30 Apr 1987 at Palatka, Putnam County, Florida. Buried at Palatka, Oak Hill cemetery, Putnam County, Florida. James Reid and Margaret Arnold had issue, which was the tenth generation in America:

B4347341. Edwin Orris Reid, first child and first son of James Reid and Margaret Arnold, born 10 May 1930 at Palatka, Putnam County, Florida. Married 29 Jun 1955 to Rachel V. Chesser.

B4347342. Ronald Elon Reid, second child and second son of James Reid and Margaret Arnold, born 19 Nov 1933 at Palatka, Putnam County, Florida. Married 15 Sep 1953 to Barbara Jernigan.

B434735. Ethelle Burnia Reid, fifth child and fourth daughter of Elizabeth Pounds and Thomas Reid, born 1 Jan 1893 in Lincoln County, Georgia and died 8 Nov 1989. Married 25 Dec 1910 to George L. Sumner.

B434736. Henry Hatcher Reid, sixth child and second son of Elizabeth Pounds and Thomas Reid, born 18 Sep 1896 at Lithonia, DeKalb County, Georgia and died 1968. Married Clara Synett.

B43474. Alexander Johnston Pounds, fourth child and first son of James Pounds and Elizabeth Johnston, born 6 Jun 1858 in Lincoln

County, Georgia and died 15 May 1908. Buried at Troy, Hober Baptist Church cemetery, Mccormick County, South Carolina. Married 8 Jan 1905 to Josie Lee McCrey. Alexander Pounds and Josie McCrey had issue, which was the ninth generation in America:

B434741. Claudia Pounds, first child and first daughter of Alexander Pounds and Josie McCrey, date and place of birth unknown.

B43475. Thomas Peter Pounds, fifth child and second son of James Pounds and Elizabeth Johnston, born 14 Oct 1859 in Lincoln County, Georgia and died 22 Aug 1913 at Cordele, Crisp County, Georgia. Buried at Cordele, Sunnyside cemetery, Crisp County, Georgia. Married Alice Ward. Thomas Pounds and Alice Ward had issue, which was the ninth generation in America:

B434751. Winina Pounds, first child and first daughter of Thomas Pounds and Alice Ward, date and place of birth unknown.

B434752. Ross Pounds, second child and first son of Thomas Pounds and Alice Ward, date and place of birth unknown.

B434753. T.P. Pounds, third child and second son of Thomas Pounds and Alice Ward, date and place of birth unknown.

B43476. William Henry Pounds, sixth child and third son of James Pounds and Elizabeth Johnston, born 28 Nov 1861 at Bradley, Greenwood County, South Carolina and died 16 Feb 1950 at Houston, Harris County, Texas. Buried at Palatka, Oak Hill cemetery, Putnam County, Florida. Married 24 Dec 1885 at Double Branches, Lincoln County, Georgia to Minnie Lee Fleming, daughter of Hilliard Benjamin Fleming and Lavinia J. Moseley, born 16 Jan 1870 at Double Branches, Lincoln County, Georgia and died 30 May 1928 at Palatka, Putnam County, Florida. Buried at Palatka, Oak Hill cemetery, Putnam County, Florida. William Pounds and Minnie Fleming had issue, which was the ninth generation in America:

B434761. Clinton L. Pounds, first child and first son of William Pounds and Minnie Fleming, born 29 Jul 1887 at Augusta, Richmond County, Georgia and died 15 Jul 1949 at Houston, Harris County, Texas. Buried at Dorough cemetery,

Crisp County, Georgia. Married 25 Dec 1910 in
Georgia to Alma Dorough, born 30 Jul 1893 at
Penia, Crisp County, Georgia and died 18 Oct 1934
in Georgia. Clinton Pounds and Alma Dorough had
issue, which was the tenth generation in America:
B4347611. Maxine Pounds,
first child and first daughter of Clinton Pounds
and Alma Dorough, date of birth unknown at
Cordele, Crisp County, Georgia and date of death
unknown at Cordele, Crisp County, Georgia.
B4347612. Doris Pounds,
second child and second daughter of Clinton Pounds
and Alma Dorough, date of birth unknown at
Cordele, Crisp County, Georgia. Married Woodrow
Cone. Doris Pounds and Woodrow Cone had issue,
which was the eleventh generation in America:
B43476121. Lillian Ann
Cone, first child and first daughter of Doris
Pounds and Woodrow Cone, date and place of birth
unknown.
B43476122. Sonny Cone,
second child and first son of Doris Pounds and
Woodrow Cone, date and place of birth unknown.
B434762. Hilliard Fleming Pounds,
second child and second son of William Pounds and
Minnie Fleming, born 5 May 1889 at Augusta,
Richmond County, Georgia and died 8 Feb 1963 at
Houston, Harris County, Texas. Buried at Houston,
Forest Park cemetery, Harris County, Texas.
Married 11 Jul 1909 to Linnie Lou Sangates, born
12 Nov 1892 and died 24 Dec 1984. Buried at
Houston, Forest Park cemetery, Harris County,
Texas. Hillard Pounds and Linnie Sangates had
issue, which was the tenth generation in America:
B4347621. Charles W. Pounds,
first child and first son of Hilliard Pounds and
Linnie Sangates, date and place of birth unknown.
Married Lillie ---.
B4347622. Alice Pounds,
second child and first daughter of Hilliard Pounds
and Linnie Sangates, date and place of birth
unknown. Married Joe Brown. Alice Pounds and Joe
Brown had issue, which was the eleventh generation
in America:
B43476221. Annette
Brown, first child and first daughter of Alice

Pounds and Joe Brown, date and place of birth unknown.

B43476222. Joe Brown, Jr., second child and first son of Alice Pounds and Joe Brown, date and place of birth unknown.

B4347623. Hilliard Henry Pounds, third child and first son of Hilliard Pounds and Linnie Sangates, date and place of birth unknown. Married Betty ---.

B4347624. Mary Pounds, fourth child and second daughter of Hillard Pounds and Linnie Sangates, date and place of birth unknown.

B434763. Thyrza Luvenia Pounds, third child and first daughter of William Pounds and Minnie Fleming, born 11 Apr 1891 at Augusta, Richmond County, Georgia and died 1967 at Palatka, Putnam County, Florida. Buried at Palatka, Oak Hill cemetery, Putnam County, Florida.

B434764. Robert Raymond Pounds, fourth child and third son of William Pounds and Minnie Fleming, born 17 Feb 1893 at Lincolnton, Lincoln County, Georgia and died 8 Jul 1917 at Glenrock, Converse County, Wyoming. Buried at Thomasville, Laurel Hill cemetery, Thomas County, Georgia.

B434765. Albert Johnston Pounds, fifth child and fourth son of William Pounds and Minnie Fleming, born 14 Jan 1895 at Augusta, Richmond County, Georgia and died Dec 1950 at Trinidad, British West Indies. Married Dolly (Collie) Proudfoot. Albert Pounds and Dolly Proudfoot had issue, which was the tenth generation in America:

B4347651. Steve Pounds, first child and first son of Albert Pounds and Dolly Proudfoot, born about 1933 at Trinidad, British West Indies.

B4347652. Sally Pounds, second child and first daughter of Albert Pounds and Dolly Proudfoot, born 1938 at Trinidad, British West Indies.

B434766. Mary Elizabeth Pounds, sixth child and second daughter of William Pounds and Minnie Fleming, born 8 Jan 1898 at Cordele, Crisp County, Georgia and died 28 Apr 1986 at Galax, Carroll County, Virginia. Buried at Galax,

Carroll County, Virginia. Married 9 May 1929 to Carlisle Frank Carpenter, born Mar 1896 in Carroll County, Virginia and died 21 Sep 1980 at Lynchburg, Appamattox County, Virginia. Buried at Galax, Carroll County, Virginia.

B434767. Agnes Estelle Pounds, seventh child and third daughter of William Pounds and Minnie Fleming, born 29 Jul 1899 at Cordele, Crisp County, Georgia and died 1974 at Houston, Harris County, Texas. Buried at Houston, South Park cemetery, Harris County, Texas. Married 6 Apr 1919 in Georgia to Thaddeus Crayton Johnson, born 1888 and died 1940 at Houston, Harris County, Texas. Buried at Houston, South Park cemetery, Harris County, Texas. Agnes Pounds and Thaddeus Johnson had issue, which was the tenth generation in America:

B4347671. Thaddeus Crayton Johnson, Jr., first child and first son of Agnes Pounds and Thaddeus Johnson, born at Thomasville, Thomas County, Georgia and died in Germany. Buried at Houston, Harris County, Texas.

B4347672. Ruth Johnson, second child and first daughter of Agnes Pounds and Thaddeus Johnson, born about 1930 at Miami, Dade County, Florida. Married James Gillespie. Ruth Johnson and James Gillespie had issue, which was the eleventh generation in America:

B43476721. Darla Gillespie, first child and first daughter of Ruth Johnson and James Gillespie, born about 1945 at Houston, Harris County, Texas.

B434768. Jeannette Johnston Pounds, eighth child and fourth daughter of William Pounds and Minnie Fleming, born 8 Nov 1901 at Cordele, Crisp County, Georgia and died 22 Mar 1967 at Houston, Harris County, Texas. Buried at Houston, Brookside Memorial Park, Harris County, Texas. Married 31 Mar 1923 at Palatka, Putnam County, Florida to Paul Lesley Curtis, Sr., son of James Caldwell Curtis and Louisa Jane Wilcox, born 17 Sep 1901 at Morton's Gap, Hopkins County, Kentucky and died 14 May 1957 at Houston, Harris County, Texas. Buried at Houston, Brookside Memorial Park cemetery, Harris County, Texas. Jeannette Pounds and Paul Curtis had issue, which was the tenth generation in America:

B4347681.   Barbara   Jean
Curtis, first child and first daughter of
Jeannette Pounds and Paul Curtis, born 18 Aug 1925
at Lake Worth, Palm Beach County, Florida.
Married 17 Jun 1945 at Houston, Harris County,
Texas to Wallace Eck Collins, born 21 Mar 1924 at
Galveston, Galveston County, Texas.   Barbara
Curtis and Wallace Collins had issue, which was
the eleventh generation in America:

B43476811.   Vickie Lee
Collins, first child and first daughter of Barbara
Curtis and Wallace Collins, born 8 Dec 1946 at
Houston, Harris County, Texas.   Married 14 Jul
1973 at Clute, Brazonia County, Texas to Gary Gene
Miles.

B43476812. Wallace Craig
Collins, second child and first son of Barbara
Curtis and Wallace Collins, born 12 Mar 1951 at
Houston, Harris County, Texas.

B43476813.   Leslie Jean
Collins, third child and second daughter of
Barbara Curtis and Wallace Collins, born 15 Sep
1953 at Freeport, Brazonia County, Texas.

B4347682.   Paul L. Curtis,
Jr., second child and first son of Jeannette
Pounds and Paul Curtis, born 7 Oct 1926 at Lake
Worth, Palm Beach County, Florida. Married 16 Feb
1947 at Houston, Harris County, Texas to Reba Fern
Briggs.

B434769.   Annie Wallace Pounds,
ninth child and fifth daughter of William Pounds
and Minnie Fleming, born 17 Nov 1905 at Cordele,
Crisp County, Georgia.   Married 27 Apr 1930 to
Harry Alfred Dale, born 18 Aug 1904 at St.
Augustine, St. Johns County, Florida.   Annie
Pounds and Harry Dale had issue, which the
tenth generation in America:

B4347691. Freddie Dale, first
child and first son of Annie Pounds and Harry
Dale, date and place of birth unknown.

B43477. Jeannette Pounds, seventh child
and fourth daughter of James Pounds and Elizabeth
Johnston, born 22 Nov 1865 in Lincoln County,
Georgia and died 31 Oct 1891 at Augusta, Richmond
County, Georgia.   Buried at Augusta, Magnolia

cemetery, Richmond County, Georgia. Married 15 Nov 1883 to Samuel McClellan, born 1858 and died Jun 1886.

B43478. Robert Sims Pounds, eighth child and fourth son of James Pounds and Elizabeth Johnston, born 20 Mar 1867 in Lincoln County, Georgia and died 12 Oct 1871.

B43479. James Madison Pounds, ninth child and fifth son of James Pounds and Elizabeth Johnston, born 11 Jul 1871 at Lincolnton, Lincoln County, Georgia and 20 Oct 1932 at Palatka, Putnam County, Florida. Buried at Palatka, Oak Hill cemetery, Putnam County, Florida. Married 20 Jan 1904 to Leticia Chatham Rankin, born 6 Dec 1885 in Georgia and died 11 Jul 1979 at Palatka, Putnam County, Florida. Buried at Palatka, Oak Hill cemetery, Putnam County, Florida.

B4348. Madison Pounds, eighth child and eighth son of James Pound and Keziah Simms, born 1821 in Columbia County, Georgia. Married about 1842 in Warren County, Georgia to Martha T. ---, born about 1820 in Georgia. Madison Pounds and Martha --- had issue, which was the eighth generation in America:

B43481. Elizabeth M. Pounds, first child and first daughter of Madison Pounds and Martha ---, born 1843 in Warren County, Georgia.

B43482. Nathan Pounds, second child and first son of Madison Pounds and Martha ---, born 1844 in Warren County, Georgia.

B43483. Rachel R. Pounds, third child and second daughter of Madison Pounds and Martha ---, born 1846 in Warren County, Georgia.

B43484. John E. Pounds, fourth child and second son of Madison Pounds and Martha ---, born 1849 in Madison County, Georgia.

B435. Isham (1) Pounds, fifth child and fourth son of of Samuel Pound and Sarah Walker, born 10 Jan 1782 in Onslow County, North Carolina and died 5 Apr 1820 in Columbia County, Georgia. Married 5 Apr 1808 at the home of David Walker in Columbia County, Georgia to Sarah Hendley. The following information is found in the Court Records of Hancock County, Georgia Book A B page 272, January 23, 1793:

THIS INDENTURE WITNESSETH that Samuel Pound, late of Georgia in the County of Washington hath bound and by these presents doth bind his son Isham to James Britten and his wife Liddy, citizens of the County and State above written to serve them from the day and date hereof until he shall arrive to the age of twenty years, during all which time he the said Isham Pounds his said Master shall faithfully serve, his secrets keep, his lawful commands every where gladly obey, he shall do no damage to his said Master nor see it to be done by others without letting or giving notice thereof to his said Master, he shall not waste his Master's goods nor lend them unlawfully to others, he shall not commit fornication nor contract matrimony within the said term, at cards, dice or any unlawful game he shall not play, whereby his said Master may be damaged with his own goods or the goods of others during the said Term without license of his said Master, he shall neither buy nor sell, he shall not absent himself day or night from his Master's service without his leave nor haunt ale houses, taverns or play horses but in all things behave himself as a faithful Indenture ought to do during the said Term and the said Master shall give the said Isham Pounds one year schooling also furnish him the said Isham Pounds with sufficient meat, drink, apparel, washing and lodging fitting for an Indenture during the said Term and for the true performance of all and any the said covenants and agreements either of the said parties bind themselves unto the other by these Presents. IN WITNESS WHEREOF they have interchangeably put their hands and seals this 23rd day of January one thousand seven hundred and ninety three and in the seventeenth year of the sovereignty and Independence of America:
Test: Harmon Runnels, J.P.

                                             his
                                   Samuel   X   Pound
        SEAL
                                           mark

B436. Leroy Pound, sixth child and fifth son of Samuel Pound and Sarah Walker, born 1795 in Onslow

552

County, North Carolina.

B44. William Pound, fourth child and fourth son of John Pound IV and his Indian wife, born about 1749 in Culpeper County, Virginia, died about 1823 in Culpeper County, Virginia. William married Frances Underwood, daughter of Lott Underwood and Mary Hackley. Through Frances Underwood, there is what might be termed a left-handed connection of the Pound family to our nation's thirty-third President. Let us back up and show the relationship as follows:

George Mott married Elizabeth ---
Ellen Mott married Richard Shippy
Jael Shippy marrried William Underwood
Lott Underwood married Mary Hackley
Frances Underwood married William Pound
> One of Ellen Mott's sisters enters the picture

Margaret Mott married Alexander Doniphan
Mott Doniphan married Rosanna Anderson
Alexander Doniphan married Magdaline Monteith
Richard Shipp married Elizabeth Doniphan
William Truman married Emma Shipp
Anderson S. Truman married Mary J. Holmes
John A. Truman married Martha E. Young
Harry S Truman was their son.

John Anderson Truman married Martha E. Young and their son later in life became the nations thirty-third President. Harry's parents wanted to honor both grandfathers by giving their son a middle name that began with an S, but they couldn't agree on which grandpa to honor, so they compromised with just plain S with a period.

And on another note, Frances Underwood's grandfather, William Underwood, was a member of the House of Burgesses in 1652 and married a great-granddaughter of Pocahontas. It was said that Frances Longworth Underwood showed strongly marked Indian features.

William Pound and Frances Underwood had issue, which was the sixth generation in America:

B441. Lott Underwood Pound, first child and first son of William Pound and Frances Underwood, married on 8 Jun 1798 in Culpeper County, Virginia to Patsy Faulconer, born about

1780 in Virginia.

B442. Molly Pound, second child and first daughter of William Pound and Frances Underwood, married Tarpley Sisson on 26 Jul 1798 in Culpeper County, Virginia.

B443. Richard Pound, third child and second son of William Pound and Frances Underwood, born 1781 in Fairview, Spotsylvania County, Virginia and died in 1812 in Fairview, Spotsylvania County, Virginia. Buried at Fairview cemetery, Spotsylvania County, Virginia. He married in 1801 in Spotsylvania County, Virginia to Ann (Nancy) Lyon of Spotsylvania County, Virginia, daughter of James Lyon and Mary Longwill. Ann was born 1782, at Falmouth, Stafford County, Virginia, and died 31 Dec 1860 at Chancellorville, Spotsylvania County, Virginia. Buried Fairview Cemetery, Spotsylvania County, Virginia. Ann Lyon, widow of Captain Richard Pound, married secondly in 1814 George Chancellor, of "Chancellorsville", Spotsylvania County, Virginia. Ann Lyon Pound and George Chancellor had issue, which was the seventh generation in America:

B4430. Melzie Sanford Chancellor, first child and first son of Ann Lyon Pound and George Chancellor, date and place of birth unknown. Melzie Chancellor married Lucy Fox Frazier. Melzie Chancellor and Lucy Frazier had issue, which was the eighth generation in America:

B44301. Mary Edwards Chancellor, first child and first daughter of Melzie Chancellor and Lucy Frazier, date and place of birth unknown.

B44302. Annastasia Chancellor, second child and second daughter of Melzie Chancellor and Lucy Frazier, date and place of birth unknown.

B4430. Melzie Sanford Chancellor, first child and first son of Ann Lyon Pound and George Chancellor, date and place of birth unknown. Married secondly to Bettie W. Caldwell. It was after George Chancellor's death that the large brick "Chancellorsville House" was built. It was built by William Lorman of Baltimore for his half-sister, Ann Lyon Pound Chancellor. The

House was built to be used as an inn, for the
Plank Road ran though the estate, the main road
between Orange, Madison, and all those rich up-
country counties and Fredericksburg, the head of
navigation. The house was partially destroyed in
May 1863 and totally destroyed in November 1927.
Richard was a Captain in the War of 1812. He
lived at Fairview, Spotsylvania County, Virginia
and died intestate, leaving 4 infant daughters.
After his death, administration of his estate was
granted to his wife Ann. Richard Pound and Ann
(Nancy) Lyon's issue was the sixth generation in
America:

B4431. Frances (Fannie) Longwill
Pound born 22 Jul 1803 in Spotsylvania County,
Virginia, first child and first daughter of
Richard Pound and Ann Lyon, died 9 Jul 1892 in Oak
Grove, Spotsylvania County, Virginia. Buried at
Fairview cemetery, Spotsylvania County, Virgiania.
Fannie married 8 Jan 1823 at Forest Hall,
Spotsylvania County, Virginia to Major Sanford
Chancellor, born 8 Jan 1791 at Forest Hall,
Spotvylvania County, Virginia, and he died 1860 at
Forest Hall, Spotsylvania County, Virginia.
Buried at Fairview cemet4ery, Spotsylvania County,
Virginia. He was a son of John Chancellor and
Elizabeth Edwards, in Spotsylvania County,
Virginia. Fannie and Sanford had issue, which was
the eighth generation in America:

B44311. John Andrew Chancellor,
first child and first son of Fannie Pound and
Sanford Chancellor, born 31 Dec 1823 in
Spotsylvania County, Virginia; died 28 Sep 1838
Spotsylvania County, Virginia.

B44312. Julia Decarto Chancellor,
second child and first daughter of Fannie Pound
and Sanford Chancellor, born 13 Jul 1825 in
Spotsylvania County, Virginia and died 26 Mar 1904
in Stafford County, Virginia. Married 29 Jan 1846
to Thomas Rogers Chartters, born Cherry Grove,
Stafford County, Virginia; son of William
Chartters and Elizabeth Rogers.

B44313. Mary Edwards Chancellor,
third child and second daughter of Fannie Pound
and Sanford Chancellor, born 7 May 1827 in
Spotsylvania County, Virginia and died 14 Oct 1922

in Spotsylvania County, Virginia. Married Jan 1875 in Virginia to John Thomas Frazer, son of Thomas Fox Frazer and Margaret Magee.

B44314. William Cooper Chancellor, fourth child and second son of Fannie Pound and Sanford Chancellor, born 15 Jan 1829 in Spotsylvania County, Virginia; died 9 Mar 1838 in Spotsylvania County, Virginia.

B44315. Charles William Chancellor. fifth child and third son of Fannie Pound and Sanford Chancellor, born 19 Feb 1832 in Spotsylvania County, Virginia; died 3 Jan 1915 in Baltimore, Baltimore County, Maryland. Married 18 Mar 1863 to Mary Archer Taliaferro, daughter of Alexander Gault Taliaferro and Agnes Marshall, date and place of birth unknown, but she died 24 Mar 1864 in Virginia. Charles William married secondly 18 Feb 1867 at New Orleans, Jefferson Parish, Louisiana to Martha Ann Butler, daughter of William Ormond Butler and Martha Ann Hale. Charles and Mary had issue, which was the ninth generation in America:

B443151. Leah Seddon Chancellor, first child and first daughter of Charles Chancellor and Mary Taliaferro, married H.G. Willis.

B44315. Charles William Chancellor, fifth child and third son of Fannie Pound and Sanford Chancellor, born 19 Feb 1832 in Spotsylvania County, Virginia and died 3 Jan 1915 in Baltimore, Baltimore County, Maryland. Married secondly 18 Feb 1867 to Martha Ann Butler, daughter of William Ormond Butler and Martha Ann Hale. Charles and Martha had issue, which was the ninth generation in America:

B443151. Son Chancellor, first child and first so of Charles Chancellor and Martha Butler, date and place of birth unknown.

B443152. Daughter Chancellor, second child and first daughter of Charles Chancellor and Martha Butler.

B44316. Ann Elizabeth Chancellor, sixth child and third daughter of Fannie Pound and Sanford Chancellor, born 30 Aug 1834 in Spotsylvania County, Virginia; died 17 Nov 1921 at Atlanta, Fulton County, Georgia.

B44317. Jane Hall Chancellor, seventh child and fourth daughter of Fannie Pound and Sanford Chancellor, born 10 Apr 1837 in Spotsylvania County, Virginia; died 1894 in Atlanta, Fulton County, Georgia. Married in Atlanta, Fulton County, Georgia to Henry M. Abbett.

B44318. Frances Douglas Chancellor, eighth child and fifth daughter of Fannie Pound and Sanford Chancellor, born 3 Feb 1840 in Spotsylvania County, Virginia; died 19 Aug 1864 in Chancellorville, Spotsylvania County, Virginia.

B44319. Penelope Abbett (Abbie) Chancellor, ninth child and sixth daughter of Fannie Pound and Sanford Chancellor, born 31 Dec 1841 in Spotsylvania County, Virginia; died 19 Aug 1864 in Chancellorville, Spotsylvania County, Virginia.

B44320. George Sanford Chancellor, tenth child and fourth son of Fannie Pound and Sanford Chancellor, born 31 Mar 1845 in Spotsylvania County, Virginia; died 17 Feb 1878.

B44321. Susan Margaret Chancellor, eleventh child and seventh daughter of Fannie Pound and Sanford Chancellor, born 19 Feb 1847 in Spotsylvania County, Virginia; died 28 Dec 1935 in Spotsylvania County, Virginia. Buried at Fairview cemetery, Spotsylvania County, Virginia. Married 8 Mar 1893 in Virginia to Vespian Chancellor, son of Melzie Sanford Chancellor and Lucy Fox Frazer, born about 1838 in Virginia and died 28 Apr 1908 in Virginia. Buried at Fairview cemetery, Spotsylvania County, Virginia.

B4432. Margaret Lyon Pound, second child and second daughter of Richard Pound and Ann Lyon, born 13 Aug 1806 in Spotsylvania County, Virginia; died 15 Mar 1881 in Spotsylvania County, Virginia. Married 12 Jan 1831 Spotsylvania County, Virginia to Charles C. Bailey, born 1802 at Mill Dale, Spotsylvania County, Virginia. Died 1882 in Virginia. Buried at Fairview cemetery, Spotsylvania County, Virginia.

B4433. Elizabeth Richard Pound, third child and third daughter of Richard Pound and Ann Lyon, born 1808 Spotsylvania County, Virginia;

died 1863 at Chancellorville, Spotsylvania County, Virginia. Married 21 Aug 1834 in Spotsylvania County, Virginia to William Addison Grady, born 1808 in Spotsylvania County, Virginia and died 1862 in Virginia.

B4434. Mary Ann Pound, fourth child and fourth daughter of Richard Pound and Ann Lyon. born 1810 at Chancellorville in Spotsylvania County, Virginia; died 1852 at Chancellorville, Spotsylvania County, Virginia. Buried at Chancellorville, Spotsylvania County, Virginia. Married 5 Nov 1835 to Jacob E. Appler, born 1812 in Virginia and died 1894 in Virginia. Jacob E. Appler married secondly to Ann Monroe Chancellor, daughter of George Chancellor and Ann Lyon Pound Chancellor, born 1882 at Chancellorville, Spotsylvania County, Virginia and died 1895 at Columbus, Muscogee County, Georgia.

B444. Reuben Pound, fourth child and third son of William Pound and Frances Underwood; born about 1780 in Virginia. Reuben married a lady whose name is unknown. This couple was survived by two daughters. These two daughters were the seventh generation in America:

B4441. Reubena Pound, first child and first daughter of Reuben Pound and unknown wife, date and place of birth unknown, married John Hawkins 25 Jun 1850 in Page County, Virginia.

B4442. Ellen Pound, second child and second daughter of Reuben Pound and unknown wife, date and place of birth unknown, married Morgan Bixler 22 Apr 1851 in Page County, Virginia.

B45. Peter Pound, fifth child and fifth son of John Pound and his Indian wife, born about 1752 in Orange County, Virginia.

B46. Richard Pound, sixth child and sixth son of John Pound and his Indian wife, born about 1754 in Orange County, Virginia. Married Ally --

B5. Deborah Pound, fifth child and second daughter of John Pound, Jr. and Deborah Lewis, born 9 Feb 1716 at North Farnham Parish, Richmond County, Virginia.

C. Thomas Pound

C.   Thomas Pound, third child and second son of
John Pound and Elizabeth Joy, born 1687 in North
Farnham Parish, Richmond County, Virginia and died
4 Mar 1718 in Halifax County, Virginia.   Thomas
Pound died in 1718, a little earlier in the same
year that his brother John Pound, Jr. died.   That
left one other brother, Samuel Pound, to survive.
In about 1735, Samuel Pound moved from Richmond
County, Virginia to Germanna, the county seat of
Orange County, Virginia and it is believed that
with his own family he took his nephew John Pound
(3) and raised him as his son.   John began
appearing in the records of Orange and Culpeper
Counties in 1737.   Comparing the death date of
Thomas Pound; the date that Margaret Pound, widow,
applied to be administraror of the estate of
Thomas Pound, Sr., and the birthdate of Elizabeth,
their youngest daughter, it seems that Elizabeth
was born after her father's death, or one or the
other's death date is wrong.   Thomas Pound married
about 1716 in North Farnham Parish, Richmond
County, Virginia to Margaret Bradley.   Thomas
Pound and Margaret Bradley had issue, which was
the fourth generation in America:
   C1.   Sarah Pound, first child and first
daughter of Thomas Pound and Margaret Bradley,
born possibly in North Carolina.
   C2.   Anny Pound, second child and second
daughter of Thomas Pound and Margaret Bradley,
born possibly in North Carolina.
   C3.   Jane Pound, third child and third
daughter of Thomas Pound and Margaret Bradley,
born possibly in North Carolina.
   C4.   Rachel Pound, fourth child and fourth
daughter of Thomas Pound and Margaret Bradley,
born possibly in North Carolina.
   C5.   Ruth Pound, fifth child and fifth
daughter of Thomas Pound and Margaret Bradley,
born possibly in North Carolina.
   C6. Thomas Pound, Jr., sixth child and first
son of Thomas Pound and Margaret Bradley, born 7
Apr 1717 possibly in North Farnham Parish,
Richmond County, Virginia and died 1763 in
Rockingham County, North Carolina.   Thomas Pound

married Jean (Jane?) --- and they had issue, which was the fifth generation in America:

C61. Thomas Pound, first child and first son of Thomas Pound and Jean ---, born about 1730 in Rockingham County, North Carolina and died 10 Apr 1822 in Rockingham County, North Carolina. Married about 1751 to Ann ---. Thomas Pound and Ann --- had issue, which was the sixth generation in America:

C611. John Harvey Pound, first child and first son of Thomas Pound and Ann ---, born in Rockingham County, North Carolina and died about 1838 in Weakley County, Tennessee. Buried in Weakley County, Tennessee. Married 13 Apr 1822 in Rockingham County, North Carolina to Lucy Roach, daughter of James Roach and Lucy Spyres, born about 1801 in Rockingham County, North Carolina and died 9 Dec 1881 in Idlewild, Gibson County, Tennessee. Buried at Idlewild, Pounds cemetery, Gibson County, Tennessee. Lucy had married first, 20 Dec 1820 to Edward Godsey. John Pound and Lucy Roach had issue, which was the seventh generation in America:

C6111. Elizabeth R. Pound, first child and first daughter of John Pound and Lucy Roach, born about 1823 in Rockingham County, North Carolina. Married 3 Aug 1842 in Gibson County, Tennessee to William Harrison.

C6112. James M. Pound, second child and first son of John Pound and Lucy Roach, born 1825 in Rockingham County, North Carolina and died Feb 1850 in Gibson County, Tennessee. Married 4 Feb 1846 in Gibson County, Tennessee to Nancy Sherron.

C6113. Thomas L. Pound, third child and second son of John Pound and Lucy Roach, born 1826 in Rockingham County, North Carolina. Married 29 Feb 1848 in Gibson County, Tennessee to Eliza Jane Connell, born 1833 in Gibson County, Tennessee. Thomas Pound and Eliza Connell had issue, which was the eighth generation in America:

C1131. Elizabeth Pound, first child and first daughter of Thomas Pound and Eliza Connell, born 1848 in Gibson County, Tennessee. Married --- Conelly.

C1132. Providence Pound, second child and second daughter of Thomas Pound and Eliza Connell, born 1850 in Gibson County, Tennessee. Married --- McKelvey.

C1133. Amanda (Amy) Pound, third child and third daughter of Thomas Pound and Eliza Connell, born 1852 in Gibson County, Tennessee. Married --- Taylor.

C1134. Mary Pound, fourth child and fourth daughter of Thomas Pound and Eliza Connell, born 1853 in Gibson County, Tennessee. Married --- Bannister.

C1135. John Pound, fifth child and first son of Thomas Pound and Eliza Connell, born 1855 in Gibson County, Tennessee.

C1136. Louisa Leona Pound, sixth child and fifth daughter of Thomas Pound and Eliza Connell, born 1856 in Gibson County, Tennessee. Married --- Taylor.

C1137. Newton Pound, seventh child and second son of Thomas Pound and Eliza Connell, born 1858 in Gibson County, Tennessee.

C1138. Eliza Clarenda Pound, eighth child and sixth daughter of Thomas Pound and Eliza Connell, born 30 Sep 1861 at Bradford, Gibson County, Tennessee and died 30 Jul 1927 at Fort Worth, Tarrant County, Texas. Buried at Denison, Fairlawn cemetery, Grayson County, Texas. Married 15 Oct 1878 in Gibson County, Tennessee to John Henry Akin, born 2 Jul 1852 at Milan, Gibson County, Tennessee and died 25 Dec 1897 at Blue Ridge, Collins County, Texas. Eliza Pound and John Akin had issue, which was the tenth generation in America:

C11381. Roscoe Sheridan Akin, first child and first son of Eliza Pound and John Akin, born 13 Dec 1879 at Milan, Gibson County, Tennessee. Married Nov 1900 to Eppsie Ann Shaw.

C11382. Bonnie Dee Akin, second child and first daughter of Eliza Pound and John Akin, date and place of birth unknown. Married A.S. Patterson.

C1139. James Pound, ninth child and third son of Thomas Pound and

Eliza Connell, born 1864 in Gibson County, Tennessee. Married 18 Sep 1884 in Gibson County, Tennessee to Sarah L. McCleary.

C1140. Willie Pound, tenth child and fourth son of Thomas Pound and Eliza Connell, born 1866 in Gibson County, Tennessee.

C1141. Monroe Pound, eleventh child and fifth son of Thomas Pound and Eliza Connell, date and place of birth unknown.

C6114. Julia Ann Pound, fourth child and second daughter of John Pound and Lucy Roach, born 1829 in Rockingham County, North Carolina and died 30 Jul 1896 in Gibson County, Tennessee. Buried at Idlewild, Pounds cemetery, Gibson County, Tennessee. Married 8 Jan 1846 in Gibson County, Tennessee to Wiley A. Waldrop, son of John Waldrop, born 5 Jun 1823 in Gibson County, Tennessee and died 28 Sep 1855. Julia Pound and Wiley Waldrop had issue, which was the eighth generation in America:

C61141. John Waldrop, first child and first son of Julia Pound and Wiley Waldrop, born 1847 in Tennessee.

C61142. James Waldrop, second child and second son of Julia Pound and Wiley Waldrop, born 1848 in Tennessee.

C6115. John Harvey (Harve) Pound II, fifth child and third son of John Pound and Lucy Roach, born 1832 in Rockingham County, North Carolina and died 1880 at Idlewild, Gibson County, Tennessee. Buried at Idlewild, Pounds cemetery, Gibson County, Tennessee. Married 15 Mar 1859 in Gibson County, Tennessee to Mary C.N.A.C. (Cassandra Nancy Alabama Clay) Johnson, born 1835 in Tennessee and died 1875 in Weakley County, Tennessee. Buried at Idlewild, Pounds cemetery, Gibson County, Tennessee. John Pound and Mary Johnson had issue, which was the eighth generation in America:

C61151. William Everett Pounds, first child and first son of John Pound and Mary Johnson, born 30 Dec 1863 in Gibson County, Tennessee and died 1932. Married 1 Mar 1885 in Gibson County, Tennessee to Martha (Mattie) Thetford, born 1868 in Tennessee and died

1940.

C61152. John Harvey (Pap) Pounds III, second child and second son of John Pound and Mary Johnson, born 2 Feb 1865 at Cades, Gibson County, Tennessee and died 23 Jun 1938 at Mt. Pleasant, Gibson County, Tennessee. Buried at Idlewild, Pounds cemetery, Gibson County, Tennessee. Married 27 Feb 1885 at the John Thetford home, Gibson County, Tennessee to Anna Della (Dell) Sanders, daughter of James Lafayette Sanders and Mary Caroline Pounds, born 27 Nov 1865 in Gibson County, Tennessee and died 20 Mar 1951 at Mt. Pleasant, Gibson County, Tennessee. Buried at Idlewild, Pounds cemetery, Gibson County, Tennessee. John Pounds and Anna Sanders had issue, which was the ninth generation in America:

C611521. Gideon Moses Pounds, first child and first son of John Pounds and Anna Sanders, born 18 Jan 1886 at Bradford, Gibson County, Tennessee and died 9 Dec 1967 at Union City, Obion County, Tennessee. Buried at Idlewild, Pounds cemetery, Gibson County, Tennessee. Married 10 Oct 1910 to Esther Ellen Butler.

C611522. John Harvey Pounds IV, second child and second son of John Pounds and Anna Sanders, born 27 Mar 1887 at Idlewild, Gibson County, Tennessee and died 29 May 1969 at Milan, Gibson County, Tennessee. Buried at Idlewild, Pounds cemetery, Gibson County, Tennessee. Married 8 Jan 1911 to Ruby Bridges, born 27 Feb 1893 and died 20 Jul 1971 at Milan, Gibson County, Tennessee. Buried at Idlewild, Pounds cemetery, Gibson County, Tennessee. John Pounds and Ruby Bridges had issue, which was the tenth generation in America:

C6115221. Jay Harvey Pounds, first child and first son of John Pounds and Ruby Bridges, born 9 Jan 1914 at Skullbone, Gibson County, Tennessee. Married Ada Mildred Wheatley.

C6115222. Audey Bee Pounds, second child and first daughter of John Pounds and Ruby Bridges, born 18 Aug 1915 at Bradford, Gibson County, Tennessee. Married

Bernard Hanes.

C6115223. R.P.
Pounds, third child and second son of John Pounds
and Ruby Bridges, born 4 Mar 1917 at Bradford,
Gibson County, Tennessee. Married Alta May Knott.

C6115224.
Katie Aline Pounds, fourth child and second
daughter of John Pounds and Ruby Bridges, born 25
Oct 1918 at Bradford, Gibson County, Tennessee.
Married Clyde Hyde.

C6115225.
Maurine Pounds, fifth child and third daughter of
John Pounds and Ruby Bridges, born 8 Mar 1921 at
Bradford, Gibson County, Tennessee.

C6115226. John
Henry Pounds, sixth child and third son of John
Pounds and Ruby Bridges, born 17 Jul 1923 at
Bradford, Gibson County, Tennessee. Married
Maydell Wright.

C6115227.
Boone Bouthit Pounds, seventh child and fourth son
of John Pounds and Ruby Bridges, born 28 Dec 1824
at Bradford, Gibson County, Tennessee. Married
Dolores Vanlinder.

C6115228.
James Willard Pounds, eighth child and fifth son
of John Pounds and Ruby Bridges, born 11 Nov 1928
at Bradford, Gibson County, Tennessee. Married 5
Sep 1947 in Corinth, Alcorn County, Mississippi to
Mae Willis, born 27 May 1931 in Dyer County,
Tennessee. James Pounds and Mae Willis had issue,
which was the eleventh generation in America:
C61152281. Mary Ann Pounds, first child and first
daughter of James Pounds and Mae Willis, born 24
Oct 1948 at Bradford, Gibson County, Tennessee.
C61152282. James Duwayne Pounds, second child and
first son of James Pounds and Mae Willis, born 3
Jun 1950 at Chicago, Cook County, Illinois.
C61152283. Kerry Lane Pounds, third child and
second son of James Pounds and Mae Willis, born 7
Aug 1957 at Los Angeles, Los Angeles County,
California.

C6115229.
Evelyn Faye Pounds, ninth child and fourth
daughter of John Pounds and Ruby Bridges, born 27
Aug 1930 at Bradford, Gibson County, Tennessee.

Married Harlis Verble.

C6115230.
George Washington Pounds, tenth child and sixth
son of John Pounds and Ruby Bridges, born 22 Feb
1932 at Bradford, Gibson County, Tennessee.
Married Betty Jean Edwards.

C611523. Lewis Lee
Pounds, third child and third son of John Pounds
and Anna Sanders, born 22 Feb 1889 at Idlewild,
Gibson County, Tennessee and died 20 Mar 1968 at
Milan, Gibson County, Tennessee. Buried at
Idlewild, Pounds cemetery, Gibson County,
Tennessee. Married 10 Dec 1912 to Nora Ann
Parker, born 15 Sep 1893 and died 21 Apr 1975.
Lewis Pounds and Nora Parker had issue, which was
the tenth generation in America:

C6115231.
Claude Pounds, first child and first son of Lewis
Pounds and Nora Parker, date and place of birth
unknown.

C611524. Hess
Lafayette Pounds, fourth child and fourth son of
John Pounds and Anna Sanders, born 24 Jan 1891 in
Gibson County, Tennessee and died 24 Mar 1981 in
Gibson County, Tennessee. Buried at Idlewild,
Pounds cemetery, Gibson County, Tennessee.
Married 17 Dec 1911 to Lockie M. Knott, born 19
Mar 1892 and died 8 Nov 1979.

C611525. Mary Sally
Viona Pounds, fifth child and first daughter of
John Pounds and Anna Sanders, born 17 Dec 1892 at
Idlewild, Gibson County, Tennessee and died 19 Mar
1984 at Martin, Weakley County, Tennessee. Buried
at Idlewild, Pounds cemetery, Gibson County,
Tennessee. Married 26 May 1918 in Tennessee to
Doss C. Cribbs, son of William E. Cribbs and
Leathy S. Akins, born 31 Mar 1885 at Hollyleaf,
Gibson County, Tennessee and died 23 Apr 1922 at
Trezevant, Hart's Mill farm, Carroll County,
Tennessee. Buried at Cribbs cemetery, Gibson
County, Tennessee. Married 13 Aug 1925 in
Tennessee to John Franklin Pope. Mary Pounds and
Doss Cribbs had issue, which was the tenth
generation in America:

C6115251.
Dossey Clyde Cribbs, Sr., first child and first

son of Mary Pounds and Doss Cribbs, born 15 Jun 1919 at Hart's Mill farm, Carroll County, Tennessee. Married 18 Mar 1949 at Millington, Shelby County, Tennessee to Ruby Lucille Thomas, born 31 Jul 1925 at Tieplant, Granada County, Mississippi. Dossey Cribbs and Ruby Thomas had issue, which was the eleventh generation in America:

C61152511. Ann Thomas Cribbs, first child and first daughter of Dossey Cribbs and Ruby Thomas, born 18 Jan 1952 at Sangley Point, NAS Hospital, Phillippines.

C61152512. Jane Sanders Cribbs, second child and second daughter of Dossey Cribbs and Ruby Thomas, born 1 Apr 1954 at Millington, NAS Hospital, Shelby County, Tennessee.

C61152513. Dossey Clyde Cribbs, Jr., third child and first son of Dossey Cribbs and Ruby Thomas, born 5 Sep 1961 at Millington, NAS Hospital, Shelby County, Tennessee.

C6115252. Bud Harvey Cribbs, second child and second son of Mary Pounds and Doss Cribbs, born 6 May 1921 at Trezevant, Carroll County, Tennessee. Married 13 Jul 1947 at Vernal, Uintah County, Utah to Lorene Fausett, born 24 Jul 1932 at La Point, Uintah County, Utah. Bud Cribbs and Lorene Fausett had issue, which was the eleventh generation in America:

C61152521. Jackie Doss Cribbs, first child and first son of Bud Cribbs and Lorene Fausett, born 29 Feb 1948 at Vernal, Uintah County, Utah.

C61152522. Ray Harvey Cribbs, second child and second son of Bud Cribbs and Lorene Fausett, born 18 Nov 1950 at Vernal, Uintah County, Utah.

C61152523. Irene Cribbs, third child and first daughter of Bud Cribbs and Lorene Fausett, born 29 Dec 1952 at Rock Springs, Sweetwater County, Wyoming.

C61152524. Clayton Bud Cribbs, fourth child and third son of Bud Cribbs and Lorene Fausett, born 16 Aug 1954 at Vernal, Uintah County, Utah.

C61152525. Eileen Cribbs, fifth child and second daughter of Bud Cribbs and Lorene Fausett, born 22 Mar 1960 at Farmington, San Jacinto County, New Mexico.

C61152526. Aaron Leroy Cribbs, sixth child and fourth son of Bud Cribbs and Lorene Fausett, born 10 May 1961 at Farmington, San Jacinto County, New Mexico.

C61152527. Colleen Cribbs, seventh child and third daughter of Bud Cribbs and Lorene Fausett, born 12 Feb 1963 at Farmington, San Jacinto County, New Mexico.

C61152528. Kristeen Cribbs, eighth child and fourth daughter of Bud Cribbs and Lorene Fausett, born 7 Nov 1972 at Farmington, San Jacinto County, New Mexico.

C61152529. Kaylene Cribbs, ninth child and fifth daughter of Bud Cribbs and Lorene Fausett, born 3 Oct 1975 at Soldotna, Kenai Peninsula, Alaska.

C611525. Mary Sally Viona Pounds, fifth child and first daughter of John Pounds and Anna Sanders, born 17 Dec 1892 at Idlewild, Gibson County, Tennessee and died 19 Mar 1984 at Martin, Weakley County, Tennessee. Buried at Idlewild, Pounds cemetery, Gibson County, Tennessee. Married secondly 13 Aug 1925 in Tennessee to John Franklin Pope. Mary Pounds and John Pope had issue, which was the tenth generation in America:

C6115251. John Poundsie (Johnny) Pope, first child and first son of Mary Pounds and John Pope, born 28 Jan 1925 at Greenfield, Weakley County, Tennessee. Married Mary Dorthula (Dot) Carroll.

C611526. Kate Cleo Pounds, sixth child and second daughter of John Pounds and Anna Sanders, born 15 Jul 1895 at Skullbone, Gibson County, Tennessee and died 2 Feb 1974 at Milan, Gibson County, Tennessee. Buried at Mt. Pleasant cemetery, Gibson County, Tennessee. Married 29 Sep 1912 to Roy Holmes, Sr.

C611527. William (Bill) Jennings (twin) Pounds, seventh child and fifth son of John Pounds and Anna Sanders, born 11 Jun 1897 at Mt. Pleasant, Gibson County, Tennessee and died 21 Mar 1984 at Milan, Milan Hospital, Gibson County, Tennessee. Married 8 Aug 1944 to Essie Barker.

C611528. Daisy May (twin) Pounds, eighth child and third daughter of

John Pounds and Anna Sanders, born 11 Jun 1897 at Mt. Pleasant, Gibson County, Tennessee and died 7 Apr 1898 at Bradford, Gibson County, Tennessee.

C611529. Thomas Reuben (Rube) Pounds, ninth child and sixth son of John Pounds and Anna Sanders, born 13 Mar 1899 at Mt. Pleasant, Gibson County, Tennessee. Married Jewell Allen. Married secondly 15 Feb 1950 to Ruth Osteen. Married thirdly to Jennie Ruth Sutton.

C611530. Teola (Duck) Pounds, tenth child and fourth daughter of John Pounds and Anna Sanders, born 2 Oct 1900 at Mt. Pleasant, Gibson County, Tennessee. Married 14 Aug 1923 to Lonnie Osteen.

C611531. Roxie Lou Pounds, eleventh child and fifth daughter of John Pounds and Anna Sanders, born 31 Jul 1903 at Bradford, Gibson County, Tennessee. Married 25 Dec 1925 to Buford Lassiter.

C61153. Fanny (Vinsone) Pounds, third child and first daughter of John Pound and Mary Johnson, born 1864 in Gibson County, Tennessee. Married Jim Parker.

C61154. Lee Pounds, fourth child and second daughter of John Pound and Mary Johnson, born 1868 in Gibson County, Tennessee and died 1959. Married George Swaim.

C61155. Luther Pounds, fifth child and third son of John Pound and Mary Johnson, born 19 Jan 1870 in Gibson County, Tennessee and died 2 Sep 1954. Married Pesis Emerson.

C6116. Sarah A. Pound, sixth child and third daughter of John Pound and Lucy Roach, born 8 Aug 1833 in Rockingham County, North Carolina and died 25 Apr 1912 at Bradford, Gibson County, Tennessee. Buried at Idlewild, Pounds cemetery, Gibson County, Tennessee. Married 12 Mar 1851 at Bradford, Gibson County, Tennessee to John R. Thetford.

C6117. Nathaniel Newton Pound, seventh child and fourth son of John Pound and Lucy Roach, born 1836 in Rockingham County, North Carolina. Married 21 Sep 1862 in Gibson County, Tennessee to Amanda McKelvey, born 1836.

Nathaniel Pound and Amanda McKelvey had issue, which was the eighth generation in America:

C61171. John Pounds, first child and first son of Nathaniel Pound and Amanda McKelvey, born 1865 in Tennessee.

C61172. Decie Pounds, second child and first daughter of Nathaniel Pound and Amanda McKelvey, born 1866 in Tennessee.

C61173. Julia Pounds, third child and second daughter of Nathaniel Pound and Amanda McKelvey, born in Tennessee. Married 9 Jun 1867 in Gibson County, Tennessee to Wiley A. Waldross.

C6118. Louisa M. (Lucy Jane) Pound, eighth child and fourth daughter of John Pound and Lucy Roach, born 1838 in Gibson County, Tennessee. Buried at Concord cemetery, Gibson County, Tennessee. Married 5 Jan 1858 in Gibson County, Tennessee to William Lewis Sanders, Jr., born 1836 in Gibson County, Tennessee and died 31 Dec 1862 in the Civil War. Buried at Sanders cemetery, Gibson County, Tennessee. Louisa married 9 Jun 1867 in Gibson County, Tennessee to John Wesley Waldrop, Jr. Married 22 Mar 1883 to Abe Lewis. Louisa Pound and William Sanders had issue, which was the eighth generation in America:

C61181. Mahulda Sanders, first child and first daughter of Louisa Pound and William Sanders, born 24 May 1858 in Gibson County, Tennessee and died 20 Aug 1863 in Tennessee. Buried at Milan, Sanders cemetery, Gibson County, Tennessee.

C61182. Lucy Ann Sanders, second child and second daughter of Louisa Pound and William Sanders, born 1859 in Gibson County, Tennessee. Married 7 Feb 1878 in Tennessee to Robert Jones. Lucy Sanders and Robert Jones had issue, which was the ninth generation in America:

C611821. Edgar Jones, first child and first son of Lucy Sanders and Robert Jones, date and place of birth unknown.

C611822. James Jones, second child and second son of Lucy Sanders and Robert Jones, date and place of birth unknown.

C611823. Clopton

Jones, third child and third son of Lucy Sanders and Robert Jones, date and place of birth unknown.

C611824. Cyrus Jones, fourth child and fourth son of Lucy Sanders and Robert Jones, date and place of birth unknown.

C611825. Tyree Jones, fifth child and fifth son of Lucy Sanders and Robert Jones, date and place of birth unknown.

C611826. Esther Jones, sixth child and first daughter of Lucy Sanders and Robert Jones, date and place of birth unknown.

C611827. Etta Jones, seventh child and second daughter of Lucy Sanders and Robert Jones, date and place of birth unknown.

C611828. Ether Jones, eighth child and third daughter of Lucy Sanders and Robert Jones, date and place of birth unknown.

C611829. Edie Jones, ninth child and fourth daughter of Lucy Sanders and Robert Jones, date and place of birth unknown.

C611830. Zula Jones, tenth child and fifth daughter of Lucy Sanders and Robert Jones, date and place of birth unknown.

C611831. Birtie Jones, eleventh child and sixth daughter of Lucy Sanders and Robert Jones, date and place of birth unknown.

C611832. Blanche Jones, twelth child and seventh daughter of Lucy Sanders and Robert Jones, date and place of birth unknown.

C611833. Margie Jones, thirteenth child and eighth daughter of Lucy Sanders and Robert Jones, date and place of birth unknown.

C611834. unknown name Jones, fourteenth child and ninth daughter of Lucy Sanders and Robert Jones, date and place of birth unknown.

C611835. unknown name Jones, fifteenth child and tenth daughter of

Lucy Sanders and Robert Jones, date and place of birth unknown.

C6119. Mary Caroline Pound, ninth child and fifth daughter of John Pound and Lucy Roach, born 20 Feb 1841 in Gibson County, Tennessee and died 17 Nov 1888 at Milan, Gibson County, Tennessee. Buried at Milan, Sanders cemtery, Gibson County, Tennessee. Married 9 Feb 1862 in Gibson County, Tennessee to James Lafayette Sanders, son of William Lewis Sanders and Matilda Mahulda Yarbrough, born 2 Feb 1842 in Gibson County, Tennessee and died 15 Mar 1931 in Gibson County, Tennessee. Buried at Idlewild, Walnut Grove cemetery, Gibson County, Tennessee. James Lafayette Sanders married secondly 14 Sep 1892 in Gibson County, Tennessee to Nancy Adeline (Reaves) Waugh, born 19 Nov 1860 in Carroll County, Tennessee and died 1940 at Idlewild, Gibson County, Tennessee. Buried at Idlewild, Walnot Grove cemetery, Gibson County, Tennessee. On 16 Jul 1927, James L. Sanders gave a sworn statement in the Court Records of Gibson County, Tennessee as follows: "J.L. Sanders, after being duly sworn by and before H.P. Webb, a Notary Public in and for the County and State aforesaid, duly commissioned and qualified and residing at Milan, makes oath in due form of law, that he is now eighty five years old since 22nd day of January 1927, that he entered the Civil War during the month of May 1861 and that he was continually in the Army for a period of more than six months, and honorably discharged in 1862. And that during the month of September 1862 he joined the Cavalry and was in the Cavalry and in prison until the surrender. Both records are shown in Parole at Washington, D.C." Mary Pound and James Sanders had issue, which was the eighth generation in America:

C61191. George Washington Newton Sanders, first child and first son of Mary Pound and James Sanders, born 31 Dec 1862 in Gibson County, Tennessee and died 19 Mar 1951. Married 22 Nov 1882 to S.E. Butler. Married 23 Mar 1892 to S.E. Davis. Married 7 Jan 1897 to Lula Hopkins. Married 5 Jun 1898 to Banana Williams. Married 27 Aug 1899 to Lessie Patterson.

C61192. Lou Ella Sanders, second child and first daughter of Mary Pound and James Sanders, born 14 Jun 1864 in Gibson County, Tennessee and died 1941. Married John Quincy Adams (Tobe) Butler, born 8 Apr 1862 in Gibson County, Tennessee and died Nov 1939. Lou Sanders and John Butler had issue, which was the ninth generation in America:

C611921. John Arthur Butler, first child and first son of Lou Sanders and John Butler, born 25 Sep 1882 at Idlewild, Gibson County, Tennessee.

C611922. Roscoe Butler, second child and second son of Lou Sanders and John Butler, born 11 Feb 1884 at Bradford, Gibson County, Tennessee.

C611923. Addie Mary Butler, third child and first daughter of Lou Sanders and John Butler, born 28 Jan 1886 at Bradford, Gibson County, Tennessee.

C611924. Fannie Neat Butler, fourth child and second daughter of Lou Sanders and John Butler, born 7 Aug 1891 at Brazil, Gibson County, Tennessee.

C611925. Lillie Elizabeth Butler, fifth child and third daughter of Lou Sanders and John Butler, born 31 Dec 1893 at Brazil, Gibson County, Tennessee.

C611926. Jessie May Butler, sixth child and fourth daughter of Lou Sanders and John Butler, born 26 Dec 1896 at Brazil, Gibson County, Tennessee.

C611927. Fonza William Butler, seventh child and third son of Lou Sanders and John Butler, born 27 Nov 1898 at Brazil, Gibson County, Tennessee.

C611928. Charley Hartley Butler, eighth child and fourth son of Lou Sanders and John Butler, born 16 Oct 1900 at Brazil, Gibson County, Tennessee. Married Ruth Edwards. Married secondly Blanche Freeman. Charley Butler and Ruth Edwards had issue, which was the tenth generation in America:

C6119281. Charles Edward Butler, first child and first son

572

of Charley Butler and Ruth Edwards, born 1 Oct 1921 in Chester County, Tennessee.

C6119282. Frances Marie Butler, second child and first daughter of Charley Butler and Ruth Edwards, born 18 Aug 1929 in Obion County, Tennessee.

C6119283. James Harvel Butler, third child and second son of Charley Butler and Ruth Edwards, born 8 Mar 1934 in Gibson County, Tennessee.

C611929. Quincy Adams Butler, ninth child and fifth son of Lou Sanders and John Butler, born 30 Sep 1903 at Brazil, Gibson County, Tennessee.

C611930. Katie Bell Butler, tenth child and fifth daughter of Lou Sanders and John Butler, born 1 Jul 1906 at Brazil, Gibson County, Tennessee.

C61193. Anna Della (Dell) Sanders, third child and second daughter of Mary Pound and James Sanders, born 27 Nov 1865 in Gibson County, Tennessee and died 20 Mar 1951 at Mt. Pleasant, Gibson County, Tennessee. Buried at Idlewild, Pounds cemetery, Gibson County, Tennessee. Married 27 Feb 1885 at the John Thetford home, Gibson County, Tennessee to John Harvey (Pap) Pounds III, previously entered as C61152, son of John Harvey Pounds II and Mary C.N.A.C. (Cassandra Nancy Alabama Clay) Johnson, born 2 Feb 1865 at Cades, Gibson County, Tennessee and died 23 Jun 1938 at Mt. Pleasant, Gibson County, Tennessee. Buried at Idlewild, Pounds cemetery, GIbson County, Tennessee.

C61194. Mary Etta (Bunch) Sanders, fourth child and third daughter of Mary Pound and James Sanders, born 29 Jun 1867 at Milan, Gibson County, Tennessee and died 7 Apr 1967 at Marmaduke, Greene County, Arkansas. Buried at Gainesville, Greene County, Arkansas. Married 3 Dec 1882 in Gibson County, Tennessee to John William Hill, born 3 Aug 1846 at Idlewild, Gibson County, Tennessee and died 26 Dec 1912 at Gainesville, Greene County, Arkansas. Buried at Gainesville, Gainesville cemetery, Arkansas. Mary Sanders and John Hill had issue, which was the ninth generation in America:

C611941. Nora Lee Hill, first child and first daughter of Mary Sanders and John Hill, born 16 Feb 1884 in Gibson County, Tennessee and died 29 Sep 1918. Married 21 Jan 1900 to Gus Crocker.

C611942. Olie Bee Hill, second child and second daughter of Mary Sanders and John Hill, born 24 Aug 1885 in Gibson County, Tennessee and died 27 Jun 1985. Married 18 Dec 1910 to James Thomas Workman.

C611943. Linnie Vee Hill, third child and third daughter of Mary Sanders and John Hill, born 11 Apr 1887 in Gibson County, Tennessee and died 18 May 1907. Married 14 Dec 1905 to Bufford Skinner.

C611944. Bossie Beulah Hill, fourth child and fourth daughter of Mary Sanders and John Hill, born 16 Dec 1888 in Gibson County, Tennessee and died 1915. Married 10 Dec 1905 to Sam Skinner.

C611945. Ora Vina Hill, fifth child and fifth daughter of Mary Sanders and John Hill, born in Gibson County, Tennessee and died in infancy.

C611946. Leonard Homer Hill, sixth child and first son of Mary Sanders and John Hill, born 15 Feb 1893 in Gibson County, Tennessee. Married 24 Dec 1922 to Emma Smott.

C611947. John Coleman Hill, seventh child and second son of Mary Sanders and John Hill, born 21 Feb 1895 in Gibson County, Tennessee. Married 15 Jun 1918 to Mary Lou Mason.

C611948. Herbert Luke Hill, eighth child and third son of Mary Sanders and John Hill, born 10 Dec 1897 in Gibson County, Tennessee. Married 9 Dec 1922 to Erphie Shearer.

C611949. Oather Learline Hill, ninth child and sixth daughter of Mary Sanders and John Hill, born 2 Jan 1900 in Gibson County, Tennessee. Married 12 May 1918 to Alvin Luther Starnes.

C611950. Jessie Lorene Hill, tenth child and seventh daughter of

Mary Sanders and John Hill, born 16 Feb 1902 in Gibson County, Tennessee. Married 14 Aug 1925 to Hubert Cleo Pinkston.

C61195. Lewis Bedford Lee Sanders, fifth child and second son of Mary Pound and James Sanders, born 22 Feb 1869 in Gibson County, Tennessee and died 19 Oct 1873 in Tennessee. Buried at Milan, Sanders cemetery, Gibson County, Tennessee.

C61196. Willie Elizabeth Sanders, sixth child and fourth daughter of Mary Pound and James Sanders, born 23 Dec 1870 in Gibson County, Tennessee and died 23 Oct 1918 in Gibson County, Tennessee. Buried in Gibson County, Tennessee. Married 27 Nov 1887 in Gibson County, Tennessee to Israel Anderson Powell, born 1 Dec 1870 in Gibson County, Tennessee and died 28 Feb 1945 in Gibson County, Tennessee. Buried in Gibson County, Tennessee. Willie Sanders and Israel Powell had issue, which was the ninth generation in America:

C611961. Ida Powell, first child and first daughter of Willie Sanders and Israel Powell, born 27 Sep 1888 at Idlewild, Gibson County, Tennessee and died 17 Mar 1936. Married 19 Feb 1905 to John Vick.

C611962. Eddie Powell, second child and first son of Willie Sanders and Israel Powell, born 14 Mar 1890 at Idlewild, Gibson County, Tennessee.

C611963. Eula Powell, third child and second daughter of Willie Sanders and Israel Powell, born 3 Jul 1892 at Idlewild, Gibson County, Tennessee and died Nov 1963. Married 1910 to Willie Butler.

C611964. Lottie Powell, fourth child and third daughter of Willie Sanders and Israel Powell, born 10 Feb 1896 at Idlewild, Gibson County, Tennessee. Married 1912 to Earnest Taylor.

C611965. Ovie Powell, fifth child and fourth daughter of Willie Sanders and Israel Powell, born 10 Aug 1898 at Idlewild, Gibson County, Tennessee and died 15 Aug 1918. Married 1914 to John Baker.

C611966. Cassie

Powell, sixth child and fifth daughter of Willie
Sanders and Israel Powell, born 24 Jan 1902 at
Idlewild, Gibson County, Tennessee. Married Nov
1918 to Odis Campbell.

C611967. Finis J.
Garrett Powell, seventh child and second son of
Willie Sanders and Israel Powell, born 18 Apr 1903
at Idlewild, Gibson County, Tennessee. Married 26
Apr 1924 to Lillie Yates.

C611968. Mary Etta
Cleo Powell, eighth child and sixth daughter of
Willie Sanders and Israel Powell, born 24 Sep 1905
at Idlewild, Gibson County, Tennessee. Married 20
Mar 1921 to Guy Carlton Trimble.

C611969. Horace
Powell, ninth child and third son of Willie
Sanders and Israel Powell, born 11 Mar 1907 at
Idlewild, Gibson County, Tennessee.

C611970. Linell
Powell, tenth child and seventh daughter of Willie
Sanders and Israel Powell, born 13 Jan 1910 at
Idlewild, Gibson County, Tennessee. Married 18
Sep 1926 to Frank Reynolds.

C61197. Albert Monroe
Sanders, seventh child and third son of Mary Pound
and James Sanders, born 11 Sep 1872 in Gibson
County, Tennessee and died 19 May 1955 at Memphis,
John Caston hospital, Shelby County, Tennessee.
Buried at Shiloh, Shiloh cemetery, Montgomery
County, Tennessee. Married Arie Belle Rice, date
of birth unknown but she died NOv 1960 at Memphis,
Shelby County, Tennessee. Buried at Shiloh,
Shiloh cemetery, Tennessee. Albert Sanders and
Arie Rice had issue, which was the ninth
generation in America:

C611971. Stanley
Clifford Sanders, first child and first son of
Albert Sanders and Arie Rice, date of birth
unknown in Missouri.

C611972. Mary
Alberta Sanders, second child and first daughter
of Albert Sanders and Arie Rice, born 24 Apr 1901
in Missouri.

C611973. Herman
Fonzy Sanders, third child and second son of
Albert Sanders and Arie Rice, born 24 Jul 1903 in

Missouri and died 7 Nov 1957.

C61198. Thomas Franklin Lafayette Sanders, eighth child and fourth son of Mary Pound and James Sanders, born 16 Apr 1875 in Gibson County, Tennessee and died 5 Mar 1963 at St. Louis, St. Louis County, Missouri. Buried at Greenway, Mitchell cemetery, Clay County, Arkansas. Married Jun 1894 at Trenton, Gibson County, Tennessee to Ava Ann Tucker, born 16 Jan 1875 in Gibson County, Tennessee and died 24 Feb 1916 at Greenway, Clay County, Arkansas. Buried at Greenway, Mitchell cemetery, Clay County, Arkansas. Thomas Sanders and Ava Tucker had issue, which was the ninth generation in America:

C611981. Jesse Sanders, first child and first son of Thomas Sanders and Ava Tucker, born 18 Mar 1895 at Bradford, Gibson County, Tennessee. Married Paralee Bradford. Married secondly 9 Nov 1922 to Clara Bradford.

C611982. Hobart Sanders, second child and second son of Thomas Sanders and Ava Tucker, born 17 Mar 1897 at Milan, Gibson County, Tennessee. Married 1922 to Etta Peeler.

C611983. Mary Sanders, third child and first daughter of Thomas Sanders and Ava Tucker, born 27 Feb 1904 at Greenway, Clay County, Arkansas and died Nov 1953. Married 1921 to J.D. Anderson.

C611984. Geneva Sanders, fourth child and second daughter of Thomas Sanders and Ava Tucker, born 4 May 1908 at Bradford, Gibson County, Tennessee. Married 1924 to A.J. Huckalby.

C611985. Lucille Sanders, fifth child and third daughter of Thomas Sanders and Ava Tucker, born 14 Apr 1911 at Piggott, Clay County, Arkansas. Married 1929 to B.L. Robison.

C61199. Minnie Pearl Sanders, ninth child and fifth daughter of Mary Pound and James Sanders, born 16 Oct 1877 in Gibson County, Tennessee and died 6 Nov 1924 in Gibson County, Tennessee. Buried in Gibson County, Tennessee. Married 10 Sep 1893 to Thomas

Elmer Mount, born 7 Sep 1871 in Gibson County, Tennessee and died 9 May 1946 in Gibson County, Tennessee. Buried in Gibson County, Tennessee. Thomas Mount married secondly Caroline Blankenship, born 3 Aug 1888 and died 13 Jan 1951.
Minnie Sanders and Thomas Mount had issue, which was the ninth generation in America:

C611991. Thomas Irby Mount, first child and first son of Minnie Sanders and Thomas Mount, born 17 Jun 1895 in Gibson County, Tennessee. Married 29 Aug 1917 to Bessie F. Flippin.

C611100. James Hampton Sanders, tenth child and fifth son of Mary Pound and James Sanders, born 1 Dec 1879 in Gibson County, Tennessee. Married Florence Knott.

C611101. William L.B. Sanders, eleventh child and sixth son of Mary Pound and James Sanders, born 10 Aug 1882 in Gibson County, Tennessee. Married 28 Jul 1901 in Gibson County, Tennessee to Ethel Waugh, born 12 May 1880 in Gibson County, Tennessee and died 19 Sep 1911 in Gibson County, Tennessee. Buried at Idlewild, Walnut Grove cemetery, Gibson County, Tennessee. William Sanders and Ethel Waugh had issue, which was the ninth generation in America:

C6111011. Robert Sanders, first child and first son of William Sanders and Ethel Waugh, born in Gibson County, Tennessee. Married Edna Warner.

C6111012. Mary Sanders, second child and first daughter of William Sanders and Ethel Waugh, date and place of birth unknown. Married Burman Reed.

C6111013. Birtio Sanders, third child and second daughter of William Sanders and Ethel Waugh, date and place of birth unknown. Married Charlie Williams.

C6111014. Lee Roy Sanders, fourth child and second son of William Sanders and Ethel Waugh, date and place of birth unknown.

C6111015. Aubry Sanders, fifth child and third son of William Sanders and Ethel Waugh, date and place of birth unknown.

C611102. Virgie Missouri Sanders, twelth child and sixth daughter of Mary Pound and James Sanders, born 27 Mar 1888 in Gibson County, Tennessee. Married 21 Apr 1907 to George Lewis Pratt, born 20 Dec 1884 and died 1 Feb 1959 at Trezevant, Carroll County, Tennessee. Buried at Trezevant, Campground cemetery, Carroll County, Tennessee. Virgie Sanders and George Pratt had issue, which was the ninth generation in America:

C6111021. Chester Maybell Pratt, first child and first daughter of Virgie Sanders and George Pratt, born 3 Mar 1908 in Gibson County, Tennessee. Married Bryan Galloway.

C6111022. Ester Adell Pratt, second child and second daughter of Virgie Sanders and George Pratt, born 9 Apr 1910 in Gibson County, Tennessee. Married Ray Maynard.

C6111023. Hubert Paul Pratt, third child and first son of Virgie Sanders and George Pratt, born 30 Oct 1911 in Gibson County, Tennessee. Married Jeffie Abbott.

C6111024. Claude Hall Pratt, fourth child and second son of Virgie Sanders and George Pratt, born 16 Feb 1913 in Gibson County, Tennessee and died 28 Jul 1932.

C6111025. Mark H. Ethridge Pratt, fifth child and third son of Virgie Sanders and George Pratt, born 16 Jul 1914 in Gibson County, Tennessee and died 7 Aug 1932.

C6111026. G.A. Clark Pratt, sixth child and fourth son of Virgie Sanders and George Pratt, born 19 Jun 1917 in Gibson County, Tennessee. Married Kathryn McBroom.

C6111027. Effie Genella Pratt, seventh child and third daughter of Virgie Sanders and George Pratt, born 18 Jun 1919 in Gibson County, Tennessee. Married Louis Cooper.

C6111028. George Lewis Pratt, Jr., eighth child and fifth son of Virgie Sanders and George Pratt, born 2 May 1929 in Carroll County, Tennessee. Married Pauline Sutties.

C612. Elizabeth Pound, second child and first daughter of Thomas Pound and Ann ---, born about 1783 in Rockingham County, North Carolina and died in Kentucky. Married John E. Pound, born about 1775 in Halifax County, Virginia and died in Kentucky, not known to be related at this point.

C613. Sarah Pound, third child and second daughter of Thomas Pound and Ann ---, born about 1773 in Rockingham County, North Carolina and died 1826 in Kentucky. Married 6 Jul 1801 in Rockingham County, North Carolina to Joseph Asbridge, born 1750 in Maryland and died 1835 in Kentucky. Sarah Pound and Joseph Asbridge had issue, which was the seventh generation in America:

C6131. child Asbridge, first child of unknown sex, date and place of birth unknown of Sarah Pound and Joseph Asbridge.

C6132. child Asbridge, second child of unknown sex, date and place of birth unknown of Sarah Pound and Joseph Asbridge.

C6133. child Asbridge, third child of unknown sex, date and place of birth unknown of Sarah Pound and Joseph Asbridge.

C6134. child Asbridge, fourth child of unknown sex, date and place of birth unknown of Sarah Pound and Joseph Asbridge.

C6135. child Asbridge, fifth child of unknown sex, date and place of birth unknown of Sarah Pound and Joseph Asbridge.

C6136. child Asbridge, sixth child of unknown sex, date and place of birth unknown of Sarah Pound and Joseph Asbridge.

C6137. Samuel Asbridge, seventh child of Sarah Pound and Joseph Asbridge, born 1812 in North Carolina. Married in Kentucky to Jane Bonner, born 1814 in Tennessee and died 1871 in Missouri. Married secondly Elizabeth Hagler, born 1844 in Illinois. Samuel Asbridge and Jane Bonner had issue, which was the eighth generation in America:

C61371. child Asbridge, first child of unknown sex, date and place of birth unknown of Samuel Asbridge and Jane Bonner.

C61372. child Asbridge,

second child of unknown sex, date and place of birth unknown of Samuel Asbridge and Jane Bonner.

C61373. child Asbridge, third child of unknown sex, date and place of birth unknown of Samuel Asbridge and Jane Bonner.

C61374. child Asbridge, fourth child of unknown sex, date and place of birth unknown of Samuel Asbridge and Jane Bonner.

C61375. child Asbridge, fifth child of unknown sex, date and place of birth unknown of Samuel Asbridge and Jane Bonner.

C61376. child Asbridge, sixth child of unknown sex, date and place of birth unknown of Samuel Asbridge and Jane Bonner.

C61377. child Asbridge, seventh child of unknown sex, date and place of birth unknown of Samuel Asbridge and Jane Bonner.

C61378. Sidney L. Asbridge, eighth child of Samuel Asbridge and Jane Bonner, born 1 Jun 1873 in MIssouri. Married H. Pewett.

C61379. Rachel Melvina Asbridge, ninth child of Samuel Asbridge and Jane Bonner, born Aug 1875 in Missouri.

C61380. child Asbridge, tenth child of Samuel Asbridge and Jane Bonner, born and died in Missouri.

C6138. child Asbridge, eighth child of Sarah Pound and Joseph Asbridge, sex unknown, date and place of birth unknown.

C614. Anny Pound, fourth child and third daughter of Thomas Pound and Ann ---, born about 1775 in Rockingham County, North Carolina. Married 31 Jan 1809 in Rockingham County, North Carolina to Travis Barber.

C615. Jane Pound, fifth child and fourth daughter of Thomas Pound and Ann ---, born about 1777 in Rockingham County, North Carolina. Married Robert Dobbins.

C616. Rachel Pound, sixth child and fifth daughter of Thomas Pound and Ann ---, born about 1781 in Rockingham County, North Carolina. Married 17 Feb 1810 in Rockingham County, North Carolina to James McNeely.

C617. Daniel Walker Pound, seventh child and second son of Thomas Pound and Ann ---, born 1783 in Rockingham County, North Carolina and died 1876 in Amite County, Mississippi. Married Celia ---.date and place of birth unknown but she died 12 Oct 1813 in Rockingham County, North Carolina. Married secondly 9 May 1817 in Stokes County, North Carolina to Julia Ann Clayton, born 1801 in Virginia. Daniel Pound and Celia --- had issue, which was the seventh generation in America:

C6171. Thomas Walker Pound, first child and first son of Daniel Pound and Celia ---, born 5 Apr 1811 in Rockingham County, North Carolina and died 24 Dec 1884 at Danville, Yell County, Arkansas. Married 1838 in Amite County, MIssissippi to Lucinda Hall, daughter of John Hall and Penelope ---, born 11 Nov 1817 in Mississippi and died Feb 1875 at Danville, Yell County, Arkansas. The following is a portion of the obituary of Thomas Walker Pound. "Honorable Thomas Walker Pound died the 24th day of December, 1884 at his home in Danville, Yell County, Arkansas, aged 73 years, 8 months and 19 days. He was born in Rockingham County, North Carolina on the 5th of April 1811. When a boy, he emigrated with his father to Kentucky, and grew to manhood in that state, and west Tennessee, went to Amite County, Mississippi in the year 1835. There he married Lucinda Hall. In 1844, he came to Danville, Yell County. He had seven children of whom two daughters and a son are dead. One of his deceased daughters was the first wife of Honorable Thomas Boles, now Marshall of the Western District of Arkansas. Her name was Julia. The other, Penelope, was the wife of J.R. Smith. The eldest son was Americus, who died in 1881. Three daughters, Miss Ellen, Mrs. Littlejohn, and MRs. Bumgarner, and one son, Joseph Warren Pound, are still living. His wife departed this life in November 1875. In 1846, he was elected Clerk of the Circuit Court, and ex-officio clerk of the County and Probate Courts, and Recorder of Yell County, which office he held 14 years, when he retired from the office and began the practice of law in Danville which he continued, excepting a few years of the War, until his death. He was made a Free Mason in the State of Mississippi, and had in that state, taken all the degrees up to and including the Council degree. He took the Templar degrees at Little Rock on the night of December 11, 1866. At the time of his death he was a member of Danville Lodge No. 41, Dardanelle Chapter No. 64, and Palestine Commandery No. 7 K.T. at Russellville, having been a petitioner for, and a charter member of each. He was the first Master of Danville Lodge No. 41, and was a member of that Lodge ever since its organization in 1850." Thomas Pound and Lucinda Hall had issue, which was the eighth generation in America:

C61711. Americus Hall Pound, first child and first son of Thomas Pound and Lucinda Hall, born 15 Oct 1838 in Mississippi and died 26 Dec 1856 in Arkansas. Buried at Danville, Yell County, Arkansas.

C61712. Ellen Ernestine Pound, second child and first daughter of Thomas Pound and Lucinda Hall, born 3 Mar 1841 in Mississippi and died 20 Aug 1901 in Arkansas. Married 5 Jul 1885 in Yell County, Arkansas to Dr. J.H. McCargo.

C61713. Joseph Warren Pound, third child and second son of Thomas Pound and Lucinda Hall, born 12 May 1843 in Mississippi and died 19 Feb 1901 in Yell County, Arkansas. Buried at Yell County, Arkansas. Married 16 Jul 1868 in Danville, Yell County, Arkansas to Melezeren Reagan, born 1846 in Tennessee and died 1928 in Yell County, Arkansas. Buried at Yell County, Arkansas. Joseph Pound and Melezeren Reagan had issue, which was the ninth generation in America:

C617131. Thomas Lovick Pound, first child and first son of Joseph Pound and Melezeren Reagan, born 1870 in Yell County, Arkansas and died 11 Jan 1926 in Yell County, Arkansas. Married 1900 to Lillie McCarrell, born 1880 in Arkansas and died in Arkansas. Married secondly to Lucille Craig. Thomas Pound and Lillie McCarrell had issue, which was the tenth generation in America:

C6171311. Joseph Carroll Pound, first child and first son of Thomas Pound and Lillie McCarrell, born 1901 in

Arkansas and died in Arkansas. Married Adele Newson.

C6171312. Nellie Pound, second child and first daughter of Thomas Pound and Lillie McCarrell, born 1903 in Arkansas and died in Arkansas. Married in Pennsylvania to Richard Cuenco.

C6171313. Thomas Richard Pound, third child and second son of Thomas Pound and Lillie McCarrell, born 1906 in Arkansas and died in Arkansas. Married Helen Keithley.

C6171314. Woodrow Pound, fourth child and third son of Thomas Pound and Lillie McCarrell, born 1912 in Arkansas and died 1931 in New York.

C6171315. Maurine Pound, fifth child and second daughter of Thomas Pound and Lillie McCarrell, born 1909 in Arkansas and died 1913 in Arkansas.

C6171316. Ruth Pound, sixth child and third daughter of Thomas Pound and Lillie McCarrell, born 1915 in Arkansas. Married at Little Rock, Pulaski County, Arkansas to Olen Thomas.

C6171317. Mary Jean Pound, seventh child and fourth daughter of Thomas Pound and Lillie McCarrell, born 1921 in Arkansas. Married at Norman, Cleveland County, Oklahoma but the spouse's name is unknown. Married 1948 to Walter Scott Murphy, Jr., son of Walter Scott Murphy, Sr., and Sydney Vivian Briggs, born 1920 in Oklahoma. Mary Pound and Walter Murphy had issue, which was the eleventh generation in America:

C61713171. Michael S. Murphy, first child and first son of Mary Pound and Walter Murphy, born 1945.

C61713172. Nancy Murphy, second child and first daughter of Mary Pound and Walter Murphy, date and place of birth unknown.

C617132. Mary Lucinda Pound, second child and first daughter of Joseph Pound and Melezeren Reagan, born 1872 in Yell County, Arkansas and died 1947 in Yell County, Arkansas. Married 1888 in Yell County,

Arkansas to William Walter Briggs, born 1874 in Arkansas. Married secondly 1936 to Henry Melton. Mary Pound and William Briggs had issue, which was the tenth generation in America:

C6171321. Sydney Vivian Briggs, first child and first daughter of Mary Pound and William Briggs, born 1889 in Arkansas. Married 1905 at Norman, Cleveland County, Oklahoma to Walter Scott Murphy, Sr., born 1885 in Texas and died 1966 in Oklahoma. Sydney Briggs and Walter Murphy had issue, which was the eleventh generation in America:

C61713211. Myrtle Marie Murphy, first child and and first daughter of Sydney Briggs and Walter Murphy, born 1909 in Texas and died 1928 in Oklahoma.

C61713212. Walter Scott Murphy, Jr., second child and first son of Sydney Briggs and Walter Murphy, born 1920 in Oklahoma. Married 1948 to Mary Jean Pound, born 1921 in Arkansas, previously listed as C6171317.

C61713213. Joseph Lee Murphy, third child and second son of Sydney Briggs and Walter Murphy, born 1930 in Oklahoma. Married 1948 to Betty Jo Sterling.

C6171322. Meda Atha (Mae) Briggs, second child and second daughter of Mary Pound and William Briggs, born 1892 in Arkansas. Married at Danville, Yell County, Arkansas to Hays Scisson. Meda Briggs and Hays Scisson had issue, which was the eleventh generation in America:

C61713221. Virginia Scisson, first child and first daughter of Meda Briggs and Hays Scisson, born 1919. Married 1935 to Haynes A. Harmon.

C61713222. Lula Marie Scisson, second child and second daughter of Meda Briggs and Hays Scisson, born 1929 in Arkansas. Married Bill F. Lewis.

C61714. Julia Elizabeth Pound, fourth child and second daughter of Thomas Pound and Lucinda Hall, born 16 Oct 1845 in Yell County, Arkansas and died 21 Mar 1872 in Arkansas. Married 15 Aug 1866 in Yell County, Arkansas to Judge Thomas H. Boles.

C61715. Mary Lavina Pound, fifth child and third daughter of Thomas

Pound and Lucinda Hall, born 14 Apr 1847 in Yell County, Arkansas and died 17 Jul 1885 in Yell County, Arkansas. Married 25 Jan 1872 at the Thomas Pound home, Danville, Yell County, Arkansas to James David Littlejohn, born 21 Jun 1845 in Union County, South Carolina and died 22 Jun 1889 in Yell County, Arkansas. Buried in Yell County, Arkansas. Mary Pound and James Littlejohn had issue, which was the ninth generation in America:

C617151. Arthur R. Littlejohn, first child and first son of Mary Pound and James Littlejohn, born 27 Oct 1871 in Yell County, Arkansas. Married 10 Oct 1895 in Arkansas to Maggie A. Pledger.

C617152. Di Littlejohn, second child and second daughter of Mary Pound and James Littlejohn, born 21 Dec 1875 in Yell County, Arkansas and died 1 Jan 1875 in Yell County, Arkansas.

C617153. Lucinda Albertine Littlejohn, third child and third daughter of Mary Pound and James Littlejohn, born 25 Aug 1876 in Yell County, Arkansas and died 9 Nov 1901 in Arkansas. Married --- Matheny.

C617154. STI Littlejohn, fourth child, sex unknown but thought to be female, of Mary Pound and James Littlejohn, born 3 Oct 1878 in Yell County, Arkansas.

C617155. James Marcellus (twin) LIttlejohn, fifth child and second son of Mary Pound and James Littlejohn, born 26 Mar 1880 in Yell County, Arkansas and died 10 Aug 1955 in Arkansas. Married 28 Oct 1903 to Lula Mary Pledger.

C617156. Thomas Marvin (twin) Littlejohn, sixth child and third son of Mary Pound and James Littlejohn, born 26 Mar 1880 in Yell County, Arkansas.

C617157. Lydia Fostina Littlejohn, seventh child and fifth daughter of Mary Pound and James Littlejohn, born 10 Feb 1883 in Yell County, Arkansas and died 8 Dec 1953 in Arkansas. Married John E. Chambers.

C617158. Louvinia Pearl LIttlejohn, eighth child and sixth daughter of Mary Pound and James Littlejohn, born 20 Mar

1885 in Yell County, Arkansas. Married Oscar Clements.

C61716. Rachel Virginia Pound, sixth child and fourth daughter of Thomas Pound and Lucinda Hall, born 10 Oct 1851 in Yell County, Arkansas and died 28 Aug 1928 in Oklahoma. Married 1871 in Arkansas to Thomas D. Bumgarner.

C61717. Penelope Americus Pound, seventh child and fifth daughter of Thomas Pound and Lucinda Hall, born 14 Aug 1857 in Yell County, Arkansas and died 25 Dec 1877 in Arkansas. Married 13 Jan 1876 in Arkansas to J. Rhodes Smith.

C617. Daniel Walker Pound, seventh child and second son of Thomas Pound and Ann ---, born 1783 in Rockingham County, North Carolina and died 1876 in Amite County, Mississippi. Married secondly 9 May 1817 in Stokes County, North Carolina to Julia Ann Clayton, born 1801 in Virginia. Daniel Pound and Julia Clayton had issue, which was the seventh generation in America:

C6171. Daniel Milton Pound, first child and first son of Daniel Walker Pound and Julia Ann Clayton, born 5 Oct 1832 in Tennessee and died 29 Dec 1904 in Pike County, Mississippi. Buried at Magnolia, Pounds family cemetery, Pike County, Mississippi. Married about 1856 in Mississippi to Jane Olivia Leggett, born 22 Dec 1834 in Mississippi and died 16 Mar 1916 in Pike County, Mississippi. Buried at Magnolia, Pounds family cemetery, Pike County, Mississippi. Daniel Pound and Jane Leggett had issue, which was the eighth generation in America:

C61711. Julia Elizabeth Pound, first child and first daughter of Daniel Pound and Jane Leggett, born about 1857 in Pike County, Mississippi. Married Monroe Simmons. Julia Pound and Monroe Simmons had issue, which was the ninth generation in America:

C617111. Howard Simmons, first child and first son of Julia Pound and Monroe Simmons, date and place of birth unknown.

C617112. Lucius Simmons, second child and second son of Julia

Pound and Monroe Simmons, date and place of birth unknown.

C617113.   Lizzie Simmons, third child and first daughter of Julia Pound and Monroe Simmons, date and place of birth unknown.

C61712.   Daniel Wright Pound, second child and first son of Daniel Pound and Jane Leggett, born 16 Mar 1859 in Pike County, Mississippi and died 12 Nov 1904 in Pike County, Mississippi. Buried in Pike County, Mississippi. Married 28 Nov 1882 in Pike County, Mississippi to Agnes Kizziah Simmons, born 25 Feb 1860 and died 4 Jan 1933 in Pike County, Mississippi. Buried at Magnolia, Pounds family cemetery, Pike County, Mississippi. Daniel Pound and Agnes Simmons had issue, which was the ninth generation in America:

C617121.   Julia Annie Pound, first child and first daughter of Daniel Pound and Agnes Simmons, born 8 Oct 1883 in Pike County, Mississippi and died 12 Apr 1939 in Pike County, Mississippi. Buried at Magnolia, Pounds family cemetery, Pike County, Mississippi. Married 26 Jan 1904 in Mississippi to Robert Lee Shoup, born 28 Sep 1870 and died 14 Jun 1927 in Pike County, Mississippi. Buried at Magnolia, Pounds family cemetery, Pike County, Mississippi. Julia Pound and Robert Shoup had issue, which was the tenth generation in America:

C6171211. Jewel Agnes Shoup, first child and first daughter of Julia Pound and Robert Shoup, born 3 Nov 1905 in Pike County, Mississippi and died 12 Apr 1939 in Pike County, Mississippi.

C6171212. William Lee Shoup, second child and first son of Julia Pound and Robert Shoup, born 4 Sep 1907 in Pike County, Mississippi and died 28 Sep 1914 in Pike County, Mississippi.

C6171213. Robert Eugene Shoup, third child and second son of Julia Pound and Robert Shoup, born 22 Jul 1909 in Pike County, Mississippi. Married Alyne Young.

C6171214. Ruby May Shoup, fourth child and second daughter of Julia Pound and Robert Shoup, born 28 Nov 1911 in

Pike County, Mississippi and died 27 Apr 1913 in Pike County, Mississippi.

C6171215. George Latimore Shoup, fifth child and third son of Julia Pound and Robert Shoup, born 25 Feb 1914 in Pike County, Mississippi and died 17 Dec 1917 in Pike County, Mississippi.

C6171216. Daniel Edwin Shoup, sixth child and fourth son of Julia Pound and Robert Shoup, born 17 Aug 1916 in Pike County, Mississippi and died 18 Jun 1921 in Pike County, Mississippi.

C6171217. Linda Blanche Shoup, seventh child and third daughter of Julia Pound and Robert Shoup, born 9 Mar 1919 in Pike County, Mississippi and died 14 Jun 1924 in Pike County, Mississippi.

C6171218. Ora Nell Shoup, eighth child and fourth daughter of Julia Pound and Robert Shoup, born 4 Jun 1924 in Pike County, Mississippi. Married M.A. Wilkinson. Ora Shoup and M.A. Wilkinson had issue, which was the eleventh generation in America:

C61712181. Bobby Wilkinson, first child and first son of Ora Shoup and M.A. Wilkinson, date and place of birth unknown.

C61712182. Henry Norman Wilkinson, second child and second son of Ora Shoup and M.A. Wilkinson, date and place of birth unknown.

C61712183. Delores Wilkinson, third child and first daughter of Ora Shoup and M.A. Wilkinson, date and place of birth unknown.

C61712184. Linda Wilkinson, fourth child and second daughter of Ora Shoup and M.A. Wilkinson, date and place of birth unknown.

C6171219. Evie Jane Shoup, ninth child and fifth daughter of Julia Pound and Robert Shoup, born 13 Jun 1926 in Pike County, Mississippi. Married Albert Parker. Evie Shoup and Albert Parker had issue, which was the eleventh generation in America:

C61712191. Glenda Parker, first child and first daughter of Evie Shoup and Albert Parker, date and place of birth unknown.

C617122. Joseph Solomon (twin) Pound, second child and first son of Daniel Pound and Agnes Simmons, born 29 Jan 1885 in Pike County, Mississippi and died 17 Jul 1885 in Pike County, Mississippi.

C617123. Thomas Daniel (twin) Pound, third child and second son of Daniel Pound and Agnes Simmons, born 29 Jan 1885 in Pike County, Mississippi and died 6 Jun 1885 in Pike County, Mississippi.

C617124. Benjamin Wright Pound, fourth child and third son of Daniel Pound and Agnes Simmons, born 12 Mar 1886 in Pike County, Mississippi and died 10 Jan 1969 in Pike County, Mississippi. Married 24 Dec 1916 in Mississippi to Eunice Helen Tucker, born 13 Sep 1896 at Pascagoula, Jackson County, Mississippi. Eunice Tucker Pound, widow of Benjamin Wright Pound, married secondly 3 Jul 1943 at Pascagoula, Jackson County, Mississippi to B.W. Coffey. Her parents were W.B. and Billie Sue Tucker. Benjamin Pound and Eunice Tucker had issue, which was the tenth generation in America:

C6171241. Benjamin Tucker Pounds, first child and first son of Benjamin Pound and Eunice Tucker, born 26 Oct 1917 in Pike County, Mississippi and died 24 Jan 1940 while on duty with the Armed Forces. Buried at Magnolia, Pike County, Mississippi.

C617125. Lillian Sophronio Pound, fifth child and second daughter of Daniel Pound and Agnes Simmons, born 5 Mar 1887 in Pike County, Mississippi and died 4 Apr 1922 in Pike County, Mississippi. Buried at Magnolia, Pounds family cemetery, Pike County, Mississippi. Married 21 Dec 1908 in Pike County, Mississippi to Iverson (Ive) Paul Allen, born 1 Jan 1882 in MIssissippi and died 26 Oct 1957 in Pike County, Mississippi. Buried at William Allen cemetery, Mississippi. Lillian Pound and I. Paul Allen had issue, which was the tenth generation in America:

C6171251. Carroll Allen, first child and first son of Lillian Pound and I. Paul Allen, born in Pike County, Mississippi. Married Ella Mae Kennedy. Carroll Allen and Ella Kennedy had issue, which was the eleventh generation in America:

C61712511. Bobby Ive Allen, first child and first

son of Carroll Allen and Ella Kennedy, date and place of birth unknown. Married Claudia Elizabeth Simmons. Bobby Allen and Claudia Simmons had issue, which was the twelth generation in America:

C617125111. Thomas Paul Allen, first child and first son of Bobby Allen and Claudia Simmons, date and place of birth unknown.

C617125112. Richard Carroll Allen, second child and second son of Bobby Allen and Claudia Simmons, date and place of birth unknown.

C617125113. Teresa Malinda Allen, third child and first daughter of Bobby Allen and Claudia Simmons, born 13 Jun 1957 in Mississippi.

C61712512. Carol Ann Allen, second child and first daughter of Carroll Allen and Ella Kennedy, date and place of birth unknown. Married Jimmy Alford.

C6171252. Irma Allen, second child and first daughter of Lillian Pound and I. Paul Allen, born in Pike County, Mississippi. Married Isaac Carter. Irma Allen and Isaac Carter had issue, which was the eleventh generation in America:

C61712521. Glen Carter, first child and first son of Irma Allen and Isaac Carter, date and place of birth unknown. Married --- ---. Glen Carter and --- --- had issue, which was the twelth generation in America:

C617125211. Glenn Allen Carter, first child and first son of Glen Carter and --- ---, date and place of birth unknown.

C61712522. William Carter, second child and second son of Irma Allen and Isaac Carter, date and place of birth unknown.

C61712523. Nina Carter, third child and first daughter of Irma Allen and Isaac Carter, date and place of birth unknown. Married Bobby Graves.

C6171253. Ethel Allen, third child and second daughter of Lillian Pound and J. Paul Allen, born in Pike County, Mississippi. Married R. Eldridge McKinney. Ethel Allen and R. Eldrige McKinney had issue, which was the eleventh generation in America:

C61712531. Robert McKinney, first child and first son of Ethel Allen and Eldridge McKinney, date and place of birth unknown.

C61712532. Patrick Allen McKinney, second child and second son of Ethel Allen and Eldridge McKinney, date and place of birth unknown.

C61712533. James Perry McKinney, third child and third son of Ethel Allen and Eldridge McKinney, date and place of birth unknown.

C61712534. Charles Avery McKinney, fourth child and fourth son of Ethel Allen and Eldridge McKinney, date and place of birth unknown.

C617126. Maud Olivia Pound, sixth child and third daughter of Daniel Pound and Agnes Simmons, born 19 Mar 1888 in Pike County, Mississippi and died 1946 in Pike County, Mississippi. Buried at Silver Creek cemetery, Pike County, Mississippi. Married 28 Feb 1904 in Mississippi to J. Walter Holmes, born 1876 in Mississippi and died 1953 in Pike County, Mississippi. Buried at Silver Creek cemetery, Pike County, Mississippi. Maud Pound and J. Walter Holmes had issue, which was the tenth generation in America:

C6171261. Berniece Holmes, first child and first daughter of Maud Pound and J. Walter Holmes, born 1905 in Pike County, Mississippi. Married Herbert N. Morgan, born 1902 in Mississippi and died 1965 in Mississippi. Berniece Holmes and Herbert Morgan had issue, which was the eleventh generation in America:

C61712611. Helen Morgan, first child and first daughter of Berniece Holmes and Herbert Morgan, date and place of birth unknown. Married James Dunnaway.

C61712612. Donald Wayne Morgan, second child and first son of Berniece Holmes and Herbert Morgan, date and place of birth unknown.

C61712613. Diane Morgan, third child and second daughter of Berniece Holmes and Herbert Morgan, date and place of birth unknown.

C6171262. Bessie Mae Holmes, second child and second daughter of Maud Pound and J. Walter Holmes, born about 1907 in Pike County, Mississippi. Married John O'Connor. Bessie Holmes and John O'Connor had issue, which was the eleventh generation in

America:
C61712621. Johnnie O'Connor, first child and first son of Bessie Holmes and John O'Connor, date and place of birth unknown.
C61712622. Jimmie O'Connor, second child and second son of Bessie Holmes and John O'Connor, date and place of birth unknown.
C61712623. Patricia O'Connor, third child and first daughter of Bessie Holmes and John O'Connor, date and place of birth unknown.
C61712624. Michael O'Connor, fourth child and third son of Bessie Holmes and John O'Connor, date and place of birth unknown.
C61712625. Robert O'Connor, fifth child and fourth son of Bessie Holmes and John O'Connor, date and place of birth unknown.

C6171263. Jamie Holmes, third child and first son of Maud Pound and J. Walter Holmes, born about 1909 in Pike County, Mississippi. MArried Mavis Martin. Jamie Holmes and Mavis Martin had issue, which was the eleventh generation in America:
C61712631. Eddie Martin, first child and first son of Jamie Holmes and Mavis Martin, date and place of birth unknown.
C61712632. Ronnie Martin, second child and second son of Jamie Holmes and Mavis Martin, date and place of birth unknown.

C6171264. Walter Herman Holmes, fourth child and second son of Maud Pound and J. Walter Holmes, born 11 Mar 1911 in Pike County, Mississippi and died 10 Nov 1913 in Pike County, Mississippi.

C617127. Oscar Cicero Pound, seventh child and fourth son of Daniel Pound and Agnes Simmons, born 9 Apr 1890 in Pike County, Mississippi and died 19 Feb 1940 in Pike County, Mississippi. Married 19 Apr 1908 in Mississippi to Lula B. Holmes. Oscar Pound and Lula Holmes had issue, which was the tenth generation in America:

C6171271. Vera Pounds, first child and first daughter of Oscar Pound and Lula Holmes, date and place of birth unknown. Married Bryan Webb. Vera Pounds and Bryan Webb had issue, which was the eleventh

generation in America:

C61712711. Frank Pounds Webb, first child and first son of Vera Pounds and Bryan Webb, date and place of birth unknown.

C61712712. Theresa Ann Webb, second child and first daughter of Vera Pounds and Bryan Webb, date and place of birth unknown. Married Alcy Campbell. Theresa Webb and Alcy Campbell had issue, which was the twelth generation in America:

C617127121. Darrell Ray Campbell, first child and first son of Theresa Webb and Alcy Campbell, born 24 Mar 1956 at Roxie, Franklin County, Mississippi.

C6171272. Wright Pounds, second child and first son of Oscar Pound and Lula Holmes, date and place of birth unknown. Married Lucy Conerly, born 20 Feb 1907 in Walthall County, Mississippi and died 30 Mar 1955 in Mississippi. Wright Pounds and Lucy Conerly had issue, which was the eleventh generation in America:

C61712721. Helen (twin) Pounds, first child and first daughter of Wright Pounds and Lucy Conerly, date and place of birth unknown. Married Curtis E. Cade. Helen Pounds and Curtis Cade had issue, which was the twelth generation in America:

C617127211. Lucy Darlene Cade, first child and first daughter of Helen Pounds and Curtis Cade, born 3 Jul 1957 in Mississippi.

C61712722. Di (twin) Pounds, second child and second daughter of Wright Pounds and Lucy Conerly, date and place of birth unknown.

C61712723. Jeanine (twin) Pounds, third child and third daughter of Wright Pounds and Lucy Conerly, date and place of birth unknown.

C61712724. Jeanette (twin) Pounds, fourth child and fourth daughter of Wright Pounds and Lucy Conerly, date and place of birth unknown.

C61712725. Cathryn Pounds, fifth child and fifth daughter of Wright Pounds and Lucy Conerly, date and place of birth unknown. Married Louis Hart, born at Chestnut, Winn Parish, Louisiana.

C6171273. Vivian Pounds, third child and second daughter of Oscar Pound and Lula Holmes, date and place of birth unknown.

594

C6171274.
Cecil Wayne Pounds, fourth child and second son of
Oscar Pound and Lula Holmes, born 14 Jul 1925 in
Kentucky and died Dec 1983 in Villa Park, Dupage
County, Illinois.
C6171275. Earl
Pounds, fifth child and third son of Oscar Pound
and Lula Holmes, date and place of birth unknown.
Married Ruby Mote.
C6171276. Vada
Lee Pounds, sixth child and third daughter of
Oscar Pound and Lula Holmes, date and place of
birth unknown. Married Charles Franklin Webb.
Vada Pounds and Charles Webb had issue, which was
the eleventh generation in America:
C61712761. Charles Franklin Webb, Jr., first
child and first son of Vada Pounds and Charles
Webb, date and place of birth unknown but he died
Jan 1962. Buried at Mt. Zion Church cemetery,
Mississippi.

C61712762. Jan Annette Webb, second child and
first daughter of Vada Pounds and Charles Webb,
date and place of birth unknown.
C61712763. Karen Rowena Webb, third child and
second daughter of Vada Pounds and Charles Webb,
date and place of birth unknown.
C61712764. Robert Wayne Webb, fourth child and
second son of Vada Pounds and Charles Webb, date
and place of birth unknown.
C6171277. Otto
Clyde Pounds, seventh child and fourth son of
Oscar Pound and Lula Holmes, date and place of
birth unknown. Married Mary B. Gibson, date and
place of birth unknown, but she died 23 Sep 1955
in Warnerton, England. Buried at Mt. Zion church
cemetery, Mississippi. Married secondly to Rose
Simmons. Otto Pounds and Mary Gibson had issue,
which was the eleventh generation in America:
C61712771. Oscar Clyde Pounds, first child and
first son of Otto Pounds and Mary Gibson, born 15
Dec 1947.
C61712772. Elizabeth Lorraine Pounds, second
child and first daughter of Otto Pounds and Mary
Gibson, born 12 Jun 1950 in Alaska.
C61712773. Susan Daisy Pounds, third child and

second daughter of Otto Pounds and Mary Gibson, date and place of birth unknown.

C61712774. Daniel Griffin Pounds, fourth child and second son of Otto Pounds and Mary Gibson, date and place of birth unknown.

C6171278. Eunice Pounds, eighth child and fourth daughter of Oscar Pound and Lula Holmes, date and place of birth unknown. Married Lloyd Rudolph Freeman. Eunice Pounds and Lloyd Freeman had issue, which was the eleventh teneration in America:

C61712781. Sylvia Lynn Freeman, first child and first daughter of Eunice Pounds and Lloyd Freeman, date and place of birth unknown.

C61712782. Lloyd Rudolph Freeman, Jr., second child and first son of Eunice Pounds and Lloyd Freeman, date and place of birth unknown.

C6171279. Inez Pounds, ninth child and fifth daughter of Oscar Pound and Lula Holmes, date and place of birth unknown.

C6171280. Brentis Pounds, tenth child and sixth daughter of Oscar Pound and Lula Holmes, date and place of birth unknown. Married M.L. Westbrook.

C617128. George Eugene Pound, eighth child and fifth son of Daniel Pound and Agnes Simmons, born 8 Nov 1891 in Pike County, Mississippi and died 1947 in Mississippi. Buried at Magnolia, Pounds family cemetery, Pike County, Mississippi. Married Janie Statham. Janie Statham married secondly Charlie Weaver. George Pound and Janie Statham had issue, which was the tenth generation in America:

C6171281. Catherine Pounds, first child and first daughter of George Pound and Janie Statham, date and place of birth unknown. Married Homer Webb. Catherine Pounds and Homer Webb had issue, which was the eleventh generation in America:

C61712811. Jane Webb, first child and first daughter of Catherine Pounds and Homer Webb, date and place of birth unknown.

C617129. William Boyd Pound, ninth child and sixth son of Daniel

Pound and Agnes Simmons, born 28 May 1894 in Pike County, Mississippi and died 14 Nov 1950 in Pike County, Mississippi.

C617130. Milton Ivy Pound, tenth child and seventh son of Daniel Pound and Agnes Simmons, born 30 Jan 1896 in Pike County, Mississippi. Married 4 Mar 1922 in Mississippi to Hazel Simmons. Milton Pound and Hazel Simmons had issue, which was the tenth generation in America:

C6171301. Willard Pounds, first child and first son of Milton Pound and Hazel Simmons, date and place of birth unknown. Married Dimple Heinz. Willard Pounds and Dimple Heinz had issue, which was the eleventh generation in America:

C61713011. Wilton Pounds, first child and first son of Willard Pounds and Dimple Heinz, date and place of birth unknown.

C61713012. Allen Pounds, second child and second son of Willard Pounds and Dimple Heinz, date and place of birth unknown.

C6171302. Margaret Pounds, second child and first daughter of Milton Pound and Hazel Simmons, date and place of birth unknown. Married Herk Neil. Margaret Pounds and Herk Neil had issue, which was the eleventh generation in America:

C61713021. Sammie Sue Neil, first child and first daughter of Margaret Pounds and Herk Neil, date and place of birth unknown.

C61713022. Claudia Neil, second child and second daughter of Margaret Pounds and Herk Neil, date and place of birth unknown.

C61713023. Burk Neil, third child and first son of Margaret Pounds and Herk Neil, date and place of birth unknown.

C6171303. Peggy Ann Pounds, third child and second daughter of Milton Pound and Hazel Simmons, date and place of birth unknown. Married John William Teel, Jr.

C617131. Albert Felder Pound, eleventh child and eighth son of Daniel Pound and Agnes Simmons, born 14 Mar 1897 at Magnolia, Pike County, Mississippi. Married 11 Sep 1922 in Pike County, Mississippi to Olive

Allen, born 4 Feb 1889 in Pike County, Mississippi and died 4 Feb 1963 in Pike County, Mississippi. Albert Pound and Olive Allen had issue, which was the tenth generation in America:

C6171311. Norma Jean Pounds, first child and first daughter of Albert Pound and Olive Allen, born 4 Feb 1927 in Pike County, Mississippi. Married 4 Nov 1944 in Mississippi to Anthony W. Fordine.

C6171312. Merle Pounds, second child and second daughter of Albert Pound and Olive Allen, born 1930 in Pike County, Mississippi. Married Donald Matthews.

Merle Pounds and Donald Matthews had issue, which was the eleventh generation in America:

C61713121. Charles Raymond Matthews, first child and first son of Merle Pounds and Donald Matthews, date and place of birth unknown.

C61713122. Bennie Matthews, second child and second son of Merle Pounds and Donald Matthews, date and place of birth unknown.

C61713123. Brenda Matthews, third child and first daughter of Merle Pounds and Donald Matthews, date and place of birth unknown.

C61713124. Barbara Lynn Matthews, fourth child and second daughter of Merle Pounds and Donald Matthews, date and place of birth unknown.

C617132. Edwin Ray Pound, twelfth child and ninth son of Daniel Pound and Agnes Simmons, born 28 Mar 1899 in Pike County, Mississippi and died 1965. Married 30 Apr 1918 to Marie Kennedy. Edwin Pound and Marie Kennedy had issue, which was the tenth generation in America:

C6171321. Horace Mitchell Pounds, first child and first son of Edwin Pound and Marie Kennedy, date and place of birth unknown. Married Rosa Gianforte. Horace Pounds and Rosa Gianforte had issue, which was the eleventh generation in America:

C61713211. John Ray Pounds, first child and first son of Horace Pounds and Rosa Gianforte, born in 1948 in Mississippi.

C61713212. Judith Ann Pounds, second child and first daughter of Horace Pounds and Rosa

Gianforte, born 1950 in Mississippi.

C6171322.
Bernon Ray Pounds, second child and second son of
Edwin Pound and Marie Kennedy, date and place of
birth unknown. Married Wilma Fae Barr. Bernon
Pounds and Wilma Barr had issue, which was the
eleventh generation in America:
C61713221. Brenda Fae Pounds, first child and
first daughter of Bernon Pounds and Wilma Barr,
born 1950 in Mississippi.

C617133. Mae Pound,
thirteenth child and fourth daughter of Daniel
Pound and Agnes Simmons, born 6 Oct 1900 in Pike
County, Mississippi.

C61713. STI Pound, third
child sex unknown of Daniel Pound and Jane
Leggett, stillborn 1861 in Pike County,
MIssissippi.

C61714. STI Pound,
fourth child sex unknown of Daniel Pound and Jane
Leggett, stillborn 1863 in Pike County,
Mississippi.

C61715. Virginia
(Jennie) A. Pound, fifth child and second daughter
of Daniel Pound and Jane Leggett, born 22 Sep 1864
in Pike County, Mississippi and died 29 Dec 1913
in Pike County, Mississippi. Buried at Magnolia,
Pounds family cemetery, Pike County, Mississippi.
Married Amon A. Kennedy. Married secondly John
Roach.

C61716. Lucy Pound,
sixth child and third daughter of Daniel Pound and
Jane Leggett, born 1868 in Pike County,
Mississippi. Married 12 Dec 1889 in Mississippi
to John B. Statham. Lucy Pound and John Statham
had issue, which was the ninth generation in
America:

C617161. Janie
Statham, first child and first daughter of Lucy
Pound and John Statham, date and place of birth
unknown. Married George Eugene Pound, son of
Daniel Wright Pound and Agnes Kizziah Simmons,
born 8 Nov 1891 in Mississippi and died 1947 in
Mississippi. Buried at Magnolia, Pike County,
Mississippi. Janie Statham and George Pound had

issue, which was the tenth generation in America:

C6171611. Catherine Pound, first child and first daughter of Janie Statham and George Pound, date and place of birth unknown. Married Homer Webb. Married secondly Charlie Weaver. Catherine Pound and Homer Webb had issue, which was the eleventh generation in America:

C61716111. Jane Webb, first child and first daughter of Catherine Pound and Homer Webb, date and place of birth unknown.

C61717. Nettie Pound, seventh child and fourth daughter of Daniel Pound and Jane Leggett, born 19 Jan 1871 in Pike County, Mississippi and died 31 Aug 1947 in Pike County, Mississippi. Buried at Magnolia, Pounds family cemetery, Pike County, Mississippi. Married 5 Feb 1891 in Pike County, Mississippi to E. Adolph Raiborn, born 22 May 1864 in Mississippi and died 26 May 1941 in Pike County, Mississippi. Nettie Pound and E.A. Raiborn had issue, which was the ninth generation in America:

C617171. Floy Raiborn, first child and first daughter of Nettie Pound and E.A. Raiborn, born and died 21 Jan 1895 in Pike County, Mississippi.

C617172. Mollie Raiborn, second child and second daughter of Nettie Pound and E.A. Raiborn, born 6 Sep 1898 and died 7 Sep 1898 in Pike County, Mississippi.

C617173. Wilma Raiborn, third child and third daughter of Nettie Pound and E.A. Raiborn, born and died 7 Dec 1905 in Pike County, Mississippi.

C617174. Carey Raiborn, fourth child and fourth daughter of Nettie Pound and E.A. Raiborn, date and place of birth unknown.

C61718. Carrie Pound, eighth child and seventh daughter of Daniel Pound and Jane Leggett, born 15 Jan 1875 in Pike County, Mississippi and died 4 Jul 1898 in Pike County, Mississippi.

C61719. Maggie Pound, ninth child and eighth daughter of Daniel Pound and Jane Leggett, born 1877 in Pike County,

Mississippi. Married 16 Jan 1897 in Mississippi to Oscar Holmes.

C618. Ruth Pound, eighth child and sixth daughter of Thomas Pound and Ann ---, born about 1787 in Rockingham County, North Carolina. Married 25 Mar 1813 in Rockingham County, North Carolina to James Barber.

C619. Thomas Pound, ninth child and third son of Thomas Pound and Ann ---, born about 1791 in Rockingham County, North Carolina.

C62. John Pound, second child and second son of Thomas Pound and Jean ---, born about 1738 in Halifax County, Virginia. Married before 12 Dec 1802 in Halifax County, Virginia to Drucilla Lacy.

C63. William Pound, third child and third son of Thomas Pound and Jean ---, born 1749 in Mecklenburg County, Virginia and died 1814 in Chatham County, North Carolina. Buried in Chatham County, North Carolina. William Pound was an American Revolutionary War veteran, having served in Colonel Gibson's Virginia regiment and was a corporal in Captain Valentine's company, 1st Virginia National Regiment. He was discharged at Philadelphia, Pennsylvania on December 23, 1779 after three years service. On his way home he was authorized to draw sixteen days rations. He drew two days rations at Lancaster, Pennsylvania, four days at York, Pennsylvania and three days at Frederick Town (Frederick, Maryland). William Pound drew two hundred acres of land in Kentucky as a Revolutionary solder (Warrant No. 1934 - 200 acres, Virginia State Line, 3 years, October 30, 1783, page 247. Sons of the Revolution, Kentucky Society, 1913.(Virginia Land Office.) In location book, Warrant No. 1937 under another name is a mistake which the research worker (A.V.D.F.) states proves that the location of the 200 acres was in Kentucky. His war pension is recorded in the pension office in Book C. Volume 1, page 184 and was inscribed on the roll of Fayetteville, North Carolina March 4, 1831. William Pound married about 1774 in Mecklenburg County, Virginia to Mary Elizabeth Tune, daughter of James Tune and Amanda Cary, born 19 Apr 1756 in Mecklenburg County, Virginia and died Sep 1846 in Chatham

County, North Carolina. Buried in Chatham County, North Carolina. The following data were obtained from the Veterans Bureau in reference to William Pound, and is contained in an affidavit filed by Elizabeth (Tune) Pound, for a pension: "She was resident of the County of Chatham, North Carolina. Mary Elizabeth Pound, at the time of filing the application, was then 87 years old, her date of birth being April 19, 1756. William Pound, she states, served two year and upwards in the Virginia State Line during the Revolutionary War and that she was married to him prior to this service in Mecklenburg County, Virginia by the Rev. William Campbell in 1774. They resided in Mecklenburg County, Virginia, during the Revolutionary War and until the year 1803, when they settled in Chatham County, North Carolina, where she now resides, and that her husband William Pound died in 1814, and she has remained a widow. She stated that the records of the family have been lost." These statements of Mary Elizabeth Pound were attested to by Nathan Williams, Justice of the Peace.

An additional statement of Mary Elizabeth Pound states she was "born in Mecklenburg County, Virginia in 1756 and was married there in 1774. Their first child was born in 1776 (Jane)." Their second child, Samuel, was born June 26, 1778 while Elizabeth was residing temporarily in North Carolina. Elizabeth's pension certificate No. 3940 for $40 per month began November 15, 1843 and ended September 4, 1846, presumably at her death. William Pound and Mary Elizabeth Tune had issue, which was the sixth generation in America:

C631. Jane Pound, first child and first daughter of William Pound and Elizabeth Tune, born 1776 in Mecklenburg County, Virginia.

C632. Samuel Pound, Sr., second child and first son of William Pound and Elizabeth Tune, born 26 Jun 1778 in Chatham County, North Carolina and died about 1878 in Hancock County, Illinois. Married --- ---. Samuel Pound married secondly to Sarah Williams, daughter of Joseph T. Williams, who served as a Revolutionary War soldier with the 8th Virginia Regiment from August 3, 1777 to 1782. Joseph T. Williams was born in

Pittsylvania County or Halifax County, Virginia, but migrated to Jackson County, Illinois, where he died in 1832.

Samuel Pound, according to Naomi Pounds Cooper, was acquainted with his wife Sarah, not only in Illinois, but when a boy in North Carolina and Virginia. It seems quite probable that Mecklenburg County, North Carolina was the site of the early acquaintance of the Williams and Pound families. Also according to Naomi Pounds Cooper, Joseph Williams, father of Joseph T. Williams, had been married twice to sisters, Sarah and Rebecca Lanier. He married Sarah, his first wife and mother of Joseph T. Williams, on June 3, 1766 in Granville County, North Carolina. Naomi Pounds Cooper, in relating incidents of family history, told the story of how one set of grandparents of her grandfather Williams came from Germany. This was the tale she told: A gardener's son at the baron's castle fell in love with the baron's daughter. The baron's daughter reciprocated this affection and eventually they eloped, were married, and escaped to America. Of the names and dates, there is no record.

Samuel Pound, as noted in the old Pounds family Bible now in the Nebraska Historical Museum at the state capitol, Lincoln; was born June 26, 1778 in North Carolina. It appears that Mecklenburg County, Virginia is not far distant from Chatham County, North Carolina, and the Pounds women folk moved back and forth during the Revolutionary War, living with various relatives. During one of these sojourns in NOrth Carolina from Virginia, Samuel Pound was born. His mother, as noted heretofore, was Mary Elizabeth Tune Pound. Shortly after he grew to young manhood, Samuel migrated to the then Northwest - Ohio, Indiana and Illinois. His migration trek was by way of Maryland, Pennsylvania, Ohio and Indiana. Evidently he stopped on the way to visit kinsmen in Pennsylvania as there is a family tradition as told by Naomi Pounds Cooper that soon after the orgiinal immigration of the Pounds to Jamestown, Virginia, many of them went north to Maryland and Pennsylvania. The name of Samuel Pound's first wife is unknown, but it believed that eight

children were born of that marriage. During the
period Samuel was in Ohio and Indiana, according
to his daughter Naomi, which was the period of the
War of 1812, Samuel was associated with the
American forces as a scout and guide. Apparently,
he did not enlist, but frequently guided and led
the American troops against hostile Indians and
British troops. Samuel Pound had by this time
added an "s" to his name, becoming Pounds. These
data were also told by Samuel's daughter, Naomi.
Samuel married Sarah Williams, daughter of Joseph
T. Williams, also a Revolutionary War soldier.
This marriage probably took place in 1811 or 1812
in Ohio. The family Bible, above mentioned,
recorded also the following legible data as to
births of the children of Samuel and Sarah Pounds:

      Samuel - born November 14, 1813
      Charity - born January 16, 1816
      Benjamin - born 1817
      Thomas - born 1817
      Joseph - born May 21, 1821
      Naomi - born 1823
      Isaac - birthdate unknown
      William - birthdate unknown
      John - birthdate unknown

Samuel was said to have lived to the age of 100
year and six months, which would make his death in
1878, in Hancock County, Illinois. Samuel Pounds
and Sarah Williams had issue, which was the
seventh generation in America:

               C6321. Samuel Pounds, Jr.,
first child and first son of Samuel Pounds and
Sarah Williams, born 14 Nov 1813 in Ohio. Samuel
Pounds, Jr. was killed when cutting timber by
having a tree fall on him while saving two young
children from being killed by the falling tree.
He died from the effects of this injury two days
prior to his approaching marriage.

               C6322. Charity Pounds, second
child and first daughter of Samuel Pounds and
Sarah Williams, born 16 Jan 1816 in Ohio. Married
in Guernsey County, Ohio to Robert Andersen.
Charity Pounds and Robert Andersen had issue,
which was the eighth generation in America:

               C63221. Emma Andersen,
first child and first daughter of Charity Pounds

and Robert Andersen, date and place of birth unknown. Married --- Bell.

C63222. Lucretia Andersen, second child and second daughter of Charity Pounds and Robert Andersen, date and place of birth unknown.

C63223. Edith Andersen, third child and third daughter of Charity Pounds and Robert Andersen, date and place of birth unknown.

C63224. Sarah Andersen, fourth child and fourth daughter of Charity Pounds and Robert Andersen, date and place of birth unknown.

C63225. George Andersen, fifth child and first son of Charity Pounds and Robert Andersen, date and place of birth unknown.

C63226. Bird Andersen, sixth child and fifth daughter of Charity Pounds and Robert Andersen, date and place of birth unknown.

C63227. Robert Andersen, Jr., seventh child and second son of Charity Pounds and Robert Andersen, date and place of birth unknown.

C6323. Benjamin Pounds, third child and second son of Samuel Pounds and Sarah Williams, born 1817 in Ohio. Married --- ---. Benjamin Pounds early moved to Kansas and was a frontiersman and died there. Benjamin Pounds and --- --- had issue, which was the eighth generation in America:

C63231. Thomas Pounds, first child and first son of Benjamin Pounds and --- ---, date and place of birth unknown. Thomas Pounds was a Union soldier during the Civil War. Married --- ---. Thomas Pounds and --- --- had issue, which was the ninth generation in America:

C632311. George Benjamin Pounds, first child and first son of Thomas Pounds and --- ---, born 1861 in Missouri and died 1941 in Oklahoma. Married --- ---. George Pounds and --- --- had issue, which was the tenth generation in America:

C6323111. Thomas Franklin Pounds, first child and first son

of George Pounds and --- ---, born 1891 in Missouri and died 1966 in Oklahoma. Married --- - --. Thomas Pounds and --- --- had issue, which was the eleventh generation in America:
C63231111. Archie McClellan Pounds, first child and first son of Thomas Pounds and --- ---, born 1918 in Oklahoma.

C63232. Elias Pounds, second child and second son of Benjamin Pounds and --- ---, date and place of birth unknown.

C63233. Benjamin Pounds, Jr., third child and third son of Benjamin Pounds and --- ---, date and place of birth unknown. Benjamin Pounds was killed at Vicksburg while serving in the Union army.

C63234. Amos Pounds, fourth child and fourth son of Benjamin Pounds and --- ---, date and place of birth unknown.

C63235. James Pounds, fifth child and fifth son of Benjamin Pounds and --- ---, date and place of birth unknown.

C63236. Rachel Pounds, sixth child and first daughter of Benjamin Pounds and --- ---, date and place of birth unknown and she died in Illinois. Married 21 Sep 1870 in Mason County, Illinois to John (Jack) Wallace, date and place of birth unknown, and he was a half-brother of Theodore Long Cooper. He died in Jewel City, Kansas. Rachel moved back to Illinois.

C6324. Thomas Pounds, fourth child and third son of Samuel Pounds and Sarah Williams, born 1817 in Ohio.

C6325. Joseph Pounds, Sr., fifth child and fourth son of Samuel Pounds and Sarah Williams, born 21 May 1821 in Muskingum County, Ohio probably near Zanesville and died 24 Jan 1855 at Durham, Hancock County, Illinois. Married 12 Oct 1845 in Mason County, Illinois to Mary Jane Ackison, born 29 Nov 1827 in Zanesville, Muskingum County, Ohio and died 16 Sep 1916 in Red Oak, Montgomery County, Iowa. Mary Jane Ackison Pounds married secondly 15 Aug 1856 at Durham, Hancock County, Illinois to Daniel Horner, date of birth unknown but he died 14 Jun 1900 at Dallas City, Hancock County, ILlinois. Joseph and his wife moved to Washington County, Iowa and later to Hancock County, Illinois. During his life, Joseph was sheriff of Hancock County for a time. Family reports had it that he was rather severe on the Mormons then living in Hancock County and was instrumentatl in compelling them to move out of the county as much stealing of stock was laid at their door. Anyway, Joseph was once compelled to flee for his life on horseback, having been attacked by a mob of Mormons. Much of this Mormon disturbance occurred at Pontoosuc, Illinois. It was also said that Joseph saw Joseph Smith, the Mormon leader, died at Carthage, Illinois. Joseph Pounds was an active churchman (Methodist). He was a trustee of the local church at Durham, Illinois and superintendent of the Sunday School. He was looked up to as a leader in the community and was intensely loyal to his religion. He was an energetic and intelligent man, physically powerfully built. It was told that he could not cross his legs in comfort. Joseph died January 1855 at 34 years of age, and was buried at Durham, Hancock County, Illinois. THe cause of his death was said to be brain fever, probably epidemic cerebro-spinal meningitis. He had rather extensive land holdings in Mason and Hancock Counties, Illinois at his death, though this has not been verified. Joseph Pounds and Mary Ackison had issue, which was the eighth generation in America:

C63251. William Henry Pounds, first child and first son of Joseph Pounds and Mary Ackison, born 29 Sep 1846 in Hancock County, Illinois and died at Bladen, Nebraska. William Henry Pounds served in the Union army diring the Civil War. His home, up to the time of his death, was at Bladen, Webster County, Nebraska. Married --- ---. William Pounds and --- --- had issue, which was the ninth generation in America:

C632511. Sidney Pounds, first child and first son of William Pounds and --- ---, born at Bladen, Webster County, Nebraska.

C63252. Joseph Pounds, Jr., second child and second son of Joseph Pounds and Mary Ackison, born 15 Feb 1848 in Hancock County, Illinois and died 11 Nov 1913 in Ogallala, Keith County, Nebraska. Married --- ---. Joseph Pounds and --- --- had issue, which was the ninth generation in America:

C632521. Roy Pounds, first child and first son of Joseph Pounds and --- ---, date and place of birth unknown.

C632522. Joseph Pounds, second child and second son of Joseph Pounds and --- ---, date and place of birth unknown.

C632523. Chase Pounds, third child and third son of Joseph Pounds and --- ---, date and place of birth unknown.

C632524. Walter Pounds, fourth child and fourth son of Joseph Pounds and --- ---, date and place of birth unknown.

C632525. Clarence Pounds, fifth child and fifth son of Joseph Pounds and --- ---, date and place of birth unknown.

C632526. Dewey Pounds, sixth child and sixth son of Joseph Pounds and --- ---, date and place of birth unknown.

C632527. Lloyd Pounds, seventh child and seventh son of Joseph Pounds and --- ---, date and place of birth unknown.

C632528. Louisa Jane Pounds, eighth child and first daughter of Joseph Pounds and --- ---, date and place of birth unknown.

C632529. Pearl Pounds, ninth child and second daughter of Joseph Pounds and --- ---, date and place of birth unknown.

C632530. Cretie Pounds, tenth child and third daughter of Joseph Pounds and --- ---, date and place of birth unknown.

C632531. Addie Pounds, eleventh child and fourth daughter of Joseph Pounds and --- ---, date and place of birth unknown.

C63253. Louisa Jane

Pounds, third child and first daughter of Joseph Pounds and Mary Ackison, born 29 Oct 1850 in Hancock County, Illinois. Married Sidney H. Smith. Louisa Pounds and Sidney Smith had issue, which was the ninth generation in America:

C632531. Ervin Smith, first child and first son of Louisa Pounds and Sidney Smith, born at Crete, Saline County, Nebraska.

C632532. May Smith, second child and first daughter of Louisa Pounds and Sidney Smith, born at Crete, Saline County, Nebraska.

C632533. Milton O. Smith, third child and second son of Louisa Pounds and Sidney Smith, born at Crete, Saline County, Nebraska.

C63254. James Reynolds Pounds, fourth child and third son of Joseph Pounds and Mary Ackison, born 20 Apr 1852 at Durham, Hancock County, Illinois and died 5 Mar 1934 at Emporia, Lyon County, Kansas. Married 30 Jun 1880 at the home of Dr. Alexander Taylor, Ashland, Cass County, Nebraska to Sarah Taylor. At the death of his father, Joseph Pounds, James Reynolds Pounds and his younger sister, Mary Ann (Naomi) Pounds were taken and raised by their paternal aunt, Naomi Pounds Cooper. As his mother would not sign the legal papers necessary, James did not legally take the name of Cooper until he was of age, when proper documents were secured at the earnest desire of his aunt Naomi and his uncle, Theodore Long Cooper, and James became James Reynolds Cooper. After the Civil War, the Coopers lived in Nebraska where a homestead was filed on a quarter section of land, some nine miles southeast of Tecumseh, Nebraska. There the hardships of early frontier life were experienced. Poor crops, grashopper plagues, hot winds in summer, blizzards in winter. James told of an average yield of three bushels of wheat per acre and using dead branches of trees to harrow the plowed ground. The long haul to market from Tecumseh to Nebraska City by wagon train, their making a living by hunting rabbits, quail, prairie chickens, with an occasional buffalo or antelope were all part of these hardships. Theodore Cooper, the foster father of James, seems to have had an "itchy foot", as the family moved frequently; for a time living in Peru, Nemaha County, Nebraska, where Theodore and Naomi ran a students boarding house and saw that James attended the state normal school there, graduating late in the 1870s, probably '77 or '79. While at Peru, James met Sarah Taylor, and married her at the home of her parents, Dr. and Mrs. Alexander Taylor, at Ashland, Nebraska on June 30, 1880. James Cooper and Sarah Taylor had issue, which was the ninth generation in America:

C632541. Theodore Reynolds Cooper, first child and first son of James Cooper and Sarah Taylor, born 18 Apr 1881 at Jewell, Jewell County, Kansas and died 28 Mar 1943 in Lone Pine, Inyo County, California. Married Jun 1908 at Bellevue, Sarpy County, Nebraska to Harriett Fletcher. Theodore Cooper and Harriett Fletcher had issue, which was the tenth generation in America:

C6325411. Kenneth James Cooper, first child and first son of Theodore Cooper and Harriett Fletcher, born 1907 in Nebraska.

C6325412. Hugh Alexander Cooper, second child and second son of Theodore Cooper and Harriett Fletcher, born 1910 at Biggs, Butte County, California.

C6325413. Theodore Reynolds Cooper, Jr., third child and third son of Theodore Cooper and Harriett Fletcher, born 1912 at Biggs, Butte County, California.

C6325414. Betty Cooper, fourth child and first daughter of Theodore Cooper and Harriett Fletcher, born 1913 at Biggs, Butte County, California.

C632542. Alexander Taylor Cooper, second child and second son of James Cooper and Sarah Taylor, born 8 Apr 1883, at Yutan, Saunders County, Nebraska. Married 5 Feb 1910 at Atlantic City, Atlantic County, New Jersey to Charlotte Carter Baker. Alexander Cooper entered the Medical Corps of the Regular Army and served on active duty from Oct 1, 1909 until he retired from active service January 31, 1940. After retirement, he and his wife elected to live in San Juan, Puerto Rico. Alexander Cooper and Charlotte Baker had issue, which was the tenth generation in America:

C6325421. David Cooper, first child and first son of Alexander Cooper and Charlotte Baker, born 29 Jan 1918. David Cooper served on active duty with the U.S. Army during World War II. Married 3 Sep 1942 at West Point, Post Chapel, New York to Patricia Magner, born in New York.

C6325422. Quentin Cooper, second child and second son of Alexander Cooper and Charlotte Baker, born 4 Oct 1923. Quentin Cooper served with the U.S. Army during World War II.

C632543. Lucille Maude Cooper, third child and first daughter of James Cooper and Sarah Taylor, born 24 Sep 1884 at Yutan, Saunders County, Nebraska and died at Escondido, San Siego County, California. Married 1906 at Auburn, Nemaha County, Nebraska to Arthur E. Oberman.

C63254. James Reynolds Cooper, fourth child and third son of James Pounds and Mary Ackison, born 20 Apr 1852 at Durham, Hancock County, Illinois and died 5 Mar 1934 at Emporia, Lyon County, Kansas. Married secondly May 1891 in Nebraska to Grace Baird, born at Blystone, Nebraska and she died 1921 at Emporia, Lyon County, Kansas. James Cooper and Grace Baird had issue, which was the ninth generation in America:

C632541. Paul Baird Cooper, first child and first son of James Cooper and Grace Baird, born 5 Jan 1893 at Auburn, Nemaha County, Nebraska. Married about 1917 at Emporia, Lyon County, Kansas to May Boughton. Paul Cooper and May Boughton had issue, which was the tenth generation in America:

C6325411. Warren Cooper, first child and first son of Paul Cooper and May Boughton, date and place of birth unknown.

C6325412.
Clarice Cooper, second child and first daughter of
Paul Cooper and May Boughton, date and place of
birth unknown.

C632542.   Robert
Curry Cooper, second child and second son of James
Cooper and Grace Baird, born 12 Feb 1895 at
Auburn, Nemaha County, Nebraska.

C632543.   Warren
Cooper, third child and third son of James Cooper
and Grace Baird, born 1897 and died in infancy at
Auburn, Nemaha County, Nebraska.

C632544. Anna Naomi
Cooper, fourth child and first daughter of James
Cooper and Grace Baird, born 1899 at Auburn,
Nemaha County, Nebraska. Married at Emporia, Lyon
County, Kansas to Tracy Boughton. Anna Cooper and
Tracy Boughton had issue, which was the tenth
generation in America:

C6325441.
Kenneth Boughton, first child and first son of
Anna Cooper and Tracy Boughton, date and place of
birth unknown.

C6325442.
Murice Boughton, second child and first daughter
of Anna Cooper and Tracy Boughton, date and place
of birth unknown.

C6325443. Dean
Boughton, third child and second son of Anna
Cooper and Tracy Boughton, date and place of birth
unknown.

C632545.   Katherine
Cooper, fifth child and second daughter of James
Cooper and Grace Baird, born 1901 at Auburn,
Nemaha County, Nebraska.

C632546.   Dwight
Harold Cooper, sixth child and fourth son of James
Cooper and Grace Baird, born 1903 at Auburn,
Nemaha County, Nebraska. Married --- ---Dwight
Cooper and --- --- had issue, which was the tenth
generation in America:

C6325461. Jack
Cooper, first child and first son of Dwight Cooper
and --- ---, date and place of birth unknown.

C6325462.

Eleanor Cooper, second child and first daughter of Dwight Cooper and --- ---, date and place of birth unknown.

C632547.   Lois Cooper, seventh child and third daughter of James Cooper and Grace Baird, born 1907 at Auburn, Nemaha County, Nebraska.

C632548.   Helen Cooper, eighth child and fourth daughter of James Cooper and Grace Baird, born 1911 at Auburn, Nemaha County, Nebraska.

C63255. Mary Ann (Naomi) (Mollie) Pounds, fifth child and second daughter of Joseph Pounds and Mary Ackison, born 3 Nov 1853 in Hancock County, Illinois and died 1921 in Lincoln, Lancaster County, Nebraska.   Buried at Lincoln, Lancaster County, Nebraska.   Married William J. Blystone. Mary Ann was christened Mary Ann according to her older sister, Louisa, but later her name was changed to Mary Naomi, after her aunt Naomi who was raising her. She lived for the first part of her married life with her husband on his farm some nine miles southeast of Tecumseh, Nebraska. The latter part of her life she and her husband lived in Lincoln, Nebraska. She died in the early fall of 1921 from pneumonia, and was buried at Lincoln, Nebraska. During her life, she was an indefatigable worker, actice in church and social circles.   Mary Ann Pounds and William Blystone had issue, which was the ninth generation in America:

C632551.   Samuel Cooper Blystone, first child and first son of Mary Pounds and William Blystone, born at Tecumseh, Johnson County, Nebraska.

C6326. Naomi Pounds, sixth child and second daughter of Samuel Pounds and Sarah Williams, born 1823 in Ohio. Married Cecil White, early in adult life, who died shortly after marriage during the days of 1849 in California. Married secondly Theodore Long Cooper. Married thirdly --- Elyea. Shortly after the death of her brother, Joseph Pounds, Naomi, who was childless and then married to Theodore Long Cooper, with her mother's permission, took Joseph's two youngest children, James and Mary Ann (Mollie) to live with

her temporarily.   THeir mother, Mary Jane, never
regained   the   custody   of   these   two   youngest
children.   It developed into a quarrel between the
two women as to who would have them.   Louisa
Pounds Smith, an older sister, told how these two
young children were practically kidnapped by their
aunt Naomi, who claimed that Joseph, their father,
had promised them to her should anything happen to
him (Joseph).   Naomi retained them by moving away
promptly and practically going into hiding in
frontier Nebraska and Kansas, out of reach of Mary
Jane, their mother.   No adoption papers were ever
taken out during childhood as Mary Jane refused to
sign the necessary documents.   James and Mollie
grew up as the children of Theodore L. Cooper and
his wife, their aunt Naomi.   After he arrived at
maturity (age 21), proper adoption papers were
written up and James, urged by Theodore L. Cooper,
became officially, James Reynolds Cooper.   Mollie,
marrying before she was twenty-one years, wed as
Mollie Pounds.   Naomi would never discuss this
action of hers with Alexander Cooper and would
never talk to James or his family about it.
James' older siste, Louisa, related the facts as
stated.   James lived within less than 100 miles of
his mother for years and was unaware of it.   (Red
Oak, Iowa and Auburn, Nebraska).   They had lost
track of each other. Naomi Pounds Cooper married
late in life, after the death of her second
husband, Theodore Long Cooper, a Mr. Elyea.   Mr.
Elyea became mentally unbalanced in his old age
(senile dementia) and Naomi died from a hatchet
blow at his hands.   Naomi Pounds and Theodore
Cooper did not have issue, but adopted an infant
female, who was considered to be in the eighth
generation in America:
                              C63261.   Alice Cooper,
adopted child of Naomi Pounds and Theodore Cooper,
date and place of birth unknown.   Alice, adopted
in infancy, who grew to womanhood and cared for
Naomi in her old age.   Alice grew into a comely,
vivacious young woman.   She was remembered with
affection as a talented and charming individual.
She later went to India as a teacher missionary
for the Lee Memorial Mission at Calcutta.   Here
she met a missionary by name of Rev. P.G.

614

Hastings, married him and had two children. Upon her return to this county, they lived in Newburg, New York where her husband was pastor of the Reformed Episcopal Church.

C6327. Isaac Pounds, seventh child and fifth son of Samuel Pounds and Sarah Williams, born about 1825 in Ohio. Isaac Pounds was a trapeze performer. He fell and hurt himself, dying from the effects of this fall at thirty years of age.

C7328. William Pounds, eighth child and sixth son of Samuel Pounds and Sarah Williams, born about 1827 in Ohio. William Pounds diex unmarried in young manhood of exposure on the western plains.

C6329. John Pounds, ninth child and seventh son of Samuel Pounds and Sarah Williams, born about 1829 in Ohio.

C633. William C. Pound, third child and second son of William Pound and Elizabeth Tune, born about 1781 in Chatham County, North Carolina and died in Kansas. Married 15 Apr 1815 in Pittsboro, Chatham County, North Carolina to Jane Hadley, daughter of Jeremiah Hadley and Mary Dickey, born 17 May 1785 in Chatham County, North Carolina and died in Kansas. William Pound and Jane Hadley had issue, which was the seventh generation in America:

C6331. James L. Pounds, first child and first son of William Pound and Jane Hadley, born 1814 in North Carolina. Married 1 Jan 1843 in Hendricks County, Indiana to Emaline Purcell.

C6332. Mary Ann Pounds, second child and first daughter of William Pound and Jane Hadley, born 8 Sep 1816 and died 18 Apr 1892 in Morgan County, indiana. Buried at West Union cemetery, Indiana. Married 19 Jan 1835 in Morgan County, Indiana to Jesse Brooke Johnson.

C6333. William Henderson Pounds, third child and second son of William Pound and Jane Hadley, born 18 Mar 1822 in Ohio and died 13 Jul 1900 at Pawnee Township, Smith County, Kansas. Buried at Womer cemetery, Kansas. Married 20 Mar 1844 in Morgan County, Indiana to Martha Ruth Anderson, daughter of Eli Johnson and

Mary Thatcher, born 2 Nov 1827 at Wilmington, Clinton County, Ohio and died 16 Feb 1916 at Smith Center, Smith County, Kansas. Buried at Fairview cemetery, Smith Center, Kansas. William Pounds and Martha Anderson had issue, which was the eighth generation in America:

C63331. Anderson (Ans) Pounds, first child and first son of William Pounds and Martha Anderson, born 23 Feb 1845 in Morgan County, Indiana and died 23 Apr 1915 in Smith County, Kansas. Married 21 Mar 1866 in Oskaloosa, Mahaska County, Iowa to Catherine Ann Hughes.

C63332. Mary Jane Pounds, second child and first daughter of William Pounds and Martha Anderson, born 1 Jan 1847 in Indiana and died before 1916 in Missouri. Married 27 Oct 1864 in Morgan County, Indiana to Lemuel Faulkner, born 1837 in North Carolina. Mary Pounds and Lemuel Faulkner had issue, which was the ninth generation in America:

C633321. Anna D. Faulkner, first child and first daughter of Mary Pounds and Lemuel Faulkner, born 1868 in Indiana.

C633322. Maggie P. Faulkner, second child and second daughter of Mary Pounds and Lemuel Faulkner, born 1872 in Indiana.

C633323. Clarie B. Faulkner, third child and third daughter of Mary Pounds and Lemuel Faulkner, born 1876 in Iowa.

C633324. Rawilo Faulkner, fourth child and fourth daughter of Mary Pounds and Lemuel Faulkner, born Jan 1880 in Kansas.

C63333. Thatcher M. Pounds, third child and second son of William Pounds and Martha Anderson, born 16 Sep 1849 at Monrovia, Morgan County, Indiana and died after 1924 at Beloit, Mitchell County, Kansas. Married 18 Nov 1875 in Oskaloosa, Mahaska County, Iowa to Maria Elwood.

C63334. Alonzo Pounds, fourth child and third son of William Pounds and Martha Anderson, born 1 Mar 1852 in Indiana and died 11 Jul 1852 in Indiana.

C63335. Allie Pounds,

fifth child and second daughter of William Pounds and Martha Anderson, born 17 Jul 1853 in Indiana and died 29 Jun 1854 in Indiana.

C63336. Eva Mae Pounds, sixth child and third daughter of William Pounds and Martha Anderson, born 20 May 1855 at Monrovia, Morgan County, Indiana and died at Red Cloud, Webster County, Nebraska. Married 9 Dec 1877 in Indiana to Arthur Stevenson.

C63337. Charles Freemont Pounds, seventh child and fourth son of William Pounds and Martha Anderson, born 2 Nov 1857 in Indiana and died 15 Sep 1924 at Smith Center, Smith County, Kansas.

C63338. Joel Dayton Pounds, eighth child and fifth son of William Pounds and Martha Anderson, born 27 Nov 1859 in Morgan County, Indiana and died 18 Sep 1847 at Yuma, Yuma County, Colorado. Buried at Yuma cemetery, Yuma County, Colorado. Married 2 Oct 1881 at Thornburg, Smith County, Kansas to Elizabeth Bruce, daughter of (Seth) Thomas McIntyre Bruce and Martha Jane Windsor, born 5 Jul 1863 at Holton, Ripley County, Indiana and died 4 May 1942 at Yuma, Yuma County, Colorado. Buried at Yuma cemetery, Colorado. Joel Pounds and Elizabeth Bruce had issue, which was the ninth generation in America:

C633381. Beckie (Nelsie Faye) Pounds, first child and first daughter of Joel Pounds and Elizabeth Bruce, born 31 Jul 1882 at Thornburg, Smith County, Kansas and died 30 Mar 1965 at Smith Center, Smith County, Kansas. Married 4 Aug 1901 in Smith County, Kansas to Chester Vinton Burgess, date and place of birth unknown but he died in 1930. Beckie Pounds and Chester Burgess had issue, which was the tenth generation in America:

C6333811. George Dayton Burgess, first child and first son of Beckie Pounds and Chester Burgess, born 22 Mar 1903 in Smith County, Kansas and died 12 Jun 1960.

C6333812. Doris Faye Burgess, second child and first daughter of Beckie Pounds and Chester Burgess, born 27 Aug 1905 in Smith County, Kansas and died

26 Jun 1946.

C6333813. Elma Twila Burgess, third child and second daughter of Beckie Pounds and Chester Burgess, born 29 Sep 1908 in Smith County, Kansas. Married 3 Aug 1932 in Kansas to Garth Maley Holmes.

C633814. Chester Earl Howell Burgess, fourth child and second son of Beckie Pounds and Chester Burgess, born 10 Jan 1911 in Smith County, Kansas.

C633815. Charles Leonard (twin) Burgess, fifth child and third son of Beckie Pounds and Chester Burgess, born 23 Sep 1913 in Smith County, Kansas and died 20 Jun 1974.

C633816. Clarence Henry STI (twin) Burgess, sixth child and fourth son of Beckie Pounds and Chester Burgess, born and died   23 Sep 1913 at Smith County, Kansas.

C633817. Mildred (Millie) Elizabeth Burgess, seventh child and third daughter of Beckie Pounds and Chester Burgess, born 30 May 1916 in Smith County, Kansas.

C633818. Arthur Woodrow Burgess, eighth child and fifth son of Beckie Pounds and Chester Burgess, born 1 Sep 1918 in Smith County, Kansas and died 24 May 1964.

C633819. Mary Marie Burgess, ninth child and fourth daughter of Beckie Pounds and Chester Burgess, born 3 Mar 1921 in Smith County, Kansas.

C633382. Sarah Ann Pounds, second child and second daughter of Joel Pounds and Elizabeth Bruce, born 25 Jun 1884 at Thornburg, Smith County, Kansas and died 26 May 1911 at Smith Center, Smith County, Kansas. Buried at Fairview cemetery, Smith County, Kansas.

C63383. Lewis Earl Pounds, third child and first son of Joel Pounds and Elizabeth Bruce, born 9 Jan 1888 at Thornburg, Smith County, Kansas and died 20 Feb 1965 at Coolidge, Pinal County, Arizona. Married 16 Apr 1916 at Smith Center, Smith County, Kansas to Hettie May Whitmarsh. Lewis Pounds and Hettie

618

Whitmarsh had issue, which was the tenth generation in America:

C633831. Claude Pounds, first child and first son of Lewis Pounds and Hettie Whitmarsh, date and place of birth unknown.

C633832. Dayton Pounds, second child and first son of Lewis Pounds and Hettie Whitmarsh, date and place of birth unknown.

C633833. Harry Pounds, third child and third son of Lewis Pounds and Hettie Whitmarsh, date and place of birth unknown.

C633834. Elizabeth Pounds, fourth child and first daughter of Lewis Pounds and Hettie Whitmarsh, date and place of birth unknown.

C633835. Helen Pounds, fifth child and second daughter of Lewis Pounds and Hettie Whitmarsh, date and place of birth unknown.

C63384. Charles Henry Pounds, fourth child and second son of Joel Pounds and Elizabeth Bruce, born 13 Jun 1892 at Thornburg, Smith County, Kansas and died 26 Oct 1950 at Yuma, Yuma County, Arizona.

C63385. Joel Leonard (Doc) Pounds, fifth child and third son of Joel Pounds and Elizabeth Bruce, born 9 Dec 1896 at Smith Center, Smith County, Kansas and died 26 Mar 1975 at Portland, Multnomah County, Oregon. Buried at Portland, Multnomah County, Oregon. Married 8 Dec 1917 at Smith Center, Smith County, Kansas to Flossie Belle Horsman, born 24 Sep 1898 at Amity, DeKalb County, Missouri and died 5 Jul 1983 at Portland, Multnomah County, Oregon. Joel Pounds and Flossie Horsman had issue, which was the tenth generation in America:

C633851. Margaret Lois Pounds, first child and first daughter of Joel Pounds and Flossie Horsman, born 18 Aug 1920 at Kirwin, Phillips County, Kansas. Married 26 Mar 1950 at Portland, Multnomah County, Oregon to Lloyd Preston Dawson. Margaret Pounds and Lloyd Dawson had issue, which was the eleventh

generation in America:

C6338511.   Carol Jean Dawson, first child and first daughter of Margaret Pounds and Lloyd Dawson, born 4 Oct 1951 at Toledo, Lincoln County, Oregon.   Married 16 Sep 1973 at Yachats, Lincoln County, Oregon to Michael P. Morrison.   Carol Dawson and Michael Morrison had issue, which was the twelfth generation in America:

C63385111.   Ryan Michael Morrison, first child and first son of Carol Dawson and Michael Morrison, born 15 Nov 1984.

C6338512.   Dale Alan Morrison, second child and second son of Margaret Pounds and Lloyd Dawson, born 27 Feb 1953 at Newport, Lincoln County, Oregon.   Married 13 Feb 1982 Lincoln City, Lincoln County, Oregon to Deborah Bond Hunter.   Dale Morrison and Deborah Hunter had issue, which was the twelfth generation in America:

C63385121.   Christy Lee Dawson, first child and first daughter of Dale Morrison and Deborah Hunter, born 11 Apr 1985.

C63385122.   Bruce Alan Dawson, second child and first son of Dale Morrison and Deborah Hunter, born 28 Jan 1989.

C6338513.   Linda Kay Dawson, third child and second daughter of Margaret Pounds and Lloyd Dawson, born 22 Aug 1955 at Newport, Lincoln County, Oregon.   Married 23 Oct 1976 at Yachats, Lincoln County, Oregon to Michael Leon Morrison. Linda Dawson and Michael Morrison had issue, which was the twelfth generation in America:

C63385131.   Jonathan Michael Morrison, first child and first son of Linda Dawson and Michael Morrison, born 28 Apr 1979.

C63385132.   Amanda Rose Morrison, second child and first daughter of Linda Dawson and Michael Morrison, born 9 Aug 1982.

C63385133.   Rebecca Anne Morrison, third child and second daughter of Linda Dawson and Michael Morrison, born 29 Sep 1984.

C633852. Frances Lucille Pounds, second child and second daughter of Joel Pounds and Flossie Horsman, born 18 May 1922 at Logan, Phillips County, Kansas. Married 30 Mar 1942 at Vallejo, Marin County, California to Joseph George Muench.

C633853. Wilma Marie Pounds, third child and third daughter of Joel Pounds and Flossie Horsman, born 18 Oct 1924 at Salem, Marion County, Oregon. Married 25 Feb 1943 at Roseburg, Douglas County, Oregon to James Wesley Beaver, born 3 Jul 1919 at Quenemo, Osage County, Kansas.

C63386. Flossie Elizabeth Pounds, sixth child and third daughter of Joel Pounds and Elizabeth Bruce, born 23 Aug 1899 at Smith Center, Smith County, Kansas and died 6 May 1966 at Scotts Bluff, Scotts Bluff County, Nebraska. Married 4 Feb 1920 at Yuma, Yuma County, Colorado to Thomas W. Briggs. Flossie Pounds and Thomas Briggs had issue, which was the tenth generation in America:

C633861. Agnes Briggs, first child and first daughter of Flossie Pounds and Thomas Briggs, born 10 Jan 1921 in Colorado.

C633862. Everett Briggs, second child and first son of Flossie Pounds and Thomas Briggs, born 10 Oct 1923 in Colorado.

C633863. Howard Briggs, third child and second son of Flossie Pounds and Thomas Briggs, born 31 Jan 1928 in Colorado.

C633864. David Briggs, fourth child and third son of Flossie Pounds and Thomas Briggs, born 12 Sep 1932 in Colorado.

C633865. Bernon Briggs, fifth child and fourth son of Flossie Pounds and Thomas Briggs, born 9 Dec 1936 in Colorado.

C633866. Ruth Briggs, sixth child and second daughter of Flossie Pounds and Thomas Briggs, born 29 Apr 1942 in Colorado.

C63339. John Harvey Pounds, ninth child and sixth son of William Pounds and Martha Anderson, born 10 Oct 1861 in Indiana and died 10 Feb 1919 at Dayton, Columbia County, Washington. Married 21 Nov 1886 in Smith County, Kansas to Lillie May Bruce. John Pounds and Lillie Bruce had issue, which was the ninth generation in America:

C633391.   Tina Pounds, first child and first daughter of John Pounds and Lillie Bruce, date and place of birth unknown.

C633392.   Viola Pounds, second child and second daughter of John Pounds and Lillie Bruce, date and place of birth unknown.

C633393.   Jerry Simpson Pounds, third child and first son of John Pounds and Lillie Bruce, date and place of birth unknown.

C633394.   Leland Pounds, fourth child and second son of John Pounds and Lillie Bruce, date and place of birth unknown.

C633395.   Lois Pounds, fifth child and third daughter of John Pounds and Lillie Bruce, date and place of birth unknown.

C633396.   Lona Pounds, sixth child and fourth daughter of John Pounds and Lillie Bruce, date and place of birth unknown.

C633397.   Royal Pounds, seventh child and third son of John Pounds and Lillie Bruce, date and place of birth unknown.

C633398.   John Pounds, eighth child and fourth son of John Pounds and Lillie Bruce, date and place of birth unknown.

C63340.   Amy Pounds, tenth child and fourth daughter of William Pounds and Martha Anderson, born 23 Oct 1862 in Indiana and died 3 Mar 1866.

C63341.   Willie Pounds, eleventh child and seventh son of William Pounds and Martha Anderson, born 27 Nov 1866 in Indiana and died 28 Nov 1868 in Indiana.

C63342.   Lemuel Pounds, twelfth child and eight son of William Pounds and Martha Anderson, born 19 Jan 1868 in Indiana and died 24 Aug 1868 in Indiana.

C634.   Thomas Pound, fourth child and third son of William Pound and Elizabeth Tune, born about 1794 in Mecklenburg County, Virginia.

        C635. Sarah Pound, fifth child and second daughter of William Pound and Elizabeth Tune, date and place of birth unknown.

        C636. Mary Pound, sixth child and third daughter of William Pound and Elizabeth Tune, born about 1783 in Mecklenburg County, Virginia. Married 12 Mar 1822 in Chatham County, North Carolina to Isaac Wells.

        C637. Elizabeth (Betsy) Pound, seventh child and fourth daughter of William Pound and Elizabeth Tune, born about 1787 in Mecklenburg County, Virginia. Married 23 Feb 1816 in Chatham County, North Carolina to BIshop Barker.

        C638. Lewis T. Pound, eighth child and fourth son of William Pound and Elizabeth Tune, born 12 Apr 1792 in Mecklenburg County, Virginia and died 2 Feb 1878 in Hendricks County, Indiana. Buried at Christy cemetery, Hendricks County, Indiana. Married 14 Oct 1813 in Chatham County, North Carolina to Margaret (Peggy) B. Johnston. Married secondly to Goncey Todd. Lewis Pound and Margaret Johnston had issue, which was the seventh generation in America:

        C6381. Andrew J. Pounds, first child and first son of Lewis Pound and Margaret Johnston, born 16 May 1815 in Chatham County, North Carolina and died 30 Jul 1840. Married 16 Jan 1840 to Nancy Tout.

        C6382. William Pounds, second child and second son of Lewis Pound and Margaret Johnston, born 11 Apr 1819 in Chatham County, North Carolina. Married 8 Nov 1838 to Sarah Downs.

        C6383. Henry A. Pounds, third child and third son of Lewis Pound and Margaret Johnston, born 15 May 1821 in Chatham County, North Carolina. Married 20 Sep 1842 to Harriett Hankins.

        C6384. Joseph B. Pounds, fourth child and fourth son of Lewis Pound and Margaret Johnston, born 17 Jul 1823 in Chatham County, North Carolina and died 20 Dec 1884.

        C6385. Elizabeth Pounds, fifth child and first daughter of Lewis Pound and

Margaret Johnston, born 1826 in Chatham County, North Carolina and died May 1852. Married 10 Apr 1851 to Gideon Morris.

C6386. Lewis L. Pounds, sixth child and fifth son of Lewis Pound and Margaret Johnston, date and place of birth unknown, but he died 30 Jul 1846 in the Mexican War.

C6387. Thomas E. Pounds, seventh child and sixth son of Lewis Pound and Margaret Johnston, born 1832 in Hendricks County, Indiana.

C6388. James Andrew Pounds, eighth child and seventh son of Lewis Pound and Margaret Johnston, born 14 Jan 1834 in Hendricks County, Indiana and died 19 Jul 1884. Married 3 Aug 1954 to Sarah G. Barron.

C6389. Archibald Price Pounds, ninth child and eighth son of Lewis Pound and Margaret Johnston, born 1838 in Hendricks County, Indiana and died 10 May 1888. Married 8 Jul 1860 to Susanna Todd.

C6390. --- Pounds, tenth child and sex unknown of Lewis Pound and Margaret Johnston, died in infancy.

C639. Archibald Pound, ninth child and fifth son of William Pound and Elizabeth Tune, date and place of birth unknown.

C640. Lucy Pound, tenth child and fifth daughter of William Pound and Elizabeth Tune, born about 1785 in Mecklenburg County, Virginia.

C64. Solomon Pound, fourth child and fourth son of Thomas Pound and Jean ---, born about 1742 in Richmond County, Virginia and died 1804 in Charlotte County, North Carolina. Married 28 Feb 1791 in Halifax County, Virginia to Frances Bryant.

C65. Samuel Pound, fifth child and fifth son of Thomas Pound and Jean ---, born about 1751 in Halifax County, North Carolina and died 1 Apr 1830 in Anson County, North Carolina. Samuel Pound married Sarah Rorey, born about 1754 in Virginia and died 21 Sep 1847 in Anson County, North Carolina. Samuel Pound and Sarah Rorey had issue, which was the sixth generation in America:

C651. Abraham Pound, first child

and first son of Samuel Pound and Sarah Rorey, born about 1788 in Onslow County, North Carolina. Abraham Pound married --- ---. Abraham Pound and --- --- had issue, which was the seventh generation in America:

C6511. Abram Pound, first child and first son of Abraham Pound and --- ---, born 1810 in North Carolina.

C6512. Elizabeth Pound, second child and first daughter of Abraham Pound and --- ---, born 1820 in North Carolina.

C6513. Julia Pound, third child and second daughter of Abraham Pound and --- ---, born 1827 in North Carolina.

C6514. Jacob Pound, fourth child and second son of Abraham Pound and --- --- born 1832 in North Carolina.

C6515. Clara Pound, fifth child and third daughter of Abraham Pound and --- ---, born 1837 in North Carolina.

C6516. Lydia Pound, sixth child and fourth daughter of Abraham Pound and --- ---, born 1839 in North Carolina.

C6517. Zethbey Pound, seventh child and third son of Abraham Pound and --- ---, born 1841 in North Carolina.

C6518. Margaret Pound, eighth child and fifth daughter of Abraham Pound and --- ---, born 1844 in North Carolina.

C6519. Samuel Pound, ninth child and fourth son of Abraham Pound and --- --- born 1846 in North Carolina.

C652. Elizabeth Pound, second child and first daughter of Samuel Pound and Sarah Rorey, date and place of birth unknown.

C653. --- Pound, third child presumed a daughter of Samuel Pound and Sarah Rorey, date and place of birth unknown.

C654. Samuel Pound, fourth child and second son of Samuel Pound and Sarah Rorey, born 15 Oct 1800 in Anson County, North Carolina. Married about 1828 at Brunswick, Columbus County, North Carolina to Nancy ---, born 1811 in North Carolina. Samuel Pound and Nancy --- had issue, which was the seventh generation in America:

C6541. John Pound, first

child and first son of Samuel Pound and Nancy ---
born 1829 at Brunswick, Columbus County, North
Carolina.

C6542. Amanda Pound, second
child and first daughter of Samuel Pound and Nancy
---, born 1832 at Brunswick, Columbus County,
North Carolina.

C6543. Rebecca Pound, third
child and second daughter of Samuel Pound and
Nancy ---, born 1838 at Brunswick, Columbus
County, North Carolina.

C6544. Mary Pound, fourth
child and third daughter of Samuel Pound and Nancy
---, born 1841 at Brunswick, Columbus County,
North Carolina.

C6545. Jesse Pound, fifth
child and second son of Samuel Pound and Nancy ---
, born 1844 at Brunswick, Columbus County, North
Carolina.

C6546. Margaret Pound, sixth
child and fourth daughter of Samuel Pound and
Nancy ---, born 1846 at Brunswick, Columbus
County, North Carolina.

C6547. Luiesa Pound, seventh
child and fifth daughter of Samuel Pound and Nancy
---, born 1849 at Brunswick, Columbus County,
North Carolina.

C655. Isaac Pound, fifth child and
third son of Samuel Pound and Sarah Rorey, born
1800 in North Carolina. Married about 1828 in
North Carolina to Mary ---, born 1806 in North
Carolina. Isaac Pound and Mary --- had issue,
which was the seventh generation in America:

C6551. William Pound, first
child and first son of Isaac Pound and Mary ---,
born 1829 in North Carolina.

C6552. Godenia Pound, second
child and first daughter of Isaac Pound and Mary -
--, born 1831 in North Carolina.

C6553. Elizabeth Pound, third
child and second daughter of Isaac Pound and Mary
---, born 1832 in North Carolina.

C6554. Emeline Pound, fourth
child and third daughter of Isaac Pound and Mary -
--, born 1837 in North Carolina.

C6555. John Pound, fifth

child and second son of Isaac Pound and Mary ---, born 1840 in North Carolina.

C6556. Adrian Pound, sixth child and third son of Isaac Pound and Mary ---, born 1843 in North Carolina.

C6557. Hannah Pound, seventh child and fourth daughter of Isaac Pound and Mary ---, born 1850 in North Carolina.

C66. --- Pound, sixth child and sixth son of Thomas Pound and Jean ---, date and place of birth unknown.

C67. Sarah Pound, seventh child and first daughter of Thomas Pound and Jean ---, born about 1745 in Richmond County, Virginia.

C7. John Pound, seventh child and second son of Thomas Pound, born 7 Nov 1718 possibly in North Carolina.

C8. Elizabeth Pound, eighth child and sixth daughter of Thomas Pound and Margaret Bradley, born 30 Jun 1719 possibly in North Farnam Parish, Richmond County, Virginia and died 22 Nov 1726 in North Farnham Parish, Richmond County, Virginia.

D.   Samuel Pound, fourth child and third son of
John Pound and Elizabeth Joy, born 1690 in
Richmond County, Virginia and died about 1758 in
Germanna, Orange County, Virginia. Married 1714
in North Farnham Parish, Richmond County, Virginia
to Sarah Evans, date and place of birth unknown
but she was christened 24 Dec 1726 in North
Farnham Parish, Richmond County, Virginia. Samuel
Pound moved from Richmond County, Virginia to
Germanna, which was the county seat of Orange
County, Virginia. On 14 Jun 1735, he received a
lease from Governor Alexander Spotswood for 100
acres adjoining the Courthouse. On 28 Jun 1750,
Samuel, aged about 60 years, made a deposition in
Orange County Court and stated his son William
Pound, was born 16 October 1724 and that he hired
him to John Smith, under-sheriff to William
Russell, Gentleman, and was in the said Smith's
sevice at the time the plaintiff's writ was served
on Theophelas Eddis.   (Was this John Smith the
oldest son of Margaret (Pound) Smith, Samuel
Pound's sister?).   Samuel Pound and Sarah Evans
had the misfortune to lose two of their sons in
their childhood.   After their first son Samuel
died, they named another son Samuel, most likely
to commemorate the name and memory of their first
son Samuel.   It may well be that they named a
younger son Peter after the loss of their first
son Peter, and he may be the same Peter Pound who
was in the 1790 census of Orange County, South
Carolina, and a Revolutionary War veteran.   Our
records of the first five children's birth was
recorded in records of North Farnham Parish in
Richmond County, Virginia and if Samuel and Sarah
had moved to Orange County, South Carolina, a
younger Peter would not be in the Farnham Parish
records, but elsewhere in the Parish they resided
in at the time of his birth.   If we had the war
records of Peter Pound of Orange County, South
Carolina,   they   might   give   the   necessary
information to Place him in the family chain.
Samuel Pound and Sarah Evans had issue, which was
the fourth generation in America:
    D1.   John Pound, first child and first son of
Samuel Pound and Sarah Evans, born 4 Nov 1714 in
North Farnham Parish, Richmond County, Virginia.

D2. Samuel Pound, Jr., second child and second son of Samuel Pound and Sarah Evans, born 9 Nov 1715 in North Farnham Parish, Richmond County, Virginia, and died 5 Jan 1730 in Richmond County, Virginia.

D3. Peter Pound, third child and third son of Samuel Pound and Sarah Evans, born 25 Mar 1722 in North Farnham Parish, Richmond County, Virginia, and died 23 Oct 1722 in Richmond County, Virginia.

D4. William Pound, fourth child and fourth son of Samuel Pound and Sarah Evans, born 16 Oct 1724 in North Farnham Parish, Richmond County, Virginia and died 18 May 1810 at Clarke County, Georgia. Married 17 Aug 1749 in Westmoreland County, Virginia to Martha Green. Married secondly to Elizabeth ---. William Pound and Martha Green had issue, which was the fifth generation in America:

D41. William Pound, first child and first son of William Pound and Martha Green, born 1749 and died 1883. Married --- ---. William Pound and --- --- had issue, which was the sixth generation in America:

D411. Reuben Pound, first child and first son of William Pound and --- ---, born 1780.

D412. Richard Pound, second child and second son of William Pound and --- ---, born 1781.

D42. Samuel Pound, second child and second son of William Pound and Martha Green, born 1755 in Virginia and died in Anson County, North Carolina. Married Sarah Roney. Samuel Pound and Sarah Roney had issue, which was the sixth generation in America:

D421. Samuel Pound, first child and first son of Samuel Pound and Sarah Roney, born about 1800.

D4. William Pound, fourth child and fourth son of Samuel Pound and Sarah Evans, born 16 Oct 1724 in North Farnham Parish, Richmond County, Virginia and died 18 May 1810 in Clarke County, Georgia. Married secondly to Elizabeth ---. William Pound and Elizabeth --- had issue, which was the fifth generation in America:

D41. Isham Pound, first child and first son of William Pound and Elizabeth ---, born 1775 in South Carolina and died 2 Nov 1856 in St. Tammany Parish, Louisiana. Buried at Cheraw, Marion County, Mississippi. Married 4 Mar 1860 to Margaret Yarborough, born 1791 in South Carolina and died 4 Mar 1860 in St. Tammany Parish, Louisiana. Buried at Cheraw, Marion County, Mississippi. Isham Pound and Margaret Yarborough had issue, which was the sixth generation in America:

D411. Polly Anne Pounds, first child and first daughter of Isham Pound and Margaret Yarborough, born 16 Jan 1809 in Mississippi and died 11 Oct 1854 in Mississippi. Married 26 May 1824 in Mississippi to Nathaniel Pigott.

D412. John Pounds, second child and first son of Isham Pound and Margaret Yarborough, born about 1825 in Mississippi. Married Dec 1842 in Mississippi to Mary Hennessy, daughter of Isaac Hennessy ahd Lida ---. born 1827 in Mississippi. John Pounds and Mary Hennessy had issue, which was the seventh generation in America:

D4121. George Pounds, first child and first son of John Pounds and Mary Hennessy, born 1844 in Mississippi.

D4122. --- Pounds, second child and first daughter of John Pounds and Mary Hennessy, born 1848 in Mississippi.

D413. Margaret L. Pounds, third child and second daughter of Isham Pound and Margaret Yarborough, born about 1814 in Mississippi. Married 1831 in Mississippi to William Collins, born 1808 in South Carolina. Margaret Pounds and William Collins had issue, which was the seventh generation in America:

D4131. L.J. Collins, first child and first son of Margaret Pounds and William Collins, born 1836 in Mississippi.

D4132. W.H. Collins, second child and second son of Margaret Pounds and William Collins, born 1839 in Mississippi.

D4133. M.M. Collins, third child and first daughter of Margaret Pounds and

William Collins, born 1841 in Mississippi.

D4134. J.C. Collins, fourth child and third son of Margaret Pounds and William Collins, born 1843 in Mississippi.

D4135. Thomas L. Collins, fifth child and fourth son of Margaret Pounds and William Collins, born 1845 in Mississippi.

D4136. G.E. Collins, sixth child and fifth son of Margaret Pounds and William Collins, born 1849 in Mississippi.

D414. Isham Johnson Pounds, fourth child and second son of Isham Pound and Margaret Yarborough, born 10 Jun 1815 in Mississippi and died 26 Dec 1875 in Mississippi. Married 9 May 1838 in Mississippi to Sarah Mary Keller, daughter of Henry Keller and Sophia Page, born 23 Jun 1825 in Mississippi and died 17 Mar 1898. Sarah Keller married secondly 7 Dec 1876 to Monroe Jenkins. Isham Pounds and Sarah Keller had issue, which was the seventh generation in America:

D4141. Helen N. Pounds, first child and first daughter of Isham Pounds and Sarah Keller, born 18 Oct 1844 in Mississippi. Married 12 Nov 1865 in Mississippi to M.G. Williams.

D4142. Miriam Pounds, second child and second daughter of Isham Pounds and Sarah Keller, born 31 Oct 1846 in Mississippi. Married 1 Nov 1865 in Mississippi to S.R. Pool, born 1837 in Mississippi.

D4143. Sarah Pounds, third child and third daughter of Isham Pounds and Sarah Keller, born 29 Nov 1848 in Mississippi. Married 5 Nov 1875 in Mississippi to Andrew Jackson Seals, born 1851 in Mississippi.

D4144. Joseph Leon Pounds, fourth child and first son of Isham Pounds and Sarah Keller, born 27 Feb 1852 in Mississippi. Married 24 Jan 1878 in Mississippi to Bernetta Pierce, born 24 Jan 1858 in Louisiana.

D4145. Margaret Sophia Pounds, fifth child and fourth daughter of Isham Pounds and Sarah Keller, born 4 Apr 1854 in Mississippi.

D4146. Rachel Elizabeth (Lizzie) Pounds, sixth child and fifth daughter of Isham Pounds and Sarah Keller, born 19 Sep 1856 in

Mississippi. Married 18 Dec 1876 in Mississippi to D. Karr.

D4147. Linnie Pounds, seventh child and sixth daughter of Isham Pounds and Sarah Keller, born 27 Apr 1859 in Mississippi. Married 18 Dec 1876 to --- ---.

D4148. Cathie Pounds, eighth child and seventh daughter of Isham Pounds and Sarah Keller, born 9 Jul 1861 in Mississippi. Married 9 Jan 1879 in Mississippi to Israel Magee.

D4149. Julia Isabella Pounds, ninth child and eighth daughter of Isham Pounds and Sarah Keller, born 30 Aug 1865 in Mississippi. Married in Mississippi to James Page.

D415. Joseph E. Pounds, fifth child and third son of Isham Pound and Margaret Yarborough, born 1 Mar 1818 in Mississippi and died 17 Sep 1882 in Marion County, Mississippi. Buried in Lott cemetery, Marion County, Mississippi. Married 4 Jan 1838 in St. Tammany Parish, Louisiana to Elizabeth Keller, born 14 Apr 1819 in Mississippi. Joseph Pounds and Elizabeth Keller had issue, which was the seventh generation in America:

D4151. Margaret C. Pounds, first child and first daughter of Joseph Pounds and Elizabeth Keller, born 4 Apr 1839 in Louisiana. Married 11 Oct 1855 in Louisiana to John Lott, son of Joshua Lott, born 1835 in Mississippi. Margaret Pounds and John Lott had issue, which was the eighth generation in America:

D41511. Julia M. Lott, first child and first daughter of Margaret Pounds and John Lott, born 29 Nov 1856 in Louisiana. Married --- Eubanks.

D41512. Rosanna E. Lott, second child and second daughter of Margaret Pounds and John Lott, born 26 Dec 1859 in Louisiana.

D41513. James H. Lott, third child and first son of Margaret Pounds and John Lott, born 9 Aug 1862 in Louisiana.

D41514. Leona A. Lott, fourth child and third daughter of Margaret Pounds and John Lott, born 19 Jun 1865 in Louisiana.

D41515. Lemon A. Lott,

fifth child and second son of Margaret Pounds and John Lott, born 13 Nov 1867 in Louisiana.

D41516. John H. Lott, sixth child and third son of Margaret Pounds and John Lott, born 17 Jun 1871 in Louisiana.

D41517. Sarah V. Lott, seventh child and fourth daughter of Margaret Pounds and John Lott, born 1873 in Louisiana.

D41518. Frances J. Lott, eighth child and fifth daughter of Margaret Pounds and John Lott, born 1877 in Louisiana.

D4152. Sophia A. Pounds, second child and second daughter of Joseph Pounds and Elizabeth Keller, born 14 Nov 1841 in Louisiana. Married 6 Apr 1865 in Louisiana to Morris M. Williams, born 6 Apr 1865. Sophia Pounds and Morris Williams had issue, which was the eighth generation in America:

D41521. Laura K. Williams, first child and first daughter of Sophia Pounds and Morris Williams, born 14 Sep 1867 in Louisiana.

D41522. Hardy L. Williams, second child and first son of Sophia Pounds and Morris Williams, born 28 May 1869 in Louisiana.

D4153. Johnson B. Pounds, third child and first son of Joseph Pounds and Elizabeth Keller, born 20 Mar 1844 in Mississippi. Married 15 Dec 1869 in Louisiana to Mary C. Pittman, born 1846 in Mississippi. Johnson Pounds and Mary Pittman had issue, which was the eighth generation in America:

D41531. Joseph A. Pounds, first child and first son of Johnson Pounds and Mary Pittman, born 9 Nov 1865 in Mississippi.

D4154. Joseph L. Pounds, fourth child and second son of Joseph Pounds and Elizabeth Keller, born 22 Apr 1846 in Louisiana. Married 29 Nov 1866 in Louisiana to Martha V. Pittman, born 1849 in Mississippi. Joseph Pounds and Martha Pittman had issue, which was the eighth generation in America:

D41541. Thomas E.

Pounds, first child and first son of Joseph Pounds and Martha Pittman, born 7 Dec 1867 in Marion County, Mississippi.

D41542. Mary Virolyer Pounds, second child and first daughter of Joseph Pounds and Martha Pittman, born 23 May 1870 in Marion County, Mississippi.

D41543. Emily Pounds, third child and second daughter of Joseph Pounds and Martha Pittman, born 1875 in Marion County, Mississippi.

D41544. Harrison Pounds, fourth child and second son of Joseph Pounds and Martha Pittman, born 1877 in Marion County, Mississippi.

D4155. Henry B. Pounds, fifth child and third son of Joseph Pounds and Elizabeth Keller, born 4 Mar 1849 in Louisiana. Married about 1870 in Mississippi to Mary J. ---, born 1856 in Mississippi. Henry Pounds and Mary --- had issue, which was the eighth generation in America:

D41551. Robert H. Pounds, first child and first son of Henry Pounds and Mary ---, born 29 Jul 1871 in Marion County, Mississippi.

D41552. Luella E. Pounds, second child and first daughter of Henry Pounds and Mary ---, born 7 Jun 1873 in Marion County, Mississippi.

D41553. Sarah J. Pounds, third child and second daughter of Henry Pounds and Mary ---, born 1875 in Marion County, Mississippi.

D41554. Zarel T. Pounds, fourth child and second son of Henry Pounds and Mary ---, born 1878 in Marion County, Mississippi.

D4156. Sarah E. Pounds, sixth child and third daughter of Joseph Pounds and Elizabeth Keller, born 11 Jan 1851 in Louisiana.

D416. Elizabeth Pounds, sixth child and third daughter of Isham Pound and Margaret Yarborough, born about 1820 in Mississippi. Married 1848 in Mississippi to Alexander Dairs.

D417. Minerva Caroline Pounds, seventh child and fourth daughter of Isham Pound and Margaret Yarborough, born 15 Jul 1827 at Raleigh, Smith County, Mississippi and died 7 Feb 1902 at Robert Lee, Coke County, Texas. Buried at Hayrick Lodge cemetery, Coke County, Texas. Married about 1849 in Mississippi to William Henry Kellar, son of Henry Kellar and Sophia Page, born 1827 in Meridian, Lauderdale County, Mississippi, and died 28 Nov 1905 at Robert Lee, Coke County, Texas. Buried at Hayrick Lodge cemetery, Coke County, Texas. Minerva Pounds and William Kellar had issue, which was the seventh generation in America:

D4171. John Henry George Kellar, first child and first son of Minerva Pounds and William Kellar, born about 1848 in Louisiana and died before 1905. Married 28 Feb 1878 in Williamson County, Texas to Mary Fisher.

D4172. Rose Ann Kellar, second child and first daughter of Minerva Pounds and William Kellar, born about 1850 in Louisiana.

D4173. Feliciann Asenith Kellar, third child and second daughter of Minerva Pounds and William Kellar, born 25 Mar 1852 in Rapides Parish, Louisiana and died 3 Aug 1937 at San Marcos, San Diego County, California. Buried at Phoenix, Maricopa County, Arizona. Married 25 Mar 1868 at Liberty, Liberty County, Texas to Francis Marion Green, born 20 Feb 1846 in Liberty County, Texas and died 12 Jul 1897 at Bronte, Coke County, Texas. Feliciann Kellar and Francis Green had issue, which was the eighth generation in America:

D41731. William Benjamin Green, first child and first son of Feliciann Kellar and Francis Green, born 11 Dec 1869 in Georgetown, Williamson County, Texas and died 20 Dec 1920 at Litchfield Park, Maricopa County, Arizona. Buried at Phoenix, Maricopa County, Arizona.

D41732. Minerva Caroline Green, second child and first daughter of Feliciann Kellar and Francis Green, born 5 Dec 1871 in Georgetown, Williamson County, Texas and died 13 May 1957 at Phoenix, Maricopa County,

Arizona. Buried at Phoenix, Maricopa County, Arizona.

D41733. Francis Henry Green, third child and second son of Feliciann Kellar and Francis Green, born 16 Feb 1873 in Georgetown, Williamson County, Texas and died 16 Sep 1957 at San Marcos, San Diego County, California. Buried at San Marcos, San Diego County, California.

D41734. Joseph Riley Green, fourth child and third son of Feliciann Kellar and Francis Green, born 14 Oct 1876 in Georgetown, Williamson County, Texas and died 20 Dec 1904 at Dublin, Erath County, Texas.

D41735. Mary Roseann Green, fifth child and second daughter of Feliciann Kellar and Francis Green, born 21 Nov 1879 in Georgetown, Williamson County, Texas and died 21 Dec 1967 at Prescott, Yavapai County, Arizona. Buried at Prescott, Yavapai County, Arizona.

D41736. Archie Dallas Green, sixth child and fourth son of Feliciann Kellar and Francis Green, born 23 Mar 1882 in Georgetown, Williamson County, Texas and died 27 Apr 1936 at Phoenix, Maricopa County, Arizona. Buried at Phoenix, Maricopa County, Arizona.

D41737. Ward Beecher Green, seventh child and fifth son of Feliciann Kellar and Francis Green, born 22 May 1885 in Georgetown, Williamson County, Texas and died 3 Jan 1928 at Phoenix, Maricopa County, Arizona. Buried at Phoenix, Maricopa County, Arizona.

D41738. Edward Pruitt Green, eighth child and sixth son of Feliciann Kellar and Francis Green, born 2 Sep 1886 in Georgetown, Williamson County, Texas and died 14 May 1964 at Phoenix, Maricopa County, Arizona. Buried at Phoenix, Maricopa County, Arizona.

D41739. John Carlton Green, ninth child and seventh son of Feliciann Kellar and Francis Green, born 10 Apr 1889 in Georgetown, Williamson County, Texas and died 14 May 1964 at Avondale, Maricopa County, Arizona. Buried at Phoenix, Maricopa County, Arizona.

D41740. Orr Tolliver

Green, tenth child and eighth son of Feliciann Kellar and Francis Green, born 24 Apr 1891 at Sanco, Coke County, Texas and died 4 Jan 1966 at Mesa, Maricopa County, Arizona. Buried at Phoenix, Maricopa County, Arizona.

D41741. Helen Ozelia Narcissus Green, eleventh child and third daughter of Feliciann Kellar and Francis Green, born 26 Oct 1893 at Sanco, Coke County, Texas and died 28 Nov 1969 at Phoenix, Maricopa County, Arizona. Buried at Phoenix, Maricopa County, Arizona.

D4174. William Joseph Ison Kellar, fourth child and second son of Minerva Pounds and William Kellar, born 27 Apr 1854 in Texas and died 15 May 1890 in Williamson County, Texas. Buried at Gravel Hill cemetery, Williamson County, Texas. Married 6 Dec 1876 in Williamson County, Texas to Louisa W.J. Hobbs.

D4175. Louisiana Kellar, fifth child and third daughter of Minerva Pounds and William Kellar, born about 1854. Married 22 Dec 1875 in Williamson County, Texas to L.C. Bullion.

D4176. Margrett Ann Kellar, sixth child and fourth daughter of Minerva Pounds and William Kellar, born about 1856.

D418. Robert Pounds, eighth child and fourth son of Isham Pound and Margaret Yarborough, born 1828 in Mississippi and died 2 Mar 1863 in the Civil War.

D419. Andrew Jackson Pounds, ninth child and fifth son of Isham Pound and Margaret Yarborough, born 1832 in Mississippi. Married 4 Feb 1853 in Marion County, Mississippi to Lucinda Smith, born about 1831 in Mississippi and died before 1870 in Mississippi. Married secondly 1870 in Marion County, Mississippi to Mary Boutwell. Andrew Pounds and Lucinda Smith had issue, which was the seventh generation in America:

D4191. George Pounds, first child and first son of Andrew Pounds and Lucinda Smith, born 1855 in Mississippi.

D4192. RoseAnn Pounds, second child and first daughter of Andrew Pounds and Lucinda Smith, born 1860 in Mississippi.

D4193. Leon Pounds, third

child and second son of Andrew Pounds and Lucinda
Smith, born 1861 in Mississippi and died about
1920 in Mississippi. Married 10 Aug 1885 in
Lawrence County, Mississippi to Edna Ophelia
Herrington, born 21 Aug 1860 in Lawrence County,
Mississippi and died 7 Jun 1899 in Mississippi.
Married secondly to Betty Yates. Edna Herrington
married secondly to John Polk. Leon Pounds and
Edna Herrington had issue, which was the eighth
generation in America:

D41931. Mary Pounds,
first child and first daughter of Leon Pounds and
Edna Herrington, date and place of birth unknown.

D41932. Bob Pounds,
second child and first son of Leon Pounds and Edna
Herrington, date and place of birth unknown.

D41933. Rosie Pounds,
third child and second daughter of Leon Pounds and
Edna Herrington, date and place of birth unknown.

D41934. Ophelia Pounds,
fourth child and third daughter of Leon Pounds and
Edna Herrington, date and place of birth unknown.

D41935. Agnes Elizabeth
Pounds, fifth child and fourth daughter of Leon
Pounds and Edna Herrington, born 3 Aug 1894 in
Mississippi and died 31 Mar 1986 in Mississippi.
Married 1910 in Mississippi to William Alexander
Spiers.

D419. Andrew Jackson Pounds, ninth
child and fifth son of Isham Pounds and Margaret
Yarborough, born 1832 in Mississippi. Married
secondly 1870 in Marion County, Mississippi to
Mary Boutwell, born about 1840. Andrew Pounds and
Mary Boutwell had issue, which was the seventh
generation in America:

D4191. Martha E. Pounds,
first child and first daughter of Andrew Pounds
and Mary Boutwell, born 1871.

D4192. Marion J. Pounds,
second child and second daughter of Andrew Pounds
and Mary Boutwell, born 1875.

D4193. Philamy Pounds, third
child and third daughter of Andrew Pounds and Mary
Boutwell, born 1876.

D4194. Sepphrona Pounds,
fourth child and fourth daughter of Andrew Pounds

and Mary Boutwell, born 1879.

D5. Catherine Pound, fifth child and first daughter of Samuel Pound and Sarah Evans, born about 1727 in North Farnham Parish, Richmond County, Virginia. Married 4 Jan 1817 in Halifax County, Virginia to Joseph Lovin.

D6. Samuel Pound, sixth child and fifth son of Samuel Pound and Sarah Evans, born 2 Sep 1730 in North Farnham Parish, Richmond County, Virginia and died 1805. Married Sarah ---.

Pound(s) Surname Index

This index is arranged by descendancy and the family in which the name occurs.

```
Lecil T. Pounds                        15
Lillian Pounds                         15
Richard Simpson Pounds                 15
James Garland Pounds, Sr               15
Betty G. Pounds                        15
Lora Elouise Pounds                    15
Laura Joan Pounds                      15
Charlie Wheeler Pounds                 15
James Kenneth Pounds                   15
James Garland Pounds, Jr.              15
Roy Gale Pounds                        15
Kathern Ann Pounds                     16
Charley Pounds                         16
Gaby Bedford Pounds                    16
Raleigh Pounds, Jr.                    16
Richard Pounds                         16
Gertrude Pounds                        16
Mary Elizabeth Pounds                  16
Dewey Pounds                           17
Eliza Pounds                           17
Benjamin Pounds                        17
Thomas Pounds                          17
Henry Pounds                           17
Sarah Pounds                           17
William Pounds                         17
Merryman Pounds                        17
Benjamin Pounds                        17
Mary Elizabeth Pounds                  17
Andrew Pounds                          33
Wade A. Pounds                         33
George Ann Pounds                      34
Nancy J. Pounds                        34
Alex Dock Pounds                       34
A.D. Pounds                            34
Billy Gene Pounds                      34
Robert Pounds                          34
Myrtle Lee Pounds                      34
George Pounds                          34
Newbern Pounds                         34
L.V. Pounds                            35
Lester Pounds                          35
Chester Pounds                         35
William Wade L. Pounds                 35
Jessie Jewell Pounds                   35
```

643

William Pounds	59
Hoyle Pounds	59
Donald Emerson Pounds	59
Judy Pounds	59
Dona Pounds	59
Barbara (Bo) Pounds	60
Donald Pounds, Jr.	60
John Pounds	60
William (Will) Pounds	60
James Herbert Pounds	60
James (Jimmy) Pounds	60
Steven (Steve) Pounds	60
Russell Stevenson Pounds	60
Russell Stevenson Pounds, Jr.	60
Rice Pounds	60
Mary Dial Pounds	60
Harriet Pounds	60
Narcissus Ophelia Pounds	61
Bastian Pounds	63
James Pounds	63
Augustus Young Pounds	63
James Carlus Pounds	63
James Carlus Pounds, Jr.	63
Leslie Young Pounds	63
Mary Sue Pounds	63
Rosie Pounds	64
Annie Pounds	64
Henry Pounds	64
Carlos (Shug) Pounds	64
Edna Pounds	64
Corrine Pounds	64
William Newman Pounds	64
Letha Ann Pounds	65
John William Pounds	65
William M. Pounds	65
Lonie Rufus Pounds	65
Miles J. Pounds	65
James Edward Pounds	65
Mildred Louise Pounds	65
Hortense Pounds	66
Frances Pounds	66
Richard N. Pounds	66
Martha Pounds	66
Martha Ann Pounds	66
John L. Pounds	66
Ophelia C. Pounds	66

645

Wilbert Warren Pounds	85
Leona May Pounds	85
Mildred Kathleen Pounds	85
Elizabeth Pounds	85
Sarah Jane Pounds	85
Angeline Pounds	85
James Pounds	85
William Pounds	85
Mary Pounds	86
Stephen Pounds	86
Willis C. Pounds	86
Charles M. Pounds	86
Martha Ann Pounds	86
William P. Pounds	86
Susan Pounds	86
John Sidell Pounds	86
Mary Pounds	86
Frances Pounds	86
Silas Pounds	86
Lewis Pound	87
Thomas S. Pound	87
Mary Pound	87
Jane Pound	87
Richard Kenner Pound	87
Keziah Jane Pound	87
Sarah Ann Pound	87
Serena Pound	89
Isaac Simpson Pound	89
Martha Anna Pounds	89
James Pounds	90
Thomas Henry Pounds	90
Samuel Kenner Pound	90
Nancy Caroline Pound	90
Richard Franklin Pound	90
Harriet Elizabeth Pound	90
Leroy (twin) Pound	90
Wilburn Clive Pound	91
Audra Jane Pound	91
Julian Haynes Pound	91
Cleburne Green Pound	91
Norma Jean Pound	91
Mary Ann Pound	91
Richard Leroy Pound	91
Glenn Simpson Pound	92
Allyn Vernell Pound	92
John Leroy Pound	92

651

653

657

661

665

668

676

679

www.ingramcontent.com/pod-product-compliance
Lightning Source LLC
Chambersburg PA
CBHW072058040426
42334CB00040B/1297